W9-CAD-143

THE PENETRATION OF AFRICA

THE PENETRATION
OF AFRICA

EUROPEAN EXPLORATION IN

NORTH AND WEST AFRICA

TO 1815

by

ROBIN HALLETT

FREDERICK A. PRAEGER, *Publishers*

NEW YORK · WASHINGTON

BOOKS THAT MATTER

Published in the United States
of America in 1965
by Frederick A. Praeger, Inc., *Publishers*
111 Fourth Avenue, New York 3, N.Y.,

Second printing 1967

Library of Congress Catalog Card Number: 65–25279

Printed in Great Britain

For My Parents

CONTENTS

PREFACE   *page* XIII

ACKNOWLEDGEMENTS   XX

THE AFRICAN SETTING

I. BACKGROUND   3

The Land

The People

II. THE STATES OF NORTHERN AND WESTERN   16
AFRICA IN THE EIGHTEENTH CENTURY

III. AFRICAN IDEAS ABOUT EUROPE   27

EUROPE'S KNOWLEDGE OF AFRICA IN THE EIGHTEENTH CENTURY

I. POPULAR CONCEPTIONS   37

II. SAHARA AND SUDAN   44

Classical Writers

Arab Geographers

III. GUINEA   60

The Portuguese

The English, the French and the Dutch

IV. AVENUES INTO THE INTERIOR   78

The English on the Gambia

The French on the Senegal

V. WESTERN AFRICA   92

Cartographical Impressions: 1500–1750

The Sum of Knowledge

vii

CONTENTS

VI. EXPLORERS WITHOUT RENOWN   *page* 97
Europeans in the Sahara and the Sudan:
Thirteenth to Eighteenth Centuries

VII. OTHER PARTS OF AFRICA   104
Barbary
Egypt
Nubia, Sennar and the Nile
Ethiopia
The Congo, Angola and Mozambique
South Africa
Asia and the Americas: a Brief Comparison

VIII. THE CAUSES OF IGNORANCE   125

THE BONDS OF INTERCOURSE

I. FUNDAMENTALS   137
The Outline of History
The African Trade
War and Politics

II. THE CURIOSITY OF THE AGE   146
The Cosmopolitan Spirit
The Produce of the Tropics: Interests—Practical,
Aesthetic and Scientific
The Circulation of Ideas

III. THE INFLUENCE OF GREAT MEN   156
James Cook
James Bruce
Joseph Banks

IV. THE ANTI-SLAVERY MOVEMENT   177

V. THE INTEREST OF EUROPE   184
Continental Cross-fertilizations
Paul Isert
C. B. Wadström
J. F. Blumenbach

THE AGE OF THE AFRICAN ASSOCIATION—I 1788–1802

I. THE FIRST YEARS: 1788–90   193
The Founding of the African Association
The First Explorers: John Ledyard in Cairo

viii

CONTENTS

The First Explorers: Simon Lucas in Tripoli
Widening Contacts: Ben Ali and Swediaur;
Consular Reports
The African Association: Organization, Finance
and Membership; the First Report

II. THE APPROACH FROM THE WEST: 1790–99 *page* 217
Shabeni's Story: Timbuktu and 'Housa'
Daniel Houghton
The Consul to Senegambia
Mungo Park
Park's Achievement

III. THE APPROACH FROM THE NORTH: 1797–1802   250
Frederick Hornemann
J. G. Jackson and Others in Morocco

IV. THE ENTERPRISE OF OTHERS   269
The Sierra Leone Company
The Bulama Association
W. G. Browne in Darfur

V. THE AFRICAN ASSOCIATION'S ACHIEVEMENT   285

THE ROOTS OF IMPERIALISM

I. EXPLORATION AND IMPERIALISM   297
II. FRANCE AND AFRICA   299
Senegal
Egypt
III. SPAIN AND MOROCCO   310
The Adventures of Ali Bey
IV. BRITAIN AND THE NIGER   321
The Spur of French Rivalry
Park's Second Expedition
The Death of Mungo Park
V. BRITAIN AND THE WEST COAST   346

THE AGE OF THE AFRICAN ASSOCIATION—II 1802–15

I. THE AFRICAN ASSOCIATION: 1802–15   357
II. THE APPROACH FROM THE SOUTH   361
Henry Nicholls

CONTENTS

III. THE EASTERN SUDAN   *page* 366
     J. L. Burckhardt

IV. GERMAN TRAVELLERS IN NORTH AFRICA   379
     U. J. Seetzen
     Heinrich Röntgen

V. ETHIOPIA   386
     Lord Valentia and Henry Salt

VI. 1815   397

     SOURCES AND REFERENCES   399

     INDEX   443

x

PLATES

1. Africa allegorically presented   *facing page* 90
2. Images of Africa: strange men . . .   91
3. Images of Africa: . . . and beasts as strange   106
4. Cartographical impressions: section of a map of Africa, 1525   107
5. Cartographical impressions: Blaeu's map of Africa, 1635   154
6. Cartographical impressions: D'Anville's map of Africa, 1727   155
7. Africans: Tripoli—'Officers of the Grand Seraglio regaling'   170
8. Africans: Nubia—a camel caravan in the Nubian desert   171
9. Africans: Ethiopia—'Abyssinians reposing'   266
10. Africans: Dahomey—'Public procession of the Queen's women'   267
11. Europeans in Africa: Christian slaves being tortured in Barbary   282
12. Europeans in Africa: European merchants at 'the King of Dahomey's Leveé'   282
13. Europeans in Africa: the English Fort on James Island in the Gambia River   283
14. The patron of exploration: Sir Joseph Banks, President of the Royal Society   314
15. Explorers: Mungo Park   315
16. The patron of scholarship: General Bonaparte at the Institute of Egypt, Cairo   315
17. Explorers: J. L. Burckhardt in Eastern dress   330
18. Incidents of exploration: 'Mr. Bruce enraptured at the Fountain of the Principal Source of the Nile'   330

19. Incidents of exploration: 'I saw with infinite pleasure the great object of my mission'—Mungo Park's first view of the Niger *facing page* 331
20. Incidents of exploration: The death of Mungo Park 331

MAPS

1. The States and Peoples of Northern and Western Africa in the Eighteenth Century *page* 18, 19
2. The main European Posts in West Africa in 1750 73
3. The Rivers of West Africa: according to Blaeu, 1664 93
4. The Rivers of West Africa: according to D'Anville, 1750 94
5. Mungo Park's First Journey, 1795–7 232
6. The Eastern Sudan: according to W. G. Browne, 1799 282
7. The Rivers of West Africa: according to Rennell, 1798 286, 287
8. Morocco 312
9. Mungo Park's Second Journey, 1805–6 332
10. J. L. Burckhardt's Travels in Nubia, 1813–15 373
11. The Rivers of West Africa: according to Reichard, 1803 385
12. Ethiopia 387

PREFACE

EVERY BOOK HAS A private history behind it; a personal explanation serves as the most convenient way to introduce and to account for the scope of the present study. In 1956 I found myself for the first time working in Africa. I accepted, naturally and without thinking, that well-established myth—that Africa was the continent without a history. And indeed this view seemed confirmed by all that I could see around me. The streets of Ibadan, where I was living, were splendidly alive: the proud Yorubas so confident in their gestures, so flamboyant in their dress, the clamour of trade, the blare of taxi-horns, the undimmed stridor of a hundred wireless sets—here indeed was the energy and the excitement befitting a great city, the largest in tropical Africa; but where, among those seven hills, over which the houses swarmed, mud-walled and roofed with rusting corrugated iron, where—irrelevantly perhaps, but insistently I asked myself—could one find the monuments of the past, the castles, the churches, the palaces, the quiet distinction of an elegant façade, the ancient alley-ways that Europe would have produced, that had hitherto formed the natural background of my own life, fortunate as I now realized I had been, having always lived in ancient and distinguished cities? No, Africa appeared to have no historical monuments, therefore it could have no history.

I had a good deal of time on my hands in those first months in Africa and the excellent library of the University College at my disposal. I wanted some broad sweep of history to exercise my mind. Only one subject suggested itself as relevant to my needs—for I was shortly to move to the Muslim North of Nigeria: the story of the expansion of Islam. So from their desert tents, from the famous cities of Arabia, I followed that mighty outpouring of the armies of the Prophet—eastward to Persia and to India, westward along the coast of North Africa and into Spain, where their descendants were to create so rich and fine a culture. Into al-Andalus, the Spain of the

xiii

Moors, whose stirring history I had followed in Lévi-Provençal's magnificent narrative, there had come, so I learnt, at the end of the eleventh century, a new race of conquerors, the Almoravids, Berbers veiled like the Tuareg, men whose homes lay far to the south, beyond the borders of Morocco, deep in the western Sahara. So through the unwinding of that magic cord of relevance that leads the student of history into corners of the past he never knew even existed, I was led to study the history of the people who have made the great Desert their home, and passed naturally on to their neighbours, the Negro peoples inhabiting the plains of the Sudan. Then, incredibly—for was not Africa the continent without a history?—there rose over my horizon the great empires of ancient Ghana, of medieval Mali, of the Songhai—and beyond them, farther to the east, the galaxy of the Hausa states and, by Lake Chad, its king-list stretching back a thousand years and more, Kanem-Bornu.

By this time I had left Ibadan to live in Zaria, a city five hundred years old, ringed still with its ancient walls, with mosque and palace and houses of dried mud, whose style revealed how much distinction can be achieved with the simplest of materials. Here, as in every Muslim city in Northern Nigeria, on the festival that marks the end of Ramadan, the month of fasting, the Emir sits enthroned outside his palace and the great lords and officers of the Emirate, magnificiently robed, splendidly mounted, their horses gaily caparisoned, gallop up full tilt, to the braying of long trumpets, to the excited clamour of the white-robed crowd, to perform the *jahi*, their steeds reined sharply back, curvetting in homage and in salutation. Never had I seen so superb, so exhilarating a ceremony, with people so gay, so vigorous, so rightly proud. The myth was exploded utterly, the blinkers fell at last from my eyes.

Into my mind there came now question after question—this elaborate culture, how had it come about? How were these cities founded and these states? Above all, I began to ask myself, as I travelled more widely about the country, how had this wonderful variety of peoples who make up modern Nigeria come together—peoples differing from one another in almost every conceivable way, in language, in religion, in customs, in temperament: the proud Fulani, the shrewd and humorous Hausa, the dynamic Ibo, the sophisticated Yoruba and a hundred others. There was, I came to find, much that could help me to answer these questions, the chronicles of the Hausa States and of Bornu, the oral traditions written down at last by

Nigerians or by European officials, the accounts of nineteenth-century travellers, the work of a few anthropologists and archaeologists. It became then, and for the remainder of the few years I spent in Nigeria, the exciting occupation of my leisure to try to piece this material together, to see if a coherent pattern might not emerge, as clear as the picture that has been drawn of the history of countries in Europe or in Asia. Yet one could not study these sources for long without coming to realize that this search for a pattern might be the occupation of a lifetime, without becoming aware how formidable are the qualifications a really competent student of African history should possess—intimate knowledge of the life of the people, fluency in more than one African language and—for the Muslim areas—ability to read Arabic. It was good to find that there were in Nigeria not only a handful of English scholars who had acquired these daunting accomplishments but also an increasing number of Nigerians capable of examining the past of their own people with the critical expertise of modern historical scholarship. By their work new light is being thrown every year on the history of the country; the gathering of much new material is to be expected, the solution of some tough historical problems to be hoped for.

In the course of my reading I had often touched on the first English travellers to visit the interior of Nigeria: Oudney, Denham and Clapperton, and the brothers Lander. I had taken their accounts not as the narratives of expeditions of exploration but as invaluable sources of African history, throwing light on the state of the countries through which they travelled, the personalities of the rulers whom they met. But reading their stories one could not help becoming ever more sharply aware of the personality of the writers—pedantic Oudney, bluff Clapperton, gallant Denham, Richard Lander cheerful and barely literate, John Lander looking at Africa with a romantic poet's eye. Of their courage there could never be any doubt; one came to see what other remarkable qualities they possessed—extraordinary determination, great patience and resourcefulness, an innate decency —not one of them ever fired a gun in anger or in self-defence—and a happy knack of making friends with the Africans whom they met. Nor could one help remarking the quality of the prose in which they told of their experiences, vivid, precise, compact, antithesis of the slapdash manner in which so many contemporary travel books are composed. I wanted to find out more about them, to know what induced them to become explorers, to discover what motives led the British Government to support their expeditions. Here, it seemed, was a useful subject for study and one within my powers.

Back in England, I visited the Public Record Office, expecting that I might find there one or two of the travellers' own records. A few?— there was file upon file. Here were the despatches that Denham had sent home across the desert, hidden in the robe of a courier on camel back; here that sheet on which Richard Lander with clumsy hand had written the last instructions of Clapperton, his master, as he lay dying in a hut in Sokoto. To hold such documents in one's hands was an exciting, indeed a moving experience. But I soon came to see as I worked my way through the official archives that what I had regarded as isolated expeditions were in fact part of a great movement of exploration that reached back to the year 1788, when the African Association had been founded. Yet one could not be content with this date as a starting-point; the African Association had been formed by the dozen members of a London dining club. Who were they, why had they come together, what had induced them to undertake the exploration of a continent? To answer these questions it became necessary to find out why men in the eighteenth century were interested in Africa and to discover the limits of their knowledge. This led on to a study of the sources at their command. So I found myself led back by logical degrees to the Portuguese, who had known so much and told so little, to the Arab geographers, to Ptolemy and to Pliny, and at last, to old Herodotus, Father of History, beyond whom— with relief I recognized—it was not necessary to go.

As my theme extended itself in time, so I found it expanding in space. The goals of the missions of exploration between 1788 and 1830 were simply defined: Timbuktu, the Hausa States, the course of the Niger. But the approach was made from every conceivable starting-point: from Cairo and Tripoli and Mogador in North Africa, along the Senegal and the Gambia, from Freetown, Badagry and Calabar on the West Coast, and even up the mouth of the Congo. Nor, so I found, could I afford to ignore certain missions that had taken place farther to the east; the travels of Bruce and later of Salt in Ethiopia, of Browne in Darfur, of Burckhardt in Nubia, even the French expedition to Egypt in 1798 were not without relevance to my theme. I had imagined at the outset that my scope would be limited to that area which now forms the Northern Region of Nigeria; I came to see that I should have to regard the whole northern half of Africa as my field of study.

If one is to make sense of any of the European missions of exploration, it is essential to form in one's mind a clear picture of the country
in which the mission did its work, in other words to study its history
and its geography. In my own case it became necessary to form as
clear a picture as possible of the states and societies of Northern and
Western Africa, as they existed towards the end of the eighteenth
century. A generation ago, before the revolution in African studies,
this would have been an extremely laborious undertaking; today
there are available many excellent works in French and in English
devoted to the history and to the geography of the countries in this
area. Yet I could not help but become aware once again of my own
limitations. In Nigeria I had found that actually to be living in the
country was of inestimable advantage in studying its history: it
helped one to acquire a proper grip on reality. I would have liked to
have repeated my Nigerian experience in Morocco and in Senegal, in
Egypt and in Ethiopia, to have been paddled down the Niger in the
way of Park and the Landers, to have crossed the desert along the
routes of Caillié or of Laing. This was a counsel of impossible perfection; fortunately many recent travellers have written of these
countries—from their books one can gain a measure of vicarious
experience.

By this time my ideas about the general significance of the work I
was doing had begun to change. I had thought of it originally as a
study of exploration. Yet it became clear the more deeply one bur-
rowed into the European sources that the motives behind the movement were much more complicated than the word 'exploration', with
its hint of pure scientific curiosity, implies. Why were Europeans
interested in Africa? The businessman, the philanthropist, the politician or the scholar, each would give a different answer. So one came
to see that this movement was in fact the first act in something much
larger—the penetration of Africa by the technologically more
advanced civilization of the West; here indeed one was touching the
roots of imperialism. And yet this was not the deepest significance of
the subject.

It had occurred to me when living in Nigeria that 'exploration' was
a Europo-centric expression. After all, the earliest travellers were
moving along routes that African traders had trodden for centuries,
and visiting cities and states ancient and proud of their culture. This
was a process very different from mid-twentieth-century forms of
exploration: looking for Stone Age tribes in the backwoods of the

Amazon or shooting astronauts into space. It was interesting, of course, to watch the reaction of the Europeans to new scenes and peoples; but it was equally interesting, and indeed more exciting, to find out what one could of the reaction of Africans to the first white men they had ever seen. I began to realize that it was the historian's duty to try, by an effort of the imagination, to look at the subject not only through European but also through African eyes. Here, of course, one was faced with an obvious difficulty. So far as I am aware there are only one or two written African sources that refer to the first Europeans to visit the country nor, since the movement took place a century and a half ago, is it likely that oral tradition could add anything at all. Fortunately within the European travellers' accounts are not a few references to the way in which they were regarded by their hosts, while a study of the history of African states before the coming of the Europeans and of the contacts between Europeans and Africans in the coastal establishments helps one to gain some grasp of the nature of these new relationships.

So the final, indeed—as it seems to me—the universal significance of the whole subject began to emerge. This was in fact the story of the meeting of two worlds, a theme as dramatic as any that a historian could wish to handle. The actors make it impressive, for there are great and decent men, both African and European, who have a part in it. Nor, I would like to feel, is it a story without relevance to the needs of the present. We are all now, for the first time in history, citizens of one world; the destinies of Europe and of Africa, even in this post-Imperial age, still are linked. We must learn to understand one another better—and, heaven knows, there has been precious little understanding or respect shown for Africa in Europe in the past. The surest way of getting a grasp on the realities of the present is to have some comprehension of the heritage and the burden of the past. The historian may justify his work in many ways: by none better than that, in trying to reach the truth of things, he seeks to promote a better understanding between man and man.

A word on the arrangement of this study. It is essential to have from the start the African scene clear in one's mind, hence the introductory section on the land, the people and the states of Northern and Western Africa, concluding with a chapter on African ideas about Europe.

The next section examines in some detail the extent of Europe's knowledge about the interior of Northern and Western Africa and the sources of that knowledge. It then moves on to consider more briefly what was known about other parts of the continent. This in turn leads to a consideration of the question—why was Africa the last of the continents to be known in its entirety to Europe?

The third section is concerned to analyse the variety of forces that were at work during the eighteenth century, drawing Africa and Europe ever closer together.

With the foundation of the African Association in 1788 it becomes possible to follow a straightforward course of narrative, until the year 1815 with which this volume closes.

The year 1815 has not been chosen entirely for its European significance. The first year of peace happened to mark the opening of a new era of exploration, for the British Government then adopted a policy of encouraging the penetration of the interior of Western Africa. The narrative of the seven British expeditions sent out between 1815 and 1830, together with the accounts of various French travellers, are each of them longer and more detailed than those of most of the missions before 1815. They will form the subject of a second volume designed to take the story up to 1830. At the same time I intend in the closing chapters of the second volume to pull together some of the themes implicit in the narrative that forms the second part of this volume: the nature of the African response to the European penetration, the development of the conception of the explorer, the increase in European knowledge about Africa between 1780 and 1830 and the extent to which this new knowledge modified existing ideas, the connection between European activities in these years and the rampant imperialism of the century's closing decades. The period about 1830 seems the most convenient place at which to end this detailed study. By that time most of the states in the interior of Western Africa had been visited and the greater part of the Niger's course explored. With the French conquest of Algiers, the establishment of Egyptian rule in the Sudan and the beginnings of commercial enterprise on the Niger another period opened.

ACKNOWLEDGEMENTS

THE PRESENT STUDY was begun in a cavalier mood. It would require, I imagined, the work of a few months. It has taken as many years. Little did I realize when I started how many pleasant obligations I was to incur. In meeting the expense of research I have been helped both by the Committee for Commonwealth Studies of Oxford University and by the Royal Geographical Society. The Committee for Commonwealth Studies recommended me for the award of an Oppenheimer Research grant; I have enjoyed the opportunity which the grant brought with it of becoming a temporary member of Queen Elizabeth House, Oxford. The Royal Geographical Society created a special studentship to allow me to edit the records of the African Association; I am particularly grateful to the Society's Director, Mr L. P. Kirwan, and to the Society's Librarian, Mr G. R. Crone, for their encouragement and help. I am grateful, too, to the Editor of *The Geographical Magazine* for publishing a series of articles, based on some of the material contained in the present study, under the general title 'The Lure of Africa'. To all those who have read this book in typescript, suggested improvements in structure or style, and pointed out factual errors I am deeply obliged—and especially to Mr J. G. Murray and Professor J. D. Fage. I have greatly enjoyed the opportunity of talking over certain subjects with Mr E. W. Bovill, whose writings have for a generation inspired thought and interest in the history of Northern Africa, and, more briefly, with Dr A. A. Boahen of the University of Ghana, author of a masterly thesis on British policy in the Sahara and Sudan in the nineteenth century (now published as *Britain, The Sahara and the Western Sudan, 1788–1861*). In a less personal manner, yet warmly none-the-less, I have felt grateful to every traveller and historian, the living and the dead, whose work I have read with profit, enjoyment and admiration. In the last six years I have drawn on libraries as far afield—this is fact, not fanciful alliteration—as Zaria and Zanzibar, but my greatest demands have been made on the Public Record Office, on the libraries of the Royal Geographical Society, the Royal Commonwealth Society and the British Museum, on the Hampshire County Library and on the Winchester City Library. The library services of Great Britain, run with such efficiency and such courtesy, are surely one of the finest institutions of our time. I am indebted to the Trustees of the British Museum, the Royal Geographical Society and the Royal Society for permission to reproduce maps, portraits and other illustrations from materials in their possession. It is a happy convention that allows introductions to works of scholarship to end with an acknowledgement to the author's family. I used to wonder at one time why such intimate acknowledgements were necessary; now I know.

The people of England could all read and write, and were acquainted with most other regions of the earth; but of this country alone they hitherto knew scarcely anything, and erroneously regarded the inhabitants as naked savages, devoid of religion, and not far removed from the condition of wild beasts: whereas I found them, from my personal observation, to be civilized, learned, humane and pious.

Captain Hugh Clapperton at Sokoto, 1824.

It is only today that it has become possible for the first time even to imagine a whole world consisting of peoples who have in the fullest sense entered into history and become the concern, no longer of the colonial administrator or of the anthropologist, but of the historian.

E. H. Carr.

The historian continuously asks the question, Why? and, so long as he hopes for an answer, he cannot rest.

E. H. Carr.

The study of history is a training in humility.

C. A. de Kiewiet.

THE AFRICAN SETTING

I

BACKGROUND

THE LAND

LOOK DOWN OVER AFRICA, over the northern half of the continent, over that great quadrilateral that stretches from the Mediterranean to the Gulf of Guinea and from the Red Sea to the Atlantic. The map, graspable so easily, deceives; one must use the energy of imagination to comprehend sheer size. An area here close on six million square miles, roughly twice as big as Europe or the United States: or, to take part of the whole—for one needs the emphasis of further comparison—in Libya, within its present bounds, a country nearly four times the size of France, in Nigeria nearly four times the size of Great Britain. The aeroplane has banished distance: today, in as many hours as earlier travellers required months, one can cross the Sahara. But in this study, with time rolled back, motion will be at the pace of a camel caravan or a donkey train, will involve wearing journeys made on foot, weeks and months of travel, landscapes more monotonous than variegated Europe, slowly, slowly unrolling.

Landscapes: the atlas makes it possible to take in their character almost at a glance, for Africa, so much simpler in shape than other continents with their jagged outlines, is also more regular in its features. North of the Equator, if the highlands of Ethiopia be excluded, four great belts of territory stretch in lateral bands from west to east: the Mediterranean coast, the desert, the savannah plains of the Sudan, the rain forest.

'Africa' so the geographers often say, 'begins at the Pyrenees'; but 'it would be as true', one of them has pointed out, 'to maintain that Europe terminates at the Saharan border'. And indeed it is stimulating to think of the Mediterranean as a lake which joins rather than

3

as a sea which divides, to reflect that the landscapes of Andalusia are mirrored in the sierras of Morocco, of Provence in the vineyards and olive-groves of Algeria, of Greece in the juniper-clad slopes of the Green Mountain of Cyrenaica. Yet behind the fertile coast, behind the ramparts of the great range of the Atlas, behind its eastward extension, the high plains of the Algerian Tell and the Aures mountains, lies the desert. In the Gulf of Sirte the Sahara reaches to the waves of the Mediterranean; from the southern slopes of the Atlas, at whose foot lie a string of oases, it can be seen stretching formidably away like a great white sea; in Cyrenaica, in Tripolitania and in Central Tunisia only a belt of steppe or low hills divide it from the rain-blest littoral.[1]

In popular imagination the Sahara is a vast expanse of sand, of great dunes smoothed by the wind, among which are set rare, palm-fringed oases. To the initiated it is a region of fascinating variety, possessing features so special and so strange that only the names the desert people have given them will serve to describe them. Three main types of landscape are to be distinguished: *erg*, *reg* and *hamada*. *Erg* are shifting dunes, up to two thousand feet in height, covering thousands of square miles; yet they make up no more than one-eighth of the total area of the desert. Their greatest stretches are to be found in the northern half of the Sahara. *Reg* are wind-scoured plains, strewn with pebbles; here the desert is at its most desolate, being literally waterless; in compensation *reg* present a surface ideal for travelling. *Hamada* differ from *reg* in their altitude, being plateaux covered with bare rock outcrops. Finally, there are the great massifs: Tibesti, covering an area little smaller than the Alps and with peaks as high, Hoggar, Air and some lower, smaller ranges to the west. They contain, these Saharan massifs, some of the strangest mountains in the world, even the lowest 'as bare, as twisted and as savage as the highest peaks in the Alps'.

The desert reveals other contrasts. In the northern Sahara a sharp light and fresh dawns, and the refinement of a distinct civilization in the rich oases set amid their groves of date palms; in the southern Sahara a hazier atmosphere, landscapes grander in scale but less picturesque. The western Sahara benefits from the proximity of the ocean, thick cloud often covering the sky and giving moisture even when no rain falls. In the central Sahara there is among the mountains water and some vegetation and the possibility of a tough, semi-settled life; but in the eastern desert, on the borders of Egypt, Libya

4

and the modern Sudan, lies a country as desolate as any known to man. All along the southern fringes the desert merges into steppe, the country of the *Sahel*, 'the shore', a land of tough grasses and stunted thorn trees that yet receives a little rain. Southward, the landscape slowly changes, the bush grows denser, the vegetation more varied, in more and more places crops can be raised until at last the influence of the desert fades. The traveller has reached the Sudan.

Bilad-as-Sudan—'land of the blacks'—so the Arabs came to call all the country that lies to the south of the desert and that stretches from the Senegal to the Nile. For the historian it is essential to follow Arab usage. This 'geographical Sudan' it is convenient to divide into three sectors, Western from the Atlantic to the western borders of modern Nigeria, Central reaching to Darfur, and Eastern from Darfur and Kordofan to the Red Sea.* The Sudan presents a remarkable uniformity of landscape. The great plains stretch out, a cover of long grasses and low trees forming that 'bush' which is found in so many parts of Africa—'orchard bush' in part, as some geographers have called it, remembering the gnarled and spiky look of ill-kept apple trees. Occasional outcrops of massive granite—the technical term *inselberg* is at once vivid and precise—or short ridges of laterite break the monotony of near-flatness. But the Sudan has also mountains, well defined but widely separated: the Jebel Marra in Darfur reaching up to ten thousand feet, the northern wedge of the chain of the Cameroons, the Jos Plateau with its steep escarpments, the Hombori mountains within the Niger's bend and the sandstone ranges of Bambuk. Far to the east, beyond the Nile, rise the great cliffs that guard the Ethiopian plateau, forming a frontier so nearly absolute that the traveller approaching them from the Sudan may feel that he 'has come to the end of the world'.

In the southern belt of the Sudan, the rainfall increasing, the foetid luxuriance of a truly tropical vegetation begins to appear, showing itself first in galleries of forest along the course of the streams. Here are landscapes which have been transformed by the hand of man. The rain forest once stretched a hundred miles and more to the north of its present limits. But in the open plains it has been the practice to

* There is often confusion between this use of the expression 'Sudan' and the modern use, limited to the country that lies to the south of Egypt. But it should be remembered that the modern Sudan is a creation of the twentieth century. Throughout this study 'Sudan' will be used—unless otherwise stated—according to its older meaning.

burn the bush in the dry season to clear the land for cultivation; so the edge of the forest has continually been destroyed and its mass driven back. Thus there exists, between the savannah-bush and the high forest, a natural frontier remarkably sharply defined.

The rain forest of the West Coast is roughly two hundred miles wide. It presents, at least to a European, an oppressive landscape. In the original forest trees, up to two hundred feet in height, form a canopy which shuts out the sunlight and checks the growth of other plants. When the tall trees are cut down, creepers and shrubs shoot up to create an undergrowth almost impenetrable; but round the villages the needs of cultivation have led to the clearing of many acres of ground. Nor does the forest form, as is often imagined, an unbroken line from the Cameroons to Sierra Leone. In Dahomey, in Togoland, in some of the coastal regions of modern Ghana, landscapes comparable to those of the Sudan reach to the sea. Further west, beyond the dense vegetation of the Ivory Coast and Liberia, stands the highland mass of Futa Jallon, within the forest zone but with its own characteristic features. Between Futa Jallon and the Gambia lies an area covered with a woodland quite different from that of the rain forest. North of the Gambia, between that river and the Senegal, much of the country is almost as arid in appearance as a desert.

Beyond the forest, the coast: lagoons, creeks, mangrove swamps or open beaches pounded by the surf. Offshore, hidden sand-bars masking the entrance to many of the rivers.

Western Africa contains one of the most complex river systems in the whole world. For centuries the geographers of Europe attempted to make sense of the fragmentary reports available to them; tracing the courses of the greater rivers became one of the main themes of exploration. With so many theories, so much speculation to be presented later in this study, it will be as well to see first the system as it really is. The greatest river of West Africa is the Niger, reckoned the tenth largest in the world, in length some 2,600 miles. The Niger rises among the hills of Futa Jallon and flows to the north-east for a thousand miles, being joined by many tributaries before passing through a flat and marshy area which contains one distinct lake, Debo. Near Timbuktu the river curves to the east and waters the fringes of the desert, before turning again to complete a huge bend. South-eastwards now it flows for another thousand miles, until two hundred and fifty miles from the coast it is joined by the mightiest of its tributaries, the Benue. Then the great stream, a mile wide in parts, takes its course straight to the south and the ocean, only to have its waters scattered among the labyrinthine channels of the Delta.

The Benue follows a course almost as unpredictable as the Niger: it rises on a northern flank of the Adamawa massif in the present Cameroun Republic, flows north, then west through a break in the mountains, and finally south-westwards to its confluence with the Niger. Along an early part of its course the Benue runs parallel to another great river, the Logone, the area between them being flat and sufficiently narrow to make it seem possible that the Benue may one day absorb the Logone's waters. The Logone, flowing northwards, is joined by the larger Shari, the combined streams merging into the waters of Lake Chad. The multitudinous tributaries of the Shari have their sources in a great arc of territory that stretches from Darfur to Adamawa; not far distant are streams that flow into two of the other great water systems of Africa, some southwards to the Congo, others eastwards to the Bahr-al-Ghazal and the White Nile. Chad is a large, shallow, fresh-water lake, not unlike one of the Norfolk Broads magnified many times and varying constantly in size. It is fed by one other river, the Komadugu Yobe, which enters from the west.

Of the westward-flowing rivers the longest is the Senegal, which rises not far from the Niger in the Futa Jallon massif, flows north-west to the edge of the desert, then due west to the coast; the largest of its tributaries is the Faleme, which enters it from the south. Roughly parallel in its course to the Senegal, but with two hundred miles between them, flows the Gambia, a mighty river as it enters the sea, but barely half the Senegal's length. Between the Gambia and the Niger numerous rivers empty their waters into the Atlantic. Only one of them is of considerable size, the Volta, whose three main sources, the Voltas Red, White and Black, rise in the area of the Niger's bend, six hundred miles from the coast. All the larger rivers of West Africa are easily navigable, at least by native craft; but most of them are broken by dangerous rapids. On the other hand, many of the smaller streams in the Sudan are completely dry for several months of the year, showing nothing but a sandy bed.

In northern Africa one can speak with reason of winter and summer. In January, when the western winds bring much rain, the average temperature is as cool as an English April and snow falls on the High Atlas; the summer months, by contrast, are dry and parching hot.

In Western Africa there is no summer and winter; the year is

7

divided into the wet season and the dry. The length of the season varies. One extreme may be found in the dreaded Tanezrouft, 'the region of thirst' in the central Sahara, where no rain has ever been known to fall, another in Debundscha on the western side of Cameroon Mountain, 'probably the wettest place in the world', where the average annual rainfall is over 400 inches. In the forest country there are only two Months in the year—December and January—when no rain is to be expected. An average of 45 inches falls at Ibadan in Western Nigeria, of 169 inches at Conakry in Guinea: these figures show how great a difference can exist between places lying within the same belt of territory. In the Sudan the dry season lasts between four and seven months, growing longer farther north. The rainfall also diminishes; yet it is remarkable how much rain is obtained in places often described by ignorant travellers as lying on the edge of the desert. Thus Kano, with 33 inches a year, has more rain than many parts of England. In Kano, as indeed over the whole of Western Africa, the rain comes not in gentle day-long drizzle but in sudden drenching downpours.

In the Sudan the dry season from October to April is the time for travelling, especially the months of December and January, when the *Harmattan* blows cold from the North and there is occasionally a nip in the early morning air—at its best something of the feel of a bright March day in Italy. When the rains come in April and May rivers suddenly rise in spate, marshy valleys turn into quagmires, mosquitos breed in their myriads and damps and sudden chills induce agues. But the Sudan is at its most beautiful during the rains—a verdant landscape played on by a lucid light, a contrast to the dusty browns of the dry season more dramatic than any the changing months in the greener lands of Europe can provide.

By those who have never been there, West Africa is usually regarded as being excessively hot. This is a misleading impression. Physically the heat of the tropics is no more of a hardship than the cold of temperate lands. There are, it should be remembered, great climatic variations within West Africa. In the forest belt the temperature is most unlikely ever to rise over 100° F, the average maximum being about 87° F. In the Sudan greater heat is experienced during the last months of the dry season, but in compensation there is a wider variation between night and day and between the dry season and the wet. In the desert the daily range is even more extreme, grilling days—extremes of over 130° F are reported—followed by cool, even icy nights. There is a profound difference in the quality of the heat. The sticky humidity of the forest country contrasts with the dryness of the Sudan, the intense desiccation of the desert. For Europeans the climate of West Africa has some disadvantages. It is undeniably monotonous and it cannot provide that crisply exhilarating air that adds vigour to life in the temperate zones. But in itself the climate is not dangerous to health.

For the 'unwholesomeness' of West Africa earlier writers blamed the climate. 'Do the impetuous torrents of water poured from the clouds during the rainy season in tropical countries contain what is unfriendly and injurious to health?... is the sickness of those seasons to be ascribed to the intense heat of the almost vertical sun?... is it not more probable, that as in some of those countries the earth for six or eight months of the year receives no moisture from the heavens but what falls to the ground in dews, the surface of the ground becomes hard and incrusted with a dry scurf, which pens up the vapours below, until, by the continuance of the rains for some time this crust is softened and the long pent-up vapours set free?' So in 1768 wrote James Lind, a naval surgeon with experience of the tropics and the author of a manual on tropical diseases that ran into many editions; his crescendo of questions expresses very well the contemporary spirit of baffled inquiry. The climate is to blame for the unhealthiness of West Africa, but less directly than Lind imagined. The warmth and the humidity of the tropics provide ideal breeding grounds for the microbes of horrible diseases—malaria, yellow fever, bilharzia, sleeping sickness—and for their insect vectors—the mosquito, the guinea worm, the tsetse fly. These were the unknown enemies that made the West Coast 'the White Man's Grave'. The West Coast was not the only part of the tropical world where Europeans died in their scores: Bengal, Bencoolen in Sumatra, Batavia in Java, some of the West Indian islands, part of the coast of Central America, where the Spaniards had named one of the rivers Rio de Morte—these all acquired sinister reputations. Yet West Africa surpassed every other region of the tropics in its tales of mortality. Two reasons could be suggested for this disparity: the lack of salubrious and easily accessible hill stations, such as other tropical lands possessed, and the inferior living conditions of the Europeans in their factories, forts and hulks along the coast.*[2]

* Professor P. D. Curtin has recently estimated that 'somewhere between 25 and 75 per cent of any group of Europeans newly arrived on the Coast

In North Africa Europeans of the eighteenth century were exposed to the same range of diseases as they had to face at home—with one alarming addition. The plague which had not reoccurred in England since 1665, was still a regular visitant, carrying off its victims in thousands.

THE PEOPLE

In the subtler variations of landscape and of climate the northern half of Africa cannot rival the fecund diversity of Europe; but in the variety of its people, no other comparable part of the world presents so striking a heterogeneity. Berber and Arab; Egyptian, Nubian, Beja; Tuareg, Tebu, Moor; Fulani, Wolof, Mandingo, Bambara, Mossi, Songhai; Hausa, Kanuri, Shuwa Arab, Wadayan, Fur; Baqqara, Nuba, Fung; Amhara, Galla, Somali; Susu, Mende, Akan, Ewe, Yoruba, Ibo, Ibibio. Even so brief a list of the principal peoples or 'tribes'—a complete roster would occupy pages—must appear to the reader extraordinarily confusing. There are good reasons for this confusion. In the first place most of the names are unfamiliar—an unfamiliarity that will strike Africans almost as much as Europeans; thus even today, when the opportunities for intercourse are infinitely greater than they were in the eighteenth century, a Yoruba in Ibadan or a Wolof in Dakar will probably never have heard mentioned such people as the Mossi of the Upper Volta or the Fur of Darfur. About such ignorance there is nothing surprising; how many people in England could chart the ethnography of the Balkans? In Europe, and to a large extent in Asia, nations have come to take their name from the largest group within their frontiers—England is the land of the English, Turkey of the Turks, Malaya of the Malays. Over most of Africa there exist no such convenient national groupings. Almost every

(in the eighteenth century) died within the first year. Thereafter, the death rate was much less perhaps on the order of 10 per cent per annum, but still substantial'. The basic reason for the higher mortality of West Africa— 'roughly four times as high as in India or the West Indies'—lies in the fact that 'virtually the whole of West Africa was and is still an extremely favorable environment for the mosquitoes, *Anopheles gambiae* and *Anopheles funestus*. Both are among the most effective vectors for carrying plasmodial parasites from one person to another ... *Plasmodium falciparum*, the prevalent West African parasite, is also especially dangerous, since it often kills in the first attack, while the *P. vivax* of the West Indies is more often enervating than fatal.'[3]

10

independent state or colony in Africa, its frontiers originally demarc-
ated by outsiders, contains within itself a mosaic of different 'tribes'.
Thus today, to take a particularly striking example, the Northern
Region of the Federation of Nigeria contains in its population
members of more than one hundred different tribal groups.*

To the uninitiated the very word *tribe* can be misleading. It is used,
reasonably enough, to describe those groups that may be found
among a nomadic people, where the members of each group are
bound together by a common ancestry; but it is also applied, at least
in popular usage, to people such as the Hausa or the Yoruba, who
number many million and contain within themselves the relics of
many kingdoms. A word stretched to contain such diversity becomes
meaningless. Nevertheless, one can reasonably talk of 'tribal consciousness', of the sense of belonging to some particular group of
people, who have their own name for themselves and who feel themselves different from their neighbours by reason of language or religion or social structure or custom or by a combination of all these
factors. About such 'tribal consciousness' there is nothing specifically
African. Europe was once covered with 'tribal' groups nor, even in
the twentieth century, has 'tribal' feeling completely disappeared. Ask
a Welshman what he thinks about the English, sound a Bavarian's
views on the North Germans, consider the suspicion with which an
'outsider' is regarded in any rural community. Yet in Europe centuries of increasingly centralized administration have served to wear
down local differences; over most parts of Africa such a highly
evolved system of government has only recently been established.
Local differences still flourish; since Africa physically is so much
bigger than Europe, there are inevitably more of them. The quickest
way to see the variety of people any one country may contain is to take
a stroll round one of its great markets—in Kano, for instance, or

* A minor source of confusion arises from the fact that African peoples
are called by a variety of names. Thus the widely scattered people who call
themselves *Fulbe* are called by the French, adopting a Wolof form, *Peul*,
by the Bambara *Fula*, a form also used in Sierra Leone, by the Kanuri
Fellata, by the Hausa *Filani* and by the British in Northern Nigeria *Fulani*.
Soninke or *Sarakole*, *Mandingo* or *Malinke*, *Bambara* or *Bamana*—these
are only a few examples of the variations to be encountered. To them must
be added differences in spelling; thus *Tibu* or *Tubu* are possible variations
of *Tebu*, though the people call themselves either *Teda* or *Daza*. A European
reader will find this less strange if he reflects that the expressions *Deutsch-
land, L'Allemagne* and *Germany* all refer to the same country.

Accra or Marrakesh. To comprehend this variety, one must fall drily back on classification.

The first and most obvious distinction is one of skin colour and physique. There is a sharp contrast between the blacks and the whites. The whites are the people of North Africa, Egyptians, Arabs and Berbers, the latter including the Tuareg and the Moors; to them should be added the pastoral Fulani of the Sudan. White is, of course, an imprecise term—if Northern Europeans are pinkish-grey, North Africans are olive-coloured; but a light skin carries with it a strange cachet of superiority. The people of the Forest and many of the people of the Sudan are very dark, though never, perhaps, absolutely black—chocolate-coloured would be a more exact description; but in any large group a great range of complexions, with some lighter variations, may be found. Some groups, especially in Ethiopia and countries on its borders, are neither black nor white, but brown—or rather, bronze, copper or coffee. Skin-colour is only one, though the most immediately striking, of physical differences: stature, the shape of the lips, the form of the head, the hair, the nose—all these points help to distinguish people one from another. Thus the people of the Forest tend to be shorter and stockier, with broader noses and with spiralled hair, the people of the Sudan taller, the people of the desert thinner and more wiry, with straight hair, straight noses and thin lips. The traveller in Africa soon finds himself able to recognize these physical differences.

After physique, language. Philologists have come to distinguish two great language families in Northern and Western Africa. One, for which the terms Afro-asiatic or Hamito-Semitic have been invented, embraces Arabic, Amharic, Somali, Berber and Hausa; the other, now named Nigritic or Niger-Congo, includes the great variety of languages spoken between the Atlantic Coast and the Congo—and indeed beyond, for the Bantu languages are regarded as being only a branch of this family. Certain linguistic groups have resisted this great work of simplifying classification; thus there appears to be a Central Saharan group of languages, which includes both Kanuri and Tebu, with no apparent relationship to the Afro-asiatic group which surrounds it. But this analysis, unless carried much further to points of grammar, tone and vocabulary, is not of much assistance to the European traveller; within one language family differences will be as great as those between English and Italian or Greek and Polish. More relevant to note those languages which have developed into

12

lingua franca. Of these the most important is Arabic. In North Africa, from Egypt to Morocco, this language has become the mother-tongue of the great majority of the population; today only a quarter of the people of the Maghrib speak Berber. In the western Sudan the Moors—themselves a mixture of Arab, Berber and Negro elements—have adopted Arabic completely; in the eastern Sudan, from the Shuwa Arabs who live round Lake Chad to the tribes of the Red Sea coast, Arabic is the dominant language. For the rest of the Sahara and the Sudan the position of Arabic in the eighteenth century was not unlike that of Latin in medieval Europe. Those who travelled to North Africa or to Mecca had the opportunity of acquiring a fluent knowledge; learned men were able to maintain a sometimes stilted conversation; many Arabic words had been absorbed into the vernaculars; but the language itself was incomprehensible for the mass of the people. In the Sudan certain other languages had come to be widely understood: Mande or Mandingo with its various dialects in the western Sudan, Songhai on the Niger Bend, Hausa in the central Sudan, Kanuri round Lake Chad. But there was no *lingua franca*, until the introduction of the languages of the European powers, to bridge the gap between the Sudan and the Forest.

The spread of Arabic was intimately connected with the expansion of Islam. Between A.D. 640 and 730 the irresistible armies of the Caliphate had borne their religion across Christian North Africa and on into Spain. Later, Muslim traders carried the creed southwards along the trade-routes of the Sahara to the countries of the Sudan. Inevitably, therefore, it was the people living in the northern belt of the Sudan, from the Wolof on the Senegal to the Fung in Sennar, who came to be most strongly influenced by the new religion. Yet in Western Africa the contrast has never been between a broad mass of Muslims on the one side, of pagans on the other. Some people living in the Sudan—the Bambara, for instance, or the Mossi—have spurned Islam for centuries. Indeed, even today, when the faith is more widely diffused than it was two hundred years ago, no group of people living west of Lake Chad can be accurately described as entirely Muslim. Thus among the Fulani, some of those who settled in the towns became the most ardent protagonists of the faith, while others, following the ancestral pattern of tending cattle in the bush, remained pagan. The practice of religion was more strictly observed in the towns—especially in such centres of learning as Jenne, Timbuktu or Katsina—and among the upper classes. Yet, at the end of

13

the eighteenth century, in kingdoms whose rulers were professing Muslims, ancestral pagan rites might still be officially sanctioned.

Even where the tenets of the faith appeared to have been only superficially adopted, Islam had the power to introduce striking changes into the life of its converts. They acquired the knowledge of an alphabet and therefore the prestige of literacy; they took to a white cotton robe, where before they might have been content to go semi-naked; if wealthy enough, they might adopt a new style of architecture, replacing the traditional round mud hut with its conical thatch by a square, flat-roofed structure, sometimes crowned with a skilfully wrought dome of mud. Thus, even to an outsider, the distinction between an Islamized and a pagan people was immediately apparent.

Equally obvious was the distinction resulting from different physical environments. The desert, the plains of the Sudan, the rain forest, each produced its own characteristic way of life. In the desert, away from the oases, a scanty population derived its wealth from its herds of camels or of goats, supplemented by raiding neighbours or by guiding caravans. Some of those who lived in the Sudan were also nomads, notably the pastoral Fulani, but the great majority were peasant cultivators. So, too, were the people of the Forest; yet there was a world of difference in the agricultural life of the two regions. In the forest, agriculture was an occupation to be followed all the year round, the plots rough clearings, growing yams or cassava or maize with oil-palms or bananas growing above them. In the Sudan, farming was restricted by the length of the dry season; the holdings usually the untidy furrows of shifting cultivators, but in the more densely populated areas round the larger towns regularly manured fields, in the hilly country roughly terraced strips, in marshy valleys irrigated plots. Each region had its own characteristic style of dwelling: in the desert, tents made of leather; in the Sudan, except in the most strongly Islamized centres, the round hut with roof of straw; in the Forest, a rectangular-shaped house with gabled roof made from bark or leaves. So, too, each region possessed its own distinctive craft, camel-hair weaving or leather-work or wood-carving.

There still exist today parts of the world where one may feel that the mode of life has change little in the last two centuries. Only in the remotest parts of Europe—and nowhere in England—can the traveller have this experience. But in Africa, away from the towns created by Europeans, it is possible to see almost everywhere the past pre-

14

served in the present. Peasants hoeing their fields, women carrying water from a stream, a hunter setting out with his bow and his dog, the crowds at a village market, a great man, splendidly robed and mounted, surrounded by his retainers—images such as these are immensely stimulating to the imagination of the historian. But Africa is changing fast, even as Europe has changed. Nowhere, in this age of African Revolution, is the change more marked than in the field of politics. To understand the political geography of African states two hundred years ago, one must begin by casting completely out of the mind the pattern drawn on the map during the age of European imperialism.

II

THE STATES OF NORTHERN AND WESTERN AFRICA IN THE EIGHTEENTH CENTURY

THE POLITICAL GEOGRAPHY OF AFRICA during the eighteenth century was as complicated as its ethnography. Yet one should not think that there was anything essentially African in such complexity; Europe itself in that age did not fall into the relatively simple pattern of modern nation states. Think of the galaxy of petty principalities that made up a large part of Germany, of the varied nationalities under Habsburg or Turkish rule, of Russia and its uncertain borderland to the east. All these political phenomena—small city-states, wide-flung, loosely united empires, uncharted frontiers—were to be found in a form not essentially different in North and West Africa. Yet the African pattern was made still more involved by the existence of societies for which, if one seeks a Western European parallel, it is necessary to go back to the Dark Ages or to pre-Roman times—groups of nomads or small settled communities, living in the bush or forest, on the marshy borders of rivers or lakes, or on isolated hilltops, in complete independence, owing allegiance to no man.

It is misleading to push the comparison with eighteenth-century Europe too far. In technology, in scholarship or in art, there were great differences between African societies. Morocco and Egypt, for example, had evolved styles of architecture to which the kingdoms of the Sudan or the Forest—partly perhaps for lack of the right building materials—could show nothing to compare. Even more significant was the fact that the cities of North Africa had behind them over a thousand years of a highly literate culture, while the people of the Forest were still living in pre-literate societies. Yet no part of Africa had evolved that dynamic of technological invention and economic change that was transforming the face of contemporary

16

Europe and making possible the achievements of a wonderfully rich and varied culture.

Of the five states of North Africa, only Morocco was strictly independent; the others, Algiers, Tunis, Tripoli and Egypt, were, at least nominally, under Turkish suzerainty. Morocco's boundaries were much the same as they are today; but with the great mass of the Atlas mountains running down its centre, the rulers of the country have always had to struggle against a geography that encourages fragmentation and disunity. The periods of peace and order have been broken by long stretches of 'anarchy'. One period of comparative calm occurred at the beginning of the eighteenth century with the reign of Mulay Ismail, a ferocious despot notorious in European eyes for the size of his harem—he sired over a thousand children—and for his attempt to build a palace to rival Versailles. His death in 1727 was followed by a time of troubles, terrible enough, according to Muslim historians, 'to whiten the hair of babes'. Murderous family quarrels, in which descendants of Ismail's Negro palace guard took a prominent part, undermined the power of the throne, and made it easy for the untamed Berber tribes of the mountains to press down on to the fertile plains of the Atlantic coast. Not until the reign of Sidi Muhammad (1759–90) was some semblance of order restored.[1]

East of Morocco lay the state of Algiers, blackened in the eyes of Europe by the piracy carried on by its inhabitants.* In the first half of the sixteenth century the sea ports of the Barbary coast were occupied by Turkish corsairs, in response to an appeal from the inhabitants to drive out the Spanish garrison established in their midst. For the next three centuries the Turks of Algiers remained as a governing class distinct from the Berber–Arab majority. For a century they accepted Pashas sent by the Porte, later they elected Deys from their own ranks and removed them when they showed signs of growing too oppressive. Algiers was forced to look to the sea for its wealth, but piracy, at its most successful during the seventeenth century, was a declining source of profit, the number of prizes falling sharply as the strength of European navies increased. In the interior only about a sixth of the present area of the country was under Turkish control,

* Piracy was carried on by all the maritime nations of Europe. It may be argued that the English, having more scope, were even more successful pirates than the Algerines. The practice of using prisoners as galley slaves was carried on with quite as much brutality by the French as by the Algerines.[2]

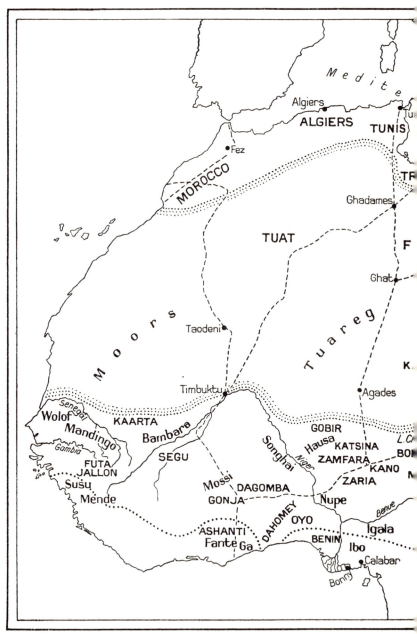

1. The States and Peoples of Northern

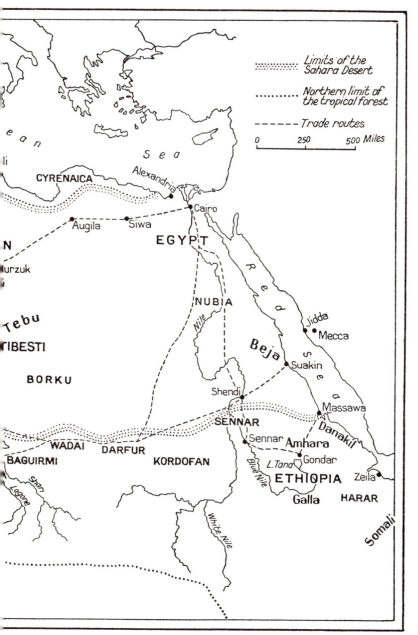

Legend:
- Limits of the Sahara Desert
- Northern limit of the tropical forest
- Trade routes

0   250   500 Miles

Sea

CYRENAICA   Alexandria

N   Augila   Siwa   Cairo

urzuk   EGYPT

Tebu   NUBIA   Red

TIBESTI   Beja   Jidda
                                         Mecca
BORKU   Suakin

              Shendi   Massawa
                        SENNAR   Danakil
WADAI   DARFUR   KORDOFAN   Sennar   Amhara
BAGUIRMI   L.Tana   Gondar
                                ETHIOPIA   Zeila
                        Galla   HARAR

Nile   Blue Nile   White Nile   Shari   Logone   Somali

stern Africa in the Eighteenth Century

19

held down by armed garrisons. In the hinterland to the south, the villages of the Aures, the nomadic tribes of the high Plateau, the maraboutic communities on the edge of the desert lived in complete independence.

In Tunis and in Tripoli, cities more congenial to Christians than the seaports of Algiers, the Turks were gradually absorbed into the population. In both countries dynasties founded by families of Turkish descent—the Husainid Deys in Tunis, the Karamanli Pashas in Tripoli—established themselves at the beginning of the eighteenth century and became virtually independent of the Porte. Tunis, hemmed in by Algiers to the west and by the desert to the south, remained a small country. But from Tripoli the Karamanlis, during the course of the eighteenth century, asserted their power over the tribes of the interior, the towns of Cyrenaica and even over the distant oasis kingdom of the Fezzan; yet it was never easy to hold in check the Bedouin tribes of the desert, and revolts were frequent.

If Tripoli suffered on occasion from the depredations of the Bedouin, the rich and populous provinces of Egypt formed for the desert tribes a much more tempting raiding ground. Conflict between the desert and the sown on the borders of the Nile Valley can be traced back to the dawn of recorded history; so long as there was an effective ruler in Egypt, the raiders could be resisted, but during the eighteenth century the country was suffering from the decay of Ottoman rule. Effective control was slipping into the hands of the Mamluk Beys, most of whom were of Caucasian descent. The quarrels of the Mamluks among themselves or with the Turkish Pashas, together with the menace of Bedouin attack, were grave causes of disorder, but sufficient power still remained in the hands of the traditional bureaucracy to prevent the country from falling completely to pieces.

The boundaries of Egypt reached nominally at least as far south as Aswan. Beyond, along the valley of the Nile, lay the country usually referred to as Nubia. Its people, settled there for millennia, were strongly influenced both in blood and in culture by the Arab tribes who for centuries past had been crossing the Red Sea or seeping down from Egypt. East of the Nile, amid the barren Red Sea Hills, moved the turbulent Beja, camel nomads differing in race and in language from the Arabs but not uninfluenced by Islamic culture. In the two most important ports of the African coast of the Red Sea, Suakin and Massawa, Turkish sovereignty, established in the sixteenth century, was still, albeit shakily, maintained.

All the states of Northern Africa from Tr\. bordered and limited by the Great Desert that 、 those other states, not incomparable in size, that la the Sudan. But the desert was not simply a ba. Several hundred thousand people—nomadic trit dwellers, caravan merchants—having their home there, their own response to that cruel environment. Among th、 four distinct groups could be recognized; the Bedouin Arat north, the Moors in the west, the Tuareg in the central Sahaι and the Tebu in the east, each group being composed of a great variety of different tribes. The Arabs were not the descendants of the original conquerors of the Maghrib in the eighth century but of those fero-cious Bedouin, the Banu Hilal and the Banu Sulaim, launched so devastatingly against the kingdoms of North Africa by the Fatimid Caliphs in the eleventh century. Some of the Arabs had mixed with the Berber tribes of the western Sahara to form the people now called Moors, whose acceptance of the Arabic language disguises the fact that they are mainly of Berber blood. The Tuareg are also a Berber people, who have been forced slowly southward in the course of the last two thousand years. Arabs, Moors and Tuareg are essentially light-skinned people and therefore quite different from the dark Tebu, who seem, at least in part, to be the descendants of some ancient Saharan race.

Moor, Tuareg and Tebu had all felt the lure of the easier environ-ment of the Sudan; some of their tribes, indeed, being driven south-ward, had taken to agriculture and slowly become absorbed, even to the loss of the most distinctive of their physical characteristics, among the larger Negro population of the settled zone. The tribes that remained in the desert based themselves on those massifs that caught a little rain and so provided grazing land for camels; thus Tibesti became a stronghold for the Tebu, Hoggar, Air and Adrar of the Iforas for the Tuareg, the Adrar of Mauretania for the Moors. Toughened by their harsh surroundings, grown rapacious through poverty, possessing exceptional mobility in their camels, all the desert tribes turned to raiding to supplement their meagre resources. The Tebu raided as far eastwards as the Nile, the Tuareg struck at all the lands between Timbuktu and Lake Chad, the Moors harried the banks of the Senegal; at the same time every tribe was prepared to make war on its neighbour or to attack any ill-protected caravan that passed through its territory.

21

arious well-trodden trade-routes led across the desert. From Morocco the direct route to Timbuktu, the most important commercial centre in the western Sudan, lay across long and desolate stretches of *erg* and *reg*, but had the advantage of passing through the salt mines of Teghaza and of Taodeni, whose product was a vital commodity in the trade with the Sudan. For traders from Tripoli and Tunis the most convenient route to Timbuktu lay through the oasis of Tuat. In the central Sahara an easier but still arduous route ran south from Tripoli to the Fezzan and on, by way of the Kawar oasis, to Bornu. From Bornu traders could pass without difficulty to the cities of Hausaland. An alternative route ran from Tripoli to Ghat, thence through the mountains of Hoggar and Air to Agades, Katsina and Kano. From the Fezzan a little-used route ran along the western flank of Tibesti to Wadai, the direct north–south route between Kufra and Wadai not coming into use until the beginning of the nineteenth century. Finally, Egypt was linked to Darfur by the *Darb-al-Arba'in*, 'the forty days' road', that left the Nile at Asyut and struck diagonally across the desert.

Though wells were to be found in the middle of the Sahara, the larger oases all lay towards the northern or southern ends of the trade-routes. The oases served both as trading centres and as victualling stations, their water making possible the cultivation of date-palms, of cereals and of some vegetables. Several of the North African oases, such as Ghadames, Ghat or Wargla, had developed into rich little towns, independent republics of merchants, desert Hamburgs. Murzuk was the capital of the kingdom of the Fezzan. Agades, then in decline, had once been a wealthy place. On the other hand, Bilma, the largest place in the Kawar oasis, though famous for its salt, was a miserable straggling village, while Taodeni was to be reckoned as possibly the most desolate place regularly inhabited by man, the poor wretches sent to work at the salt mines being dependent on passing caravans for their food and dying of hunger when the caravans failed to arrive. All the oases possessed a mixed population, the manual work invariably being performed by the large class of Negro slaves.

The trans-Saharan trade was controlled by merchants from North Africa, some of whom had come to settle in the principal towns of the Sudan. They dealt in a remarkable variety of goods: salt from the desert mines, from North Africa and Egypt embroidered dresses, copperware, perfume and occasionally horses, together with many things of European manufacture, printed cottons and silks from

France or from England, beads from Venice, paper and cutlery from Nuremberg and much else beside. These were exchanged for slaves and gold, gum, senna, ivory and ostrich feathers. By the middle of the eighteenth century slaves were the Sudan's most valuable export —though the Saharan slave trade was conducted on a much smaller scale than the trade across the Atlantic; but it was the trade in gold that had for centuries excited the imagination and the cupidity of the Mediterranean world. Gold, found in alluvial deposits or shallow mines, occurred at a number of widely separated areas in West Africa: Bambuk, lying between the Faleme and the Upper Senegal; Bure on the Upper Niger; Lobi on the Upper Volta; Ashanti and other countries in the hinterland of the Gold Coast; and in the valley of the Zamfara River in Hausa country.*

In the past three great empires, Ghana, Mali and Songhai, had risen in the western Sudan; but the last and the most powerful of them all, the Songhai Empire, had been shattered by an army sent across the desert from Morocco at the end of the sixteenth century. In the eighteenth century the most extensive state in the whole Sudan was the Empire of Bornu whose ruling dynasty, the Sefuwa, could trace their lineage back over a thousand years. The centre of Sefuwa power had originally lain in Kanem, north-east of Lake Chad; driven from their homeland in the fourteenth century, the Sefuwa had re-established their kingdom in Bornu, west of the Lake. Bornu had reached the height of its power in the sixteenth century; two hundred years later it was showing signs of weakness and decline, but the Empire still possessed great prestige, its supremacy being acknowledged by some of the Hausa kingdoms on its western borders. South of Lake Chad and at the northern tip of the Cameroon mountains lay

* The name *Wangara* came to be applied to most of the gold-bearing areas of the Sudan. Wangara was first mentioned by the twelfth-century Arab geographer, al-Idrisi. He described it as an island three hundred miles long and one hundred and fifty broad, being surrounded and regularly inundated by the waters of the 'Nile of the Sudan'. It seems likely that al-Idrisi's Wangara is to be identified with the alluvial deposits of either Bure or Bambuk, both of which are partially surrounded by rivers. Four hundred years later Leo Africanus produced the report of another Wangara on the borders of the Hausa state of Zamfara; this was probably a reference to the gold deposits in the valley of the River Zamfara. The two Wangaras of al-Idrisi and of Leo were more than a thousand miles apart, but European cartographers assumed that there was only one country of that name. By attempting to equate the two places they added greatly to their own confusion.[3]

Mandara, a kingdom small in size but strong enough to maintain its independence against Bornu.

East of Mandara, across the River Shari, were the territories of Bornu's most powerful rival, Baguirmi, a kingdom founded in the sixteenth century. Three hundred miles to the eastward lay another considerable state, the kingdom of Wadai. Until the middle of the eighteenth century, Wadai recognized the overlordship of Darfur. The heart of the kingdom of Darfur lay in the mountains, the Jebel Marra; its armies raided to the west, to the south and to the east, into the plains of Kordofan, where roamed the Baqqara Arabs with their camels and their cattle. To the east of Kordofan, between the White Nile and the Blue, lay Sennar, founded in the early sixteenth century; its ruling dynasty came from a people of mixed Arab and Negro ancestry known as the Fung. In the first half of the century Sennar's influence spread out over a wide radius; in the 1770s there began a period of desolating civil war that presaged the kingdom's utter ruin.

The Christian kingdom of Ethiopia, isolated on its high plateau, was a much smaller state that its modern boundaries would suggest. With its capital at Gondar, the Empire was confined to the three provinces of Tigre, Amhara and Gojam. The course of its history during the eighteenth century was not unlike Morocco's: after the death of a strong ruler, Iyasu I, in 1706, there followed a period of disorder that lasted many generations, real power lying not with the shadowy Emperors on the throne of Solomon but in the hands of the great provincial chiefs and military commanders. The southern half of the plateau was being increasingly settled by the Galla, originally a nomadic people who were being driven out of their grazing grounds in the Horn of Africa by the Somali. The Somali and the Danakil commanded the dry, hot plains of the Red Sea coast. There were a number of small Muslim sultanates in this area and two important towns, Harar and its port, Zeila.

To the south of all these kingdoms from Bornu to Ethiopia lay a mosaic of small independent tribes, untouched by Islam and therefore lumped together by Arab travellers and dismissed as cannibals. In fact, there was great variety among these people. Some of them, the Chamba, for instance, on the Upper Benue or the Shilluk on the White Nile, had created complex political organisations; others, following a very simple life in isolated villages or hamlets, had been forced back into mountainous or marshy country by the raids of their better-armed and more mobile neighbours to the north.

West of Bornu lay the galaxy of the Hausa states. The Hausa people, builders of cities, skilful farmers, shrewd merchants, had never united to form one great empire but were divided into many different kingdoms. Six could be distinguished in the eighteenth century: Kano, Katsina, Zaria, Zamfara, Kebbi and Gobir. The hegemony passed in the course of the century from Kebbi to Zamfara and then to Gobir. South of Hausaland and separated from it by a belt of territory occupied by a variety of more primitive peoples lay the ancient kingdom of Yauri and, on the opposite bank of the Niger, the city states of Borgu. Farther downstream lay the cities of the Nupe, joined by the eighteenth century into one kingdom, and of the Igbirra. Along the lower Benue the Jukun people had established a widely flung but loosely held empire, now entering into decline. The influence of all these different principalities was felt by their more backward neighbours, some of whom came to be absorbed into their way of life.

The great empire of the Songhais, the most powerful West African state in the sixteenth century, had been built up along the line of the Niger, the centre of its power lying on the river's bend between the cities of Gao and Timbuktu. In 1590 the empire was overthrown by a Moroccan army sent across the desert. After their cataclysmic defeat the remnants of the Songhai nobility retreated down the Niger and established a number of petty states on the right bank of the river. The descendants of the victorious Moroccan soldiery, many of them not Moors but Iberian renegades, were still to be found in the cities of Gao, Jenne and Timbuktu, where they formed a distinct caste known as the Arma. But control of their cities had passed into other hands, the Tuareg dominating Gao and Timbuktu, the Bambara Jenne.

There were two Bambara kingdoms in the eighteenth century, Segu and Kaarta, both founded after the break up of the Songhai empire. By 1750 Segu, astride the upper reaches of the Niger, had become the most powerful state in the western Sudan. Kaarta lay to the north-west, nearer to the desert; despite the ties of blood, wars between the two kingdoms were frequent during the century. To the east of Segu lay another galaxy of states, partly inhabited by the Mossi people: Yatenga, Wagadugu, Gurma, Mamprussi and Dagomba. The Fulani people were to be found with their cattle in most of the countries in the western Sudan; they had also come to form two considerable states—Futa Toro to the south of the Senegal and Futa Jallon in the

25

hills among which the Niger has its source. In between the two Futas, in the country of the Senegal and the Gambia, were a number of small kingdoms, Bondou, Wuli, Kasson, Kayor and others, created by the Wolof, the Sarakole and the Mandingo.

As powerful as any of the states of the Sudan were the kingdoms of the Forest. Of these the greatest, as it was also the most ancient, was the Yoruba kingdom of Oyo, at the height of its power in the eighteenth century. In the same period Oyo's western neighbours, Ashanti and Dahomey, were both expanding states, fighting to win for themselves a footing on the sea coast, so that they could deal directly and more profitably with the European slave traders. Benin, so prosperous when Europeans had first visited it at the end of the fifteenth century, was in decline, worn out by many wars. Farther east, in the Niger Delta and beyond, lay the city states of Brass and Warri, Bonny and Calabar, small in territory but rich from trade. Behind them lay the densely populated Ibo country, whose many independent communities were linked together and given an underlying unity by ties of trade and religion. Two hundred miles up the Niger lay the kingdom of Idah founded by the Igala. To the west of the Delta lay a chain of small principalities from Lagos and Whydah to the Fante states of the Gold Coast. The stretch of country between the Gold Coast and the Gambia, including the Ivory and the Grain Coasts and Sierra Leone, was more thinly populated, its peoples more isolated and therefore more backward.

Compared with the vigorous states of the Maghrib, the Sudan and the Forest, European establishments in Northern and Western Africa seemed remarkably weak. In the course of the eighteenth century the Portuguese were forced to surrender the last of their strongholds in North Africa, the Spaniards to withdraw from all but two of their bases. On the West Coast, the French, the English, the Dutch, the Portuguese and one or two minor powers maintained their forts, their factories or their hulks as bases for trade, through which there passed in increasing numbers African slaves to cultivate the plantations of the New World from Virginia to Brazil. Both African middlemen and European merchants drew their profits from the trade, but the Europeans held their establishments on sufferance from African rulers. Here, as over the whole of Northern Africa, effective power still lay in the hands of Africans.

III

AFRICAN IDEAS ABOUT EUROPE

WEAK THOUGH THE POSITION of Europeans in eighteenth-century Africa might be, their impact over the previous three centuries had been sufficiently strange, dramatic and powerful to have left a profound impression on the minds of those Africans who knew or heard about them. Most of this study will be taken up with European ideas about Africa; to achieve a truer understanding of the complexity of events, it is essential to adopt for a time another viewpoint, to see how Europe looked through African eyes.

It is impossible, of course, to make any simple generalizations. A sea-captain from Algiers, a Sherif from Morocco, a Muslim nobleman from Bornu, a Bambara peasant, a trader from Calabar, an Ibo slave—each of them would have formed a different image of the white men from over the seas. Moreover, these images were not static: the first impression of white on black would change with the years, as more intimate intercourse brought deeper experience. Thus there was a fundamental difference between North and West Africa in the impression created by Europeans. In West Africa no white man had ever been seen before the middle of the fifteenth century, and still in most parts of the country white men were unknown. In North Africa links with the people living on the other side of the Mediterranean, links formed through trade, war or conquest, could be traced back over three millennia. Moreover, just as in physical appearance North Africans were more closely akin to Europeans, so also in material development the gap between them was less great; indeed, in some respects parts of North Africa were more highly developed than parts of Europe. Thus North Africans never had reason to feel that instinct of inferiority which the presence, or at least the first sight, of Europeans might induce in the inhabitants of West Africa.

There was another important difference between the two parts of the continent: to West Africa Europeans had come mainly as traders, North Africa they had invaded with their armies. Consequently, in West Africa despite the slave trade, relations between Africans and Europeans were rather less strained.

For in North Africa, from Egypt to Morocco, the attitude to Europeans most commonly expressed was one of loathing and contempt. Europeans ascribed this attitude to Muslim 'fanaticism' and pride: in fact, it was the product of bitter historical memories of Christian aggression reaching back to the time of the Crusades.* Thus in Algiers an observer noted that the people showed themselves 'most inveterate against the Spaniards and Portuguese as the treacherous Usurpers of Countries formerly belonging to their Ancestors'. At the same time the presence of Christian slaves in large numbers helped to confirm the disdain which every Muslim might feel for an unbeliever: 'the Algerines, being accustomed from their Infancy, to see Slaves of all Nations, easily contract an Opinion that other People are, by Nature, designed for Servitude; this naturally tends to raise in them the utmost Contempt of all Foreigners'.[1]

In Tunis and in Tripoli Europeans were regarded with less open aversion than in Morocco or Algiers; but the Bedouin tribes of Tripolitania 'hated the name of a Christian'. 'They have not lost sight of the cause which produced that hatred in their predecessors, who were provoked by the injustice and cruelty of the crusades, when the blood of their countrymen was indiscriminately shed for following the standard of Mahomet, and since which the name of a Christian is held in abhorrence in the different countries of the Levant. The uncivilized part of their communities throughout Africa and Asia have confirmed with their latest breath their hatred to their children. Seven hundred years have not obliterated from the unlettered mind of the Arab, that agriculture, commerce, and the fine arts, were buried by the Christians under the wreck of the Saracenic empire'.[2]

This statement was made in the 1780s by an English lady, the sister-in-law of the British Consul, Richard Tully, who had lived for ten years in Tripoli. The same opinion was expressed by the Danish traveller, Carl Niebuhr, who visited Egypt in the 1760s. 'The Turks in general hate Europeans; probably from an indistinct remem-

* Christians could, of course, recall equally bloody memories of Muslim aggression from the seventh century onwards. In the late seventeenth century Central Europe had been ravaged by Turkish armies.

28

brance of the bloody wars which they have at different times waged with the inhabitants of the west. Children are, with them, as much terrified at the name of European, as with us at the name of the Turk.' Niebuhr had the advantage of being able to contrast the attitude of the Egyptians with that of the Muslims of Arabia and the Persian Gulf. 'In Yemen, Oman and Persia,' he discovered, 'an European is treated with as much civility as a Mahometan would find in Europe.' 'The Arabians,' he concluded, 'having never had any quarrels with the inhabitants of Europe, have not the same reasons for viewing them with aversion.' Between Muslims and Christians religion was not then in this period a fundamental cause of conflict. On the other hand, the part that religion could play in promoting tension was shown by the experience of European Christians in the Christian kingdom of Ethiopia.[3]

During the sixteenth century Europeans were welcomed in Ethiopia; their numbers increased greatly. But when in the early seventeenth century the Jesuits tactlessly used their influence to persuade the Emperor to adopt Catholic practices they precipitated a revolt in which national and religious feelings were fused. All Europeans were expelled from the country, whereupon some of the Ethiopians, so a contemporary historian recorded, 'ran about, Singing for joy, Chanting forth the following lines.

> At length the Sheep of Ethiopia free'd
>   From the Bold Lyons of the West,
> Securely in their Pastures feed.
>   St Mark and Cyril's Doctrine have o'recome
> The Folly's of the Church of Rome.
>   Rejoyce, Rejoyce, Sing Hallelujahs all
>   No more the Western Wolves
>   Our Ethiopia shall enthrall.

Thereafter, as later European travellers discovered, the Ethiopians became notorious for their xenophobia.[4]

In West Africa a different range of attitudes was to be encountered. By a piece of singular good fortune the narrative of a voyage made to the Senegal in the 1450s by a young Venetian, Cadamosto, contains an account of the African reaction to the very first appearance of white men in West Africa, an account which Cadamosto obtained from the first African slaves to be carried to Lisbon. 'When the negroes first saw the sails of vessels on the sea, they were of the opinion that they were large birds with white wings, and had flown thither from some foreign country; but when their sails were furled, from the distance they saw them at, they believed them to be fishes. Other supposed they were spectres and expressed great fear of them; probably because they made their excursions in the night time, and were seen from the coast the next day a hundred miles distant.' Magical beings, so again and again to those Africans, untouched by the wider knowledge and greater sophistication that came from an adherence to Islam, the first Europeans were to appear, reasonably as strange as creatures from outer space would be to our own generation.[5]

For Africans living on the coast the strange magic of that first encounter soon disappeared, as they came to make the acquaintance of the white man through many different roles, slave, concubine, trading partner or landlord. Indeed, there were few parts of the world where so vigorous and intimate an intercourse between European and non-European was maintained as on the West Coast of Africa. In all the main trading centres, in Senegal, on the Gold Coast, in Whydah or in Calabar, there were many Africans who had acquired the smattering of a European language and taken to some items of European dress; a few had mastered the art of writing—an African businessman in Calabar was keeping a diary in pidgin English at the close of the eighteenth century—and built for themselves houses designed and furnished in the European style.

The Europeans who visited West Africa were far from being the most impressive representatives of their various nations. Most of them had a stake in the slave trade, a traffic that coarsened its participants. Harsh judgements were passed on those hard-drinking sea-captains, those seedy European factors. 'With a few exceptions, the English and the Africans, reciprocally, consider each other as consummate villains, who are always watching opportunities to do mischief'. So wrote John Newton, who had been captain of a slave-ship, before becoming one of the most vigorous opponents of the slave trade. 'In short,' he added, 'we have, I fear too deservedly, a very unfavourable character upon the coast.' 'The poor Africans,' wrote Mungo Park, after living among the Muslim Mandingo, 'whom we affect to consider as barbarians, look upon us, I fear, as little better than a race of formidable but ignorant heathens.' 'The discerning Natives,' one white trader recorded, 'account it the greatest Unhappiness that they were ever visited by Europeans. They say we Christians introduced the Traffick of Slaves and that before our coming they liv'd in peace; but, say they, it is observable that where-ever Christianity comes, there comes with it a Sword, a Gun, Powder and Ball.'[6]

Repulsive though many individual white men might appear, their technically superior culture retained for many Africans its strangeness and its attractions. But how was the technical superiority of white over black to be explained? Only, most Africans must have thought, by supernatural causes. So legends developed, one of which, common on the Gold Coast and in Ashanti in the early nineteenth century, has been recorded.

> In the beginning of the world, God created three white and three black men, with the same number of women; he resolved, that they might not afterwards complain, to give them the choice of good and evil. A large box or calabash was set on the ground, with a piece of paper, sealed up, on one side of it. God gave the black men their first choice, who took the box, expecting it contained every thing, but on opening it there appeared only a piece of gold, a piece of iron, and several other metals, of which they did not know the use. The white men opening the paper, it told them every thing. God left the blacks in the bush, but conducted the whites to the waterside (for this happened in Africa), communicated with them every night, and taught them to build a small ship which carried them to another country, when they returned after a long period, with various merchandize to barter with the blacks, who might have been the superior people.[7]

Most Africans who left their native shores travelled in the hold of a slave-ship, destined for one of the plantations of the New World, where again they were presented with one of the meanest aspects of the white man's culture. But to a few favoured individuals occurred the opportunity of visiting Europe as honoured guests. In the age of their first contacts with West Africa the Portuguese made a practice of entertaining with regal hospitality the African princes and ambassadors they invited to Lisbon and of encouraging African chiefs, especially in the Congo, to send their sons to Portugal for their education. On the coast of Senegal the French, so an English trader reported at the end of the sixteenth century, were accustomed to invite Africans to come to France 'to the further increasing of mutuall love and amity'. In the eighteenth century Liverpool traders, who dealt with the West Coast, regularly brought back young Africans to England in order that they might acquire a measure of education and so prove better qualified to act as their agents. In addition there was a number of other Africans, whom the vagaries of fortune had brought to Europe; one such was Job ben Solomon. His story achieved considerably notoriety, when it was published in England in 1734. It is indeed something of a moral tale, illustrating at once the possibilities of a harmonious and fruitful relationship between the races and the utter lack of respect of innate human dignity that the slave system involved.[8]

Job ben Solomon was a Fulani, a son of the ruler of the little state of Bondou in the western Sudan. In the course of a trading expedition to the Gambia, he had been captured by a party of Mandingos and sold to a white slave dealer. Transported across the Atlantic, he was bought by a plantation owner in Maryland. Job was a devout Muslim and refused to abandon the strict practice of his religion, in spite of the jeers and the scorn with which the local whites mocked his prayers. At length, made desperate by his misery, he escaped but was recaptured. His case, however, came to the notice of certain English merchants, who visited him in prison and learnt the whole of his story. As a result of their representations the royal slave was freed and brought to England. There, having by this time acquired some knowledge of the language, he was introduced to Sir Hans Sloane, President of the Royal Society, for whom he translated some Arabic manuscripts, entertained by the Duke of Montagu and other members of the nobility, granted an audience with the Royal Family and presented by the Queen with a 'rich gold watch'. Though a devout Muslim, he was prepared—to the astonishment of those who equated Islam with fanaticism—to discuss religion 'in a very temperate and rational manner'. He developed a remarkable aptitude for mechanics. He talked philosophically about his experiences. How strange it must have seemed—though not to those of a later age who have come to know the Fulani in their homes—to find an African prince with the temperament and tastes of an English gentleman. On all who met him Job made a deep impression: 'in his natural temper there appeared a happy mixture of the grave and the cheerful, a gentle mildness guarded by a proper warmth, and a kind and compassionate disposition to all that were in distress'. When after fourteen months Job decided to return to his native land, he was presented by his English friends with gifts said to have been valued at £500. No more is known of him after his return to Bondou.[9]

If some of the people of West Africa were in daily intercourse with Europeans, and if a very few had had the opportunity of seeing for themselves the white man's country and returning to tell the tale, for other West Africans, Europe, if not utterly unknown, was presented only through garbled reports. Dupuis, who visited Ashanti in 1820, found that the King of the country thought of Europe as containing many tribes inhabiting a number of large islands; these tribes—they included the Dutch, the Danes, the Americans and the Portuguese—were all subordinate to the King of England, to whom they paid annual tribute. 'Their notions of geography,' Mungo Park wrote of the Mandingo of the Western Sudan, 'are puerile. They imagine that the world is an extended plain, the termination of which no eye has discovered—it being, they say, overhung with clouds and darkness. They describe the sea as a large river of salt water, on the farther shore of which is situated a country called *Tobaudo doo*—"the land of the white people". At a distance from Tobaudo doo, they describe another country, which they allege is inhabited by cannibals of gigantic size, called *Koomi*. This country they call *Jong sang doo*—the land where the slaves are sold. But of all countries in the world their own appears to them as the best, and their own people as the happiest; and they pity the fate of other nations, who have been placed by Providence in less fertile and less fortunate districts.'[10]

From the countries of the Ashanti and the Mandingo regular trade routes led to the European establishments on the coast; other parts of West Africa were very much more isolated. Equiano, an Ibo, who was enslaved as a young boy and later wrote an account of his experiences, told that in his own village, far from the coast, people had 'never heard of white men or of Europeans or of the sea'. The same comment could no doubt be made about most of the communities that lay away from the main trade routes.[11]

For the people of the Sahara and the central and eastern Sudan reports about Europeans filtered down from North Africa, being carried by traders or by wandering Sherifs, holy men claiming descent from the Prophet, who were to be found in most of the Muslim courts of the Sudan begging for alms. Muslim prejudice must have coloured many of the stories they told. Thus, W. G. Browne, the first European traveller to reach Darfur, was assured by one of the great officers of the Sultan that Europeans were 'a small tribe, cut off by the singularity of colour and features'—their skin was red and their eyes were green—' and still more by their impiety from the rest of mankind.'[12]

Not many Sudanese could compete with the travelling Moors in experience of a wider world; but there were always a few men living in the cities of the Sudan, whom diplomacy, trade or pilgrimage had brought to North Africa. Such was a Prince of Bornu, who passed through Tripoli in 1789 on his way to his own country from Tunis; he was accompanied by his three wives, one of whom had learnt to speak Italian. In Tripoli he was the guest at a number of parties given by the European consuls; among those who met him was the sister-in-law of the British Consul. 'The prince of Bornu,' she wrote, 'considering he comes from the interior of Africa is extremely well-informed and much acquainted with the state of Europe.'[*][13]

No African in the middle of the eighteenth century could have foretold that his country, whether Morocco or Egypt, Senegal or Calabar, would increasingly attract the interest of Europeans, nor could he have foreseen a time when white men would rule his land. To Europeans, too, of the same age such a prophecy would have seemed fantastic. Yet such was the course of history. A variety of causes were serving to draw the two continents closer together; to understand them it will be necessary to look at Africa through European eyes, and first to chart the extent of Europe's knowledge and to determine the reasons for its limitations.

* Since many Arabic books found their way to the Sudan, one would like to know if any of the Muslim scholars of Katsina or of Timbuktu ever read the great work of geography, the *Book of Roger* of al-Idrisi. Though written in the twelfth century, it conveyed an impression far less misleading than the garbled accounts of contemporary fabulists. Here, for instance, is al-Idrisi's description of England: 'a considerable island, in shape like an ostrich's head, where are to be found flourishing towns, high mountains, great rivers and plains. The country is fertile, its inhabitants brave, active and enterprising but a perpetual winter reigns there'.[14]

EUROPE'S KNOWLEDGE OF AFRICA
IN THE EIGHTEENTH CENTURY

I

POPULAR CONCEPTIONS

'AFRICA IS, AS YOU know, divided into nine principal parts, which are Egypt, Barbary, Biledulgerid, Zaara, Nigritia, Guinea, Nubia and Ethiopia.* The Africans are the most ignorant and unpolished people in the world, little better than the lions, tigers and leopards and other wild beasts, which that country produces in great numbers.' Thus wrote the fourth Earl of Chesterfield in one of a series of letters designed to provide his son with an education 'as near perfection as possible', letters which when published became one of the most popular and influential books of the age. Lord Chesterfield won fame as a politician, literateur and wit; he 'embodied', according to a biographer, 'in rare completeness the characteristics of a shrewd man of the world'. It is not unreasonable, therefore, to assume that his view of Africa was typical of that held by many highly educated men in eighteenth-century Europe. Yet one must beware of all-embracing generalizations; just as African views on Europe served to reflect a variety of experiences, so in Europe one should not expect a complete uniformity of opinion. At one extreme there must have been a vast

---

* Barbary: the states of North Africa, from Morocco to Cyrenaica. Biledulgerid, i.e. Bilad-al-Djarid 'the land of palms': Southern Tunisia and the Algerian Sahara. Zaara: Sahara. Nigritia: the western and central Sudan. Guinea: the country between the Senegal and the Cameroons. (The name Guinea, introduced to Europe by the Portuguese, was derived from the Berber word, *aguinaou* meaning 'Negro', identical therefore, with the Arabic word *Sudan*.) Nubia: the eastern Sudan. Ethiopia was divided into two parts, Inferior and Superior. Ethiopia Inferior covered the entire southern half of the continent, including the west coast south of the Cameroons; Ethiopia Superior contained the Kingdom of Ethiopia, whose size was grossly exaggerated, its boundaries being reckoned to reach the Equator.

area of ignorance; to a French peasant, a German artisan or an English farm-labourer, Africa would mean as little as Europe to a Fulani cowherd, a Bambara farmer or a Yoruba craftsman. At the other the intimate experience of those, European and African, who had traded and lived together.* African knowledge, in the absence of written records, can never be charted exactly; in Europe the position is naturally quite different. By 1750 many books about Africa enjoyed a European circulation; their contents reveal the remarkable extent of available knowledge. Yet if one is seeking to discover the popular conception of Africa, to trace the source of Lord Chesterfield's extraordinary ideas, it is worth looking first not at the original sources but at those more widely distributed types of reading material, ranging from school textbooks to encyclopaedias, for it is by works such as these that many of the general ideas of an age are formed.[1]

One may take as a sample of school textbook a work which had proved popular enough to reach its third impression in 1746, *A New and Easy Introduction to the Study of Geography by Way of Question and Answer, Principally Designed for the Use of Schools*. This was what it had to say about Nigritia:

> What is most observable in this country?
> 1. That the river Niger waters it, as the Nile waters Egypt.
> 2. The Negro trader is in the Country of great consequence.
> 3. The English have in a manner monopolized it, and transport a great number of them to their Plantations in the West Indies.

And here, rather more exciting though even less accurate, is the proper answer to the question asked about the Sahara:

> What sort of people inhabit this desert?
> The natives are undaunted and will not only face but will engage with a Lion whenever they meet one, which they frequently do. Their chief Occupation is looking after their Camels, which are very serviceable to them. The Southern part of the Country is full of Sand, the Middle full of Stones and Eastwards it is full of Morasses. From the month of August until Winter it rains continually, which causes some Grass to grow out of the Sand, for the support of the Cattle.

* To those who consider European ignorance of Africa only as an eighteenth-century phenomenon, one may commend the withering comment made in 1961 by a Committee appointed to examine the state of Oriental and African Studies in British Universities on 'the men and women, who by and large man the senior ranks of the Civil Service, the British Council, the B.B.C., commerce and the non-technical branches of industry', that 'their collective influence is as vast as their curiosity and collective knowledge about the non-western world is meagre'.

Another popular school book of the age was Salmon's *A New Universal Geographical Grammar*, designed to present 'the youth of Great Britain with the world in miniature'. Of the 770 pages in the 1782 edition, less than two were deemed sufficient to describe Africa south of the Tropic of Cancer. 'This immense territory,' the inquiring schoolboy was informed, 'is very little known; there is no traveller that has penetrated into the interior parts, so that we are ignorant not only of the bounds, but even of the names of several inland countries.'[2]

Fortunately, if a young man of well-to-do parents, undeterred by the dismal fare of his schooldays, came to feel something of the fascination of Africa, he would almost certainly find on the shelves of his father's library more than one book to fire his imagination. In every literate society books on travel have always been popular; in the eighteenth century theology, it has been reckoned, was the only subject in greater demand. 'The science of Geography is now become the most fashionable as well as the most rational amusement of the present polite and enlightened age': this was written in 1787, but it was a sentiment that could have been uttered at any time in the second half of the century. For anyone interested in the world beyond his horizon three different types of books were available: the narratives of individual travellers, collections of travels often reproducing accounts no longer in print, and systematic works of geography.[3]

Collections of travellers' tales had been known in medieval times, but it was not until the sixteenth century, the development of printing coinciding with the great age of discovery, that they became an essential part of the culture of the age. The most famous collection of that century was made by a Venetian of distinguished family, G. B. Ramusio; his book, *Delle navigationi e viaggi*, appeared in its original Italian in the 1550s. It was never translated in its entirety into English, but served as an exemplar to an English work of almost equal importance, Richard Hakluyt's *The Principall Navigations, Voiages, Traffiques and Discoveries of the English Nation, made by Sea or Over-land, to the remotest and farthest distant quarters of the Earth, at any time within the compass of these 1500 Years*. Hakluyt's collection, which appeared in its final form between 1598 and 1600, is the greatest of its kind in the English language; its qualities, 'the feeling for form and style, the editorial integrity and systematic plan', are—as two modern scholars, Mr G. R. Crone and Mr R. A. Skelton, have pointed out—'rarely seen in the compilations of the next two hundred years'.[4]

A quarter of a century later there appeared *Hakluytus Postumus or Purchas his Pilgrim*, the work of an Essex clergyman, Samuel Purchas, who drew more widely on foreign sources than his predecessor, but handled his material less adroitly. Purchas's work was the only general collection of travels to appear in seventeenth-century England, the internal troubles of the age and the lack of startling discoveries by English travellers seeming to have muted public demand. But at the beginning of the eighteenth century the outbreak of war with Spain aroused popular interest in far distant corners of the world. Thus assured of sufficient support, there appeared two new *Collections of Voyages and Travels* in large and handsome folio volumes, one brought out in 1704 by a pair of London booksellers, A. and J. Churchill, the other in 1705 by John Harris, 'a divine of some standing in the scientific world'. New and enlarged editions of both these works appeared in the 1740s—significantly during another war with Spain. In 1745 a new collection was published by another London bookseller, Thomas Astley, who was able to collect over a thousand subscribers. Astley's work was more comprehensive and better arranged than either Harris's or Churchill's; unfortunately it was broken off after four volumes, two of which had been devoted entirely to Africa. But it had achieved a European reputation, for in 1747 a French and a German translation appeared, the former the work of the Abbé Prévost (better known as the author of *Manon Lescaut*), both of which collections were continued for the space of over forty years until they each came to include twenty large volumes.[5]

These collections—Churchill, Harris, Astley, Prévost—were large, handsome, expensive folios, fit adornments for the libraries of the mansions of the aristocracy. But as wealth and education spread more widely among the urban middle class, a new audience emerged, eager to read books of travel but unable to afford such lavish publications; to meet their needs, a number of more modest collections began to appear from the 1750s onwards. One such was *The World Displayed*, for which Samuel Johnson wrote an introduction; it ran to twenty volumes. With the exception of Astley's *Collection*, none of these works had any pretensions to scholarship, but they served, with all their deficiencies, a valuable purpose, for they made accessible to a growing public the great classics of travel and discovery in an easily digested form. Africa naturally formed only a small part of their contents, varying between a tenth and a sixth; but here could be found, not too rigorously abridged, the works of the Venetian Cadamosto, who sailed with the Portuguese to Senegal in the 1450s, of the Italian-ate Moor, Leo Africanus, who visited all the states of the Sudan in the early sixteenth century, of the Englishmen Jobson and Moore on the Gambia, the Frenchman Brue on the Senegal, the Dutchman Bosman and others on the coast of Guinea.

Those who brought out collections of travels were content to let their authors speak for themselves. But travellers' tales can become tedious in the mass; nor could the critical reader fail to notice diverg-ences between them. There was then a real need for someone who could study all the existing authorities and, as one writer put it, reduce 'the mass and substance of them into the narrowest compass'. One of the earliest and most industrious of these academic geo-graphers was a Dutchman, Olfert Dapper, who produced in the second half of the seventeenth century a large number of geographical works, including a lengthy *Description of Africa*. Dapper, as his French translator pointed out, 'had had the patience to read a prodi-gious number of geographers and travellers, both ancient and modern, Latin, French, Spanish, Italian, English and Dutch'. Dapper had an English counterpart and contemporary, John Ogilby. A man as remarkable for his versatility as for his industry, Ogilby started his career as a dancing master, turned to translating Homer and Virgil, and devoted the last years of his life to producing a magnificent series of works on geography and topography. Typographically, his work on Africa, which was based largely, though not exclusively on Dapper, is one of the most beautiful books that have ever been devoted to the continent.[6]

During the eighteenth century Ogilby's and Dapper's productions served as models for a number of works which touched on all the countries of the world and were usually entitled *Systems of Geo-graphy*. These were the *Statesman's Yearbooks* of the age; 'a kind of Geographical, Historical and Political Dictionary' was the descrip-tion Emmanuel Bowen, the King's Geographer, applied to his *Com-plete System of Geography of the Known World*, published in 1747. The analogy with the handy reference volumes of our own day must not be pushed too far; Bowen's two volumes weigh over twenty pounds. Moreover, his work was designed to be read with pleasure: 'the Matter it contains,' Bowen wrote in his Preface, 'is of such Variety that there is no Danger of being quickly tired; and so instructive that it is impossible to employ many Hours in Reading without being the better for it.'[7]

Bowen's great tomes contained 1,800 double-columned pages; of these 125 are given up to Africa, 245 to America, 317 to Asia and the rest to Europe. One can hardly say that Africa was being neglected. The same proportion was maintained in the other *Systems of Geography* of the eighteenth century—Fenning's (1765), Middleton's (1779), Miller's (1782), Bankes's (1787)—their dates and number showing very clearly the growing popularity of the subject. What impression would the average reader obtain from them about Africa? By some his preconceived ideas of African barbarism would be confirmed: 'The barrenness in several places,' he would read in Middleton, 'the brutality and savageness of the natives and the ferocity of the innumerable wild beasts in most of its countries evince that the rays of the sun are here so fervid and powerful as to dry and burn up the juices of the vegetable and overheat the blood of the animal creation, so that the first is rendered futile and the latter furious.' Yet in another of the encyclopaedic works of the age, *Modern History or the Present State of the Nations*, produced in 1739 by Thomas Salmon, he would come across this challenging assertion: 'I had reason to believe from my own reading and personal observation on distant countries that there was very little to be depended on in the numerous volumes which are stuffed with relations of giants. I am also confirmed in the opinion that all men are naturally inclined to acts of humanity and benevolence and that it is only prejudice and an unhappy education which induce them to commit acts of cruelty and injustice and treat strangers with inhumanity. The title of barbarians therefore may with much more propriety be applied to those Europeans who have invaded, plundered and massacred the natives of Asia and America rather than to those people they have represented as savages'. Salmon—a prolific writer who towards the end of his life kept a coffee-house in Cambridge—had a sovereign advantage over the literary hacks of the day; a much travelled man—he even accompanied Anson on his voyage round the world—he knew the supreme worth of first-hand experience.[8]

As for the interior of the continent it was generally accepted as unknown. 'The Midland Parts,' wrote Bowen, 'were for a long while believed inaccessible and uninhabitable by Reason of their intolerable Heat, they lying mostly under the Torrid Zone. They have on that very account as well as the Savageness of the Inhabitants been little visited by any Strangers.' Yet Nigritia was undoubtedly part of the interior; Nigritia had been visited in the sixteenth century by the Moorish traveller, Leo Africanus; Leo, whose account was invariably mentioned, showed that there existed in one part at least of the interior a people that could reasonably be called civilized. How confusing this was, so confusing indeed that the ordinary reader would probably feel too perplexed to sort the matter out. But imagine a man of the century, critical, rational, humane and scholarly enough to follow up the references in these secondary accounts to the original sources. To appreciate Europe's knowledge to the full, it is necessary to find out how much information such a man could acquire, first about those areas—Zaara, Nigritia, Guinea, to use the contemporary designations—that form this study's central concern, then more briefly about other parts of the continent.[9]

II

SAHARA AND SUDAN

CLASSICAL WRITERS

IN AN AGE WHOSE culture drew so much of its inspiration from the
classical world, an age in which educated men were brought up to
read the classics fluently, a scholar with an interest in Africa would
naturally turn to those passages—in themselves all too brief—in
which the geographers of Greece and of Rome described what they
had learnt about the mysterious interior of the great continent. Nor
was it absurd to pay attention to such distant authorities. The broad
facts of geography do not change, and 'the Ancients' probably
possessed, as the shrewder minds of the eighteenth century realized,
greater knowledge of the interior than did the modern world. It was
not surprising that this should be so. For centuries the Egyptians had
traded and fought with the people beyond their borders. The Greek
and Carthaginian cities of the Libyan coast had maintained some
commerce with the interior. Finally, the Romans, bringing the whole
North African littoral under their rule, had been forced, by the usual
dynamic of imperialism, to push their frontier posts farther south
beyond the borders of cultivation.

Herodotus, 'Father of History', was the earliest writer to say anything about the interior of Africa. He visited Egypt and Libya in the
middle of the fifth century B.C. and collected a mass of information,
geographical, historical and anthropological, the accuracy and value
of which has come to be fully appreciated only in the present century,
as the areas he described have been scientifically explored. Herodotus
grasped the basic facts about Libyan geography: a belt of fertile land
along the coast, another belt where only wild beasts were to be found,
and beyond it a country 'altogether parched with sand and exceeding

drye'. But the desert did not extend indefinitely: such was the point of a story told to Herodotus by the people of the city of Cyrene, a story they themselves had heard from Etearchus, king of the oasis city of Ammon or Siwa. The heroes of Etearchus's tale were certain young men, belonging to one of the tribes of Cyrenaica, the Nasomonians; their famous adventure has never been more vigorously rendered than in the version of that anonymous Englishman, who in the reign of Elizabeth produced the first translation of Herodotus.

> Certayne yong Gentlemen, issued of the chief and most noble families of all their nation, who beeing at a reasonable age very youthfull and valiant, determined in a bravery to go seeke straunge adventures. Five of them being assigned thereto by lot, put themselves in voyage to go search and discry the wilderness and desert places of Africa, to the ende they might see more, and make further report thereof then ever any that had attempted the same. These gentlemen-travellers having made sufficient provision of water, and other vyands necessary for theyr journey, first of all passed the countreys that were inhabited; and next after that came into the wylde and waste regions amongst the caves and dennes of fierce and untamed beastes, through which they helde on theyr way to the west parte of the earth. In which manner, after they had continued many dayes journey, and travelled over a great part of the sandy countreys, they came at length to espy certain fayre and goodly trees, growing in a fresh and pleasaunt medowe, whereunto incotinently making repayre, and tasting the fruite that grew thereon, they were suddenly surprised and taken short by a company of little dwarfes, farre under the common pitch and stature of men, whose tongue the gentlemen knew not, neither was their speache understoode of them. Being apprehended, they were lead away over sundry pooles and meares into a city, where all the inhabitants were of the same stature and degree with those that had taken them and of colour swart and blacke. Fast by the side of thys city ranne a swift and violent river, flowing from the Weast to the East, wherein were to be seen very hydeous and terrible serpents called Crocodyles. . . . The Nasomonian gentlemen returned home to theyr owne country . . . (and told) how the people also of the city whether they were brought were all conjurors, and geven to the study of the blacke arte.[1]

The 'swift and violent river, flowing from the West to the East' Etearchus thought to be the Nile. Herodotus agreed with this interpretation, pointing out that it followed 'a very like and semblable course unto the river Ister'. In fact, the river which Herodotus set so symmetrically against the Danube is likely to have been either the Komadugu Yobe, as it flows into Lake Chad, or the Niger in the area of its great bend. The essential truth of Etearchus's story has been confirmed by modern archaeologists. For the Sahara has been found to be particularly rich in rock-engravings, some of which illustrate the extraordinary fact that the desert was crossed in *horse-drawn chariots* by certain Libyan people in the course of the first millennium B.C. As for the reference to 'little dwarfes', though some have taken this as evidence that the Sudan was once inhabited by pygmies, it seems more likely that the Nasomonians were speaking figuratively rather than exactly, for the Tuareg, the descendants of the Libyan tribes, are among the tallest people in the world, whereas many negroes are short and stocky.[2]

Herodotus had another passage to intrigue those who sought to learn more about the interior. The southernmost of all the tribes of Libya were the 'numerous' Garamantes. 'These Garamantes,' he was informed, 'are accustom'd to sit in Chariots, and hunt the Aethiopian Troglodytes; who are reported to be swifter of Foot than any other Nation in the World. They feed upon Serpents and Lizards, with many other Kinds of Reptiles: and their Speech resembles the shrieking of a Bat rather than the Language of Men'. The country of the Garamentes corresponds to the modern Fezzan, while in the 'Aethiopian troglodytes'—the black men who live in holes—have been seen the ancestors of the Tebu of Tibesti.[3]

For over four hundred years little was added to the report Herodotus had given of Africa. But with the establishment of Roman rule in North Africa, a number of Roman military expeditions were launched across the desert, some of which seem to have reached the borders of the Sudan. The records of these expeditions have been preserved in a few terse passages in the writings of Pliny the Elder and of Claudius Ptolemy.[4]

The earliest of these expeditions took place at the end of the first century B.C. It was commanded by Cornelius Balbus, who was granted a triumph on his return; the names of the towns which he had captured were officially recorded in a list reproduced by Pliny. Along with the towns, which included Garama, the capital of the Fezzan, and Cydamus (modern Ghadames), was mentioned the name of a river, the Dasibari. To eighteenth-century readers this name would be quite meaningless; but recently Henri Lhote, one of the greatest modern authorities on the Sahara, has pointed out that the Songhai, who live on the Niger, call the river *Isa-Beri* ('great river'), while according to their traditions *Da* was the name of the ancient inhabitants of the river valley. May it not be then that Balbus's Dasibari is a variant of *Da-isa-beri*, 'the great river of the Da'? Moreover, the very name 'Niger', with which the Romans later became familiar, seems to have been derived from a Tuareg expression *N-ger-n-gereo*, 'river of rivers'. If the Romans knew the name the Tuareg gave to the river, is it not reasonable to suppose that they were also aware of the expression used by the Songhai? And if this be the case, is it not at least possible that Balbus's legionaries once stood on the banks of the Niger? This question, to which no assured answer can ever be given, seems never to have been asked in the eighteenth century; but how strongly such a speculation would have appealed to those who felt themselves the heirs of Rome.[5]

Nearly a century after Balbus two other Roman expeditions crossed the central Sahara. 'Julius Maternus, setting out from Leptis Magna and Garama with the King of the Garamantes, who was beginning an expedition against the Ethiopians, by bearing continuously southward came within four months to Agisymba, the country of the Ethiopians where the rhinoceros is to be found.' This aggravatingly compressed account—together with one of a similar expedition led by Septimius Flaccus—is to be found in Ptolemy, the great second-century geographer of Alexandria. Ptolemy, who had obtained the stories from an earlier writer, Marinus of Tyre, confessed that he found the accounts incredible, for he could not understand how the Ethiopians came to be so far distant from the Garamantes. Modern scholars, more accurately informed on the time involved in a desert crossing, are not perplexed on this point, but have argued over the location of Agisymba and found reasons for identifying it with Air or Tibesti or Adrar of the Iforas or even with Adamawa.[6]

Both Pliny and Ptolemy were able to make use of other sources of information on 'Libya interior' and 'Ethiopia inferior', as the Sahara and the Sudan were called by classical writers. Juba, a scholarly Berber king, a friend and contemporary of Augustus, had written an account of Africa, which Pliny preserved in part. In this he put forward a startling theory about the source of the Nile—a riddle as tantalizing to the ancient world as it was to eighteenth-century Europe. The river, so Juba declared, had its source in a mountain in lower Mauritania (southern Morocco), flowed into a lake in which were to be found crocodiles and fish similar to those of the Nile of Egypt, ran underground until it emerged in another lake in a part of Mauritania corresponding to southern Algeria, resumed its subterranean course for the space of a twenty days' journey across desert country,

47

and 'so soone as he has once againe espied a man'—the words are those of Pliny's Elizabethan translator, Philip Holland—'forth he starteth (as it should seem) out of that spring, which they called Nigris. And then dividing Affrick from Aethyopia, being acquainted if not presently with people, yet with frequent companie of wild and savage beasts and making shade of wood, as he goeth, he cutteth through the middest of the Aethyopians', finally joining the Nile in the neighbourhood of Meroe. Pliny found in their similarity a good reason for believing that the two rivers were one: 'the river Nyger is of the same nature as the Nilus. It bringeth forth Reed and Papyr, breedeth the same living creatures, and riseth or swelleth at the same season'. An absurd theory it may be thought by those who have never had to grope through the mists of ignorance but as late as the 1820s there were eminent and scholarly men who believed that in joining the Niger to the Nile Pliny must be right.[7]

Ptolemy, writing a century after Pliny, knew far more about the Sahara, deriving his information partly from geographers such as Marinus of Tyre, partly, one must assume, from inquiries made among those—traders or army officers—who had passed beyond the *limes*. His geography is in fact a gazetteer; as such it lists a remarkably large number of rivers and mountains, towns and tribes. Most of these names were meaningless to eighteenth-century geographers; but every cartographer showed on his map the more prominent features mentioned by Ptolemy, while the greatest of them all, the Frenchman, D'Anville, was able, after a careful study of Ptolemy's account of the rivers of the interior, to correct one of the most glaring errors of the age. In recent years French scholars, having acquired an intimate knowledge of Saharan geography, of the dried-up wadis, the complex massifs, the desert tribes and their divisions, have been able to identify many of the places mentioned by Ptolemy and so to confirm the remarkable accuracy and the astonishing detail of his knowledge.[8]

But the increase in the Roman world's knowledge of Africa was demonstrated by Ptolemy in too arid and compressed a form. For the ancients the interior of Africa remained, as Hugh Murray, a popular historical geographer of the early nineteenth century, eloquently wrote, a region that 'inspired always emotions of wonder and curiosity, mingled with terror. It was the region of mystery, of poetry, of superstitious awe. The wild and strange aspect of man and nature, the immense tracts abandoned to wild beasts, the still more immeasureable deserts of sand beyond, and the destruction that had overwhelmed most of those who attempted to penetrate; all these formed, as it were, a fearful and mysterious barrier drawn round the narrow limits occupied by the civilized nations of the continent. Every object which appeared through the veil tended to heighten this impression —the human race, under an aspect and hue nowhere else seen on the globe; animals of strange form and magnitude; forms of society altogether uncouth and peculiar. Imagination, kept always on the stretch, created wonders, even when nature ceased to present them. No part of the interior was ever explored with such precision, as to deprive that active faculty of full scope for exertion; and the whole region was in a manner given up to fable.'[9]

Strange men: there were the Blemmyes, who 'by report have no heads but mouth and eies both in their breast' (in fact, they were the ancestors of some of the tribes of the Eastern Sudan); the Satyrs, the Goat-pans, the Strapfoots, who crawled instead of walking, and others described with more respect for probability, the Gamphasantes, for instance, who went naked, lived peacefully and avoided strangers. All these people were mentioned by Pliny, who himself drew on Herodotus and on other writers now lost. In Pliny, too, the reader avid for romantic tales could read of Atlas 'the most fabulous mountaine of all Affricke', that 'shineth often times with many flashes of fires, and is haunted with the wanton lascivious Aegipans [Goat-pans] and Satyres whereof it is full, that it resoundeth with noise of haut-boies, pipes, and fifes, and ringeth again with the sound of tabers, timbrels and cymbals'.[10]

Strange beasts: elephants and lions, cameleopards and hippopotami. How well Pliny could describe them: 'he hath a cloven foot like a boeufe; the backe, maine and hire of an horse; and he hath his neighing also. His muzzle or snout turneth up: his taile twineth like the bores, and his teeth like wise are crooked and bending downwards as the bores tusks but not so hurtfull; the skin or hide of his back unpenetrable'—could one better this concise account of a hippo? But there were other more fearsome creatures—*pegasi*, winged horses armed with horns, the *yale*, the *leucricota* and most terrible of all the *mantichora*, 'which has a triple row of teeth, meeting like the teeth of a comb, the face and ears of a human being, grey eyes, a blood-red colour, a lion's body, inflicting stings with its tail in the manner of a scorpion, with a voice like the sound of a pan-pipe blended with a trumpet, of great speed, with a special appetite for human flesh'.[11]

49

As a fiery back-cloth to these fabulous creatures, beyond Agi-symba, beyond Meroe on the Nile, there lay the Torrid Zone, 'the middle of the earth,' so Pliny called it, 'where the Sunne hath his way and keepeth his course, scorched and burnt with flames, is even parched and fried again with the hote gleams thereof, being so near'. It was an old belief—one can trace it back to Pythagoras in the sixth century B.C. and Aristotle had given it his magisterial blessing—that the world was divided up into three zones, arctic, temperate and torrid; the last was deemed uninhabitable.[12]

Here, then, were a set of concepts—the torrid zone, strange beasts and men as strange—so much more easily comprehensible than the dry and precise cartography of Ptolemy. They came to form the stock picture of the interior of Africa for the later Roman world, and passed on through the medium of Solinus, a third-century geographer, who put together a book entitled a *Collection of Wonderful Things*, to the men of the Middle Ages. Solinus drew largely on Pliny, yet included some stories of his own. 'There be ants,' he wrote in his chapter on Ethiopia, 'as big as a mastiff that have talents [talons] like Lyons, wherewyyth they scrape up sand of golde, which they keepe that no man may fetch it away and if any men adventure, they pursue them to death.' The notion which Solinus conveyed of Africa is shown by his heading to the same chapter: 'Of Aethyop, of the filthy fashion of the people of that Countrey, of their monstrous shape, of the Dragons and other wylde beastes of wonderful nature there.' There has perhaps never been a work of geography—if indeed one can dignify it with that title—that has influenced so many men's minds, for it was widely read, when Pliny and Strabo had faded out of sight, for over a thousand years. Nor, even in the eighteenth century, that avowedly rational and enlightened age, was Solinus's approach to Africa entirely disapproved. On a map of Africa published in Paris in 1761 by a certain de Mornas there appears this note: 'It is true that the centre of the continent is filled with burning sands, savage beasts and almost uninhabitable deserts. The scarcity of water forces the different animals to come together to the same place to drink. It happens that finding themselves together at a time when they are on heat, they have intercourse one with another, without paying regard to the difference between species. Thus are produced those monsters which are to be found there in greater numbers than in any other part of the world.'[13]

For the twentieth century the sights of Africa—the lip-plugged women, the pygmies with their poisoned darts, the gorilla, the okapi, the giraffe—have become the clichés of the television screen, of the tourist brochure. Yet for those Europeans—the vast majority—who, lacking first-hand experience, fail to realize that Africa is far less exotic than they care to imagine, a sense of the strangeness of Africa still remains. No one who is aware of the fatuity of many current conceptions about Africa will be surprised at the incredulity of earlier generations.

ARAB GEOGRAPHERS

In the last years of his life the historian of the decline of the Roman Empire turned his mind to the historical geography of Africa. 'The inland geography of that vast continent,' Gibbon reflected, presented 'an obscure scene which had been less invisible to the Arabian Moors than to any other nation of the ancient or modern world.' 'I have before me,' he went on, 'the Latin version of the Sherif al Edrisi and the Italian original of Leo Africanus.' al-Idrisi's great geography had been translated into Latin in 1619; an English translation, which Gibbon praised as being 'executed with no vulgar hand', was made by Francis Moore and published as an appendix to his own *Travels into the Interior Parts of Africa* in 1738. Moore had also included extensive extracts from Leo Africanus's work, which Ramusio had published in 1551 and John Pory translated into English in 1600.[1]

Today scholars are aware of the works of many other Arab geographers and historians who touched on the interior of Africa: al-Bakri, who lived in Spain in the eleventh century, Ibn Khaldun, the Berber historian of the fourteenth century, who with St Augustine is to be hailed as the greatest writer Africa has ever produced, Ibn Battuta, most energetic and inquiring of travellers, and half a dozen others. The manuscripts of these works were brought to Europe and translated, mainly by French scholars, during the course of the nineteenth century. Yet in the whole corpus of Arab writing relating to the countries of the Sahara and the Sudan, the works of al-Idrisi and of Leo still stand out as the fullest, and therefore the most valuable.

al-Idrisi—he was referred to anonymously by Moore as 'the Nubian geographer'—lived in the twelfth century. Of Spanish–Arab descent—his grandfather had been Emir of Malaga—he came to settle in the court of that remarkable patron of the arts and sciences,

51

the Norman King, Roger II of Sicily. al-Idrisi was not the first Arab writer to describe the countries beyond the Sahara—al-Bakri, also a Spanish Arab, had written a detailed account of the countries of the western Sudan a century before; but he was the only Arab geographer to gather all the information available and to present a systematic account of the whole region from the Red Sea to the Atlantic as part of his description of the entire known world. Today, even with the resources of modern scholarship, much of al-Idrisi's account, though it reads in a deceptively easy manner, has not been fully interpreted; most of the cities he mentions have disappeared, and his method of describing their location—by saying that they lie so many days' journey from such and such a place without always specifying the exact direction—makes it difficult to plot them exactly. Of these complexities earlier scholars could not be so deeply aware; from the seventeenth century onwards European cartographers did not hesitate to mark their maps with the names of cities mentioned by al-Idrisi as flourishing communities, but in their own day, if they had only known, desolate and in ruins.

Like the ancient Greeks and other Arab geographies, al-Idrisi divided his world into seven climates. The greater part of the first climate—the only section of his work which Moore translated—was taken up by the countries of the Sudan and contained eight states of some size: from west to east Tekrur, Ghana, Wangara, Kaugha, Kuku, Kanem, Zaghawa and Nubia.* The great river of the country al-Idrisi called the Nile of the Negroes; it rose from the same source as the Nile of Egypt and flowed in a straight line westwards to fall into the Atlantic. All the states and cities of which al-Idrisi had been informed lay either on the river or to the north of it, with one excep-

* Tekrur lay on the lower Senegal. Kuku was probably on the site of Gao, the great city on the Niger bend, east of Timbuktu. The location of Kaugha is uncertain. Recent archaeological research suggests that the capital of Ghana was at Kumbi Saleh on the edge of the desert, three hundred miles west of Timbuktu. The Kingdom of Ghana was founded, according to as-Sadi, the seventeenth-century Timbuktu historian, early in the first millennium A.D., the earliest rulers being white immigrants from North Africa. The empire survived under a dynasty of black rulers until the thirteenth century. On Wangara *v. supra*, p. 23n. Kanem lay to the northeast of Lake Chad; its rulers were later to move their centre of power to Bornu. The Zaghawa are today a tribe with some affinities to the Tebu, leading a nomadic life in the country to the north-west of Darfur. Nubia lay in the Nile Valley to the south of Egypt and was the site of a number of kingdoms, still Christian in al-Idrisi's day.

tion, the land of Lem-lem, whose inhabitants, he had been told, were Jews (most of them 'unbelieving and ignorant'). Of the other countries to the south of the river he had no knowledge.

Though the precise details of al-Idrisi's account might perplex cartographers, the ordinary reader would find in it much to fire the imagination. It was clear that the Sudan, as al-Idrisi knew of it, was not a land given up entirely to ignorance and barbarism. The king of Tekrur was 'a mighty Prince having many Servants and Soldiers, of known Fortitude, Power and Justice with a Country well secur'd and exposed to no Fears.' Kaugha was 'a populous City, without Walls, famous for Business and useful Arts for the Advantage of its People' (the women of Kaugha were especially noted for their skill in witchcraft). In Kuku, while the common people might 'cover their Nakedness with the Skin of Beasts', 'the Governors and Nobility are covered with Sattin'. Wangara was, 'most famous for the Excellency and Plenty of Gold'. But of all the states of the Sudan 'the largest, most populous and wealthiest' was Ghana. Its King was reported to be 'the most just of all Men'; everyday accompanied by his captains on horseback, he would pass through the streets of the city, dispensing justice to all who brought their cases to him. In his palace he possessed 'an entire Lump of Gold, not cast, nor wrought by any other Instruments, but perfectly formed by the Divine Providence only, of thirty Pounds Weight, which has been bored through and fitted for a Seat to the Royal Throne'. In addition he had 'Abundance of rich Ornaments, and Horses, with most sumptuous Trappings, on solemn Days, led before him. He has many Troops who march each with their Colours, under his Royal Banner; Elephants, Camels and various kinds of Animals, which are found in the Negroes Countries, precede him.'[2]

al-Idrisi's remarkable account was confirmed in the impression it gave of the wealth and civilization of the Sudan by Leo Africanus, whose *History and Description of Africa*, based unlike al-Idrisi's work on first-hand experience, was written four hundred years later. Leo—or to give him his proper name al-Hassan ibn Muhammad al-Wezaz—was a Moor, born in Granada a year or two after the Spanish conquest of the city in 1492. When he was still a young boy his father, a man of wealth and distinction, moved to Fez, where Leo received his education. By the time he was twenty, he was able to look back on a remarkable variety of experiences and adventures; already though so young, he had served as diplomat, soldier, lawyer, judge

53

and merchant, travelled as far afield as Tabriz in Persia and accompanied his uncle to Timbuktu on an embassy to the great Songhai Emperor, Askia Muhammad. Some time later he revisited Timbuktu and went on to make an extensive tour of the countries of the Sudan, turning first westwards to Jenne and Mali, then eastwards to Gao, Agades, Kano and Bornu, finally coming, possibly by way of Nubia, to Egypt, having spent two years on his journey.

In 1518 Leo was returning by ship from another visit to Egypt when he was captured by Italian pirates off the coast of Tunisia. The pirates decided to make a present of the distinguished young Moor to the Pope Leo X. Leo was a Medici, a son of Lorenzo the Magnificent, and noted for his patronage of the arts. Discovering the extraordinary knowledge of little known lands that his young captive possessed, he freed him, granted him a pension and persuaded him to become a Christian, giving him on his baptism his own names Giovanni Leo, though it was as Leo the African that he was generally known. Pope Leo died a year or two later, but his protégé stayed on in Italy, wrote his great work on Africa in Italian and taught Arabic at Bologna. Of his later years no certain details have been uncovered; it is not known when or where he died, but it is not unlikely that he returned to North Africa and resumed the faith of his fathers.[3]

The larger part of Leo's *History* was devoted to North Africa; but two of the nine 'books' into which his work was divided were given up to the Sahara and the Sudan. These 'books' provided the only recent description of these regions available to European readers, until the results of the various expeditions sponsored by the African Association were published at the end of the eighteenth century. Every map, every textbook that touched on Africa for over two hundred years was indebted to Leo, even though many of those who used him took only the dry outline rather than the living detail of his account.

The main features of the Sahara Leo grasped pretty well. He wrote about the oases, Wargla, Tuat, Ghadames, the Fezzan, Agades. He knew the main trade routes and the salt-mines at Teghaza. He was aware of the broad divisions among the tribes of the desert—under his nomenclature of Terga and Bardeoa can be recognized the Tuareg and the Tebu. He had seen for himself their mode of living: 'they live all after one manner, that is to say, without all lawe and civilitie'; 'they spend their whole daies in hunting and theeving, for all their indevour and exercise is to drive away the camels of their enemies'; 'it would seeme to any man incredible what hunger and scarcitie this nation will indure'. He had been inside their tents, noted their diet of camel's milk, seen the men with their veils, the women 'grosse, corpulent' but 'very civil'—'sometimes they will accept a kisse: but whoso tempted them further, putteth his one life in hazard'. He viewed them with the prejudices of the townsman against the nomad; yet he could praise them for their 'courtesie and liberalitie'. One incident in particular he liked to recall: when the caravan with which he was travelling had reached Arawan to the north of Timbuktu the local Tuareg chief, having collected the customs that were his due, invited the merchants to his tents, where he entertained them with 'wonderful and magnificent cheere'; 'roasted ostriches were brought to the table in wicker platters, being seasoned with sundrie kindes of herbes and spices'. Yet his final judgement on the Saharan tribes was a harsh one: 'all the Numidians, being most ignorant of naturall, domesticall, and commonwealth-matters are principally addicted unto treason, trecherie, murther, theft and robberie'.[4]

'I myselfe saw,' Leo wrote of the Sudan, 'fifteen kingdoms of the Negroes: howbeit there are many more which although I saw not with my own eyes, yet are they by the Negroes sufficiently knowen and frequented'. Of these fifteen cities and states, none was so important as Timbuktu, the greatest city of the wide-flung Songhai Empire, then at the height of its splendour under the greatest of its rulers. Leo gave more space to Timbuktu than to any of the other places that he visited in the Sudan, yet his account takes up less than a thousand words; short though it was, it was sufficient to cast over the city a glow that made it in the mind of Europe the most romantic of all places in the heart of Africa, a goal which young men were to dream about and one or two to give their lives to reach, a glow that has not faded yet, though modern travellers risk disillusionment when they arrive—'the first impression,' one of the most recent of them has written, 'is of a vast, grey ruin', 'the streets look grim and desolate—like an abandoned mining town.'[5]

But here is Timbuktu as Leo saw it; seminal as the passage is, it is worth a lengthy quotation.

Tombuto is situate within twelve miles of a certaine branch of Niger, all the houses whereof are now changed into cottages built of chalke, and covered with thatch. Howbeit there is a most stately temple to be seene, the wals thereof are made of stone and lime; and a princely palace also built by a most excellent workeman of Granada*. Here are many shops of artificers, and merchants, and especially of such as weave linen and cotton cloth. And hither do the Barbarie-merchants bring cloth of Europe. . . . The inhabitants, and especially strangers there residing, are exceeding rich, insomuch that the king that now is married both his daughters unto two rich merchants. . . . Corne, cattle, milke and butter this region yeeldeth in great abundance: but salt is verie scarce here; for it is brought hither by land from Tegaza, which is five hundred miles distant. . . .

The rich king of Tombuto hath many plates and scepters of gold, some whereof weigh 1,300. poundes: and he keepes a magnificent and well furnished court. . . . He hath alwaies three thousand hoursemen, and a great number of footmen that shoot poysoned arrowes, attending upon him. They have often skirmishes with those that refuse to pay tribute, and so many as they take, they sell unto the merchants of Tombutu. . . . Here are great store of doctors, judges, priests, and other learned men, that are bountifully maintained at the kings cost and charges. And hither are brought divers manuscripts or written bookes out of Barbarie which are sold for more money than any other mechandize. The coine of Tombuto is of gold without any stampe or superscription; but in matters of small value they use certaine shels brought hither out of the kingdome of Persia, fower hundred of which shels are worth a ducate. . . . The inhabitants are people of a gentle and cherefull disposition, and spend a great part of the night in singing and dancing through all the streets of the citie: they keep great store of men and women-slaves, and their town is much in danger of fire: at my second being there half the town almost was burnt in five hours space. Without the suburbs there are no gardens or orchards at all.[6]

There is the ring of truth about this account. Later travellers were to comment on the splendour with which even the rulers of petty Sudanic states surrounded themselves—the slaves, the horsemen, the magnificent robes: and indeed, one has only to visit the chief town of any Emirate in Northern Nigeria during the two great festivals of the Muslim year to see this splendour, so moving and so exciting in its reality, still. 'The gentle and cheerful disposition of the people', the nights spent in singing and dancing, the thatched mud houses, 'the shops of artificers and merchants': all these the modern traveller will find as he passes through the cities of the Sudan. So too, if he pos-

* The great mosque of Timbuktu was built for Mansa Musa, the fourteenth-century Emperor of Mali, by an Andalusian, as-Saheli, famed both as a poet and as an architect, whom the Emperor had met in Mecca on his great pilgrimage of 1324. The king to whom Leo refers is not the Emperor Askia, whose capital was at Gao, but his governor known as the Timbuktu-koi.

sesses the right introductions, will he be able to meet learned *mallams* and *alkalis* and be shown the books and manuscripts they treasure. There is nothing, therefore, improbable about Leo's account; yet it is not difficult to understand how it presented to the imagination of an age generally ignorant of the interior of Africa a picture sufficiently remarkable to make itself the stuff of legend; and, besides, the gold— its supply in our own day exhausted—was there to dazzle and to gild.

Timbuktu was only one of the places Leo described. He went to Jenne—the name is given as Ghinea in his version—'a certaine great village onely', where 'the priests and doctors of their law go apparelled in white cotton', the rest of the inhabitants being clad in black or blue cloth. In the capital of Mali he found 'great store of temples, priests and professours' and a people who 'excell all other Negros in wit, civilitie and industry'. At Gao, though the houses, the king's palace excepted, 'were but meane', he met 'exceeding rich merchants'; 'it is a woonder to see what plentie of Merchandize is dayly brought hither, and how costly and sumptuous all things be'. In the walled city of Kano he found the inhabitants to be 'rich merchants and most civill people'. In Bornu the ruler was 'a most puissant prince': 'horseman he hath in a continuall readiness to the number of three thousand, and an huge number of footmen'. Though he appeared to have no regular revenue apart from the spoils taken in war, 'the king seemeth to be marveilous rich, for his spurres, his bridles, platters, dishes, pots and other vessels wherein his meate and drinke are brought to the table, are all of pure golde: yea, and the chaines of his dogs and hounds are of golde also'.

The great princes, the wealthy merchants—Leo moved naturally in their company; but he was well aware of the state of the mass of the people. Thus in Gao he found that, apart from the capital, the kingdom 'containeth nought but villages and hamlets inhabited by husbandmen and shepherds, who in winter cover their bodies with beasts skins; but in summer they goe all naked save their privie members'. 'They are ignorant and rude people,' he added, 'and you shall scarce find one learned man in the space of an hundred miles. They are continually burthened with grievous exactions, so that they have scarce any thing remaining to live upon.' In Katsina where the people, he noted, were 'extremely black', 'they dwell in most forlorn and base cottages . . . and beside their base estate they are mightily oppressed with famine'. Zamfara, too, lying to the west of Katsina, was 'inhabited by most base and rusticall people', 'their dispositions most savage and brutish'. 'Brutish' and 'savage' were epithets that Leo applied to many of the tribes of Bornu and 'Gaoga' or Baguirmi, 'especially those that inhabite the mountaines, who go all naked save their privities'.[7]

It must have been the memory of these backward pagan people whom he would look down on with all the prejudice of an educated Muslim that led him in an earlier part of his *History*, when he was trying to summarize the vices of the inhabitants of Africa—he had just listed their virtues and was determined to show his impartiality, 'the dutie of a historiographer' being 'to set down the plaine truth in all places'—to write a sentence that must have given some of his European readers that lovely thrill of having their own prejudices confirmed by an expert. 'The Negros leade a beastly kinde of life, being utterly destitute of the use of reason, of dexteritie of wit, and of all artes. Yea they so behave themselves as if they had continually lived in a forest among wilde beasts.' This brief, rash judgement influenced his readers more, one suspects, than all the matter contained in his book on Negroland. But that book is what appeals to a modern reader. In its packed and vivid detail, so judiciously selected to reveal, on the one hand, the wealth and culture of the courts and cities, on the other, the poverty and backwardness of the countryside it stands as a little masterpiece of descriptive writing.[8]

Leo's contribution to the geographical knowledge of his age was then a very considerable one; without his book European scholars would never have heard of the group of Hausa states, Kano, Katsina, Gobir, Zamfara and Zeg-zeg (Zaria)—Leo, it should be noted, does not in fact use the word Hausa, though he remarks that all these states speak the language of Gobir—nor would they have been made aware of the division of the Saharan tribes, while their knowledge of Timbuktu, Gao and Bornu would have remained shadowy in the extreme. Unfortunately he committed geographers to one gross error about the course of the river Niger. 'The Niger,' he asserted (Pory made a hash of this passage, so one has to use a modern version), 'rises from a very large lake in the desert of the Seu in the east, and flows westward into the Ocean: and our Cosmographers assert that it is a branch of the Nile, which flows underground and on issuing forms the Lake referred to. Others assert that this river rises in some mountain in the West, flows East and forms a lake. Such, however, is not the case, for we navigated it with the current from Timbuktu to Guinea and Melli, which are to the West of Timbuktu.' This powerful testimony, which, after all, only confirmed what al-Idrisi had said, came to be very widely accepted. Most European maps produced in the seventeenth and eighteenth centuries showed the Niger flowing westwards, having a triple mouth formed of the Gambia, the Senegal and the Rio Grande. Though there were a few critical and original minds who could produce some evidence to dispute this view, it was not until a European had come to stand on the banks of the river and observe with his own eyes the direction of its flow that this drastic error was generally corrected.[9]

Leo misled the most critical of his readers in two other ways. 'Our ancient Chroniclers of Africa,' he wrote, 'to wit, Bichri and Meshudi, knew nothing of the land of Negros, but only the regions of Guechat and Cano.' In fact, Masudi, whose geography was known in Europe, makes no mention of these places, while al-Bakri's much more detailed account was not available. European scholars were therefore forced to turn to al-Idrisi. Now the only place in al-Idrisi's text which sounded like Cano was Ghana: so scholars proceeded to equate the two, though Kumbi Saleh, the site of ancient Ghana, and Kano, the Hausa city, lie over a thousand miles apart. But al-Idrisi had placed his Wangara not far from Ghana, and Leo had a Wangara not far from Kano; the two geographers had different Wangaras in mind, the one Bure or Bambuk, the other the Zamfara valley; it was impossible for even the sharpest-minded scholar to avoid being misled.[10]

These cartographical technicalities are a little boring—why bother about them? For a good reason: by tracing how mistakes arose, one can come nearer to the state of mind of European geographers of the eighteenth century and feel something of the confusion, the bafflement, the irritation they had to live with all their lives as they tried to make sense of the shape of a part of the old world, not covered, as were certain parts of the centre of Africa, in an utterly unbroken darkness, but lit by a source, brilliantly precise—according to the limits of the age—for some countries, tiresomely vague about others.

III

GUINEA

THE PORTUGUESE

LEO WAS THE LAST of the writers of Arab descent to leave a description of Africa; for by the time his book appeared, the daring mariners of Portugal had already mapped the giant outline of the continent and established their trading posts along its coast. Over Guinea the Portuguese asserted their monopoly and were strong enough in the first half of the sixteenth century to enforce it: monopoly of trade and also, in so far as they could secure it, monopoly of information. Thus some of the writings of Portuguese navigators—the *Esmeraldo de Situ Orbis* of Pachecho Pereira is one example—seem to have been deliberately censored and have been brought out of the darkness of the official archives only in recent years. But among those who sailed to the West Coast was a young Venetian, Alvise da Ca'da Mosto (Cadamosto became the English form of the name), who made two voyages to the Senegal and beyond in the 1450s. His was the first original account to be published by anyone who had sailed those fabulous seas; it appeared first in Vicenza in 1507 and was later given wider publicity by Ramusio.[1]

Cadamosto's is by any standards an excellent account, vivid, truthful, observant and concise. Here are his reflections after a visit to a Senegal chief 'the Lord Budomel' (possibly the Damel of Cayor): 'preeminence in this country does not consist in treasures or money of any sort (which they despise), but in the multiplicity of ceremonies and in the splendour and greatness of the train they are attended with.' And here a point about local markets: 'their poverty may best be known on such occasions by the trifling value of the goods they carry for sale.' And here the Wolof women: 'very gay and airy', 'much inclined to singing and dancing, but they never dance except by moonlight'. Anyone who has lived or travelled in the Sudanic belt will at once acknowledge the rightness of Cadamosto's observations.[2]

One other point in Cadamosto's narrative must be singled out— the information he gathered about the trade of the interior. He grasped very clearly the grand line of commerce in the western Sahara and Sudan, the trade in salt and gold. His Moorish inform-ants told him of the desert mines at Teghaza, 'which signifies a chest of gold, where a vast quantity of rock salt is got'. He learnt how the salt was carried in great slabs on camel-back southwards to Timbuktu and to Mali, then the capital of a great but declining empire. At Mali so intense was the heat that the people 'ran the risk of having the blood stagnated', and were preserved from 'destruction' only by drinking a daily dose of salt dissolved in water (a precaution still recommended to those who sojourn in the tropics). The slabs of the salt were broken up into small pieces and carried on men's heads a great distance to a country where it could be exchanged for gold by the mysterious ritual of the silent trade, a country whose shy inhabi-tants were extremely black, with enormous under-lips that 'hung down towards their breasts and dripped something like blood'.*
Cadamosto was a clever man to learn so much, but he was also lucky in his age, for African traders had not yet had cause to regard the Europeans who came to the West Coast as commercial rivals to be checked most easily by a conspiracy of silence. Cadamosto's know-ledge is limited enough; yet it is in some respects greater than that

* The 'silent trade' was first described by Herodotus. 'The Carthaginians say that beyond the Columns of Hercules is a region of Libya well in-habited; where when they arrive, they unload their Merchandize on the Shore, and returning again to their Ships, make great Fires: That the Inhabitants seeing the Smoak, come down to the Coast, and leaving Gold in exchange for the Goods, depart again to some Distance from the Place: That the Carthaginians at the same Time going ashore, view the Gold: and if the Quantity seem sufficient for the Goods, they take it up and sail away; but if they are not contented, they return to their Ships and continue there: That the Libyans upon this come again, and lay down more Gold to the former 'till they have satisfied the Merchants; that no Wrong is done on either part, the Carthaginians never touch the Gold, before they acquiesce in the Price; nor the Inhabitants the Merchandize, before the Gold is taken away.' Cadamosto described the trade in much the same terms, except that the trade took place on the banks of a lake or river and not on a sea-shore. It has been suggested that the area to which the mer-chants of Mali went for gold was Lobi on the upper Volta, where some of the local tribes still wear lip-discs, and where there are remains of ancient gold-workings.[4]

possessed by the European traders who worked on the coast in the eighteenth century. This is a surprising and a significant fact.[3]

After Cadamosto, the most informative account of Portuguese activities was to be found in the official history of the country's expansion, the great work, *Da Asia*, by João de Barros, a civil servant with first-hand experience of West Africa, having served as Commander of the fortress at Elmina in the 1520s. The first 'decades' of de Barros's history appeared in Portugal in the 1550s and were not reprinted until 1778; they were never translated. Those who could not read Portuguese would know nothing of the work, apart from a few brief extracts in Astley and Prévost. This was unfortunate, for de Barros's book contained sufficient information to give a pretty clear picture both of the depth and of the slenderness of the Portuguese penetration of the interior.[5]

The Portuguese, in the course of their bold probing down the unknown coast of Africa, had been lured on not only by reports of gold but also by rumours of the presence of a great Christian monarch in the interior, the fabulous Prester John, who might prove the most valuable and strategically placed of allies in their long crusade against the Muslims. In 1486 the Portuguese thought they had wind of this mysterious personage. The year before, one of their captains, Fernao do Po (the island he discovered took his name), made contact with the ruler of Benin and brought back to Lisbon ambassadors from that state. These ambassadors told their Portuguese hosts that the greatest king in their country was a certain Ogané, to whom, though he lived 'twenty moons' distant to the east of Benin, every ruler of Benin had, on his accession, to apply for investment and from whom he received 'a staff and head-piece of shining brass' and a brass cross to be worn round the neck 'as a holy and religious emblem.' This Ogané was a divine king, who never showed his face to the ambassadors of Benin, but received them, hidden behind curtains of silk, revealing nothing of himself but his foot, when the interview was at an end. Who could this Ogané be, thought the Portuguese, but Prester John himself?[*][6]

Two or three years later the Portuguese king, João II, already, according to de Barros, 'very well informed' about the geography of the interior, learnt of another powerful and possibly Christian king

* In fact, the Ogané seems almost certainly to have been the Oni of Ife, whom the Edo of Benin still call *Oghene*. Ife was the religious centre not only for Benin but also for the Yoruba of Oyo.[7]

in the heart of Africa. The information reached him in a curious way. A Wolof ruler, Bemoy, had been brought to Lisbon, after being over-thrown by a rival and taking refuge in the Portuguese factory at Arguin. In Lisbon he was received 'in every respect as a Sovereign Lord, accustomed to our civilization and not as a barbarous prince outside the law', baptized and given 'the worldly honour of knight-hood'. 'In return for this honour he had engaged himself to subject to the King every state he might conquer or possess'. From Bemoy João learnt of the existence of a ruler, 'the king of the people of Moses, whose state began beyond Timbuktu and extended towards the Orient—a King neither Moor nor gentile, with customs in many ways like those of Christian peoples'. This was probably a reference to the formidable kingdom of the Mossi people established in the area of the Niger bend; but for João of Portugal the ruler of this mysterious kingdom seemed more likely to be the Prester John, 'whom he so eagerly wished to meet'.

João therefore decided to send an expedition, made up of twenty caravels, to restore Bemoy and to establish a fort on the river Sene-gal, which might serve both as a 'door' for the penetration of the interior and as a depot to tap the gold trade. In its immediate results the expedition miscarried disastrously; the Portuguese commander accused Bemoy of treachery, stabbed him to death and returned home, leaving the fort uncompleted. But the people of Senegal, used to seeing only one or two Portuguese ships with 'poor and ill-clothed sailors', had been 'amazed' at the sight of 'so many ships, so many gallant people and such warlike equipment', all deployed in the cause of a local princeling. Several other rulers then began to seek the friendship and alliance of the Portuguese; 'this resulted in so much intercourse with these people that the King began with more confi-dence to send his agents with messages to their greatest princes, and to intervene in their affairs and wars as a known and valued friend'.[8]

Of the missions despatched by João into the interior the most important seems to have been sent to Mandi Mansa, ruler of the empire of Mali.* 'On this mission went one Rodrigo Rabelo, a squire

* Mali had been founded in the thirteenth century and reached its apogee in the next century, when the rich cities of the Niger bend were among its vassals. The site of Niani, the capital of the Empire, lies on the present frontier between the modern republics of Guinea and Mali. In the fifteenth century Mali was weakened by the rising power of the Songhai but was able to extend its influence westwards into the countries on either side of the Gambia.

of his household, Pero Reinel, gentleman of the spurs, and João Colaço, crossbow man of the chamber, with other auxiliaries, making a total of eight persons. They took him as a present horses, beasts of burden, and mules with their harnesses and several other gifts much appreciated in that land, for they had been sent before. Of them all Pero Reinel alone escaped, being more accustomed to these parts; the others died of disease.' This mission travelled by way of the Gambia; but it was possible to send another by quite a different route, northwards from Elmina on the Gold Coast. 'This Moorish king—in reply to our king's message, amazed at this novelty (according to what we have read in these letters, which are in our possession) said that none of the four thousand four hundred and four kings from whom he was descended had received a message or had seen a messenger of a Christian king.' This intercourse with Mali was renewed forty years later, when in 1534 another Portuguese mission was able to visit the capital.

Mali, in its decline ringed round with enemies, had good reason to court an alliance with the Portuguese. The Portuguese, however, did not scruple to make contact with Mali's opponents, among them a Fulani tribe under a 'fiery warrior named Temalo', who had 'rebelled in a district called Futa' and the Mossi, 'those people of Moses' of Bemoy's report, to whose ruler King João 'sent a letter by an Abyssinian called Lucas, who went by way of Jerusalem'. João also made contact with Tekrur on the Senegal and with Timbuktu; infuriatingly, de Barros, who was obviously very well informed, goes no further than mentioning the name of these places. Finally, in this period the Portuguese made an attempt to establish a factory at Wadan in the southern Sahara, with the intention of capturing some of the gold trade and gathering more information about the interior. The factory was short lived; 'the country was desert'—one must read between the lines of this terse comment of de Barros—and the local Moors would not tell the Portuguese anything about the interior.[9]

All these efforts took place in the reign of João II and were due to the king's initiative.

He was so occupied and so eager in these affairs, that his mind was never at rest, chiefly since he saw and enjoyed many things unknown to the classical writers on this part of Africa. And as a hungry lion, from whom the game hides fearfully in some thorny bush, which he prowls round and attacks on many sides, is wounded and hurt by the thorns, in entering and coming out, and tires of hurling himself upon the hidden

64

prey—so the king, continually attacking on many sides this great bush of Guiné, which until today had not been entered, exhausted by this continual expenditure of his wealth and also by the many worries arising from the affairs of the kingdom, especially at the time of the treasons, rested somewhat from this great zeal which consumed him.

This splendid and vigorous paragraph of de Barros's should serve to win for the king an honoured place among the great patrons of African exploration, to show him as a worthy successor of Prince Henry the Navigator. Yet in political terms his attempts had all ended in failure.[10]

With enterprises on hand or colonies established in Sofala and Mombasa, at Goa, in the Spice Islands and in Brazil, Portugal, a small nation heroically extended, lacked the resources to consolidate the penetration of the interior of West Africa. Indeed, with mounting difficulties at home and increasing pressure from maritime rivals abroad, official Portuguese enterprise on the West Coast declined disastrously after the end of the sixteenth century. But this did not mark the end of Portuguese influence. A Frenchman, Villault de Bellefond, who visited the coast in the 1660s, summed up the position of the Portuguese in a concise and fascinating paragraph.

> The Portuguais being overpower'd by the English and the Dutch and beaten off from the Coasts in the year 1604, they retreated further into the Countrey, and marrying with the Natives, have begot that generation of people, they call Mullettos or Olive-couler'd, and have by that means acquired such an interest amongst them, as have been the cause we have made no further discoveries there, and that they doe to this day go away with the whole Inland Trade; he that should endeavour to share with them being certain to be destroyed by their great influence and authority with the Negros; so that they have ingross'd that whole commerce to themselves, passing up and down every where as they please, and running up the Niger as far as Benin, which is more than 800 leagues.[11]

So these Portuguese adventurers had then, if Villault is to be believed, solved for their own purpose the riddle of the Niger. It is certainly not impossible that they should have done so—and why should they, any more than the officials at Lisbon, be prepared to reveal their secrets? Clearly the Portuguese knew a great deal about the interior; whether scholars in England or France in the eighteenth century realized the possible extent of Portuguese knowledge is uncertain. But at the beginning of the nineteenth century Hugh Murray commented shrewdly that 'the archives of the Portuguese monarchy must contain very important information' about the interior. 'It is probably owing to the reserved character of the Portuguese government, that the knowledge displayed by their writers does not altogether correspond to these opportunities.' Alas, the Torre do Tombo at Lisbon has never given up its secrets. 'Deliberate destruction of documents for security reasons or in the course of archival reorganization, and the accidental ravages of the Lisbon earthquake of 1755, have reduced to a fragmentary condition what must once have been an exceptionally comprehensive series of records': this is the disappointing report of a modern scholar, Dr A. F. C. Ryder, who has recently made a survey of the Portuguese archives. To the eighteenth century's knowledge of the interior of the northern half of Africa, the Portuguese had less to contribute than the Arabs.[12]

THE ENGLISH, THE FRENCH AND THE DUTCH

By the middle of the sixteenth century English, French and Dutch sailors had begun to visit the coast of Africa, which the Portuguese had maintained for a hundred years as their own preserve. With the establishment of plantation-colonies in the West Indies and the ever-growing demand for slave labour, the trade of the maritime nations of Europe with the West Coast of Africa steadily increased. This growing interest was reflected in the number of books on West Africa: a single one in the sixteenth century, a handful in the seventeenth, a shelf-full in the first half of the eighteenth.

The earliest accounts of voyages to Guinea were to be found in Hakluyt's collection, beginning in the reign of Henry VIII with 'olde M. William Haukins of Plimmouth', who 'not contented with the short voyages commonly then made onely to the knowne coasts of Europe, armed out a tall and goodly shippe of his own . . . wherwith he made three long and famous voyages unto the coast of Bresil . . . in the course of which voyages he touched at the river of Sestos upon the coast of Guinea, where hee traffiqued with the Negros and tooke of them Elephants teeth and other commodities'. The voyages described by Hakluyt were in themselves not especially remarkable; but the magnificent Elizabethan prose invests them with an epic notability, stamping certain scenes on the reader's mind with fresh and compact power. The climate of the West Coast, for instance, as described in the account of the first English voyage to Benin: 'smothering heate with close and cloudie aire, and storming weather, of such putrifying quality that it rotted the coates of their backs'; or the court of the king of Benin, 'who being a blacke Moor (although not so blacke as the rest) sate in a great huge hall, long and wide, the wals made of earth without windowes, the roofe of thin boards, open in sundry places, like unto lovers to let in the air', whose subjects bore him such 'great reverence' that 'when his noblemen are in his presence, they never looke him in the face, but sit cowring . . . upon their buttocks, with their elbowes upon their knees and their hands before their faces, not looking up until the king commands them'.[1]

The seventeenth century produced only one English work on West Africa, Richard Jobson's account of his voyage up the Gambia. Purchas included extensive extracts from Jobson in his collection of travels; he also introduced to English readers the first Dutch work describing 'the Golden Kingdom of Guinea', an account of the Gold Coast written by a trader, Pieter de Marees, at the beginning of the century. The first French narrative of a voyage to the West Coast did not appear until 1642, a superficial work by a well-to-do young man, Claude Jannequin, who had visited the Senegal as a passenger in a trading vessel. Two more serious accounts appeared in the last half of the century, one by Villault de Bellefond, the other by a surgeon, Sieur Le Maire. Villault found his countrymen being ousted by their trade-rivals, the English and the Dutch, and intended his description of 'the Coasts of Africk called Guinee' to serve as a call to action. These works could not compare in comprehensiveness with the description of Africa produced by the Dutch geographer, Olfert Dapper. Of West Africa, Dapper provided a particularly valuable account, for he made use of many works by his own countrymen that existed only in manuscript. Yet in spite of Dapper's work, another Dutchman, Bosman, writing at the beginning of the eighteenth century, could say that 'the coast of Guinea is for the most part unknown' and the 'few scraps' available in the existing books 'afford but a sorry sketch of Guinea'. He sought to remedy this deficiency by drawing on his own fourteen years' experience of West Africa to produce in 1704 *A New and Accurate Description of the Coast of Guinea*. A work with a wider scope, *A Description of the Coasts of North and South Guinea and of Ethiopia Inferior*, appeared in one of the volumes of Churchill's *Voyages* in 1732. Its author was John or Jean Barbot, a French Huguenot, who had taken up residence in England; in the 1660s he had been 'Agent-General of the Royal Company of Africa at Paris' and made many visits to the West Coast in this capacity. 'Whereso-ever I was,' he wrote in the introduction to his book, 'either at sea or ashore, I us'd to pry into every object that occur'd to the eye, and made enquiry after what I could not have the opportunity of seeing, if there was anything in it either curious or useful; and immediately noted it down in my pocket-book.' Barbot did not confine himself to what he had seen or heard himself but drew on other writers, includ-ing Bosman, usually without acknowledgement.[2]

Barbot's great tome—it runs to over six hundred folio pages—was the largest work available on West Africa to the eighteenth-century reader, but its contents could be supplemented by a number of other accounts. On the Senegal the key work was the *Nouvelle Relation de l'Afrique Occidentale*, by Pére Labat. Labat, a Dominican father, compiled a number of travel books. He had never been in Africa, but drew extensively on the memoirs of André Brue, the energetic gov-ernor of the Senegal at the beginning of the century. On the Gambia Francis Moore provided the diary, misleadingly entitled *Travels in the Inland Parts of Africa*, of his five years as a writer in the factories of the Royal African Company on the Gambia River; Moore was a man of some scholarship, capable of giving a vivid and sensible account of his experiences. Brue and Moore, like Bosman, had the advantage of having lived in Africa for a long stretch of time.[3]

Less detailed, more superficial were the books of those who had come only on trading voyages: two English ships' captains, Thomas Phillips and William Snelgrave, a French captain, des Marchais, an English surgeon, Atkins—and, in a slightly different capacity, a sur-veyor sent out by the Royal African Company to report on its forts, William Smith. Yet these books had the advantage of being more easily digested than Barbot's massive folio; inevitably they contain much that is repetitive, yet none of them is without illuminating flashes and some of them contain passages of great historical interest —Snelgrave's account, for instance, of his visit to the camp of the king of Dahomey after that ruler had conquered Whydah. All these works, except Bosman's, appeared between 1728 and 1745. In 1757 there was published the first book about West Africa by a man not connected with trade, Michael Adanson, a young naturalist sup-ported by the French East India Company—'the first philosopher', so he was called in the preface to his work, 'who adventured to visit the torrid zone for the propagation of knowledge'. Adanson spent five years on the coastal areas of Senegal, living closely with Africans and observing them with a mind unpreoccupied by the constant necessity of driving a hard bargain.

In these few books, the curious reader could find a mass of information 'describing', as William Smith engagingly put it in the title of his *New Voyage to Guinea*, 'the Customs, Manners, Soil, Climate, Habits, Buildings, Education, Manual Arts, Agriculture, Trade, Employments, Languages, Ranks of Distinction, Habitations, Diversions, Marriages and whatever else is memorable among the Inhabitants, likewise an Account of their Animals, Minerals, etc., with great variety of entertaining incidents, worthy of Observation' for that 'large Country' from Arguin to the Cameroons. Much of this material is irrelevant here, but it will be profitable to ask first with the philosopher what impression these writers might give of the nature of man in Africa, then with the geographer what information they conveyed about the interior.

If the eighteenth-century philosopher started off with a set of pre-conceptions in his mind, derived either from Hobbes or Rousseau, about the squalor or the virtue of 'primitive' society, or even if he accepted the notion that all Africans were savages, he would, if he were honest, soon find himself having to modify his views. In the first place he would have been shown that West Africa contained such a variety of tribes that it was really impossible to generalize about Africans in the mass. There was Le Maire, for instance, pointing the contrast between the Moors 'small, meager and of an uncouth mien' but with a 'genius that's free and refin'd' and the Negroes 'large, fat and well-proportioned but very silly and of shallow conceptions'. This, of course, might help to bolster up the notion of inherent white superiority, for the Moors were white-skinned—or nearly so. But was Le Maire justified in his remarks about the Negroes? The Felups, who lived in the Bissagos islands, might strike Barbot as being 'exceedingly barbarous and cruel', but Adanson had found the Wolof of Senegal 'very good natured, sociable and obliging'. Then again there was a striking contrast, as Barbot had shown, between the Africans of the Pepper coast, 'a strong sturdy, laborious sort of men', who spoke a language none could understand, so that trade had to be carried on by means of signs and gestures and those of the Gold Coast, many of whom could speak European languages, 'men of sense and wit enough, of a sharp, ready apprehension and skill in business'. Other paradoxes would strike the attentive reader and puncture his generalizations: the average African was a black man, living in a simple mud hut—a reasonable statement, surely, but how then did one account for the metropolis of Benin, a city 'prodigious large' with 'thirty very great streets' and a palace that took up as much space, according to Barbot, as the whole town of Bordeaux?[4]

If it was impossible to generalize about Africans in the mass, every author was prepared to pass judgement on the character of individual tribes. Thus Barbot on the 'Blacks' of Senegambia: 'they are genteel and courteous in their way, but leud and lazy to excess, which may perhaps proceed from the fertility of their climate, affording them all that is necessary to their support without much labour'; 'they are generally extremely sensual, knavish, revengefull, impudent, lyars, impertinent, gluttonous, extravagant in their expressions and so intemperate that they drink brandy as if it were water'. Or Bosman booming out, like the old coaster that he was, his opinion of the 'Natural Temper of the Natives': 'To begin, the Negroes are all without exception crafty, villainous and fraudulent, and very seldom to be trusted ... they indeed seem to be born and bred villains ... these degenerate vices are accompanied by their Sister, Sloth and Idleness ... they are besides so incredibly careless and stupid' ... and so on. Yet at Whydah only a little way along the coast Smith found that the natives were 'the most Gentleman-like Negroes in all Guinea, abounding in Good Manners and Ceremony to each other' and 'naturally industrious'. So, too, the people of Benin were generally regarded as being 'very civil and good natured'.[5]

On the whole, the balance of opinion about Africans was an unfavourable one: Lord Chesterfield would have found passages enough to gratify him in his prejudice. But he would also have come across a few remarks that should have made him stop and think. Moore, for instance, writing in his diary: 'The Natives really are not so disagreeable in their Behaviour as we are apt to imagine; for when I went thro' any of their Towns, they almost all came to shake hands with me, except some of the Women, who having never seen any White Men ran away from me as fast as they could.' Or Captain Phillips: 'Nor can I imagine why they should be despised for their colour being what they cannot help, and the effects of the climate it has pleased God to appoint them. I can't think that there is any intrinsic value in one colour more than another, nor that white is better than black, only we think it so because we are so, and are prone to judge favourably in our own case, as well as the blacks, who in odium of the colour, say, the devil is white and so paint him.' Or, in some ways

70

most remarkable of all the words of that old coaster, Charles Wheeler, who travelled on the same ship home as William Smith, (Astley's editor thought Wheeler's remarks a complete fabrication; on the contrary, they have a remarkable ring of truth): 'A Guinean by treading in the Paths prescribed by his Ancestors, paths naturally pleasant and diverting, is in the plain Road to be a good and happy Man; but the European has sought so many Inventions and has endeavour'd to put so many Restrictions upon Nature that it would be next to a Miracle if he were either happy or good . . . I thought that Polygamy . . . was a very bad Custom but I soon found my aversion to it was only the Prejudice of a different Education.'[6]

What sense could the stay-at-home Englishmen make of these conflicting views? He should have come to realize that in the play of generalizations, when so much depended on the eye of the beholder, there was as much to be said in defence of Africans as against them. He might have seen too that the nefarious practice of the slave trade bedevilled relations between black and white. Even Barbot, who was himself involved in the trade, recognized this: 'If the Negros be generally crafty and treacherous, it may well be said, the Europeans have not dealt with them as becomes Christians', having 'very unjustly and inhumanely, without any provocation, stolen away abundance of the people'. Later, with the development of the anti-slavery movement, the abolitionists came to ascribe all the crimes that blackened the West Coast, and especially the inter-tribal wars, to the effects of the slave trade. Yet that this was rather too simple a view the case of Dahomey, as those with a stake in the trade hastened to point out, served to show. It was during the 1720s that the army of this inland state reached the sea and made contact with Europeans. From then on a constant intercourse was maintained by European merchants; indeed, Dahomey came to be regarded, according to a writer at the end of the century, as 'the country where strangers are least exposed to insults, and where it is easy to reside in security and tranquility'. Yet civilized as the Dahomeyans appeared in their dealings with Europeans, their kings were notorious for their practice of sacrificing in great numbers prisoners captured in war.[7]

One such holocaust occurred in 1777 as the aftermath of a successful campaign; 'the insatiable thirst after blood, the barbarous vanity of being considered the scourge of mankind, and the savage pomp of dwelling in a house garnished with skulls and stained with human gore seem to be the only motives for the atrocious actions'—such was the judgement of Archibald Dalzel, who published a *History of Dahomey* in 1793 after thirty years' experience of the coast. In the same work Dalzel recorded the speech of a Dahomeyan monarch on learning that the Abolitionists in England were asserting that human sacrifice was a product of the conditions arising from the slave trade. 'In the name of my ancestors and myself I aver, that no Dahoman man ever embarked in war merely for the sake of procuring wherewithal to purchase your commodities. I have without thinking of the market killed many thousands. ... When policy or justice requires that men be put to death, neither silk, nor coral, nor brandy, nor cowries can be accepted as substitutes for the blood that ought to be spilt for example's sake.' The bloody annals of Dahomey provided the best example available for those vehement defenders of the slave trade who wished to convince the public of African barbarism. In fact, they were not typical of Africa as a whole, being the result of a convergence of forces as difficult to unravel and comprehend as those that produced the hideous massacre of the Jews in twentieth-century Germany.*[8]

The philosopher's confusion, faced with conflicting accounts of

* Herskovits, in his study of Dahomey, has pointed out that human sacrifice was a royal prerogative and 'in essense an economic phenomenon'. All Dahomeyans sacrificed to their gods; good form demanded that each man should give according to his means—from the poor man beans, from the rich man animals, from the king men. This does not fully explain why human sacrifice came to be practised on such a hideous scale in Dahomey, whereas in neighbouring Oyo it was always strictly limited. It can be argued reasonably enough that the slave trade produced in those, black or white, who were engaged in it an utter contempt for human life, and so created an atmosphere in which the enormities of human sacrifice could be accepted without demur. The history of Benin in the nineteenth century indicates that human sacrifice was employed there as a means of political repression; the same may have been true of Dahomey.

The whole subject of human sacrifice in West Africa needs to be studied by a historically minded social anthropologist. Too many Europeans have been mesmerized by the horrors of Dahomey and Benin into inflating the significance of human sacrifice in West African society; in fact, the holocausts occurred only in limited areas and in limited periods. It is salutary to be reminded of two further points. 'There are few races, and few religions,' according to the author of the article on 'Human Sacrifice' in the *Encyclopaedia of Religion and Ethics*, 'which can show a history free from the stain of human sacrifice.' 'More slaves,' as Basil Davidson has recently pointed out, 'were thrown alive into the Atlantic by slave-ship captains, sacrificing to their god of profitability, than were ever beheaded by the King of Dahomey or the Obas of Benin.'[9]

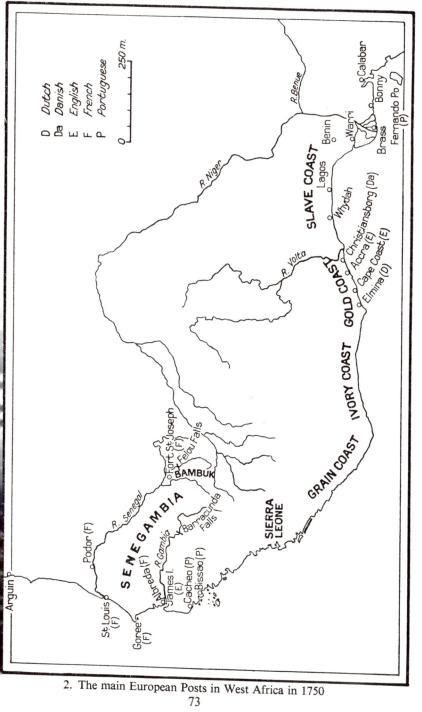

2. The main European Posts in West Africa in 1750

73

civility and barbarism, was matched by the geographer's ignorance, a sensation equally exasperating. Except on the Gambia and the Senegal, two parts that require more extensive treatment, European establishments in West Africa in the middle of the eighteenth century —the forts, factories and posts of the trading companies—were all confined to the coast. The coasts themselves, named after their staple commodities, Pepper or Ivory, Gold or Slaves, were well known, with their islands, bays, creeks, rivers, towns and villages, described and charted. But inland there lay, as Barbot and indeed all Europeans on the coast imagined, 'such wild savage countries, where the roads are, for the most part, narrow and hard to find, being in most parts hid with woods, and overgrown with shrubs: besides being every where pester'd with robbers, in many places quite desart, without any dwellings or subsistence to be found, or any carriage of horses, carts or the like'. These difficulties 'together with the treacherous disposition of the inhabitants', 'the excessive heat of the days in the summer season', 'the continual heavy rains in the winter', and the danger of 'ravenous wild beasts, which swarm in those countries' were sufficient, Barbot considered, 'to deter the boldest and most resolute man' from undertaking a journey into the interior. Ask, then, what lay no more than a hundred miles inland, seek a description of those countries which must exist in that belt of territory, close on a thousand miles in breadth, between the coast and the states of Nigritia as Leo Africanus had described them—and immediately one was confronted with the humiliating limitations of European knowledge. For no European had ever seen those countries; consequently, there was no means of checking the vague, obscure, limited accounts obtained from African sources. For such accounts did exist, the interior was not, as is sometimes suggested, absolutely blank, and yet on certain parts of the interior not a single fact seems ever to have been recorded, or at least ever to have found its way into print.[10]

Thus, on the Slave Coast, represented today by modern Nigeria, there was no conception of the fact that the labyrinth of creeks and rivers lying between Benin and Bonny formed in fact the delta of a great river, whose main stream flowed broad and clear only a hundred miles inland. East of the lower reaches of the river lay the country of the Ibo people, one of the largest of West African tribes. Yet the Ibo are mentioned by the compendious Barbot only through a single line on a map indicating that 'the Hackbous Country is some Leagues above N. Calabar'.[11]

West of the Niger, the Yoruba, lords of Oyo, the greatest and most ancient of the kingdoms of the Forest, were known not at first hand but through the reports of their neighbours, Benin and Dahomey. 'That remote inland Nation,' Barbot calls 'the Oyoes', that 'strike such a terrour at Ardra, and all the adjacent countries, that they can scarce hear them mentioned without trembling; and they tell a world of strange stories about them'.* Beyond Benin other shadowy kingdoms were reported; only their names—Jaboe, Oedoba, Issabo and others—were known.[12]

At the beginning of the eighteenth century the first Muslim merchants—Mandingo from the area covered by the ancient empire of Mali—appeared in Dahomey. Snelgrave, Smith and des Marchais all commented on the presence of these strangers, so different from the natives of the coast in appearance, 'being right East Indians, of a tawny complexion, with long black hair'; in dress, they wore 'long gowns, with a Cloth wreathed about their heads like a Turkish Turbant'; and in attainments, for they were literate in Arabic and skilled leather-workers. The Europeans were told that 'they were Malayes, which is a Nation far inland, bordering on the Moors'—a correct, if confusing designation, which led Smith to suggest that they were 'originally Natives of Mallacca, a huge Promontory in Asia', driven from their homes by Dutch oppression and settled on the coast of the Red Sea. It was evident that they could supply a great deal of information about the interior; but the European traders were

* One such story, relating to a Yoruba invasion of Dahomey, was told to Captain Snelgrave by a Portuguese mulatto in the camp of the King of Dahomey. The Yoruba army consisted of cavalry, that of Dahomey of infantry armed with guns and swords. A four-day battle took place in open country, where the advantage would certainly have gone to the invaders, 'if the unusual Noise of the Dahome's Fire-Arms had not so frightened the Horses that their Riders could never make a Home-Charge on the Enemies Foot'. At last the King of Dahomey, seeing that his soldiers were utterly exhausted, had recourse to a strategem worthy of a Münchausen. He had brought with him 'great quantities of Brandy', which he obtained from the French in exchange for slaves. This he left in his camp, which he evacuated by night. 'When Day came, the J-oes [i.e. Yorubas] thinking the Dahomes were fled, fell to plundering and destroying the Town, and drinking greedily of the Brandy; and as they seldom had tasted of that Liquor before, it so intoxicated them, that they fell asleep in great numbers on the Ground.' Thus the tide was turned, but so fearful was the King of Dahomey at the possibility of another invasion that he sent 'great Presents' to Oyo.[13]

strictly prohibited from talking to them, and a suggestion made by des Marchais's editor, Labat, that a Frenchman, possessing a good knowledge of Arabic, be sent out to accompany the 'Malayes' on their homeward journey was never followed up.[14]

The Gold Coast was the scene of the greatest European activity in West Africa. Yet traders found it impossible to travel into the interior. Nevertheless, Europeans knew more about the hinterland of the Gold Coast than they did of the countries beyond Dahomey, Benin or Calabar. Thus, Bosman was able to provide at second hand a fair description of the inland state of Denkera that lay about a hundred miles from the sea; he had also heard of the rising power of Ashanti farther north. Deeper inland lay the 'Kingdom of Mandinga', the relic of the great empire of Mali, for its rule, as Dapper had been informed, once stretched over a far wider area. The country was said to be rich in gold—a reference probably to the deposits of Bure—and to attract Arab traders from Timbuktu. The people of Mandinga, like the Oyos to the east, were known as formidable horsemen. They had recently accepted Islam; but their king, according to Dapper's report, was reputed to be a great magician with the power of calling up demons to torment his enemies. To the people of the Gold Coast the inhabitants of Mandinga appeared, so Barbot learnt, 'a sort of wild and bloody Blacks'.[15]

In all these accounts the fact of greatest interest to European traders—the exact location of the mines that gave the coast its name —obstinately eluded inquiry. Thus, from 'some rational and judicious Blacks' Barbot gathered that the gold mines were 'not very remote from the coast'. But his informants 'would never tell where, nor how they did work them; so politick and discreet they are in that point, lest foreigners should know them and be tempted to invade their country, for the sake of those subterraneous treasures'.*[16]

The country between the Gold Coast and the Gambia was more

* Barbot was probably not aware of the fact that the Portuguese had on one occasion succeeded in working a gold mine in the interior. In 1623 the Portuguese sent an expedition up the Ankobra River; fifteen miles from the coast a fort was built and a mine opened. A rich yield was obtained, until in 1636 an earthquake destroyed the mine tunnels and many of the surrounding villages. The mine had been sunk in a sacred hill; to the local people the earthquake could appear only as a sign of divine vengeance. 'They took the natural course of burying alive in the mouth of the adit all the Portuguese survivors they could catch as a sacrifice to the god.'[18]

thinly populated than the coasts to the east. Opportunities for trade were, therefore, less inviting and European establishments fewer and usually only of a temporary nature. Nevertheless, information about the interior was by no means negligible. Dapper's report was the fullest; it mentioned the names of many tribes in what is now the hinterland of Liberia and of Sierra Leone, one of the most remote being the Susu, who had their homes in a mountainous country eight days' distance from the coast.[17]

Nowhere in all the country between Calabar and Sierra Leone was any European, at least since the days of the secretive Portuguese, known to have travelled more than a few miles from the coast. But farther north, beyond the forest country, through the bush of the Western Sudan, flowed the Gambia and the Senegal. Both rivers provided possible avenues into the interior. During the seventeenth and early eighteenth centuries the English on the Gambia, the French on the Senegal made a number of attempts to penetrate into the heart of Western Africa.

IV

AVENUES INTO THE INTERIOR

THE ENGLISH ON THE GAMBIA

TO THE SEAFARER THE Gambia is the most inviting of all the rivers of West Africa. Its estuary is wide and deep, its stream tidal and easily navigable; but its course grows increasingly sinuous, and at Barracunda, only two hundred miles in a straight line from the sea, a ledge of rock, misleadingly called 'Falls', forms a barrier that larger boats cannot pass. For another one hundred and forty miles, until its junction with the Nerico, the river is navigable by canoes; thereafter it forms a 'succession of shallow rapids and pools', which no boat can get through. For the first hundred miles from the sea the river is set with mangrove swamps, then bounded by ironstone cliffs, which give way later to 'banks of waving grass, fringed with reed and melting into parkland, reminding one of an English river'. So it appears today: two hundred years ago the country was considerably wilder. A Frenchman, Golbéry, who visited the Gambia in the 1780s, described 'immense forests' covering the banks and noted that 'the great isles of the river as well as the woods are full of elephants, and a number of wild and ferocious animals', while its waters abounded with crocodiles and hippopotami.[1]

Four tribes inhabited the Gambia country: Felup, Mandingo, Wolof and Fulani. The Feloops, the earliest inhabitants, lived to the south of the river in small, primitive, fiercely independent communities. The Mandingos and the Wolofs had migrated from the east, establishing themselves in the Gambia before the coming of the Europeans. In the eighteenth century both people were coming increasingly under the influence of Islam. The Mandingos, who were the most numerous, had formed petty kingdoms of varying stability

78

on either side of the river. The Wolofs occupied the more fertile parts of the country between the Gambia and the Senegal. The Fulani possessed no state of their own, but were found in every kingdom, peaceful infiltrators, excellent farmers as well as pastoralists.[2]

The Portuguese had kept the Gambia as their own preserve for over a century; but the disasters that afflicted their country—the overwhelming defeat and death of King Sebastian in Morocco in 1578, followed by the Spanish annexation two years later—eased the entrance of the French and the English. In 1588 a certain Antonio, bastard son of a Portuguese prince and an unsuccessful claimant to the throne, arrived in England. To raise money to pay his debts he granted a concession to a group of English merchants, who sent out three ships to trade on the Senegambian coast. The English sailor found the Portuguese and Spaniards on the spot actively hostile; many of them were established on the Gambia, which they kept 'concealed' as 'a river of secret trade and riches'. A crowd of desperate ruffians they seemed to the English: 'for the most part banished men or fugitives for committing most hainous crimes and incestuous acts ... of the basest behaviour that we have ever seene of these nations in any other countrey'. A French ship had recently been seized while sailing up the Gambia; the Englishmen prudently avoided the river.[3]

An account of this voyage, written by Richard Rainolds, one of the merchants involved, was published by Hakluyt. That diligent collector was also able to gather some exciting information about the interior. By some uncertain means there had come into his hands a copy of a letter written by a Portuguese trader at Arguin, a trading post on the Saharan coast two hundred miles to the north of the Senegal. This reported that '50 leagues up into the land the Moores have many exceeding rich golde mines', in a country called 'the kingdom of Darha', which contained 'great store of towns and cities'. At Arguin 'for a small trifle they will give us a great wedge of gold'; yet the Portuguese trade was insufficient, and so the gold was carried over the desert to 'the king of Fez'. Even more intriguing was the letter sent home by Laurence Madoc, an English merchant in Morocco, in reply to an inquiry 'to discover the estate and quality of the countries of Tombotu and Gago'. He reported that the King of Morocco had recently sent across the desert an army which had without much difficulty seized these two cities. 'The report is that Mahomed the Moroccan commander bringeth with him such an infinite treasure as I never heard of; it doth appear that they have more gold then any other part of the world beside'.*[4]

Here indeed was a prospect to lure English merchant adventurers. But conditions on the coast were at first too unstable; the Portuguese monopoly had been broken by the French and the Dutch, but international rivalry soon degenerated into piracy, with the estuary of the Gambia providing an ideal hide-out for privateers. In 1619, however, a group of thirty-two shrewd English businessmen came together and formed a company to which James I gave the exclusive right to trade in Guinea and 'Binney' (Benin). It was, however, to the Gambia that the company's first efforts were directed.

The company started by sending to the river a single ship loaded with nearly £2,000 of merchandise, the supercargo being a Barbary merchant of great experience named Thompson. Thompson sailed the ship a hundred miles up the river to Kasson, then transferred to a smaller boat more easily manageable on the higher reaches. But his arrival had incensed the Portuguese traders (many of whom were, in fact, mulattoes), for it meant the end of their monopoly. As soon as Thompson disappeared up the river, the Portuguese attacked the English ship and massacred all the crew that had been left behind. When the news of this disaster reached the directors of the company they did not despair, for at the same time they had received hopeful reports from Thompson on the possibilities of trade. Quickly they fitted out a relief vessel. Within a few weeks of this ship's arrival on the Gambia, most of its crew were dead of fever.

Meanwhile the directors, ignorant of the fate of their second ship, sent out two larger vessels with Captain Richard Jobson as one of the supercargoes. In February 1621 Jobson reached the river, where he learnt that Thompson had been killed in a quarrel with his own men at Tenda over three hundred miles from the coast. Jobson himself spent a year on the Gambia; he reached Tenda but could go no farther, as the river was impassable. However, he was able to establish excellent relations with a merchant of Tenda, Bucknor Sano, from whom he learnt that a few days beyond Tenda lay a town called Tombaconda; this he wrongly assumed to be Timbuktu. He also gathered information on 'the golden trade of the Moores in Barbary'

---

* Some echo of these reports must have been in Shakespeare's mind when he was writing the second part of *King Henry IV* and made the bombastic Pistol burst out, as he announced the glad news to Falstaff that their Hal was king, 'I speak of Africa and golden joys.'

and was told that there lay 'four moons' beyond Tenda 'a great town, the houses whereof are covered only with gold'. Alluring indeed were such reports, but more valuable—though not many may have appreciated it—was a simple truth that Jobson discovered. He had been told on the coast that the people of the interior were 'a bloody and dangerous nation'; he found, on the contrary, that although the natives of Tenda had never seen white men before, they received his company with 'familiar conversation, fair acceptance and mutual amitie'. Jobson had not only treated his African hosts with tact and understanding; in African eyes he had distinguished himself sharply from other Europeans who had come to the river by strictly refusing to engage in the trade in slaves.[5]

On his return to England, Jobson, dazzled by the riches which seemed to lie just over the horizon, pressed hard to be allowed another attempt. From the Company, which had lost nearly £6,000, he obtained no support. He found other backers, but was provided with a ship that proved so unseaworthy that he had to turn back in the English Channel. Undeterred, he appealed to the most exalted quarter in the land, dedicating to the new king a pamphlet, which was never printed, entitled 'The Discovery of the Cuntry of King Solomon his rich trade and trafique within twenty daies sale of England'. 'Some I have known,' wrote Purchas, who included Jobson's account of his journey up the Gambia in his collection, 'which place Ophir neere Gambra. Of this minde was Captaine Jobson. . . . And indeed I doe easily persuade myselfe that the richest Mynes of Gold in the World are in Africa . . . and I cannot but wonder, that so many have sent so many, and spent so much in remoter voyages to the East and West and neglected Africa in the midst; which perhaps might prove as much richer as neerer, then both the Indies.' Splendid, fantastic vision: the ships of King Solomon fetching gold from the western Sudan. But English businessmen who wanted gold from Africa found it much easier to send ships to the Gold Coast, where the first English post was established in 1631. For the reign of Charles I the Gambia and its hidden treasures were ignored.[6]

Thirty years passed. In 1651 a new Company was formed under a patent from the Commonwealth government. A trader of this Company, Langley, went beyond the Barracunda Falls and picked up rumours of a mountain of gold in the interior. He died on the Gambia, while the ships sent out to support him fell into the hands of that most dashing of Royalists, Prince Rupert, who had taken to privateering in the struggle with the enemies of his king. Rupert's appearance in the Gambia River is a curious episode in the territory's history; even stranger was the establishment of a small fort near the mouth of the river by an enterprising Baltic princeling, James Duke of Courland, who sought slaves for his colony in the West Indies.

Rupert remembered what he had heard about the mountain of gold; no sooner was Charles II restored to his throne than a plan was put forward with the support of some of the highest in the land, including James, Duke of York, to reach this Eldorado. An ambitious expedition was sent out; its only lasting achievement was to drive the Courlanders from their base, which was taken and renamed James Island. This insalubrious spot, dependent always on the mainland for its drinking water, remained the principal English base on the river for the next hundred years. Only one member of the expedition concerned himself with the search for gold, Colonel Vermuyden, who set off up the river in a small boat with a crew of seven. His account indicates more expressively than any other the difficulties to be met with after Barracunda. 'Up the buffing Stream, with sad Labour, we wrought, and sometimes could not go above two Miles in a Day'; 'often in a Day we were constrained to strip ourselves, and leap into the Water, with main strength to force our Boats over the Flats'. In four months they reached farther, so he reckoned, than any boat had ever been before, but at the point where they had to turn back, Vermuyden hit gold. So much was 'the vast Proportion of Gold I discovered there,' he wrote later, that 'I was more troubled to obscure its Abundance from my Fellows, than to bring down what I got'. This perverse attitude, combined with an unwillingness to follow up his discovery, threw his whole account into discredit; in fact, the geographical details of his journey are true enough, but no one ever discovered what strange quirk of mind had led him to make such 'vainglorious exaggeration' about the gold which at the best can only have been some poor alluvial deposits.[7]

So the English on James Island had to content themselves with more prosaic commodities—slaves, ivory and hides. But in the 1680s a new attempt was made to unravel the mysteries of the interior; it was due to the energy of a tough and brutal sea-captain, Cornelius Hodges. Hodges made three journeys. In the first two, in 1681 and 1688, he kept to the river, but on the third in 1689 he determined to strike overland, taking with him sixty-eight men and a substantial quantity of trade goods, from Barracunda to Bambuk. He was able to leave Barracunda only 'after very strong disputes with ye Mandingo Chief and ye overcoming a vast many threats they put me too, upon their understanding my Designe of travelling to ye gold-mines'. Harassed by the hostility of local traders and suffering gravely from lack of provisions, he succeeded in reaching Bambuk; but when he visited the gold mines of Nettico he found that famine in the surrounding country prevented them from being worked that year. Learning, however, that much of the gold was sent to 'Tarra' 'a place in the Moors country', well known as a mart for slaves, Hodges decided to send a party of his men there, taking with them 'a reasonable cargo'. His men reached 'Tarra' after a journey of three hundred miles and found it 'very neare as bigg as ye Citty of London' with houses built of stone. Shortly after their arrival, a Moroccan army, forty thousand strong and led by the Emperor in person, appeared and laid siege to the town. Hodges's men presented themselves to the Emperor and were granted 'a very kind reception'. A battle then ensued; the visitors joined in, used their fire-arms to good effect and played a large part in the Moroccan victory. On their departure the Emperor requested them to bring their leader to him, presenting them with 'a very fine Barbary horse' and two camels for his conveyance. With this message they returned to Hodges, who had waited in Bambuk.*

Hodges prepared to set out for 'Tarra' immediately; but his enemies, the Mandingo traders, 'began to play their parts Bravely saying that since I was not satisfied with understanding ye Gold Trade, but I must make Inspection into ye Slave Trade, I should pay dearly for my experience'. Three times they tried to catch him, but he escaped and moved northwards across the Senegal, only to find himself finally surrounded by a body of four hundred horsemen. The intervention of three marabouts, 'being touched with a desire of Doeing good', saved him from being cut down on the spot; but for his boldness he was forced to pay dearly by surrendering all his goods. There was no alternative now but to return the way he had come. Famine made dreadful his passage through Bambuk; 'I had lived 5 months on wild fruites, Roots, such as I could gett in ye woods and never nearer

---

* 'Tarra' seems likely to have been Atar, a town known to have existed in the seventeenth century and today one of the most important centres in Mauritania. The credibility of Hodges's narrative is confirmed by the fact that the Emperor Mulay Ismail (1672–1727) is known to have sent several expeditions south into Mauritania.[8]

starving in all my life. Some of my people dying of hunger and the natives daily!' When he returned to Barracunda he had been away just over a year. Hodges's full report of his remarkable journey lay hidden in the files of the Royal African Company, and was not published until the present century; but his exploit was not entirely unknown, for Labat mentioned, albeit too briefly, that a certain 'Agis', an English sea-captain, had reached Bambuk from the Gambia 'with almost inexpressible fatigue'. Praise where praise is due: Hodges deserves to be remembered as the most enterprising English explorer in West Africa before the age of Houghton and of Park.[9]

For the next twenty years the English on the Gambia were too harassed by their wars with the French, in the course of which James Island was twice captured and left desolate, to think about the possibilities of the interior. But in 1720 a new attempt was made. The driving spirit was the Duke of Chandos, who had recently put a substantial amount of his money into the declining Royal African Company. Under his initiative a committee was set up to report on the state of trade. It pointed out among its recommendations that 'a Thorough Knowledge of the Inland Parts of Africa may prove of very great advantage to the Company'. An elaborate questionnaire was drawn up to be used by the company's agents in gaining information from the slaves brought down to the coast; furthermore, it was suggested that if any of the slaves be found 'of Superior Rank or better Understanding', they should be released, given samples of the Company's wares and sent back to their homes, accompanied by 'a Factor or writer with some soldiers', 'to bring back the returns of this trade or to settle, if it be found convenient a Factory in some part of the kingdom they belong to'. It seems unlikely that these excellent suggestions led to any practical results; such, of course, is not infrequently the fate of the bright ideas that emanate from Head Offices.[10]

For the expedition up the Gambia special arrangements were put in hand that would not be dependent on the vagaries of the Company's servants at their wretched stations on the coast. Since technical skill and scientific knowledge would be required in exploiting the gold mines, a band of Cornish miners was recruited, together with a botanist and a chemist. They set sail in a ship that was lost at sea. Again, as with that other Gambian expedition almost exactly a hundred years earlier, the Directors refused to give in. They prepared another ship and gave the command to Captain Bartholomew Stibbs;

he was to go 'in quest of the Gold Mines and making other Discoveries'. Arrived on the Gambia, Stibbs set out with fourteen other white men and thirty-eight Africans in five canoes. The expedition lasted less than three months. Fifty-nine miles beyond the Barracunda Falls they found it impossible to continue. Stibbs excused himself on the grounds that the local people had assured him that he had set out too long after the rains to have a chance of being able to reach Tenda by way of the river. His prolix account leaves an impression neither of energy nor of enterprise.[11]

Stibbs's expedition was the last attempt to use the line of the river as an avenue for exploration. In the next seventy years not one scrap was added to the scanty knowledge possessed of the interior, so that Francis Moore, who spent five years on the river, could still believe that the Gambia was one of the mouths of the Niger. The golden dream had faded; it would need other motives to stir men into action.*

THE FRENCH ON THE SENEGAL

The River Senegal is considerably longer than the Gambia but less easy of access, its mouth being guarded by a long and constantly shifting sand-spit that forms a dangerous underwater bar. The river itself is navigable, when in full flood during the rainy season, for a distance—taken in a straight line from the coast—of some six hundred miles; but during the long dry season it grows so shallow that boats can then only use the first three hundred miles of its course. 'There is perhaps no river in the world,' wrote Golbéry, 'which has so many turnings, circumvolutions and contortions.' But meandering was the least of its inconveniences: 'sand-banks and congeries of rocks . . . enormous trees which its waters detach and bear along with

* In the 1780s the Gambia again attracted the attention of men of affairs in Britain when it was seriously considered as a possible site for a convict settlement to replace the lost 'dumping-ground' in America. Encouraged by the statement of a former Chief Justice of Senegambia that the Gambia was 'the richest spot in Africa', the British Government purchased an island in the river over one hundred miles from the sea. Here the convicts were to be left, with tools and provisions, to fend for themselves. 'In a very few years', it was anticipated, 'they would become Planters . . . as they grow rich they naturally grow honest.' The scheme was abandoned after a stream of witnesses pointed out to a Parliamentary Committee that the Gambia was too unhealthy for settlement. Instead, largely on Sir Joseph Banks's suggestion, it was decided to send convicts to Botany Bay in New South Wales.[12]

them . . . successive hurricans and storms, which are almost always followed by dead calms; a burning atmosphere, which when not violently agitated, becomes stagnant and insupportably oppressive . . . and lastly the disagreeable exhalations, from the flowers of certain trees, which flourish in great plenty on the banks of the river and which diffuse a pleasing smell, but produce most dreadful headaches'—'such are the obstructions, the disgust and the dangers of this tedious navigation'. Dangerous indeed—for Golbéry estimated that a third of the Europeans who made the journey up the river to Galam lost their lives.[1]

The Senegal served as a frontier between two worlds: to the north lay the desert and the country of the Moors, while the fertile river valley was populated by the Wolof, a people 'deeply black, tall, corpulent and well-formed' as Cadamosto had noticed. Yet it would be wrong to stress the contrast between the desert north and the fertile south, for in fact to the south of the river there stretches almost to the Gambia a low sandstone plateau, the Ferlo, a desolate, waterless country, uninhabited save for a few Fulani and their cattle, with a vegetation as dreary as that on the edge of the Sahara.

From the middle of the sixteenth century the French had been trading on the Senegal coast. Rainolds, in his voyage of 1591, had found Frenchmen from Dieppe and 'New Haven' well established there: 'in all places generally they were well beloved and as courteously entertained of the Negros, as if they had been naturally borne in the countrey'. The French at this time were sending two 'small barks' a year up the river, but it was not until 1638 that a permanent factory was established on land. Twenty years later the foundations of St. Louis were laid on the spit at the mouth of the river. Meanwhile the Dutch had been building posts for themselves along the Senegambian coast. In 1617 they made into a base the island of Goree, lying off the Cape Verde peninsula and in sight today of booming Dakar; in 1633 they built a factory at Arguin. From these they were ejected by the French in the 1670s. Arguin and St. Louis became the most important centres for the trade in gum. Senegal gum, reckoned superior to the gum of Arabia and used in many manufacturing processes, came from a species of acacia that grew in the sandy country to the north of the river; it was collected and traded by the Brakna and Trarza Moors. In order to pay for the maintenance of the posts in Senegal, monopoly rights were granted by the French Government to companies of merchants. Between

1659 and 1798 there were four companies, each succeeding a predecessor that had lapsed into bankruptcy. Nevertheless, despite the
vagaries of company rule and the corruption and inefficiency of many
of the officials in the trading stations, the French showed themselves
capable of sustaining a policy of remarkable expansion.[2]

The first expedition to attempt to penetrate far up the river took
place about 1667; it is recorded by Le Maire. 'The Gentlemen of the
Company having mind to take the benefit of the Flood, sent some
Barks to discover the Inhabitants about the place, where the Branches
of the Niger separate; they endeavouring to Sail from the River of
Senegal to that of Gamby, of whose entrance the English are
masters.' (This passage shows how strongly held was the belief that
the Senegal and the Gambia were both arms of a great, westward
flowing Niger.) 'Since our People could no how make any Discoveries that way, but at the time of the high waters, by whose assistance
they might sail over Rocks, which at other times stood on dry
ground. They sent 30 men in these Barks, who went up near 300
leagues from our Residence, but they underwent such Fatigues, that
but five of them return'd.' Twenty years later another attempt was
made. Chambonneau, the chief official of the French Company,
succeeded in reaching Galam at the junction of the Senegal with the
Faleme and suggested, on his return, that the French should occupy
the whole of the Senegal valley, an operation reckoned to require the
use of a military force, twelve hundred strong. There was never any
possibility of raising the money for such a scheme, but the career of
André Brue, who arrived to take command of St. Louis in 1697,
showed how much could be achieved by individual initiative.[3]

When Brue finally left West Africa he allowed Père Labat to make
use of his diaries and papers. Brue owes his fame to Labat; but even
if one disregards the influence of this publicity, he is still to be regarded as one of the most remarkable Europeans ever to have
worked in West Africa, a man distinguished for his energy, his initiative and his vision. He was in his middle forties when he arrived in
Senegal, but of his earlier career nothing has been recorded; nor does
Labat provide any facts to illuminate his character, being concerned
only to describe his multifarious activities. Of these the most striking
was his establishment of French posts on the upper reaches of the
Senegal.

Brue himself made only one journey up the Senegal. This was in
1698. He found the rulers of Galam Sarakole Negroes, of 'an in-

constant, turbulent disposition', and was glad to push on up the river, past its confluence with the Faleme, until he reached Dramanet, a town with a population of about four thousand. Dramanet was an independent republic, one in a group of little city-states linked together in a practical confederation. The inhabitants were Mandingos, most of them being marabout traders. 'They are a good Sort of People,' Brue found, 'honest, hospitable, just to their Word, laborious, industrious, and very ready to learn Arts and Sciences.' 'They carry on a Commerce to all the neighbouring Kingdoms, and by this Means amass Riches, and propagate the Mohammedan Religion wherever they go.' From Bambara and Timbuktu they bought gold and slaves, which they took to the Gambia to sell to the English. Many African traders had developed an obstinate suspicion of Europeans; the men of Dramanet were different—'they love Strangers either through Inclination or on Account of the Profit they gain by them'. So cordial was their reception of the French that Brue, who must have possessed a fine diplomatic sense, was able to secure their consent to the establishment of a French post in their midst. Such a post would serve to draw into French hands the trade that had previously gone to the Gambia. This was one of his objectives; another was to discover more about the interior. From the Mandingo traders he was able to obtain details of a route to Timbuktu. Possibly, if he had not been burdened with an official position of such responsibility, he might himself have attempted to reach the famous city.[4]

With the level of the Senegal suddenly falling, Brue had to hasten back to St. Louis, but he left behind, as his agent in Dramanet, an Augustinian lay-brother named Apollinaire, a surgeon by profession. Apollinaire was instructed to try to reach the country of Bambuk, lying only a short distance to the south of Dramanet and known to be rich in gold. But though 'he was a Man of Genius and Prudence, as well as Good Morals, and capable of insinuating himself into the Esteem of those People', 'neither his Address nor his Presents could gain the End'. But when in 1701 Apollinaire returned to the coast, there were other Frenchmen to take his place, for in the previous year a permanent French post at Dramanet, known as Fort St. Joseph, had been erected.[5]

In 1702 Brue was recalled to France. His departure had dire consequences for the new post. For the marabouts of Dramanet were becoming increasingly critical of French activities, their suspicion fanned, so the French believed, by English intrigue and seemingly justified by a letter purporting to come from Sallee in Morocco, which reported that the French had been planning to join forces with an army from Morocco 'to conquer the Country, carrying all those able to bear Arms into Slavery and oblige the Rest to work in the Mines'. Brue's departure freed them from their promise of an eternal alliance. Suddenly the whole countryside rose against the French and attacked the fort. The French shot down many of their assailants and suffered no casualties themselves; but their position was hopeless. Setting fire to the buildings, the garrison made a hazardous escape down the river.[6]

Ten years passed before the French could re-establish a base in Galam. A start had already been made, when Brue returned to Senegal in 1714. He approved the rebuilding of Fort St. Joseph on a new site not far from Dramanet and the erection of a new fort, St. Pierre, at Kaynura down the Faleme. Brue himself was too busy with affairs on the coast to be able to revisit Galam himself, but he urged his subordinates to pursue an active policy.

Thus encouraged, one of the Company's agents, Sieur Compagnon, succeeded in penetrating Bambuk. 'In the Year and a half, which he spent in travelling over that Country, he crossed it so many different ways, that he seems to have left but a few Places unvisited. He viewed every Thing that had occurred with all the Exactness a Man of his Genius was capable of; especially when incited both by his own Curiosity and the Promise of large Rewards, as well as by the Desire of being useful to his Country, and doing a Service to the Company that employed him.' Compagnon's journeys were made possible only by the support he received from Farim, the chief of Kaynura, Farim considering him 'not so much as a Servant of the Company as a Virtuoso who sought to satisfy his Curiosity in visiting a Country he had heard so much of'. Farim provided Compagnon with his own son to act as a guide. Yet even this backing was not sufficient to disarm suspicion and prejudice; he found that it was generally believed in Bambuk that 'undoubtedly he must have some bad Design and wanted to steal their Gold, or conquer their Country after he had surveyed it'—a suspicion that was by no means unreasonable.

At one of the first places Compagnon visited, 'the most passionate were for knocking him on the Head'. He talked his way out of this situation by assuring them that he was an honest merchant, who could provide them 'with better Goods and at a cheaper Rate than the

Guineas and other Merchants'. 'He found, wherever he went, the same Jealousies, and almost the same Dangers. He was obliged to answer numberless Questions, to undergo tedious Examinations, and would never have been able to have opened himself a Way, but by Dint of Presents.' Nevertheless, he was able to visit the gold-bearing areas and to make a detailed report upon them. In some places, he discovered, 'it is not necessary to take the Trouble of digging. They need only scrape the Superficies of the Earth, wash it into a Bowl, and pour off the Water gently to find the Gold in Dust at the Bottom, sometimes in large Grains.' Elsewhere, in particularly rich areas, pits were dug; but since the natives had not discovered how to use ladders or how to prop up the earth, it was not possible to go deeper than eight feet.[7]

In spite of the favourable account that Compagnon sent back, the actual amount of gold that reached the French was disappointingly meagre. Yet belief in the existence of an African Eldorado was not shattered, for beyond Bambuk, several hundred leagues to the eastward, lay Timbuktu, whose riches were said to be immense. In 1716 Brue wrote to the commandant at Galam, urging him to find a European who would be willing to follow the course of the Senegal to see if the river actually joined the Niger and to discover the exact location of Timbuktu. Nothing came of this suggestion; but Brue was not the man to let the matter drop. Three years later, when a new commandant, Violaine, was appointed to Galam, he pressed him to take action. Violaine replied by elaborating the difficulties: a single European could never make the journey, a local chief who might have proved a useful ally was now dead, fighting was taking place among the states of the Bambara; in any case there was no one in his establishment who would volunteer for such a hazardous enterprise. So the project was dropped; but Violaine was able to send back some interesting information obtained from the only African he could find who had been in Timbuktu. This man, a Bambara named Malade, reported that in Timbuktu there was still a Moroccan garrison, the soldiers living in well-constructed stone forts, set with cannon. They engaged in trade and kept their own boats on the Niger, which they used for transporting slaves. They wore red robes reaching to the ground and—curious and delightful detail—never went out without a parasol or gloves.[8]

The French maintained their posts in Galam until the English conquest of Senegal in 1758. In 1720 their garrison numbered forty, in

1. Africa allegorically presented. From O. Dapper's *Description de l'Afrique*, Amsterdam, 1686

2. Images of Africa: strange men . . . (From an edition of Pliny's *Natural History*, Frankfurt, 1582)

1736 eighty-three, of whom only a small proportion were white men. Few Europeans can have led such isolated lives; for at least six months in the year the Senegal was so shallow that there could be no communication with St. Louis. To maintain themselves in so remote a district was no mean achievement; but after Brue's final departure from the coast in 1720 no practical advances were ever made, no fresh information gathered on the interior nor, though various officials were able to visit Bambuk and even to establish a post in the centre of the country, did that golden land ever fulfil the expectations so many had covetously cherished.[9]

V

WESTERN AFRICA

CARTOGRAPHICAL IMPRESSIONS, 1500,-1750

FOR EVERY PERSON WHO studied the books about Africa, there must have been a dozen others who were content to form their ideas from glancing at a map. With the development of European cartography, the impression that maps conveyed altered slightly from age to age.

At the beginning of the sixteenth century, when the first printed maps were being produced, cartographers of Western Africa had three main sources to guide them: Ptolemy, the Majorcan mapmakers of the previous century and the Portuguese. Thus in the map of Africa drawn by the German, Waldseemüller, about 1510, the outline of the coast is taken from the Portuguese, the mountains that fill up so much of the interior of West Africa are named after those which Ptolemy had described as lying in the neighbourhood of Agisymba, while the notes on the salt trade, together with the pictures of the King of 'Meli' and of a rhinoceros are probably derived from Majorcan sources.*

By the middle of the sixteenth century Ramusio had made Leo's account available. From Leo cartographers obtained much material to fill up the interior; but their lack of critical sense often led them seriously astray. A close examination of one of the best maps of the seventeenth century, the *Africae Novae Descriptio* produced by the Dutch cartographer, Blaeu, in 1665, reveals characteristic failings. Blaeu places in the interior of West Africa not only all the kingdoms that Leo had made familiar but also a surprising number of other details: all the names on the coast—mostly of rivers or of capes—are

---

* On the Majorcan school of cartography, *v.* p. 98 *inf.*

written stretching not seawards but inland, thus covering up much of
the unknown hinterland; chains of mountains, for which it would be
impossible to find authoritative evidence, are boldly depicted to give
an air of authenticity; boundaries of uncertain significance are
sketched in with a broad brush; finally, in the few empty spaces, with
the skill of a miniaturist are depicted animals ranging in size from an
elephant to a frog. Half a century later Dean Swift was to satirize
these frivolous and misleading details:

> So Geographers in Afric-Maps
> With Savage-Pictures fill their Gaps:
> And o'er unhabitable Downs,
> Place Elephants for want of Towns.

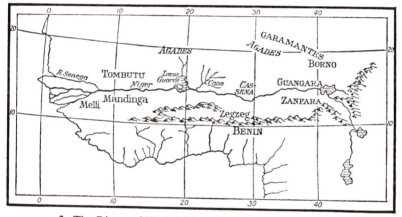

3. The Rivers of West Africa: According to Blaeu, 1664

Maps produced during the sixteenth and seventeenth centuries had
another failing: distances were calculated from the reports, often no
more than rough guesses, of travellers and navigators. Thus one of
the best cartographers of the time produced a map showing the
Mediterranean three hundred miles longer than it was in reality;
while on Blaeu's map, 'Tombutu' (Timbuktu) was placed far too far
to the west, and Benin, on which many first-hand reports were available, too far to the north. By the end of the seventeenth century the
advances in astronomy and in mathematics enabled cartographers to
devise more accurate methods of plotting location. The first to make
use of the new methods was a Frenchman, Delisle, who died in 1726
at the age of forty-one; in the course of his short life he was able to

re-examine and reform the geography of the whole globe. He was succeeded and surpassed by his compatriot, J. B. Bourguignon d'Anville, possibly the greatest cartographer the world has ever known.[1]

D'Anville was born in Paris in 1697. As a boy he developed a passion for maps, a passion that was to dominate his whole life and to keep him working with the dedicated energy of genius fifteen hours a day until the age of eighty. The whole world was his subject. Some have accounted his work on classical geography as his masterpiece,

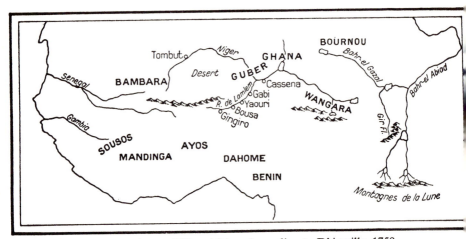

4. The Rivers of West Africa: According to D'Anville, 1750

others his maps of Italy or of Egypt or of China. But of the two hundred and eighteen maps and seventy articles that he produced, none, one may think, were of such influence and importance as those he dedicated to Africa. All D'Anville's maps are works of art, to be admired for their clean, austere beauty. Even more remarkable is the strength of mind that they reveal: the rubbish of the unconfirmed swept away, the boundaries of knowledge clearly defined. 'To destroy false ideas,' D'Anville wrote, 'even if one can put nothing else in their place is one of the ways of contributing to the progress of knowledge.'[2]

One can follow the workings of D'Anville's mind by reading his Memoir on the rivers in the interior of Africa. A single example will serve to illustrate the sharpness of his method. For two centuries every European cartographer, basing himself on Leo and al-Idrisi, had shown the Niger and the Senegal as one and the same river.

D'Anville went beyond al-Idrisi to Ptolemy, for whose information he had a very great respect; he pointed out that Ptolemy knew of a river, the Daradus, flowing in the same area as the Senegal, with which it could reasonably be equated. This river was separate from the Niger, of which Ptolemy was also informed. D'Anville then re-examined al-Idrisi's account; he checked the distances given by al-Idrisi and found that they indicated that he could hardly have known anything of countries as far west as the Senegal; therefore his account of the Niger reaching the sea was to be viewed with suspicion. Finally, he made use of the information that he had been able to obtain from a Frenchman who had served at the French fort in Galam; his report also indicated that the Niger and the Senegal were different rivers. To us the outcome of this involved chain of reasoning has the simplicity, indeed the tedium, of the obvious; to D'Anville's contemporaries it was a challenging, indeed a revolutionary proposition.[3]*

Given the information at his command, even D'Anville could not be protected from error. But his work on Africa was of the greatest importance: it forced his contemporaries to become graphically aware of the humiliating limitations on their knowledge. He himself was keenly interested in the possibilities of exploration, and was indeed involved in a project to send a suitable agent from Galam to Timbuktu, a project that for reasons outside his control failed to materialize. D'Anville died in 1783. Five years later the African Association was founded and the modern age of African exploration began. It was an age of which he, as much as any man, could claim the right to be called the father.

THE SUM OF KNOWLEDGE

It is time to pull the threads of this long inquest together and to define eighteenth-century Europe's knowledge of 'Zaara, Nigritia, Guinea'.

* D'Anville's map of Africa contains one exceptionally interesting detail. South of Gobir he shows a river, which he calls Lamlem, flowing into the Niger from the south. On this river he places the following towns: Gabi, Boussa, Yaorri, Bourgou, Gingiro, Kormachi and Kekia. Gabi is probably Kebbi, the next three are easy to identify, as their names have not changed today, though Borgu is the name of a district not of a town. Is Kormachi a corruption of Kumasi, does Gingiro refer to Gonja or Gurma? It seems likely that it was from some Tripoli source that D'Anville obtained this information, which represents the first new set of facts to be acquired about the central Sudan since Leo's account was published two hundred years earlier.

It is clearly not enough to say, as so many writers have done, that only the coast was known. The coast indeed was known with a remarkable wealth of detail, but first-hand knowledge extended deeply into the interior along the line of the Senegal, less far along the Gambia. On other parts of the interior African sources provided a rough framework of fact. On the tribes of the Sahara, on the cities and states of the western and central Sudan Leo Africanus had written a judicious introduction. In Bambuk French agents were able to pick up reports of the Bambara; in Dahomey European merchants were hearing stories of the terrible warriors of Oyo; on the Gold Coast the first information about Ashanti was filtering down to the coast. In some parts of the continent, on the East Coast, for instance, the interior could be represented as a complete blank; it was not so in Western Africa.

And yet, after all, how thin was the film of fact: the kingdoms of the Mossi, for example, known only through a single line in de Barros's *Asia*, the states of the Hausa through a few paragraphs in a book over two hundred years old. How surprising that three centuries of European enterprise should have produced so meagre a harvest of information. Why did Europe know so little? Here is a question that clamours to be answered; it cannot be done without a brief review of Europe's knowledge of other parts of the continent. But first, a necessary diversion. It has been implied that no European had ever crossed the Sahara or set foot in the cities of the Sudan. So all eighteenth-century geographers must have thought. In fact, they were wrong. On various occasions from the thirteenth century onwards Europeans had reached the interior of Western Africa; but only in the present century has there come to light—largely through the inspired research of a French scholar, M. Charles de la Roncière —the accounts of these explorers without renown.

VI

EXPLORERS WITHOUT RENOWN

EUROPEANS IN THE SAHARA AND THE SUDAN:
THIRTEENTH–EIGHTEENTH CENTURIES

AT THE BEGINNING OF the Christian era the Mediterranean could be regarded as a Roman lake. In the eighth century the Muslim conquest of North Africa sharply sundered the opposing shores. In the eighteenth century there existed between Europe and North Africa a state that might almost be described as 'cold war'. But 'throughout the Middle Ages,' as E. W. Bovill has pointed out, 'relations between the maritime peoples of southern Europe and those of the Barbary states were very close. In spite of the differences in religion and the constant state of tension caused by the hordes of Christian and Muslim pirates which infested the Mediterranean, preying relentlessly on each other's ships and shores, there was much friendly intercourse between Europe and Africa'. Christian mercenaries, 'openly recruited in their own countries', served in Muslim armies; Christian shipping frequented 'every African port from Tripoli to Agadir'; most surprising of all, Christian missionaries were allowed in Muslim cities. A Franciscan mission was established at Marrakesh in 1219; a guard of Christian soldiers was recruited for an Almohad Sultan at Sijilmassa on the Saharan side of the Atlas in 1237; and in 1283 an unknown European —one of a group of twelve sent out by a certain cardinal to report on all the countries of the world—travelled with a salt caravan across the desert to a country, possibly ancient Ghana, where the Negroes worshipped a dragon that lived on an island in the middle of a lake. And this was only a beginning.[1]

In the fourteenth century Italian merchants began to penetrate into the interior of the Maghreb; in 1320 a Venetian ambassador in

Tunis obtained permission for his compatriots to travel wherever they pleased. But as traders in the Maghreb, the Italians could not compete with that other group of non-Muslims, the Jews. The Jews had been settled for many centuries in North Africa; some had established themselves as traders in the oases of the northern Sahara; and traces of Jewish influence were even to be found, so some scholars believe, in the countries of the Sudan. It was through the Jews that some knowledge of the interior of Africa reached medieval Europe. The work of diffusion was carried on by their co-religionists in Majorca, who were developing a remarkable school of cartography. Less detailed than the maps of their Muslim contemporaries, more concerned to show the places that would be of interest to a merchant than the kingdoms whose positions would concern the scholar or the statesman, 'these Jewish maps were'—as Bovill has said—'too crude and inaccurate to have much topographical value, but they lit up, if only dimly, what had hitherto been impenetrable darkness. They gave positions to places like Timbuktu, Gao, and Mali which were already known in Europe as great and infinitely remote markets, and this gave some shape and form to a region hitherto visualized only as a repository of untold wealth'. Bovill reproduces, as the frontispiece to his work *The Golden Trade of the Moors*, the most important of these Majorcan maps. There one may see boldly drawn, on the one side a veiled Tuareg astride his camel, on the other, depicted with all the conventional symbols of Christian monarchy, the crown, the sceptre and the orb, 'Musa Mali, Lord of the Negroes of Guinea'. 'So abundant,' continues the inscription, 'is the gold which is found in his country that he is the richest and most noble king in all the land.'[2]

In the fifteenth century the Majorcan school was destroyed by the Spanish persecution of the Jews; but an interest in Africa was maintained by Italian cartographers. To the Italians reports of gold in the interior were as exciting as they were later to be to the Portuguese, the English and the French; for gold was in urgent demand to finance the growing trade with the East. The first Italian known to have attempted a journey into the interior of Africa was a wealthy Genoese merchant, Antoine Malfante.*

* In one of the fifteenth-century Chronicles of Languedoc de la Roncière came across the story of a knight of Toulouse, Anselm d'Ysalguier, who was said to have visited the city of Gao on the Niger, married an African lady of noble lineage, and returned to France in 1413, accompanied by his wife,

In 1443 Malfante arrived in Tuat, the oasis in the North Central Sahara; a copy of a long letter that he wrote from Tuat to a friend in Genoa has been preserved. Malfante started his journey from Honein, then the port of Tlemcen, on the north coast; he reached Tuat in twelve days, travelling on horseback. No Christian had ever been seen in the oasis before. 'On my first arrival they were scornful of me, because they all wished to see me, saying with wonder, "This Christian has a countenance like ours"—for they believed the Christians had disguised [*contrafactum*] faces. Their curiosity was soon satisfied, and now I can go alone anywhere, with noone to say an evil word to me.' Malfante enjoyed the protection of the wealthiest lord in Tuat, a man 'who had been for thirty years at Timbuktu' and 'for fourteen years in the land of the blacks'. 'Every day he tells me wonderful things of these peoples. He says that these lands and peoples extend endlessly to the south; they all go naked save for a small loin-cloth to cover their private parts.' 'When the blacks catch sight of a white man from a distance, they take to flight as though from a monster, believing him to be a phantom. They are unlettered and without books. They are great magicians, evoking by incense diabolical spirits, with whom, they say, they perform marvels.'

'Such,' Malfante told his friend, 'were the stories which I heard daily in plenty.' But he was also able to send back more precise information. He wrote of the Jews of Tuat, 'who lead a good life here', enjoying 'very secure social standing'—'trade is in their hands and many of them are to be trusted with the greatest confidence'; and of 'the Philistines' (the Tuareg), 'fair, strong in body, and very handsome in appearance', 'great warriors, continually at war among themselves'. He listed the names of the twelve Muslim cities or states of which he had heard in the country of the blacks; he mentioned the existence of a very great river in the interior, that passed by Timbuktu and flowed on to Egypt, that would indeed have been navigable all along its route, were it not that 'at a certain spot it falls 300 cubits over a rock'. Finally, he reported on the trade: the familiar reference to salt, but also a note that 'the copper of Romania' (the Byzantine Empire), which came by way of Alexandria, was in great demand among the blacks. Was it gold that had brought Malfante to

three Negresses and three eunuchs, one of whom became a famous doctor. The story is so engaging that one would like it to be true. Unfortunately a local historian in Toulouse has found convincing reasons for doubting its authenticity.[3]

Tuat? 'I often enquired where the gold was found and collected: my patron always replied, "I was 14 years in the land of the Blacks, and I have never heard nor seen anyone who could reply from definite knowledge".' This was not the only disappointment Malfante had to face; 'the people here will neither sell nor buy unless at a profit of one hundred per cent ... for this reason, I have lost, Laus Deo! on the goods I brought here, two thousand *doubles*'.[4]

Commercially, then, Malfante's journey had been a failure; yet his experience did not damp the ardour of his compatriots. His letter passed into Florentine hands. Florence in the mid-fifteenth century, under Lorenzo the Magnificent, was at the height of its glory, a city not only of artists but also of those who made the artists' achievements possible, tough, exuberant businessmen. In 1406 Pisa had been conquered; the control of a sea-port made possible the development of overseas trade. In North Africa the Florentines secured special concessions. It seems likely that several of their businessmen succeeded in reaching the markets of the Sudan; there has survived the record of only one of them, Benedetto Dei, a member of the great banking house of the Porsinari. He had travelled previously in the Levant, partly to find a way of attacking the Turks. His narrative is brief and curious. 'I was at Beirut, the year I brought back to Florence a snake with a hundred teeth and four legs ... at Carthage the year I secured a chameleon that lives on air ... I have been at Timbuktu, a place south of the kingdoms of Barbary, in a very arid country, and I sold there broad cloth and serges made in Lombardy.' This was in 1470; perhaps other Florentines followed Dei, but the movement cannot have lasted for long. Already a new and bloodier era in the history of the Maghreb had begun.[5]

For centuries the Iberian Peninsula had been torn by warfare between Muslim and Christian. By the beginning of the fifteenth century most of the country was in Christian hands. In 1415 the Portuguese carried the war across the straits and captured Ceuta on the African mainland. In 1492 Granada, the last Muslim stronghold in the Peninsula, fell to the Spaniards. Meanwhile the Portuguese were extending their control over the Moroccan coastlands as far south as Agadir, while their plundering expeditions reached to the walls of Marrakesh. The Spaniards, too, carried their crusade into their enemies' territory: in 1509 they made Oran the first of their conquests; in the next half-century they held, even if only for limited periods, both Tunis and Tripoli. These offensives provoked a Muslim reaction. In Morocco, with the fury of a holy war, a new dynasty, the Sa'adian, emerged; in 1578 the Portuguese were crushingly defeated on the battlefield of Alcazar. Farther east, a new force had appeared: Turkish corsairs aided the coastal towns, notably Algiers, in their struggle against the Spaniards and transformed them into bases for waging maritime war. The seventeenth century was the great age of the 'Barbary pirates'. In Algiers alone, it was reckoned, were to be found no less than 35,000 Christian slaves. It is therefore not surprising that the next mention of Europeans in the Sudan refers to slaves or renegades in the service of North African rulers.

In 1590 the Sultan of Morocco Mulay Ahmad al-Mansur sent an army across the Sahara to conquer the great empire of the Songhais. Its leader, Judar, was a eunuch, a Spaniard by birth, who had been captured as a child and brought up in the royal palace. Of his four thousand men, only fifteen hundred were natives of Morocco; some were Andalusians—Moors from Spain, others were probably Turks, but a very substantial proportion were either renegades or Christians; most of them must have been of Spanish or Portuguese descent, but it is not impossible that there were Frenchmen or Englishmen among them. Thirty years later—by which time Moroccan garrisons had been firmly established at Timbuktu and Gao—reports reached Europe that a French sailor, Paul Imbert, had visited Timbuktu as a slave and acted as a guide to his caravan, being skilled in navigating by the stars.[6]

It was not only in the cities of the Niger that European slaves might be seen at this period. In 1636 ambassadors from Bornu came to Tripoli to renew certain treaties, bearing with them magnificent gifts, including a massive bracelet of gold; in return the Pasha of Tripoli sent to the Mai or Sultan of Bornu fifteen young Christians, armed with muskets. So high was the reputation gained by these slaves 'de valeur et d'addresse' that twenty years later another Mai wrote to another Pasha asking for another such present, a request that was duly granted. This story was written down by a French surgeon, who spent some years in comfortable captivity in Tripoli; he acquired a considerable amount of information about Bornu, but never published it, his notes lying forgotten in the French archives until the present century.[7]

Tripoli was indeed the best place in North Africa in which to pick up information about the interior. On several occasions in the seventeenth and eighteenth centuries French or English consuls were able to send home detailed reports on the Saharan trade. One of the French consuls, d'André, ended a report written in 1779 with a stirring call to action. 'What glory would cover the merchant, who by gradual stages extended his business to Gingiro in Cafreria. The path is already well-trodden; the route I wish to open is by no means an imaginary one; we know that caravans come and go from Fezzan to Timbuktu, from Timbuktu to Lybia, and from Lybia to Bornu. There is no information on the possible relations between Bornu and the Kingdom of Gingiro but the advantage would go to whomsoever could establish communication between them. Thus the whole of Upper Ethiopia would be covered. To the Dutch in the Cape of Good Hope could be left the task of completing the chain by way of Lower Ethiopia.'* D'André's grandiose proposal was put forward at a time when there was not a single French or English merchant residing in Tripoli—and for good reason: the place did little trade with the outside world, such trade as there was lying firmly in the hands of the Jews. Little wonder, then, that the Chamber of Commerce in Marseilles should greet his suggestion with an ironical riposte.[8]

It was not only commercially minded consuls who looked with curiosity to the lands south of the desert; at the beginning of the eighteenth century the kingdom of Bornu had excited the interest of the Catholic Church. In 1707 two sons of the King of Bornu had arrived in Cairo; they told of a powerful kingdom named Canorfa, a hostile neighbour to their own country, whose people, they said, were 'Christians', with crosses on their churches and houses.† This story inspired the Catholic missionary body, the Propaganda Fide, which

* What did d'André have in mind when he talked about Gingiro? D'Anville knew of a Gingiro, which he placed on his river Lamlem beyond Borgu. But there was another Gingiro, as the Jesuits had discovered, a pagan kingdom on the southern borders of Ethiopia. Many cartographers accepted absurdly inflated ideas about the size of Ethiopia and made the country stretch south of the Equator. One suspects that d'André may have heard of d'Anville's Gingiro and equated it with that other kingdom in Ethiopia.
† It is not clear what is meant by 'Canorfa', as no kingdom of this name is known in the neighbourhood of Bornu. It may be a reference to the kingdom of Baguirmi, south-east of Lake Chad, which was consistently hostile to Bornu. Faint traces of Christian practices have been reported from various parts of the Sudan between Lake Chad and Darfur; it is possible that they were introduced by refugees from the Christian kingdoms of Nubia, which were not conquered by the Muslims until the fourteenth century.

maintained a convent in Tripoli, to send a mission to Bornu. Two Italian fathers, Carlo Maria and Severino di Salesia, were appointed, the former being given the title 'Prefect to the Mission to Bornu'. From Tripoli they travelled to the Fezzan, where they found that the direct route to Bornu was blocked 'in consequence of the multitude of robbers and other impediments'. Undeterred, they set out along another caravan trail that brought them to Agades. Here, in this metropolis of the Southern Sahara, they were not allowed to preach, but they were informed that 'in the kingdom of Cassina they would have an opportunity of exercising their spiritual office, particularly in some village or other of that kingdom but not in the capital'. Their hopes were to be cruelly disappointed. Shortly after their arrival in Katsina, 'it so happened through the malignity of the water there, the Father Prefect grew sick, being attacked with the swelling of the whole body, and in eight days gave up his spirit to God'. The dead man's possessions were promptly seized by the ruler of Katsina. When Father Severino protested he was told that they would be restored to him only if he would become a Muslim. This, of course, was unthinkable. 'Begone then,' the king said to him, 'and for thy deeds thou shalt die like thy companion.' The royal curse was dreadfully effective. Within two weeks the brave Father succumbed to the same sickness—it must have been dysentery—that carried off his companion. The news of their fate was brought back to Tripoli by a Muslim merchant who had accompanied them on part of their journey.[9]

So here are a handful of Europeans who had seen the countries of the western and central Sudan long before the days of Park or Denham and Clapperton: two Italian priests, a number of European slaves and renegades, possibly a company of Roman legionaries. Perhaps there were others; the historian, after all, only knows a minute fraction of what has happened. But if there were others, then one must say that they were not historically important, because they left nothing behind them, because their experience was not of a kind to stir others to action.

VII

OTHER PARTS OF AFRICA

BARBARY

'OF ALL THE PEOPLE with whom Europeons have any continued intercourse,' wrote the translator of a French work on Morocco, published in the 1780s, 'those who inhabit the coast of Barbary seem to be the least known.' 'Least known,' perhaps, in an exact sense, but not infrequently discussed: 'a great deal is everywhere said'—this comment was made in the first half of the century—'about the Algerines, their Cruelties and the Chastisement they deserve'. No other countries, indeed, in the whole world were painted by the popular imagination of Europe in shades so black as the states of Barbary, especially Morocco and Algiers. Not without reason. They had been—for by the eighteenth century their power was declining—inveterate and successful pirates: 'War,' in the tense judgement of one who knew them well, 'is the very Soul of the Algerine Government.' They refused to observe the ordinary decencies of international behaviour: 'What need have I of thy king?' the Dey of Algiers once told the ambassador of a European power. 'He sends me ambassadors and presents, I ask him nothing, and I send him nothing; he purchases my friendship; I care very little for his.' They were said to treat their Christian captives abominably: of Mulay Ismail, most powerful Emperor of Morocco in the eighteenth century, one who had been a slave in his dominions, wrote, 'How many poor Christian Slaves hath he run through with Launces, Shot, thrown to the Lyons, and caused to be burnt alive in burning Lime-kilns.' The Government of Morocco seemed a despotism as cruel and barbarous as any in the world; nor was Algiers much better. 'The Practices of the Deys of Algiers to maintain their Sovereignty are

104

very justly accounted abominable; for many Persons of valuable Qualifications are put to death upon slight Suspicions, forced Accusations or if they show any Opposition to the Measures in Vogue. Some Deys also have been so sanguinary as to behead their Enemies with their own Hands, or to have them murdered in their Presence.' As for the people, 'the Barbarians are more Jealous and Lazie than the Native Irish'; with this judgement made by one who had lived among them as a slave and whose account was given to the world by a Professor of Arabic at Cambridge in 1713, few would find much cause to disagree. Finally—and this for Europeans was hardest of all to bear—'a general Dissoluteness of Manners, Pride and Rudeness towards Strangers are the Characteristic of the Inhabitants of the whole Kingdom of Algiers', and, it might be said, of Morocco as well.[1]

Three causes brought Europeans to reside in the Barbary states, trade, diplomacy and the need to redeem Christian captives. The merchants of the Italian city states were well established in many towns of North Africa in the fifteenth century. They lost their predominant position in the years of active warfare between Moor and Portuguese, Turk and Spaniard—except in Tunis, where in the middle of the eighteenth century the Genoese and the Venetians were reckoned to have by far the greater share of trade. Farther west, however, in Algiers and Morocco trade had fallen to the hands of newcomers to North Africa, English, French, Dutch and Baltic merchants. Yet one must avoid exaggeration; compared to other parts of the world, the Barbary trade was reckoned to be 'but trifling'. Indeed, it is possible that it stood at a lower level in the eighteenth than in the sixteenth century, when English merchants in Morocco sold cloth, munitions and naval stores in exchange for sugar-cane and saltpetre, and English technicians—'goldsmiths, plumbers, carvers, and polishers of stone and watchmakers'—found employment in the court of the Emperor, while the French enjoyed excellent relations with the Turks of Algiers.[2]

Trade might be of minor importance (though the English looked to Morocco to supply corn for their garrison in Gibraltar), but the piratical practices of the Barbary states could never be forgotten. No power could count on immunity for its shipping, though naturally it was the smaller nations, the Italian and the Baltic states, that suffered most. Force was expensive and impractical: the French had bombarded Algiers several times unsuccessfully during the reign of Louis

XIV, while Morocco was almost invulnerable. In the petty crises that constantly occurred a great deal depended on the abilities of the men on the spot: 'in critical junctures,' wrote Thomas Shaw, the English chaplain at Algiers in the 1730s, 'the ground is to be maintained by the nice management and address of our consuls; by knowing how to make proper application to the particular passions of those who have the Dey's ear; by flattering one, placing confidence in another, and especially by making proper use of those invincible arguments, money, Kaf-tans and gold watches'. Finally, there were the needs of the Christian captives, whose numbers were very much less in the eighteenth century than they had been a hundred years earlier. In Morocco 'Spain maintained a Franciscan hospital to console and relieve the captives'. In Algiers there were a number of similar religious houses; some had been established by the great St Vincent de Paul in the 1620s. The European population might also be said to include, apart from the slaves, a number of renegades (the Pasha of Tripoli's naval commander at the end of the century was a Scotsman), and a few technicians—among those in Morocco, an architect, a gardener and a painter, sent out by the King of Denmark.[3]

For information on the Barbary states the eighteenth-century reader would find Leo Africanus's *Description* still the most detailed and comprehensive account. During the great age of Barbary piracy the narratives of former slaves enjoyed a popularity comparable to that of escape stories in the twentieth century. More substantial were the latest works on North Africa. Best known to English readers was Thomas Shaw's account of Algiers and its hinterland (1738). A man of great erudition, a naturalist and a classical scholar, Shaw was also a daring traveller; he went from the chaplaincy at Algiers to become Head of an Oxford College and Regius Professor of Greek. There were other books to be recommended: the serviceable accounts of Morocco written by two consuls, Host, a Dane (1779), and Chenier, a Frenchman (1788), the lively narrative of an English army surgeon, Lemprière, who had travelled through Morocco to attend the son of the Emperor (1791), the letters of a French botanist, the Abbé Poiret, who described with a fine romantic verve his experiences among the Bedouin of northern Tunisia (1788).[4]

The most remarkable of all the books on Barbary was one which was published anonymously in England in 1750. *A History of the Piratical States of Barbary*. The original edition had appeared in

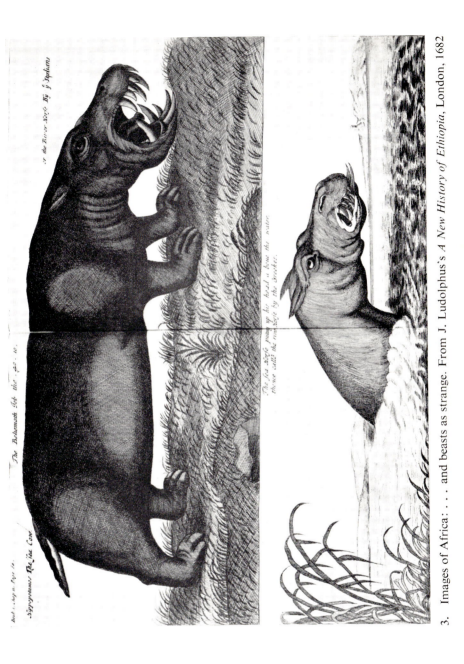

The Behemoth. Job this c.40. v.10.

Hippopotamus The Sea Cow.

n the River Nile. By y̆ Inham

The Sea Horse pawing his head above the water throws out the water by the Nostrils.

3. Images of Africa: . . . and beasts as strange. From J. Ludolphus's *A New History of Ethiopia*, London, 1682

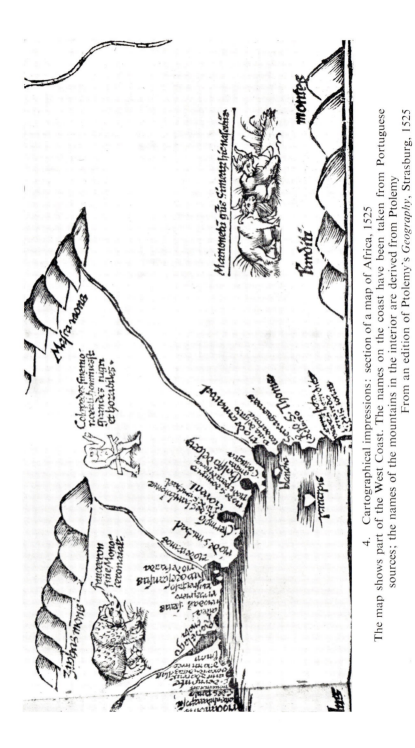

4. Cartographical impressions: section of a map of Africa, 1525

The map shows part of the West Coast. The names on the coast have been taken from Portuguese sources; the names of the mountains in the interior are derived from Ptolemy

From an edition of Ptolemy's *Geography*, Strasburg, 1525

France quarter of a century earlier; it was the work of a Frenchman, Langier de Tassy, who had lived for many years in Algiers in the service of the king of Spain. De Tassy was a man with a shrewd and philosophical turn of mind; he believed in advance of the general opinion of his age that 'what we call Virtues and Vices are only Modifications, varying according to Education, Laws, Customs, Climate and Constitution'. This belief led him to look for what was good in Algerine society; he praised the degree of equality existing among the Turks, the speed with which justice was administered, the reasonable treatment experienced—contrary to popular belief—by most Christian slaves. His attitude led him also to take a more balanced view of Barbary piracy: 'It must be confessed, that a Rover is a very infamous profession; but wherein do they exceed the Subjects of Christian princes when at War? . . . What original Right had the Europeans to their vast Acquisitions in both East and West Indies? . . . Can anything surpass the Perfidiousness and Cruelty of the Spaniards in Peru? Is not this the worst kind of Piracy?'[5]

Certainly there were gaps in Europe's knowledge; the valleys of the High Atlas, for instance, seem never to have been described by a European traveller. But taking all the works on Barbary together, it is clear that the inquiring reader could make himself pretty well informed.

EGYPT

Hallowed by biblical, gilded by classical associations, no country in Africa presented so obvious a claim for study as the land of Egypt. Few countries in the whole world could compare with Egypt in the magnificence of its monuments from the past, few also, alas, in the misery and the misgovernment of the present. Only towards the end of the eighteenth century, as its strategic significance dawned on the new imperialists of the West, did contemporary Egypt begin to arouse the interest of men of affairs.

The ties between Egypt and the Western World, formed first in Roman days, had never been broken. But for the European, at least until the reign of Muhammad Ali, travelling in the country was never without dangers; the 'Frank' must always expect to be cheated, to be reviled, to be assaulted by those in whose minds undimmed memories of the Crusades had bred a passionate loathing of his race. Even the consuls of the European powers could not count on diplomatic immunity; in 1749 the English Consul was thrown out of his house in Cairo, in 1777 the French Consul was murdered in Alexandria—for these and many other incidents there was no means of redress. Nevertheless, there always remained a few permanent European residents in the country, living in Cairo or in Alexandria, merchants for the most part but also a few Catholic missionaries; their presence facilitated the visits of their compatriots.[1]

Egypt, indeed, was able to attract a type of traveller to be found nowhere else in North Africa—the tourist, scholarly or urbane, who came inspired solely by curiosity. One such at the beginning of the seventeenth century was George Sandys, a gentleman of literary tastes and son of an Archbishop of York; the account of his travels, part of which was published by Purchas, achieved great popularity. Another was an Oxford don, John Greaves, famed as a mathematician, distinguished as an orientalist, who visited Egypt in 1638 and measured the great Pyramid. They moved, as did all other travellers of the age, within a familiar and limited field, whose bounds were Cairo, Alexandria, Sinai, along roads the medieval pilgrims had trodden. But in the century after 1650 an important extension took place in Europe's knowledge of the country. Some travellers greatly daring, pushed up the Nile and reported on the almost unknown parts of Upper Egypt: the earliest to make the journey was a German priest, Father Vansleb, sent out by the great French Minister Colbert in 1672 to collect manuscripts and medallions; the most renowned, a Danish naval officer, Frederick Norden, supported by a pension from his king, Christian VI, who reached the border of Nubia in 1737. Meanwhile, more detailed reports became available on those parts of the country frequently visited: the most informative was the *Description de l'Égypte*, written by Benoit de Maillet, who had spent sixteen years in Cairo as French Consul, spoke fluent Arabic and showed an appreciation for Muslim architecture almost unique in his age; the most magnificent were the great folios, profusely illustrated, of Norden and of another gentlemanly traveller, Richard Pococke, an English clergyman, later a bishop. Norden and Pococke introduced to their age the splendours of Egyptian architecture, though viewed through classical spectacles that softened and embellished the stern lines of that hierophantic art.[2]

But even as the intellectual interest quickened, the links of trade between Egypt and the West seemed to be falling apart. So chaotic

had grown the internal state of the country, so turbulent its government that the English withdrew their consul from Cairo in 1757, the
French theirs twenty years later, while the number of French mercantile houses declined from fifteen in 1770 to three in 1785, a year in
which there was not a single English factor in that most populous city
of Africa. A country's fate is not seldom decided by forces over which
it has no control; the more frequent signs of weakness in the Ottoman Empire together with the growing importance of European
establishments in the East made the statesmen of England and of
France begin to realize that Egypt was a country of strategic importance to themselves. The philosopher Leibnitz had presented Louis
XIV with a plan for the annexation of Egypt; this idea was reconsi-
dered by French ministers in the 1770s; it was put into action before
the century was over. In the same period the possibility of using
Egypt as a quicker route between Europe and India came to be
explored. For two centuries the Turks had kept the northern half of
the Red Sea closed to infidel shipping; in the 1770s this prohibition
was relaxed. So, though there were still many obstacles to be surmounted, servants of the East India Company began to use the
route that lay through Suez; several of them wrote accounts of their
experiences on crossing the Egyptian desert.[3]

Interest in Egypt, then, was growing; so it was fitting that there
appeared in the 1780s two studies of the country, both the work of
young Frenchmen, which superseded and in popularity surpassed
anything that had been written before. Savary and Volney—they
make a nice diptych: both in their twenties when they visited Egypt;
both scholarly and devoted travellers; each with the courage of an
explorer (Volney indeed, after a bookish education, spent a year
toughening himself for his visit, sleeping in the open and learning
how to ride bareback), though neither broke new ground; both looking on the same scenes—but with what different eyes. Of them M.
Carré, the author of an elegant and stimulating study of French
travellers in Egypt, has written 'Volney verra l'Égypte en noir, ou du
moins en gris, Savary la voit en rose.' For Volney the philosophe,
'spectacles of barbarism and devastation', for Savary, the romantic,
the pleasures of the picturesque. Their accounts, both so lucidly
written, so well composed, the one so cool, so impersonal, the other
so spontaneous, so fresh, had the power to stir the thoughts of their
contemporaries—yet in such different ways. When the French expeditionary force set out for Egypt in 1798 young officers carried Savary's

Letters in their knapsacks, but Volney's *Travels* was the manual fit for a Bonaparte.*[4]

NUBIA, SENNAR AND THE NILE

South of Egypt, along the course of the Nile, lay the country usually known as Nubia. Leo had produced a characteristically succinct account; by the beginning of the eighteenth century, it could be supplemented by the impressions of a number of European travellers. In 1698 there arrived in Cairo an emissary of the Emperor of Ethiopia, who sought the services of a European physician. A French druggist, Poncet, residing in the city, offered himself; he set out accompanied by a Jesuit priest, Father de Brevedent, who went disguised as his servant. They travelled south, until they arrived at Sennar, the capital of the largest kingdom in the eastern Sudan. There they resided for three months, being 'very honourably entertained by the king, before going on to Ethiopia, where de Brevedent died.[1]

Others followed in their footsteps. Between 1699 and 1710 a number of Catholic missionaries, mainly Franciscans, took this route to Ethiopia; finding themselves unwelcome in that Christian kingdom, they spent the greater part of their time in Sennar. Meanwhile the French Government, strongly urged by de Maillet, the consul in Cairo, decided to follow up Poncet's visit with a full-scale mission to Ethiopia. This was entrusted to de Maillet's vice-consul, Noir du Roule. It ended disastrously. Du Roule and his companions were murdered in the streets of Sennar, the climax of some obscure intrigue.

The narrative of these events was reasonably well known. Poncet's account was published in 1700, while later events in Sennar were described by a French writer, Legrand. Yet the most informative work on Nubia and Sennar seems to have escaped completely the notice of its age. It was written by a German Catholic missionary, Theodor Krump, and bore the confusingly allegorical title, *The High and*

* Savary, who also published a translation of the Koran, died at the early age of thirty-eight in 1788, his last days saddened by the spiteful attacks Volney had made upon his book. Volney had a distinguished career, was made a Count by Napoleon and wrote a large number of scholarly works.

Another French traveller visited Egypt at this time, C. S. Sonnini, a naval officer turned naturalist and explorer. His interesting account, much longer than either Volney's or Savary's, was not published until 1799, and so was soon superseded by the works of the officers who accompanied Bonaparte.[5]

Fruitful Palm-Tree of the Holy Evangelist. Published in Augsburg in 1710, it was brought to the notice of African scholars only a few years ago, when the late O. G. S. Crawford discovered a copy in the British Museum. It is a long work with over five hundred double-columned pages, containing much curious information.[2]

On the course of the Nile Ptolemy, as D'Anville with his customary acumen pointed out, was still the best authority. Drawing on information derived from merchants who had visited the East Coast of Africa, the Greek geographer placed the source of the river in two lakes, fed by the snow-water of the Mountains of the Moon. A later generation, learning of Lake Victoria and the Ruwenzori, would find this less far-fetched than it must have seemed to the men of the eighteenth century. The classical world had learnt something else about the Nile, for the Emperor Nero had sent out two centurions to discover the river's source. These earliest of African explorers travelled down the White Nile until they found their path blocked by marshes that stretched endlessly into the distance. The significance of this expedition was hardly appreciated, for to most eighteenth-century geographers it was the Blue Nile, rising as the Jesuit traveller, Father Paez, had shown in the mountains of Ethiopia, that seemed the main stream. But there were reports that mentioned the Blue Nile's confluence with the White; once again it was D'Anville who stressed contemporary ignorance of the greater of the two rivers.[3]

ETHIOPIA

For the greater part of the eighteenth century Poncet's narrative of his mission to Ethiopia provided the only recent account of that country. The Frenchman had been an honoured and yet an unpopular guest; he had attended the Emperor in his court at Gondar and accompanied him on his tours, yet all the time he had been kept in seclusion and had often found himself in danger of his life, for the monks of the Ethiopian church were 'implacable enemies of all Franks'. It had not always been so; indeed, less than a century before, Ethiopia had been more open to European influence than any other country in Africa.

In the later Middle Ages Europeans first became aware of the existence of Ethiopia as the land of the Prester John, a great Christian kingdom, 'cut off by deserts, distance and Islam'. Information may have filtered through from the Italian merchants in Egypt, some

111

of whom had travelled as far south as Dongola, one of the cities of the then still Christian kingdom of Nubia. In the first half of the fifteenth century an Italian, Pietro Rombulo, reached Ethiopia and spent thirty years in the country. In 1441, nine years before Rombulo's return to Italy, two Ethiopian delegates arrived in Florence to attend a Council of the Church. Thereafter the exchange of visits between Ethiopia and Italy become more frequent.[1]

Stronger, however, than the links of religion were the political and economic forces at work to draw the two countries together. For the trade-routes of Asia had, at the beginning of the century, been broken by the conquests of Tamerlane; only along the Red Sea could the spices of the Orient now be brought to the Mediterranean. Yet in between lay the toll-gate of Egypt; pepper bought for 50 dinars in Cairo was sold to Europeans at Alexandria for 130 dinars. To the Venetians an alliance with Ethiopia seemed the only way 'to loosen the stranglehold of the Egyptian middlemen'. The Ethiopians, too, had Muslim enemies, that group of states, Adal or Zeila, Harar, Ifat, that formed a semicircle around the southern and eastern flanks of the great plateau, on to which they had begun to thrust their harassing raids. It was not the Venetians but the Portuguese who cemented this community of interest into a practical alliance. In the 1480s the sea-captains of Portugal were inquiring after the Prester John on the coasts of West Africa; but that passionate geographer, João II, was also pushing his researches in other directions, for he sent envoys to Jerusalem to seek information. They returned with a report that only travellers with a knowledge of Arabic would be able to visit the country of that long-sought-for monarch. To this end João commissioned two envoys, of whom one, Pedro da Covilhām, reached Ethiopia, was highly honoured by the Emperor, rewarded with lands and riches but never allowed to return home; he was still alive thirty years later, when in 1520 the first substantial Portuguese mission arrived in the country from the new settlements in India. The mission marked the opening of a hundred years of ever-increasing intercourse.[2]

The mission spent six years in the country. Three years after it had left, the heart of Ethiopia was ravaged by the most formidable commander the Muslim states had yet produced, Ahmad ibn Ibrahim Gran (the left-handed). It was the darkest hour in Ethiopia's history. 'They dominated the Ethiopian church,' a contemporary chronicler wrote of the Muslim invaders, 'they had been conquerors in all the battles to the East, to the West, to the North, to the South; they had destroyed all the churches; they had put to the sword a great number of Christians. . . . Many believers had embraced Muhammedanism, hardly one in ten maintained his religion.' There had remained in Ethiopia one member of the Portuguese mission, João Bermudez; he was now sent to Europe to beg for aid. Assistance came at last in 1541, a small Portuguese expeditionary force, four hundred strong, commanded by a young man, Christopher da Gama, brother of the Viceroy of India and a son of the great Vasco. After a year of heavy fighting, in the course of which da Gama was captured and beheaded, the Muslims were defeated in the most decisive battle in the country's history; 'with the death of Gran' (who fell in the battle), 'the serious Muslim menace to Ethiopia had been removed for ever'.[3]

'So important a service rendered the Portuguese considerable at the court of Aethiopia.' Poncet's account of the course of events over the next ninety years has the merit of brevity. 'Many of them planted themselves there and enjoyed the principal employs. Their number increased, corruption of manners crept in, and they gave themselves such liberties that they rais'd a jealousie in the Aethiopians that they designed to make themselves masters of their country and subject it to the crown of Portugal. Upon this suspicion the people were in a fury against the Portuguese. They took up arms in all places and made a terrible slaughter of them, at the time they thought themselves most securely established in that Empire.' (In 1625 the Emperor, worked on by Jesuit missionaries, declared himself a Catholic; the tactlessness of the Jesuits' attack on the old religion provoked the popular revolt against them.) 'Those who escaped from this first commotion had a liberty allow'd to retire. There departed out of Aethiopia seven thousand Portuguese families,* who dispers'd themselves thro' the Indies and upon the coast of Africk.'[4]

Yet there remained from this disaster one obviously enduring

---

* It is difficult to see how Poncet reached this surprisingly large figure. In the 1540s about one hundred of the survivors of da Gama's expedition stayed on in Ethiopia, while in 1628 when Catholic influence was at its height there were no more than nineteen Jesuit priests in the country. Poncet's figure no doubt includes the offspring of Portuguese marriages with Ethiopian women. In another work (Hallett 1964, 3) I have stated, with Poncet's remark in mind, that 'several thousand Portuguese lived in Ethiopia'; on second thoughts it would have been more prudent to have substituted for 'thousands' 'hundreds' or even 'scores'. It would be interesting to know if Portuguese archives in Goa or Mozambique provide any evidence for the arrival of refugees from Ethiopia in 1630s.

monument—the books the Portuguese had composed. The earliest of them was written by Father Francisco Alvarez, who took part in the mission of 1520; Ramusio gave it European fame, and later Purchas introduced it to English readers. Purchas also made use of an abridged translation of Bermudez's account of his experiences. But it was the Jesuits who provided Europe with information more precise than that available on any other part of Africa. 'They reached the southern parts of the country, into which Europeans did not again penetrate until the present century. They studied the language of Ethiopia and its history—laboriously pieced together from fragmentary indigenous chronicles. They investigated the physical, social and ethnic conditions which had never before been studied or described.' A summary of their discoveries was put together by Father Balthazar Tellez and published in English translation in 1710; another Jesuit work, *A Voyage to Abyssinia*, by Father Jerome Lobo, was translated from a French version by an obscure young man named Samuel Johnson. (It was Johnson's first published work; a quarter of a century later he was to use Ethiopia as the setting for his fable *Rasselas*.) But the greatest name in Ethiopian studies was that of one who had never visited the country, the German scholar, Job Ludolf, who died at the age of eighty in 1704. Working for a time in collaboration with one of the Ethiopian monks who were to be found in Rome (the Vatican had bought a house for their use in 1539), he produced not only a monumental, yet entertaining history of the country, but also dictionaries and grammars of Ge'ez and Amharic, his work being, in the judgement of a modern scholar, Professor Ullendorf, 'of an importance far transcending his own time'. In a generation such as the present, which has seen such an exhilarating extension of African studies, Ludolf deserves to be remembered as the first true Africanist. He had no immediate successors; not until the end of the eighteenth century was Ethiopia to be brought vividly once again to the attention of educated society in Europe through the adventures of that most remarkable traveller, James Bruce of Kinnaird.[5]

THE CONGO, ANGOLA, MOZAMBIQUE

Strung out along the coast of Guinea were numerous European forts and factories, yet the roads to the interior seemed barred; south of the equator there were far fewer coastal establishments, yet the Portuguese in the Congo, Angola and Mozambique, the Dutch in South Africa, had penetrated deeply into their hinterlands. Such a contra-distinction requires explanation.

In 1483 the first Portuguese ship reached the mouth of the river Congo. Its captain, Diego Cão, carried back with him to Lisbon four Africans, hostages for the safety of four of his own men, not yet re-turned from a mission to the chief of the country. It was a time when the king João II was obsessed with the search for Prester John; pos-sibly the great river might lead directly to his country. So the four Africans were entertained with regal hospitality and returned to their homes to tell of the marvels they had seen, Diego Cão accompanying them as the bearer of appropriate presents and of a message to the ruler of the Congo, urging him to accept the Christian faith. Thus was inaugurated an alliance that seems, in contrast to the behaviour of Europeans in other parts of Africa, 'a model of diplomatic under-standing and restraint'.[1]

The Manicongo—such was the Portuguese version of the ruler's title—was 'paramount chief of a loose confederation of tribal organizations'; the centre of his powers lay to the south of the river, in territory that now forms part of northern Angola. Not unnaturally he welcomed these surprising bearers of surprising presents and asked that there be sent to him 'missionaries, builders and farmers to in-struct his people'. His request was granted; in 1491 there arrived in Mbanza, his capital, a small Portuguese mission, 'four priests, a number of lay brothers, and several Portuguese soldiers who had instructions to discover a route leading to Prester John and India'. 'So great was the multitude who ran to see the Portuguese Christians' —so runs a Portuguese narrative written a century later—'that it seemed as if the whole country were covered with people, who loaded them with kindness, singing and making sounds with cymbals and trumpets and other instruments.' The Manicongo was baptized and took the Christian name of his royal supporter; later, however, he began to grow restive under the new religion. Nevertheless, he allowed his son and heir, Afonso, to receive a complete education from the Portuguese fathers. A devout Christian, 'versed in the foreigner's language and familiar with Portuguese history and tradi-tion', Afonso became a ruler, 'whose counterpart', as a recent his-torian has pointed out, 'may be found in some of the Oxford-educa-ted African princes of the twentieth century'. His policy was to develop peaceful and profitable contacts with the Portuguese. To his 'royal brother', Manuel of Portugal, he addressed a stream of requests, for doctors, for a ship of his own, for church ornaments, for a loan to finance a mission to the Holy See. To Portugal he despatched the sons of his nobility to receive their education; from Portugal he received a high official to act as his adviser, together with an expert on legal reform, and many missionaries.

Yet 'this moderate programme of co-operation and development' fizzled out in black confusion. The island of São Tomé, far out in the Atlantic, had become a base for Portuguese slave-dealers; to them the comparatively densely populated Congo offered a fruitful field for exploitation. Even some of the missionaries sent out to aid Afonso were not averse to acting as their agents. In 1526, twenty years after he had succeeded his father. Afonso was writing to Manuel: 'We cannot reckon how great the damage is, since the merchants daily seize our subjects, sons of the land and sons of our noblemen and vassals and our relatives. ... They grab them and cause them to be sold; so great, Sir, is their corruption and licentiousness that our country is being utterly depopulated.' '*It is our will,*' he ended, underlining the crucial sentence for emphasis, '*that in these kingdoms there should not be any trade in slaves or market for slaves.*' Vain command: the slave-dealers were too powerful a vested interest to be restrained, even if the rulers of Portugal, distracted by greater imperial responsibilities in Brazil and in the Indies, had felt concerned to try to maintain the rights of an African prince of no international significance.[2]

Afonso died in 1543. Missionary activity continued at first unabated; in 1548 the first Jesuits arrived, at whose suggestion the name of the capital was changed to São Salvador. But the state of the country grew ever more dismal; to the struggles of Afonso's descendants were added the rivalries between different groups of the Portuguese and their mulatto offspring. 'By 1615 most traces of Christian life had disappeared; the white population had died, fled or been absorbed. The Congo chiefs became more and more despotic and the unity of the kingdom crumpled. São Salvador was a deserted city in 1690, its twelve churches in ruins, its walls and fortress in ruins.'[3]

By that time the Portuguese had gained compensation in the establishment of their power in Angola. Luanda, founded in 1576, was reckoned a century later to be 'fine and beautiful enough', 'having many fair Houses, Churches and Cloisters'; it was indeed the finest, in a sense the only European city in the whole continent. The most important slaving port south of the equator, it was also a centre

116

for missionary enterprise, the Italian Capuchins being particularly
active in the country and also in the Congo in the seventeenth
century. Above all, it served as a base for the advance into the
interior. Inland, up the Cuanza River, there were said to be silver
mines: this rumour proved false, but the interior certainly produced
slaves—incentive enough, yet not to be obtained without a struggle,
for the Kimbundu people under their ruler, the Ngola, proved re-
doubtable opponents. So the 'bloody monotony' of frontier wars,
with which, for two centuries, the annals of the colony were filled. But
gradually there came to be established up-country, two hundred, three
hundred, even seven hundred miles from the sea, trading posts, military stockades, lonely outposts of a seemingly decaying empire,
staffed by solitary white men, who married African wives and whose
mulatto offspring would lose within a generation or two every vestige
of Portuguese culture.[4]

In 1487 Bartolomeu Dias rounded the Cape of Good Hope. Ten
years later Vasco da Gama was sailing up the East Coast of Africa,
his crews gazing in amazement at the chain of rich Muslim cities, in
material culture the equal of their own towns, that stretched from
Sofala to Mogadishu. 'They are merchants,' wrote one of da Gama's
companions of the people of Mozambique, the first city which they
visited, 'and they trade with the white Moors, four of whose vessels
were here at this place, carrying gold, silver and cloth, and cloves,
pepper and ginger, and rings of silver, with many pearls and seed-
pearls and rubies and the like.' Gold: there lay the secret of these
cities' wealth, for it was gold above all other commodities, ivory or
pearls or slaves, that brought the merchant-sailors down from
Arabia, from India, even possibly from China. Gold: al-Idrisi, three
centuries earlier, had learnt that 'in quantity and in size the gold of
Sofala surpasses that of any other country'. Gold: were not those
mines hidden in the interior the site of Ophir, from which King
Solomon had drawn his wealth, that country, whose identity represented one of the most tantalizing mysteries of Christendom? Gold:
what lodestone could have such power?[5]

From the first there was violence. In the harbour of Mozambique
da Gama, too hasty in his suspicions of Muslim treachery, had let off
his cannon: ill-omen for the future. Within twelve years, with brute
and naked force, the Portuguese had shattered a civilization, sacked
Kilwa, richest of all the cities, plundered Mombasa and made their

sovereignty acknowledged from Sofala to Malindi. At Sofala they built a fort; through it they hoped would pour the gold of the interior, for they had not realized how easily the flow could by tribal wars or by reluctant middlemen be obstructed. When the gold came only in a trickle, a certain Antonio Fernandez decided to set out alone to look for the mines; he was an ex-convict and illiterate, but he has been esteemed by a modern historian as 'in some ways the greatest of the explorers of the interior of Southern Africa'. In the years before 1514 Fernandez travelled over three hundred miles into the country, visited many of the mines in the kingdom of Monomotapa (which lay partly within the borders of modern Southern Rhodesia) and 'acquired in the process so much renown among the natives that he came to be reverenced by them almost as a god'. On his return he advised his superiors that the easiest way into the interior lay along the line of the Zambezi, north of the route he had taken. As a result, the Portuguese came to build their first bases in the interior on the banks of the great river, first at Sena over a hundred miles inland, then at Tete two hundred and sixty miles from the sea. From Tete freelance traders pushed on up-country, the most famous of them, Antonio Caiado, 'a one-time Coimbra don', establishing himself at the capital of the kingdom of Monomotapa, as unofficial adviser to the ruler. His influence secured a welcome for the Jesuit missionary, Gonçalo da Silviera. Within a few months Silviera had baptized the whole court, but his success aroused the hostility of the Swahili traders. They told the king that he was both a spy and a sorcerer. They achieved their end: Silviera was strangled at the king's command.[6]

To avenge this martyrdom and at the same time 'to extend his dominions by means of new conquests', the new king of Portugal, Sebastian, a 'moody, headstrong and devout' young man, decided to send a large expeditionary force against Monomotapa. It was led by Francisco Barreto, a former Governor-General of India, and contained a thousand volunteers, many of noble birth. This brave display of imperial might ended in a squalid fiasco. The original force reached little farther than Sena; within two years, worn out by skirmishes with local rulers or sickened by the fevers of the Zambezi valley, Barreto and most of his men were dead. It was a salutary lesson in the difficulties of campaigning in tropical Africa.[7]

Forty years later, in 1608, another expedition was sent into the interior, this time to occupy some silver mines said to exist at Chichoa a hundred miles beyond Tete. Though Chichoa was reached, no mines were discovered; quarrels among local officials caused the force to withdraw. The province of Mozambique was indeed too poor to support 'imperial exploitation on a grand scale'. 'Malaria, unrest among the Africans, dispersal of authority, and the essential poverty of the region conspired to thwart all ambitious plans for development.' The golden dream faded. Within the last half of the seventeenth century the Portuguese lost their possessions north of Cape Delgado to the Omani Arabs, their hegemony of the Eastern Seas to the Dutch, the English and the French. Imperial interests concentrated on Brazil. Mozambique, isolated and ignored, with its 'scandalous priests', its corrupt officials, its lawless half-caste settlers on their great fiefs, seemed to have reached the nadir of seedy decay.[8]

The search for a shorter route to Prester John had led the Portuguese up the Congo; later with their establishments in Angola and Mozambique on roughly the same latitudes, it was natural for them to think of seeking a land-route across the continent to join their two colonies. Their maps were encouraging but misleading; they showed Africa to be narrower at this point than in fact it was, and they indicated a great lake in the centre where both the Zambezi and the rivers of Angola had their source. How far the Portuguese penetrated in the sixteenth and seventeenth centuries is uncertain; but it would seem that none of the plans—and there were many—for striking deep into the continent led to any significant achievement until the end of the eighteenth century, when there took place the remarkable expedition of Dr Francisco José de Lacerda.[9]

Lacerda, outside his own country, is almost unknown. He deserves to be remembered as one of the great African explorers. Born in Brazil, he spent ten adventurous years surveying frontier districts before he transferred to Angola, where he travelled widely in the interior. It was this experience that led him to propose the feasibility of a trans-continental route. The advantages, as he pointed out in an official memorandum, would be both commercial and political. 'Ships from Asia would discharge cargo at Mozambique and goods could be carried overland to Benguela [in southern Angola] without the danger and the delay of doubling the Cape of Storms. Thus the custom house duty would increase and the industry of the whites as well as of the blacks would be fostered.' 'The new possessors of Table Bay—the English', he went on to suggest with prophetic insight, 'require careful watching, or our want of energy will enable them to extend northwards.'[10]

Lacerda gained the official support he required. In July 1798 he set out from Tete on the Zambezi with twenty Portuguese and fifty African soldiers. Three months later he reached the kraal of the great chief Cazembe, on the shores of Lake Mweru. There, stricken by fever, he died; but his companions returned to the East Coast with his diary and a map that extended detailed knowledge of the interior by several hundred miles. Sixteen years later the continent was crossed in a hazardous journey, that involved a three-year detention at Cazembe's, by two *pombeiros*, bush traders, whose Portuguese names, Baptista and José, concealed their mainly African ancestry. Yet they were literate enough to keep a rough journal of their achievement.[11]

Some nineteenth-century Portuguese scholars and their English supporters, understandably chagrined by the contemptuous references to their compatriots' achievements in Africa, came to refer to the contemporary exploration of Africa as 'the Rediscovery of a Lost Continent'. Park and Livingstone, it could be suggested, were following paths where other white men—the Portuguese—had been before. There is a certain amount of truth in this suggestion; yet it must be recognized that there were large parts of the interior, especially in East and Central Africa, which were completely unknown to the Portuguese, while the reports of their journeys in West Africa were in fact so meagre as to constitute no addition to geographical knowledge. Yet indisputably, in many parts of the continent, in the western Sudan, on the marches of Ethiopia, in the Congo forest, on the plateaux of Angola or on the Rhodesian veld, the Portuguese can claim to have been the first Europeans to have set foot. This is an achievement as remarkable in its way, though far less widely recognized, as their great circumnavigation of Africa.[12]

In the twentieth century the Portuguese territories have been, at least for English readers, the least known part of the continent; not until the appearance of James Duffy's excellent survey (1959) has there been any comprehensive work available in English. The eighteenth-century reader was somewhat better served, at least in respect of the West African colonies. Thus the editor of Astley's *Collection* was able to devote two hundred double-columned pages to Angola and the Congo. Purchas had already published two important accounts, one by Duarte Lopez, a Portuguese merchant whom the Manicongo sent to Rome as his ambassador in the 1580s, the other the 'strange adventures' of Andrew Battell, an English sailor, who was captured by the Portuguese and kept for eighteen years in

Angola. More recent information was to be found in the detailed descriptions of a number of Italian Capuchins who had come as missionaries to the Congo and Angola and in the account of a voyage to the Congo, written by James Barbot and included in his uncle's massive folio on Guinea.[13]

On the East Coast the English reader was not so well provided, unless he could read Portuguese. Only two Portuguese works relating to East Africa had been translated. Purchas published an abridgement of the *Ethiopia Oriental* of João dos Santos, a Dominican priest who served in Mozambique from 1586 to 1595, while John Stevens brought out in 1695 a translation of the *Asia Portuguese* of the seventeenth-century historian, Manuel de Faria y Sousa. Another work, which contained interesting information on the East Coast, was the *Voyages* of Jan van Linschoten. Van Linschoten, a Dutchman who spent nine years in Portuguese service in the East Indies, wrote a detailed account of the lands of the Indian Ocean. An English translation appeared in 1598. From 1591 English sailors visited the coast of East Africa on their way to India. The earliest English accounts were published by Hakluyt; compared to van Linschoten or dos Santos, they were superficial. The eighteenth century added nothing to contemporary knowledge. Astley's editor produced only a few pages on the East Coast; he quoted from the work of Alexander Hamilton (1727). Hamilton had spent thirty-five years as a trader in the Indian Ocean; he devoted little attention to East Africa. This neglect was not surprising; in the eighteenth century the East Coast was a backwater. Adequate contemporary accounts of Sofala and Mozambique, Mombasa and Zanzibar did not appear until the first decades of the nineteenth century.[14]

SOUTH AFRICA

South Africa was the last part of the continent to attract Europeans. Not until 1652 did the Dutch, needing a victualling station on the route to the East Indies, establish at the Cape the first permanent settlement on that coast. From the start settlers, working either privately or with official support, began pushing into the interior, seeking to buy cattle—for as yet they had none of their own—from the Hottentots, seeking also to reach golden Monomotapa, which contemporary maps showed as stretching far to the south. Later, there was reports of copper to the northwards; in 1681 Governor van der Stael led an expedition to seek for the mines among the Nama-quas.[1]

During the eighteenth century this movement of expansion and exploration developed; the search for new grazing grounds, the quest for ivory led many a farmer to break away and trek deeply into the sparsely populated hinterland. In 1760 reports were received of the Orange River, four hundred miles north of the Cape. By that time European readers had reason to be familiar with the Dutch colony. 'There is scarce any place in the world,' Astley's editor noted, 'more frequently described in books of travel than the Cape of Good Hope.' Before the century ended there appeared a number of excellent works describing the interior. Two were written by Swedes, Andrew Sparrman (1783) and Carl Thunberg (1788), another by an English army officer, William Paterson (1789), the last by a French naturalist, Le Vaillant (1790). All four of them were professional and well-qualified travellers, who had come to South Africa with a scholarly desire to study the country. It is unlikely that any of them covered ground where no Dutch farmer had been before them; but they were able to bring back to Europe a mass of detailed information on the topography, the people and especially on the natural history of the parts they visited.[2]

ASIA AND THE AMERICAS: A BRIEF COMPARISON

To see the eighteenth-century's knowledge of Africa in proper perspective, it is essential to compare it with that possessed of Asia and the Americas.

The mighty land-mass of Asia with its vast distances, its deserts and towering mountains presented a physical challenge to European travellers quite as formidable as the deserts, swamps, and forests of Africa; yet by the middle of the eighteenth century a remarkable amount was known about the continent. Once European powers had obtained command of the Eastern seas it was easy for them to visit all the countries of Eastern Asia; but sea-power was in no way a key to the interior, to the great steppes of Siberia, the mountains of Tibet, or the cities and rivers of China. Of these areas, Siberia was almost completely unknown to Europe at the beginning of the seventeenth century; yet before that century was over, the successive rivers that flow into the Arctic Ocean had been traversed, intercourse established with the Chinese Empire by way of Manchuria, the

Pacific coast reached, a start made to the exploration of Kamchatka, while Behring was soon to discover the straits that bear his name and to explore part of Alaska. This magnificent achievement was entirely the result of Russian enterprise, private or official: the fur-traders pushing farther and farther eastwards, the bands of adventurers founding the settlements, Yakutsk or Anadyrsk or Albazin, that became bases for further exploration, the Government itself encouraging a policy of expansion and supporting individual explorers.

The credit for laying the foundation of a sound geography of the great empire of China lay almost entirely with the Jesuits. From 1600 Jesuit missionaries had been established in Peking, where they were welcomed not for their faith but for their learning—and especially for the scientific knowledge that they were able to impart. A century later the fathers were entrusted by the Emperor, Kang-Hi, with the task of mapping the whole empire. The information thus gathered was published in Paris in 1735 together with an atlas of maps prepared by the masterly D'Anville.

Tibet has been regarded as one of the most inaccessible of countries; yet during the first half of the eighteenth century it was frequently visited by Catholic priests, after the Jesuits and the Capuchins had succeeded in establishing, if only for a decade, their missions in the holy city of Lhasa. Even the remote areas of Central Asia were not completely unknown. In the Middle Ages European travellers, among them Marco Polo, taking advantage of the administrative unity imposed by the Mongol Empire, had crossed those deserts and those steppes. The empire fell, the trade-routes grew too dangerous, Polo's road was closed. But there were still cases of Europeans making remarkable journeys into the remote heart of the continent; in 1604 the Jesuit de Goes, for instance, went from India into China, crossing the Pamirs and passing through Yarkand.

Of the other countries of Asia, India, Persia and the countries of the Turkish Empire were by the standards of the time comparatively well known. The interior of Arabia naturally held nothing to attract travellers; but Mecca had been seen by Europeans, and agents of the various European East Indian companies had established posts in the ports of the eastern coast of the Red Sea.

The New World, the twin continents of the Americas, presented to Europe a task even greater than the elucidation of the geography of the other two continents. For Asia and Africa were Europe's neighbours; historical associations, war and trade bound the continents of the Old World together. But the Americas had risen over the horizon of the Western Ocean, fabulously unexplored, having a land area larger by far than Africa, with a coastline of great complexity, together with high mountains and some of the densest and least-penetrable forests in the world to impede those who sought to traverse them. Yet within two hundred and fifty years of Columbus's landfall, many of the most striking geographical problems of the New World had been solved, the coast, the bays, the great rivers and lakes charted, and flourishing centres of European civilization established from Lima to Quebec.

One motive stands out above all others in the extraordinary outrush of energy that led to the establishment of Europe in the New World—the search for wealth, for wealth in its most obvious, hard and glittering form: thus Pizarro seeking the capital of the Incas, Raleigh in quest of El Dorado, the Spaniards in Mexico striking northwards lured by the golden mirage of the Seven Cities. And if not gold, then some other metal or furs or slaves; no part of the globe could compare with these part-virgin lands as a jackpot for adventurers. Yet some were led to them for different reasons—not least by the fretfulness that ignorance provokes, the desire to find out whether some theory be true or false: so in Canada the *couriers des bois* were drawn ever westward by the reports of some great sea. And in the Americas, as in Asia, in Canada, in Paraguay, on the upper reaches of the Amazon, Catholic missionaries—the Jesuits above all—were to be found among the foremost in the discovery of new lands.

Certainly there were gaps in Europe's knowledge of these continents, on many regions only sketchy reports were as yet available. Nevertheless, the amount that was known was by 1750 clearly sufficient, as it would not have been a century earlier, to throw into sharp relief the extent of Europe's ignorance of a continent whose shores almost touched her own.

VIII

THE CAUSES OF IGNORANCE

A SURVEY OF EIGHTEENTH-CENTURY Europe's knowledge of Africa reveals it to be more extensive than later generations have assumed. It was not only the coasts that were known; on many inland countries information was available, on Ethiopia, Morocco or Angola, along the upper Senegal, the upper Nile, the upper Zambezi. Yet, as D'Anville's map graphically revealed, vast areas of the interior were still blank. Why was this so? Why, after three hundred years of intensive intercourse with Africa, the nearest of all the continents to their own, had Europeans been unable to penetrate more deeply?

To this question one answer has come to command almost universal assent: the physical deterrent. The classic exposition of the theory is to be found in a passage written in 1790 by Major James Rennell, the greatest English geographer of his day.

> Africa stands alone in a geographical view! Penetrated by no inland seas, like the Mediterranean, Baltic or Hudson's Bay; nor overspread with extensive lakes, like those of North America; nor having, in common with the other continents, rivers running from the centre to the extremities: but, on the contrary, its regions separated from each other by the least practicable of all boundaries, arid deserts of such formidable extent, as to threaten those who traverse them, with the most horrible of all deaths, that arising from the thirst! Placed in such circumstances, can we be surprised either at our ignorance of its interior parts, or of the tardy progress of civilization in it?

The lack of navigable rivers, the dreadful barrier of the Sahara—these are not the only obstacles that have been detected. 'The West African forest repelled Europeans,' writes Professor R. J. Harrison Church, the author of the most recent, as it is also the best-informed, of text-books on the geography of West Africa, 'just as it had the

125

Arabs. To the difficulties of penetrating the forest were added those of an inhospitable coast, difficult to approach and land upon. Beyond lay the fly-ridden forest, where animals could not be kept and where the wheel was unknown.'[1]

Not one of these statements, except the irrelevant reference to the wheel, is strictly in accord with historical fact. For two thousand years and more, regular trade-routes have existed across the Sahara; certainly the physical difficulties of desert travel have always been severe, yet one may wonder whether the Saharan crossing was in fact a greater ordeal than the infinitely tedious sea-passage round the Cape from Europe to the Indies. The tropical forest of the Guinea coast presented to the European imagination a picture of dreadful gloom; yet its perpetual shade had for centuries been broken by many clearings, its dense growth traversed by many well-trodden paths. Only indeed in parts of the Congo, as Stanley found in his herculean expedition of 1874–77, did the forest impose a really formidable, though even then not an insuperable barrier. In West Africa the first Europeans to pass through the forest belt—Bowdich in 1817 or Clapperton in 1826—found the physical difficulties of travel, leaving aside the ravages of disease, by no means excessive. As for the lack of navigable rivers, it is curious to find an eighteenth-century encylopaedist writing of the continent, 'it is furnished with the greatest and most convenient navigable rivers and perhaps with as many as any other of the chief parts of the world'. This must be taken as a reference to the Senegal and the Gambia and also possibly to the creeks and inlets of the Slave Coast.[2]

About the rivers of West Africa two points need to be made, one bearing on the Niger, the other on the Gambia. It may seem incredible that Europeans, after three hundred years' experience, were unable to recognize that the creeks between Warri and Bonny formed part of the delta of a great river; yet anyone who has seen the Delta for himself and tried to find his way through that labyrinth of waterways will not be surprised at their failure, especially as the dense vegetation of the mangrove swamps gave to the Niger's outlet an appearance quite different from those other great deltas—the Rhine's or the Nile's—with which Europeans might have been familiar. As for the Gambia, a glance at a map showing the density of population in West Africa will reveal a peculiarly significant fact: the districts that surround the upper reaches of the Gambia are the most thinly populated of any in the western Sudan. With their arid and unpromising soil, they seem to have acted in much the same way as that desolate Nyika which forms the immediate hinterland of the East African Coast and which increased so greatly the rigours of intercourse with the interior. It was in these parts that Captain Hodges and his men had almost died of starvation. Yet even here, as over the whole of West Africa, there were regular trade-routes; where Africans could move with ease, Europeans could follow.

Nevertheless, the environment did impose one indisputable danger —and from an unrecognized enemy, the anopheles mosquito. There is in de Barros's great history a peculiarly striking passage. He has been writing in glowing terms of the Portuguese position in Guinea: 'it is so peaceful, meek and obedient an estate, that, without our having one hand holding a lighted lunt on the touch-hole of a gun and the other hand holding a lance, it gives us gold, ivory, wax, hides, sugar, pepper, malagueta; and it would give us more things if we would only penetrate into the hinterland. . . . But it seems that for our sins, or for some inscrutable judgement of God, in all the entrances of this great Ethiopia that we navigate along, He has placed a striking angel with a flaming sword of deadly fevers, who prevents us from penetrating into the interior to the springs of the garden, whence proceed these rivers of gold that flow to the sea in so many parts of our conquest.' *The flaming sword of deadly fevers*—only in our own day has that weapon been wrested from the angel's hand. It was not until the nineteenth century that the phrase, 'The White Man's Grave', was to be coined and popularized, but from the first every visitor to the West Coast had commented on the 'unwhole-someness' of the climate. And yet how formidable was this really as a deterrent?

> Beware and take care
> Of the Bight of Benin,
> For one that comes out
> There are forty goes in.

So ran the macabre sea-shanty that English sailors sang on the West Coast run. Yet despite the appalling decimation of disease, Europeans continued to come to the coast in increasing numbers; some of them, toughened and immunized by many fevers, were able to live there for many years at a stretch. It is clear that disease made large-scale European settlement in West Africa impossible, but it was never a barrier to intercourse nor, as later events were to show, an absolute deterrent to the initial penetration of the interior; the journeys of

Park, of Clapperton and of the Landers were all made before anyone realized the efficacy of quinine as a prophylactic.[3]

The physical deterrent was then in itself less powerful than has often been suggested. And yet the idea of it existed and strongly influenced men's minds. Barbot's conception of the interior—'wild savage countries', 'woods pester'd with robbers', 'ravenous wild beasts'—provides one illustration; another may be found in the experience of the early-nineteenth-century poet, Leigh Hunt. Hunt, as he recounts in his *Autobiography*, was making a sea-journey to Italy. After Gibraltar, the passengers caught sight of the coast of Africa. 'The first sight of Africa is an achievement . . . "Africa", they look at it, and repeat the words, till the whole burning and savage territory, with its black inhabitants and its lions, seems put in their possession.' *Burning and savage territory*—how vividly that old illusion of the terrible Torrid Zone still haunted men's imagination.[4]

More significant, undoubtedly, than climate, topography or disease was the power possessed by African states to keep Europeans from penetrating the interior: the human deterrent, which had as its converse the weakness of the Europeans. This weakness needs emphasizing; one could find no franker avowal than the statement made in 1758 by the Board of Trade to the English Prime Minister, William Pitt, who had received a suggestion that the English should buy all the land containing gold mines in Guinea. 'The British interest, both in Possession and Commerce, depends chiefly, if not entirely, on the good Will and Friendship of the Natives, who do not allow us even those Possessions, limited as they are to the bare spots on which our Forts and Factories are situated, without the Payment of an annual Quitrent. . . . The Natives have ever expressed great Jealousy at every attempt made by Europeans to discover the Nature and Produce of their Country and particularly their Gold.' Nor was it only on the Gold Coast that such conditions existed; Snelgrave had found in Dahomey thirty years earlier that it was not wise to ask questions about the interior. Similarly in North Africa, though for different reasons, it was virtually impossible for a European to travel in the interior of the country. May one not invoke the jargon of the mid-twentieth century and talk of a curtain surrounding Northern and Western Africa, a curtain woven from the 'fanaticism' of North African Muslims and from the suspicions of West African middle-men? A curtain, not a wall, for there were ways round it and through it. The French had penetrated deeply into the interior from their base on the Senegal; two Italian fathers had found a way of passing from Tripoli to Katsina. The future was to show that no great deployment of force was to be required to send European travellers to many parts of the interior.[5]

But why, one must ask, was this effort not made earlier? To answer this question it is necessary to consider more closely the motives behind Europe's exploration and penetration of the remote areas of the world. It is tempting to think of exploration only in terms of the individual explorer.

> For always roaming with a hungry heart
> Much have I seen and known; cities of men
> And manners, climates, councils, governments. . . .
> Yet all experience is an arch where thro'
> Gleams that untravell'd world, whose margin fades
> For ever and for ever when I move.

So Tennyson's Ulysses, the archetypal traveller—and poor indeed is the man who has never felt himself in the grip of a passionate curiosity, who has never experienced the excitement of the unknown. But curiosity, one may think, is a universal quality, a part of the human condition; and indeed we are all, in the profoundest sense, explorers. But the experiences of individual travellers are of no historical significance unless they are bound up with or lead to the deployment of political power. Three motives above all led the men of Europe to tramp the five continents and sail the seven seas: the search for wealth, the search for political advantage, the search for souls to save.

'No part of the world,' wrote the author of the article *Africa* in the 1778 edition of *Encyclopaedia Britannica*, 'abounds with gold and silver in a greater degree . . . and it is surprising that neither the ancient or modern Europeans notwithstanding their extraordinary and insatiable thirst after gold and silver, should have endeavoured to establish themselves effectively in a country much nearer to them than either America or the East Indies and where the object of their desires are to be found in equal, if not greater plenty.' The encyclopaedist was wrong; he cannot have thought of the ardent expeditions of Jobson and other Englishmen on the Gambia, or Compagnon and other Frenchmen in Bambuk, of Fernandez and other Portuguese on the Zambezi. But the gold of Bambuk and of Monomotapa was disappointingly meagre; the richest deposits in the continent, before the discoveries in South Africa in the 1880s, lay on the Gold Coast, the mines only a few miles inland but effectively guarded by their African possessors.[6]

Besides gold, what had Africa to offer? Slaves, of course, in lucrative quantities; but the slave trade had become efficiently organized at the ports; except in Angola there was no necessity for Europeans to go hunting men in the interior. After slaves, gum—a profitable trade, but again effectively organized; Europeans could have no incentive to conquer the arid territory on the very edge of the deserts, where the gum trees grew. Besides, the European market for gum was a limited and a specialized one; so too with West African timber and ivory. As for North Africa the commercial possibilities were meagre in the extreme. Apart from the slave trade, how could this part of the world compare as a field for profitable investment in an age of restricted capital with the Americas, their sugar or their furs, with Asia and its spices?

Strategic necessity—the need to harass or supplant a rival—has frequently been a powerful motive leading governments to support exploration. Drake or Anson circumnavigating the world to plunder the Spaniards, the French and the English sending out rival expeditions to discover that mythical Southern Continent, the *Terra Australis*, the scientists of Russia and America battling to reach the moon: though separated by centuries one may detect a common pattern in all these events. Strategic significance does not remain constant: it changes in accordance with the shifting balance of international power. For a brief moment in the late fifteenth century the interior of West Africa had a strategic importance for the Portuguese, when they believed that among the 'peoples of Moses' was to be found that Prester John whose alliance they sought in their struggle with the Muslims of North Africa. Later the squabbles of European traders on the coast were to be drawn into the pattern of world rivalry between the Dutch and the Portuguese, the English and the French. Alarm at French activity on the Upper Senegal was one of the motives behind Hodges's expedition to Bambuk. This theme was to develop: during the Napoleonic War Park's second expedition into the interior of Africa was supported by the British Government as a counter to a possible move by the French.

Finally, that impulse—so strange to most non-Christians—to save souls. Often enough there has been cause to refer to missionary endeavour: in North Africa, in Ethiopia, in the Congo, in Mozambique. And indeed in Asia and the Americas, as in Africa, it is extraordinary how often the hero of some remarkable journey turns out to be a Catholic priest. Only in West Africa does the figure of the missionary explorer not appear. There are some obvious but not entirely conclusive reasons for this. Many of the coastal settlements were in the hands of Protestant powers, English, Dutch or Danish. The Protestant missionary movement was in time to produce in the person of David Livingstone the paragon among African explorers; but it was not until the 1790s that the missionary societies which were to do so much for Africa were founded. Among the Catholics the Propaganda Fide, the Church's central missionary body, encouraged the establishment of a number of stations staffed by Capuchins on the West Coast. They were to be found in Benin, on the Gold Coast and in Dahomey, but none of them lasted for more than a few years. Missionary activity, indeed, reflecting the temper of the age, was at a low ebb in the eighteenth century when compared to its vigour in the century that was past or in the century that was to come.[7]

It would appear, then, that there existed in the first half of the eighteenth century no motive sufficiently powerful to make Europeans want to penetrate the interior of West Africa. But this inquiry cannot be concluded without some examination of the conditions that facilitate exploration.

Efficient organization in the home country is, if not an absolute necessity, undoubtedly a great advantage. This organization can be constructed in various ways and by different bodies—by the Government or by some perpetual corporation such as the Church or by a well-established trading Company or by a group of private individuals. To be effective the organization must provide three things: money, information and publicity to attract the right sort of recruits for its work. Portugal has provided the world in the persons of Prince Henry the Navigator and King João II with the supreme examples of official patrons of exploration. In the brilliant exploits of members of the Society of Jesus may be seen the advantages of ecclesiastical patronage—the measure of continuity in a policy worked out over centuries and whose aims are conceived as eternal. Much less effective was the support which a group of individual businessmen could give, as Jobson had found on his return from the Gambia. And even large trading organizations, such as the successive French companies which had developed the policy of penetrating along the Senegal, were forced to keep a close watch on their profit and loss account. In the penetration of new lands there was room, under certain conditions, for purely individual enterprise: so the *pombeiros* showed in Angola, the *trek-boers* in South Africa. These conditions—notably a sparse and scattered indigenous population—did not prevail in Western and Northern Africa. Yet even there much could be achieved by the individual, self-financed traveller, as time was to show in the exploits of Bruce in Ethiopia, of Browne in Darfur and, most remarkable of all, of Caillié on the road to Timbuktu.

For ease of travel in an unknown country certain ideal conditions can be envisaged. One is that the country should be thinly populated by a primitive people: such was the case in parts of South Africa, of North and South America, and of Siberia. Alternatively, it is an advantage if the country forms one great empire with a strong ruler at the centre, as in Ethiopia, in China or on a smaller scale in the Congo. So long as they could be assured of the ruler's support, Europeans—in practice mainly Catholic priests—could travel widely over large areas. One may contrast Father Lobo's travels in the highlands of Ethiopia with the impasse he faced when he landed at Juba on the East African coast and was told by the Gallas that there were 'no fewer than nine nations between us and Abyssinia, who were always embroiled amongst themselves or at war with the Abyssinians and enjoyed no security even in their own territories'. A not dissimilar situation prevailed in West Africa, where there were, as Bosman reported, 'innumerable Kingdoms and several Commonwealths'. It would be wrong to think of all these states as being constantly engaged in fighting and raiding one another; but there were frequent hostilities and as a result much mutual suspicion. Yet even in times of peace such a variety of sovereign bodies made travelling difficult, for each petty ruler required to be propitiated in a suitable manner; this called for a mixture of generosity and tact, qualities not every European traveller might possess.[8]

Finally, one may note that the existence of some easily defined goal, preferably invested with an air of mystery, helps to focus popular interest on an unknown region: in the Arctic the North-West Passage, in the South Seas the *Terra Australis*, in West Africa the riddle of the Niger's course, in East Africa the unknown sources of the Nile. Yet intellectual curiosity in itself cannot lead to continuity of action, without the support of practical incentives. The North-West Passage would serve as a shorter route to the East, the Niger once charted would reveal a commercial highway into the interior:

on advantages such as these the advocates of exploration were to lay great stress.

One returns at the end to the original question—why was Africa the last continent to be penetrated by Europeans? The argument has been involved; it will be as well to summarize it briefly. The physical deterrent imposed by the desert and the forest and by disease was not quite so formidable as it was represented; nevertheless, it did raise frightening images in men's minds. The political or human deterrent provided by African states was strong enough to serve in some key places—on the Gold Coast and in Morocco—as a barrier to European penetration, but not every possible line into the interior was blocked in this way. Europeans, for their part, had no compelling motives to try to establish their power away from the coast, except in some gold-bearing areas; in any case their own capital resources were fully extended in other more lucrative portions of the globe. Finally, the multiplicity of states in the interior increased the difficulties and dangers a traveller would have to face; and yet, given favourable political conditions and sufficient incentive, it was not impossible, as the Portuguese had discovered in the sixteenth century, to send isolated missions to the very heart of the West African interior.

So, one may say, there existed in the year 1750 two worlds, the cities and states of the interior of Western Africa and the nations of Western Europe, moving on their own courses, largely unaware of each other's existence. Yet already there were at work, shaping men's thoughts and influencing their actions, forces which were destined to send travellers from Europe into the heart of Africa, forces which were at once extending, diversifying and strengthening the bonds of intercourse between the two continents.

THE BONDS OF INTERCOURSE

I

FUNDAMENTALS

THE OUTLINE OF HISTORY

IF IN THE YEAR 1750 a European historian had set himself to make an extensive review of the development of his continent's contacts with Africa he could hardly fail to be impressed by the progress that had been achieved in the last three centuries. In 1450 Europe's knowledge of Africa was less than that possessed by the classical world. By 1550 the Portuguese had followed up their great circumnavigation by establishing posts on many of the coasts of the continent. By 1650 the maritime nations of Western Europe, England, France and Holland, had come to develop a flourishing trade with West Africa. In the course of the last hundred years there had been no startling advances, but European knowledge had increased both in South Africa and on the Senegal, and the links between Africa and Europe had been progressively strengthened.

Of the ties between the two continents the most obvious was that of commerce; but Africa was also coming to acquire a political significance in the struggles between the nations of Western Europe. Trade and politics were of fundamental importance; they helped to generate other interests. Between 1700 and 1750 more than three times as many books had been published containing accounts of Africa as in the whole of the preceding century. This could be interpreted as evidence of Europe's growing wealth, but it was also a sign of an increasing and more widely diffused curiosity, a curiosity that at its most pointed implied an attitude of rational inquiry to every aspect of creation. In the study of botany and of natural history, of geography and of ethnology important advances were taking place; many a different path could lead the scholarly mind to Africa.

Forty years later, in 1790, a European observer would have been aware that more people were talking, thinking and reading about Africa than ever before. New influences had contributed to this growth in interest. From the end of the Seven Years War in 1763 there could be detected the beginning of a movement for the systematic exploration of the unknown regions of the world; foremost among those who by their achievements had roused the interest of Europe were Captain James Cook, Joseph Banks, Cook's companion on his first voyage and now President of the British Royal Society, and James Bruce, 'the Abyssinian traveller'. For such a movement the unknown interior of Africa would seem an obvious focus. At the same time, a variety of different intellectual currents, the cult of the 'noble savage', the revolutionary belief in human equality, the first scientific study of racial differences, the emergence of the Protestant missionary spirit, were combining to produce a more humane attitude to a people whom many Europeans had regarded as fit only to be slaves. Indeed, the slave trade itself, the basis of Europe's commerce with Africa, accepted as part of the normal order of things by generations of God-fearing Europeans, and steadily increasing year by year, had now come under attack both in England and in France by a small body of dedicated idealists, who with skilful propaganda were engaged in rousing the conscience of their compatriots and making the fate of Africa a matter for private argument and public debate.

This entire movement needs, however, to be seen in a proper perspective. Africa has never been, even today in its age of revolution, a subject of abiding interest for the majority of educated Europeans. Yet slight shifts of opinion, caused by the action and advocacy of a handful of single-minded individuals, can precipitate those changes that serve to mark the course of history. So through the life-work of traders and of politicians, of travellers and of scientists, the ties that bound Africa and Europe ever more closely together were multiplied. Such is the broad outline of a movement that influenced in greater or lesser degree all the educated societies of Western Europe; it is worth illustrating its course in more detail from the experience of that country which was to take the leading part in the penetration of the interior of Africa.

THE AFRICAN TRADE

In 1720 sixty-five ships, whose total tonnage was less than 6,000 tons, left England for African ports, taking in their holds £130,000 worth of trade goods. In 1772 the comparable figures were one hundred and seventy-five ships, over 19,000 tons and exports valued at £866,000. In fifty years the trade had increased more than six times in value. In the relationship between England and West Africa this is a fact of cardinal importance.[1]

The West African trade formed one arm of that triangular traffic across the Atlantic: English and Indian manufactured goods to West Africa; slaves from Africa to the West Indies; sugar and other tropical crops from the West Indies to England. 'How vast,' wrote an anonymous pamphleteer in 1772, 'is the importance of our trade to Africa, which is the first principle and foundation of all the rest; the main spring of the machine, which sets every wheel in motion.' And Malachi Postlethwayt, one of the best known economic journalists of his day, asked in a series of rhetorical questions:

> Are we not indebted to those valuable People, the Africans, for our Sugars, Tobaccoes, Rice, Rum and all other Plantation Produce? And the greater the Number of Negroes imported into our Colonies, from Africa, will not the Exportation of British Manufactures among the Africans be in Proportion; they being paid for in such Commodities only? The more likewise our Plantations abound in Negroes, will not more Land become cultivated, and both better and greater Variety of Plantation Commodities be Produced? ... May we not say therefore ... that the general Navigation of Great Britain owes all its Encrease and Splendor to the Commerce of its American and African Colonies?[2]

Far-reaching indeed were the consequences of this commerce. 'By 1750,' Eric Williams has pointed out in *Capitalism and Slavery*, that work of penetrating and passionate scholarship, 'by 1750 there was hardly a trading or a manufacturing town in England which was not in some way connected with the triangular or direct colonial trade. The profits obtained provided one of the main streams of that accumulation of capital in England which financed the Industrial Revolution.' 'Every brick in this infernal town is cemented with an African's blood', a drunken actor on a Liverpool stage is said to have told his hissing audience. And certainly in Liverpool, greatest of the slave ports, Liverpool, whose population had risen from 5,000 in 1700 to 34,000 in 1773, while the number of its ships trading with

Africa had increased from fifteen in 1730 to eighty-nine in 1772, in Liverpool, where busts of blackamoors and elephants adorned the town-hall and slaves were publicly auctioned in the Customs' House, Africa was very close.[3]

From Liverpool, from Bristol, its supplanted rival, from London the ramifications of the trade spread out. Clothiers in East Anglia and the West Country, gunsmiths in Birmingham, cotton manufacturers in growing Manchester, all had a stake in the West African market. To naval officers—and, of course, to armchair strategists—the increase in shipping represented a valuable reserve for time of war, while the slave trade, whose ships required larger crews, could be described in one of the clichés of the age as 'a nursery for seamen'. The trade itself was always a chancy business, probably the most risky investment the eighteenth century afforded. Sugar was safer, and it was in sugar that some great fortunes were made. Retired planters or absentee landlords returned to England to establish themselves with a country estate among the ranks of the gentry, to mingle with the aristocracy and to buy themselves, if they could afford it, a seat in a Parliament, where the West Indian interest formed one of the most powerful of pressure groups.

Listening to the words of a successful, though barely literate slave-dealer named Owen, whose journal has been preserved, one finds oneself almost overhearing one of those conversations by which an interest in Africa could be spread. If a man made his fortune in the slave trade, 'that very perticular,' wrote Owen, 'hides all other infirmities, then you have hapes of frinds of all kinds thronging and wateing for your commands. Then your known by the name of the "African Gentleman" at every great man's house and your discourse is set down as perticular as Cristopher Culumbus's expedition in America.' How many 'African gentlemen' there were in English society, how many 'West Indians' has never been estimated; but here at least was a substantial leaven, here were men who could talk about Africans, whether they had dealt with them as merchants on the West Coast or as slaves in Barbados or Jamaica, from first-hand experience. Here, too, were men wealthy enough to buy the new books that were appearing on Africa and so to make possible their production.*

* It would be an interesting, though laborious, study to analyse in detail the subscription lists of books relating to Africa published in the eighteenth century. Dalzel's *History of Dahomey* (1793), to give one example, had 260 subscribers. Of these seventy gave their address as Liverpool and 105 Lon-

Finally, here were men who could be expected to keep an eye open for any new commercial possibilities Africa might present.[4]

In fact, apart from the slave trade, Africa did not present an encouraging field for trade and investment. But this was not always the view of contemporaries. In 1745 Malachi Postlethwayt was prepared to write of the 'immense treasures wherewith Africa abounds'. 'If the trade to the Spanish Indies and the Brazils is so inviting,' he suggested in one of his pamphlets, 'it is equally certain that the Inland Trade, duely extended upon the Continent of Africa ... may be rendered little inferior to either, if not equal to the united Advantages of them both. The Continent of Africa is of great extent, the Country extremely populous, and this Commerce, by Reasons of its Discouragements hitherto, but yet in its Infancy.' 'If we could so exert our commercial policy among these people,' he wrote some years later, 'as to bring a few hundred thousand of them to cloath with our commodities, and to erect buildings to deck with our furniture, and to live something on the European way, would not such traffic prove far more lucrative than the slave-trade only.' 'Trade and navigation exciting to the advancement of arts and sciences necessary thereto, these have naturally civilized men.' 'Were this country planted by the Europeans in colonies and settled habitations, towns and cities built, and people brought out to inhabit as in the American plantations, something like what the Portuguese have already done in Africa, the whole commerce of this part of the world might, in all probability, be considerably more extended among those people than it has ever yet been.' Commerce, Colonization, Civilization—the trinity for nineteenth-century imperialists: Postlethwayt was indeed a prophet born before his time.[5]

But Postlethwayt was not a man with first-hand experience of Africa or even, it seems likely, of business at home. The men on the spot took a less sanguine view of the possibilities of the interior. Half a century later a British naval officer in the West African squadron, a man with a keen interest in exploration, wrote of the traders: 'They have neither the talent, enterprize, activity or inclination for such an undertaking [the penetration of the interior]; few of them leave their store or shop during the day, it is their natural occupation, nor can it be expected that they will sacrifice their own interest and health for

don; most of the London subscribers had addresses either in the City or in the Docks. Some subscribers were to be found as far afield as West Africa, the West Indies and Canton.

the general good.' Make the effort to imagine the conditions under which the traders lived: the enervating climate, bad food, indifferent accommodation, the degrading routine of the commerce in slaves, the constant demands on business acumen and diplomatic skill in dealing with African merchants and princes, above all, the steady kill, kill, kill of the fevers of the coast—it would be uncharitable and unjust to censure men living under such a strain for not showing greater initiative.[6]

WAR AND POLITICS

'Trade,' wrote Daniel Defoe, summing up in a few words one of the leading ideas of his age, 'is the Wealth of the World; Trade makes the difference as to Rich and Poor, between one Nation and another.' 'When trade is at stake,' said the young William Pitt in 1739, 'it is your last entrenchment; you must defend it or perish.' Trade was wealth, wealth was power, and the defence or the extension of power and of wealth meant war.[1]

In a sense traders on the West Coast had always realized this; ever since the sea-powers of Western Europe had broken the Portuguese monopoly there had been local violence. But it was not until the middle of the eighteenth century that the strategic importance of West Africa was grasped by English politicians and by none with such assurance as William Pitt, who, as the monument appropriately raised to him in the Guildhall of London proclaimed, raised 'his nation to a high pitch of prosperity and glory . . . by commerce for the first time united with and made to flourish by war'.

'In those places where we have forts, we carry on trade with the natives; where other nations have forts, and we have none, we are excluded the right to trade.' So Postlethwayt summed up the English position on the West Coast. In another work he provided a pointed illustration of the working of this rule: 'Before the French got possession of the forts upon the Coast of Africa, on the river Senegal and on the islands of Arguin and Goree, the English traded freely and uninterruptedly to all places on the said coast. Since the French have possessed the said Forts, they have absolutely excluded the British nation from those parts, and taken and confiscated all British ships as have ventured to trade there.' Nor was it only on the Gum Coast that French obstruction was to be feared. Their factory at Albreda on the Gambia was a constant vexation to the English settlement on

James Island; their traders were unpleasantly active in the bays of Sierra Leone and at Whydah on the Slave Coast. Should it come to war, the British forts, administered by a Company of Merchants with the support of a Government subsidy, were in a perilously weak state, their garrisons often consisting of soldiers so old and decrepit that they were said to require nurses to look after them. But the French settlements at St. Louis and Goree were in fact not much better off. It was clear that the struggle would be decided in favour of the first power able to send a strong naval force into West African waters.[2]

In 1756 France and England were again at war. After months of disasters, Pitt was called to power. He had not been many weeks in office, when he was approached by a Quaker merchant, Thomas Cumming, with an extraordinary story to relate. Seven years earlier a group of Moors had been kidnapped by a Dutch trader, taken to the Cape Verde Islands and, since none would buy them as slaves, left to fend for themselves, until an English sea-captain had given them a passage to London. There, in one of the streets of the City, Cumming had seen them, mistaking them first for Turks on account of their eastern dress, talked to them, befriended them, helped them to return to their native land and been given for his pains a cordial invitation to visit them in their homes. Five years later Cumming found himself on the Gum Coast, was given an affectionate welcome by his Moorish friends and introduced to their chief. This man, 'Amir Sultan, King of Legibbilli', told him that not only was he anxious to trade with the English but, so great was his hatred of the French, he would gladly help their rivals to capture St. Louis and Goree.[3]

Pitt was immediately attracted by the prospect of successful action that Cumming's story revealed and gave orders for an expedition to be prepared. After many delays the force sailed in March 1758. Cumming went with it and played a vital part in the success of the operation by piloting the ships' boats across the bar at the mouth of the Senegal. Confronted by such a force, the garrison at St. Louis did not hesitate to surrender. Goree beat off one attack but fell to the British before the year was over.

Goree, to Pitt's fury, was returned to the French under the terms of the Treaty of Paris; but St. Louis remained in English hands. It was joined in 1765 to James Island on the Gambia to form 'the province of Senegambia'. How imposingly reads the constitutional establish-

ment of this, the first colony of the British Crown in tropical Africa—
Governor, Chief Justice, the Council with its members, the two
official chaplains; how seedy was the reality. Seedy—the epithet has
been applied, not without an insular sneer, to the possessions of other
European powers in the Tropics; it can be applied with equal justice
to this first British colony in Africa, with its corrupt, quarrelsome and
often brutal officials. It would be ungenerous—remembering the
isolation, the discomfort, the boredom of life in this outpost of
Empire—to speak too critically, and yet there was much to repre-
hend. When the French, having joined the American rebels in the
war against the English, sent a naval force to West Africa the garrison
of St. Louis was reduced to twenty-one men, only twelve of whom
were fit to bear arms. Yet this wretched dozen were actually engaged
in fighting one another in a quarrel over their commanding officer,
when the French ships hove in sight and forced them to surrender. It
was the end of Senegambia.[4]

The English had held the colony for twenty years, yet they had
never been able successfully to re-establish the posts the French had
built up the river. Worge, the first military governor of St. Louis, had
sent three missions up to Galam; on each occasion the officer in
command had died in the course of the journey, and though a
detachment was established in Galam after the evacuation of the
French, it soon had to be withdrawn. O'Hara, who was governor of
Senegambia from 1766 to 1775, showed in the first few weeks after
his arrival an intense interest in the interior. He spoke in his despatches of the gold mines of Galam as being the richest in the world
and pointed to the great and unexplored market for English manufactures to be found in Galam itself and in the countries farther east.
He suggested that the Consuls in North Africa should send agents
with the Saharan caravans to report on the commercial possibilities
of the interior and sought permission to re-establish a post at Galam,
to be followed by further posts reaching ever more deeply into the
hearts of the continent. These imaginative schemes faded away under
the hard grind of office; there were too many difficulties—lack of the
necessary funds, the danger of excessive casualties from disease and
too many distractions, above all, the irrepressible activity of the
French on the Gum Coast. But there were some English traders who
ventured occasionally as far as Galam in their ships. One might
speculate on what would have happened if the English had produced
a man with the knowledge and ability of Brue. Had they done so the

whole course of a part of West African history might have been different.*[5]

In the negotiations that led up to the Treaty of Versailles in 1783, the fate of the West African colonies was made the subject of lengthy diplomatic bargaining. The English were in a weak position; they had to accept the loss of St. Louis and to return the island of Goree, which they had captured; their only gain was the right to trade on the Gum Coast. By now it was abundantly clear that no statesman in England or in France could afford to disregard the place of West Africa should war once again break out between the two most powerful states of Europe.[7]

* O'Hara's predecessor as Governor of Senegambia, Barnes, who was appointed by the Company of Merchants before the Government took the colony over, sent back one interesting piece of information. 'At the head of the River Senegal there is a ridge of mountains beyond which, according to the natives, there is a great river, which runs eastwards into a great lake, around which there are settlements of white people.' He suggested that 'this valuable country might very easily be explored by means of some of the natives of Senegal'.[6]

II

THE CURIOSITY OF THE AGE

EIGHTEENTH-CENTURY ENGLAND WAS 'FULL'—the comment is G. M. Trevelyan's—'of creative intellectual power both in the sciences and the arts'. 'It was a century,' another historian has pointed out, 'in which knowledge was made known to far wider circles than had ever been the case previously, and was applied, moreover, in every possible direction, in order to improve the conditions of human life.' Among the ramifications of the rich and complex intellectual activity of the age there were two lines of development that would serve to draw men's attention to the least known of the continents: the cosmopolitan spirit in literature and in scholarship, and the curiosity that played on the natural products of lands outside Europe.[1]

The popularity of works of travel has already been noted. The information that travellers brought back encouraged imaginative writers to introduce exotic scenes or characters of different race into their novels, plays or poems. Indeed, it is remarkable that in the work of almost every major English writer there can be found some reference to Africa and its people: Shakespeare's *Othello*, Johnson's *Rasselas*, Blake's *Little Black Boy* are only the most obvious of examples. Before the century was over, the generous passions roused by the campaign against the slave trade were to inspire not only great poets like Cowper or Coleridge but also many lesser writers to express their emotions in poetic or dramatic form; one may note such titles as *Zembo and Nila—An African Tale, The Guinea Voyage, The Wrongs of Africa* and *The Princess of Zanfara*, the last a play which was performed at many provincial theatres.[2]

146

More remarkable than these ephemeral productions were three books that appeared in the 1780s from the hands of African authors, all of them freed slaves living in England: Ottobah Cugoano, Olaudah Equiano, and Ignatius Sancho. Cugoano was a Fante; his work on the slave trade revealed a keen, scholarly and logical mind. Equiano, an Ibo, had been taken as a slave at the age of ten, yet the memories of his home were so vivid, his mastery of English so assured that he was able to produce in the first chapter of his autobiography a masterly vignette of African village life and to present with a restrained, yet heart-rending poignancy the misery the slave trade inflicted on its individual victims.[3]

Ignatius Sancho had been born on a slave-ship during the voyage to the West Indies. Brought to England at the age of two, he was to make the country his home for the remainder of his life, becoming for a time butler to the Duke of Montagu and later being helped by the Montagu family to set up a business as a London grocer. 'A commerce with the Muses'—in the words of his English biographer—'was supported amid the trivial and momentary interruptions of a shop.' Two plays, some poems and a work on the Theory of Music issued from his pen and he was able to count among his friends Garrick, the greatest actor, and Sterne, one of the greatest writers of the age. After his death in 1780 his letters were collected and published with an introduction written anonymously by Joseph Jekyll, a Member of Parliament, well-known as a man-about-town. They are worthy of a place in any anthology of English letters.*[4]

So great was the demand for Sancho's letters that the subscription

* Brief quotations give some taste of the quality of both Equiano's and Sancho's style.

Equiano. We are almost a nation of dancers, musicians and poets.
       As our manners are simple, our luxuries are few.
       In our buildings we study convenience rather than ornament.
Sancho. If I knew a better man than yourself—you wou'd not have had this application—which is in behalf of a merry—chirpy—white tooth'd—clean—tight—and light little fellow;—with a woolly pate—and face as dark as your humble;—Guiny-born, and French bred—the sulky gloom of Africa dispelled by a Gallic vivacity—and that softened again with English sedateness—a rare fellow!
   I say it is with reluctance, that I must observe your country's conduct has been uniformly wicked in the East—West—Indies—and even on the coast of Guinea—The grand object of all English navigators—indeed of all Christian navigators—is money—money—money—for which I do not pretend to blame them.[5]

list for them was said to have been of a length unknown since the appearance of the first number of the *Spectator*, over fifty years earlier. Equiano's work was equally popular; its subscription list was headed by a Royal Duke, and within five years it had passed through eight editions. The moral of these books was brought out by Jekyll: 'He who could penetrate the interior of Africa, might not improbably discover negro arts and polity, which could bear little analogy to the ignorance and grossness of slaves in the sugar-islands, expatriated in infancy, and brutalized under the whip and the task-master. And he who surveys the extent of intellect to which Ignatius Sancho has attained by self-education, will perhaps conclude that the perfection of the reasoning faculties does not depend on a peculiar conformation of the skull or the colour of a common integument.' Among the factors that induced Englishmen to take an interest in Africa, the influence of these three long-forgotten books should certainly be counted.[6]

If Ethiopia and Egypt be excepted, the development of truly African studies, of a scholarly interest in the achievements of African peoples, is a product of the latter half of the nineteenth century. It was natural when so much was to be explored that European scholars should turn first to those parts of the world which could show in their literature the heritage of a great culture. Orientalists and Africanists in the absorption of their respective studies may feel that they have little in common; yet their work springs from a common motive—a desire to understand more deeply people whose way of life is utterly different from that of Europe. It may not then be entirely irrelevant—in illustration of the cosmopolitan spirit of the age—to say something of the development of Oriental studies in eighteenth-century England.[7]

The movement had started a century earlier with the establishment of Chairs of Arabic at Cambridge in 1632 and at Oxford four years later. The seventeenth century produced a number of great scholars, the earliest of them William Bedwell, a contemporary of Shakespeare's who pointed out the practical value of a knowledge of Arabic as being 'the only language of religion and the chief language of diplomacy and business from the Fortunate Isles [the Canaries] to the China Sea'. In the early eighteenth century two important works appeared, the *History of the Saracens*, by S. Ockley, the first account of Arab expansion to be based on original sources, and an excellent translation of the *Koran*, by George Sale, a work that came to enjoy for many years a European reputation.

A generation later the seven great Odes of pagan Arabia were translated by a young English lawyer, William Jones. Jones was to become one of the greatest orientalists Europe has ever known; to an extraordinary flair for languages—he was said to have known thirteen thoroughly and twenty-eight fairly well—he could add a wide-ranging curiosity, an elegant style and a peculiarly amiable manner. In 1784 he went out to India as a judge of the Supreme Court at Calcutta. The next year he was one of the founder members of the Asiatic Society of Bengal, whose purpose was to inquire into 'the history and antiquities, arts, sciences and literature of Asia'. In Bengal Jones met a kindred spirit, Charles Wilkins, who in 1785 published the first translation of the *Bhavadgita*. Before his tragically early death in 1794, Jones, with Wilkins's help, had laid the foundations of modern Sanskrit studies. Farther east, another servant of the East Indian Company, William Marsden, a young officer at the factory in Bencoolen, was gathering material for a history of Sumatra, which he published on his return to England in 1783. For the next forty years of his life, Marsden, who later became a senior civil servant at the Admiralty, occupied his leisure in gathering material for a dictionary and grammar of the Malay language.

All these men were amateurs, whose works had to be written in the time left over from other careers. In reading their lives one cannot help being moved by their passionate devotion to scholarship even in the face of real suffering and hardship. Thus Ockley, who wrote his history as a poor country parson and found himself little better off when he was elected Professor of Arabic at Cambridge, had to finish off the second edition in Cambridge Castle, where he was imprisoned for debt; while Castell, who produced a huge dictionary of oriental languages in the seventeenth century, sacrificed a fortune of £12,000 to finance the work.

THE PRODUCE OF THE TROPICS:
INTERESTS—PRACTICAL, AESTHETIC AND SCIENTIFIC

The rational curiosity of the best minds of the eighteenth century knew no artificial bounds; not for them 'the two cultures' of an age of specialization, the utterly distinct intellectual worlds of the historian and the scientist, each burdened, as scholars two hundred years ago could never be, by the sheer mass of available knowledge. So, as they turned to consider lands beyond Europe, it was not only the cultures of little-known people that claimed their attention, not only the simple delineation of new countries on the map, but also their natural products in all their variety. Thus Thomas Shaw, travelling in North Africa, made detailed notes on Roman inscriptions, on the manners of Bedouin Arabs and on the flora of the country.

The practical, the aesthetic, the scientific—three distinct motives induced men to take an interest in the products of distant lands, their fruits and trees and flowers and, to a lesser extent, their animal life. The best evidence of a practical interest was to be found in the increasingly important part that the products of the tropics were coming to play in the economy of Western Europe. Furniture manufacturers were turning from native woods to tropical timbers—especially to mahogany, which from the middle of the century increased steadily in popularity; most of the mahogany was imported from Central America, but a certain quantity—usually referred to as Redwood—was obtained in West Africa. The importance of gum senegal, used most of all in the process of silk manufacture, has already been mentioned. The healing properties of tropical herbs and barks—most of them derived from South America—were increasingly appreciated by druggists and by apothecaries. But, above all, the diet of the well-to-do was being transformed by the acceptance as necessities of tropical products such as sugar and rice, coffee and tea, which an earlier generation regarded as expensive luxuries. As the price grew cheaper, the taste for these commodities spread through ever-wider circles of the population. Meanwhile other tropical products were being introduced as luxuries or as curiosities. The tomato, for instance, or 'love-apple', as it was usually called, was first cultivated not for its flavour but for the singularity of its appearance as a decorative garden plant. To the tables of Europe, West Africa had as yet nothing to contribute, but the practical interest in tropical crops was bound to turn attention to the West Coast as a possible source of supply, and before the end of the century more than one attempt was to be made to set up some form of agricultural settlement in that part of Africa.[1]

If some plants were of interest to Europe for their practical value, many more—as the case of the tomato shows—were introduced solely for their decorative qualities. For the eighteenth century, the most splendid period in the history of domestic architecture, was also, at least in England, a great age of gardening. One quite remarkable set of figures will indicate the energy with which Englishmen sought for new plants: by 1700, it has been reckoned, not more than a thousand exotics had ever been brought into the country; within the course of the next century the number of new species introduced amounted to not less than five thousand. Naturally most of these new plants came from temperate lands, but the development of the artificially heated greenhouse—one of the minor inventions of the age—made it possible to rear tropical plants as well. Indeed, a number of English noblemen gained fame for their collections of tropical exotics, mostly obtained from the West Indies.[2]

The practical concern of wealthy landowners in the improvement and embellishment of their estates led some of them to a practical interest in the study of botany and of zoology, two sciences in which, through the genius of one man, a great advance had taken place. Carl Linnaeus was a Swede, with an international reputation. Born in 1707, the son of a poor country clergyman, in 1741 he became Professor of Botany at the University of Uppsala, where he remained until his death in 1778. Linnaeus has been called 'the great organizer', the man who took the wonderful variety of living things and described and classified them more effectively than any of his predecessors. 'God has endowed him with the greatest insight into natural knowledge, greater than any has ever gained': the words are his own judgement on himself—nor were they misplaced. To the superb intellectual powers of a great scientist was added the enthusiasm of an inspired teacher. 'No modern naturalist has impressed his own character with greater force upon his pupils . . . . He imbued them with his own intensive acquisitiveness, reared them to close and accurate observation, and then despatched them to various parts of the globe.'[3]

As a young man he had proved himself as a botanical explorer. 'In my youth,' he wrote of himself, 'I penetrated into the wilds of Lappland, . . . I lived solely on water and meat, without bread or salt: I risked my life on the mountains of Skulberget in Finnmark, on the alpine glaciers, or by shipwreck, or amidst the clouds; wandering on foot I forced my way through forests and mountainous regions, and all this with the aim of collecting plants belonging to the meagre Lappland Flora. . . . What pains, what research could be more tiring and laborious than botany, if it were not that the enchantment of a strange will, which I myself cannot explain, often drove us in this direction, so that love of plants vanquishes love of ourselves?' Inspired by his teaching and by his example, several of Linnaeus's best students set out to collect plants in some of the most distant parts of the earth. Thunberg and Sparrman, both of whom travelled in South Africa, have already been mentioned; another, Hasselquist, visited Egypt in 1750 and died in Syria two years later. He was not the only disciple of Linnaeus to pay for his scientific enthusiasm with his life.[4]

Linnaeus's influence came to spread far beyond the circle of his students at Uppsala. 'Botany,' wrote one of the first historians of English gardening, 'was a chaos of unarranged facts ... until the mastermind of Linnaeus resolved its confusion and discord to harmony.' As a result, it became possible for a man to acquire in a few months a degree of knowledge that before would have required the work of a lifetime. More than this, Botany was made respectable; 'Linnaeus's system gave a final blow to the invidious line of distinction which had existed between the Gardener and the Botanist and completed the erection of the Art of the former into a Science. . . . From being merely practised by servants, it became more extensively the study and delight of many of the most scientific and noble individuals of the country.'[5]

In 1760 two events of peculiar significance occurred. The Dowager Princess of Wales established the Royal Botanical Gardens at Kew, and D. C. Solander, one of Linnaeus's favourite students, arrived in England. At Kew there was established, through the influence of the Earl of Bute, the finest collection of exotics in Europe. As for Solander, he became so enamoured of England that he never returned to his native Sweden. Some time after his arrival he made the acquaintance of a wealthy young man with a passion for botany, Joseph Banks. In 1768 Linnaeus's student agreed to join the scientists that Banks was taking at his own expense on Captain Cook's first expedition to the Pacific. So the names of the three men—Linnaeus, Banks and Cook—who were to do more than anyone else in their generation to make the educated public of Europe aware of the lands beyond their shores, came thus intimately to be joined.[6]

THE CIRCULATION OF IDEAS

There is one other element in the culture of the eighteenth century of such relevance to this study that it cannot be ignored: the greatly improved machinery for the circulation of ideas.

The remarkable increase in the printed word provides the most obvious evidence. Newspapers, first appearing as irregularly issued sheets a century earlier, were established in the eighteenth century as an essential part of life. Their numbers multiplied, their circulation rose; nor were they confined, as in an earlier generation, to the metropolis; the provincial Press had become an effective vehicle for the wider distribution of information. Equally important were the periodicals: sixty different reviews and magazines appeared in London in the half century before 1780, the greatest among them the *Gentleman's Magazine*, founded in 1731 and within a few years selling 15,000 copies, and the *Annual Register*, started in 1758 with Edmund Burke as its first editor.[1]

Growing wealth and wider advertisement stimulated the demand for books. Rapidly there developed a taste for a new literary form, the novel; some of the most popular contemporary works of fiction— *Robinson Crusoe* was an obvious example—were based on narratives of adventures in exotic lands. The interest in works of travel has already been remarked. The *Systems of Geography*, published in the second half of the century, catered to a demand for encyclopaedic works already well established. John Harris, known also as the compiler of a *Collection of Travels*, brought out the first English encyclopaedia in 1704. A quarter of a century later Ephraim Chambers brought out his *Cyclopedia*; the work ran into seven editions in twenty years and inspired French scholars to produce the great *Encyclopédie*, generally regarded as the most influential work of the whole century. In 1768 the *Encyclopaedia Britannica* appeared; its second edition, published a decade later, was four times the length of the first. These great works could be bought only by the well-to-do. For the less opulent, the establishment of lending libraries—another innovation of the age—was a great advantage. But the taste for books and reading was not confined only to the upper and the middle classes. 'All foreigners,' Dr Johnson noted with pride, 'remark that the knowledge of the common people of England is greater than that of any other vulgar.'[2]

Not only through the printed word did new ideas, new knowledge spread: conversation, too, had its part. Facilities for wider social intercourse were greater than ever before. This was due, in great part, to better communications: travelling was easier, quicker, safer. For stimulating conversation London was as ever the centre. The taverns and the coffee-houses of the metropolis—for the great age of London clubs had not yet begun—were the places where men met, where a group of acquaintances, brought together by some common interest or simply by pleasure in one another's company, could hire a private room and form themselves into a dining club. One such club will occupy a central place in this study; its members were to dedicate themselves to the exploration of Africa.

Of formal societies there was in mid-century only one, the Royal Society, 'beyond dispute', according to its early-nineteenth-century historian, 'the most magnificent and liberal establishment of the kind which has ever been formed'. Founded in 1660, its interests concentrated on, but were not confined to, the physical sciences. Of the four thousand articles that had appeared in the Society's *Transactions* by 1800, about one-fifth had been devoted to Natural History and nearly seventy to Geography. In the cause of science the Society was prepared to finance expeditions to distant lands. Thus in 1761 astronomers were sent both to St Helena and to Sumatra to observe the transit of Venus. The Royal Society was not alone in its concern to extend the bounds of knowledge; in 1764 a highly exclusive dining club, the Society of Dilettanti, founded thirty years earlier by a group of rich young men with an interest in Italy and the arts, organized a successful archaeological expedition to Ionia. Here were precedents not without relevance for the future.[3]

The Philosophical Transactions of the Royal Society was the first learned journal to appear in England. Its importance was well put by the Society's historian: 'Formerly a philosopher could not well appear before the world, unless he had a complete treatise to publish. But at present through these periodical channels, every idea and new fact may be easily and advantageously communicated. The experimenter runs but little risk of losing his labour by investigating what has already been ascertained; while, by the multiplicity of co-operation, emulation and industry are more likely to be maintained.'[4]

One other manifestation of the mental energy of the age requires attention—the mania for collecting. 'In those days,' wrote Augustine Birrell in an essay on the Bodleian at Oxford, 'there were learned men in all works of life, and many more, who if not learned were endlessly curious. The great merchants of the City of London instructed their agents in far lands to be on the lookout for rare things, and transmitted them home to find a resting place in Bodley's buildings. All sorts of curiosities found their way there—crocodiles, whales, mummies and black negro boys in spirits.' It was at Oxford that the first public museum was founded, named after the collector, Elias

154

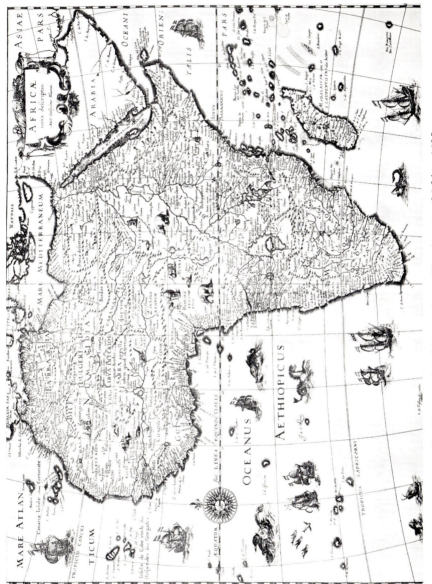

5. Cartographical impressions: Blaeu's map of Africa, 1635

6. Cartographical impressions: D'Anville's map of Africa, 1727

Ashmole, who presented to the University 'twelve cartloads of curiosities'. Ashmole himself had inherited the collection from John Tradescant, a Dutchman who became gardener to Charles I; most of the pieces came either from Virginia or from Algiers.[5]

The greatest collector of the early eighteenth century was Sir Hans Sloane, already mentioned for the interest that he took in Job ben Solomon, the princely slave from Bondou. Sloane was a very remarkable man. Born in 1660, he studied both medicine and botany. In his twenties he went to the West Indies, where he made a scholarly study of tropical flora. On his return to England, he set up in practice in London; so successful was he that he was able to make and spend a fortune on the magnificent collection that he built up over fifty years. A brief, incomplete catalogue illustrates the range of his interests: fifty thousand books and manuscripts, twenty-three thousand coins and medals, over a thousand pieces of antiquarian interest, nearly two thousand 'quadrupeds and their parts', over five thousand insects, together with a vast number of geological and botanical specimens. In 1727 Sloane succeeded Isaac Newton as President of the Royal Society; he held this influential office for twenty-six years, until his death at the age of ninety-three in 1753. In his will he bequeathed his great collection to the nation. It became the foundation of the British Museum, which opened its doors to the public for the first time in 1759.[6]

Here, then, is evidence enough that the curiosity of the men of the eighteenth century was as exuberant as that of the Elizabethans, yet better directed and more rational, therefore more conscious of the extent of its ignorance. When such curiosity played upon the world, what could be more provoking than the map of Africa, what more challenging to the manifest power of the age than the blanks of that mysterious interior?

III

THE INFLUENCE OF GREAT MEN

JAMES COOK

THE SEVEN YEARS' WAR of 1756–63 was the most profitable and exhilarating struggle in which the British people have ever been engaged. 'They had won a victory,' J. C. Beaglehole has pointed out, 'that had enlarged without exhausting the national spirit; they were self-congratulatory but they were unsatisfied; and the next three decades, the golden age of Georgian culture, was a period of astonishing activity, and of personalities no less astonishing.' 'The unconquerable spirit,' wrote James Bruce, himself among the most remarkable personalities of the new age, 'raised in this nation by a long and glorious war, very naturally at the return of peace resolved itself into a spirit of adventure and enquiry.' That spirit manifested itself in many fields—in literature, in art, in mechanical invention, in political thought, in imperial expansion, not least in exploration. In exploration a similar outburst of energy occurred in that later aftermath, the years that followed Waterloo. Then Africa and the Arctic presented the challenge of the unknown; in the 1760s it was the far Pacific that held men's minds.[1]

No sudden craze accounted for this interest. More than sixty years earlier William Dampier had brought out his *New Voyage Round the World*, the record of twelve years drifting from job to job in every corner of the tropics. It was a seminal work, setting the fashion for books of travel, rousing Englishmen to the lure of the South Seas and inducing the Government to sponsor for the first time a voyage of exploration, with Dampier in command; it appeared, too, at a propitious time, for the outbreak of war with Spain in 1701 gave a strategic significance to that distant ocean. As more reports became available during the next half century, geographers grew increasingly aware of the extent of their own ignorance. Nothing definite was known of the southern latitudes of the globe. Was it not possible that there might be found some great, temperate continent, *Terra Australis*, whose discovery would be of incalculable importance to the expanding nations of Europe ?[2]

In the years immediately after the Seven Years' War three expeditions, two British and one French, were despatched to the Pacific; they added little to existing knowledge. In 1768 the desire to observe the transit of Venus from the other side of the world provided the pretext for a fourth expedition. Its single ship was commanded by James Cook, a former warrant officer, who had proved his ability as a marine surveyor. In the course of the next ten years, in three successive voyages, Cook charted New Zealand and the eastern coast of Australia, became the first man to cross the Antarctic Circle, and, on his last expedition, before his death in Hawaii, mapped the northwestern coast of America. Never before, in the whole course of human history, had one man brought about so tremendous an accession to geographical knowledge.

The wonderful achievement of James Cook served in a variety of ways to stimulate exploration. There was, first, the example of his personality, the inspiration of his career. Cook was a self-made man, son of a farm labourer; without the advantage of a lengthy education, he had made a mark for himself in the Navy through his resolute industry in mastering his profession as a marine surveyor, his infinite capacity for taking pains. His first expedition developed his character as a leader of men. Practical and unfailing care for the well-being of his crew, unruffled cheerfulness in the most trying conditions, a strict sense of discipline, these qualities won him the affection and respect of all who sailed with him. The power and charm of his spirit was felt not only by those of his own race; among the people of Tahiti his tact, fearlessness and decency won him a reputation near-divine. Practical and unassuming though he always remained, his personality had a magnetic influence on his contemporaries: Boswell, for instance, confessed that he found himself, after talking to Cook, seized by an 'enthusiasm of curiosity and adventure'. His life indeed seemed shaped—how forcefully one can still feel this—by the heroic simplicity of greatness.

Equally stimulating was the lesson of his method. In the new lands that he reached Cook took the greatest care to chart the coastline accurately, showing always a scholarly hesitation in his reluctance to theorize about places he had never seen. But the knowledge acquired on his voyage was not confined to cartography nor was it collected by Cook alone. On his first voyage Cook had been accompanied by a wealthy young man, Joseph Banks. Banks had the backing of the Royal Society, but he went at his own expense, taking with him Dr Solander, Linnaeus's student and probably the best botanist to be found in England, together with a team of three artists and a naturalist. 'The number of natural productions discovered on this voyage,' Banks wrote after his return, 'is incredible; almost one thousand species of plants that have not been described by any botanical author; five hundred fishes; as many birds; with insects, sea and land, innumerable.' Nor were the human inhabitants disregarded; wherever he landed, Banks made extensive notes on the natives and their way of life. Banks and Cook were not the only pioneers of scientific exploration; in 1768 the Russian Government instructed the Academy of St Petersburg to select explorers capable of making a detailed survey of the little-known regions of Siberia and Central Asia. But the great success achieved by Cook and by Banks may be said to have established a standard and a model; the two men never sailed together again, but on his second and third voyages Cook was accompanied by men with scientific knowledge, while Banks was able to use the prestige he had acquired to further the cause of detailed and intensive exploration.[3]

Cook's success showed very clearly that effective, large-scale exploration could best be undertaken when supported and financed by the Government. This lesson could naturally best be appreciated by the Admiralty, the Government Department most closely involved in the preparations for his expeditions. That the Government should sponsor exploration by land as well as by sea was an idea that would have to wait longer for acceptance. But in the Admiralty, at least, something of a tradition had been established, to be maintained by the initiative and enthusiasm of individual officers and civil servants. In the course of the next half century, in the Arctic and in the Antarctic, in Australia and on the Pacific Coast of North America, in East Africa and in North Africa, on the Congo and in the Central Sudan, British naval officers, more than any other single class of men, were to play a leading part in the charting of the unknown areas of the world.*

* Among naval officers who made a name for themselves as explorers and surveyors were Vancouver and Broughton in the North Pacific in the

Finally, there was the challenge of Cook's achievement. The clear light which his discoveries had thrown on some of the remotest countries of the world showed up in provoking contrast Europe's ignorance of many much nearer lands.

Of the objects of inquiry which engage our attention the most, there are none, perhaps, that so much excite continued curiosity, from childhood to age; none that the learned and unlearned so equally wish to investigate, as the nature and history of those parts of the world, which have not, to our knowledge, been hitherto explored. To this desire the Voyages of the late Captain Cook have so far afforded gratification, that nothing worthy of research by Sea, the Poles themselves excepted, remains to be examined; but by Land, the objects of Discovery are still so vast, as to include at least a third of the habitable surface of the earth: for much of Asia, a still larger proportion of America, and almost the whole of Africa, are unvisited and unknown.

This statement was made ten years after Cook's death; its author was Henry Beaufoy, Secretary of the newly founded Association for Promoting the Discovery of the Interior Parts of Africa.[4]

Others interested in Africa felt stirred by Cook's triumph. In 1785 a young Frenchman, Silvester Golbéry, went to the Senegal as aide-de-camp to the Governor. He became an ardent advocate of colonial expansion. The times were not propitious; in that troubled, pre-revolutionary decade no one at Versailles showed any interest in Africa. Such indifference seemed to Golbéry the more inexcusable, because, as he wrote some years later, 'our rivals the English had just gained a vast accession of glory from the last voyages of Captain Cook. His achievement should have excited the emulation of France to whom her establishments in Africa . . . presented the most eligible opportunities . . . of attaining considerable discoveries in the interior.'[5]

So the influence of a great man's actions spread, ripple upon ripple, to touch the minds of men in times and in places far removed from the day and scene of his own achievements.

JAMES BRUCE

'It was a golden age, which united humanity and science, exempted men of liberal minds and education, employed in the noblest of all 1790s; Flinders in Australia from 1795 to 1803; and after the end of the Napoleonic War, Tuckey on the Congo, Smyth, Beechey and Lyon in North Africa, Clapperton in the Central Sudan, Owen in East and West Africa, Weddell in the Antarctic, and Franklin and Parry in the Arctic.

occupations, that of exploring the distant parts of the globe, from being any longer degraded, and rated as little better than the Bucanneer or pirate, because they had, till then, in manners been nearly similar.' The sentiment might have been expressed with Captain Cook in mind; but those words were written by one who was profoundly conscious of his own contribution to this change in opinion. They occur in the 'Dedication to the King', with which James Bruce opened the five massive volumes of his *Travels to Discover the Source of the Nile*, the book which established his fame as the first great African explorer of modern times.[1]

Bruce was born in 1730, the eldest son of a Scottish country gentleman, the Laird of Kinnaird. At the age of eight he was sent to school in London; he did not return to Scotland until he was seventeen. For a year he dabbled in law at Edinburgh University, then used the excuse of a serious illness to break off his studies. Returning home, he spent several pleasantly uneventful years, absorbed in the recreations of country life, hunting, shooting and fishing. Forced at last to think of earning a living, he returned to London with the idea of seeking a post in the East India Company's service. Instead, he met the daughter of a London wine-merchant, married her and became a partner in her father's business. 'Many persons of distinction honoured him with their friendship', and he might have settled down to the agreeable routine of a comfortably established man-about-town, had not tragedy befallen him. Eight months after their marriage, his wife died of consumption in peculiarly harassing circumstances. After her death Bruce lost much of his interest in business and began to devote himself increasingly to the study of foreign languages, especially Spanish and Portuguese, and to the art of drawing, preparing himself for the time when he could travel abroad 'in the character of a merchant, with the taste and science of a scholar'. In 1757 he left England and spent two years on the Continent, developing an interest in Arabic culture in Spain and a taste for military adventure in Germany, where he was a spectator at the battle of Crevelt.[2]

He returned to England in 1759, as heir, after his father's death, of a considerable estate. With a shrewd eye for business, he became a partner in the newly opened iron-works at Carron and the owner of several coalfields, thus securing for himself a substantial income. But he still hankered after 'adventures more congenial to the spirit of his ancestors'. This spirit led him, with the outbreak of war between England and Spain in 1761, to submit to the Government a plan for a commando raid on the Spanish naval base of Ferrol, of which he had made careful drawings four years earlier. The plan was turned down, but not before Bruce had been granted an interview with the Prime Minister himself to explain his views. Disappointed, he decided to return to Kinnaird, there to console himself with his private studies, studies which had led him to make a serious attempt to learn Arabic and to acquire an interest in Ge'ez, the classical language of Ethiopia. Once again, however, fortune intervened.

In the discussions that took place over his plan for the attack on Ferrol, Bruce had made the acquaintance of Lord Halifax, one of the Secretaries of State. Halifax 'laughed at his design for retiring so early in life' and suggested that 'the way to rise in the present reign was by enterprise and discovery and that his Majesty's love of the arts was a sure and effectual introduction to patronage. He observed that Africa, though almost at our very door, was yet unexplored; that Dr Shaw, a writer of undoubted credit, had spoken of magnificent remains of architecture existing in the kingdom of Tunis and Algiers and that something should now be done to preserve them by drawings for the king's collection.' Halifax went on to mention that the post of consul in Algiers was at present vacant, and affirmed that if Bruce were to accept the post he would be given leave to appoint a vice-consul and thus free himself to make tours of the interior. Bruce had a number of conversations with Halifax over Africa, conversations in which Robert Wood, the Under-Secretary, himself an experienced traveller in the Middle East, joined.* In the course of these discussions, frequent reference was made to a problem that since the dawn of history had baffled the civilized world, the location of the source of the Nile. 'Hints were obliquely thrown out,' wrote Bruce's biographer, Alexander Murray†, 'that the discovery of these "coy sources" could not

* Robert Wood spent several years in the Levant, led there by a desire 'to read the Iliad and the Odyssey in the country where Achilles fought, where Ulysses travelled, where Homer sang'. In the 1750s he produced two superb volumes which introduced his countrymen to the magnificence of Palmyra and of Baalbek. He died in 1771.³

† Alexander Murray, Bruce's biographer, was a person sufficiently remarkable to deserve more than a bibliographical mention. He was born in 1775 the son of a Scotch shepherd but came to display such a genius for learning languages that he was able to make his way into the University, where one of his contemporaries remembered him as 'a little shivering creature, gentle, studious, timid and reserved'. He taught himself Ge'ez and was probably the only person in Great Britain able to read Amharic. As a result, Constable, the Edinburgh publisher, engaged him to edit the

be expected from any ordinary traveller, much less from one who had not any experience in those difficulties which must accompany an enterprise of such magnitude and glory; and it was insinuated that, if any Briton should fulfil in this particular the wishes of every age, he needed not, under such a monarch and in a period so auspicious to discovery and learning despair of a high reward.'[4]

In 1762 Bruce received his appointment as consul in Algiers, was introduced to the king and promised to make drawings for the royal collection. His friend, Wood, 'intent on promoting the study of art and science, had employed all his influence with the ministry to procure for his friend a residence of a few months in Italy for the purpose of improving his taste and of qualifying him to collect with greater ability the remains of antiquity in the southern parts of the Roman Empire'. With such support Bruce was able to spend nine pleasant months in France and in Italy. In March 1763 he arrived in Algiers. Whatever Halifax and Wood may have implied, Bruce soon found that the consulship was no sinecure. No vice-consul was ever appointed, so it was impossible for him to leave his post to visit the interior; the ruling Dey, though not ill-disposed to Bruce personally, was bitterly hostile to the country he represented; finally, certain individuals at home, whom he had offended by his plain speaking, began to intrigue to have him removed. His enemies were successful: after two years in Algiers Bruce found his appointment suddenly terminated. He can hardly have regretted this outcome, for his dismissal left him free to gratify to the full his taste for travel and adventure.[6]

In 1765 Bruce was thirty-five years old and eminently qualified for the role he had cast for himself. His appearance was striking. 'He is the tallest man you ever saw in your life—at least, *gratis*': so young Fanny Burney described her 'Man-mountain', as she mockingly called him. 'However,' she added, 'he has a very good figure, and is rather handsome.' 'His walk was stately, his air'—so Murray was informed—'stately and commanding': a family trait, for he had inherited from his father 'the love of magnificence, the dignity and stately deportment not unsuitable to the heir of an ancient family'. His hair was dark red; his voice was loud and strong; but his laugh, so Miss Burney noted, 'when his dignity is off its guard, is a chuckle

second edition of Bruce's *Travels*. In 1812 Murray, who had become a country clergyman, was appointed to be Professor of Oriental Languages at Edinburgh University; he died the next year at the early age of thirty-seven.[5]

of delight that shines his face of a bright scarlet, and shakes his whole vast frame with a boyish ecstasy'. 'He was attentive to his dress and was particularly successful in wearing that of the nations through which he passed in an easy and graceful manner.' To the manner of a Grand Seigneur he added the mind of a scholar and the accomplishments of a man of action. He was an enthusiastic sportsman, an excellent shot, skilled, too, from his practice among the Barbary Arabs at wielding the javelin and the lance; moreover—this for his African hosts was to be among the most impressive of his qualities— he was a magnificent horseman. He had spent ten years in the study of languages and could speak Arabic with ease; he was a competent draughtsman, a good amateur astronomer and not unversed in medicine; he had acquired a first-hand experience of business and of diplomacy; he had moved with assurance in the world of the great. Finally, he possessed that scholarly curiosity about every facet of experience that is one of the most striking qualities of the best minds of his age. In England, 'his robustness of conviction and expression', his open intolerance, his love of talking about his own ancestry, 'the curvetting, strong pride'—as Archbishop Mathew has called it—'of his haughty manner' made him many enemies. In the courts of African princes such manners might prove less ill-esteemed; in any case Bruce knew how to keep himself in check when he was seeking the support of some influential man, an essential preliminary, as he understood from the start, to any of the journeys he planned to undertake. James Bruce possessed then, one may fairly say, the grand traits of character of the complete man. By birth possibly the most distinguished, in material means certainly the most fortunately endowed, he was also, in character and training, the best equipped of all the African explorers with whom this study will be concerned.[7]

On leaving Algiers in 1765, Bruce obtained permission to visit the interior, passed through the Jebel Aures and came to Tunis. From Tunis he followed the pilgrim road to Tripoli and Bengazi, took a ship but was wrecked on the shores of Cyrenaica, losing most of his equipment and being cruelly treated by the Arabs into whose hands he fell.* Eventually he reached Crete and went on to the Levant,

* Bruce did not make use of the extensive notes he had made in North Africa when he wrote his *Travels*; but some of his notes were published by Colonel Playfair, the scholarly English Consul at Algiers, in 1877. Bruce was mainly interested in Roman antiquities, of which he made many highly competent sketches, but he also collected some information about the geography of the interior and can claim the distinction of being the first

where he settled for a time in Aleppo. He played now with the idea of going to Armenia to observe that same transit of Venus that was serving as the cause of Cook's first expedition; but finding that it would be impossible quickly to replace the instruments he had lost in the shipwreck, he turned his mind to that other project Halifax and Wood had suggested to him in London five years before—the discovery of the source of the Nile.

Arriving in Egypt he took to Arab dress, 'gave out that he was going to India and seldom appeared in public except in the guise of a Dervish who was skilled in magic and cared for nothing but Study'. His skill in medicine and in prophecy won him the friendship of Ali, the most powerful of the Mamluk Beys, and of that greatest of ecclesiastics in the Ethiopian Church, the Patriarch of Alexandria; from them he obtained letters of introduction to many of the important people he should meet on his journey to Ethiopia, where, so he was convinced, the solution of the mystery of the river was to be found.[9]

From Cairo he passed down the Red Sea to Jidda, then crossed to Massawa, where he needed all his skill to extricate his party from the clutches of a murderous Governor. At last, on February 15, 1770, after a dangerous and exhausting journey, he reached Gondar, capital of Ethiopia.

The situation which he found in the country was one of desperate and bloody confusion: a ruling family torn by savage feuds, provincial governors quick to seize any opportunity of asserting their independence, a countryside devastated by the raids of the pagan Gallas. The annals of the time are tedious with revolt, intrigue and massacre. Tedious as annals—but as recounted in the cool, lucid and precise prose of a humane observer, the years Bruce spent in Ethiopia assume an epic quality: the clash of character, the tenderness of friends, the cruelty of enemies, the uncertainty of fortune, in the palace of a king, the camp of a warrior, the violence and the laughter —this is the stuff of Homer and of Shakespeare, though set on a stranger stage, in the remotest kingdom of Christendom. To have caught so superbly the grandeur and misery of those times—this, one may think, is the most enduring of Bruce's achievements. He was able to write as he did, only because he had come to know intimately the great people of his day: Ras Michael, the cruel and immensely

European to have mentioned the existence of Kufra, loneliest of Saharan oases, five hundred miles south of Cyrenaica. A century passed before Kufra was visited by a European, the German traveller Rohlfs in 1879.[8]

powerful old war-lord and kingmaker; his beautiful and spirited wife, Ozoro Esther; the pale, composed young Emperor, Tecla Haimanot; the venerable and imposing Queen Mother—these and many others. To them all he commended himself by his upright character and his practical skill, whether with horse or gun or medicine chest. He was given royal office as commander of the household cavalry, rode with Ras Michael and the Emperor on their campaigns and suffered in their reversals. Yet in the end he came to be disgusted with Ethiopia, the insensate cruelty, the ghastly punishments, the summary executions. To depart from the country proved as difficult as it had been to enter it. Bruce chose the route by way of Sennar and the Nubian desert; after many adventures he reached Cairo in January 1773. So long had he been lost completely to the world that when after an absence of ten years he returned to Europe, he seemed as a man risen from the dead.

In the main object of his expedition he considered that he had succeeded, for he had reached the springs of Geesh, where the Blue Nile has its source, and had reflected, 'standing in that spot which had baffled the genius, industry and inquiry of both ancients and moderns' that he 'though a mere private Briton' had triumphed, where the kings and their armies had failed. A dramatic but not, alas, an accurate conclusion, for a century and a half earlier, the Portuguese Jesuit, Father Paez, had been to Geesh, as Bruce unreasonably attempted to disprove. Moreover, the Blue Nile was by no means so great a river as the White Nile, on whose further course Bruce had gathered no information. Indeed, if the main task of an explorer be to chart lands hitherto unknown, Bruce had little to contribute. On the other hand, the material with which he returned was more substantial than that ever before acquired by any traveller in the interior of Africa, comprising, as it did, manuscripts for the historian, vocabularies for the philologist, drawings of animals and birds for the zoologist, plants for the botanist, cartographical and meteorological data for the geographer, together with much information about the manners and the mode of life of little-known peoples. Not without reason Bruce could claim, in typically magniloquent phrase, that he had come to 'fill a great chasm in the history of the Universe'.[10]

His reception on his return to Europe was in fitting accord with his achievement. In Rome he was 'not insensible' to the pleasure 'with which the ancient Nobility enjoyed his fame'. In Paris, 'his travels became a subject of general conversation; his company was courted everywhere and by persons of the first distinction in point of learning and quality'. In London 'every person of distinction or learning who had any curiosity to know the wonders of foreign countries, sought his acquaintance'. And yet, set against the backcloth of his experiences in Algiers or in Cairo, in Gondar or in Sennar, London and its society must have appeared a little effete. Moreover, the adventures he had undergone had swollen his self-confidence and his already intense pride. Why should he bow down before the self-appointed pundits of the day? Why restrain the 'open, free and animated' course of conversation, if some were too squeamish to stand his descriptions of the savage manners of the Gallas, the bloody feasts of the Abyssinians? Yet one cannot deliberately shock English society with impunity. Nor was this his only offence; 'when he observed men deficient in moral conduct, he usually expressed his contempt for them in unqualified terms'. This was splendid; but it made him many enemies, enemies who attacked him first by questioning his veracity in specific details, then by insinuating that he had never been to Ethiopia at all. To a man of his independence of mind such critics were beneath contempt: he might have discredited them straightaway had he published his memoirs soon after his return. But he had his own private affairs to consider. He returned to Scotland and married a second time.[11]

'Happy in his family and satisfied that he had done or at least suffered as much as any man then alive in order to instruct and gratify the public, he allowed his mind an interval of repose between the toils of travelling and the vexations of appearing before the public as a candidate for literary fame.' Murray puts the matter too obliquely. In fact, had his wife not died after ten years of married life, Bruce might never have written up his experiences. Thirty years earlier the death of his first wife had led him to seek distraction in foreign travel; now, urged on by his closest friends, he sought consolation in his memories of Ethiopia. So, seventeen years after his return to Europe, there appeared in 1790 the five great volumes of his *Travels*. They met with a mixed reception. 'Everyone is looking into Bruce's Travels,' Lord Sheffield wrote to his old friend, Edward Gibbon. 'Part takes the attention but they are abominably abused. Banks objects to the Botany, Rennell to the Geography, Cambridge to the History, the Greeks to the Greek etc., etc.; yet the work is to be found on every table.' Of course his critics had their reasons: the old man had not been as scrupulous in quoting his sources as a true scholar should, and sometimes, as he sat there in misty Kinnaird reliving his adventures in sweltering Massawa or among the mountains of Ethiopia, he had allowed his imagination a little licence. Today, not troubled by the recollection of that disturbing physical presence, we can make allowance for these foibles and see in Bruce not only a superb Africanist but also one who will always—as Richard Garnett once put it—'remain the poet, and his work the epic of African travel'.[12]

Who can ever accurately assess the influence of a great book? For most of his readers Bruce must have opened new windows on the world, supplied them in the blurb of the age with 'a great fund of instruction and entertainment'. But there were some who were more deeply moved. One of his most attentive readers was an Oxford undergraduate named Browne; he suspected that Bruce must be wrong over the Nile and decided to go out to Africa to set him right. And there were other young men destined to win fame as African explorers, Park and Hornemann, Röntgen and Burckhardt, who were excited and inspired by Bruce's adventures.

The great movement in exploration directed by the African Association had already begun when Bruce's work appeared. He was not directly involved in it, but watched with interest the progress of the Association's travellers. Their greatest achievements he did not live to see. One April day in 1794 he was hurrying down the stairs of his house in Kinnaird to see a lady into her carriage, when he slipped, fell and was picked up unconscious. He died the next day. For one whom Providence or his own sagacity had preserved through so many and great dangers, it was an ironic ending.[13]

JOSEPH BANKS

Whether he was playing the part of Yagoube the English Dervish in the halls of Ethiopia or stalking through the drawing-rooms of London Society as 'His Abyssinian Majesty', James Bruce was always, one suspects, a great outsider. But Joseph Banks was unquestionably one of the central figures of English life, 'the Great Panjandrum of British Science', as J. C. Beaglehole has called him, 'the president, the organizer, the lord justice of appeal'; were he alive today, one could not refrain from breathing the word *Establishment*. For Banks, indeed, possessed to the full the characteristic virtues of the English Establishment at its best—great energy, a shrewd common-sense judgement, a wide range of interests, the practical sense of knowing

THE BONDS OF INTERCOURSE

how to get things done, the social sense that goes with the capacity to draw the most out of a wide range of acquaintances extending through every class. Yet he has suffered the fate that history seems to reserve for the Establishment; having been for half a century one of the best known and most highly esteemed persons of his age, he is today, for all but the specialist, forgotten and unknown. Such perhaps will always be the lot of those whose work, seemingly diluted by being spread through so many fields, leaves behind it no impression of passionate and single-minded originality. Yet as one comes to make his further acquaintance, there emerge the lineaments of an impressive and an inspiring figure, a great and decent man.[1]

He was a man on whose birth fortune had smiled, for he came of a line of well-to-do country gentlemen and was left at the age of eighteen—he was born in 1743—the heir of a fine estate, Revesby Abbey in Lincolnshire, and the possessor of a considerable fortune. Wealthy, handsome, assured, fond of hunting and shooting, passionately devoted to fishing, one trait alone would seem to distinguish him from his contemporaries at Eton and Oxford: at the age of fourteen, in a moment of almost mystical revelation, he had decided to become a botanist.* This interest in natural history led him, at an age when other rich young men were enjoying the pleasures of the continental Grand Tour, to sail in a Fisheries Protection vessel to Newfoundland and Labrador, where he made a collection of plants that formed the foundation of a great herbarium. On his return he was elected a Fellow of the Royal Society. He was thus well placed to learn of the preparations that were being made for Cook's expedition and to secure the Society's backing for his proposal to accompany Cook in a private capacity and at his own expense.

* At the end of his life Banks told his old friend, Sir Everard Home, how he first came to develop a passion for botany. One summer evening, when he was fourteen and had been a year at Eton, he was returning from a bathe, 'walking leisurely along a lane the sides of which were richly enamelled with flowers, he stopped and looking round, involuntarily exclaimed, How beautiful! After some reflection, he said to himself, it is surely more natural that I should be taught to know all these productions of Nature, in preference to Latin and Greek'. Whereupon he resolutely set himself to learn all that he could about flowers, gaining much information from the old women he met 'culling simples' in the Eton lanes to sell to London druggists and apothecaries. When he came to Oxford he found that the Professor of Botany never gave lectures; undismayed, Banks went off to Cambridge, where he was able to engage the services of a competent botanist to come and lecture in Oxford.[2]

Banks's three years with Cook laid the foundations of his fame. Such a voyage could not fail to be a gruelling test of a man's character. A test in the first place of personal relations: on the one hand, the dilettante young scientist with his £6,000 a year, on the other, the self-made naval officer, resolutely practical in his manner—what room, as indeed the history of other expeditions could show, for petty complaints, for sarcasm, for nagging quarrels. Instead there developed on board the *Endeavour* a complimentary intercourse of remarkable minds. The careful student of Cook's journal can trace how during the course of the voyage he came to acquire 'a greatly heightened sense of the scope of human thought', his eyes turning, through the example of Banks and, equally important, of Solander, to observe more carefully the new strange scenes, his mind coming, through the two gentlemen's lively talk (was not the affable Solander known in London Society as the 'philosophical gossip?'), to speculate on questions of ethno-history that can have worried few straightforward mariners in the past. If Cook gained and grew in stature, surely Banks, fifteen years his junior, must have absorbed as much, learned lessons about the practical character of great leadership which would be remembered as an inspiration throughout his life.*[3]

The voyage was a test in other ways. Not many men of Banks's class—unless they took to the army as a career—were called upon in that uncataclysmic age to face danger, to run the risk of sudden death. The expedition on which Banks had embarked—though the superb management of its commander disguised this fact—was as perilous an enterprise as any in the history of maritime exploration. On the icy hillsides of Tierra del Fuego, where his two Negro servants were frozen to death, on the beaches of New Zealand with the cannibal Maori brandishing their spears, on the reefs of Australia, when the *Endeavour* was holed by coral and nearly wrecked, on the homeward run from Batavia, when many of the crew and several of Banks's own party died in agony of a virulent dysentery, when he himself lay wracked with fever in his cabin, on all these occasions Banks came to know how it felt to have one's life put to the test. Nor was it merely a case of refusing to shirk the ordinary perils; in any emergency he was always to the fore, in any encounter with the

* The influence of Solander on Banks should not be ignored. 'We may well think,' Beaglehole has written, 'that in this intoxicating morning of his powers he had in Solander ten years older, so much better trained, a solid base, a standard of reference, a centre of professional integrity.'[4]

natives it was to him that Cook invariably turned for advice. During those three years with Cook, Banks displayed, as Cuvier, the great French naturalist, pointed out in his obituary oration, 'an astonishing activity'. 'Fatigue does not depress him, nor danger deter him. We see him in Brazil sneaking ashore like a smuggler, in order to seize upon some specimens of the natural production of that rich country, in spite of the stupid jealousy of the governor. At Otaheite [Tahiti] he allowed himself to be painted black from head to foot in order that he might join in a funeral ceremony which he would not otherwise have been allowed to witness; and it was not simply by *seeing*, but by *observing*, that he displayed his true character.'[5]

Above all, Banks had proved himself an outstanding and highly professional explorer. He had started off primarily as a botanist, his cabin lined with the latest works on natural history, the hold filled with the impedimenta of a naturalist, equipment on which he had laid out several thousand pounds. But Banks had only to find himself in a strange land to be excited into inquiring about every aspect of the life he saw around him. In our own day he would have made a superb anthropologist. In Tahiti he proved himself to have the happy knack of being able to win the confidence and the affection of the natives; he learnt their language, slept in their huts, shared their meals, observed every custom, every practice, every craft, and tried, so far as his knowledge of the language would allow, to probe their deepest thoughts about religion. Such an attitude was based on a profound humanity. There was an occasion when the *Endeavour* first made landfall in New Zealand and four Maoris were killed in an attack on one of the ship's boats. It was, Banks wrote in his journal, 'the most disagreeable day my life has yet seen; black be the mark for it, and Heaven send that such may never return to embitter future recollection'.[6]

Back in England, Banks, who was not yet thirty, stepped ashore to instant fame. He was frequently received by the king and established with the sovereign a friendship that was to endure the course of their lives. 'The curiosities brought home, by Mr Banks and Dr Solander,' noted a London newspaper only six weeks after their return, 'have already been seen by most of the nobility.' Most flattering of all, if Banks could have known it, was the compliment paid him by the great Linnaeus in a letter to an English friend: 'I cannot sufficiently admire Mr Banks who had exposed himself to so many dangers and bestowed more money in the service of Natural Science than any

7.   Africans: Tripoli—'Officers of the Grand Seraglio regaling'
     from Tully's *Letters*, London, 1817

8. Africans: Nubia—a camel caravan in the desert. From T. Krump's *Hoher und Fruchtbahrer Palm-Baum*, Augsburg, 1710

other man. Surely none but an Englishman would have the spirit to do what he has done.'[7]

Cook returned to the South Seas a year later. From the start Banks was determined to accompany him; for this purpose he gathered a larger and even more imposing team—Solander, of course, now employed as Banks's librarian, was to be of the party, together with Joseph Priestley, the great chemist, Zoffany, the artist, and Lind, the leading authority in England on tropical diseases. But Banks allowed his enthusiasm ('his dictatorial wrongheadedness', so Beaglehole calls it) to run away with him. In order to accommodate his party in the comfort he expected, it would have been necessary to have altered Cook's ship to such an extent as to endanger its sea-worthiness. The Admiralty, reasonably enough, would not accept the suggestions of a landsman on nautical matters; Banks, to his life-long disappointment, was forced to withdraw. He consoled himself with a brief but fruitful trip to Iceland. It was his last journey abroad. Six years later, at the unusually youthful age of thirty-five, he was elected President of the Royal Society. He remained in that distinguished chair for a span of forty-two years.*[8]

* Not everyone approved of Banks's exploits; some found them in thoroughly bad taste. Horace Walpole, fastidious among the books and the bric-à-brac of Strawberry Hill, referred to 'that wild man Banks'. Another derogatory comment came from that engaging and quintessentially English traveller, John Byng, Viscount Torrington, who passed Banks's Lincoln-shire home one day in the 1780s: 'the park is flat, dismal and unimproved; the house mean and uncomfortable with a horsepond in front, with no gardens or comforts but when a man sets himself up for a wild eccentric character and (having a great estate with the comforts of England at command) can voyage it to Otaheite and reside in a corner seat of Soho Square, of course his country seat will be a filthy, neglected spot'. Later, however, Banks came to pay great attention to his estate and always resided for a few months every year in Revesby. After Banks's election as President of the Royal Society another group of detractors emerged in the mathematicians of the Society. Their views on Banks's occupations were expressed in a satire composed by 'Peter Pindar'.

> To hunt for days a lizard or a gnat.
> And run a dozen miles to catch a bat;
> To plunge in marshes, and to scale the rocks
> Sublime, for scurvy grass and lady smocks
> Are matters of proud Triumph to be sure
> And such as Fame's fair volume should secure:
> Yet to my mind it is not such a feat
> As gives a man a claim to Newton's seat.[9]

171

The election forms the central event of Banks's life. As a young man he had won fame as a traveller: as Peter Pindar, a contemporary satirist put it,

> I'm honoured, stared at, whereso'er I go
> Soon as a room I enter, lo! all ranks
> Get up to complement Sir Joseph Banks. . . .
> 'Lord, that's Sir Joseph Banks, how grand his look
> Who sailed all round the world with Captain Cook.'

In middle and old age he was to play a different part. It is the mark of a wise man that his intellectual interests, narrow through inexperience when he is young, should come with the years to develop and branch out. So it was with Banks. Botany, the passion of his younger days, remained a source of delight throughout his life, even though the many calls made upon his time left him with no opportunity to engage in detailed research, so that he published next to nothing—not even the journal of his voyage with Cook—and came modestly to refer to himself as a 'botanizer' rather than a botanist. Besides, botany was for him never a subject to be studied in isolation; it came rather to be the seed-bed in which other ideas germinated, from which other interests sprung. Botany led Banks to become an explorer. His experience of exploration drew his mind both to the problems of geography and to the practical issues of colonization—issues which in turn produced a concern for the politics of imperialism, and a consideration of what would now be called the processes of economic development, both as they affected his own country and more distant lands. But one cannot make a simple chart of the development of any man's mind, least of all a mind so constantly throwing off new shoots of interest so vigorously as Banks's. Certain fields of thought and experience—abstract speculation, imaginative literature, political gossip—seem not to have attracted him: to this extent his mind was a limited one. But whatever was of practical import in promoting man's knowledge and mastery of his environment secured his enthusiastic support.*[10]

A biographer trying to decide on the most significant achieve-

---

* Banks was created a baronet in 1781. In 1795 he was made a Knight of the Bath. After this honour, whenever he took the Chair at the Royal Society, he would appear wearing the star and the broad red sash of his Order, not out of personal conceit, but out of respect for his high office. So he appears in Thomas Phillips's portrait. In 1797 he was appointed a member of the Privy Council.

ments of Banks's middle age might point to three things: his services to agriculture and horticulture by encouraging the transfer of useful plants from one part of the world to another; the part he played in the founding of the first British settlement in Australia; his work as the most prominent of the founder members of the African Association. Yet these were only three strands among many in a life of remarkable richness. The prestige of his high office as President of the Royal Society gave him a wonderful opportunity to play a distinguished part in the public life of his age: to use this opportunity to the full he was pre-eminently fitted, not only by the amplitude of his private means, the width of his interests and the practical bent of his mind, but also by the warmth, the range and the generosity of his hospitality. In 1776 he had bought for himself a town house in Soho Square: here he housed the collection of plants, insects and fishes he had brought back from his travels, here he built up his great library of Natural History, reckoned at the time to be the largest of its kind in the world. To any who could profit from them, to any scientist no matter what his country, the library and the collection were always open. So 32 Soho Square became, as a French visitor described it, 'the rendezvous for those who cultivate the sciences'. 'Foreigners are always received there with politeness and affability. They assemble every morning in one of the apartments of an extensive library. . . . There all the journals and public papers relative to the sciences are to be found; and there the members of the party communicate to each other such new discoveries as they are informed of by their respective correspondents or which are transmitted by the learned foreigners who visit London and who are all admitted to this society. A friendly breakfast of tea and coffee maintains that tone of ease and fraternity which ought universally to prevail among men of science and letters.'*[11]

The quality and range of Banks's friendships have been vividly described by Dr H. C. Cameron, his most recent biographer.

> Nearly all his friendships were based on a community of interests and to become his intimate a candidate must profess proficiency in at least

---

* Banks's Library, which is now in the British Museum, contained among other things a magnificent collection of works of travel, covering every continent of the world. On Africa there were about one hundred and forty different volumes at the time of his death; this number may seem small by modern standards, but at the time it included every book of any importance that had been written on that continent.

one of the subjects necessary for qualification. London Society, never more exclusive than then, looked a little askance at one of their number who mixed freely on the most friendly terms with all sorts and conditions of men. Without distinction, if they shared his interests, he made friends with all, from Farmer George, King of England to the tough sea-dog who ventured his life in his service. Sailors commissioned and sailors uncommissioned, farmers and breeders of sheep, explorers and adventurers, men who grew plants, men who drew and painted plants, country clergymen who loved their gardens, doctors, whether successful or undistinguished, men of science and great men with an interest in science, all these Banks welcomed to his house with a warm clasp of the hand or a hearty clap on the back and immediately his great voice began to boom in eager discussion over some new project or the possibilities of the latest discoveries. All were put at ease because he himself was so entirely at ease in their company. So long as there was a topic to debate he could give animation to a discussion on a vast range of subjects and the quality of his table-talk, especially when it turned upon the travels and adventures of his youth, was long remembered.

As President of the Royal Society or of some other learned body he dominated the assembly as long before he had dominated the natives of Tahiti and of New Zealand. Sitting silent and motionless in the chair, his immobility seemed to stifle opposition, but if need arose there came a formidable heave of his ponderous bulk and a lowering of his great eyebrows as he turned to face a disturber of the peace. Yet in society in the ordinary sense he was the shyest of men. For Banks had no small-talk and no interest in the little trivial intriguing things of life. With no topic on the agenda to discuss at the moment, and among those who had no understanding of his many interests and no part to play in them, he felt lost and embarrassed.

Thus Fanny Burney, meeting him at a tea-party, found him, as she noted in her diary, 'so exceedingly shy that we made no acquaintance at all. If instead of going round the world he had fallen from the moon he could not appear less versed in the usual modes of a tea-drinking party.'[12]

Impatience with trivialities is a characteristic usually to be found in those who live well-organized lives. Few lives, one may feel, have been better organized than Joseph Banks's. For to the Presidency of the Royal Society, to the membership of many committees, to the practical hospitality so generously dispensed there came as a natural corollary a vast and fruitful correspondence carried on with friends and scholars all over the world. From this correspondence it is possible to trace the growth of his interest in Africa.

Banks's first-hand experience of Africa was limited to a few weeks spent at Cape Town in 1771, on his way home with Cook. Significantly, in the next year, a young botanist from Kew Gardens, Francis Masson, a Scotsman, was sent out to the Cape to make a collection of plants. Masson spent three years in South Africa and returned again ten years later; on each occasion he made long and adventurous journeys into the interior. In 1780 Banks made contact with West Africa, when he was one of a group of wealthy subscribers who sent William Brass, the gardener to the Duke of Northumberland, to Cape Coast on the Gold Coast for 'botanical exploration'. Brass found his task a rewarding but a dangerous one; on one occasion he was attacked by the Dutch and lost all his books and papers, but he was able eventually to send back a collection of plants that was divided among those who had financed his mission.[13]

Three years later Banks received an interesting suggestion from one of his correspondents in the West Indies, Henry de Ponthieu, a merchant in Antigua. Ponthieu told Banks that he had come across Negroes and occasionally Moors possessing a good knowledge of Arabic, who had been brought as slaves across the Atlantic. 'From them,' he suggested, 'I think a better account could be attained than we have yet got (if indeed we have any) of the interior parts of Africa.' He went on to propose that a group of subscribers purchase three or four such Arabic-speaking slaves, have them brought to England to be questioned at one of the Universities and then sent back to Africa to collect further information; such an operation would not cost more than a few hundred pounds. There is no evidence that Banks acted directly on this proposal; but it must have served to sharpen his interest in the little-known continent.[14]

Certainly by the middle of the 1780s Banks had come to be regarded as one directly interested in Africa. In 1785 Isert, a German surgeon working in the Danish Fort Christianborg on the Gold Coast, wrote to Banks telling him of his plan to make a journey into the interior and asking for his support. Two years later Captain Thompson, a naval officer acting as escort to the first party of settlers bound for the new colony of Sierra Leone, wrote to say that he would be willing to undertake 'any observations or research' that Banks might care to suggest. In 1774 Banks made the acquaintance of James Bruce on his return from Ethiopia. From 1787 he was able to secure first-hand information on another part of Africa, after he had obtained the appointment of one of his protégés, James Matra, whom he had known as a midshipman with Cook on the *Endeavour*, as Consul in Tangier. Matra held this difficult post until his death in

1806; during these nineteen years he kept up a regular correspondence with Banks and sent him much useful information about Morocco.*[15]

It is clear then from the fragmentary evidence available that towards the end of the 1780s one of the most influential and practical-minded men in Europe was thinking increasingly about Africa. There were others whose minds were moving in the same direction and at the same time—but for different reasons.

* J. M. Matra was born in America in 1746, entered the Navy and sailed with Cook and Banks. Later he obtained a post as secretary to the British Embassy in Constantinople, but was not happy there and wrote to Banks in 1779 asking for his help in obtaining another post. In 1783 he was in London, leading as he wrote to Banks, 'the life of a solitary fugitive'. In the same year he drew up an elaborate plan for a settlement in New South Wales as a refuge for American loyalists. His plan, which Banks approved, was considered by the Government but not adopted. He served nineteen years in Morocco and died there in 1806. His consular despatches show him to have been a most able, enterprising and conscientious diplomat in a post of difficulty and discomfort; they provide an excellent picture, far more detailed than any published work, of Moroccan life and politics. They also show how scurvily Matra was treated by his superiors. Matra had a brother, Perkins, who preferred the name Magra. The latter had reached the rank of Major in the Army when in 1789 he was appointed Consul in Tunis. Luckier than his brother, he escaped from Barbary in 1804 and became equerry to the Duke of Sussex.[16]

IV

THE ANTI-SLAVERY MOVEMENT

BANKS'S INTEREST IN AFRICA centred at first not on the people, not even on the geography, but on the natural products of the continent: it was, at this stage, strictly scientific. But there was among his contemporaries a small band of men and women who had come to be passionately concerned with the fate of Africans as individual human beings. During the 1780s they founded the Anti-Slavery movement, a movement that hindsight reveals as the fountain-head of that great stream of philanthropic and missionary interest in Africa which did so much to open up the 'dark' continent and to define the civilizing mission of the European powers.

For a hundred years and more isolated voices had been raised in protest against both the institution of slavery in the European settlements of the New World and the Atlantic slave trade. Indeed, the critics of the system included almost every writer or philosopher of distinction in England and in France: Locke and Montesquieu, Pope and Defoe, Adam Smith and Condorcet, Tom Paine and Dr Paley, each in his different way attacked the servitude of Africa. At the same time, there had developed the concept of the 'noble savage', of whom Defoe had drawn a model in his Man Friday, while Rousseau, by suggesting that in virtue primitive people might be the superior of civilized Europeans, had pointed the moral. This concept was not only a salutary corrective to crude notions generally entertained about the 'savages' of Africa and America; it also provided a link between the less civilized people of the world and the refreshing and liberating ideas that were beginning to stir Europe. From the brotherhood of man, from the notion of human equality, the black man was not to be excluded. But these were only words and ideas; it was

177

to be the glory of a few dedicated young men to translate them into action.*

Yet it would be a mistake to consider the movement to abolish the slave trade and to stamp out slavery solely in terms of a great crusade. To dwell excessively, as most writers have done, on the individual abolitionists is to ignore those great political and economic changes which made abolition a practicable cause. Had the American colonies not broken away in 1776, the vested interests in favour of the trade would have proved, as American history subsequently showed, vastly more formidable. American independence was indeed the first step in the ruin of the British West Indian influence. Even more significant were the economic forces beyond the planters' control that steadily eroded their power. In the 1780s the production of the French West Indian islands, by virtue of more fertile soil, sur-

* The 'noble savage' of eighteenth-century literature, whose parentage can be traced back to Montaigne—or even, some would say, to Tacitus and his Germans—was usually a man of American Indian or Carib stock. With Man Friday Defoe was at pains to point out that 'his hair was long, not curled like wool . . . the colour of his skin not quite black . . . his mouth small, not flat like the Negroes'. Yet sensitive minds began to see in the Negro too images of pristine virtue. 'I beheld a perfect image of pure nature; an agreeable solitude bounded on every side by charming landscapes; the rural situation of cottages in the midst of trees, the ease and indolence of the Negroes, reclined under the shade of their spreading foliage; the simplicity of their dress and manners; the whole revived in my mind the idea of our first parents, and I seemed to contemplate the world in its primitive state'. The passage comes from Adanson's *Voyage to Senegal*; it is quoted as a note to a poem, *The Dying Negro*, written in 1775 by Thomas Day, a poem 'noteworthy for its enthusiastic attitude towards the Negroes'.

> In the wild wastes of Afric's sandy plain
> Where roams the lion thro' his drear domain,
> To curb the savage monarch in the chace,
> There too Heav'n planted Man's majestic race
> Bade Reason's sons with nobler titles rise
> Lift high their brow sublime and scan the skies . . .
> What though no rosy tints adorn their face,
> No silken tresses shine with flowing grace
> Yet of ethereal temper are their souls
> And in their veins the tide of honour rolls.

The third edition of this poem was dedicated, significantly, to Rousseau. Day was a remarkable man of advanced views and eccentric behaviour. He died in 1789 but came on account of his writings to be 'anathemized as a Jacobin' during the reactionary 'nineties.[1]

passed their Caribbean rivals. Meanwhile, as the total volume of British trade developed, the relative importance of the West Indies in the imperial economy declined, and the restrictions imposed by West Indian influence, the narrowly mercantilist conceptions of the sugar planters, came to seem increasingly irksome. Manufacturers in Birmingham could see no point in subsidizing planters in Jamaica by paying an unnecessarily high price for their sugar when the same product could be bought more cheaply in other tropical markets, markets which would, moreover, be glad to take the wares Birmingham was making. The future lay, of course, with Birmingham and not with Jamaica: the West Indian slave owners were by the end of the eighteenth century a doomed class. To contemporaries, however, they appeared one of the most powerful vested interests in the country. Many humane men must have thought despairingly—as some may think of *apartheid* in South Africa today—that the slave system was invulnerable to change; to attack any part of it required passionate conviction, remarkable audacity and a high sense of dedication.

The first blow was struck by a young civil servant named Granville Sharp, born in 1735 to a cultured and well-to-do family. In 1765 the iniquity of slavery was forcibly brought before Sharp's eyes, when in his brother's consulting room he saw a Negro, Jonathan Strong, who had been savagely beaten by his master and thrown into the street. Sharp played the good Samaritan, had the slave looked after, and found him a job when he was recovered. There the matter might well have ended, had not Strong's former master, Lister, run into his ex-slave by chance two years later, claimed him as his property and sold him to a friend for thirty pounds. To make sure of his purchase, the friend had Strong locked in jail, but was not able to prevent him from smuggling a message out to Sharp. Sharp was able to secure Strong's release; Lister and his friend promptly brought a law-suit against him for damages, but Sharp fought the case tenaciously and forced them to drop their charges.

By now Sharp was alive to the principles involved. There were at that time over ten thousand Negro slaves in England (a figure indicating that the proportion of people of African stock in the total population was almost as high in the 1760s as it is two hundred years later). They had been brought over as servants by American and West Indian planters, men who found it natural to advertise slaves for sale or to offer rewards for runaways in English newspapers. But could there be any legal sanction for such behaviour? Could English law be held to tolerate a state of slavery in England? With these questions in mind, Sharp decided to concentrate on the cases of runaway slaves recaptured by their masters. After a long, hard battle he secured from Lord Chief Justice Mansfield the momentous judgement that 'the state of slavery is so odious that nothing can be suffered to support it but positive law'. This was in 1772; six years later a similar judgement was reached in Scotland; thus from 1778 the state of slavery ceased to exist in the British Isles.

But if slavery was to be regarded as 'odious' in Britain, what justification could be found for accepting it as natural in the British territories overseas? The times were propitious for so challenging a question. After the humiliations of the American war, a wind of change was in the air; with talk of Parliamentary reform at home, of free trade abroad, of a new deal in India, the post-war years after 1783 seemed remarkably hospitable to new and liberal ideas. There were signs of change, too, within the Established Church. For forty years the poorer people of England had been responding to Wesley's preaching with its call for a life of good works and more intense religion. Now, when the break between Wesley's Methodists and the Established Church was complete, something of Wesley's spirit had begun to touch the hearts of some of the Anglican clergy and laity. In the 1780s there was beginning to form a small group of devout laymen, whom their contemporaries nicknamed the Evangelicals or Saints; their combination of wealth, social standing, energy and intelligence were to transform them into one of the most influential pressure groups in English society.

Of all English sects, the Quakers had the longest record of opposition to slavery, both in England and in America. In 1783 the Quakers took a decisive step in the attack on the slave system by establishing a committee of six to work by means of the written and the spoken word for 'the relief and liberation of the Negro slaves in the West Indies and for the discouragement of the Slave Trade on the coast of Africa'. The committee was soon at work, lobbying M.P.s, getting newspaper editors to accept their articles and producing pamphlets for wide distribution. Others joined the movement: among them Granville Sharp and a remarkable young man, just down from Cambridge, named Thomas Clarkson. At the University Clarkson had won a prize for a Latin essay on the subject, 'Is it right to make men slaves against their will?' He had embarked on the essay as an academic exercise, but the facts he had come across in gathering material affected him so seriously that he decided in a moment of sudden revelation that 'if the contents of the essay were true, it was time some person should see these calamities to their end' and that to this task he should dedicate his life. In 1787 the original Committee was expanded, with Sharp elected as Chairman. The members now decided to concentrate their attack not on slavery itself but on the trade in slaves. To ensure success they would have to continue to stir up public opinion; yet public opinion alone would be too crude a force without the advocacy and the support of influential members of Parliament.

To fight for Abolition in the House of Commons was too difficult a task for any obscure back-bencher, too invidious an undertaking for any party leader with the sentiments of his followers to consider. Yet by a twist of fortune that must have seemed to the Abolitionists truly Providential, exactly the right man was available—William Wilberforce. Young—he was not yet thirty, wealthy, blessed with a wit and gaiety that made him one of the most popular figures in fashionable society, an excellent debater—'the nightingale of the House', they called him in the Commons, remembering the remarkable quality of his voice, at once the contemporary and the intimate friend of the young Prime Minister, William Pitt, Wilberforce seemed to have the world at his feet. Yet even as he was enjoying the bright world of politics and society to the full, the thought shadowed his mind that it was all a sham. 'My conscience told me,' he wrote in his diary, 'that in the true sense of the word, I was not a Christian. . . . For months I was in the deepest depression from strong conviction of guilt.' For spiritual comfort he turned to one of the most powerful preachers of the day, John Newton, 'the old African blasphemer' as he called himself, for he had served, before his conversion, as the captain of a slave-ship. This was in 1785. In the course of the next year Wilberforce thought seriously of retiring from politics, but from Newton and from other friends he gained an insight into the fight against the slave trade. Finally, one day in June 1787, when he was staying with Pitt in his country house, his friend suggested that he should take up the battle in the House of Commons. This suggestion coming from the Prime Minister, who was himself sympathetic to the cause, was decisive. From that day on Wilberforce was committed to the crusade that was to be his daily concern for the remaining forty-six years of his life.

The Abolitionists' campaign was skilfully planned. It was essential for them to be sure of their facts. To this end Clarkson set out in the winter of 1787 on the first of his country-wide tours to gather evidence about the slave trade. The task sounds prosaic: in fact, it demanded a passionate spirit of dedication in the face of obstruction, abuse, disappointment and real physical danger—for some of the slave-dealers would have been happy to have caused the death of this obstreperous busy-body. Clarkson is indeed the real hero of the Abolitionist movement. All the material that he had collected Wilberforce set himself to master, while the Committee made certain that the dreadful facts uncovered were widely known by distributing over fifty thousand pamphlets in the course of the year. By the summer of 1788, Clarkson wrote later, 'the nature of the Slave Trade had, in consequence of the labours of the Committee and of their several correspondents, become generally known throughout the kingdom. It had excited a general attention, and there was among people a general feeling on behalf of the wrongs of Africa. . . . Not only had the traffic become the general subject of conversation but public meetings had taken place in which it had been discussed.'[2]

Constantly from 1788 to 1792 the question of abolition was before the House, or the evidence on the trade was being sifted by one or other of the Parliamentary Committees established for that purpose. In those years, too, ably stimulated and directed by the Abolitionist Committee, there developed a crescendo of popular support that reached its peak in 1792, when three hundred thousand people resolved to boycott the use of West Indian sugar and over five hundred towns and cities submitted petitions to Parliament demanding the abolition of the trade. Yet the West Indian merchants and the Liverpool slave-dealers, no less skilful as lobbyists than their opponents, could count on the support of the stolid, unimaginative mass of landed proprietors, who filled the back benches of the Commons and flooded the House of Lords. 'The property of the West Indians is at stake and though men may be generous with their own property, they should not be so with the property of others.' The M.P. who thus delivered himself voiced the general opinion; or, as Horace Walpole sardonically reported, 'commerce chinked its coin and the sound is generally prevalent with the majority'. Against this sublime logic the eloquence of Pitt, of Burke, of Fox—for that great trio were resolute in their opposition to the trade—beat itself in vain.[3]

So the motion for abolition was defeated in 1791, and even though a compromise resolution for gradual abolition was accepted in 1792, there was little prospect of it ever being enforced. For the times had grown inclement for liberal measures: the war with France, the bloody events in Paris, the even bloodier scenes on the French West Indian island of Saint Domingo, where the slaves had risen and massacred their masters—all these combined to make effective abolition for another decade an impossible cause. Yet the Abolitionists had done their work well. They had organized and shown the power of liberal public opinion. They had roused to an interest in Africa many who would otherwise never have concerned themselves with that remote continent. They had preached the need for a more humane understanding of the people of Africa. They had urged the advantage of legitimate commerce. They had in Sierra Leone begun a remarkable experiment in colonization.* They became the inspiration of that remarkable wave of missionary enthusiasm which developed during the latter half of the 1790s. Commerce, Christianity, Colonization—these were to be the grand lines of so much of the coming century's enterprise in Africa: in the thoughts and words of the Abolitionists this new approach was for the first time made fully explicit.

* On the founding of a colony of freed slaves in Sierra Leone, see p. 269.

V

THE INTEREST OF EUROPE

CONTINENTAL CROSS-FERTILIZATIONS

TRADE AND POLITICS, SCHOLARSHIP and philanthropy were serving to direct the attention of Englishmen to Africa. But this great movement must not be considered only within national bounds; it was a European phenomenon. Throughout most of Western Europe the same forces could be detected: an expanding economy, improved communications, a growing interest in overseas trade, a vigorous intellectual life—all were to have among their consequences a greater awareness of the fact of Africa. In the counting-houses of the slave-traders of Nantes and Bordeaux, in the cabinets of French statesmen, in the salons of the *philosophes*, in the libraries of the splendid palaces of some of the German princes, in all these different places might be heard from time to time speculation about the land, the products and the peoples of Africa.

More easily than ever before ideas and information could pass from state to state. The field of African studies illustrates very clearly the working of this process of European cross-fertilization. Bruce, it will be recalled, on his return from Ethiopia had been fêted by high society in Paris and in Rome. Banks was in correspondence with scholars from many countries and was elected an honorary member of their Academies. Clarkson was enthusiastically welcomed by the leaders of the Revolution when he visited Paris in 1789. Almost all the books written in English or in French about Africa were translated into one or the other language and also into German. Thus there was available a fund of common knowledge about Africa on which anyone with a good library could draw. To this fund the greatest contribution had been made by English and French travellers and

184

geographers—but not exclusively by them: during the 1780s the work of a German surgeon in Danish service, a Swedish philanthropist and a German university professor received a measure of international recognition. In the development of new ideas about Africa these three men, Isert, Wadström and Blumenbach, played a not insignificant part.

PAUL ISERT

Of the massive European forts that still stand along the Gold Coast, one of the most imposing is Christiansborg on the outskirts of Accra. It had been built by the Swedes in 1652, only to fall five years later into the hands of the Danes, who held it for close on two hundred years. It was not strange that the Danes should have a stake in West Africa: they had acquired island colonies in the West Indies, and therefore were as much interested in the Atlantic trade as their more powerful neighbours.

To Christiansborg there came in 1783 a young German doctor, Paul Isert. Isert was a Berliner; starting life as an apothecary, he had developed a passion for natural history; having no means of his own, he decided that only by qualifying as a doctor could he satisfy his craving for foreign travel and gain the opportunity of making original discoveries in his chosen field. From Copenhagen he obtained an appointment as first physician to the Danish settlements in Africa, only to find that his official duties allowed him no time to pursue his own researches. After two years on the Gold Coast he wrote to Sir Joseph Banks—it is a remarkable indication of Banks's international prestige that he should have done so—telling him of his hopes and frustrations. 'It would afford me,' he confided, 'a great deal of pleasure to make a voyage up into the heart of the country.' He asked Banks to help him obtain a post in English service with a salary of £500 to cover the expenses of African travel. Banks's reply has not survived; but it seems unlikely that he could render any practical assistance.[1]

A year later, however, Isert secured the opportunity he had been waiting for. A sister of the King of Ashanti had come to Accra to consult him on a malady for which the native doctors could provide no remedy. Isert cured her, won her confidence and secured an invitation to visit her brother's kingdom, that powerful nation in whose territory no white man had ever yet set foot. Indeed, no European was known to have passed beyond the line of hills that bounded so provokingly the horizon to the north of Accra. Isert set out, climbed the hills, and without difficulty reached Aquapim, sixty miles inland. Dreadful rumours about the ferocity of the inhabitants of the interior prevailed on the coast; but the people of Aquapim received Isert with a courtesy and a hospitality in shining contrast to the manners of the Africans he had known at Accra. Nothing prevented his further progress, when an order reached him from Christiansborg requiring his instant return. Shortly afterwards he was struck down by fever; recovering, he experienced so intense a revulsion against Africa that he decided to throw in his hand.

But back in Europe Isert learnt how insistently Africa pulls at the heart-strings. A project was put forward for establishing an agricultural colony in the interior of the Gold Coast; the King of Denmark gave practical support, and Isert, who had published an account of his earlier experiences, agreed to take charge of the venture. He returned to the West Coast in 1789 and laid the foundations of a new settlement in the Aquapim Hills. There, a few months later, struck down once again by fever, he died.*†

C. B. WADSTRÖM

Many different motives have induced Europeans to interest themselves in Africa; few so strange as that which inspired a Swedish engineer, Carl Bernard Wadström. Born in 1746, he had risen to hold the office of Controller of Gold and Silver. In 1779 he came under the influence of the mystical philosophy of Swedenborg and joined a society whose members planned to establish a Utopian community, where the master's ideals of 'social order and happiness' might be achieved. Europe offered them no opening, so they turned to Africa and obtained from the King of Sweden a charter to establish a colony on the West Coast. Visionary concepts combined with practical con-

* The settlement at Aquapim was maintained for some years after Isert's death. A Danish botanist was sent out and had some success in growing coffee. Later local wars led to its abandonment, until the 1830s, when it became the site of a mission station founded by German missionaries with Danish support.[2]

† One other German traveller deserves brief mention. In 1785 there arrived in Tripoli a German nobleman, the Baron de Haslien. He had left in Tunis two of his brothers, who planned to cross the Sahara to the Guinea coast; he himself hoped to visit the Fezzan. An outbreak of plague forced him to abandon the attempt. It would be interesting to know more about de Haslien and his brothers and to discover what induced them to turn their energies to African exploration.[3]

siderations: Africans possessed, according to Swedenborg, a strange capacity to receive the heavenly teaching, those living in the heart of the continent having been 'taught by angels the doctrine of the New Jerusalem'.[1]

To spy out the land, Wadström decided to make a voyage to West Africa, in co-operation with a French merchant who was planning an expedition up the Senegal in search of gold. The mention of that metal immediately aroused the interest of the King of Sweden; he decided that Wadström should be accompanied by Sparrman, famous as a naturalist after his travels in South Africa, and Arrhenius, an artillery officer and mineralogist. There was talk of trying to cross Africa from west to east; for such a purpose few expeditions could have been so ill devised. 'The king,' so Wadström wrote afterwards, 'loved gold, my worthy companions loved natural science, and I loved colonization.'[2]

With French assistance the three travellers reached Senegal. It was impossible to travel up the river; local traders refused their help and there was war in the interior. After sailing down the coast—Wadström noting on the way that Cape Verde, recently purchased by the French, would have made an ideal site for his colony—the party returned to Europe.

Wadström and Sparrman stopped off in England, where their evidence on the slave trade provided the Abolitionists with some of their most effective material. Indeed, so absorbed did Wadström become in the Abolitionist crusade that he decided to stay on in England. He never revisited Africa—a projected mission under English auspices fell through; but 'the liberty of Africans' became 'the favourite project of his mind'. With passionate interest he watched the development of the attempts at philanthropic colonization made by the Sierra Leone Company and the Bulama Association; their experience he used as the basis for a vast and rambling work, entitled *An Essay on Colonization.**[3]

* There is some evidence that Wadström himself did not in fact write the major part of the *Essay on Colonization*. The copy of that work in the Library of the Royal Geographical Society, London, contains on the title page a note written by William Dickson, LL.D. 'This work was really compiled by me; and I claimed it in the Monthly Magazine for December 1799. I hold Wadström's Bill for £126, being balance due to me. The whole was £208. 10.—poor pay for 15 mos hard fagging—I also compiled in 1789 his Voyage to Guinea—a still more troublesome piece of work for its size—Such a temper and such notions as those of W. no human being

'To accomplish this magnificent design'—the civilization of Africa, 'let us,' he urged, 'form agricultural colonies on its coast. . . . Let us kindly mix with the inhabitants, and assist them in cultivating their fertile soil. . . . Let us give them a manly and generous education, which will make them feel the nobility of their origin and show them of what great things they are capable—an education which will teach them no longer to suffer themselves to be dragged from their simple, but improveable and beloved societies. . . . Thus on the wreck of tyranny let us build altars to humanity and prove to the Negroes that the Europeans, become just from sound policy, and generous from a sense of their true interests, are at last disposed to make some atonement for the irreparable mischiefs their perverted system of commerce has occasioned in Africa.'[4]

Some time after publishing this book, Wadström, who was naturally in sympathy with the ideals of the Revolution, moved to France, where he died in 1799. 'His heart,' wrote a friend after his death, 'seemed more enlarged than his understanding, his feelings were always in the right, but his judgement sometimes erred.' Today one might be inclined to reckon him a prophet born before his time, for what in fact was he advocating but those ideals of enlightened colonialism that in a later age so many Europeans were to hold before themselves during their service in Africa?[5]

J. F. BLUMENBACH

During the nineteenth century there came from the states of Germany a great line of African explorers—Hornemann, Burckhardt, Barth, Nachtigal and Rohlfs—men who displayed a remarkable combination of audacity and intelligence. This movement of interest in Africa began long before the new German Empire had secured a colonial foothold on the continent (the factories established by the Brandenbergers on the Gold Coast in the seventeenth century had been maintained for only a few decades); it was inspired solely, in its early stages, by scientific curiosity; it can be traced back to its source in the life and work of a very remarkable man, Johann Frederich Blumenbach.

ever had— "None but himself could be his parallel"—But he was a most zealous Abolitionist, and a generous man—too generous to be just—A *courtier* too tho' *republican.* Mr. W. furnished only a small part of the materials namely the contents of his voyage, the commercial questions and certain Swedenborgian doctrines.'

Blumenbach was born in Gotha in 1752, the son of a schoolmaster with an infectious interest in geography and natural history. As a student Blumenbach attended the recently founded University at Göttingen, stayed on as a lecturer and was appointed Professor of Medicine in 1778. Göttingen remained his home for over sixty years until his death in 1840. Blumenbach's career represents the academic life at its best. All living things were of interest to him, and his mind was constantly active, enriched by continuous reading and by intercourse with the liveliest intellects of the age. Natural history, anatomy, geology, biology, medicine—to all these fields of science he made substantial contributions, but he is best remembered as the founder of modern ethnology, for he was the first to work out a classification of the races of mankind on a scientific basis.*

Not only was Blumenbach an outstanding scientist, he was also a brilliant lecturer—indeed probably the greatest teacher of his day. In the testimony of a younger colleague, he 'drew the natural sciences out of the narrow circle of books and museums into the cheerful stream of life' and 'made the results of his own persevering researches intelligible and agreeable to any educated person'. As a result, 'he soon came to be regarded as the supporter and representative of natural science and collected crowds of young men about him and by words as well as deeds continued to exercise an increasing influence upon the entire circle of study for many decades'.[1]

Blumenbach was led by two different lines of study to take an interest in Africa. From his father he had inherited a passion for geography, his familiarity with books of travel being reckoned quite remarkable. Thus when Bruce's *Travels* appeared in a German translation in 1790 it was Blumenbach who wrote the introduction, a piece of work that reveals very clearly at once the scholarly breadth of his reading and the critical sharpness of his mind.[2]

Geography provided one path to Africa; even more important was the interest derived from his work on ethnology. Blumenbach lived in an age when many people imagined that there must exist different *species* of man (even the great Linnaeus had described the orang-utan as *homo silvestris*), and when it was common form to compare

* Buffon, the great French naturalist, a little earlier had worked out a system of classification based on colour; but Blumenbach took other physical factors into consideration—and especially the shape of the cranium. To aid him in his research, he built up a remarkable collection of skulls, drawn from almost every country in the world.

Africans with beasts. Against these terrible misconceptions Blumenbach asserted the fact of the fundamental unity of mankind. 'Although there seems to be so great a difference between widely separate nations that you might easily take the inhabitants of the Cape of Good Hope, the Greenlanders and the Circassians for so many different species of man, yet when the matter is thoroughly considered, you see that all do so run into one another, and that one variety of mankind does so sensibly pass into the other, that you cannot mark out the limits between them.' So he wrote at the age of twenty-three in his thesis *De Generis Humani Varietate Natura*, a book that in its various editions was to acquire a European reputation and become one of the seminal works of the age. 'It has been asserted,' he wrote elsewhere, 'that the Negroes are specifically different in their bodily structure from other men and must also be placed considerably in the rear, from the conditions of their obtuse mental capacities ... I am acquainted with no single distinctive bodily character which is at once peculiar to the Negro, and which cannot be found to exist in any other nation.'*[3]

Scientific integrity led Blumenbach to these conclusions. Precise and practical his mind always showed itself, but it was also generous and humane. When the poet Coleridge visited Göttingen in 1799 Blumenbach showed him 'a complete little Library of his own collecting, consisting of books written entirely by African Blacks'—'books in every Science, Astronomy, pure and mixt Mathematics, Medicine, Theology, Poetry, Belles Lettres etc'. No dilettante interest in *négritude* inspired this collection, but a profound belief in African capacity. In an essay which began with a list of Negroes who had achieved distinction in many fields, Blumenbach gave it as his opinion that 'there is no so-called savage nation known under the sun which has so much distinguished itself by such examples of perfectibility and original capacity for scientific culture and thereby attached itself so closely to the most civilized nations of the earth as the Negro'. These were words written with authority and so read with attention. Therefore among the influences that were shaping men's minds for a new approach to Africa must be placed the teaching of this good, wise man.[4]

* Old ideas die hard—and not only the crudities of 'black apes' and down from the trees'. Very many educated people in Europe still assume that African backwardness is due to biological differences and not to the influence of environment. Blumenbach's ideas are as important today as ever they were in his own lifetime.

THE AGE OF THE AFRICAN
ASSOCIATION—I 1788-1802

I

THE FIRST YEARS: 1788-90

THE FOUNDING OF THE AFRICAN ASSOCIATION

GREAT MOVEMENTS RISE FROM small beginnings: a single man turning over new ideas in his mind, a group of men coming together, talking and resolving on action. So it was with the movement to explore Africa, to penetrate into the unknown interior, to break down the barrier between two worlds.

Among the various clubs to be found in London during the 1780s was one so informal—its function was confined to a dinner three or four times a year—and so exclusive—its membership was limited to twelve—that no note of its foundation or of its early history has been preserved: it was called the Saturday's Club, and it held its meetings in the St Albans Tavern off Pall Mall.* Of its twelve members one has already been brought forward—Sir Joseph Banks; the others will require introduction.[1]

The oldest member was General Conway, then in his late sixties. He had recently retired after a lifetime of public service, having held high office both in the Army and in politics—in the 1760s he had been one of the Secretaries of State. Though not of the first ability, he was universally liked and respected for his unflinching honesty; today he is remembered as the lifelong friend and correspondent of Horace Walpole.

Of the other members of the Club, the two youngest, Lord Rawdon and Sir John Sinclair, both in their middle thirties, were to become the best known. Rawdon was the son of an Irish peer, the Earl of

---

* The St Albans Tavern was in St Albans Street, which was removed in 1815 to make room for Regent Street and Waterloo Place. It was celebrated during the eighteenth century for political and fashionable dinners.

Moira, whom he succeeded in 1794; this was not the last of his trans-
formations—in 1817, when Governor-General of India, he was
created Marquess of Hastings, by which name he is now remembered.
He had started his career as an army officer and served with some distinction in the American war. On entering Parliament, he had become
an intimate friend of the Prince of Wales. Some people found him
conceited, pompous, cold and ambitious, and suspected that his
friendship with the Prince was a move to secure high office on the
King's demise. Sinclair also struck people as having an inflated impression of his own worth. He was a Scottish landowner, who had
been rewarded with a baronetcy by Pitt, then turned against him. He
and Rawdon were close political associates, and were trying, without
significant success, to form a third force—it was nicknamed 'the
armed neutrality'—between the supporters of Pitt and of Fox.
Sinclair was a man of unremitting industry—'the most indefatigable
man in Britain', a Frenchman once called him—who wrote on a great
variety of subjects relating to the country's economy, was a pioneer
in the science of statistics—indeed he was said to have invented that
term—and became the first President of the Board of Agriculture.[2]

Sinclair was one of the six Scotsmen in the Club. Two of the others
like him possessed large estates north of the border: the Earl of
Galloway, a friend of Wilberforce, whose Evangelical faith he shared,
and Sir Adam Ferguson, regarded as the best type of Scottish
country gentleman, 'kindly, cultured, shrewd, methodical, and
public-spirited'. William Pulteney, born Johnstone, was the heir of a
Scotch baronetcy, but had assumed his present name when his wife
succeeded to the vast estates of her father's first cousin, William
Pulteney, Earl of Bath. This piece of singular good fortune made him
a millionaire and the richest commoner in England. Pulteney must
have been closely associated with another Scotsman in the Club,
Andrew Stuart, as he took Stuart's widow for his second wife four
years before his own death. Stuart was a lawyer, who had served for
three years, from 1779 to 1782, as a member of the Board of Trade.
Finally, there was Sir William Fordyce, a successful doctor, well
liked for his hospitality and generosity.[3]

Of the three remaining members, one was an Irish peer, the Earl of
Carysfoot, 'esteemed a good and elegant scholar'. The others were
both Englishmen of less aristocratic antecedents. Henry Beaufoy was
a Quaker and the son of a London wine merchant. Richard Watson,
Bishop of Llandaff, was one of the most remarkable self-made men

of his age. Having been appointed at Cambridge first to the Chair of Chemistry—he possessed no prior knowledge of the subject, but remedied the omission by shutting himself up in a laboratory for a year—then of Divinity, in 1783 he was given the see of Llandaff by his political friends. There in this poorest of the bishoprics Watson stuck, for his patrons fell from office and his views were uncomfortably independent. He contented himself with acquiring numerous minor livings, together with a large estate in Westmorland, where he spent his old age, thus acquiring in the eyes of a more censorious generation a shocking reputation as a pluralist and a non-resident.[4]

What was it that brought these twelve men together? In the year 1788 eight of them were Members of Parliament, with seats in the Commons or places in the Lords. Stuart had been an M.P. and was to return again to the House after a six years' interval in 1790, when Lord Carysfoot was also to be elected. Thus Fordyce and Banks were the only two not directly involved in politics. Of the politicians, Sinclair and Rawdon were the most active. Sinclair had recently gathered together a group of independent M.P.s who met in the St Albans Tavern and called themselves the St Albans Club; Rawdon, Pulteney and Watson were probably members. Furthermore, the members of the Saturday's Club held similar views on some of the great questions of the day: they had opposed the war with the American colonies, and most of them were to support the campaign to abolish the slave trade. They were men of liberal mind, open to the new ideas of the age.[5]

A similarity of political views enabled the members of the Saturday's Club to find each other's company more congenial; but it cannot have been the basic reason for their coming together, if only because Sir Joseph Banks, the most prominent man among them, was one to whom party politics were of no attraction. There was, however, one subject that aroused in all the members a lively response: the practical application of the scientific ideas of the age to the development of natural resources. Banks, Carysfoot, Ferguson, Galloway, Sinclair and Watson were, as landowners, noted for the improvements they were making on their estates, while Banks and Sinclair had recently been engaged, with royal encouragement and support, in plans for the introduction of Merino sheep from Spain. Both Pulteney and Conway had made reputations for themselves as botanists, while Conway had recently—with that splendid eighteenth-century versatility—amused himself in his retirement by inventing a

195

furnace for the use of brewers. Fordyce was, as might be expected from a doctor, the author of a number of medical works; but he had also to his credit an essay on Rhubarb—awarded a gold medal by the Society of Arts. Beaufoy, though a Londoner, was deeply interested in fisheries. These varying achievements had earned for half the members—Beaufoy, Carysfoot, Conway, Pulteney, Sinclair and Watson—election to the Royal Society, of which distinguished body Banks had now for ten years been the President.[6]

These, then, were the men, who, with Sinclair, Carysfoot and Watson temporarily absent, came together in the St Albans Tavern on June 9, 1788, a day worthy to be commemorated in the annals of history, to pass the following momentous and grandly worded resolution:

> That as no species of information is more ardently desired, or more generally useful, than that which improves the science of Geography; and as the vast Continent of Africa, notwithstanding the efforts of the Ancients, and the wishes of the Moderns, is still in a great measure unexplored, the Members of this Club do form themselves into an Association for Promoting the Discovery of the Inland Parts of that Quarter of the World.

Then, being eminently practical, they straightway proceeded to draw up the rules for the new Association. Each member of the Club was to pay a subscription of five guineas a year for three years and 'to recommend, for the approbation of the Club, such of his Friends as he shall think proper to be admitted to the new Association'. A Committee of five was to be elected from the members of the Club; to it was to be entrusted 'the choice of the persons who are to be sent on the Discovery of the Interior Parts of Africa, together with the Society's Correspondence, and the Management of its Funds'. On the receipt of any interesting information, the Secretary was to convene the Members of the Association and communicate to them 'such parts of the said intelligence as, in the opinion of the Committee, may, without endangering the object of the Association, be made public'.[7]

Before they broke up that day the members elected their Committee: Beaufoy as Secretary, Banks as Treasurer, together with Rawdon, Watson and Stuart. A permanent Chairman the Association never found it necessary to appoint.

The first step had been taken; it is worth asking how it had come about. Banks's growing interest in Africa has already been described. None of the others had had the opportunity to become so directly involved in the continent, though Conway, in his term as Secretary of State a quarter of a century ago, had had some dealings with Senegambia, and Beaufoy and Galloway, as friends of Wilberforce, were in a position to acquire an intimate insight into the struggle against the African slave trade. But all of them were men excited by the progress of the age; all of them must have listened to and participated in conversations about the unknown continent; all of them were convinced—as Beaufoy was to write in the prospectus he prepared for the Association—that 'while we continue ignorant of so large a portion of the globe, that ignorance must be considered as a degree of reproach upon the present age'.[8]

'Sensible of this stigma,' he continued, 'and desirous of rescuing the age from a charge of ignorance, which, in other respects, belongs so little to its character, a few Individuals, strongly impressed with a conviction of the practicability and utility of thus enlarging the fund of human knowledge, have formed the Plan of an Association for promoting the Discovery of the Interior parts of Africa.' *The utility of enlarging the fund of human knowledge*—there in a phrase of fine precision lay their motive: scientific curiosity one may call it—but curiosity applied to practical ends. They were all men of affairs; as they looked to Africa, their vision was not distorted by the crude images of strange men and strange beasts that bemused so many of their contemporaries; rather they speculated on the products that unknown interior might reveal, the markets those teeming millions —it was a common fallacy to exaggerate Africa's population— might afford for the growing manufactures of Great Britain.

As they discussed these matters among themselves, one of them must have suggested that they themselves should take up the task of sponsoring exploration. To Henry Beaufoy is probably due the credit for first putting forward this idea; after his death, Rennell, the geographer of the Association, writing in praise of Beaufoy, spoke of 'the researches in Africa being a path of his own choosing; a path which, more than any other person, he had contributed to open and to render smoothe'. Certainly the energy with which he threw himself into his work as Secretary is a proof of his passionate belief in the importance of the new Association. In this he was enthusiastically seconded by Sir Joseph Banks.[9]

One may attempt to reconstruct some of the arguments they would use. It was unlikely, they could point out, that the Government, especially under the economical Mr Pitt, would agree to vote money for so speculative a project but, with royal approbation—Sir Joseph basked in the sun of royal favour—and with the influential contacts that members possessed in high places, a measure of official co-operation and support could be guaranteed. No businessman at this stage would wish to risk his capital on such a venture. But Mr Bruce had recently shown to the world how much could be achieved, at no great expense, by a single individual. Moreover, there was the example of the Dilettanti Society, with their highly successful archaeological expedition to Ionia in 1764, to show what a dining club could achieve as a patron of research; Sir Joseph Banks was well placed to draw attention to this point, for he had been secretary to the Society for the last ten years. Already, he could go on to say, he had acquired some experience of sending travellers to Africa—there had been Brass's mission on the West Coast and Masson's in South Africa; he could refer also to the offer made by Isert, the suggestion received from de Ponthieu. So far, with some assurance, one can proceed. For the rest, it is wise to pause and let imagination do its work, straining to overhear those ardent conversations in which the seeds of the great idea were sown, to catch the tones, sceptical or enthusiastic, speculative or reminiscent, fanciful or practical, of the voices of a dozen men of the world, sitting round a dining-table in a tavern off Pall Mall, drawing up plans for the exploration of a continent.[10]

THE FIRST EXPLORERS: JOHN LEDYARD IN CAIRO

How should they set about their self-appointed task? So, with the map of Africa spread out before them, the members of the Saturday's Club must have asked themselves. The *Plan of the Association* which Beaufoy composed and had printed for members to show to their friends makes it possible to follow the course of their speculations.[1]

Every expedition needs a goal, yet with the interior of 'that vast continent' 'still but a wide extended blank', it was not easy to find an object that could be defined with precision. The first step was to decide which part should first receive their attention. On South Africa, Sparrman's narrative had recently 'furnished important information', Paterson's *Travels* were 'already in the Press', and, 'if a description of the still more extended Travels of Colonel Gordon, the present Commander of the Dutch troops at the Cape of Good Hope, should be given to the public, the southern extremity of the

African peninsula may perhaps be justly considered as explored'*. On Eastern Africa, too, much new information should be available when Mr Bruce's account, at last being prepared for the Press, was made available.

But perhaps the most interesting part of the interior was that 'on which the Geographer, on the authority of Leo Africanus, and of the Xeriss Edrissi the Nubian Author, has traced, with a hesitating hand, a few names of unexplored rivers and of uncertain nations'. There flowed the great Niger, whose course, 'the places of its rise and termination, and even its existence as a separate stream', remained 'undetermined'. More than half a century had passed since Brue had pushed up the Senegal and Moore described the Gambia; yet nothing had been added to the information their accounts contained. Nor had advantage been taken of the fact, long though it had been known, that 'even on the western coasts of Africa, the Mahometan faith is received in many extensive districts from the Tropic of Cancer southwards to the Line', that the 'Mussulman Priests' understood Arabic and 'must from the nature of their religion possess, what the Traders to the coast ascribe to them, intercourse with Mecca'.

With these general ideas in mind, the members of the Committee set to work; and already at their first meeting, held only four days after the inauguration of the Association, Beaufoy was able to announce that no less well qualified a person than Simon Lucas, Oriental Interpreter at the Court of St James, had offered himself, if the Committee could secure his release on full pay, as the first of the Association's travellers. Lucas could claim to possess a deeper first-hand knowledge of North Africa than almost any other man in England. Born the son of a London wine-merchant, he had been sent as a youth to Cadiz to learn the trade, only to be captured by Moorish pirates. For three years he had been a slave in the Imperial Court of Morocco, an experience that proved the making of his future career, for on his release he was appointed Vice-Consul in Morocco, a post he held for sixteen years. Through his official position as interpreter, Lucas had recently come to make the

* Colonel R. J. Gordon, an officer in the Scotch Regiment in the service of the United Provinces of the Netherlands, travelled in South Africa in the early 1770s and returned as second-in-command of the garrison in 1777. Between 1777 and 1779 he made three journeys into the interior in company with William Paterson and reached the large river which he named the Orange in honour of the Stadtholder.

acquaintance of Haji Abd-ar-Rahman, Foreign Minister of Tripoli, who had visited London in 1786 on an official mission and spent fifteen months in the capital. This was an invaluable contact, for Tripoli lay at the end of one of the trade-routes across the Sahara and maintained an intermittent intercourse with the great Empire of Bornu. Lucas offered to proceed from Tripoli to the Fezzan. With Banks's influence reaching to the highest in the land, there was no difficulty in securing his release from his official duties.[*2]

Less than a week later, on June 17, the Committee met again to hear another exciting piece of news. A day or two earlier there had appeared at Soho Square, asking for Sir Joseph, a tough individual, dressed in rags, and speaking with a colonial accent. Banks knew him well: he was a thirty-seven-year-old American, John Ledyard, who had been lost to the world for the last two years on an astonishing adventure. Beaufoy, on being introduced to him, was immediately struck by 'the manliness of his person, the breadth of his chest, the openness of his countenance and the inquietude of his eye'. An English gentleman could not help remarking in him the raw matiness of a colonial: 'little attentive to differences of rank, he seemed to consider all men his equals and as such he respected them', but his manner, 'though unpolished', was 'neither uncivil nor unpleasing'. Moreover, though a man of little formal education, he possessed a lively and well-stocked mind. Above all, he was ideally suited for the purpose that the Association had in mind: 'adventurous beyond the conception of ordinary men, yet wary and considerate and attentive to all precautions, he appeared to be formed by Nature for achievements of hardihood and peril'.[4]

Adventurous indeed—few men of his age could have claimed to have lived so exciting a life. As a boy he had thought of becoming a missionary among the Red Indians, but after running away from his seminary to spend some months alone in the backwoods, he developed

* It was as well that Banks did not know the opinion that was held of Lucas by the English community in Morocco. 'I hear that my friend Lucas is the person you rely on,' Matra wrote to Banks from Gibraltar in February 1789. 'He never has, nor never will, nor can he if he pleased, tell you one word of the truth about the country—he is a good-natured, obliging fellow who means harm to no one, but by being brought so early among the Moors has got such a determined habit of lying that he is quite a proverb not only over all Barbary, but at this place.' As both Beaufoy's and Lucas's fathers were London wine-merchants, it is possible that there was some connection between them.[3]

a taste for a roving life among primitive people that was never to leave him. Forced to earn his living, he went to sea—his father had been a sea-captain—came to English and enlisted in the Marines in time to volunteer to accompany Cook on his last expedition. Thus he came to know the forests and fjords of the American North-West, and to be with Cook when he was killed in Hawaii. After his return Ledyard published the journal of his experiences and, through the book's success, won an introduction into distinguished society in both London and Paris, making the acquaintance of Sir Joseph Banks and counting among his friends Jefferson, then American Ambassador in France, and the dashing Lafayette. But the wild still called him—and especially the remote North-West, for he was convinced that if only he could return there, he would be able to develop a profitable trade in furs with China. But ill-fortune upset all his schemes and partnerships. At length, in 1786, penniless but for a small sum given him by Banks, he set out on a fantastic expedition, planning to reach his goal by going overland across Russia and Siberia. He walked round the Gulf of Bothnia in mid-winter, and reached Yakutsk in Eastern Siberia, when an officer arrived from Moscow with orders for his instant return under police escort. Six weeks later he was dumped at the Polish frontier. Using Sir Joseph's name to draw money, he travelled straight to London and called immediately at Soho Square.[5]

Banks received him warmly, told him of the plans of the newly formed Association and was delighted to find that Ledyard, quite of his own accord, had already turned his mind to Africa. In Siberia, dreaming about the future, he had confided to his journal that he intended first to cross America from West to East—'and then, thy glowing climate Africa explored, I will lay me down'. A day or two later Ledyard called on Beaufoy. 'I spread the map of Africa before him,' Beaufoy wrote of that first meeting, 'and tracing a line from Cairo to Sennar and from thence westward in the latitude and supposed direction of the Niger, I told him that was the route by which I was anxious that Africa might, if possible, be explored.' Asked when he would be prepared to leave, Ledyard replied without hesitation, 'Tomorrow morning'.* For Beaufoy the scene was

---

* Beaufoy omitted one fact when he came to write this account. The Committee's Minutes show that Ledyard's instructions were to proceed by way of Cairo to Mecca; 'from thence (unless insuperable difficulties shall occur) he shall cross the Red Sea and taking the route of Nubia shall

magnificently dramatic, for Ledyard the heroic role peculiarly congenial. Writing to his mother in America to tell her of his new enterprise, he could say that he felt himself an instance of God's goodness: 'I have tramped the world under my feet, laughed at fear, derided danger. Through millions of fierce savages, over parching deserts, the freezing north, the everlasting ice, and stormy seas have I passed without harm. How good is my God! What rich subjects I have for praise, love and admiration!'[6]

The Committee were anxious to set both explorers on their way without delay. To provide the necessary funds, the members, 'too conscious of the importance and dignity of their undertaking to canvas for subscriptions', decided to advance £430 from their own pockets. Of this money some went on a proper set of clothes for ragged Ledyard, some on instruments for both men, some on passage money. At Cairo Ledyard was to receive £50 for his journey into the interior, with the possibility of another £30 being advanced later. It was not merely shortage of funds that led to this parsimonious decision, for the Committee felt 'persuaded that in such an undertaking poverty is a better protection than wealth'. Barely three weeks after his arrival in England, Ledyard was off. At the beginning of August he was in Alexandria, being entertained by Baldwin, the British Consul, and already, so he wrote back, possessed of information about caravans coming to Cairo, whose traders appeared to make contact somewhere in the interior with other merchants, whose home was 'near the shores of the Atlantic'. Lucas left England somewhat later and arrived in Tripoli in mid-October; his instructions considerably exceeded his own proposals, for after reaching the Fezzan, he was expected to return 'by way of the Gambia or by that of the coast of Guinea'.[8]

By the time Lucas reached Tripoli, Ledyard had been settled for some weeks in Cairo. He put up at the Catholic convent, the usual hostel for European travellers. Knowing no Arabic and staying where he did, it was impossible for him to adopt any form of disguise. It would have been better if he had been able to do so, for popular feeling against all 'Franks' ran high in the city, and Ledyard, taunted

traverse the Continent of Africa as nearly as possible in the direction of the Niger'. That the Committee should have suggested a detour to Mecca at the start of the journey is an indication of their ignorance of the realities of African travel. It is clear, too, that they accepted the idea of a westward-flowing Niger.[7]

by jeers and malicious glances as he walked the streets, found his position disagreeable and humiliating. But he was not prevented from making preparations for his journey. The Venetian Consul, who acted as British chargé d'affaires in Cairo, secured him an introduction to Aga Muhammad, the confidential minister of one of the most powerful of the ruling Mamluk Beys, from whom he obtained a promise of protection to the limit of Mamluk territory and letters of introduction to the rulers of the interior. At the same time he frequented the slave-markets of the city to pick up information both from the travelling merchants and from their property, for slaves—over twenty thousand of them that year he reckoned—reached Cairo from Darfur and the various kingdoms of the Upper Nile. Asking some slave-women from Darfur if he would be well treated in their homeland, he was ingenuously delighted with their reply that they would make a king of him and regale him with all the delicacies of the country.

On November 15 he wrote to Jefferson that he would be leaving Cairo in a few days' time: 'from Cairo I am to travel S.W. about three hundred leagues to a black king. There my present conductors will leave me to my fate. Beyond, I suppose I shall go alone. I expect to cut the continent between the parallels of twelve and twenty degrees of North latitude.' By the end of November Ledyard was still in Cairo, confined to his bed by a bilious complaint. To cure himself he obtained some vitriolic acid, a common, if drastic, remedy in that age. Somehow, by mistake, he poured himself an overdose. The best doctors in the city were summoned to his bedside; they found it impossible to save him. So died John Ledyard: a wretched end for so ambitious and adventurous a man. But there can be little doubt that he would never have succeeded in his attempt to cross the continent from east to west. Darfur seems to have been the goal of the first stage of his journey. He might, as another traveller was to prove a few years later, have reached it without excessive difficulty. But beyond Darfur there lay the turbulent country of Wadai, whose Muslim inhabitants were noted for their fanaticism. Ill-equipped as he was, he would almost certainly have been murdered—such was the fate of the first explorers to reach Wadai in the 1850s and 1860s—or died of disease. As it was, he died too early to prove anything, too suddenly to have had time even to send back all the information that he had collected.[9]

THE FIRST EXPLORERS: SIMON LUCAS IN TRIPOLI

Bitterly disappointing though the news of Ledyard's sudden death must have been, the members of the Association could still place their hopes in Simon Lucas in Tripoli. Since Tripoli was to serve as the starting-point for many expeditions into the interior during the next hundred years, it is worth looking at the city more closely. Fortunately, the sister-in-law of the British Consul of the day, Richard Tully, was a most intelligent and observant lady, whose long letters home were subsequently published; one could not wish for a better account of life as seen by a European in that small Muslim principality.*

The traveller approaching Tripoli from the sea would hold in his memory the view spread out before him as he sailed into the little bay. Along the low-lying land of the coast there stretched for mile upon mile plantations of date-palms; framed in their green, the city lay, its square-shaped houses of a dazzling whiteness, a strong wall girding it round, its sky-line broken by the domes and minarets of the mosques and by the massive bulk of the Pasha's castle. Ashore, the traveller, wandering through the town, found that blending of squalor and splendour that was coming to be associated with the east: the streets narrow and uneven from the accumulated rubbish of centuries, suffocatingly dusty at the passing of a mule-train or a laden camel, the dark, roofed-over alleys of the *suq* heavy with the pungent reek of musk and other odours. The throat and the nose might suffer: the eye found much to delight in—the open booths with their rich display of merchandise, ranging even to gold and pearls and precious stones; the little plantations of date-palms and of fig trees, like rich gardens surrounding the mosques; the mosques themselves with sentences from the Koran inscribed in painted relief above their doorways; the coffee-houses, green arbours set with marble benches, covered with costly rugs, where the chief men of the city were to be found at certain hours, sitting cross-legged and attended by their slaves.

Few towns in the Mediterranean contained so varied a population.

* It is irritating to have to refer to the writer of the letters by a cumbersome circumlocution, but her name is not known. On the title-page the letters are described as being 'in the possession of the family of the late Richard Tully'; in the Preface the writer is described only 'as the sister-in-law of the late Richard Tully'. One imagines that she must have been Tully's wife's sister.

There was the nobility, mostly of Turkish descent, though usually described as Moors, superbly attired in flowing robes of satin or of velvet, richly embroidered or adorned with costly furs. In cruel contrast were the pieces of brown cotton, looking like dirty blankets, worn by the poor, either Arabs or Berbers, many of whom, though free, were worse off than the slaves. Slaves, brought from all the countries of the central Sudan, formed a substantial portion of the city's population; not a few among them had risen to places of esteem and affection in their masters' households. To this medley was added a sizeable minority of Italians, Jews and Maltese. Their presence served to accustom the Muslim majority to the sight of infidels. Tripoli, indeed, was the only town in North Africa where a Christian could count on being well received by the upper classes and likely to be little molested as he moved around the streets.[1]

A small state lying in the middle of an area of conflict between greater powers, Tripoli in its history had had to suffer many changes. In the Middle Ages it had been under the suzerainty first of the Almohads of Morocco, then of the Hafsids of Tunis. In the sixteenth century the Spaniards and the Knights of Malta each in turn occupied it for a generation, but in 1551 the city fell into the hands of the Turkish admiral, Darghut Pasha. For a hundred and fifty years Turkish Pashas, sent from Constantinople every three years, ruled in Tripoli, until in 1711 a member of the local nobility, Ahmad Karamanli, disposed of the Turkish garrison by the not unprecedented ruse of inviting its officers to a banquet and having them murdered as they sat, appeased his impotent suzerain with suitable presents and established himself as the founder of a dynasty. Under the rule of the Karamanlis, Tripoli came to be regarded as the most civilized of the Barbary states, the government of the country, when compared to the 'despotic tyranny' of Morocco, being reckoned extremely mild. But this mildness may have been due more to impotence and to poverty than to intention. The ruling family was constantly torn by internecine quarrels (Tully's sister-in-law records in her letters several horrifying murders); the Arab tribes who roamed the hinterland were frequently in revolt; and though the Pasha claimed that the Fezzan and even distant Bornu were tributary to him, the tribute was little more than the occasional despatch of presents as a gesture of friendly relations; finally, the country, so much of it desert, was frequently struck by famine and suffered in the 1780s a decimating outbreak of plague.[2]

205

Lucas, on his arrival in Tripoli, stayed with the British Consul. He was shocked to find that Tully was deep in debt and constantly harassed by creditors; 'the misery of his wretched situation beggars description', he wrote back to his superiors in Whitehall. Yet in spite of these debts (they had formed one subject of Abd-ar-Rahman's mission to England), Tully, who had lived twenty years in Tripoli, remained on the most friendly terms with the Pasha and his family and was able to provide Lucas with the right introductions. The Pasha, Ali Karamanli, 'a short robust old man with an affable joyous disposition', was surprised when Lucas said that he wished to visit the Fezzan and told him that no Christian had ever made the journey before. To this Lucas gave the disingenuous reply that he had heard of certain Roman antiquities and hoped also to collect various medicinal plants not known in Europe. The Pasha was satisfied with this explanation, and promised to send Lucas on his way as soon as the opportunity of a safe conveyance presented itself; at the moment, however, the road to the south was extremely insecure, for the Arab tribes were in revolt and had recently attacked a caravan. Lucas accepted this explanation; indeed, his own opinion, reached after a few days in Tripoli, was that the Government of the country was fast dwindling into insignificance.[3]

Three weeks later Lucas's hopes revived, when his friend Abd-ar-Rahman, whom Tully's sister-in-law praised as 'a most enlightened man' having been repeatedly at the chief courts of Europe', with 'so excellent a character that he is universally beloved by Christians as well as by Moors', introduced him to two emissaries recently arrived from the Fezzan. The younger of the two was tall and copper-coloured, a son-in-law of the ruler of the country; the elder, Imhammed, was short and black and a most entertaining conversationalist. Both men were Shereefs and claimed that the reverence paid to them as descendants of the Prophet secured them from attack on their journeys. They told Lucas that they would be as delighted to escort him across the desert as they knew their sovereign, who had never set eyes on a Christian traveller, would be to welcome him. The Pasha, less confident of the Shereefs' chances of immunity, could not help being aware of the complications that would arise if so distinguished a personage as the Interpreter to the King of England were to be assaulted in his territory; he therefore asked Lucas to defer his journey until the campaign just launched against the rebels had been successfully concluded.[4]

When they heard of the delay, the Shereefs were indignant, for they had already sent a messenger to the Fezzan to announce that Lucas was coming. Eventually the Pasha was persuaded to change his mind. So on February 1, 1789, Lucas and the Shereefs set out from Tripoli, accompanied by a few merchants and some freed slaves returning to their homeland, in a small caravan of twenty-one camels. Lucas himself rode on a handsome mule that the Pasha had given him, wore Turkish dress and had let his hair grow long so that he was beginning to look, he wrote in one of his letters home, 'like a London Jew in deep mourning'. In his baggage were the presents for the King of the Fezzan: fine clothes and strong brandy, of which the king was said to be inordinately fond, together with a letter of recommendation from the Pasha.[5]

The caravan took the coast road as far as Mesurata. Here they were on the point of turning inland, when they were stopped by the Governor. He warned them that they would need more camels to cross the desert and that these could be obtained only from the Arab tribes who were now in revolt. The tribesmen, it appeared, would not be willing to provide any animals for fear lest they should be detained by the Pasha's son, who had taken the field against them; the Bey, for his part, was not prepared to give an assurance that he would in fact refrain from taking the animals. Faced with this dilemma, Lucas decided to wait until the campaign was over. Time wore on; the days grew warmer; the hot season was at hand, when it seemed better not to attempt a desert crossing. Eventually the Shereefs, exhausted by Lucas' dithering, decided to leave him and return to their summer residence in the hills above Tripoli. Lucas felt that there was no alternative but to return to England.[6]

A more resolute man would have stayed on and found a way through; but Lucas was middle-aged, not accustomed to hard living or strenuous exertions, nor—from the complaints about gout in his letters—did he enjoy the best of health. It is not difficult to understand his feelings. Moreover, he could claim that his mission had not been without practical results. The days of waiting at Mesurata had been profitably spent, for he had found that Imhammed, the elder of his two companions, was a mine of information on the countries to the south of the Fezzan, especially on Bornu, which he had often visited on official business. Hesitant to arouse suspicions by asking too many direct questions, Lucas hit on the ruse of bringing out a map, which he was intending to present to the King of the Fezzan and asking Imhammed to help him to correct it, for he suspected that it contained many mistakes. For that talkative old man no work could be more congenial, sweetened as it was by Lucas's promise to present him with a special copy of the complete map.[7]

In this way Lucas was able to obtain on Bornu and the Fezzan a more detailed and accurate account than any that had previously been available. He also secured the first specific report on Tibesti, whose inhabitants, according to Imhammed, were a wild and savage people; they possessed the best camels to be found in Africa, and frequently raided the caravans that passed between Bornu and the Fezzan. Of the states lying to the west of Bornu, 'Cashna' (Katsina) was 'until of late esteemed the first in power'; but though it contained a thousand towns and villages, it was still far inferior to Bornu. Of the other Hausa states, curiously enough, Imhammed had nothing to report, apart from a brief mention of Zamfara. The Niger was described as forming the southern boundary of Cashna and as flowing from east to west with such rapidity that no vessel could navigate it. Farther south, in a country remarkable for 'the vast variety' of its fauna and its flora, but where 'the raging heat of the torrid zone increases', lay many other states with towns surrounded by walls, whose Pagan inhabitants traded amicably with the Muslims. Here, between the Niger and 'the Kingdom of Tonouwah, which borders on the coast of the Christians and of which the town of Assente is said to be the capital', was to be found 'a succession of hills, among which are mountains of stupendous height'. Despite a few gross errors—the westward-flowing Niger, the 'mountains of stupendous height'—there was much that was of value here. Lucas could pride himself on having made, at little cost to himself or to his employers, the most substantial contribution to the geography of the interior since Leo Africanus had written his account two hundred and sixty years earlier.[8]

Lucas was to return to Tripoli, for in 1793 he was appointed Consul, in succession to Richard Tully, on whose debts he had reported to his superiors. Indeed, it is not impossible that he was intriguing to obtain this post at the time of his first visit to Tripoli. In 1799 he married 'a Dame of easy virtue belonging to Barbary', only to divorce her after a short espousal. It was at this time that the latest of the African Association's explorers, Frederick Hornemann, found himself in Tripoli, having already visited the Fezzan. After he had made Lucas's acquaintance, he wrote back to the Association: 'I don't know if the Committee believe his excuses for returning to England or if they give them so little credit as I do myself.' On May 4, 1801, Simon Lucas died in Tripoli, Africa thus claiming him, as it claimed many braver explorers, at the last.[9]

WIDENING CONTACTS: BEN ALI AND SWEDIAUR; CONSULAR REPORTS

While Lucas was still abroad, the members of the Committee busied themselves looking round for other sources of information. From a certain Dr Thomson they learnt that there was living in London a Moor, named Ben Ali, who had visited the countries south of the Sahara twenty years earlier. Beaufoy arranged to interview this man, using a Barbary merchant named Dodsworth as interpreter. The information thus obtained confirmed and supplemented the report that Lucas had secured from Imhammed. But Ben Ali went further than giving information; he offered to escort two travellers on a trading expedition to Timbuktu, if the Association would provide £300 for the purchase of trade-goods and agree to try to obtain for himself a pension of £200 a year on his return. Dodsworth had a hand in this proposal, which the Committee was prepared to consider seriously until Beaufoy, examining the matter further, found that the scheme was 'equally inconsistent with the state of our funds and with the common maxims of mercantile prudence'. Moreover, he suspected both Dodsworth and the Moor of being rogues.[1]

At this point, however, a middle-aged doctor, Francois Xavier Swediaur, heard of the scheme. Born in Austria of Swedish parents, Swediaur had come to practise in London, where he had gained the friendship of Fordyce and the acquaintance of Banks. He now offered to proceed into the interior with Ben Ali, accompanied by a friend, Mr Hollen Vergen. Banks trusted Swediaur, and felt that Ben Ali might be attached to him as 'a useful but subordinate partner'. The terms Swediaur asked for his friend and himself were reasonable; a London businessman, Philip Sansom, 'a gentleman of great commercial knowledge', offered to send out a supercargo with trade-goods to the value of £500, which would be forwarded to the explorers as soon as they had reached Timbuktu; the route along the Gambia suggested by Ben Ali seemed less hazardous than the Saharan crossing—properly developed, it might 'eventually prove of the greatest importance to the commercial interest of Britain'. With such considerations before them, the Committee had no hesitation in accepting Swediaur's offer and in advancing him a substantial sum for his preparations. No sooner had this decision been reached, when a note arrived from Dodsworth to say that Ben Ali had disappeared and that there was reason to fear that he had made away with himself. Whether he died then or later is not certain; but within a few months his death was confirmed and the Committee found themselves being approached to pay his debts. The expedition might still have gone on without him; but that autumn Swediaur was taken seriously ill and decided to withdraw. Though ending in fiasco, this episode was of considerable importance in the development of the African Association, for it opened the eyes of the members of the Committee to the possibilities of commercial advantage that might arise from an intercourse with the countries of the interior of Western Africa, countries that had originally been chosen through the working of a rational curiosity as a goal for their explorers.[2]

In the spring of 1789 the Association received two valuable pieces of information from official sources. In October 1788 Lord Sydney, one of the Secretaries of State, had ordered all the Barbary Consuls to send in a report on the caravan trade to the interior.* Banks's friend, Matra, in Tangier, and Robert Traill, the acting Consul in Tunis, took this directive seriously, and after several months' research were able to send back some extremely interesting facts. Matra reckoned that the Moorish merchants went no farther than Timbuktu, 'the capital of Negroland' as he called it. His report on the great city was brief but encouraging: the people 'civilized and quiet', justice 'administered with great integrity', the surrounding

* The Consuls were also asked by Sydney to report on the slave trade with the interior. Matra found that the trade had much diminished since the days of Mulay Ismail and his Negro army; he reckoned that between three and four thousand slaves were brought across the Sahara annually, all of them speaking the same language. Among them were eunuchs from Bambara, whose king was prepared to exchange twenty or thirty of these unfortunates for a single horse. Traill reported that the Ghadames traders usually procured their slaves from 'the Twerkians' (probably Tuareg, though Traill gave the name of the 'despotic prince' of 'Eghalir' as 'Tworkia') to the number of twelve to thirteen hundred. Some of the slaves were sold on the return journey or at Ghadames, but a thousand slaves were brought every year into 'the dominion of Tunis', 'among them not above 100 or 150 men and boys and no eunuchs'. The traders also brought with them senna from Air, gold dust, ostrich feathers and ivory.

country 'fruitful', with an abundance of corn and rice, cattle and sheep. All this was some confirmation of Leo Africanus.[3]

Traill was able to go even farther. Traders from Ghadames, the independent oasis some four hundred miles south of Tunis, were accustomed, so he had learnt, to make a journey which took them from the Mediterranean almost as far as the Bight of Benin. Their route lay across the desert by way of Ghat and Air on to 'Eghalir, a very extensive country governed by a despotic prince' (probably Gobir), Katsina and Yauri 'where they procure the castrated negroes'. '10 days further is Burgu and 20 days beyond that a very extensive forest called Gabba which produces great quantity of dye woods which are usually sent to Giorback a seaport 8 days distance from the forest where they are sold to Christians who go to the coast of Guinea'.[4]

Had any geographer been in a position to understand the veracity of this remarkable document, he would have been able to make more accurately narrow the great blank that on contemporary maps separated the states of Guinea from the kingdoms described by Leo Africanus. But two men at least seem to have seen the importance of Ghadames. In the winter of 1789/90 a Dr Crammond and a Mr Walwyn presented the African Association with a statement of their plan to go to Ghadames and on into the interior; the Committee agreed to send them £100 as soon as they had passed Ghadames. Again disappointment; at least no more was heard of them. Thirty-five years had to pass before an English explorer—Major Laing—visited that rich, lonely oasis peopled by such enterprising traders.[5]

So gradually through merchants, through Moors picked up in the streets of London, through consular officials, the Association built up its essential network of contacts.

THE AFRICAN ASSOCIATION: ORGANIZATION, FINANCE AND MEMBERSHIP; THE FIRST REPORT

So many activities involved considerable expense. Ledyard's expedition had cost the Association £237 10s. and Lucas's £400. Ben Ali had been given twenty-one guineas for his services and Dodsworth as many pounds. A highly efficient part-time clerk had been engaged, Thomas Ivatts, who worked in Mr Stuart's office: he received £15 a year. Incidental expenses—mainly postage and stationery—were kept low, never more than a few pounds every year.

211

But in January 1790 it was resolved at a special General Meeting to publish the Association's proceedings: this involved a bill of £226 16s. 3d. The only source of revenue—leaving out the temporary loan advanced by members of the Committee—lay in the five-guinea annual subscription of members: this brought in £315 in 1788/89 and £472 10s. in 1789/90, membership having increased from sixty to ninety.[1]

Entrance to the Association was controlled by the Saturday's Club, those wishing to join having first to obtain nomination by one of the Club's members. To be elected, a nominee had to secure the vote of two-thirds of the members present at any one meeting. In April 1789 members chivalrously resolved that 'as the Improvement of Geographical Knowledge is not unworthy the attention or undeserving the encouragement of the Ladies of Great Britain, the ballot should not be applied to the fair sex'; in fact, not more than half a dozen ladies took advantage of this concession. Nor indeed is there any instance, according to the Club's minute book, of any nominee failing to secure the necessary votes. The privilege of membership was limited to the right to receive the Association's publications and to attend the annual General Meeting, usually held on the last Saturday in May. At the General Meeting in 1789, the only one for which records of attendance have survived, of the twelve founder members, eight were present, of the sixty-one ordinary members, only thirteen: those with any experience of the running of voluntary societies will not be surprised at these figures.[2]

All power lay in the hands of the Committee. Of its five members, the Bishop of Llandaff was unable to attend a single meeting in the first two years. Stuart's influence is impossible to gauge from the records. Rawdon, who made an imposing Chairman at the General Meetings, could be relied on to throw up an occasional suggestion. But the donkey-work fell, as in any voluntary society, on the Secretary and the Treasurer. In the first years Beaufoy played a more active part than Banks, being responsible for conducting the detailed negotiations with Ben Ali, Swediaur and others, and for writing the report. But it is clear that no decision was made, no traveller engaged, without the assent of Sir Joseph Banks. It was Banks who came to be regarded, in the words of Beaufoy's successor, Bryan Edwards, as 'the life and soul of the Association'.[3]

The African Association was from the start a deliberately exclusive body. Yet the eighteenth-century Establishment, the class that governed England, was far more varied in its composition than the expression *aristocracy* is usually held to imply. A study of the membership of the Association not only serves to indicate those quarters in which an interest in Africa was to be found but also provides a richly detailed impression of the most influential section of English society.[4]

The list of members of the Association published in 1790 contains, including the founders, ninety-five names. These could be divided into three different groups. The first was made up of members of the titled aristocracy: three dukes, eleven earls, four barons, two peeresses and two heirs to earldoms. Famous names occurred among them. There were two former Prime Ministers: the Duke of Grafton, said to be making up for the dissipations of his youth by a devotion to the Unitarian faith, and that forgotten favourite, the Earl of Bute, consoling his last years with a passion for botany and the collection of a magnificent library in his home at Luton Hoo. That nastily ambitious lawyer, Alexander Wedderburn, was there, recently ennobled as Lord Loughborough and soon to achieve the prize of the Lord Chancellorship; and Gibbon's friend, John Holroyd, Lord Sheffield, highly esteemed for his knowledge of commerce and of agriculture; and that princely dignitary of the Church, the Earl of Bristol, Bishop of Derry, using his vast wealth to transform the landscape of his Irish see. Rawdon had brought in some of his friends, the Duke of Northumberland, once an army officer in America, now in the Prince of Wales's circle, and another member of that clique, the dissolute Cholmondeley, notorious as a gambler—and some of his relations, his father Moira, his uncle Huntingdon, his sister the Countess of Aylesbury. There were two remarkable young men, Lord Daer, Selkirk's heir, recently back from Paris, where he had made friends with the leaders of the Revolution and accepted their radical ideas, which bravely he was to hold until his sadly early death, and the Honourable Frederick North, already something of a traveller. (In the course of the next thirty years North was to hold office in Corsica and in Ceylon and to become so ardent a philhellene that he was to be received into the Greek Church and to devote his last days, in Byron's age, to the founding of a University in Corfu.) Many of these noblemen were Fellows of the Royal Society and so within the range of Banks's canvass. They were all wealthy—some of them fabulously so—and had been born in an age when patronage was one of the duties of wealth.

213

The second group contained distinguished professional men, doctors, industrialists and scholars. Gibbon was there and John Hunter, the greatest surgeon of his age, and William Marsden, whose *History of Sumatra* had recently established him as one of the outstanding British Orientalists. There, too, were those two great pioneers of the Industrial Revolution, Josiah Wedgwood the potter and John Wilkinson the iron-master, both Staffordshire men, and that forgotten figure, Dr Lettsom, who, strict to his Quaker faith, had freed the slaves on his West Indian estate, settled in London and spent the profits of his lucrative practice in building up a museum and a botanical garden in his home at Camberwell. A solitary don represented the ancient Universities, Harwood, Professor of Anatomy at Cambridge, with service as a surgeon in India behind him, esteemed 'a popular bon-vivant'.

The third group—most of its members brought in, no doubt, through Beaufoy's advocacy—consisted of liberal Members of Parliament, businessmen and bankers. Wilberforce was the most prominent name, followed by that other intimate friend of the Prime Minister, whom one day he was so ineffectively to succeed, Henry Addington, through Pitt's influence elected Speaker of the House of Commons at the age of thirty-two. Many of Wilberforce's other associates had joined: all of them, except for that retiring clergyman, Thomas Gisborne, Members of Parliament, among them William Smith, James Martin, Sir Charles Middleton, that evangelical naval officer, later Lord Barham, and William Morton Pitt, a distant relative of the great Pitts, noted for his passionate interest in schemes for promoting the welfare of the poor. There were two M.P.s with experience of India: Sir John Call, now a banker, who had served there as a military engineer, and a Scottish landowner, Colonel Fullarton, who had raised his own regiment and commanded it with distinction in the recent campaign against Mysore. Naturally there was a group of Quakers, three Hoares, all London bankers, two Barclays, one a brewer, and two other Beaufoys, one of whom, Mark, having achieved the distinction of being the first Englishman to ascend Mt Blanc, had become the founder of a Society for the Improvement of Naval Architecture. Finally, there were a number of wealthy men from the City: Richard Neave, Chairman of the West Indian Merchants, Thomas Coutts, that popular and determinedly original banker, who had married a chambermaid and was to succeed her with an actress, and Paul le Mesurier, a Director of

the East India Company, who was to be the most prominent supporter of that extraordinary philanthropic affair, the Bulama
expedition.*

Tracing the careers of these men, one comes to appreciate the
insight, sympathy and balance of those sentences recently written
by Dr Steven Watson on the high society of the late eighteenth
century.

> What was most attractive in the life of this small knot of 'natural'
> rulers was their lively intellectual energy. It was a society where everyone
> knew everyone else and where argument on arts and politics, within the
> accepted framework, was both personal and pertinent. In it the qualities
> of true citizens by Aristotle's definition were realized. They had leisure
> for intellectual pursuits, yet they were sufficiently in touch with practical
> needs—through the stewards of their estates or their service in Parlia-
> ment—to avoid speculation which was purely abstract. They were rarely
> professionally competent in any field but possessed sufficient acquaint-
> ance with many skills to interest themselves in many forms of excellence.
> ... It would be wrong to idealize the picture of this society. Much of its
> leisure was devoted to drink or gaming rather than to connoisseurship.
> Yet few societies have had as living an intellectual life or as strong a
> common culture.[5]

In 1790 members received the Association's first report, a handsome quarto volume, some knowledge of whose contents reached a
far wider audience, for it was the subject of a lengthy review in the
Gentleman's Magazine. The report contained full details of Ledyard's
and Lucas's expeditions, together with a long essay on the significance
of the information that had been gathered. This was written by Major
James Rennell, the leading English geographer of the day, soon to
be elected the first honorary member of the Association.† But perhaps
the most exciting part of the report was the stirring set of

* On the Bulama expedition, see p. 274.

† James Rennell was born in 1742, joined the Navy as a boy during the
Seven Years' War, went to the East Indies and later transferred to the
East India Company, by whom he was appointed at the age of twenty-one
Surveyor-General of Bengal. He laid the foundations of the modern
cartography of the Indian sub-continent. In 1774, in the course of his
duties, he was attacked by fakirs and so severely wounded that he had to
retire. Returning home to England, he made his home in London, where
his house in Suffolk Square became a meeting-place for travellers from all
over the world. His interest in African geography seems to have been
derived from the detailed study of Herodotus on which he was engaged in
these years.[7]

215

Conclusions, with which it ended; Henry Beaufoy, their author, wielded a stylish pen, nor was he afraid of the grand manner.[6]

To the 'British traveller', who felt 'a desire of exchanging the usual excursion from Calais to Naples, for a tour more extended and important', Beaufoy recommended a journey with the merchants of Fezzan to Bornu or Timbuktu. Here was an opportunity for the gentleman of adventure; for the businessman with an eye for commercial gain there was another possibility. An association of Englishmen should set out for the upper reaches of the Gambia; 'there is reason to believe that countries new to the fabrics of England and probably inhabited by more than a hundred millions of people may be gradually opened to her trade.' Here, indeed, was the proof of the practical advantages of better knowledge: it would lead to 'the extension of the Commerce and the encouragement of the Manufactures of Britain'. Fire-arms were reported to be in special demand, and there was gold and cotton to be taken in exchange. Nor was there any need to fear the effects of the climate: 'The long descent of the rivers is a proof that the level of the inland country is raised above the level of the coast and consequently that the climate is much more temperate and probably more salubrious.'

These alluring prospects were gilded and sanctified in the final paragraph of the report: 'In pursuit of these advantages and by means as peaceful as the purposes are just, the conveniences of civil life, the benefits of the mechanic and manufacturing arts, the attainments of science, the energies of the cultivated mind and the elevation of the human character may in some degree be imparted to nations hitherto consigned to hopeless barbarism, and uniform contempt.' So there appears, couched in the smooth and balanced phrases of a classical prose, the grand motives of much of European endeavour in tropical Africa for the next hundred and seventy years. The reference to 'hopeless barbarism' is a sign certainly of European ignorance and self-satisfaction; but would it not be churlish to deny after a review of the progress of modern Senegal or Ghana or Nigeria that much of Beaufoy's prophesy has been fulfilled?

II

THE APPROACH FROM THE WEST
1790-99

SHABENI'S STORY: TIMBUKTU AND 'HOUSA'

TO COUNTRIES 'INHABITED BY more than a hundred millions of people' Beaufoy had referred in his report. This highly improbable figure he adopted after making the acquaintance of a young Moorish merchant named Shabeni. Shabeni had found himself in England through sheer accident. He was a merchant from Tetuan, who had travelled by sea to Hamburg to buy linen and other trade-goods for himself. On his way back he was captured in the North Sea by a ship manned by Englishmen but flying Russian colours, whose captain claimed that his Imperial Mistress was at war not only with the Turks but with all Muslims. Fortunately Shabeni was set ashore at Ostend, where the British Consul helped him to get to England. He arrived at Dover in December 1789. Some months later a Jew brought him to Beaufoy's notice; Lucas was called in as interpreter. Shabeni told them that at the age of fourteen he had gone with his father to Timbuktu, where he had lived for over seven years. His account of the city was sensible and realistic; but one remark was seized on—'some of the inhabitants,' he had told Beaufoy, 'are amazingly rich', making their wealth by lending out gold dust and slaves to foreign merchants at high interest rates; 'the dress of the common women,' he added, 'had been often worth 1,000 dollars'. Some concubines, no doubt, wearing gold bracelets: puff out this fact a little and what a picture there is to fire the imagination. 'We have heard of a city called Tombuctoo,' Sir John Sinclair wrote after hearing this report, 'gold is so plentiful as to adorn even the slaves'; 'if we could get our manufactures into that country,' he added, 'we should soon have gold enough.' But Timbuktu, according to Shabeni,

217

was not the greatest of the cities of the Sudan; farther east, along the banks of the Niger, lay a great and thickly populated empire, whose capital, Housa, was almost as large as London or Cairo, so large indeed that Shabeni in the two years that he had spent there had not been able to see the whole of it, the wall of the king's palace alone being 'seven or eight miles in circumference'. The government of the country, Beaufoy gathered, was 'monarchical, yet not unlimited', its justice 'severe but directed by written laws', while the art of writing was widespread, though in characters different from Arabic.[1]

Could Shabeni's story be accepted? It seems likely that he was in fact describing the powerful Hausa state of Gobir, whose hegemony over the other states of Hausaland was within the next twenty years to be violently overthrown, even as its capital, Alkalawa, was to be razed to the dust. Beaufoy seems to have had no hesitation about accepting the truth of what Shabeni had told him; but James Matra in Morocco was sceptical, until he himself three years later obtained confirmation from an Arab, who had been in Timbuktu and described Housa as 'one of the first cities in the world'. A few months later he obtained more information from a merchant in Fez, who traded with the city. Housa produced, so Matra was told, 'linen of exquisite fineness', 'in such abundance that in one day you may procure as much as would load 50 *large ships*'. The Government was stricter than anything to be found in Barbary, but foreign traders were 'very well treated' and travellers could 'sleep in the greatest security'.[2]

Here indeed, then, was a prospect to exhilarate both the scholar and the man of affairs. In an age of ever-widening knowledge it was extraordinary to discover that there should exist in a part of Africa by no means the most remote from Europe 'a very considerable Empire arrived,' as Matra described it, 'at a high state of civilization'. What secrets might it not contain? Was it not possible that something of the 'knowledge and language of ancient Egypt' was still to be found there? Might not descendants of the Carthaginians, 'lost to the world'—in Beaufoy's rotund phrase—'in the vast oblivion of the desert', have preserved there the arts and sciences for which their forebears had been famed? Was Matra right when he speculated that the present inhabitants were sprung from 'such Greeks and Vandals as were routed by the entrance of the Arabs'?[3]

Not since the days of Cortez had a more dazzling opportunity, one may think, thus revealed itself. But the gentlemen of the African Association were civilized, generous and humane, not bloody-minded conquistadors. Soon, Beaufoy reflected, 'the people of the inland regions of Africa may be united with Europe in that great bond of commercial fellowship, which the mutual wants and the different productions of the other continents of the globe have happily established'. The new relationship would be of benefit to both sides. 'Much, undoubtedly, we shall have to communicate', but, having noted that the merchants of Barbary asserted that 'the people of Housa have the art of tempering their iron with more than European skill', with proper humility he added, 'something we may have to learn'.[4]

DANIEL HOUGHTON

With Lucas and Ledyard the Association had planned to make a grand bisection of the northern half of the continent. The report on Timbuktu and Housa focused attention on the Niger. Nothing certain was known about the course of the river, yet it was clear that in part at least it was a navigable stream. Only prove that it could be easily reached from the sea and a great highway into the centre of Northern Africa would be revealed. The Committee was aware, from their discussions with Dodsworth, Ben Ali and others in the summer of 1789, that the Gambia appeared to provide the easiest route into the interior. Now in July 1790 a man with exactly the right experience for this approach offered his services to the Association; he was a fifty-year-old Irishman, a retired and bankrupt Major, Daniel Houghton by name.[1]

Houghton came of a military family. He had joined the Army in 1758 and seen active service in the West Indies. In 1772, while stationed at Gibraltar, he had been sent on a mission to the Imperial Court of Morocco, after the British Consul had been forced to flee the country; he had succeeded, so he claimed, in bringing the Emperor to reason, but had received no recognition for his services, as his patron, Lord Cornwallis, had died shortly afterwards. Indeed, he had fallen so heavily in debt that he had been forced to sell the company that he had recently purchased. Six years later he made an attempt to retrieve his fortunes by accepting a post as engineer with the Nawab of Arcot. He never reached India. War with the French broke out soon after the commencement of his journey and the ship in which he was travelling was diverted to Goree, the base off the coast of Senegambia, which the French had recently evacuated. Houghton let himself be persuaded to take on the post of fort-major on the island. He spent over three years there, learnt to speak Mandingo and 'became intimate with several of the kings of the province'. But at the end of the war Goree was returned to the French and Houghton found himself not only without a job but without a pension, all his appeals to be put on the half-pay list being rejected. By this time he was married; his wife was a woman of some means, but Houghton had the mortification of seeing her fortune seized by his creditors. In 1783 he wrote to the Government, offering his services to explore the sources of the Gambia and the Faleme; he was anxious to exploit the mines of the country, and proposed engaging miners from 'Friburg' in Saxony for that purpose. But the Government had no interest in the Gambia in the 1780s except as a possible convict station. News of the founding of the African Association raised Houghton's hopes; little more than a month after the inaugural meeting his name had been recommended to Banks by Sir William Musgrave. Again he was disappointed. Now at last, eight years after he had left West Africa, his hour had come.[2]

It was not only Houghton's experience that impressed the Committee; they noted 'the order of his mind and the strength of his constitution' and found his 'zeal' remarkably exemplified in the smallness of the sum which he asked for the expedition, compared with that which other candidates for employment required. For Houghton estimated his expenses at less than £300, two-thirds of which was to be spent on trade-goods, and made no stipulation about any reward on his return. Was there an element of Irish fecklessness in his character? For he left behind him his wife and three children, living, so the Committee were informed, in 'circumstances of great distress'. To Mrs Houghton was given a gratuity of £10, 'the utmost which the Committee conceive themselves at liberty to afford'; a hard logic determined this meagre sum, for, as Banks wrote later, the Committee felt that 'as an Association, they were not justified in appropriating money subscribed for the purposes of discovery to the maintenance of individuals, who happen to be connected with those whom they employ'.[3]

Houghton's offer was accepted on July 5. By mid-October he was on his way. He took with him a set of Moorish clothes returned by Lucas, a young companion, Cyprian Dufaud, whose presence was not mentioned to his employers, the memory of an interview on the day of his departure with the Prime Minister himself, and a letter of instruction drafted by Beaufoy. This last was a far longer document than any Lucas or Ledyard may have received, even as its terms were more precise. Housa was named as the explorer's objective, his starting-point to be the Falls of Barracunda on the Gambia. *En route* he was to gather information—Beaufoy set out a long questionnaire to help him—on 'the rise, the course and the termination of the Niger, as well as of the various Nations that inhabit its borders', and to attempt to visit Timbuktu. It was hoped that he might find it possible to return by one of the Saharan caravans.[4]

Houghton reached the Gambia at the beginning of November. It was the start of the dry season and therefore the most favourable time for travelling. Dufaud fell ill almost at once. Houghton left him behind at the mouth of the river, took advantage of a lift in a trading vessel and pushed on to Pisania, where Dr Laidley, one of the few Englishmen to maintain a trading establishment on the river, had a factory. There he bought a horse and five asses to carry his trade-goods, engaged a servant and an interpreter, and set off immediately for the interior. His first objective was Medina, the capital of the small state of Wuli. He did not reach it without adventures; native traders, fearing that the white man had come to steal their trade, laid a plot against him. By chance he heard of their plans and escaped by swimming his caravan across the river and following the southern bank to a point where the King of Wuli could send an escort to meet him.[5]

Englishmen were not unknown in Medina, for a Captain Littleton had recently spent four years in the town; he had done so well from the trade in wax and slaves that he was able to retire, but he still sent his ships to trade in the river, and made a profit that Houghton reckoned to be as high as eight hundred per cent. The King of Wuli was eager to strengthen his connection with the English and wanted to see an English fort built in his territory. 'I am greatly caressed here,' Houghton wrote to his wife on March 10, 'on account of my coming to make a settlement in their country, which will enrich them all by trade and I hope myself too.' Indeed, to a man in his circumstances there was much to be said for settling in Medina: 'You may live here almost for nothing,' he wrote in the same letter, 'ten pounds a year would support a whole family with plenty of fowls, sheep, eggs, butter, honey, bullocks, fish and all sorts of game: I am tired of killing them. I want for none of these things and wish I could send you only what I have to spare which would more than supply your family at home.'[6]

This idyllic interlude was spoilt by a singularly unfortunate series of accidents. A disastrous fire broke out in Medina, and within an hour most of the town was destroyed, including the hut in which Houghton was staying. He lost many of his possessions, among them all his arms and ammunition and 'the broad beaver hat I bought at Beavan's to keep off the sun'. A few weeks later a trade-gun he had purchased to replace his own exploded in his hands, inflicting a nasty wound. Finally, as a crowning blow, his inter-preter disappeared, taking with him the horse and three of the asses. Yet from his letters Houghton gave no impression of being daunted by the prospect before him. Timbuktu was far from being unknown to the people of Medina, individual traders passed between the Niger and the sea, and the king assured Houghton that he would be able to reach the great city 'with only a stick in his hand'. To his wife Houghton had written in March that the king had promised to send some of his own people to escort him to Timbuktu; but this promise seems to have broken down, for it was in the company of a slave-dealer that he finally left Medina on May 8, 1791.

Did he realize when he set out the full extent of the difficulties that lay ahead of him? He was making his journey at the start of the rains-season of fevers and swollen rivers and impassable tracks—and he would have to pass through a succession of states frequently at war one with another. Indeed, a war was in progress at this moment between the kingdoms of Bondou and Bambuk, which ended, so Houghton learnt on reaching the Faleme, the river that formed the border between the two kingdoms, in the victory of Bondou. In these circumstances he thought it advisable to go out of his way to pay his respects to the victor. This gesture was ill-received, for the King of Bondou ordered him to surrender most of his goods, includ-ing the blue coat he was keeping to wear 'on the day of his introduc-tion to the Sultan of Tombuctoo'. Fortunately the king did not detain him long.

From Bondou Houghton returned to the valley of the Faleme, where the slave trader with whom he was travelling had a rice farm. His companion had his own interests to consider; finding that his family were threatened with famine, he decided to postpone the journey to Timbuktu until he had provided for them. Houghton, therefore, decided to go on alone to Ferbanna, the capital of Bambuk. The King of Bambuk gave him a friendly reception. He explained that his recent defeat had been due to lack of ammunition; in the past the French traders at Fort St Joseph had kept him well supplied, but now they had abandoned their post, meanwhile his rival of Bondou was able to buy all that he required from the English traders on the Gambia. This remark gave Houghton the opportunity to suggest that it would be in the King's own interest 'to encourage the English to open a trade by way of his dominions to the populated cities on the banks of the Niger'. His conversations with native rulers showed very clearly that an African explorer needed, among other qualities, to possess the instinct and tact of a diplomatist; but Houghton had no authority to conclude commercial treaties, his task was to reach Timbuktu. In Bambuk an 'old and respectable' merchant offered to take him on horseback to the great city and back to the Gambia for a sum of £125 to be paid at the end of the journey. This seemed an excellent offer; Houghton accepted it eagerly. To facilitate travelling he changed all his trade-goods into gold dust and exchanged his two asses for a horse. Before leaving he sent a letter, dated July 24, which safely reached the Secretary of the African Association in London.

The contents of this letter were read to the members at the General Meeting of May 1792. There existed, Beaufoy wrote in his report, some 'assurance of success'. 'A natural intrepidity of character that seems inaccessible to fear, and an easy flow of constitutional good humour, that even the roughest accidents of life have no power to subdue, have formed him,' so he said of Houghton, 'in a peculiar degree, for the adventures in which he is engaged: and such is the darkness of his complexion, that he scarcely differs in appearance from the Moors, whose dress in travelling he intended to assume.'[7]

Some months later, news came from Dr Laidley; he had received the following note.

Simbing   September 1st.
Major Houghton's compliments to Dr Laidley, is in good health on his way to Tombuctoo, robbed of all his goods by Fenda Bucar's son.

Months later, Laidley wrote again saying that traders from the interior had reached the Gambia with reports that the white man was dead, either murdered, so the first rumours had it, by the King of Bambara, or, according to more probable later versions, struck down by dysentery. When a year had passed with nothing to deny these accounts the Association accepted 'with inexpressible concern' the loss of their traveller. But Mrs Houghton refused to believe that her husband was not still alive. The mystery of his fate was not to be solved until another traveller had followed in his footsteps.[8]

Today Houghton is almost forgotten, his achievement over-shadowed by that of his more fortunate successor: it is the usual lot of the pioneer, of the man who fails to reach the goal. He deserves to be better remembered, for he had succeeded in penetrating deeper into the interior than any European since the days of the Portuguese; nor had his experience been so discouraging as to daunt others. Moreover, he had made one very substantial contribution to geographical knowledge, for the information that he had acquired and been able to send back to London made it clear that the Niger was indeed a quite separate river from the Senegal, that it had its rise in mountainous country somewhere to the south-east of Bambuk, and that it flowed eastwards, not westwards, past the great cities of Jenne and Timbuktu. Other reports obtained from North Africa confirmed this drastic reversal of the traditional conception of the Niger's course; but the new knowledge was not to become generally accepted until a European had stood on the banks of the great river and seen with his own eyes the direction of its flow.[9]

Houghton's death posed the Association with a problem they had not anticipated. For his grieving family were left utterly destitute, and in 1794 his widow was thrown into the debtors' prison. The Committee received her appeals for aid somewhat coldly, being under no legal obligation to help her. But in time more charitable counsels prevailed, a fund was established to pay for the education of her sons, and a pension of £30 a year was obtained from the King's Bounty.[10]

THE CONSUL TO SENEGAMBIA

When the African Association held its General Meeting in May 1792 its members were informed of the letters received from Major Houghton, the last of which described his favourable reception by the King of Bambuk. They also had before them 'specimens of the vegetable productions of the countries on the south of the desert', which had been procured by Perkins Magra, the Consul at Tunis. It was therefore in a mood of practical optimism that the members passed a resolution empowering their Committee 'to make whatever applications to the Government they may think advisable for rendering the late discoveries of Major Houghton serviceable to the Commercial interests of the Empire'. There is nothing surprising about such a resolution coming from a body that contained among its members many more politicians and businessmen than pure scholars.[1]

Discussing the matter among themselves and with other men of affairs, the Committee came to the conclusion that they should recommend to the Government the establishment of a British consul in Bambuk. Nothing definite was done, however, until the beginning of May 1793, when Beaufoy was approached by a certain James Willis, who had heard him talk about the scheme and had come to regard it as 'sufficiently attractive to interest his Ambition or his Passion for honourable Fame'. Willis was a man of about thirty, 'at present a Governor of the Turkey Company'—Beaufoy dashed off these details to Banks in 'the interval afforded by a dull Speech' in the House—'his attainments Classical and in some degree Scientific', 'his Understanding of no ordinary Class'. Willis had thought the project out carefully and talked about it to 'a particular Friend of his', who was 'so much captivated with the plan as to promise to recommend it to Government with the utmost earnestness and with the greatest probability of success'. Willis's friend, 'the best of all Solicitors' and 'really possessed of a great interest in the quarter in which it seems the most indispensably requisite', was Alexander Brodie, M.P., a Scotsman who had made a large fortune in business in India, returned home, married his daughter to the heir of the Duke of Gordon, acquired a seat in Parliament and become one of the closest political associates of Henry Dundas, the Prime Minister's right-hand man. Apart from the support of this highly influential advocate, 'several merchants of great wealth in the City,' Willis told Beaufoy, 'had offered to vest a large sum in the adventure to Bambuk', as soon as they were assured that the plan was being given official support.[2]

Three weeks later, at the Association's General Meeting, the Committee was specifically requested to confer with Dundas as Secretary of State for Foreign Affairs and to urge on the Government 'the Experimental and Temporary Appointment of a Consul to Senegambia'.* Beaufoy immediately set about drafting a persuasive memorandum to show to Dundas. He pointed out that the Barbary states carried on an extensive trade with the nations on the banks of the Niger, a trade conservatively estimated to be worth a million pounds a year, maintained in the face of 'the hazards of a land carriage of 1,200 miles across the Desert of Zahara' and in despite of 'the frequent and varying exactions of the Barbary Governments'. Now, from the information that the Association had obtained, it appeared that the Niger was navigable at a distance of not more than three hundred and fifty miles from the higher reaches of the Gambia. Compare this distance with that of the desert crossing, almost four times as great. Bear in mind that the country between the Niger and the Gambia was in the hands of a ruler—the King of Bambuk—who had shown himself eager to trade with the English. Recall that Bambuk produced gold, which the king would exchange for fire-arms. Reflect that the intrigues of the slave traders, whom Houghton had accused of plotting against him, could only be 'resisted by persons who carry with them the Sanction of a Public Character'. Was it not clear then that the establishment of a consul in Bambuk ensuring the protection of British merchants 'would soon transfer to Great Britain the trade which is now carried on by the Barbary States'? Might it not then be suggested that such a development, viewed in the light of history, would come to represent a revolution not incomparable to that effected by the Portuguese when they discovered the sea route to the Indies?[3]

Logical such an argument might appear to anyone unacquainted with African realities. Dundas was persuaded and so was Pitt, when Beaufoy talked the matter over with them at the end of June. Willis was afire with the scheme and had already acquired a considerable knowledge of Mandingo. He now drew up a detailed set of proposals. In the kingdom of Wuli at Fatetenda, which Houghton in one of his letters had mentioned as a suitable site, a mud fort should be built as a base; this should be held by a garrison of fifty European soldiers, with two forty-ton sloops to ensure communications with the sea. As soon as the fort was completed,

* No doubt for security reasons—the country was now at war with France—the vaguer term *Senegambia* was used in all references to the Consulate. Although the French had never re-established themselves on the upper Senegal, they could regard Bambuk as lying in their sphere of influence.

the Consul should send a messenger to the King of Bambuk, to find out his terms for protecting the trade between the Gambia and the Niger. When satisfactory arrangements had been made, the merchants in London were to be informed. The annual cost of the entire enterprise Willis estimated at £3,000; this sum included his own salary, which he fixed at £600 (per annum). After chewing over the matter for a whole winter, the Government gave this ambitious, plausible, reckless plan their blessing. On April 10, 1794, Willis was appointed His Majesty's Consul in Senegambia and the sum of £3,000 per annum was appropriated to meet all expenses for two years. Willis planned to leave for the Gambia in time to arrive at the beginning of the dry season.[4]

The scheme had mushroomed into something too big and too expensive for the Association to handle; but even if successful, it would not upset their own plans. For beyond Bambuk lay Timbuktu and Housa, which still required to be explored by a European. By this time the Committee were convinced that Houghton must be dead. Discussing among themselves the course of his expedition, they found in his own behaviour some reasons for his failure. 'It would seem from various information'—possibly the first-hand account of Dr Laidley, who was in London at that time—'that this unfortunate gentleman was no favourite of the natives in general.' Houghton had made another mistake: 'contrary to all the suggestions of prudence and the remonstrances of his friends in England, the Major had encumbered himself with an assortment of bale goods, which presented to the ignorant Negroes such temptation as savage virtue could not resist'. Nevertheless, the difficulties, they concluded, were not insuperable; 'on the contrary, there is reason to believe that a traveller of good temper and conciliating manners who has nothing with him to tempt rapacity, may expect every assistance from the natives and the fullest protection from their chiefs'.[5]

Who was to serve as Houghton's successor? It is likely that there was no shortage of volunteers, for there exists among Banks's papers a scrap of paper, unfortunately undated but written about this time, containing the names of ten persons interested in becoming African explorers, none of whom were subsequently chosen. Instead, in July 1794, a young man, who was already something of a protégé of Banks, offered his services: his name was Mungo Park. Park had been introduced to Banks three years earlier by his brother-in-law, James Dickson. Dickson was a London market-gardener, a scholarly, self-educated man, who, in the course of his profession, had come to acquire a considerable knowledge of botany, written several books on the subject, and thus come to the notice of Sir Joseph. In 1789 Dickson had visited Scotland to call on his father-in-law, a farmer living near the small lowland town of Selkirk. There he made the acquaintance of Mungo, one of his wife's younger brothers (the family contained thirteen children), found that the lad shared his own passion for natural history and took him on a botanizing tour of the Highlands. Park was eighteen at that time; for the last three years he had been apprenticed to a local doctor named Anderson and was now on the point of leaving to study medicine at Edinburgh University. On finishing at the University, young Park had followed the example of so many of his compatriots and come to London to seek employment. He was fortunate in being able to stay at his sister's house and even more fortunate—in an age when appointment depended so much on influence—in being introduced by his brother-in-law to Sir Joseph Banks. Banks was impressed by the young Scotsman and helped him to secure a post as surgeon on an East India Company ship bound for Bencoolen in Sumatra, a voyage that would give him some opportunity to carry on research into natural history.[6]

Park left England early in 1792 and was away about a year. He had been back in England a year and a half before he offered his services to the African Association. How he spent this time is uncertain; but it is evident that his own ideas about what he wanted to do in life were becoming clearer. The medical profession he found irksome; his true interest was in natural history. Had the conditions of the age allowed it, he might have become a full-time naturalist. Of his ability in this field there can be no doubt; the paper which he read to the Linnean Society on 'Eight small fishes from the coast of Sumatra' was a highly professional piece of work. When his mind first turned to Africa, what contribution the conversation of Sir Joseph made to his resolve, there is no means of knowing; but it would seem that it was no sudden decision. 'I had a passionate desire,' he wrote later, 'to examine into the productions of a country so little known and to become experimentally acquainted with the modes of life and character of the natives.' Of the dangers that he would have to face from the climate he was well aware: 'I relied on my youth and the strength of my constitution to preserve me.' The Committee, for their part, after interviewing him on July 23, judged

228

him to be 'a young man of no mean talents' and 'finding him sufficiently instructed in the use of Hadley's quadrant to make the necessary
observations; geographer enough to trace his path through the
Wilderness and not unacquainted with natural history, accepted his
offer'. It was agreed that he should receive a salary of 7s. 6d. a day
to commence on August 1 and to be doubled from the day of his
arrival in Africa, together with an additional sum of £200 to cover
his expenses: by the rates of the age these were by no means ungenerous terms.[7]

Park was twenty-three years old at the time of his appointment.
He was a tall, good-looking young man. A later biographer, gazing
on his portrait, has rhapsodized on 'the fine brow', 'the prominent,
finely chiselled nose', 'the eyes that look forth so calmly, aglow with
truthfulness, self-possession and confidence'. Others may find it more
revealing to know that as a schoolboy he was regarded as being
'silent, studious and thoughtful' and that later his manner displayed
'a certain coldness and reserve'. But it was the reserve of a man absorbed in his own thoughts, for he had a sharp, active, rational
mind and could feel intensely the excitement that comes from the
pursuit of knowledge: it was indeed the mind of a scientist. Added
to this, he possessed a well-developed sense of ambition: he predicted to his brother before leaving for Africa that he would 'acquire
a greater name than any ever did'. With ambition went the faith of a
Calvinist: 'I have now reached that height,' he wrote to his former
master, Dr Anderson, in 1793, 'that I can behold the tumults of
nations with indifference, confident that the reins of events are in
our Father's hands. I wish you may be able to look upon the day
of your departure with the same resignation that I do on mine'.
Ambition and faith fused to produce an intense self-confidence, no
quality more valuable for an explorer faced with the perils of an
unknown continent.[8]

Park expected to leave England, together with Willis, a month or
two after his engagement. But as the autumn of 1794 wore on, Willis
found one reason after another to delay his departure. Beaufoy,
writing to Banks on October 17, had to report nothing but 'Official
embarrassments'. Captain Barbauld, who was to command the
troops, found it difficult to recruit the fifty men needed; but it
appeared that he himself had no desire to leave England that winter,
as he was using his commission 'to smoothe his way to a fortunate
matrimonial connection'. The War Office had been approached;

they had other vastly more important campaigns to worry about and could offer no more than ten or fifteen deserters and 'twenty rogues of comparatively fair Characters' from the convict prison at Portsmouth. Meanwhile Willis's brother had put up a hair-brained scheme for recruiting a corps of Cornish miners to work the gold deposits of Bambuk. Beaufoy was able to get Willis to abandon his brother's idea and to secure the services of a recruiting agent, who was soon able to provide fifty excellent men, but only at the cost of paying them a greatly increased bounty. This forced Willis to revise his estimates: so greatly had costs risen, that he found that he would need not £3,000 but £7,357. These figures Willis submitted to Dundas on February 27; a month elapsed before Dundas passed them on to the Treasury.[9]

For Park these delays—reasonable enough though they may have seemed to others preoccupied with the demands of a major war—must have been exasperating. Learning that a small trading vessel was due to sail for the Gambia in May, he sought and obtained the Committee's permission to set out alone. It was as well that he did not wait for Willis, for the Consul never reached Senegambia, never indeed left England. In June he obtained the extra funds that he required. It was now necessary to delay until the rainy season was over on the West Coast. In November he reported to Dundas that he was ready to set out and required only his instructions. These were issued two months later, but Willis was told that before he left he must submit the accounts of his already considerable expenditure to be examined by the Committee of the African Association. Meanwhile reports had reached England of three French privateers in the Gambia; their presence constituted a serious danger. So serious, indeed, did the Committee consider it that they recommended that the expedition should be abandoned until a time 'when Peace returns and when Prosperity incites Merchants to employ their capital on Speculations of Adventure and Novelty'. Dundas, to Willis's mortification, accepted this advice. The fiasco had cost the country over £8,000—almost as large a sum as the African Association spent in the whole of its existence. Willis, however, had protected himself from loss; more than half the total amount found its way into his own pockets, partly as salary, partly as fair compensation for the hire of two ships purchased with his own money. The Association's Committee, examining Willis's accounts, could find no legitimate grounds for censure.[10]

MUNGO PARK

Park reached the Gambia towards the end of June and went up the river to Pisania, where he was hospitably received by Dr Laidley. His instructions were the same as Houghton's: 'to pass on to the River Niger . . . ascertain the course and, if possible, the rise and termination of that river . . . visit the principal towns or cities in the neighbourhood, particularly Tombuctoo and Housa'. Since it was inadvisable to set out until the rains were over, he waited for five months in Pisania, a profitable interlude, giving him the opportunity to acquire a fair knowledge of Mandingo, the *lingua franca* of the Western Sudan, to study the local flora, to undergo a first spell of fever and in general to accustom himself to Africa. His attempt to gather information from the slave-dealers who travelled down from the interior met with no success. They seemed 'extremely unwilling' that he should prosecute his journey, while their accounts of the interior 'contradicted each other in the most important particulars'. 'These circumstances increased my anxiety to ascertain the truth from my own personal observation.'[1]

With the advent of the dry season Park prepared to leave. As interpreter, he engaged an ex-slave named Johnson, who had lived both in Jamaica and in England. For a personal servant, Laidley provided him with one of his own slaves, a 'sprightly youth' named Demba, who was promised freedom on his return. Park bought a small horse for himself and a couple of donkeys for Johnson and Demba. His baggage was as light as possible: two day's provision, an assortment of trade-goods—beads, amber and tobacco—for buying food, several changes of linen, some guns and a few essential instruments. On the news of his departure four other Africans attached themselves to him, one of them a blacksmith, who had worked for Laidley and was returning to his home in Kasson. Thus prepared, Park set out from Pisania on December 2, 1795, reflecting, after he had said good-bye to Laidley, that he had 'perhaps quitted for ever the comforts of Christian society' and that there lay before him 'a boundless forest, and a country, the inhabitants of which were strangers to civilized life, and to most of whom a white man was the object of curiosity or plunder'.

The first stage of his journey, however, passed comparatively easily. At Medina, the capital of Wuli, the old king received him as affectionately as he had received Houghton and 'tenderly entreated' him to go no farther, 'for the people of the east had never seen a white man before and would certainly destroy' him. At Fatteconda, the capital of Bondou, the king, who had treated Houghton so roughly, proved more civil than Park had anticipated. Nevertheless, he needed to be well humoured with presents, while his wives provided Park with his first experience of African colour-consciousness. 'They rallied me with a good deal of gaiety on different subjects, particularly upon the whiteness of my skin and the prominency of my nose. The first, they said, was produced when I was an infant, by dipping me in milk; and they insisted that my nose had been pinched every day till it had acquired its present unsightly and unnatural conformation.'

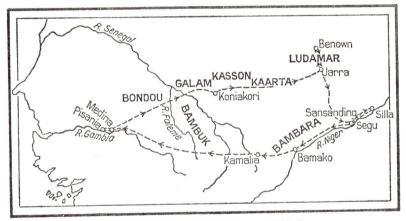

5. Mungo Park's First Journey, 1795-7

From Bondou Park travelled north-eastwards to the kingdom of Kajaaga, better known as Galam. Here, in the small town of Joag, the first unpleasantness occurred. A party of horsemen from the king of the country arrived in the middle of the night, accused Park of breaking the law by failing to make to their master the usual present, declared all his goods forfeit and demanded that he return with them immediately. His companion, the blacksmith, strongly advised him to not fall into the king's hands. It proved possible to buy off the royal ministers: by allowing them, after hours of wrangling, to make off with half of his goods.

A few days later this experience was repeated, when one of the great men of the neighbouring kingdom of Kasson, who had escorted Park from Kajaaga, demanded as the price for his protection the right to ransack his belongings. So he found himself, with only a third of his outward journey behind him, deprived of two-thirds of the goods that were essential both for buying food and for propitiating local rulers; Johnson, the interpreter, 'laughed at the idea of proceeding without money'. Fortunately a moment of relief was at hand.

They had reached Jumbo, the home-town of the blacksmith, and were invited to stay for the delightful celebrations that marked the return of the wanderer. There followed two happy days of feasting and of merriment. One incident above all others stamped itself on Park's memory, the greeting given to the blacksmith by his old blind mother. 'From this interview I was fully convinced that whatever difference there is between the Negro and European in the con-formation of the nose and the colour of the skin, there is none in the genuine sympathies and characteristic feelings of our common nature.' It is a lesson that every European in Africa has to learn for himself.

From Jumbo, Park moved to Koniakori, the capital of Kasson. The king, a kind, elderly man, had helped Houghton on his journey and was equally willing to assist Park. He provided a guide to the neighbouring kingdom of Kaarta, but warned Park that great dangers lay ahead, for Kaarta was on bad terms with its eastern neighbour, Bambara, and a Bambaran army was said to be on the point of invading the country. No sooner, indeed, had Park reached Kaartan territory than signs of approaching conflict became alarmingly evident, the roads being full of refugees flying to Kasson for safety. Disregarding the nervousness of his servants, Park pushed on to the capital. The king gave him a sympathetic reception, pointed out that if he went straight to Bambara he would undoubtedly be taken for a spy and told him that his most prudent course would be to return to Kasson and wait until the war was over. Such a delay Park was unwilling to accept. There was then, the king suggested, one other route he could attempt: north of Kaarta, on the edge of the desert, lay the Moorish kingdom of Ludamar; by crossing Ludamar—a journey not without difficulty—he would come circuitiously to Bambara.*

---

* Park's Ludamar was not strictly a kingdom, but the name of a tribe of Moors, the Oulad Mbareck. Park's Bambara is now known to historians as the kingdom of Segu. Both Segu and Kaarta were inhabited by Bambara people.[2]

How dangerous a journey through Moorish territory might prove, Park had some opportunity of judging as he travelled northwards to the frontier town of Jarra. Of all the people in the western Sudan, the Moors had the most ferocious reputation. In character and in appearance they differed sharply from their Negro neighbours. Their skin was light brown, their hair black and bushy, their features struck Park as showing 'a disposition towards cruelty and low cunning', while 'from the staring wildness of their eyes a stranger would immediately set them down as a nation of lunatics'. They lived with their herds of cattle and camels on the edge of the desert, coming south during the dry season and moving north during the rains. For the Negro people, who bordered their territory, they were the most pestilential of neighbours. In one Kaartan town Park witnessed a typical incident: a herd of cattle was grazing near the walls; five Moors galloped up and drove off sixteen of the finest beasts; a young herd-boy threw a spear at the robbers and was promptly shot and killed; five hundred of the townspeople, gathered by the walls, could do nothing but let off a brief fusillade from four muskets badly primed with locally made gunpowder.

Before reaching Jarra, Park passed the village of Simbing, from which Houghton had written his last note. Shortly afterwards he learnt the details of his predecessor's death. On the borders of Ludamar, Houghton, deserted by all his servants, had fallen in with a party of Moorish traders on their way to some salt-pits in the desert. He must have thought that they were going to Timbuktu; when he discovered that they were deceiving him he tried to return to Jarra. His companions would not let him go until they had robbed him of all he possessed, leaving him to make the journey back on foot. He reached a place where the Moors came to water their cattle; there he stayed, begging in vain for food. How the end came—from hunger or a knife-thrust—was uncertain; but Park was shown from a distance the place in the bush where his corpse had been left to rot.

Even grimmer, after such a story, the prospect before him; but if Park had ever seriously thought of turning back it was now too late to do so, for the army of Bambara had invaded Kaarta and was engaged in ravaging the whole kingdom. So he came to Jarra, a fair-sized town, whose Negro inhabitants paid tribute to the Moors. There he met a merchant, Daman Jumma, who knew Laidley well, a man of scrupulous honesty, for he gave Park some gold in payment of a debt that he had incurred with Laidley five years earlier. From

Jarra Park sent a messenger to Ali, King of Ludamar, requesting permission to cross his territory; fourteen days later he received a favourable reply. Then Johnson told him that, terrified of being enslaved by the Moors, he would go no farther; young Demba, to Park's surprise, insisted on accompanying his master.

For five days Park travelled through Ludamar. The Moors, whom he encountered, gave him evidence of their 'rudeness and barbarity' by spitting in his face and pilfering his possessions, but they did not detain him. Indeed, the worst seemed over, he had begun to feel confident enough, as he enjoyed the touching hospitality of a Negro village, to imagine himself standing on the banks of the Niger, when a party of Moorish horseman rode in. They came with orders from the king to bring him to the royal residence of Benown. Fatima, the king's wife, had heard many stories about Christians and wished to see one for herself. There was no alternative but to submit.

Benown, reached four days later, was not a town but an encampment, made up of a large number of 'dirty-looking' tents, among which moved herds of camels, goats and cattle. It lay on the edge of the desert, 'a hot sandy country covered with small stunted shrubs'. There in a large tent Ali held his court. He was an old man with a long white beard, whose cruel sullen face showed that in character he was in no way superior to his subjects. He greeted the Christian with a savage practical joke, offering him a wild hog for his supper; Park prudently refused to touch a beast so repugnant to the devout Muslim. The next day Ali took him and set him in a hut with a hog tried to a stick as companion; round this novel spectacle the crowds gathered, 'the boys to beat the hog and the men and women to plague the Christian'. 'Never did any period of my life,' Park wrote afterwards, 'pass away so heavily; from sunrise to sunset I was obliged to suffer with an unruffled countenance the insults of the rudest savages on earth.'

And this was only the beginning. Day followed day, but Park could get no clue to his fate. Once he heard that the king had decided that the Christian's eyes should be pulled out, as they 'resembled those of a cat'; another time Ali himself told him that he would be free to leave as soon as Fatima, who was away from Benown, had returned and seen him. Escape was impossible in such a desolate country and at the hottest time of the year; in any case, he was too well guarded, and Ali had given orders that he was to be shot on sight if he attempted to leave the camp. After Park had been a few days in Benown, Johnson suddenly appeared, brought in under arrest from Jarra; he was not the most cheerful of companions, both he and Demba spending most of the day 'stretched upon the sand in a sort of torpid slumber'. Soon to the burden of monotony and discomfort were added the pains of hunger, for Ali's slaves sometimes forgot to bring them food, hunger which Park found was followed by such a feeling of weakness and lassitude that it became a littler easier to bear.

He had been a month in Benown when the camp was thrown into confusion by a report that the King of Bambara, angered by Ali's refusal to help him in the war against Kaarta, was marching on Ludamar. Hastily the Moors evacuated Benown and moved northwards to Bubaker, another camp where Fatima was staying. For Park the change was for the worse, the heat more intense, water more scarce. 'Day and night the wells were crowded with cattle, lowing and fighting each other to come at the troughs.' Park and his servants, not being allowed to draw water for themselves, were forced to go round begging a drink from the Negro slaves. One night, grown almost delirious with thirst, after pleading for water in vain all day, Park could relieve himself only by drinking with the cattle from their trough. And always there was the fear of a worse fate awaiting him, for soon with the start of the rains the Moors would begin their annual migration to the desert.

Suddenly after a month of this purgatory a ray of hope appeared. Park had received a few kindly gestures from the Queen Fatima and noted that she possessed great influence over her husband. Ali was planning to visit Jarra; through Fatima's intercession Park and his servants were given permission to accompany him. But before they reached Jarra, Demba was ordered to return to Bubaker, as Ali was now to be his master. 'Shocked beyond description at the idea of losing the poor boy,' Park hastened to Ali's tent; his passionate protest was received with a 'haughty air and malignant smile'. Would that he could have had the chance 'to rid the world of such a monster'!

At Jarra Park lodged with Daman, his former host. His attempts to secure Demba's release being of no avail, he felt himself justified in planning his own escape. In this he was aided by Ali's decision to return to Bubaker, leaving him at Jarra. But his situation was still desperate. He was determined to reach the Niger, but he would have to travel absolutely alone—Johnson thought only of returning to the

Cambia—without a guide and without the means of buying food, for the Moors had left him only his horse and a change of clothes. He decided to stay with Daman until the rains had broken and there were pools of water in the bush.

These plans were interrupted by a sudden crisis. An army from Kaarta was marching on Jarra. Fearful of being mistaken for a Moor and cut down in the confusion, Park joined the refugees who were streaming out of the town. With Daman and Johnson he settled in a village some distance away. Two days later a party of Moors appeared, led by Ali's chief slave; by getting two boys to eavesdrop on their conversation, Park learnt that they had come to take him back to the king. This news was a 'stroke of thunder'; there was no alternative but to escape at once.

That night, just before dawn, he mounted his horse—reduced during his captivity to 'a perfect Rosinante'—and slipped away. After travelling for a few hours a sudden halloo alarmed him. Three Moors, 'whooping and brandishing their double-barrelled guns', were galloping towards him. There could be no escape; hearing them say that he must return with them to Ali, Park noted that his sensation, faced with the very worst that could happen to him, was 'a sort of gloomy relief'. Suddenly, as they were riding back, his captors demanded the cloak that he was carrying. Having taken this garment, they dropped their hold and rode off. Their talk of Ali had been a bluff: they were simple robbers.

After this escape Park felt himself 'like one recovered from sickness'. 'I breathed freer; I found unusual lightness in my limbs; even the desert looked pleasant'—but not for long. After riding all morning through a flat and dismal landscape of bush and white sand, he found that his thirst had grown so unbearable that he was close to fainting. By sunset his horse seemed too exhausted to carry him. He stopped and painfully hauled himself up a high tree that was growing near by; the view that unrolled itself before him was as cheerless as that from the ground. As he climbed down, a wave of giddiness swept over him, he fell on the sand, feeling himself on the point of death. But the fainting fit lasted only a few minutes; coming to his senses, he summoned his strength and resolved to push on. Soon on the horizon he saw the lightning of an approaching storm; but it was sand, not rain that the wind brought first—so violent a sand-storm that he had to halt under a bush to prevent himself getting suffocated. At last the rain came too; he caught it in the only way possible by spreading out all his clothes until they were saturated, then sucking them avidly.

The next day he obtained some food from a charitable old woman in a Fulani village, but he had to spend two more nights in the bush, slaking his thirst in the pools of rain-water, tormented by mosquitoes and alarmed by the howling of wild beasts, until he reached a small town on the borders of Bambara. There his fortunes improved: the country fertile, the people curious but friendly, the headmen hospitable. For two weeks he travelled from town to town in the company of a party of refugees from Kaarta. Then at last, on July 20, 1796, seven and a half months after leaving Pisania, with the smoke over Segu, the capital of Bambara, clearly visible in the distance, as he and his Kaartan companions were riding over some marshy ground, one of them called out, 'See the water'. 'Looking forwards, I saw with infinite pleasure the great object of my mission—the long sought for majestic Niger, glittering to the morning sun, as broad as the Thames at Westminster, and flowing slowly *to the eastward*. I hastened to the brink and, having drunk of the water, lifted up my fervent thanks in prayer to the Great Ruler of all things for having thus far crowned my endeavours with success.' It is one of the great moments of African exploration. Though Park himself was by this time not surprised at the direction of the river, for he had made many inquiries about its course on his way, he admitted that on leaving England he had been 'in great hesitation on this subject and rather believed that it ran in a contrary direction'. Many geographers had thought the same; now on this point there could be no further doubt. But on reaching the Niger, Park's mission was only half completed; Timbuktu and Housa remained as his goal.

The city of Segu which he was now approaching was one of the largest in the Western Sudan. It lay on either side of the river, a great concourse of canoes plying between the two banks. High walls surrounded it; behind them stood fine mud-built houses, many white-washed, some two stories high. The population of the city Park reckoned to be thirty thousand. Around it there lay a densely cultivated countryside, so that the view which he saw before him 'formed altogether a prospect of civilization and magnificence which I little expected to find in the bosom of Africa'.

Mansong, the King of Bambara, had his palace on the opposite side of the river; he had heard of the white man's approach and sent one of his officials to tell the stranger that he would not be allowed into the city until the king had learnt the purpose of his visit. The next day Park was told by the villagers among whom he had spent the night that the king had spent much time in discussing his case and that the Moors and the Gambian traders had been engaged in stirring up suspicion against him. The traders' attitude, Park realized, was by no means unreasonable; he had said that he had come simply to see the great river, yet who could believe that any man would have faced such difficulties to look at something—were not all rivers much the same?—he could see just as well in his own country? Was it not more likely that the white man had been sent by his people to gather information which would help them to gather all the trade of the country into their own hands? By entertaining Park, Mansong would only have provoked a domestic crisis. So, after three days of indecision, he sent a messenger to say that the white man must leave immediately; he tempered this command by making him a present of five thousand cowries, sufficient to buy fifty days' provisions. The king, in Park's own opinion, had wisely combined generosity with prudence.

From Segu Park travelled on for a week to Silla, another town on the Niger. There he was forced to recognize that he could go no farther. The rains were at their height; the Niger was in flood; a canoe was the only practicable form of transport—and he lacked the means to hire one. Nights spent on the mosquito-infested ground near the river had brought on a sharp attack of malaria. Finally—and this was decisive—Timbuktu was reliably reported to be in the hands of those 'merciless fanatics', the Moors. Were he to travel on and lose his life, all that he had discovered would perish with him.

The first days of his return journey provided a clear indication of the difficulties still to be overcome. The roads, in the heavy rains, were almost impassable. In one village he was marooned by a heavy downpour for three days. Elsewhere he had to struggle to pull his horse through swamps where the water reached his chest—always tired, usually hungry, sometimes dazed with fever. Meanwhile a report had gone about Bambara that he was a spy; many headmen refused to receive him; he was forced to keep away from Segu and seek lodging only in the more remote villages. Beyond Segu it was necessary to decide on his route to the sea. Clearly it was impossible to go back the way he had come; by crossing the Niger and striking south, he might reach the Gold Coast—but this would involve travelling through completely unknown country, among tribes whose language he would not understand; the only alternative was to follow the Niger upstream and then strike westwards. So he came to Bamako, now the capital of the Republic of Mali, then only a 'middling town', though a wealthy trading centre; there a Gambian merchant advised him to leave the river and travel to the west.

Two days later, while passing through a lonely country of steep and rocky hills, he was set upon by a band of robbers. They took away his horse and left him only the clothes in which he stood—and his hat, whose crown was stuffed with his precious notes. 'After they were gone, I sat for some time looking around me with amazement and terror. Whichever way I turned, nothing appeared but danger and difficulty. I saw myself in the middle of a vast wilderness in the depth of the rainy season, naked and alone; surrounded by savage animals and men still more savage. I was five hundred miles from the nearest European settlement. All these circumstances crowded at once on my recollection; and I confess that my spirits began to fail me. I considered my fate as certain and that I had no alternative but to lie down and perish.' It was the nadir of his fortunes. Suddenly his eye was caught by 'the extraordinary beauty of a small moss'; if this in its perfection was proof of the Divine care, 'how could that Being . . . look with unconcern upon the situation and sufferings of creatures formed after His own image?' Strengthened by this reflection, he travelled on.

His trust in Providence was not misplaced. At the next town the headman received him with great kindness, straightaway took steps to recover his stolen property and helped him to get accommodation in a neighbouring village. But now the fever, which he had felt ever since the start of the rains, attacked him with extreme violence; moreover, the country to which he had come was afflicted with famine. As soon as his stolen goods had been discovered—the horse, now useless in its emaciation, he gave away, but the spare clothes were essential, for his only shirt was worn as thin as muslin—weak though he was, he decided to push on.

Seven days later he reached the small town of Kamalia, where he was introduced to a Gambian trader, Karfa Taura. For Karfa so far different was this ragged stranger with his long beard and his skin yellowed by fever from the white men he had known on the coast that he doubted whether he could be a European; but Park was able to prove his identity when Karfa produced a small volume that was none other than a Book of Common Prayer. Then Karfa offered him all the assistance in his power, pointed out that it would be absolutely impossible for him to travel on alone across the wilderness that lay ahead, and suggested that he stay in Kamalia until the end of the rains, when he would be able to join the caravan he himself would be taking to the Gambia. 'As for payment,' Karfa added, 'wait until you are safely in the Gambia and give me whatever seems to you proper.' 'Thus,' wrote Park, 'was I delivered by the friendly care of this benevolent Negro from a situation truly deplorable.'

Deplorable indeed: for there can be little doubt that had Park travelled on alone he would have died. Shortly after his arrival in Kamalia he suffered another violent attack of fever. For five weeks he lay in his hut, passing 'the lingering hours in a very gloomy and solitary manner'. But as the rains drew to an end the fever gradually abated, yet left him so weak he could hardly stand. His convalescence was aided by 'the benevolent and simple manners of the Negroes and the perusal of Karfa's little volume'.

Park stayed in Kamalia from September to April; this intimate experience of African life enabled him to gather much information of an anthropological nature. Part of his time was spent in the house of a gentle-mannered Muslim schoolteacher; by his host's love of reading, by the pleasure he derived from teaching and by the responsiveness of his students Park was deeply impressed. How wonderful, he could not help reflecting, would be the effect of an 'easy introduction to Christianity' translated into Arabic and 'elegantly produced'; distributed at various points along the coast, it might become 'one of the school books of Africa' and so dispel many of the erroneous ideas held by African Muslims about European Christians.

At last after many delays—*losing time*, so Park discovered, was a European rather than an African concept—Karfa's caravan was ready to set out. The slaves to be sold numbered thirty-five, mostly Kaartan prisoners captured by the Bambaran army and sent down the river for sale. Some bore their fate with 'amazing fortitude'; the majority, though not badly treated, sat all day 'in a sort of sullen melancholy with their eyes fixed upon the ground'. They plied Park with questions about the fate of black men across the salt water; many of them were convinced that the white men were cannibals and bought slaves only to devour them later. When he told them that they would be set to work in the fields, one of them asked him, 'Have you really got such ground as this to set your feet upon?' As the journey proceeded, Park's respect for his wretched companions

241

grew deeper; often, quite of their own accord, they would bring him water to drink and collect branches for his bed and 'amidst their own infinitely greater sufferings' commiserate his own.

The distance from Kamalia to the coast was about five hundred miles; the journey was made in two months. The caravan passed through territory which Park had not seen before, much of it uninhabited; each town in this region was independent, for there were no states here comparable to Bondou or Bambara. Fortunately the land was at peace and the caravan passed unmolested on its way; but it was a long, tough journey made at the hottest time of year, with short rations and across difficult country. At last, on June 11, 1797, after an absence of eighteen months Park reached Pisania, where Laidley received him 'as one risen from the dead', for it had been widely rumoured that he had been murdered by the Moors. To Karfa Park gave a present of goods to the value of two prime slaves, double the amount he had originally promised him; the good trader, 'overpowered by this unexpected token of gratitude', parted from him 'with great tenderness'.

Six months later Park arrived in England. Early on Christmas morning he reached London. No news of his coming had gone before him. Not wishing to disturb his relations at such an early hour, he strolled the streets until he came to the gardens of the British Museum, of which his brother-in-law had charge; seeing one of the gates open, he walked inside. By chance James Dickson had gone to the gardens early that morning and so saw coming towards him in the dull light of a December dawn what in the first moment must have seemed an apparition, his wife's young brother, mourned as dead, two years having passed without news of him. It was a nicely dramatic ending to Park's great adventure.

PARK'S ACHIEVEMENT

To the members of the African Association, and especially to Sir Joseph Banks, Park's return must have been a matter of scarcely less rejoicing than it was to his relatives. At last the time and money spent during the past ten years was seen to have been truly justified; at last an English traveller had penetrated deep into the heart of Africa and conclusively solved one of the great riddles of African geography. It was necessary now to get Park's discoveries down in print as soon as possible. Beaufoy, the Association's able Secretary, had died in 1795; as so often in voluntary societies, it proved difficult to find a replacement, and for two years Banks had acted as Secretary. But in 1797 a gentleman named Bryan Edwards agreed to take on the post. Edwards had spent most of his life in the West Indies. He was a man of considerable means and scholarly attainments, being the author of an excellent history of the West Indies. In 1796 he had entered Parliament, where he soon made a name for himself as one of the most vigorous opponents of the Abolitionists. During the early months of 1798 Edwards and Park were closeted together to prepare an abstract of the latter's travels, while Rennell worked on the geographical significance of the new discoveries. Their combined work was then printed for the members of the Association.

In the summer of 1798 Park was free to visit his family in Scotland, but he was back in London that autumn in order to start writing a longer and more personal account of his travels, again in collaboration with Edwards. Meanwhile Banks had suggested to Park a cherished project of his own for the exploration of Australia, a project which Park appeared to welcome. On his return from Scotland, however, he told Banks that he had changed his mind. He gave as reason the lowness of the salary offered him: 'pecuniary concerns,' he wrote to Banks, 'however contemptible in themselves serve as a good criterion by which to estimate the importance or inutility of any office or pursuit.' This may not have been the real reason; Dickson, who found his brother-in-law very 'close' about the whole matter, told Banks that his wife thought a love-affair had been the cause of his decision. Banks was exceedingly chagrined by his withdrawal and referred to Park in a letter to a third party as 'that fickle Scotsman'. The quarrel, of interest in the light it throws on the character of the two men, was only a temporary estrangement. Within a month Edwards, who had commiserated with Banks on Park's 'fickle and perverse conduct', was writing to tell of the good progress he was now making with his book. In the earlier chapters Edwards gave Park some help in arranging his materials; but in January he could write to Banks: 'Park goes on triumphantly—he improves in his style so much by practice that his journal now requires little correction; and some parts which he has lately sent to me are equal to anything in the English language.'[1]

Park's book appeared in the spring of 1799. It achieved all that he can have desired: it established his fame for posterity and it secured him a nice pot of money. The first edition consisted of 1,500 copies at one and a half guineas each; it sold out within a week and was quickly followed by a second and a third edition. Authors' royalties were more generous in that age; George Nicol, his publisher, told Banks that on the first edition alone Park could expect a thousand guineas 'clear profit'. To this considerable sum, which later editions must have doubled, Park could add his accumulated salary from the African Association, continued until May 1799 in order to allow him the opportunity to finish his book; the total salary amounted to £774 15s.[2]

Even before his book appeared, Park had experienced the consequences of fame, moving as Sir Joseph's protégé through the salons and dinner parties of London society. It was not an experience he seems to have relished; nor does he seem to have made a particularly good impression. That formidable young hostess, Lady Holland, wrote in her diary after meeting him: 'He has neither fancy nor genius and if he does fib, it is dully'—a waspishly intellectual comment. Another lady, more romantically inclined, felt that he had 'the manners and dignities of his Niger kings'. His conversation is recorded as being 'neither animated or remarkable'. Indeed, to all but his intimates he appeared to present 'a cold and reserved exterior'. The tall, aloof, obviously disdainful young man moving uneasily through the drawing-rooms of the London aristocracy: it is a strange, yet convincing contrast to the African explorer, dirty, ragged, bearded, the friend of slaves, the protégé of a slave-dealer. With such memories behind him one can understand Park's attitude to high society.[3]

Before Park returned to Scotland he was present at the Association's General Meeting held on May 25, 1799. Bryan Edwards was ill and unable to attend; Banks took his place and delivered to the members a lengthy report, of which fortunately a verbatim account exists. His speech was an exceedingly remarkable one; indeed, it deserves to be regarded as one of the most significant utterances of the age, for it gives expression to the idea, never before conceived, that the English should establish themselves in the interior of Africa. Here indeed one finds oneself watching the dawn of modern imperialism in the least known of the great continents.[4]

'We have already,' Banks declared, 'by Mr Park's means opened a Gate into the Interior of Africa into which it is easy for every nation to enter and to extend its Commerce and Discovery from the West to the Eastern side of that immense continent.' The distance between the Gambia and the Niger was comparatively short; five hundred chosen troops 'would soon make the road easy'. If two hundred of them armed with field guns were to embark on the Niger they would be able to overcome 'the whole Forces which Africa could bring against them'.

What an opportunity lay here. The Moorish trade was already reckoned to be worth a million pounds a year; much of this trade was in gold *dust*. 'If Science,' Banks suggested, 'should teach these ignorant savages that Gold which is Dust at the mouth of a river must be . . . in the form of Pebbles when near the place from whence it was originally washed . . . is it not probable that the Golden Harvest that they are already in the habit of gathering might be increased a hundredfold?' 'As increased Riches,' he continued, 'still increase the wants of the Possessors, and as Our Manufacturers are able to supply them, is not this prospect, of at once attaching to this country the whole of the Interior Trade now possessed by the Moors, with the chance of an incalculable future increase, worth some exertion and some expense to a Trading Nation?'

It would require an outlay of £30,000 a year for four or five years, Banks reckoned, in order to establish British merchants in forts on the banks of the great river. He ended with a plea for urgent action. 'If this Country delays much longer to possess themselves of the Treasures laid open to them by the exertions of this Association, some Rival Nation will take possession of the banks of the Joliba [Niger] and assert by arms the right of Prior possession.'*

These were stirring words. Park had his own to add to them, for he assured members that although he was now returning to Scotland, he would hold himself in readiness at all times to proceed again to the Niger, should Government 'think fit to establish a colony on its banks'. How exciting it must have been to have found oneself at such a meeting! With what elation the members must have phrased and voted on the accompanying motion!—a motion that required the Committee 'to take into its consideration the Plan of appointing a Consul for the District of Senegambia; and sending there a sufficient force to take possession of the banks of the Joliba, and explore the Interior from thence'. Several years were to pass before the consequences of this motion were revealed.

As for Park, it is clear that Africa still retained its lure, however

* Park had reported that the name given to the Niger by the people of Bambara was *Joliba*, 'the great water'.

245

cruel the scars it had inflicted, for his privations left him afflicted with 'an inveterate dyspepsia', and his sleep was troubled by hideous nightmares from which he would awake shuddering, believing himself still in the hands of the savage Moors. Nevertheless, for the present there was no call upon his services. So he went back home to Scotland. There in the summer of 1799 he married Ailie Anderson, the daughter of his old mentor, the surgeon of Selkirk.

Before taking leave of Park for a while, it is worth trying to make a sober appraisal of his achievement on his first journey, and of the book in which he recorded his experiences. One stresses the word *sober*, for Park was to be turned, during the course of the nineteenth century, into one of the textbook heroes of British history, and his book, continuously in print ever since its first publication, into a classic of adventure; adulation is not conducive to exact appreciation. Thus among West African explorers he has come to secure a pre-eminence that his achievements do not absolutely justify. During the next eighty years others were to make even longer journeys through unknown country, others to provide much greater contributions to Europe's knowledge of the interior, others to face dangers as numerous and as great, others to show much greater ingenuity in disarming suspicion—yet how many schoolboys have ever heard of Hornemann and of Burckhardt, of Denham and Clapperton, of the brothers Lander, of Laing and of Caillié, of Barth, of Nachtigal and of Rohlfs? and how many general readers have ever found it possible to procure their works, most of which were never reprinted? But this is a dissatisfying exercise; the historian's job is to understand, not to award celestial examination marks. Better to turn to a practical question: could Park have achieved more than he did? could he have avoided some of the hardships he found himself having to face?

Looking back on his journey, it is clear that the crucial event was the war between Kaarta and Bambara. Had the war not broken out, Park would have avoided the disastrous détour he was forced to make through Ludamar. But even if he had reached Segu more easily and been received by Mansong in person, would he have been able to travel farther down the Niger than the point he actually reached? Travel by land along the course of the river for any considerable distance would have been virtually impossible because of the increasingly marshy nature of the country; but since in any circumstances he would have reached Segu almost penniless, travel by river would have been equally impossible, for he would have lacked the means of hiring a canoe or paying for paddlers. Even if he had been able to overcome these difficulties, he would still have had to face the Moors of Jenne and of Timbuktu; the experience of later travellers provides no evidence to suggest that they would have treated him more lightly than their compatriots of Ludamar had done. In reaching Silla, Park had indeed touched the utmost limit of the possible and revealed in so doing quite exceptional powers of resolution.

As to the manner in which he travelled, the experience of later explorers suggests that had he adopted a different attitude in matters of dress and language and stressed his own profession as a doctor, he might have incurred less hardship. One suspects that it would have gone against his principles to have disguised himself as a Muslim, as Hornemann, Burckhardt and Caillié so successfully were to do. But it would surely have been an advantage if he had adopted native dress from the start, and so rendered his appearance less conspicuous. When he set out he possessed a considerable knowledge of Mandingo, and he must have acquired greater fluency in the course of his travels; but it would have paid him, especially when he was in Moorish hands, to have possessed some knowledge of Arabic and to have shown a greater understanding of Islam. Finally, it is curious to observe that although he was trained as a doctor, he should make no mention of ever practising his profession on his journey; had he effected a few simple cures, he would have added greatly to his own prestige and might have secured a warmer welcome in some of the towns and villages in which he stayed. Travelling avowedly as a Christian and a European, possessing no obvious skills or knowledge, with an object before him incomprehensible to his African hosts, Park could not possibly avoid exciting suspicion.*

Of the book in which he recounted his adventures, Park himself provided the most disarming appreciation. 'As a composition,' he wrote in the Preface, 'it has nothing to recommend it but *truth*. It is a plain unvarnished tale, without pretensions of any kind, except that it claims to enlarge, in some degree, the circle of African geo-

---

* Among those who found themselves mystified by Park's purpose was the friendly merchant Karfa, especially when he had seen something of European wealth and manners in Dr Laidley's house. 'He would ask me with great seriousnesss,' Park wrote, 'what could possibly induce me, who was no trader, to think of exploring so miserable a country as Africa.'

graphy.' Unlike some other African explorers, Bruce or Denham or John Lander or, in a later age, Richard Burton or Mary Kingsley, Park was not a man of literary inclinations. He was no master of the brilliant phrase, the sudden, illuminating image that brings a scene to life and engraves it on the memory; he never acquired the skill of presenting a character in the round, with the result that one remembers hardly any of the individuals he met on his journey; nor does he ever attempt to dramatise his story, to introduce into his narrative that tension of excitement that makes a reader want to gallop from page to page. Given such a subject, his book is in some ways a little dull. Yet at the same time one can praise his style for dignity, precision and restraint, his composition for its shape and brevity: Park's *Travels* is indeed the shortest of the great narratives of African exploration—this may be one reason for its success. But, above all, the modern reader with an interest in Africa should admire the book for its truthfulness: it is a model of exact observation. For many of his contemporaries, and indeed for many later readers, it must have been their first book on Africa; few others provide so clear and well balanced an account of African life. And here one should note the excellence of those chapters in which he describes the manner of life of the Moors and the Mandingos; they make it clear that Park had the capacity to become a first-rate anthropologist—one cannot make the same claim for all his successors.

His observations were made under conditions of exceptional difficulty and hardship. Indeed, it would not have been surprising if he had developed a grudge against Africans for the sufferings he had met with at their hands; yet his attitude throughout his book is both generous and understanding. Discussing the Mandingos' 'insurmountable propensity' to steal from him nis few possessions, he suggests that 'before we pronounce them a more depraved people than any other, it were well to consider whether the lower order of people in any part of Europe would have acted, under similar circumstances with greater honesty towards a stranger, than the Negroes acted towards me'. The laws of the country gave him no protection, the goods he carried were as valuable to a Negro as gold or diamonds would have been to a European: 'Let us suppose a black merchant of Hindostan to have found his way into the centre of England with a box of jewels at his back, and that the laws of the country afforded him no security; in such a case, the wonder would be, not that the stranger was robbed of any part of his riches, but that any part was left for a second depredator.' Moreover, if some had robbed him, others had treated him kindly: 'It is impossible for me to forget the disinterested charity and tender solicitude with which many of these poor heathens sympathized with me in my sufferings, relieved my distresses, and contributed to my safety.' Among the men 'the hardness of avarice' and 'the blindness of bigotry' had sometimes 'closed up the avenues to compassion', 'but I do not recollect a single instance of hard-heartedness towards me in the women'; 'in all my wanderings and wretchedness, I found them uniformly kind and compassionate'.

These sensible and humane judgements must have been welcomed by the friends of Africa in Europe; but on one important subject Park fell sharply foul of the liberal opinion of his day. One of the most interesting chapters of his book is entitled 'Observations concerning the state and sources of slavery in Africa'. After discussing the different ways in which slaves were obtained—especially through warfare between states—and pointing to the antiquity of the practice, he ends with the challenging and unequivocal assertion 'that in the present unenlightened state of their minds' the effect of abolishing the European slave trade would 'neither be so extensive or beneficial as many wise and worthy people fondly expect'. Though provocatively expressed, this was a shrewd judgement; the state of much of the Western and Central Sudan, devastated by slave-raiders long after the trade on the coast had been abolished, would serve convincingly to support it. But made at a time when the controversy on the trade was at its height, Park's statement came inevitably to be seized on by supporters of the trade as clear evidence in their favour; while to the Abolitionists it seemed that Park had been completely led astray under the malign influence of Bryan Edwards. In fact, Park had seen enough of Africa at first hand to appreciate that there could be no glib and easy solution of its problems.

To courage and to resolution Park added, then, intelligence and magnanimity. There have been many men, brave, wise and good, whose lives have never entered the chronicles of history; but Park's story in its bare outline was peculiarly fitted to appeal to the popular imagination. He was the first European in modern times to penetrate deep into the interior of unknown Africa, he was young, he went alone, he suffered greatly, he achieved in reaching the Niger one great thing—and he lived to face a tragic sequel. Not unfittingly, therefore, he stands as one of the archetypes of an explorer.

249

III

THE APPROACH FROM THE NORTH
1797-1802

FREDERICK HORNEMANN

THE AFRICAN ASSOCIATION, EVEN before any definite news had been received of Park's progress, had decided to accept the services of another explorer. Now, with Park safely home, the attention of members could concentrate on the latest of their 'emissaries', a young German named Frederick Hornemann. One may wonder how a German came to be engaged by an English society; the story provides yet another indication of the value of the international prestige enjoyed by Sir Joseph Banks.

In 1791 Professor Blumenbach, that eminent scientist whose interest in Africa has already been described, paid his first visit to England. From Banks, to whom he was already well known, he must have received an enthusiastic account of the African Association; on his return to Göttingen, Blumenbach did everything in his power to ensure that the work of the Association should come to the notice of his countrymen. Among those who read the Association's reports most avidly was young Hornemann. He had been born in 1772, the son of a Lutheran pastor in the North German town of Hildesheim. In 1791 he came to Göttingen to study theology, spent three years at the University and left to take up a teaching post. In 1795 he returned to Göttingen to seek out Blumenbach, whom he had never met personally before; he told him that he had decided to offer his services to the African Association and asked for an introduction to Sir Joseph Banks. In a sense this was a decision that he had been working towards all his life. At an early age he had developed a passionate desire to see the unknown parts of the world; at school he had fascinated his fellows with stories about tropical

250

lands, drawn from the books he had read; at the university he had devoted his spare time to gathering information about Africa. Blumenbach soon realized that his visitor was of the stuff from which explorers are made. To his knowledge and his single-mindedness he added other valuable qualities: he was very tough—'a young robust man of an athletic bodily constitution', so Blumenbach described him in a letter to Banks—keeping himself in good shape by regular exercises and long rambles through the woods and over the hills of his native land; he was clever with his hands; he had a cheerful, friendly manner and got on well with people of every class; he was devoted to his widowed mother and scrupulous in money-matters. Blumenbach agreed to give him all the support in his power.[1]

By the spring of 1796 Hornemann had drawn up a plan of action to submit to the African Association. He would start from Cairo and accompany a caravan to Murzuk in the Fezzan; there he expected to meet the two Shereefs, whom Lucas had found so helpful; with their assistance he would travel southwards across the desert to Katsina, which he made his goal. In order to prepare himself fully for the task ahead, he was anxious to spend a few months in Göttingen. Blumenbach, in a covering letter to Banks, explained that Hornemann would spend his time 'principally with our Orientalists for the Arabian language, with our mathematicians and astronomers'; he would also acquire 'some necessary practical knowledge of Domestic Medicine and Surgery and employ a part of the time in perfectioning [sic] himself still more in drawing'. Blumenbach himself 'would furnish him with notices of natural history', while his brother-in-law, Heyne, the Professor of Classics, and Heyne's son-in-law, Heeren, a brilliant young historian, would also contribute to his education.* This was an eminently practical programme designed to leave Hornemann better equipped than any of his predecessors in the Association's service; nor would it involve a heavy expense, for £8 a month was reckoned to be sufficient for his needs during his stay in Göttingen. These proposals were considered and accepted by the Association's Committee on June 3.[2]

---

* Heeren was one of the pioneers in the study of social and economic history; he developed a special interest in North Africa and published in the 1820s a study of *The Politics, Intercourse and Trade of the Carthaginians, Ethiopians and Egyptians*. This was the greatest work on the historical geography of North Africa that the nineteenth century produced; it may still be read with pleasure for its fine scholarship and lucid presentation.

Nine months later Hornemann arrived in London. On March 20, 1797, he was introduced to the Committee and received his instructions and his conditions of service: he was to be paid an annuity of £200 a year for five years, his expenses during his stay in London and on his journey being met by the Association, together with the cost of certain basic pieces of equipment, including a telescope and a watch. Hornemann requested that £60 of his salary be sent direct every year to his mother.[3]

One serious practical difficulty remained. To reach Egypt it was necessary to travel through France; but with the war raging, passports were almost impossible to obtain. Fortunately Sir Joseph Banks was probably the only man in England who possessed the right sort of influence. It was his fervent belief that there should exist 'during the horrors of a war unprecedented in the mutual implacability of the parties engaged, an unconditional armistice for science'. This view he had put forward to the Government in the course of an incident that afforded a remarkable proof of his magnanimity, when he arranged, at no little cost to himself, for the return to France of the valuable collection of plants made by the French botanist, Labillardière, captured while on expedition to the East Indies. Now, with Charretié, the French commissioner in London responsible for the exchange of prisoners, acting as intermediary, Banks was able to obtain the sanction of the French Government for Hornemann's journey.[4]

Inevitably these negotiations took time, and Hornemann was impatient to get off. 'The naked Majesty of an African state will certainly have more interest for me than Great Britain in all its glory,' so he wrote to Heeren on June 26, a few days before his departure. By the middle of July he was in Paris. Banks had given him an introduction to his friend, Lalande, a distinguished astronomer. No young explorer at the start of his travels could have enjoyed so gratifying a reception: in the ten days he spent in Paris Hornemann attended a meeting of the recently founded *Institut National*—the republican counterpart to the Royal Society, made the acquaintance of many distinguished men of science and was put in touch with consular officials with experience of North Africa. But the most fruitful of his encounters was not with a Frenchman, but with a Turkish gentleman from Tripoli, Muhammad D'Ghies. This was a contact of inestimable importance, for D'Ghies was not only one of the most influential men in his own country but also well disposed to help European travellers. 'Never shall I forget,' Hornemann told Banks, 'the kindness and complaisance of this bearded Gentleman.' D'Ghies was strongly critical of his plan to go to Cairo and told him that if he wished to reach the interior of Africa 'the only possible and the most easy way for a Christian was by Tripoli and Fezzan'; he offered to send Hornemann 'by his recommendation so secure to Fezzan as he thought to travel from here to Marseilles'. Tempting though this offer must have seemed, Hornemann felt himself bound to follow the letter of his instructions; but he was able to obtain from D'Ghies a cordial letter of recommendation to one of his friends in Cairo, a man who knew many of the merchants from the interior. 'I think it is good and favourable,' Hornemann wrote in his letter to Banks, 'to make the acquaintance of Mohammedans by Mohammedans.'[5]

By the middle of September Hornemann was in Alexandria. He was received by Baldwin, the British Consul, and passed on to Rossetti, the chargé-d'affaires in Cairo. After staying for a few weeks with Rossetti, Hornemann moved to the Catholic convent, threw himself into the study of Arabic with a Greek Catholic priest as his teacher and set about gathering information on the interior. Before the year was out he had made another valuable acquaintance, a German from Cologne, named Joseph Frendenburgh. Ten years earlier, in circumstances that Hornemann does not relate, Frendenburgh had been forced to become a Muslim; by now, having become fluent in Arabic and in Turkish, and performed the pilgrimage three times, he had become perfectly accepted in Muslim society. Hornemann had originally engaged Frendenburgh only as an interpreter, since the latter was talking of returning to Germany; but a friendship developed between the two of them and Frendenburgh agreed to accompany Hornemann to Murzuk as his servant.[6]

It must have been during the course of his conversations with Frendenburgh that Hornemann hit upon a brilliant idea, never before adopted: he would pass himself off as a Muslim. At first sight the plan seemed outrageously daring; but on closer inspection it appeared perfectly feasible. Dress: this was the least of difficulties— soon after his arrival in Cairo Hornemann had described himself to Banks as being 'dressed as a very Turk'. Complexion: the presence in Cairo of Turks and Mamluks, some of European descent, had accustomed the population to light-skinned Muslims. Language: he had not yet achieved fluency in Arabic, but any Muslim who had performed the pilgrimage would know that there were many devout members of the faith who could not speak Arabic correctly. Circumcision: the merchants with whom he would travel were men of too much delicacy to demand ocular proof of this operation.[7]

During the spring of 1798 Hornemann made contact, possibly through D'Ghies's friend, with a party of merchants who were preparing to set out for the Fezzan. He was never to write down a detailed account of his adventures, and so his experiences during the next few months are a little confusing to follow, but it seems that at this stage he had not definitely decided to adopt a Muslim disguise. A cataclysmic turn of events forced this line of action upon him. In April there was a serious outbreak of plague in Cairo; the merchants of the Fezzan caravan scattered, while Hornemann adopted the only precaution possible, shutting himself up in his house for days on end until the epidemic had run its course. No sooner had this threat abated than Hornemann found himself facing an even greater danger. At the beginning of July news reached Cairo that an army of infidels—it was in fact Bonaparte's Egyptian Expedition—had landed at Alexandria. The population of Cairo had always been notorious for their fanatical hostility to Europeans; here was a shock to goad them into frenzy. To prevent a massacre the Turkish authorities humanely decided to intern all Europeans, Hornemann among them, in the castle until the French arrived. At the end of July the French Army entered Cairo, and Hornemann was released. But his plans were shattered; not only were his banking arrangements dislocated (he could, of course, achieve nothing without sufficient funds), but as an unprotected European he had to face the danger of a sudden murderous knife-thrust—many French soldiers died that way—whenever he moved out of doors. The first difficulty was the easier one to surmount. Bonaparte had brought with him to Egypt a remarkable team of *savants*; it was to the leaders of this party, the scientists Berthollet and Monge, both members of the *Institut National*, that Hornemann, given confidence by his reception in Paris, now introduced himself. They welcomed him cordially and immediately brought him to the notice of their young commander. Bonaparte was much impressed by Hornemann's courage, but, like all other Europeans who knew of his plans, thought his project a mad one. 'The most hideous spectacle of savage man it is possible to imagine,' so he had described the Bedouin in one of his despatches to the Directory; it was through country terrorized by these ferocious tribes that Hornemann would have to make his way. But since he was determined to set out, Bonaparte agreed to help him in every way he could, gave him a passport to take him through the French pickets, offered to forward any of his letters to the African Association in London and allowed his officers to help him procure the funds —he took with him the considerable sum of £312—that he needed.[8]

Of the other side of his life in Cairo during these last weeks, he wrote little more than one cryptic sentence. 'When I took advantage of the disturbances in Cairo and its environs to get introduced as a Mahommedan to the caravan, I could not indeed speak readily either Turkish or Arabic; but in this I flattered myself that the assumed character of a young Mameluke might be my excuse.' 'I regard the day of my departure,' he wrote to the Secretary of the African Association, 'as a day of great festival, because I have had to overcome more obstacles than I would care to describe, especially during the last three months.' His movements in that time one can only attempt to imagine, the subterfuge, the careful covering of former traces, the anxious recital of an invented story, the knowledge that a single slip could set a crowd of fanatics baying for his blood. But for a vivid impression of the background to his adventures there exists a description of Cairo in the August of that extraordinary summer written in the diary of a French Army officer, Brigadier General Detroye.[9]

In my daily walks I realize more and more that everything here tires the senses of a European. Leaving Cairo on the Suez side, one finds an arid, white desert; fine sand and a burning wind obscure the vision and interfere with breathing; a smell of rotting corpses offends the nostrils. The Bedouins' huts spread over the plain remind you of the lot of so many of your compatriots—an early assassination. . . . Returning to Cairo, what is there to see? Narrow streets, unpaved and dirty; houses in ruins and of sombre appearance; public buildings like prisons, shops like stables, an atmosphere heavy with dust and dirt; blind men, one-eyed men, bearded men covered with rags, crowded together in the streets or sitting down, their pipes in their mouths, like monkeys in the opening of a den; a few of the women of the people, in other countries nature's masterpieces, here hideous and disgusting, concealing skinny bodies beneath stinking rags and showing hanging breasts through the rents of their clothing; yellow and sickly children, covered with sores and eaten by flies; an insupportable odour resulting from the dirtiness of the dwellings, the stirring up of the dust, and the frying of bad oil in the unventilated bazaars. After this stroll, you go into the house you are living in; you will find no comfortable arrangement of rooms and no room pleasant to be in. Flies and gnats and a thousand insects are waiting to take possession of you during the night. Wringing wet with perspiration, exhausted with fatigue, you pass the time of repose in martyrdom to rashes and itching. You get up fit for nothing, swollen-eyed, exhausted, with a nasty taste in the mouth and spots or rather ulcers all over the body, to face a day that will be a repetition of the one before.

Living in circumstances such as these, Hornemann's strict adherence to his instructions reveals a quite exceptional degree of courage and of resolution.[10]

So, at the beginning of September 1798, Hornemann set out with the caravan for the Fezzan, taking for himself the name Yusuf, a Muslim, a Mamluk, a merchant, travelling in some style with a train of camels under the care of his servant Frendenburgh. The worst was over; but difficulties still remained. It was essential to conceal his ignorance of the etiquette of a caravan; yet on the very first evening he committed a *faux pas*, sitting idle while his dragoman prepared the meal, behaviour which brought down on him the reproaches of an elderly Arab and a lecture on the virtues of self-reliance in desert travel. He took the lesson to heart and won favour in the future by helping in every way he could.[11]

The dreaded Bedouin did not prove the danger his European friends had predicted. One of their bands was sighted; it did not molest the caravan. Later came grisly evidence—the track lined with the corpses of dead camels—of the robbers' depredations; again the caravan escaped attack. Hornemann's most alarming experience arose in another way; he had not thought himself completely into his disguise. During the caravan's lengthy halt at Siwa, the famous oasis visited by another European traveller, W. G. Browne, five years previously, he came close to betraying himself by his interest in the ruins of what he rightly suspected to be the great temple of Jupiter Ammon.* 'You are unquestionably still a Christian,' a group of Siwans told him after watching him making sketches and taking measurements, 'or why else should you come so often to visit these works of infidels.' Worse was to follow.

A few days later, after they had left the oasis, the caravan was overtaken by a party of a hundred Siwans mounted on asses. Their intentions were perfectly friendly, the newcomers declared, they had come to protect the caravan against a possible Bedouin attack. The caravan halted; the merchants conferred with the Siwans; Horne-mann, suspecting nothing, sat down on his baggage, but sent

* For W. G. Browne's visit to Siwa, p. 277.

Fredenburgh over to see what the conference was about. After some time Fredenburgh returned, looking very frightened. 'We are both lost,' he told Hornemann, 'the Siwans have accused us of being Christians and spies.' Immediately he began to fumble in his baggage for the fire-arms. 'Don't be a fool,' Hornemann replied, 'put your gun away. If you behave like that, you will only confirm their suspicions. In any case you yourself have nothing to worry about, everyone knows you are a Muslim.'

For Hornemann there was only one thing to do. With a magnificently cool show of courage he went over to the assembly and greeted the Siwans; they did not return his salutation, but straightway accused him, saying, 'You are one of the new Christians from Cairo come to explore our country.' Hornemann paid no attention to these remarks, but sat down and turned to address one of the chiefs who had often visited him in his tent: 'For ten days we dwelt in your midst as friends; yet now you pursue us with a hundred armed men. Do you not know that it is a great sin to tell one of the faithful that he is an infidel?' The chief, impressed by the young man's assurance, replied that he himself had never accused him; but some of his followers still muttered their suspicions. 'Hold your tongues,' Hornemann burst out, 'why if I could speak Arabic better, I would ask you enough questions to prove that you are less well instructed in the faith than I am.' 'But what about the papers,' they replied, 'the papers the infidels have written?' It was then that Hornemann realized how their suspicions had been aroused; Frendenburgh must have unwittingly shown them one of the passports they had received from the French. It was useless to disguise the papers, so Hornemann went to his baggage to fetch them; he returned with the passports and a Koran, Frendenburgh, who had by now recovered his nerve, accompanying him. 'Can anyone here read them?' the chief of the Siwans asked, looking at the passports. 'Can you,' he turned to Hornemann, 'say what it contains?' Hornemann shook his head. 'We were told only that it would allow us to leave Cairo in peace,' he replied—'but this,' Frendenburgh burst out, seizing the Koran from Hornemann's hand, 'but this is the book I understand.' The two Germans went on to demonstrate their knowledge of the Holy Book and Hornemann to prove his skill in writing Arabic. Their accusers were dumbfounded, the young Mamluk's prestige rose immensely; no one would ever dare to call his faith in question again. He was jubilant about his success—but there was one aggra-

257

vating consequence of the incident; Frendenburgh, in his moment of panic when Hornemann had left him to go to face the Siwans, had taken all his precious notebooks out of the baggage and given them to a servant to bury; it proved impossible to recover them.

The idea of crossing deserts with a camel caravan may have a superficial appeal to the romantic; in fact, it is an uncomfortable, not necessarily dangerous but above all insufferably monotonous undertaking. There is variety—rocky hills, dunes or gravelly plains —but of a kind that unrolls itself too slowly. Hour after hour, day after day, the eye is subjected to the same vista, made infinitely more irksome under the ferocious glare of the sun. There are few scenes to endear themselves to the mind or impress themselves on the memory —only perhaps the strange shape of the hills at sunrise or the sight of a few palm trees around a well at the end of a tedious day's journey. The whole of Hornemann's route from Cairo to the Fezzan lay through desert. From Siwa the caravan travelled to Augila, an ancient oasis mentioned by Herodotus, consisting only of a few mean houses. Here they waited twelve days while a guide was sent ahead to check up on the wells on the next stage of the route. From Augila sixteen days was required to reach the confines of the Fezzan, the route lying through a country of rocky hills, fascinating to the geologist, but black and dreary to the traveller.

At last Temissa, the first town in the Fezzan, was reached and 'all was gladness and felicitation,' the merchants congratulating themselves on their safe arrival and being greeted by their friends with long-drawn-out salutations, while the women assembled outside the walls sent up a joyful shout to which the caravan replied by firing their muskets in the air. At Zuila the same greetings, the same festivity. Finally, on November 17 they reached Murzuk, the capital of the Fezzan. There the Sultan, who had already, to the chagrin of the merchants, sent his officers to claim customs duty, came outside the walls to greet them. He seated himself on a small rise with his court around him, white Mamluks and Negro slaves standing with drawn swords, behind them half-naked Negroes with old-fashioned lances and halberds, his subjects, the people of Murzuk, drawn up in an oval to his left and to his right. One by one the merchants approached, barefoot, to kiss the Sultan's hand, taking then their seats behind him; 'lastly entered the Sheikh of the pilgrims with his sabre drawn and a kettledrum and a green flag of Mecca borne before him . . . the pilgrims followed chaunting praises to God who had so far conducted them in safety and continued their hymns until the Sultan was pleased to dismiss their leader with a gracious promise of sending his royal presents of dates and meats to every tent'.

Hornemann spent seven months in Murzuk. He was not the first European to visit the Fezzan: the Sultan's Mamluks, who held much power in their hands, were mostly of Greek or Genoese descent; but he was the first to visit it with the intention of bringing back information. That which he acquired during this time was exceedingly valuable, throwing a clear shaft of light on to the people and states of the central Sahara and central Sudan, confirming much that Leo Africanus and Lucas had reported before him, and supplementing their accounts with some new facts. On the Fezzan he wrote detailed notes, describing its government and its economy and noting in its people a marked 'want to energy', which he ascribed to their tyrannical form of government, their poverty and their almost meatless diet. He was able to contrast the Fezzanese with their neighbours, for many different people came to Murzuk either to trade or as slaves; thus he had the opportunity of making the acquaintance of the Tebu and the Tuareg, of men from the Hausa states, and men from Bornu.

The Tebu, the wild inhabitants of Tibesti, struck him as possessing 'much natural capacity' but with little opportunity of improving it, being 'surrounded by barbarous nations and corrupted by intercourse with the Arabs'. By the Tuareg, Hornemann, like so many Europeans after him, was deeply impressed: 'a mighty people' he called them, 'cultivated and enlightened, their natural abilities would render them perhaps one of the greatest nations upon earth'. 'Their caravans, give life to Murzuk which without them is a desert, for they like the Soudanians [Negroes] love company, music and song.' Of the Hausa also he formed a high opinion, regarding them as 'the most intelligent people in the interior of Africa'. 'They are distinguished from their neighbours by an interesting countenance; their nose is small and not flattened and they have an extraordinary inclination for pleasure, dancing and singing. Their character is benevolent and mild.' In short, Hornemann concluded, summing up his impressions of the Negro states that bordered the Sahara, 'we have a very unjust idea of these people, not only with respect to their culture and natural ability but also of their strength and the extent of their possessions'.

On the geography of the states of the central Sudan, Hornemann was able to obtain a remarkably accurate impression from a map which a Marabout drew at his request. As for the Niger, 'the river seen by Park flows southwards,' he was informed, 'from Hausa. It waters Nyffe [Nupe] and Gabi [Kebbi] where it is called Julbi, and runs eastwards into the District of Burnu where it takes the name of Zad, which means the great water.' Most of the people from the central Sudan, whom he asked about the river, agreed that it 'ran through the country of the heathen by Sennar, others affirmed that it passed Darfur and flows to Cairo'. This tangle of half-truths, in which, despite the obvious errors, one may detect references to the Niger, the Benue and the Shari-Logone, no doubt represents accurately enough the confused impression that Africans themselves possessed of the complex river-system of the central Sudan. Without maps to guide them, men, after all, can go only by what they have seen with their own eyes, supplemented by the reports, often hopelessly garbled in the retelling, of other travellers. One may detect the limitations of ocular evidence in the report Hornemann received of Zad; this was in fact Lake Chad, but though it was described as 'the great water', Hornemann did not realize it was a lake, having been told that it was only a mile wide, except during the rains, when its breadth increased to that of a day's journey.[12]

Murzuk proved a dreadfully unhealthy place. Hornemann was ill for weeks with fever, and poor Frendenburgh died there, 'led astray,' so Hornemann wrote to his mother, 'by wine and women'. By the time he himself had recovered, it was too late to join a caravan for Bornu. Rather than spend the whole of the summer in Murzuk, 'after the caravan had left, the most disinteresting town I ever saw', he decided to go north to Tripoli, where he would be able to send back letters to Europe and procure additional funds. He reached Tripoli in August and spent four months in the city. There he met his invaluable acquaintance, Muhammad D'Ghies, and was introduced to the Pasha. The Pasha knew from D'Ghies the secret of his identity; but whatever his private thoughts about the propriety of an infidel passing himself off as a Muslim and travelling through his domains, it was diplomatically imperative for him to remain on good terms with the English, whose navy dominated the central Mediterranean and afforded the only protection against a French attack; he therefore told Hornemann he would be willing to help him in every way.[13]

The British Consul in Tripoli was that unsuccessful traveller,

Simon Lucas, of whose abilities Hornemann formed, as there has already been cause to note, so poor an impression. Elated by his own achievement, his contempt for his predecessor's failure is understandable. In letters to Banks he voiced his own self-assurance in no uncertain terms. 'Pray, Sir,' he wrote on November 29 a few days before leaving Tripoli, 'do not look on me as a European but as a real African—my books I turned overboard, excepting three but replaced them by an Alcoran and some other holy books of that kind.' 'I look upon my travels done,' he added, 'as upon the work of an apprentice—not I think I have the experience at least of a young Master. It is a new plan to travel as a Mohammedan in these countries, dangerous between superstitious people leaded [sic] by fanaticism and intolerancy, but dangerous only for the beginning, afterwards it is safer and better.' His intention, he told Banks, was to travel from the Fezzan to Bornu, then westwards to Katsina, and on to Timbuktu; he expected to be back in England in two years' time and suggested that it would be better for the Association not to send out any other travellers until he had returned.[14]

By the middle of January Hornemann was back in the Fezzan. During his previous residence in Murzuk he had made the acquaintance of a Shereef from Bornu, a great traveller and a very honourable man; it was in his company that he proposed to cross the desert. But it was not until April 6 that the Bornu caravan was ready to set out. A few hours before he left Hornemann wrote a last letter to Sir Joseph Banks. 'Being in an excellent state of health, perfectly inured to the climate, sufficiently acquainted with the Arabic language, and somewhat of the Bornu tongue, and being well-armed and not without courage, and under the protection of two great Shereefs, I have the best hopes of success in my undertaking.' His original plan had been modified, no doubt as a result of the information he had acquired at Murzuk; he no longer spoke of Timbuktu, but of making his way from the Hausa states to the coast; 'I will not put my discoveries to the hazard, by exposing myself to long and unnecessary residence and delays in any one place.' In a letter to his mother written on the same day, he breathed the same supreme confidence: 'I am a complete African and feel quite at home here. Nevertheless I am coming back and I shall not bring a local beauty with me.'[15]

Hornemann's letters from Murzuk reached England safely and were read out at the Association's General Meeting in 1801. In the meantime, the British Government, at Banks's request, had sent an order to all consular officials in Africa, requiring them to pay any drafts they might receive from Hornemann. In 1802 Hornemann's account of his journey from Egypt to the Fezzan was published; with the agreement of the Association's General Meeting, a special copy was presented to General Bonaparte during that interlude of peace, in which so many English people flocked to Paris. In 1804 the Danish Consul in Tripoli met a merchant from the Fezzan who told him that Yusuf had gone to 'Gondash'—possibly a corruption of Gonja, a state to the north of Ashanti—on his way to the coast. The next year another report reached England; Macdonagh, the acting British Consul in Tripoli, had learnt from a 'very respectable Moorish merchant' that Yusuf had been in Katsina in June 1803 and had been highly respected as a Marabout. No further news reached the Association; but as late as 1808 members were told that there was 'still a faint hope' that Hornemann might be alive.[16]

In fact, Hornemann had disappeared without a trace; his fate was a complete mystery. But not for ever. In 1819 the Fezzan was once again visited by European travellers, the two British explorers, Ritchie and Lyon. In Murzuk they chanced to make the acquaintance of a man who had been Hornemann's companion on the caravan from Murzuk to Bornu. He told them that Hornemann had spent three or four months in Bornu; later they had travelled together to Katsina and on to Nupe, where they had stayed in a town named Bakkanee in the house of a Fulani named Ali.* At Bakkanee he had left Hornemann and returned to Katsina; shortly after he reached that town, he learnt that Hornemann had died of dysentery in Bakkanee—a report that surprised as much as it distressed him, for when they had parted he had been in excellent health and was planning to travel south-westwards on the well-trodden route that led across the Niger to Dagomba and Ashanti. 'It was Hornemann's custom,' Lyon was told, 'to note the bearings of every tree, mountain and village he saw, by which means he might be more easily enabled to know his road again, without a guide.' 'The people became greatly attached to Hornemann,' his travelling-companion reported, 'on account of his amiable deportment and skill in medicine and he was

---

* It is possible that 'Bakkanee' is identifiable with Bokani, a town in the present Niger province of Northern Nigeria, lying on an old trade-route that led from Katsina to Raba, an important market on the Niger. I am indebted to Mr A. R. Allen of Ahmadu Bello University, Zaria for this suggestion.

generally considered a Marabout.' It was as good an epitaph as any traveller could wish for.*[17]

That is all there is to know about Frederick Hornemann's great journey. One is left, as so often in life, with an aggravating sense of loss. If he had lived, Hornemann would surely have written one of the classic narratives of African exploration, a book, moreover, which would have come today to have possessed a very special value for the historian of the central Sudan, for he would have described the Hausa states in the last years of their independence before they were overwhelmed by the avalanche of the Fulani *jihad*. One might have gained too, had Hornemann lived, a rather sharper impression of his character and an answer to that beguiling question provoked by his remarkable adventure: what does it feel like to lead a double life for years on end? Did he, the theology student, the son of a Lutheran pastor, constantly having to act the Muslim, not find himself becoming insensibly converted to Islam, or was the reputation that he acquired as a learned and a holy man only the result of a brilliant piece of deception?

Fame requires documentation; if Hornemann has received less than his due it is only because too little can be known of his achievement. Yet unlike Park, unlike some other later explorers, Hornemann never seems to have made Fame his goal, nor an overweening ambition his goad. He was moved, one suspects, as Ledyard had been moved, by the spirit of pure adventure. If this was so, he had his reward—for in the last months of his life there could have come to him the proud and comforting reflection that he had lived his life in accordance with the dreams of his youth and in the process performed a feat unrivalled by any other European traveller.

J. G. JACKSON AND OTHERS IN MOROCCO

Tripoli, Cairo and the Gambia were not the only possible starting-points for the interior. There was another route that might commend

* Another interesting piece of information about Hornemann was picked up in 1824 by Hugh Clapperton in Kano, where he met two wealthy merchants from the Fezzan who had been with Hornemann at the time of his death. 'He passed himself off as an English merchant, professing the Mahometan faith, and had sold two fine horses here.' Clapperton tried to recover Hornemann's papers but was informed that Hornemann's host, 'a learned man of the country', 'had been burned in his own house, together with all Mr Hornemann's papers, by the negro rabble, from a superstitious dread of his holding intercourse with evil spirits'.[18]

itself to the adventurous: to set out from Mogador on the Atlantic coast of Morocco and strike the ancient and much-frequented caravan road that ran southwards to Timbuktu. To outsiders, Morocco, its inhabitants farouchely hostile to all Europeans, appeared the most barbarous of the states of North Africa, seemingly abandoned to a perpetual anarchy. This impression contained a large measure of truth; since the death of the formidable Mulay Ismail in 1727, no Emperor had found it possible to control the whole country. But during a large part of the reigns of Sidi Muhammad from 1757 to 1790 and Mulay Sliman from 1792 to 1818, the people of the coastal plains enjoyed some measure of settled government, even if the tribes of the Atlas remained irrepressible and threateningly independent. With bitter memories behind them of Portuguese and Spanish aggression, the rulers of Morocco might have preferred to isolate their country from the outside world; but self-interest forced them to attend to one line of contact—foreign trade, if skilfully controlled, might provide lucrative duties for a meagre exchequer. With this purpose in mind Sidi Muhammad had founded in 1765 the town of Mogador as an entrepôt for European trade. He made use of the services of a French engineer for designing the ground-plan, and of an English renegade for superintending the fortifications, with the result that Mogador, set, as Terrasse has described it, 'in a vast and wonderful landscape of sea, of sand-dunes, and of sky', became, as it remains today, 'one of the most astonishing and alluring cities in Morocco, where Europe and Islam, the Atlantic and the Orient are successfully brought together in a manner both strange and marvellous'.[1]

Mogador never achieved the success the Emperor had hoped. Most of the European consuls preferred to reside in the greater security of Tangier, while the volume of European trade continued to run at a very modest level. There was, however, at least one Englishman who thought there was a possibility of a more fruitful intercourse between his country and Morocco. His name was James Grey Jackson. His antecedents are uncertain; he first appears established as a merchant at Mogador in the early 1790s. Morocco and the countries to the south were to absorb his attention for the next thirty years.

Jackson published an account of Morocco in 1809; to it, with characteristic conceit, he placed as frontispiece his own portrait. It shows a determined face, dominated by a remarkably bony nose, and crowned with a shock of hair. Tiresome and pedantic, muddled and self-opinionated—such is the impression his published works convey; and it is confirmed by his surviving letters. A restless expatriate, a misfit in English society, a man with a chip on his shoulder, so— one trusts not too unsympathetically—one reads his character.

Jackson was a friend of that specious young man, James Willis. To Willis he wrote from Mogador in May 1792 to tell him of a grandiose plan of his own devising: the British Government should purchase the town of Agadir, make it a commercial centre for the trans-Saharan trade and so 'command the whole commerce of the Sudan, at the expense of Tunis, Tripoli, Algiers and Egypt, not at the expense of Morocco, because an equivalent, or what the emperor would consider as an equivalent would be given in exchange for it'. This scheme he put forward in one form or another for many years to come.[2]

In 1795 he was back in England, submitting to the Government, no doubt with Willis's encouragement, his view 'of a certain and probable trade to be established to Timouctou [sic] and the adjacent country'. In this memorandum he reckoned that Morocco exported goods worth £200,000 to the Sudan and received in exchange imports —including gold dust and 'drugs of various kinds whereof some are unknown in England'—to the value of £1,000,000. At the same time he introduced himself to Sir Joseph Banks and seriously considered entering the service of the African Association. Indeed, it seemed likely that he would have been one of the Association's explorers, if he had not changed his mind so often and thus allowed Hornemann to get in before him.[3]

In 1797 he was back in Morocco. He had decided to make his own fortune out of the Timbuktu trade, and had committed to a Moorish merchant a large assortment of goods to take across the desert; in exchange he expected to receive, so he informed Willis, four thousand ounces of gold dust, spices and five or six hundred slaves. At the same time he had thought of what seemed an easy way of getting a European to Timbuktu; he would travel with a Moorish merchant as his renegade servant, the Moor to be rewarded with a suitable sum—Jackson reckoned £250 would suffice—on their safe return. Matra, the British Consul in Tangier, to whom Jackson revealed his plan, was extremely sceptical; he himself had seen too much of Moorish treachery. Nevertheless, Jackson continued to play with the idea for several years. In 1799 he was in Tangier. 'As he has nothing to do here,' Matra wrote to Banks, 'and is a little heated with the subject, I should not be surprised if at last he undertook it himself.' Jackson, however, was not of the stuff of which explorers are made.[4]

He was not the only person to play with the idea of reaching Timbuktu by way of Morocco. In the same year, 1799, there arrived in Mogador a party of four English adventurers. 'The captain of the gang', as Matra informed Banks, was a Mr Waugh, who had served as captain of a packet in the East Indian service and been in Egypt and Arabia; his companions were another ship's captain, a surgeon and a botanist. They gave out that they had been sent by the African Association. Their expedition ended in fiasco; they quarrelled with each other, aroused the suspicion of the Moorish authorities, and were soon on their way back to Europe.[5]

More enterprising was the exploit of an English army doctor named Weales. One of the most important chiefs in Morocco was a certain Ben Nasser, who controlled most of the south of the country. Matra, who was a master of diplomatic intrigue, was particularly anxious to secure his friendship. When, therefore, Ben Nasser asked for the services of an English doctor he recommended to Lord St Vincent, in command at Gibraltar, that the request be met. Weales, a young man of twenty-five, was accordingly sent. He proved an excellent choice, for he 'showed a most happy turn for winning Moors and Arabs'. While he was with Ben Nasser, he made the acquaintance of some traders from Timbuktu. 'Without knowing the least of your views,' Matra wrote to Banks in November 1799, 'he returned here more than red-hot with a determined resolution to get there somehow or other.' Moreover, he had a friend, Quarter-Master Macks, an excellent draughtsman, 'whom he has bitten completely'. Weales was so keen that he talked of going with his own resources to Algiers to prepare himself for the journey, and was even willing to allow himself to be circumcised. This was just the sort of man the African Association was looking for; Matra recommended him whole-heartedly. There was, however, one slight snag: Weales's regiment, the 37th Foot, was due to sail shortly for the West Indies. Matra suggested that Banks would not find it difficult to pull the necessary strings.[6]

Banks was attracted by this suggestion. He was not anxious for Weales to go to Timbuktu, 'as this would be anticipating Horne-mann, whom we must protect and encourage as much as possible', and he did not care for the idea of explorers travelling in pairs,

9. Africans: Ethiopia—'Abyssinians reposing.' From H. Salt's *A Voyage to Abyssinia*, London, 1814

10. Africans: Dahomey—'Public Procession of the Queen's Women'
from A. Dalzel's *The History of Dahomy*, London, 1793

pointing out that one would inevitably get involved in the other's diffi-culties. Instead he proposed that Weales should undertake a shorter mission to 'those nations called Tippoo'—a reference presumably to the Tebu of Tibesti, though Banks places them erratically to the west of the Fezzan—'an ingenious people whose manner would be a curious discovery'. But by the time Banks's letter reached Matra, Weales had already sailed for the West Indies. Eight months later, news reached Matra that he had been killed in a duel in St Vincent.[7]

Jackson seems to have left Morocco by 1804; in that year he was in London, applying for the consulship of Algiers. In spite of Banks's unhesitating support—'if he succeeds,' Banks wrote to Lord Hawkes-bury, who controlled the appointment, 'it will be considered as a great advantage to the African Association'—he was not appointed. Some months later he received overtures from the French to go to Paris 'as Arabic and Moorish Commissary'—a strange offer to be made in time of war to an Englishman. In 1806 he was in England again, once more seeking the help of Sir Joseph. It had struck him that there was no one in London who could speak Arabic fluently so that letters had to be sent to the University to be translated, while the consular officials in North Africa were, in his opinion, incom-petent; 'this difficulty, viz., of finding a man, competent to speak fluently the Arabic and Moorish languages and to communicate with Mahommedans of all nations is now done away with by my safe arrival in England and my offer to become thus serviceable to my country'.[8]

What answer Jackson received to this modest self-presentation, either from the Government or from Sir Joseph, is not known, but some years later he took to describing himself as Professor of African Arabic. In 1809 he brought out his *Account of the Empire of Marocco* (the spelling is a characteristic piece of pedantry), with enlarged editions in 1811 and 1814. The most valuable chapter in the book is that which deals with the trade-routes from Morocco to the western Sudan, on which he had indeed secured much valuable information. Meanwhile he still cherished the idea of capturing for his country the trans-Saharan trade. As late as 1819 he issued a prospectus for a 'North African or Sudan Company', for which he sought a capital of £100,000: the company would erect a factory somewhere on the 'western coast of the Sahara', probably at Agadir, to which, in ways none too clearly specified, would be drawn all the trade with Timbuktu. In 1820 he published a rag-bag of a book, the most valuable part of which is Shabeni's account of Timbuktu and Hausa in a manuscript written by Beaufoy nearly thirty years earlier. That is the last one hears of him; one would not be surprised to learn that he ended up his days in a workhouse or a debtor's prison, a garrulous, half-crazy old man still talking about Morocco.[9]

There is no indication that his schemes for commercial enterprise ever received serious consideration; nor, indeed, did they deserve to be supported, for he had failed to examine the obvious difficulties. But his book on Morocco had a decisive influence on the life of one man; so the career of Heinrich Röntgen will reveal.

IV

THE ENTERPRISE OF OTHERS

WHILE THE AFRICAN ASSOCIATION was concerning itself with the approach to the Niger and the central Sudan by way of Cairo, Tripoli and the Gambia, another development of equal significance for the eventual penetration of the interior was taking place farther down the West Coast—the foundation of the colony of Sierra Leone. Sierra Leone had its origin in the social problem created by the famous judgement of 1772 that slavery was illegal in Britain. As a result, over ten thousand slaves found themselves free men; many of them eventually became destitute. To meet their needs a Committee was established 'for relieving the black poor', with Jonas Hanway, a London merchant who for thirty years had supported every philanthropic cause, as its Chairman. It soon became evident, however, that a permanent solution of the problem would require more than simple charity.[1]

At this stage the Committee was approached by Dr Henry Smeathman, a Londoner who had spent several years on the West Coast and gained some reputation as a naturalist. Smeathman suggested that Sierra Leone offered an opportunity for making 'a permanent and comfortable establishment in a most pleasant, fertile climate'. 'Such are the mildness and fertility of the climate and country,' he asserted in a pamphlet setting out a *Plan of a Settlement*, 'that a man possessed of a change of clothing, a woodaxe, a hoe and a pocketknife, may soon place himself in an easy and comfortable situation.' Smeathman was willing to put his ideas into practice, but he died in London in 1786; the Committee, however, accepted his plan, and the Government gave the scheme its blessing by providing free transport for the settlers.[2]

Accordingly, there sailed from Portsmouth in February 1787, some three hundred and fifty black settlers accompanied by seventy white women of dubious reputation. This ill-chosen company was landed in St George's Bay on the coast of Sierra Leone, where Captain Thompson, the commander of their naval escort, obtained for them a grant of land from a neighbouring chief, King Tom, and left them to their devices. Inevitably, the first two years were disastrous. Eighty settlers had died on the voyage to Sierra Leone, and many more expired during the first rainy season; there was no disciplined system of government; many of the settlers preferred to take the easy way of picking up jobs at the depots of neighbouring European slave traders, all of whom were naturally hostile to a scheme calculated to undermine their interests; finally, in 1789 the settlement was overrun and destroyed by a local chief.

For the Abolitionists at home the new colony had come to be regarded as an experiment in which all their most cherished ideas were being put to the test: it was to serve as a positive contribution to the civilization of Africa and as a clear proof of the advantages of legitimate trade. It was impossible, therefore, for them to accept a failure. Already, before the worst news reached England, Granville Sharp had been working on a scheme to give the colony a sounder financial backing by engaging 'several respectable merchants and gentlemen to form a company in order to carry on an honourable trade with the coast of Africa'. His plan bore fruit in 1791 in the grant of a charter for the Sierra Leone Company. The Company aimed to achieve a nice balance between profit and philanthropy. 'The foundations of happiness to Africa' and 'future prosperity to the Company'—such, declared the Directors in their first report, were their objectives; they looked forward to 'considerable and growing profits directly resulting from the general and increasing prosperity of the country'. It is a remarkable indication of the interest that Africa was now arousing that almost two thousand people were willing to buy shares to the value of £235,280 in a company that offered no chance of immediate profit. A glance down the list of subscribers reveals that they came from every part of England, that the majority of them were middle-class people (not permitted, in that punctilious age, the title of *esquire*), and that signally few members of the aristocracy bought shares. Socially

270

there was a world of difference between the African Association and the Sierra Leone Company.[3]

Meanwhile events in Sierra Leone had taken a slight turn for the better. In 1790 reinforcements had been sent out under Alexander Falconbridge;* he had succeeded in gathering together the few remaining original colonists and in founding a settlement on a new site. This was now taken over by the Sierra Leone Company. In 1791 the Company sent out a hundred Europeans, most of them engaged in the Company's service, together with wives and children; later they welcomed the arrival of twelve hundred Negroes from Nova Scotia, where they had been unhappily settled after serving on the English side in the American war. As Governor of the colony the Directors appointed Thomas Clarkson's brother John, a naval lieutenant. He was succeeded by Zachary Macaulay, remarkable father of a more famous son.

To Clarkson and Macaulay, both young men still in their twenties, the credit for seeing the colony through its early difficulties is chiefly due. Many of the Company's servants were inefficient, many of the Negro colonists quarrelsome; such squabbles beset any pioneer community, here they were exacerbated by the unhealthiness of the climate. Nevertheless, the foundations of a decent society had been truly laid, when the colony was subjected to a cruel disaster. On September 28, 1794, a squadron of French ships, encouraged by a hostile American slave trader, sailed up to Freetown, as the settlement was now called, and pillaged it ruthlessly. The colonists were resilient enough to recover; the story of their further vicissitudes will be briefly recounted in a later chapter.

Meanwhile one aspect of Sierra Leone deserves more detailed attention: its importance as a base for journeys into the interior. In the first years of its existence the new colony had attracted, besides its two able young governors, a number of other enterprising men. One of them was a certain James Watt, who had entered the Company's service as a surveyor. He had worked as a plantation

* Falconbridge had first-hand experience of West Africa, gained as surgeon on a slave-ship. Turning violently against the slave trade, of which he published an account in 1788, he had helped Clarkson to collect evidence. He took with him to Sierra Leone his young wife. The couple were soon estranged. Falconbridge died in 1792, his health undermined by hard drinking. Mrs Falconbridge married again, returned to England and published a frank, shrewd and critical account of the early days of the colony.[4]

manager in the West Indies; it is possible that conversations with Negro slaves first fired him with the ambition to see for himself countries in the interior where no white man had ever been. In 1794 he gained his opportunity, when there arrived in Freetown messengers from the Fulani ruler of Futa Jallon, who declared himself anxious to establish intercourse with the colony. Watt promptly volunteered to proceed on a mission to Timbo, the capital of Futa Jallon, taking as his companion a Mr Winterbottom, brother to the colony's doctor.[5]

The two travellers started off up the coast, till they reached the Rio Nunez, which they followed to Kakundy. Here guides had been sent to lead them over two hundred miles to Timbo. The journey was performed with a remarkable absence of difficulty. In every town through which they passed they found themselves 'always most hospitably received', 'the utmost satisfaction as well as surprise' being expressed at the appearance of white men, of whom none had ever been seen even at a distance of a few days' journey from the coast. Timbo proved to be a substantial town with seven thousand inhabitants, its people far superior to the coastal tribes 'in most branches of civilisation'. They built excellent houses and carried on many crafts in iron, silver or cloth; most surprising of all, to those previously unaware of the civilizing influence of Islam, the Fulani of Futa Jallon revealed themselves as a literate people, their chief men possessing books on divinity and law, their children taught to read in the schools which were maintained in almost every town.

The Fulani ruler gave the two travellers a cordial welcome, listened mildly while they harangued him on the evil of making war to catch slaves, explained that only by selling slaves could his people obtain European trade-goods at the factories on the coast, and asserted that if he could obtain guns, powder and cloth in exchange for ivory, rice and cattle he would soon have done with the slave trade. The speech appeared as a complete vindication of the Company's policy. Moreover, the king gave grounds for hoping that fruitful intercourse could be carried further. He said he had no objection to a European settling in his territory, and would readily provide him with land and cattle; this might serve, the two travellers suggested, as an opportunity for introducing the plough, an instrument not known in that country. The great men of Futa Jallon were as friendly as their sovereign, two of them even going so far as to say that they wished to send their sons to England for education.

The travellers returned to Sierra Leone by a different route, accompanied by an escort of five hundred men. Some of the leading Fulani came with them to Freetown, where they discussed further the possibilities of trade; they returned home 'full of admiration of what they had seen, and gratified in the highest degree by their visit'.

After such an auspicious beginning Watt was anxious to proceed immediately on another more arduous enterprise. At Labé, the second town of Futa Jallon, he had learned that a 'free communication subsisted with Tombuctoo', the great city being placed four months' journey distant on a route that passed through six different kingdoms. The people of Labé had even heard of mysterious Katsina, though the way thither was described as hazardous. To Timbuktu Watt now resolved to go. Poor Winterbottom had been drowned in a boating accident two months after his return, so Watt now chose as his companion John Gray, the Company's accountant. Their plan was to go by way of Timbo to Timbuktu, then east to Katsina and north across the desert to the Mediterranean. They would travel 'more like mendicants than merchants or men of science', taking with them, as guides and interpreters, one or two Muslims from the Gambia of the universally respected class known as Yamara, if suitable men could be found with a knowledge of Arabic and English. In these plans they could count on the enthusiastic support of the Governor of the colony.[6]

While they were still engaged in making preparations, the French attacked the colony. Gray lost all his equipment. Six months later Watt died. Gray talked of carrying on with the project. But a suitable opportunity never arose. Thirty years passed before a young Frenchman, Réné Caillié, travelling indeed very like a mendicant, succeeded in showing the soundness of Watt's project, going from Sierra Leone by way of Futa Jallon to Timbuktu and northwards across the desert to Morocco.

The Sierra Leone Company and the African Association were naturally not indifferent to one another's activities, but it was the Company which showed the greater interest, more than half its Directors being members of the Association, while not one member of the Saturday's Club was to be found among the shareholders of the Company. Sir Joseph Banks, however, was quite willing to render the Company appropriate assistance. Thus in 1792 he procured for Sierra Leone the services of a young Swedish naturalist, Adam

Afzelius.* Gray became Afzelius's 'particular friend', and on the latter's suggestion wrote to Banks telling him of the plans to reach Timbuktu. He wrote again six weeks after the French attack, saying that without help from the African Association he would be unable to proceed with the expedition. Financial help Banks could not offer; 'no doubt' he suggested, 'the Sierra Leone Company will supply you amply with common necessities'. But he went to the trouble of advising him not to attempt to cross the whole continent, gave him the latest news of the African Association's activities and sent him copies of the Association's papers. Such acts of kindness to unknown young men had rightly earned Sir Joseph the reputation of being, as Gray in his first letter somewhat fulsomely declared, 'the father of research, the laborious advocate of enquiry and the friend of the adventurous traveller'.[7]

THE BULAMA ASSOCIATION

Sierra Leone was not the only new European colony to be established on the West Coast in those years. In 1792 the island of Bulama, one of an archipelago that lies off the coast of the territory that is now Portuguese Guinea, half-way between Sierra Leone and the Gambia, was the scene of one of the most curious episodes in the history of European intercourse with West Africa.

In 1791 a young naval Lieutenant, Philip Beaver, who had seen active service at sea since the age of eleven, found himself without professional employment and with a taste for adventure that de-

* Afzelius was like his compatriot, Wadström, a Swedenborgian. He spent four years in Sierra Leone. On one of his excursions from Freetown he met three men who came down from the interior: 'the countenances of these men were beautiful and comely, their voices were sweet and sonorous, their gestures mild and engaging, and they had frequent and open communication with the spiritual world and its inhabitants; even while Mr Afzelius was with them they declared they saw angelic spirits, which it seems was no uncommon case with these men'. So, in his chance encounter with Fulani or Mandingo traders, the vision of the Master seemed confirmed.

Another Swedenborgian to come to Sierra Leone was Augustus Nordenskiold, famed as an alchemist and a dreamer. Appointed as mineralogist by the Sierra Leone Company, he arrived in Freetown in 1792, set off immediately for the interior, but was stricken by fever and died a few months later. His belief that Africa contained hidden stores of wealth was by no means an illusion; on one of his surveys he discovered diamonds in the Susu country.[8]

manded to be satisfied. Three projects attracted him: he would try to reach the North Pole; he would cross Africa from South to North or from West to East, or he would 'coast the world'. In this receptive frame of mind, he was introduced to a certain Mr Dalrymple, who had served in Goree during the last war and had just been offered the post of Governor by the Sierra Leone Company. Beaver immediately offered to accompany him; 'all I knew was, that a colony was to be established: and among uncivilized tribes: and that was enough for me'. Unfortunately, Dalrymple quarrelled with the Company and lost his job. Beaver was bitterly disappointed, but as he was talking things over with Dalrymple, the latter mentioned Bulama, an island of enticing fertility where the French had once thought of making an establishment. 'Let us colonize it ourselves,' Beaver exclaimed. 'With all my heart,' Dalrymple replied. 'And thus' —with what schoolboyish zest—'originated the expedition to Bulama.'[1]

A fantastic expedition it was to prove—and yet the purpose behind it was both practical and generous: practical in that the intention was 'to cultivate tropical productions on the cost of Africa by means of its free natives', generous because it was hoped that this experiment would disprove the idea of those 'who boldly asserted that the Africans were incapable of enjoying freedom, or being in any great degree civilized'. Dalrymple and Beaver set to work with the energy of youthful enthusiasm. Within six months they had formed two committees, one in London, the other in Manchester, gained the support of Paul le Mesurier, M.P., the Lord Mayor of London and other influential men, raised £9,000 in capital by selling shares of land in the new colony at £60 for 500 acres, attracted nearly three hundred colonists, ranging from a baronet to down-and-outs, and including fifty-seven women and sixty-four children, drawn up a constitution, which had to be scrapped as they had omitted to obtain Parliamentary sanction, bought three ships and set sail from Portsmouth.[2]

In July 1792 the first of the ships, with Dalrymple in command, reached Bulama. A party landed on the island, built a flimsy store in which they piled their arms and then, since they were a thoroughly undisciplined crowd and Dalrymple was quite unable to keep order, set off to amuse themselves, 'some on the shore fishing among the rocks, others taking oysters from the Mangrove branches', while many went inland, 'botanizing and hunting after lizards and chasing some

—butterflies, some—elephants'. Suddenly they were attacked by a war canoe manned by natives from the neighbouring archipelago of the Bissagos; their assailants seized the store of arms, shot down six of the colonists and retreated, taking with them four women and three children. So horrified were most of the settlers at this incident that they decided, after the captives had been redeemed, to sail back to England.[3]

Dalrymple was among those who left, but Beaver stayed on in charge of those who remained. He established reasonable relations with the natives, and started to build a fort and to clear the bush for cultivation. He had with him at the start eighty-six colonists, nearly half of whom were women and children; six months later the numbers had fallen to twenty-seven, thirty-seven having died and the remainder deserted; after a year on Bulama there were only nine colonists left, all of them sick men except for Beaver; finally, in November 1793 Beaver himself was forced most reluctantly to throw in his hand, when the last of the settlers refused to carry on. The failure of the expedition Beaver ascribed partly to faulty planning—they had arrived at Bulama at the beginning of the rainy season and had not brought proper building material with them—but mainly to the character of the colonists: 'the major part of our people,' he told his supporters at home on his return, 'were drunken, lazy, dishonest, impatient cowards.' But he felt that what he had done with a handful of men in clearing fifty acres and growing sufficient vegetables for fifty times their number had proved the feasibility of the scheme.[4]

History is not greatly interested in failures; but some failures may be historically significant. Of such a kind was the Bulama expedition, for it had shown the vast practical difficulties of establishing European colonies in West Africa; this was a lesson that many people, in an age interested in establishing European communities in other parts of the world, would take to heart.

W. G. BROWNE IN DARFUR

In the previous generation James Bruce had shown how much the private traveller could achieve in Africa; by contrast, all the explorers of the 1790s had the advantage of a society, whether the African Association or the Sierra Leone Company, to back them—with one exception. In 1798 there arrived back in London an Englishman named Browne. He had been away for six years, but during his absence some news of his adventures reached his friends; it appeared that he had lived for three years in the kingdom of Darfur, that country of the eastern Sudan, lying five hundred miles to the west of the Nile, of which hitherto nothing but the bare name was known. Browne's story was a remarkable one.

Remarkable, too, was the personality of him who told it. In 1798 William George Browne was aged thirty. His father had been a London wine-merchant, who came of an old Cumberland family and possessed an estate in that county. A studious, reserved and delicate youth, he had been educated privately and at Oriel College, Oxford. After leaving the University, he studied law with the intention of a public career, for he had been deeply stirred by the French Revolution and had become an avowed free-thinker; but he had always been interested in foreign lands and looked forward from an early age to the opportunity of travel. These youthful aspirations were revived by reading Bruce's great volumes and the first report of the African Association. The next year, 1791, his father's death left him a modest competence and thus the means of transforming his dreams into reality. He dropped his legal studies and booked a passage to Egypt. Before leaving London, he called on Banks and on Beaufoy; finding neither gentleman at home, he made no further efforts to contact them.[1]

In January 1792 he reached Alexandria. Bruce had stirred him more than Lucas or Ledyard, but he believed him to be wrong in describing the river whose source he had visited as the true Nile. He planned, therefore, to explore the White Nile, which Bruce had ignored. Should this prove beyond his resources, then he would visit Ethiopia and check Bruce's other questionable statements. On this extraordinary enterprise Browne embarked with grave disadvantages. Indeed, of all the African explorers of this period, none was so ill prepared. He had never been abroad before, he knew no Arabic, he had no one at home to support, encourage or advise him; but he possessed enormous obstinacy and a mind unpalsied, one suspects, by a vivid imagination.

Soon after his arrival in Egypt he set out on a preliminary canter of exploration. There had been much speculation in scholarly circles about the exact site of the famous temple of Jupiter Ammon. Ancient Ammonium was thought by some scholars to be the same as the modern oasis of Siwa. But Siwa, lying three hundred miles west of the Nile surrounded by a 'burning' desert haunted by robber tribes, seemed quite inaccessible to any European traveller. With remarkable audacity Browne decided to make Siwa his first objective. It took him six weeks to see the oasis and to return, unscathed, to Alexandria. He failed to identify the remains of the ancient temple; nevertheless, the comparative ease of this dangerous journey must have greatly increased his self-confidence.

Browne spent the summer of 1792 in Cairo. He found the few Europeans in the city singularly uncongenial: 'if the Turks are liars,' he wrote to a friend, 'these are more shameless liars; if the Turks are slaves, these are more despicable slaves'. He busied himself learning Arabic and left in September for Ethiopia, taking with him a Greek as an interpreter. They got no farther than Aswan in Upper Egypt, where news of a war raging to the south forced them to turn back. Browne consoled himself by exploring a route to the Red Sea coast. Back in Cairo, he refused to renounce his self-appointed task. He had heard much talk in the city of the kingdom of Darfur, from which came regular caravans of slaves. Would it not be possible, he asked himself, to reach Ethiopia by way of Darfur, thus making a vast detour to avoid the war-torn regions between Sennar and Aswan? The attempt seemed worth trying.[2]

Every year a caravan left Egypt for Darfur along that ancient route, *Darb-al-Arba'in* (the 'Forty Days Road'), that cuts diagonally, south-westwards from the Nile across the desert. Such a caravan Browne now prepared to join. He provided himself with a considerable quantity of merchandise, bought a string of camels and engaged an agent, for he had been told that all commerce in Darfur was carried on by barter and it would be necessary for him to take someone who knew the country. His agent, Ali, was a former slave-dealer, reputed honest. At the end of May the caravan set out; it reached the confines of Darfur two months later, after a long and dreary journey made at the hottest time of the year. To add to the vexations of desert travel, Browne soon discovered that his agent was a rogue; so insultingly did he behave that Browne once had to threaten to shoot him. On arrival at Swein, the first town in Darfur, Ali, plotting revenge, sent a friend to the Sultan to say that Browne was an infidel and a dangerous character, who should be kept under constant observation. Browne was himself to blame for the suspicion he aroused, for he had persisted throughout the journey in taking notes and asking questions. 'The Soltan of the English,' it was widely rumoured in Darfur, 'had undoubtedly sent him to inquire after these countries.' This opinion of Browne came to the ears of another European explorer, J. L. Burckhardt, travelling in Upper Egypt, disguised as a Muslin, over twenty years later. Browne came to recognize his mistake, for he himself urged Burckhardt, who had come to him for advice, to adopt the greatest circumspection when making notes.[3]

From Swein, Browne moved to Cobbe, where most of the foreign merchants resided. There a letter from the Sultan reached him, saying that he was to stay in Cobbe and reside in the house of Ibrahim, the friend Ali had perfidiously sent to the Sultan. Some weeks passed, before Browne gained some inkling of his predicament, on finding that the merchants in whose company he had travelled were leaving Cobbe on their own business. He had heard in Cairo that the Sultan of Darfur was friendly to Christians, and had expected to find himself received as an honoured guest; possibly, with Bruce's adventures in mind, he saw himself enjoying the privileges of intimacy with African royalty. But he was a much younger man than Bruce had been in Ethiopia; he had seen much less of the world; he could emulate neither the grand manner nor the physical prowess of his great exemplar. Moreover, he was in a Muslim, not a Christian, country. Coptic traders had once been welcome in Darfur, but a new ruler, Abd-ar-Rahman, recently come to the throne, was distinguishing himself by the sternness of his orthodoxy, which drove him to expel or imprison all non-Muslims. Finally, Darfur was a country even more isolated from the rest of the world than Ethiopia; nothing of the wealth and progress of Europe was known there.

At Cobbe Browne had his first attack of malaria. After he had recovered, he was given leave to proceed to El Fasher, where the Sultan held his court. Nothing came of this visit: he fell ill again, the Sultan's officers seized a large part of his goods, and the Sultan refused to grant him an interview. There was no alternative but to return to Cobbe, where he spent the winter in virtual captivity, for he was prevented from making excursions to the surrounding countryside. He diverted himself by bringing up a lion-cub and listening to the conversation of the 'graver' men; their talk 'contained few sallies of wit, much less profundity of observation, yet it was carried on without ill-humour, with mutual forbearance and on the whole in an equable course'. Unfortunately, apart from these two brief hints—the lion-cub and the old men's talk—Browne's published account tells nothing about his daily life in Darfur. He lacked the art of picking on the sudden illuminating detail and admitted in his Preface that 'a more creative imagination would have drawn more animated pictures'; nor does he seem to have possessed that interest in the vagaries of human character that would have helped him to bring to life in his writing the people whom he met—they remain, Ali, Ibrahim and the rest, little more than names.

In 1794—he is not precise about dates—Browne returned to El Fasher, where he lodged in the house of a certain Musa, son of a former Sultan and 'one of the most upright and disinterested men' he had met among Muslims. Again he was denied an audience with the Sultan and might never have come into his presence but for a curious incident. One day, sitting outside his house, Browne was jesting with a slave-girl. Unintentionally, so he says, he caught her loin-cloth and pulled it off. Hosein, her owner, happened to be passing, saw the incident and accused Browne of violating the girl. Straightaway he demanded ten slaves in compensation. Shortly afterwards Browne decided to return to Cobbe. By a regrettable coincidence he had left his goods in Cobbe stored in the house of Hosein, the owner of the slave-girl; Hosein now refused to release the goods until Browne had paid the compensation he demanded. Some merchants who were friendly to Browne told the Sultan of his predicament. The Sultan summoned Browne into his presence at El Fasher, vindicated him and ordered Hosein to drop his claim. But Browne was still unable to obtain compensation for the goods taken by the Sultan from him nearly two years ago.

At last, however, Browne felt secure enough to inquire about the future course of his journey. The information he obtained from the Melek Musa, the royal officer in charge of the affairs of foreign merchants, was extremely depressing: to the east the route to Sennar was impassable, as it led through Kordofan, whose tribes were bitterly hostile to Darfur; to the south there were only pagan tribes, whom the people of Darfur raided for slaves; to the west lay the kingdom of 'Bergoo' (Wadai), whose people would never receive a Christian in their midst. There was nothing misleading about this information: by coming to Darfur Browne had entered a cul-de-sac.

He found himself forced to spend another eighteen months in the country. It was possible to return to Egypt only on the caravan. But the Sultan, seeking to control the traffic for his own advantage, had given orders that no Egyptian merchants were to leave. During this long delay Browne divided his time between Cobbe and El Fasher, where he made himself acceptable by practising as a doctor. His terse account gives no clue to his feelings, but he seems to have suffered no special hardship or illness. At last, in March 1796, the road was opened, a caravan formed and Browne was allowed to join it. He reached Cairo safely, then travelled on, in leisurely manner, through Syria and Asia Minor to Constantinople. Not until the autumn of 1798 did he reach England; he had been absent over six years.

Browne's account of his experiences, published soon after his return, was not well received. He had anticipated some of the criticisms: 'a journey of the sort here described,' he wrote in his Preface, 'furnishes but few personal gratifications; and if agreeable sensations are sometimes excited in its course they at least are not profusely scattered nor of daily occurrence'. 'The hopes with which he undertook the voyage,' he confessed to his readers, 'even without being very sanguine, contrasted with the disappointment with which he now sits down to relate its occurrences, allow him little satisfaction from what has been executed.' This off-beat honesty is appealing, but it does not redeem the book from dullness. Indeed, Browne's *Travels* must be reckoned among the least enjoyable works in this genre that the age produced, 'the faithful registry of observation and occurrences' being, as a later critic has pointed out, 'rarely enlivened by any gleam of descriptive power'. Browne, though a man of great intelligence, seems, possibly through excessive self-absorption, to have lacked omnivorous curiosity. Thus—to take one striking example—he dismissed the history of Darfur, which he interpreted only in terms of the genealogy of its rulers, as a matter of 'small import'. Bruce, his critically regarded model of an African traveller, would have acted differently.[4]

Nevertheless, Browne could pride himself on having made an outstanding contribution to the geography of the interior, for he had gathered much information on the country round Darfur and thus filled a large blank on the map. In his self-appointed task of tracing the White Nile to its source he had not succeeded; but the reports that he had obtained suggested that the great river rose in mountainous country south of Darfur. These were not entirely mistaken, for the river of which he had heard, though not the White Nile, was to prove to be the greatest of its tributaries, the Bahr-al-Ghazal. This indicated how much remained still to be discovered.

281

To the general public there was nothing dramatic in such a report, but Browne could enjoy the scholar's satisfaction of finding his contribution appreciated by those best equipped to understand and

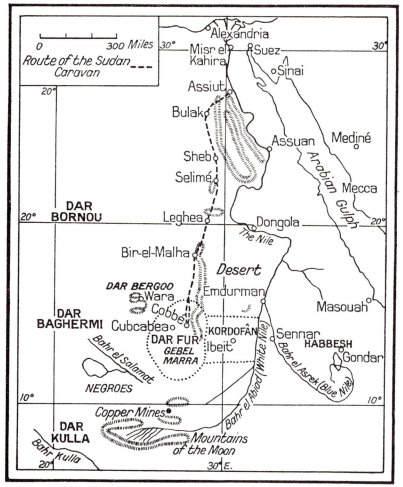

6. The Eastern Sudan: according to W. G. Browne, 1799

assess it. Banks became his friend, and Major Rennell, the outstanding African geographer in the whole of Europe, spoke of his achievement with admiration and respect.

Browne's book has another interest. One of his last chapters was entitled a 'Comparative View of Life and Happiness in the East and

11. Europeans in Africa: Christian slaves being tortured in Barbary from O. Dapper's *Description de l'Afrique*, Amsterdam, 1686

12. Europeans in Africa: European merchants at 'the King of Dahomy's Levée' from A. Dalzel's *The History of Dahomy*, London, 1793

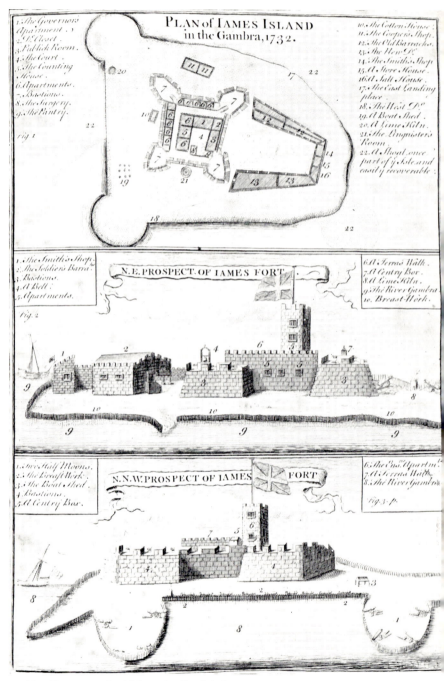

PLAN of IAMES ISLAND in the Gambra, 1732.

1. The Governor's Apartment.
2. D.º Closet.
3. Publick Room.
4. The Court.
5. The Counting House.
6. Apartments.
7. Bastions.
8. The Surgery.
9. The Pantry.

Fig 1

10. The Cotton House.
11. The Cooper's Shop.
12. The Old Barracks.
13. The New D.º
14. The Smith's Shop.
15. A Store House.
16. A Salt House.
17. The East Landing place.
18. The West D.º
19. A Boat Shed.
20. A Lime Kiln.
21. The Linguister's Room.
22. A Shoal once part of y.º Isle and easily recoverable.

N.E. PROSPECT OF IAMES FORT.

1. The Smith's Shop.
2. The Soldier's Barra.ᵗ
3. Bastions.
4. A Bell.
5. Apartments.

Fig.2

6. A Terras Walk.
7. A Centry Box.
8. A Lime Kiln.
9. The River Gambra.
10. Breast-Work.

N.N.W. PROSPECT OF IAMES FORT.

1. Two Half Moons.
2. The Breast Work.
3. The Boat Shed.
4. Bastions.
5. A Centry Box.

Fig.3.p.

6. The Ens.ⁿ Apartm.ᵗ
7. A Terras Walk.
8. The River Gambra.

13. Europeans in Africa: the English fort on James Island in the Gambia River. From T. Astley's *A New General Collection of Voyages and Travels*, London, 1745

in Europe'. To his contemporaries this appeared 'an eccentric encomium of eastern manners and customs at the expense of the civilisation of Europe'. In fact, it contains a remarkably sympathetic appreciation of Eastern culture, revealing in him who wrote it a quality of understanding that would be rare at any time and seems almost unique in that age when both Christians and Muslims were arrogantly convinced of their own superiority. Browne contrasts the 'impatience, activity and sanguine hope' of Europeans with the 'indolence, gravity and patience' of Orientals, and he concludes that the fatalism of Islam is likely to prove a greater source of happiness. He makes many other shrewd points. He points out that the backwardness of the east is due not to any congenital deficiency but to the evils caused by foreign invasion. He shocks the conventional by finding it 'deeply to be regretted that religion, intended to conciliate mankind, should be the chief cause of their ferocity against each other'. He has a crack at the Europocentricity of the classicists, informing his readers that 'the Arabian and Persian histories and romances abound with traces of magnanimity, of generosity, justice and courage, in no way inferior to, but in some instances exceeding those of other nations. The Greeks and ourselves have indeed stigmatized them with the name of barbarians, but impartial inquiry pronounces that they are susceptible of all that is admired in a polished people'.*5

Browne, indeed, is one of the first of those Englishmen who have found themselves temperamentally more in accord with the ways of life in the East than in their own country. This is brought out very clearly by his subsequent career. After two years in England he went abroad again, travelling through Asia Minor and the Levant to Egypt. Africa still held its lure for him. 'My warm wishes to promote the discovery of the interior of Africa,' he wrote to Banks from Cairo in September 1801, 'would infallibly conduct me to that country

* Here is another of Browne's observations; its acuteness will be appreciated by all those who have lived in a Muslim country. 'In complacency, ease and a disposition to associate, it might be imagined that the superiority would be found on the side of the Europeans. Yet such is not the fact. He who draws near a company of strangers in any place of public resort, finds a sufficient introduction to them in the simple and friendly salutation, *salam aleikum* and converses afterwards with them on terms of manly equality and freedom. We in vain desiderate in Europe some such easy and general introduction. A stranger, in a similar situation, is regarded as an intruder and viewed with the scowling eye of jealousy and mistrust.'6

were it not for the existence of some impediments which I cannot discover the means to surmount.' What these impediments were he declined to reveal. Returning to England in 1802, he put behind him for good his hopes of making another contribution to African discovery.[7]

For the next nine years he settled in London, leading the life of a scholarly recluse. 'An unusually grave and silent man' he appeared, whose manners seemed 'extremely cold and repulsive'. In society, so one contemporary noted, 'he conversed slowly and sparingly, never descended to familiarity, observed each and all of the company as if with jealousy and suspicion; but when this wore off and intimacy was established, he was exceedingly communicative and readily discussed the subjects about which he was most anxious and best qualified to impart information'. 'His demeanour', this same observer recorded, 'was precisely that of a Turk of the better order.' An appropriate and perhaps a deliberately induced similitude, for the Turkish lands attracted him ever more strongly and he taught himself to speak the language like a native. In 1811 he left England again, planning to reach the heartland of the Turkish race in the country beyond the Caspian. Once again he failed to reach his goal. On the road from Tabriz to Teheran he and his servant were set upon by a band of Kurdish robbers. He pleaded with the robbers to let his servant go, but gave himself up to them. They took him and strangled him and left his corpse stripped naked by the roadside. It was a wretched but not unheroic end to a brave and melancholy man.[8]

When the news of his death reached England, his will was opened. In it was a scrap of paper with a quotation from one of the Odes of Pindar in Browne's writing. A contemporary translation runs as follows:

> In the paths of dangerous fame
>   Trembling cowards never tread;
> Yet since all of mortal frame
>   Must be number'd with the dead,
> Who in dark unglorious shade
>   Would his useless life consume
> And with deedless years decay'd
>   Sink unhonoured to the tomb?
> I that shameful lot disdain,
>   I this doubtful list will prove.

The lines may stand not only as an epitaph but as a revelation of the flame that burned beneath that grave exterior.[9]

V

THE AFRICAN ASSOCIATION'S ACHIEVEMENT

'IT MAY BE JUSTLY remarked that the course of a few years has solved many of the questions respecting the geography and natural history of Africa that appeared the most important and curious, during a series of ages; and it may be added that the physical geography of Africa turns out to be more remarkable than was ever supposed.' So Major Rennell wrote in 1802; he went on—his observations forming an interim balance sheet of the Association's achievements—to enumerate what he regarded as the most significant geographical discoveries of the preceding fourteen years.[1]

The first place he gave to the establishment of the direction of the Niger's course. The majority of geographers had believed that the river flowed from east to west; Park's eye-witness account had showed conclusively that this view was wrong. Next in importance, so Rennell considered, was the information brought back by Browne about the Nile, suggesting that the river had its rise in the country south of Darfur. He then went on to list certain points of interest only to the classical geographer—in particular, Hornemann's discovery of the site of the temple of Jupiter Ammon at Siwa and Park's identification of the original lotus-plant of antiquity:* such a list suggests rather too donnish a sense of values; no doubt Rennell was influenced by the fact that he was absorbed in the study of Herodotus.[2]

Of the questions that remained the most interesting was un-

---

* In the sandy country of the *Sahel* Park had found a small shrub growing in great profusion; it produced 'small farinaceous berries of yellow colour and delicious taste'. The local people dried the berries, pounded the pulp and from it formed little cakes, which resembled 'in colour and flavour the sweetest gingerbread'. The stones could be put in water, which they would turn into a 'sweet liquor'. A similar shrub was reported from Tunis; 'there can be little doubt,' Park concluded, 'of its being the lotus mentioned by Pliny as the food of the Libyan Lotophagi'.[3]

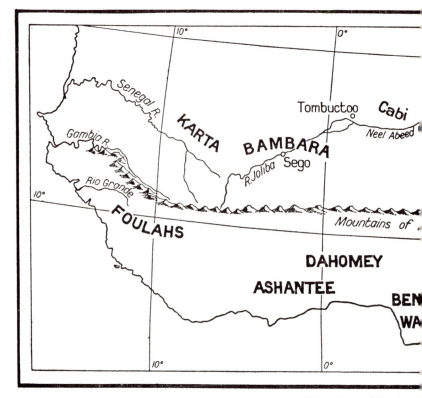

7. The Rivers of West Af

doubtedly that on the further course of the Niger. Two theories held
the field. The first was a resurrection of the idea put forward in
classical times that the Niger and the Nile were in fact one river.
Hornemann claimed to have gathered evidence that the two streams
were connected, while the ever-fanciful Jackson had picked up a
story from a Moor who had been in Timbuktu, telling how a party
of Negroes travelled all the way from Timbuktu to Cairo by canoe,
except for one short stretch over a cataract. Rennell never accepted
this theory; he pointed out that there was bound to exist a difference
in level between the two rivers which would make their junction
impossible, and found confirmation in the reports that Browne
brought back from Darfur, which contained no hint of a great river
flowing from west to east but described the rivers to the south-west
of Darfur as flowing in a westerly direction.[4]

286

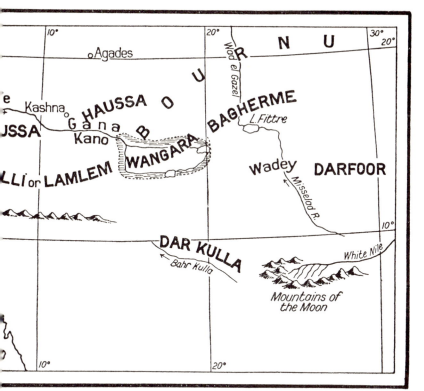

cording to Rennell, 1798

The other theory was put forward by Rennell himself and maintained for the rest of his long life. 'On the whole,' he wrote in 1798,
'it can scarcely be doubted that the Niger terminates in lakes, in the
eastern [*sic*] quarter of Africa: and those lakes'—here he was drawing on al-Idrisi—'seem to be situated in Wangara and Ghana.' A third
possibility—which no European scholar had yet supported—was
suggested by the Moor, Shabeni, who said that 'he always understood
that the Nile [i.e. the Nile of the Negroes or Niger] empties itself in
the sea, the salt sea or the great ocean'. This seems a sufficiently
categorical statement, but Rennell twisted it to his own purpose,
explaining that 'by the word *sea* (*bahr*), it is well known, the Arabs
mean to express a lake also'. Rennell's theory of the Niger ending in
a great lake somewhere in the central Sudan was buttressed by his
belief that there existed 'a belt of mountains extending from west to

east' between the tenth and eleventh degree of latitude. It was clear that the Niger, the Senegal and the Gambia rose in mountainous country to the south of Bambara and Bambuk; Lucas, it will be remembered, had secured reports of 'a succession of hills' between the Niger and Ashanti, 'among which are mountains of stupendous height'; there were a great number of streams that flowed into the Gulf of Guinea and must have their source in higher land in the interior: surely this was evidence enough to suggest the existence of a mountain chain. Such a chain Rennell came to mark in bold hatching on his maps, giving to it the name of Kong, for some of the hills seen by Park to the south of Bambara had borne that name, though in fact *Kong* is merely the Mandingo word for *mountain*. Rennell was, of course, entirely wrong; the Niger does not end in a lake, nor do the highlands of Futa Jallon stretch across West Africa. The errors of the eminent prove both ironical and instructive; the controversy over the Niger's course continued for another thirty years. Few episodes provide so clear a lesson of the necessity for the scholar of keeping an open mind and of being able to judge how much evidence must be acquired before a theory can be put forward with assurance—and of the difficulty of doing so.[5]

Careful examination of Rennell's maps of Africa of 1790, 1798 and 1802 reveals other errors, for which, given the evidence at his disposal, he could hardly be blamed. Thus Bornu covered far too large an area, and Katsina and the other Hausa states were placed at least four degrees of latitude too far to the north, with the result that the unknown country between Katsina and the sea was shown as a much wider belt than in fact it was. There was, of course, no conception of the Niger's bend, but the location of Timbuktu was approximately correct; Park, however, had exaggerated his distances, and Segu was placed too far to the east. Nevertheless, one has only to compare Rennell's map of 1802 with D'Anville's produced half a century earlier to see how considerable had been the advance; on the Fezzan and the central Sahara, on Darfur and its neighbouring countries, on the states between the Senegal and Niger a great deal of new information had been acquired in the space of ten years.[6]

'At no period of time has the spirit of enterprise been more active than the present, nor at any time has the eagerness for discoveries been more amply rewarded.' So proclaimed a writer in the *European Magazine* for June 1799, an issue which contained the first serial instalment of Park's *Travels*. *The eagerness for discoveries*—here was another aspect of the Association's achievement: its work was serving to excite public opinion. How far those who were not members of the Association discussed its activities, it is impossible to say; there are no references to its work in any of the published contemporary diaries or collections of letters. But anyone who read the reviews of the day would come across reports of its activities; thus the *Annual Register* of 1797 printed almost verbatim the Association's report for that year. In 1799 the Association received another advertisement from an unexpected quarter, when there was published in Edinburgh at the price of five shillings—the first edition of Park's *Travels* had cost six times as much—a little book entitled *A Historical and Philosophical Sketch of the Discoveries and Settlements of the Europeans in North and West Africa.* Most of the book was taken up with an account of the various expeditions that had been undertaken in the preceding ten years. No name appeared on the title-page, but it became known that the author was a young Scotsman, John Leyden.

Leyden demands a brief measure of attention. An extremely remarkable man, whom many of his contemporaries regarded as a genius, his career at one stage illustrates the influence of Africa on a vigorous and imaginative mind. He was born in 1775, the son of a Lowland shepherd. Despite his humble birth, his passion for knowledge enabled him to make his way to the University. Before long he made a name for himself in Edinburgh society, where Walter Scott became one of his closest friends. At the University he distinguished himself as a linguist; later he won a reputation as a poet and a collector of old ballads; all his life he was to display remarkable intellectual versatility. His energy was extraordinary: he prided himself as much on physical as on mental prowess—and became a formidable boxer. In any company, his spirits 'generally at full flood', this tough, shaggy young man liked to assert himself, his manner boisterous, his voice 'naturally loud and harsh' but his mood always good-humoured and his actions generous.[7]

In the memoir written after Leyden's early death Walter Scott described what Africa came to mean to his friend. His thoughts turned

towards the history of Africa in which he found much to enchant an imagination that loved to dwell upon the grand, the marvellous, the romantic, and even the horrible; and which was rather fired than appalled by the picture of personal danger and severe privations. Africa, indeed, had peculiar charms for Leyden. He delighted to read of hosts, whose arrows intercepted the sunbeams; of kings and leaders, who judged of the numberless number of their soldiers by marching them over the trunk of a cedar and only deemed their strength sufficient to take the field when such myriads had passed as to reduce the solid timber to impalpable dust—the royal halls, also of Dahomey, built of skulls and cross-bones and moistened with the daily blood of new victims of tyranny;—all, in short, that presented strange, wild and romantic views of what have been quaintly entitled "the ultimities and summities of human nature", and which furnished new and unheard-of facts in the history of man, had great fascination for his ardent imagination. And about this time he used to come into company quite full of these extraordinary stories, garnished faithfully with the unpronounceable names of the despots and tribes of Africa, which anyone at a distance would have taken for the exorcism of a conjuror.

Here indeed, one may feel, is a classic expression of the Romantic view of Africa, not uncoloured, one suspects, by Scott's own imagination, for Leyden's book is a strictly factual account.[8]

The triumphant return of his contemporary and compatriot, Mungo Park, had a powerful influence on Leyden. In 1800 he had been ordained a Minister of the Church, but his real vocation, he felt, was to travel, to extend 'the bounds of literary and geographical knowledge'; 'the discoveries of Mungo Park haunted his very slumbers'. His friends cannot have been surprised when in 1802 he offered his services to the African Association; but they were deeply distressed at his willingness to embark on 'an enterprise which sad examples have shown no little better than an act of absolute suicide'. To divert his mind they set about procuring him a post in India; the only vacancy that could be found was as a surgeon. Leyden was attracted and within six months, working from scratch, succeeded in passing all his qualifying exams. He sailed for the East in 1803. He never saw Scotland again, for he died of fever in Java in 1811. But in the space of eight years he made his reputation as an outstanding Orientalist, the equal, possibly, had he lived, the superior of the immortal William Jones. For he had 'nearly effected a classification of the various languages of Asia and their kindred dialects', thus achieving in less than a decade and in addition to his official duties 'as much for Asia', so one authority has claimed, 'as the combined scholarship of centuries had done for Europe'.[9]

In 1802 Leyden's *Historical Sketch* was translated into German; this shows the interest that Africa could arouse in a part of Europe that had no direct stake in the continent.* Another indication of German interest is provided by the extraordinary success of a book that appeared in Germany in 1801, entitled *Travels through the Interior of Africa from the Cape of Good Hope to Morocco*. This professed to tell the adventures of a cabinet-maker named Damberger, who had enlisted in the Dutch East India Company as a soldier, been posted to the Cape of Good Hope, deserted and decided to make his way home overland, since it would be impossible to get a passage by sea. In this way he had come to travel through Angola and the Congo into Housa and across the Sahara. At first sight the book has a convincing air about it. Damberger's adventures are not improbable, and the references to the narratives of other travellers, such as Park or Le Vaillant, are cunningly introduced to show where they went wrong in their descriptions; it is not surprising that many people were taken in. For in fact the work was soon revealed as an elaborate hoax, perpetrated by a printer of Wittenberg with the aid of a scholar named Junge. It was a hoax that achieved an international reputation, for the book was translated into French and English. Hoaxes should be more entertaining; perhaps the most damning comment one can make on Damberger's *Travels* is that they serve to prove the old adage that fiction is much less interesting than fact.

The best evidence of a scholarly German interest in Africa is to be found in the pages of the monthly journal, *Allgemeine Geographische Ephemeriden*. This had been founded in 1798 by an astronomer, von Zachs; its purpose was to bring together the latest discoveries in Geography, Statistics and Economics. It was not the first publication of its kind, for two similar periodicals had appeared in Germany in the 1780s: these were probably the earliest geographical journals in the world. Von Zachs was a friend of Blumenbach, who gladly passed on to him all the information he received about the work of the African Association. There seems indeed to have been nothing

---

* In fact German interest in Africa seems to have been steadily increasing in the 1790s. In 1791 a biblical scholar, P. J. Bruns, set about compiling his *Neue systematische Erdbeschreibung von Afrika*. Bruns was exasperated with the unscholarly methods used by the compilers of encyclopaedic works on Africa and laid special stress on the importance of citing the source for every piece of information. His work, completed in 1799, provided the most accurate and the most comprehensive account of the continent available at that time. But it does not appear to have been translated into any other language.

relating to the progress of African discovery that missed the vigilant editor's attention.

In 1804 Sir William Young, the Secretary of the African Association, was able to tell members that 'by their example they have become (as it were) the founders of new societies established in other countries with similar views and purposes'. The plural was hardly justified; in fact, the only country that appeared to have followed the English example was France. French interest in Africa will be considered in some detail in the following chapter; here it will be sufficient to notice that shortly after a special copy of Hornemann's *Journal* had been presented to the First Consul there was established in Paris *La Société de l'Afrique interieure et de Découvertes*. It proved a still-born child; shortly after its foundation, the resumption of the struggle with England made it impossible to put the new society to any service.[10]

Finally, as Sir William Young told members, even Spain, where 'a jealous and distrustful spirit of government hath ever monopolized and arrogated to itself the powers, the means and the direction of every public pursuit', had turned to their Association and sought the advice of 'their respected Treasurer [Sir Joseph Banks] for a traveller they were planning to send to the interior'. On this occasion Sir William stated that he was not at liberty to disclose the traveller's name; there will soon be cause to make his acquaintance.[11]

France and Spain were hostile powers when Sir William made his statement. Nevertheless, he stated that the Association would be willing to show any institutions concerned with the exploration of Africa 'the road to success, not regarding them as rivals, but as coadjutors and allies, in an undertaking of mutual and general advantage'. In a country flushed with the fever of war this was a gesture at once generous and bold.[12]

When they looked back, then, on the first fifteen years of their activity the members of the African Association had reason to be satisfied. Their travellers had made the most substantial contribution to the geography of Africa that Europe had received since the days of the Portuguese. It could be argued—as one of the bright young men of the newly founded *Edinburgh Review* pointed out in a malicious article on the Association's *Proceedings* for 1802—that these discoveries had led to no practical results and that there was no convincing evidence to show that a profitable trade could be developed with the interior; it would be fairer to say that the possibilities of intercourse had not yet been fully explored. The beginnings of a new approach to Africa can be traced back to a generation before the founding of the Association; but the supporters of the Association could rightly feel that they had done much at once to advertise, to stimulate and to make explicit this movement of humane and scholarly interest in the last great continent to be subjected to the curiosity of Europe.[13]

They could feel, too, that their activities were in accord with the most elevated spirit of the age. 'A new and nobler passion than the thirst of either gold or conquest was enlisted in the service of navigation and discovery. Travels and voyages were undertaken with no other view than that of ascertaining the real figure of, and perfecting the knowledge of the globe; the study and nature of man; the alleviation of human miseries and the multiplication of human comforts and employments, even among the most remote and barbarous tribes often not only ungrateful but jealous and hostile to their disinterested benefactors.' Such was the view taken by the author of a 'Summary Review of the Eighteenth Century' that appeared in the *Annual Register* for 1800. A later generation, endowed with the easy superiority of hindsight, might be inclined to doubt the sincerity of those words and to mock their afflatus. To do so is unfair; an intelligent European, living in the year 1800, had reason to feel proud of the century's progress, a century in which, as the same writer pointed out, 'the intercourse of men' became 'more extensive than at any former period' and 'the progression of knowledge more rapid'. The world, indeed, was coming to be knit together and for the benefit of the majority of its people. But the old Adam of gold and conquest had not been banished: the 'remote and barbarous tribes' often had reason to suspect those who came among them, even bearing gifts. In the meeting of Europe and Africa there was to be, together with a new peace and a new prosperity, much suffering and much loss. The sum of it all, the ultimate balance of good and evil, no human mind can calculate; the utmost that the historian can do is to try to understand how things happened. Here, then, at the beginning of a new century that was to bring such vast changes to the world, one may detect a foretaste of things to come and see in the movements of some explorers, the decisions of some politicians the roots of a new imperialism.[14]

THE ROOTS OF IMPERIALISM

I

EXPLORATION AND IMPERIALISM

'TRAVELS WERE UNDERTAKEN WITH no other view than that of
perfecting the knowledge of the globe': it is the conventional interpretation of European exploration, an interpretation peculiarly
flattering to European self-esteem. And certainly if one recalls the
impulse that drove a handful of young men, Park and Hornemann
and Browne, to win fame as African explorers, it is clear that
passionate curiosity was their strongest motive. But among those who
sponsored exploration, as the detailed history of the African Association indicates, curiosity, though always powerful, was by no means
the only motive that gave constancy to their endeavour; men of the
world with an interest in commerce and in politics, they were quick
to appreciate, even if with too sanguine an assurance, the practical
advantages that might accrue from a better knowledge of the interior
of Africa. Already, too, as Banks's remarkable speech on the
significance of Park's discoveries revealed, there were some who
foresaw that these practical advantages could be ensured only by
an act of conquest, by the extension of European rule.

In a later age, when many an explorer set out for Africa as the
agent of his government, seeking not only to map but also to claim
the unknown stretches of the interior, the connection between
imperialism and exploration became explicit. Then, within a generation, almost the whole of Africa was divided up between the powers
of Europe. Various causes gave birth to that frantic movement:
growing interest in the commercial possibilities of the continent;
philanthropic concern to extinguish the slave trade and to protect
missionary endeavour; above all, the intense rivalry of the nation
states of Europe, impelled by fear of one another to claim dominant
rights for their own nationals over vast blocks of Africa.

297

The Scramble for Africa began in the 1880s; yet the first signs of that movement can be detected in the opening decade of the century. The exploits of a French Army in Egypt, the adventures of a mysterious Spaniard in Morocco, the plans drawn up by the British Government for a mission to the Niger, the deeper involvement of the British in the affairs of the West Coast, all these different episodes indicate the development of a new relationship, of vast consequence for the future, between Europe and Africa.

II

FRANCE AND AFRICA

SENEGAL

IN THE LATTER HALF of the eighteenth century the French had
the same reasons as the English for being interested in West Africa;
for both powers their bases on the West Coast formed one corner in
the triangle of the Atlantic trade. But the French were weaker than
their rivals; they were, indeed, worse off than they had been in the
earlier half of the century, for the losses of the Seven Years' War
were not made good until long after 1815. In 1763 their possessions
were confined to Goree and Albreda; sixteen years later they recovered St Louis; but they were not able to re-establish themselves
on the Upper Senegal. In 1787 a French agent named Rubault made
an adventurous journey from St Louis across the Ferlo to Tambacunda and on to the Faleme and Galam. Establishing himself in the
ruins of Fort St Joseph, he began to trade and had soon acquired a
good store of gold and ivory, together with one thousand slaves.
Lacking the means of escorting this human merchandise to the coast,
he sent to St Louis for a convoy. The convoy arrived too late;
Rubault was dead, murdered by his chattels, who had broken their
fetters and risen against him. Thirty years passed before a Frenchman
was seen again in the countries of the Upper Senegal.[*1]

* Another Frenchman, Saugnier, made the trip up the Senegal to Galam
in the 1780s. He had already had one adventure in Africa; on his first
voyage from France he had been shipwrecked on the Saharan coast,
captured by Moors, taken across the desert and held for some months as
a slave in Morocco. He published an account of his experiences in 1791.
In the Preface to this work he announced his intention, if he could obtain
sufficient backing, of undertaking a journey across Africa. From Senegal
he would proceed to Timbuktu and then move either eastwards to Ethiopia

With the outbreak of the Revolution St Louis fell upon evil days; the politicians neglected to succour it—at one time the officers were reduced to drinking water instead of wine—and when in 1793 the slave trade was formerly abolished the factory lost half its value. Not till 1802 did the Government adopt a more positive attitude towards the colony; in the instructions given in that year to the Governor Blanchot one may catch the tone of a Bonaparte.* 'Up to now Senegal has been regarded only as a factory limited to exploiting certain branches of trade native to the country. Citizen Blanchot will lift his thoughts above such narrow bounds. The power of the metropolis of France grows daily under the hands that govern it; it is necessary for the colonies to feel the same dynamic. It is not enough for Senegal to exist as a mere stake for the republic in the rich territories of Africa; it must serve as a growing point, making use of every possible form of contact.' Fort St Joseph was to be refounded as a centre for the restored slave trade, and the Governor was required to do all he could to establish 'every sort of practicable relationship between the Senegal and the interior of Africa'.[3]

These instructions could not be fulfilled. In 1805 the French were involved in a war with Futa Toro which debarred them from moving up the Senegal. Goree had been in English hands, with one short break, since 1800, and the garrison at St Louis, lacking control of the sea, were blockaded. The English assault was delayed until 1809; it met with no resistance. St. Louis remained in English hands until 1817.[4]

The French inability to control the sea-routes of the world imposed a fatal limitation on their colonial policy; all their overseas campaigns in twenty years of war with the English ended in failure. But this was a lesson that could be learned only from cruel experience; in the years 1797–1802 a dynamic colonial policy seemed perfectly feasible. These years witnessed a remarkable development in French

or southwards towards Mozambique. What happened to him after the publication of his book is not known, but there is no evidence that he ever embarked on so grandiose an expedition.[2]

* Blanchot had been Governor from 1788 to 1801 and had done a remarkable job in holding the garrison together. In 1801, at the age of sixty-six, he returned to France. His successor proved so corrupt that there was a riot against him and he was driven out and had to take refuge with the English. Blanchot was then reappointed and remained at St Louis until his death in 1807.

ideas about colonialism, culminating in that extraordinary adventure, the Egyptian expedition.[5]

During the first years of the Revolution the West Indies presented the changing rulers of France with one of their most intractable problems. The complexities of the situation led to a revulsion against colonialism; Robespierre's cry 'Perish the colonies rather than our principles' became one of the watchwords of the Revolution. By 1797, with the worst excesses of the Revolution over, a new and more sober spirit was emerging. In July of that year, Talleyrand, that much travelled, widely read, brilliantly intelligent and highly unscrupulous ex-bishop, recently returned from exile, chose as the subject of a paper read to the *Institut National*: 'The advantage to be gained from new colonies in the present circumstances.' As stimulating as it was lucid, the address possessed more than academic significance, for a few weeks later Talleyrand was appointed Foreign Minister. To Talleyrand colonies had a double importance: they were a means of increasing the nation's wealth and they were safety-valves for dis-content, channels for the excess energy France so evidently possessed. He was pessimistic, as well he might be, about the future of the West Indies; hence his anxiety for new colonies. But where should they be founded? In tropical countries he suggested, countries which would provide both the products and the markets needed by France. In particular, he directed his listeners' attention to West Africa and to Egypt.[6]

Touching briefly on West Africa, Talleyrand referred to the British colonies on Bulama and at Sierra Leone, and mentioned the sugges-tion recently made by a certain citizen Montlinot that the French should establish a colony on the islands of the Bissagos archipelago to the south of the Gambia. Public interest in West African coloniza-tion was carried further by that indefatigable Swedish idealist, Wadström, who had recently transferred his activities from London to Paris. In 1798 he printed a *Précis* of his account of Bulama and Sierra Leone. This work created so much attention that a special committee of the legislature was appointed to go further into Wadström's ideas. The committee decided against any attempt to establish a colony in West Africa at the present; after all, if Freetown had been unable to defend itself against attack by French privateers, would a French colony be able to count on immunity from the British? But there was another more powerful reason why Wadström's suggestions should be turned down; Frenchmen, in the spring of

1798, when their government's plans were still a secret, were beginning to recognize the wonderful attraction of Egypt.[7]

EGYPT

Even before the Revolution, Frenchmen had played with the idea of annexing Egypt. In 1769 that powerful minister, the Duc de Choiseul, looking prophetically to the future, had considered the decline of French power in the Caribbean as inevitable and seen in Egypt a possible compensation. The American Revolution gave added meaning to this line of thought. Moreover, in the 1780s the Ottoman Empire was beginning to show serious symptoms of decline; should Austria and Russia be allowed to seize all the rich provinces of the Turks for themselves? Those two highly readable books, Savary's *Letters* and Volney's *Travels*, served to increase popular interest in the land of the Nile. But a government, threatened with bankruptcy and revolution, was in no position to enter into any wild adventures.*[1]

Talleyrand was not the only influential Frenchman whose eyes had turned to Egypt in 1797. In Italy Bonaparte, that dazzling young conqueror, had recently annexed the Ionian Isles for the Republic, thinking of them as stepping stones to the East. In September Talleyrand wrote to Bonaparte, 'Egypt as a colony would soon replace the products of the Antilles, and as a route would give us control of the trade with India.' Later that year Bonaparte, back in Paris to command the Army of England, said to one of his associates, 'My glory has already disappeared. This little Europe does not supply enough of it for me. I must seek it in the East: all great fame comes

* Volney was strongly opposed to any attempt to annex Egypt. In a pamphlet which he wrote at the time and which deserves a place among the classics of anti-imperialism he elaborated on the obstacles the French would have to face: the hostility of the Turks, of the English, and of the Egyptians themselves, combined with the difficulties of administration— 'the characters of both nations being diametrically opposite in every respect, would become mutually odious', the climate and the corruption that inevitably attended all colonial enterprises. 'It is at home,' he argued, 'and not beyond the seas, we should look for a Egypt and for Caribee Islands. We should think rather of improving than of enlarging our possessions—we should learn to enjoy the riches in our hands rather than employ in a foreign climate those pains we neglect to take at home.' But the experts differed: Magallon, who had been French Consul in Egypt and spent thirty-five years in the Levant, was one of the most ardent advocates of an expedition to Egypt.[2]

from that quarter.' The French lacked the means, as Bonaparte discovered when he inspected the Channel ports, to mount a direct invasion against England; but could not the islanders be crippled by a blow at their possessions in the East? In Bonaparte's mind that winter strategic arguments fused dynamically with the impulse of a restless ambition.[3]

Talleyrand gave shape to these grandiose dreams by submitting to the Directory on February 14 a memorandum proposing an attack on Egypt. 'Egypt,' he proclaimed in his first paragraph, 'was a province of the Roman Republic; it must become a province of the French Republic. The Romans robbed Egypt of kings illustrious in arts and sciences: the French will rob them of the most atrocious tyrants [the Mamluk Beys] who have ever existed.' A blow against England, a means to glory, a moral act: by such specious arguments the Directory was won over. Within three weeks the order had been given to prepare for the expedition.

In the weeks of preparation those who were in the secret could let their minds swell with the grandeur of their project. 'One cannot indeed calculate,' Talleyrand had written, 'the immense advantages that *La Grande Nation* would derive from this country.' But he had gone on to suggest some of them: Egypt would be restored to her ancient wealth and splendour; trade, agriculture and industry would flourish; the old route across the Isthmus of Suez, barred for so many centuries by the Turks, would come into use again, the importance of the long sea-route to the Indies would disappear, and the English would suffer a blow comparable to that which crippled the Venetians, when the Portuguese discovered the sea-route to the Indies. This was not all: French influence would spread from Egypt westwards across the North Coast of Africa, eastwards to the countries of Asia; 'we will penetrate into every part of the immense continent of Africa and discover there the rivers of the interior, the mountains and the mines of iron and of gold in which that country abounds'. The gentleman of the African Association in London were dreaming of gathering into their country's hands the rich trade of the Sahara; how modest that great project seems when set beside the extravaganzas of the French.[4]

The story of the Egyptian Expedition has often been told; here the briefest of narratives will suffice. Bonaparte left Toulon on May 19, 1798 with thirty-five thousand troops. Six weeks later, having eluded Nelson and his warships and captured Malta on their way, the

French soldiers landed in Egypt. Within a month they had captured Alexandria, advanced on Cairo and in a battle fought against the backcloth of the Pyramids—the first of those encounters, to be repeated on many a dusty field, in which the chivalry of Africa, with immense bravery, hurled themselves in vain against the disciplined fire-power of Europe—shattered the military might of the Mamluks. But if the French were now masters of Egypt, the English controlled the sea-routes to France, for Nelson had destroyed the French fleet while it lay at anchor in Aboukir Bay.

Bonaparte spent six months in Cairo, organizing his new conquest. In February he set out for Syria, where the Turks were massing against him. Gaza fell before him, and Jaffa; the whole of Palestine was nearly his. But Acre, defended by Turkish soldiers and British sailors, held out and robbed him of that crushing victory that might have opened the way to Constantinople. His army reduced by plague, he returned to Egypt. In July he defeated a sea-borne invasion mounted by the Turks. In August he was on his way back to France; events in Europe had taken a serious turn and provided him with the justification for abandoning his army.

The French troops remained in Egypt another two years, first under the command of General Kléber, who died at the hand of an assassin, and then of General Menou, who married an Egyptian girl and became a Muslim. But it was impossible to hold out against the combined attacks of the Turks and the English, who had drawn troops from the Cape and from India. In August 1801 the French surrendered.

Seen thus—and this is the conventional view—the Egyptian Expedition is a highly dramatic but politically sterile episode in the career of Europe's Man of Destiny. But from an African angle the Egyptian Expedition has a deeper significance. For this was the first time since the days of ancient Rome that a European power had brought entirely under its control an African state. Here, in microcosm, were displayed all the characteristic problems of imperial rule; and in the centre of the stage was one who possessed, according to the hyperbole of one great historian, 'the grandest intellectual gifts ever vouchsafed to man', who revealed, as even his critics would admit, a mind at once inexhaustively fertile and supremely practical. For the student of imperialism, what episode can possess greater fascination.[5]

Bonaparte's first task was to justify his assault in Egyptian eyes; he did so by posing as a liberator and as a friend of Islam. 'Peoples of Egypt,' so ran the proclamation issued as he landed in the country, 'you will be told that I have come to destroy your religion; do not believe it! Answer that I have come to restore your rights and punish the usurpers, and that, more than the Mamluks, I respect God, his Prophet and the Koran.' This was not all bluff: Mamluk rule could be represented as an oppressive foreign tyranny; and Bonaparte was genuinely sensitive to the attractions of Islam. Moreover, he realized from the start that if he was to establish his rule he would need to gain the support of the leaders of opinion. His plans were cracked by what a later writer has called 'the ineradicable conviction of all Egyptians, bred into them by their centuries of suffering, that in the end all foreign rule is bad'. The French occupation provoked some Egyptians to use the means of resistance with which the mid-twentieth century has become so familiar; French soldiers were murdered in the streets of Cairo, and in October there was a serious revolt in the capital. The French retorted with summary executions, which served only to increase the populace's hatred of the invaders. And yet it is clear that the Egyptians alone would not have been able to eject the French; without the British and Turkish intervention, Egypt would have remained a French colony.[6]

For three years, in fact, Egypt was a French colony. How was it governed? Later imperialists had precedents to guide them—Lugard, for instance, in Northern Nigeria could draw on British experience in India. The French in Egypt had no such advantages, but they possessed, like Marxists in a later age, tremendous intellectual assurance, the ideas of the Revolution providing them with the blue-print of a good society. These ideas Bonaparte proceeded to apply with remarkable tact. 'We must gradually accustom these people to our ways and our outlook,' he told his army commanders on their landing in the country, 'and meanwhile we must allow them plenty of latitude between themselves in their internal affairs.' A year later, on his departure from Egypt, he expressed himself with the insight of one who has accepted the modifications produced by experience: 'it is impossible for us to expect to exert direct influence over peoples to whom we are such strangers. In order to rule them we have need of intermediaries.' Here indeed, one may think, is one of the classic expressions of the theory of Indirect Rule. But in the next sentence Bonaparte went on to assert, 'we must give them leaders or they will choose their own'; this indeed is a drastic twist, which transforms the whole theory.[7]

305

Bonaparte had come to deliver the Egyptians from their Mamluk oppressors; the Mamluk Beys had been overthrown—who was to take their place? 'The Egyptians will be called upon to hold all offices,' he had promised in his first proclamation, 'the wisest and most learned and most virtuous will govern, and the people will be happy.' Already he was clear in his mind where these paragons were to be found—in the religious leaders of the country, the muftis and the sheikhs, that local aristocracy whom the Mamluks had systematically excluded from office. This was the class Bonaparte both flattered and respected. To associate Egyptians more closely in the work of government he created a framework of assemblies or Divans, both at provincial and at national level. Their members were nominated by the French commandants, being selected from those 'who are the most distinguished in the country by their enlightenment, their talents, and the way they received the French'. The functions of the Divans were purely consultative, but there was a serious, indeed a liberal, purpose behind them. On the one hand, they would serve 'to try to accustom the notables of Egypt to the ideas of assembly and government'; on the other, they would keep the French informed on what the people of the country thought and desired. Thus at the first meeting of the Grand Divan Bonaparte put before the notables a series of questions touching on every aspect of administration; he explained that he wanted to learn what needed to be done 'for the good of the people'. Anyone who has studied the constitutional development of an African colony during the twentieth century will appreciate the fundamental soundness of many of Bonaparte's ideas about colonial administration and the wonderful clarity with which they were expressed.[8]

The French had come to restore the wealth and splendour of Egypt. Administrative reform was therefore to be accompanied by plans for economic development; such plans demanded expert knowledge. Bonaparte, it is not always recognized, was himself an intellectual; 'the true conquests, the only conquests that cost no regret,' he had said on his election to the *Institut National* the year before, 'are those achieved over ignorance'. It was this splendid principle that led him, before leaving France, to form a Commission of Arts and Sciences to accompany him to Egypt. The one hundred and sixty-seven *savants*, who comprised that body, formed a brilliant company. At their head came Monge and Berthollet, both in their fifties and men with much experience of public service, the one

famed as a mathematician, the other as a chemist. There were other
older men among them, Vivant Denon, the artist, who had been a
court favourite under Louis XV and who produced the most vivid
personal account of the expedition, Venture de Paradis, once interpreter at the Consulate in Egypt, now distinguished as an Orientalist,
and Dolomieu, the geologist, whose name is immortalized in one of
the great mountain ranges of Europe. Beside them was a group of
brilliant young men, drawn from the great educational institutions
of Paris, many of whom were to win fame in later life. Antiquaries,
architects and astronomers, civil engineers and composers, men of
letters and musicians, printers and pharmacists, surveyors and
zoologists—every field of knowledge, every facet of technology was
represented there.[9]

In Egypt the leading members of the Commission established an
Institute, for which the *Institut National* in Paris served as a model.
The Institute was housed in Cairo. To its members Bonaparte constantly referred questions of practical importance; thus at the very
first session he sought their advice on 'the means of improving the
baking of bread, of building wind or water mills, of purifying the
Nile water, and of collecting views on the native jurisprudence,
judicial system and education'. But members were encouraged to do
research on subjects of interest to themselves. Observations on the
wing of an ostrich, memoir 'on the optical phenomenon known as
the Mirage', notice on ophthalmia, project for the establishment of
an agricultural research station, extracts from a fifteenth-century
geography of Egypt, memoir on the caravans which arrive from
Darfur and Sennar—these are a few of the subjects to be found in the
Mémoires of the Institute later published in Paris. Nor was this the
end of their work. When the members of the Commission were back
in France, after the final surrender, they put together all that they
had discovered in a truly monumental work: *Description de l'Égypte
ou Receuil des Observations et des Recherches qui ont été faites
pendant l'Expédition de l'Armée Française.*[10]

In the field of African studies the *Description de l'Égypte* remains
without a peer; indeed, there has perhaps never been a comparable
work devoted on such a scale to a single country. It consists of nine
massive folio volumes of text and twelve of plates, so large that a
special reading desk was made to be sold with them. Every aspect of
the country's life was covered, its antiquities, its present state, its
natural history. Such a work, which took quarter of a century to

produce, could not fail to serve as a stimulus to further discovery. The section of maps represented a standard of cartography that had been achieved for no other country in the world. The careful descriptions and engravings of antiquities laid the foundations of the science of Egyptology, while the discovery of the tri-lingual Rosetta stone—later captured by the English—provided a key to the hieroglyphs. The treasury of Arabic manuscripts brought back to France provided Marcel and Jomard, the expedition's orientalists, with occupation for a lifetime. Here indeed was a 'true conquest'—and one which modern scholars would do well to make themselves aware of; the twentieth century has not yet produced a comparable work.

Leaving aside the work of the Institute, the expedition to Egypt was in practical terms a failure; yet few failures have exerted so potent an influence over the future. For the Egyptians the coming of the French was, it should not be forgotten, a brazen act of aggression, associated with the hardships and the indignities of foreign occupations; yet the consequences were not wholly bad. From the French they could learn something of the organizing ability and technical expertise of modern Europe; no printing-press, to give but a single example, had ever been seen in Egypt before those which the French brought with them. For better and for worse Egypt's isolation was broken down, the stagnation of the centuries of Mamluk rule violently disturbed. The way was in some degree prepared for the economic and administrative reforms to be introduced by the Albanian adventurer, Muhammad Ali.*

* One may learn how the Egyptians regarded the French by reading the Journal of the Sheikh al Gabarti, published in a French translation in 1838; it reveals very clearly the darker side of the French occupation, the fear and the hatred, the executions and the forced levies. Hornemann, too, has an apposite comment: 'it is incredible how deep and strong an impression the expedition of the French has made on the minds of the pilgrims to and from Mecca; dispersed to their several homes, they will carry an aggravated prejudice against Christians far and wide, and to the very heart of Africa'.

On the other hand, Gabarti showed a generous appreciation of the work of the *savants* at the *Institut*. The effect of French influence at its best can be seen in the career of one of the younger Sheikhs at Al-Azhar, Hasan ibn-Muhammad al-Attar. 'He was thirty-two when the French entered Egypt and threw himself without reserve into the arms of the French soldiers and scholars.' In exchange for Arabic lessons, they taught him 'the arts of their countries'. He would come away from these lessons with heart and mind brimful of the new learning. ' "Our countries must change,"

For the French the expedition marked the beginning of an attachment to Egypt that was to become one of the guiding principles of their diplomacy throughout the nineteenth century. More than that: 'glorious through its military achievement, the expedition,' a modern French historian has declared, 'revealed the great colonizing ability to be found in the general officers and their staffs and showed once more the skill possessed by the French people in adapting themselves to new climates, in living among strange peoples, and in establishing the framework of an administration suited to their manners and their customs.' Was it not in Egypt, then, that the concept of *la mission civilisatrice* was born, a mission that was, in a later age, to draw within the charmed circle of French culture many an African, many a Muslim from the Senegal to the Congo, and from Morocco to the Nile?[12]

he was accustomed to say, "and we must take from Europe all the sciences which do not exist here." He told his friends about the books produced by the French and commented enthusiastically upon the wide range of their knowledge.' al-Attar later became Rector of al-Azhar and left a deep impression on his students.[11]

309

III

SPAIN AND MOROCCO

THE ADVENTURES OF ALI BEY

FRANCE WAS NOT THE only European nation attracted by the idea of establishing a colony in North Africa. In Spain identical arguments were used to stimulate a similar line of action. For Spain, like France, had colonies in the Americas that were threatening to break away; new colonies, nearer at hand and therefore more easily controlled, would serve to replace their loss. But if France fastened on Egypt, Spain looked naturally, across a narrower sea, to Morocco. Morocco could provide, so the argument ran, much that the Americas produced. Moreover, since imperialism always requires the veil of morality, in bringing to that 'barbarous' nation the 'blessings of civilization' Spain would be rendering a 'service to humanity'. But between Spain and France there were important differences: not only was Spain, a great power in decline, less well equipped for imperial adventures than its neighbour, but the Spaniards, unlike the French, had acquired during the course of the past three hundred years much practical experience in the difficulties of direct action on the Barbary Coast. Nevertheless, in the year 1803 the Spanish Government decided to support an attempt to transform to its own advantage the state of Morocco; it would be difficult to find in the annals of African history an episode more fantastic.[1]

In June 1803 there arrived in Tangier a very strange person. A man of 'highly polished manners', of middling height, with a long, thin head, black eyes, a large nose and a long, black beard, he appeared to be about thirty years of age. His name, he said, was Ali Bey al Abbassi; he was a Syrian, born in Aleppo, the son of a prince. This regal descent seemed to be confirmed by the 'Eastern magnifi-

310

cence' with which he surrounded himself. Strangely enough, though he spoke English and Spanish very well and French 'with great elegance and correctness', in Arabic, his mother tongue, he was 'scarcely intelligible'. This deficiency he explained by recounting the story of his life: while he was still an infant his father and all his family had taken refuge in England, bringing with them all their property; his parents had died shortly afterwards, but his father's friends had looked after his fortune and seen that he obtained a good education; since he had grown up, he had spent all his time in travelling through Spain, France and England; now, however, it was his desire to return and spend the remainder of his days in the religion of his ancestors. Certainly he was proving himself 'ostentatiously punctual' in all the observances of the faith: he was roused in the middle of the night to say his prayers, and he performed all the obligations of charity enjoined by the Koran, 'giving alms right and left, placing water in all the streets for the conveniency of the inhabitants and daily feeding and clothing twelve of the poorer people of the town'.[2]

His arrival excited widespread speculation. Within twenty-four hours the rumour began to circulate that he was a brother of the notorious Corsican. Soon throughout the whole of Morocco Ali Bey was known as 'Bonaparte'. Among those who watched him most closely was that indefatigable protector of his own country's interests, the British Consul James Matra. Matra was convinced from the start that the Syrian was an impostor; but if so, where did he come from and what was his purpose? It was hardly likely that he was a Spanish agent, so Matra informed his superiors at home, 'because there is scarce any temporal advantage in my opinion could induce the Court of Madrid to send a Christian here to apostatize'; moreover, the Spaniards probably knew as much about the state of Morocco as the Moors themselves. 'By his impudence I conclude he is a Frenchman; probably one of the savants who had been with Bonaparte in Egypt'; but whatever his identity, he surely could be 'no common traveller'.[3]

Ali Bey spent two years in Morocco; in all that time Matra, though a master-hand at securing information through his network of contacts spread throughout the country, was not able to probe his secret. Matra himself died in 1806; he would have been astonished to learn Ali Bey's true identity and even more seriously disturbed had he known the real purpose of his mission. Ali Bey was in fact a

Spaniard, Dominigo Badia y Leblich. He had been born in 1766 of unrecorded ancestry, and had developed those many-sided intellectual interests so characteristic of his age. Among the subjects which he studied with special attention were Arabic, geography and natural history; these naturally combined to direct his attention to Africa. His studies led him to the conclusion that 'North Africa is

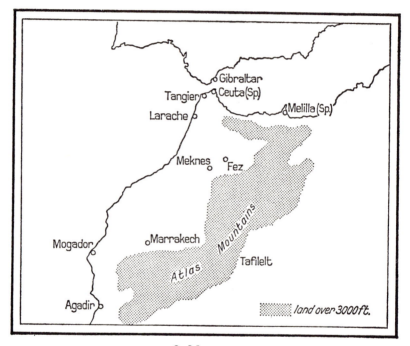

8. Morocco

the natural colony of Europe'. But how could the present situation be turned to his country's advantage? It was true that Spain maintained two footholds at Ceuta and Melilla on the African mainland; but practical experience had shown that armed expeditions were invariably fruitless. Mulling over the problem, Badia came to devise a remarkable plan.[4]

If only, he reflected, one could find a Muslim ruler who had absorbed and appreciated the modern ideas of Europe and was willing to introduce into his country the advantages of civilization. In order to achieve this end, such a man would need to be persuaded to establish 'a wise constitution' and at the same time to allow

312

Europeans to settle in part of his country, where they could teach the people 'the arts, the sciences and the artificial needs of civilization'. But what if, as seemed probable, no such enlightened Muslim ruler could be found? Would it not then be possible to find a European who could transform himself into a complete Muslim and pass himself off as a prince? And who, after all, would be better suited to carry out such a plan than he who had devised it? At this point, so Badia later confessed, he suffered from some qualms of conscience; was there not something repugnant about an act of such deception? And yet, so it struck him on deeper reflection, could it not also be argued that this 'innocent ruse' would procure immense advantages for millions of men? His qualms vanished, his heart was assured, he decided to go ahead with his plans.[5]

In 1801 Badia went straight to the source of power, submitting a memoir to the *de facto* ruler of his country, that 'gross, domineering and deceitful man', Manuel de Godoy. Godoy approved his plans, and Badia started to prepare himself in earnest for his great adventure. In 1802 he visited Paris, where he was entertained by the members of the *Institut National*. The next year he was in London, where he gave himself out as a prospective African explorer. Among those who received him warmly were Sir Joseph Banks and Sir William Young; he was anxious to meet Mungo Park, but there is no evidence that he was able to do so. While in London he was said to have been circumcised, an essential part of his disguise.*[6]

Back in Spain, Badia completed his preparations. The Government provided him with all the money he required and arranged for an army of ten thousand men, under a commander of his own approval, to be massed at Algeriças, to move at his request. As soon

* As Badia had met Sir Joseph Banks in London and as Banks and Matra were in regular correspondence, it is curious that Matra never learnt of Ali Bey's true identity. In fact, there exists a copy of a letter that Banks wrote to one of the Consuls in North Africa recommending Badia to his attention; as no address is given, it is not certain that this letter was for Matra —it is possible that Badia carried it with him as a letter of introduction. Badia did in fact seek Matra's acquaintance on his arrival in Tangier; 'considering him as an adventurer and being indisposed, I had not,' Matra wrote afterwards, 'paid great attention to the marvellous tales the Moors reported of him, yet gave an answer agreeably to his wishes. The Emperor arrived shortly after with whom he went to Mequinez, and we never met, which at the time I did not much regret.' Five of Matra's letters written to Banks after Badia's arrival have been preserved, but in none of them is there any mention of Ali Bey.[7]

as he landed in Morocco, he was to start working on the people, infecting them with his revolutionary ideas; then he was to move to the eastern part of the country to gain support among the Bedouin tribes; finally, he was to return to the Spanish base at Melilla, summon the Spanish Army and start military operations against the Emperor. The classic arguments of imperialist aggressors were to be used to justify this naked act of force: the ill-treatment of Spanish subjects and the appalling state of the country. 'I could only see in the Emperor of Morocco,' Badia wrote afterwards, 'a brigand at the head of ten thousand armed slaves, revelling in the miseries, with which he afflicted several million inhabitants. Let it not be said that those inhabitants liked this state of affairs; they groaned, they bewailed the evils of the slavery which they had to bear; they sighed for a change in the situation.' Does not this casuistry have a familiar ring? Fortunately Badia was to prove a more generous and less ruthless agent of revolution than the tight-lipped conspirators of the twentieth century.[8]

The first stage of his plan succeeded brilliantly. Despite the disconcerting nickname he had acquired, no one attempted to call his bluff; indeed, as Matra observed, 'the more absurd the tale, the more readily it was believed by Moors of every class'. During his time in Tangier, Ali Bey was occupied, according to Matra, either in conversing with Muslim divines or in 'examining all the batteries and the neighbouring Country'; every evening he received a visit from the Spanish Vice-Consul, but Matra was unable to discover what passed between them, as all the servants were regularly turned out of the house at that time.[9]

It would naturally take several months to build up his prestige; during this period Badia was anxious to avoid meeting the Emperor. But he could not avoid the consequences of his spreading fame; later in the year the Emperor, Mulay Sliman, arrived in Tangier and showed himself anxious to meet one whose piety, wealth, distinguished ancestry and curious education had aroused so much interest among his subjects. Soon Ali Bey had made another conquest; 'the Emperor overwhelmed me with brilliant proofs of his attachment'. The Emperor's friendship posed a difficult moral problem: would it not be unworthy to receive his generosity and yet continue to intrigue to bring about his downfall? Would it not also prove impossible to plan a successful revolution, while living in court, for the Emperor had invited him to accompany him to

14. The Patron of exploration: Sir Joseph Banks, President of the Royal Society. The portrait by Thomas Phillips in the possession of the Royal Society

15. Explorers: Mungo Park
From M. Park's *Travels*, London, 1799

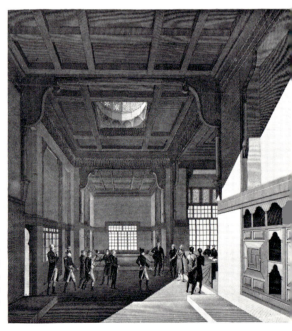

16. The Patron of scholarship: General Bonaparte (centre, in cocked hat) at the Institute of Egypt, Cairo
From *Description de l'Égypet*, Paris, 1809

Meknes, Fez and Marrakesh? Badia decided to change his plans; he reverted to his original idea and started to work on the Emperor's mind, enlightening him 'as to his own real interest'.[10]

So Ali Bey set out from Tangier with the imperial cortège on a grand tour of the country. He made no attempt to conceal certain of his interests: 'In his journey to Mequinez under the very eye of the Emperor,' so Matra was informed, 'he sounded all the rivers, measured their breadth and examined the roads and mountains with the accuracy of a Quartermaster-General.' His skill in astronomy added greatly to his prestige, especially when he was able to predict an eclipse successfully. 'I had become the veritable ruler of the country,' Badia wrote afterwards, 'because one word from my mouth was received as an oracle.' This may have been an excessive claim; but there was no doubt of his growing ascendency. 'The Moors,' Matra wrote, 'are petrified by his assurance, the Emperor seems to be blinded by his piety and Charities, by his abandoning of Christianity and voluntarily coming to this country to embrace the Religion of Mahomet, by the very valuable presents he made him, and his being in want of nothing from the Treasury, yet I believe that H.I.M. [His Imperial Majesty] is not without his suspicions.'[11]

Ali Bey spent about a year in the Emperor's company. He received practical proof of the imperial favour, being presented with a splendid estate at Semelalia, near Marrakesh, and certain privileges in the town of Mogador. In pressing his ideas about a Constitution on the Emperor, he found a powerful ally in the Emperor's brother, Mulay Abdsulem; but his policy naturally roused the hostility of other members of the court, particularly the Vizier Salawi. Nevertheless, there were other allies whom he could call in to his support. 'At Morocco [Marrakesh] his chief study is to obtain a Character for great sanctity and an utter contempt for money, in both of which points he has succeeded most wonderfully'; this report on his activities made in January 1805 by Matra provides incontrovertible evidence of his success. He had indeed made a point of cultivating the support of the influential class of the learned and the holy; he had also gained the support of other important men, and claimed to have ten thousand horsemen at his disposal. At the same time he continued to correspond with the Spanish Consul, and received from him the money he required. Matra estimated that his expenses could not be less than £4,000 a year, but he was prepared to accept Ali Bey's story that this was his own money—he gave out that he had a quarter of a million pounds invested in London—and that he used the Spanish consulate only as a post office. Although Matra had evidence from other sources that the Spaniards were up to some intrigue in Morocco, he had to confess that 'with all my vigilance I have not been able to trace the most distant connection between him [Ali Bey] and what I do most unquestionably think the Spaniards to be effecting here'. To have bamboozled Matra so successfully was not the least of Badia's achievements.[12]

The great plan was maturing in a way that must sometimes have astonished even its author, when Badia was struck off balance by a bombshell from the least-expected quarter. A letter reached him from the King of Spain ordering him to abandon the whole escapade. In his consternation he called to mind the story of Cortez; should he not follow the great conquistador's example, flatly disobey his sovereign's command and go on to win a pardon with the gift of an Empire? He reckoned that he now possessed sufficient resources to carry the plan through to a successful consummation. One reason alone, if his own account is to be believed, led him to reject this line of action; it appeared that the king had been led to his decision by scruples of conscience, after his confessor had pointed out to him that it was a great sin for a Christian to live as a Muslim. So through the word of a priest the great design was ruined.

Nevertheless, even if he obeyed the royal command, it was not going to be easy to extract himself from his present position. Besides, Badia was an ambitious man; he did not want to return to his country without some great achievement to his credit. Soon his fertile mind had hit upon a way of escape; he would undertake the Pilgrimage and so visit the holy cities of Arabia, a detailed description of which had never been brought back to Europe. These new plans met with the approval of his royal master. He now had to get rid of his crowd of supporters; he did so by shutting himself up in his castle at Semelalia and giving out that he was moved by disgust of worldly things. For six months he lived the life of a recluse; for half this time he was prostrate with a violent fever, brought on in part by the fury of frustration. At the end of this period he received another letter from Spain; the country had declared war on England, the whole complexion of events was changed, it had been decided that he should continue with his original plan.

Badia cursed the vacillating statesmen of Madrid, but accepted their command. His position, however, was far weaker than it had been six months earlier; he had lost many of his adherents, and he was conscious that the strangeness of his conduct had aroused suspicion. But he was soon able to resume many of his former contacts and so to build up once again his own party. One incident gave him particular pleasure. In the absence of the Emperor, the Pasha of Marrakesh gave a fête in his honour. At the end of the dinner everyone who was present started to shout, 'Sidi Ali Bey, the Constitution, the Constitution.' 'Yes,' Badia replied, fixing his eyes sharply on his audience, '*the* Constitution, it will be made—in one way or another.' These few words unleashed a tremendous enthusiasm; a moment later he found himself surrounded by Moors, pressing forward to seize his hand and swearing to one another, 'Sidi Ali Bey will give us a Constitution.'

Shortly afterwards the Emperor returned to Marrakesh. During Ali Bey's retirement he had turned against the idea of a Constitution and was now obstinately opposed to it, but he still seemed affectionate and trusting. As a proof of his regard, he offered Ali Bey two women, one white and the other black. To the astonishment of the courtiers Ali Bey refused to accept this gift until a Constitution had been granted. Later, however, he took the women, one of whom was later to bear him a son. Matra learnt that the Emperor had given Ali Bey the women to discover whether he was a true Muslim; one of them reported the damning fact that Ali Bey had not been properly circumcised. By that time Badia was increasingly conscious of the suspicion gathering round him. He therefore determined to transfer his activities to eastern Morocco. His plans for going on pilgrimage gave an excuse for moving to that part of the country.

At last fortune began to turn against him. He had made his first propitious contacts with the mountain tribesmen of the East, when he was detained by an escort sent by the Emperor, ostensibly to protect but, in fact, to seize him. Still treated with great honour, he was brought to the sea-port of Larache. There he found his old enemy, the Vizier Salawi, who told him that a ship from Tripoli was in the harbour ready to conduct him on the first stage of his pilgrimage. Ali Bey was accompanied by his usual train of attendants; he expected to take them with him. To his fury no sooner had he gone on board than Salawi arrested all his followers. This perfidious act filled his heart with rage as he sailed away from Morocco.

A lesser man would have considered that by now he had done enough; but Badia was irrepressible. He made his way to Egypt and in 1807 performed the pilgrimage. After a narrow escape from the fanatical Wahabis in Arabia, he moved northwards to Syria and Turkey. Three years later another European traveller, J. L. Burckhardt, who also achieved remarkable success by travelling disguised as a Muslim, met a couple of Persian dervishes who had known Ali Bey in Damascus; they said that he was indeed 'suspected of being a Christian, but his great liberality and the pressing letters which he brought to all the people of consequence stopped further inquiry.[13]

In 1809 he was back in Europe. He was soon introduced to Napoleon and urged him to use the French Army in Spain for his Moroccan adventure; the Emperor of the French listened attentively, and might possibly have accepted Badia's proposals, had his attention not been distracted by the Spanish revolt. Badia now proceeded to show how little there was in him of the Spanish patriot by attaching himself to Joseph Bonaparte, the French-imposed King of Spain. For the next five years he held a number of important posts, but he had to pay the price of his collaboration; when Napoleon was overthrown and the Bourbons restored he found himself permanently banished from his native land.

France then became the country of his adoption. In 1814, with official support, the account of his *Travels*, was published in Paris. The book contained much interesting material on Morocco and on the Holy Cities of Arabia, but made no mention of the dramatic story of his grand intrigue. There was a good reason why Badia did not wish to give away his secret; he was planning to resume his Moroccan adventure. Though it was ten years since he had left the country, he had not abandoned all his contacts. He was in correspondence with the Emperor's brother, his friend and ally Mulay Abdsulem, and had been invited by him to return. He had met another of the Emperor's brothers in Cairo, found him in a destitute condition and helped him in many practical ways, knowing that when reported in Morocco, this act of charity would redound to his advantage. He had agents and correspondents in many towns, by whom he had recently been informed that his castle at Semelalia was now 'revered as a Temple'. Finally—and this may have been the strongest pull of all—there was in Morocco a boy named Othman Bey, his own son, whom he had never seen, born of one of the women the Emperor had given him and then so cruelly snatched away.

Accordingly, in the autumn of 1815 Badia presented a long

memorandum to the French Government. In it he told the full story
of his adventures; they had been performed in the service of Spain,
now he offered himself to France. 'Through me,' he asserted,
'France can have colonies in Africa without paying the cost of a
drop of French blood; I (and I alone) can guarantee the security
and tranquillity of these colonies.' It is not surprising that this bold
offer met with no response; no time in recent French history could
have been less propitious for foreign adventure than the first months
of the Restoration. Moreover, one might well ask how Badia hoped
to preserve the secret of his identity after the publication of his book;
for although it had been given out as the *Travels of Ali Bey*, many
people in Paris and in London knew that Badia and Ali Bey were
one and the same person.[14]

For so restless, ambitious and adventurous a man, life in a Paris
gloomy with defeat, saddened by the memories of the lost, imperial
splendour, must have become increasingly irksome. Besides, Africa
still called him—and with reason: for in Africa had he not been the
friend of an Emperor, the companion of princes, by learned men
honoured, by the people revered? He would never, now, become
the founder of a European colony; but there was one enterprise
which would crown his name with glory—he could penetrate into
those parts of the continent which no European had ever yet seen.
He would resume his old disguise, go to Syria and there join the
pilgrim caravan to Mecca; in the Holy City he would recruit a new
band of servants, who would be able to vouch for his character as a
Muslim; thus prepared, he would cross the Red Sea and set out to
traverse the continent from East to West, making the Senegal his goal.
This new plan he submitted to the French Government in November
1817. It found immediate favour; within a month the royal approval
had been given. Badia was to be allowed 10,000 francs a year for a
period of three years.

At the beginning of January 1818 Badia left France. Six months
later he was in Syria, where the French Consul was an old friend.
Already there were alarming symptoms that his health was breaking
down. Nevertheless, he refused to give up his plan. At the beginning
of August he joined the pilgrims' caravan. He travelled in a litter
carried by his servants. Soon it was apparent that he was suffering
severely from dysentery. This report was brought back by a Polish
gentleman, the Count Rzevuski, who had come to Syria on a mission
to buy Arab horses for the Queen of Württemberg. Rzevuski was the

last European to see him alive. On the morning of September 1 his servants drew the curtains of the litter; to their horror they found their master dead. A party of Moroccan pilgrims in the caravan had already shown their hostility to Ali Bey by accusing him of being a sorcerer who had used his spells to bewitch their Emperor. When the body of the dead man came to be washed they found proof of their suspicions in a golden cross that hung on a chain round his neck; they used this as an excuse for performing on the corpse revolting mutilations. Such was the story the French Consul eventually uncovered; but he also learnt that Ali Bey had at length been given a decent burial. Not all the members of the caravan had shared the Moroccans' animosity; 'other pilgrims praised him for his piety, his charity and his good nature', while those who knew him best of all honoured him for his knowledge, his courage and his wisdom. Badia could not have had a better epitaph.[15]

IV

BRITAIN AND THE NIGER

THE SPUR OF FRENCH RIVALRY

IF SOME FRENCHMEN WERE looking covetously to Egypt and some Spaniards to Morocco, in England there existed an influential group anxious to capture the trade of those hitherto unvisited states of the interior, Timbuktu and Housa. At their General Meeting in May 1799 the members of the African Association, it will be remembered, had urged that an attempt be made 'to take possession of the banks of the Joliba'.

Shortly afterwards Banks had written to his old friend Lord Liverpool, President of the Board of Trade; he enclosed a copy of the Association's resolution, asked that it be brought to the attention of other members of the Cabinet and stressed at some length its significance. 'As the Trade with the Negroes for manufactured goods is already firmly established and as Gold the home investment is found in abundance in all the Torrents which fall into the Joliba, I feel strongly impressed with the hope of success should the project be fairly tried.' The Government's first step must be 'to secure to the British throne, either by Conquest or by Treaty the whole of the Coast of Africa from Arguin to Sierra Leone; or at least to procure the cession of the River Senegal as that River will always afford an easy passage to any rival nation who means to molest the Countries on the banks of the Joliba'. Should an expedition be undertaken, there could be 'little doubt that in a very few years a trading Company might be established under immediate control of the Government, who would take upon themselves the whole expense of the measure, would govern the Negroes far more mildly and make them far more happy than they are now under the tyranny of their arbitrary princes,

321

would become popular at home by converting them to the Christian Religion by inculcating in their rough minds the mild morality which is engrafted on the tenets of our faith and by effecting the greatest practicable diminution of the Slavery of Mankind, upon the principles of natural justice and commercial benefit'. How clearly Banks's letter illuminates the different strands of thought and impulse behind modern imperialism: the desire for gain, the fear of a rival, the sense of moral superiority, the self-justification of a civilizing mission. Nine years earlier, in the concluding paragraphs of the African Association's first report, the theory of the civilizing influence of commercial intercourse had been eloquently advanced. Then there was no suggestion of annexation or of the direct government of African peoples. Now there was; war, sharpening the sense of rivalry with France, had brought about this change.[1]

What influence Banks's letter had on a Government deeply pre-occupied with more urgent matters, it is not possible to discover· But it may not be entirely a coincidence that the next year was marked by the first major British achievement in West Africa since the opening of the war, the capture of the island of Goree. This success was followed by preparations for an attack on Senegal; these had to be called off at the conclusion of the Peace of Amiens. Under the terms of that treaty, Goree was to be returned to the French; but the British cunningly found excuses for delaying the withdrawal of their garrison; when the war was resumed, Goree was still in British hands.[2]

Among those who were following events in West Africa with as keen an interest as Sir Joseph was Mungo Park. Park had spent the first year of his return to Scotland in idleness, comfortably supported by the proceeds of his book. He had played with the idea of farming, only to find that the high price both of cattle and of farm rents rendered his capital insufficient. As soon as he heard of the capture of Goree, he wrote to Banks pointing out the importance of the island as a base for the exploration of the interior; if the Government shared this view he hoped that 'my exertions in some shape or other may be of use to my country'.[3]

The next year the project of a mission to New South Wales was revived. Park had rejected it three years earlier; now he responded eagerly, for he was beginning to grow seriously worried over his failure to find suitable employment. Early in the year he came down to London to discuss plans with Banks. A letter that he wrote to his wife at this time has survived. 'I am happy to know you will go to New South Wales with me, my sweet wife. You are everything I could desire; and wherever we go, you may be sure of one thing, that I shall always love you. . . . My darling, when we meet I shall be the happiest man on earth.' Only his family and his most intimate friends knew of the warmth and tenderness that were hidden behind the coldness and the reserve showed to strangers.[4]

Once again the project fell through. 'I left London, as you may easily suppose, a little down-hearted,' Park wrote to Banks in October, 'the romantic village which my fancy had erected on the shores of New Holland, as a habitation for myself and my family, had completely disappeared and I journeyed towards my native country with the painful but not degrading reflection that I must henceforth eat my bread by the sweat of my brow.' Shortly after his return he found that there was a vacancy for a surgeon in the neighbouring town of Peebles; 'tired of a life of indolence' he decided to take it. But he embarked on his new career with no enthusiasm: 'a country surgeon is at best but a laborious employ- ment and I will gladly hang up the lancet and plaister ladle whenever I can obtain a more eligible situation'. His letter to Banks ended with a direct appeal: 'I hope my friends will not relax in their endeavours to serve me.' Within a few weeks he had received a moderately reassuring reply. In consequence of the peace, Banks wrote, the Association would certainly revive the project of sending a mission to Africa; if Government support could be obtained, Park would be recommended as a suitable person to be employed.[5]

For more than half a year nothing further seems to have been done. Then in the late summer of 1802 Banks found a highly suitable stick with which to prod the Government. There had just come into his hands a book published in Paris, *Fragments d'un Voyage en Afrique*; by Sylvester Golbéry. Golbéry, some of whose impressions have already been quoted, had been in Senegal in the 1780s and had become an ardent advocate of a policy of expansion in West Africa; the turbulent decade of the nineties had allowed him scant opportun- ity to present his views, but now, under the new order of Bonapartis, imperialism, the times seemed exceptionally propitious. He considered that the whole coast from the Senegal to Cape Palmas (on the eastern border of modern Liberia) should lie within the sphere of French influence. 'Let there,' he wrote in his opening chapter, 'be conceived a plan of operations in this part of Africa; let the execu-

tion be confided to one sole administration, firm, wise and enlightened,
. . . let there be a well-organized land-force and a very active maritime one. These will concur to give us an importance in Africa, and secure to us the success of any enterprises which we may undertake in this part of the world.'[6]

On August 1 Banks wrote to John Sullivan, the Under-Secretary of State at the Colonial Office. He gave a brief review of Golbéry's book, in which he criticized the author for glossing over the unhealthiness of the country and so 'painting a picture, which every poor and industrious man in France cannot but contemplate with a wish to enjoy the comforts of so productive and so agreeable a Country'. Golbéry's assertion that West Africa was potentially more fertile than the West Indies, Banks was willing to accept. 'I am clear,' he concluded, 'that H.M. Ministers should be aware of the contents and hold in mind what will happen, which is that whoever Colonizes in that part of Africa with Spirit will Clearly be able to sell Colonial Products of all kinds in the European market at a Cheaper price than any part of the West Indies can afford it.'[7]

Sullivan took Banks's warning seriously to heart. The information that was reaching the Government from other parts of the world, from Europe, from the Mediterranean, from the West Indies, was making it increasingly clear that Bonaparte was only using the peace as an opportunity to broaden and strengthen his own power. Suppose that he turned his attention seriously to West Africa; how could the French danger most effectively be met? And, further, how could the English secure for themselves the advantages of trade with the interior? With these two questions in mind, Sullivan decided to seek the advice of three men well qualified to help him reach an answer, Captain Beaver, Zachary Macaulay and Major Rennell.

Beaver, the hero of the Bulama expedition, had recently returned to England after a long spell of active service in many waters. He was still keenly interested in the possibilities of development afforded by the islands at the mouth of the Rio Grande, recommended that one of them should be made into a base and gave it as his opinion that the river provided the easiest highway to the interior. Later he was moved to give public expression to his views by publishing the Journal he had kept on Bulama, together with various other papers in a book entitled *African Memoranda*; the map attached to this work showed with vivid colouring the part of Africa that Golbéry had claimed for France.[8]

Macaulay had spent six years in Sierra Leone; since his return to England in 1800 he had been working as Secretary of the Sierra Leone Company; there was probably no one in the whole country so well qualified to comment on West Africa. He answered Sullivan's inquiry with an exhaustive memoir. He considered that there was a reasonable possibility of being able to develop trade with the countries on either side of the Gambia, but he pointed out that the five hundred miles separating the Gambia from the Niger would prove 'very unfavourable to a regular trade' with the interior. Nevertheless, he felt it would be worth establishing 'a confidential and intelligent person who should possess a knowledge of Arabic and Mandingo' as high up the Gambia as he could securely reside, with the task of collecting information and making treaties with neighbouring chiefs; he recommended that this post should be established without delay, for Islam was advancing in this region and the distrust of Christians was growing. The Rio Grande Macaulay dismissed as a possible highway, the tribes at its mouth being 'savage and intractable'; nor did he see in the rivers to the south any better alternative. He ended by listing with admirable realism the difficulties that had to be faced in trying to establish regular trade: lack of information, the distrust of the inhabitants, the general state of insecurity and the prevalence of disease. Of these difficulties Major Rennell, though he had no first-hand experience of the West Coast, showed himself equally well aware; but he suggested in his paper that a resident should be appointed to be based on Bambuk.[9]

Thus informed, Sullivan prepared a lengthy memorandum. He suggested that the French threat could best be met by the reoccupation of the fort on James Island in the Gambia, which had been completely abandoned after its destruction by the French a century before, and by the establishment of factories as high up the river as it was navigable. 'There is no room to doubt,' he concluded, 'that a a most important commercial intercourse with the various nations who inhabit the vast extent of the interior of Africa might be established through the agency of these two societies [the Sierra Leone Company and the Bulama Association] or by their union under the protection and direction of Government and in co-operation with the factories that may be formed on the Gambia.'[10]

This discussion took place in the autumn of 1802, but it was not until a year later, by which time the country was once again at war with France, that the first practical steps to send an expedition into the interior were taken. Sir Joseph Banks was asked by Lord Hobart, the Colonial Secretary, to get in touch with Park and summon him to London. 'I have every reason to believe,' Banks wrote to Park in a letter dated October 10, 'that the expedition which is on foot, of which I am not allowed to acquaint you with the particulars, will suit your wishes.' As soon as he received the letter, Park hurried down to London for an interview with Hobart. The Government, Hobart told him, wanted him 'to take another trip into the centre of Africa to discover the termination of the Niger'; he would not have to travel alone, but would be provided with an escort of twenty-five soldiers; for pay he would receive 10s. a day and a gratuity of £200 per annum. Before accepting this proposal, Park felt he must return to Scotland to talk the matter over with his wife; at the same time he wanted to take the advice of Sir Joseph Banks, who was out of London when he arrived. He posted a letter to Banks on his way back to Scotland. Within a few days he had Banks's reply, 'I by all means advise you to return to London.'[11]

Men without children—Banks's marriage had been a childless one —are apt to be insensitive to the family responsibilities of others. In fact, the decision with which Park now found himself confronted was a movingly difficult one to make. He was happily married; he had become the father of three young children; the dangers of another journey into the interior, the chances of never returning no one knew better than himself; if he died, what would become of his family? Against all this must be set his pride, his ambition, his intellectual curiosity and his dissatisfaction with his present occupation. It would be humiliating, after having talked so much of returning to Africa, to refuse now; besides, what was there to be gained by spending his life as a doctor in Peebles? When one of his nearest relatives tried to dissuade him by stressing the dangers he would have to face, he calmly replied that 'a few inglorious winters of country practice at Peebles was risk as great, and would tend as effectively to shorten life, as the journey which he was about to undertake'. To Walter Scott, whose acquaintance he had made during his last months in Scotland, he said that 'he would rather brave Africa and all its horrors, than wear out his life in long and toilsome rides over the hills of Scotland, for which the remuneration was hardly enough to keep body and soul together'. The impulses that lead to heroic action are not necessarily admirable.[12]

In the late autumn of 1803 Park returned to London with the

expectation of setting out for Africa within a few months. Perhaps he would have done so, had Hobart's original plan been followed. But during the winter of 1803 schemes of a more ambitious nature found favour in the Colonial Office. They were advanced by a certain Colonel Stevenson. Stevenson's regiment, the York Rangers, was under orders to sail for the West Indies. Though he himself seems never to have been in Africa, he had begun to interest himself in the strategic possibilities of that continent. It is not clear how he succeeded in getting the Colonial Office to pay attention to his views.[13]

The plan which Stevenson put forward was based on two premises: that in war one can do things impossible in peace; and that the country between the Senegal and the Niger was, on account of its gold, 'unquestionably the richest in the world'. The objective was, therefore, to seize this region and divert its trade to the Gambia. The gold thus obtained would more than cover the cost of the expedition. In this way Britain would achieve something of much greater worth than the most brilliant victories in Europe or the West Indies. The necessary force would be provided mainly by black troops recruited in the West Indies. The campaign would be conducted in three stages. In the first dry season the force would advance from the Gambia to Segu, building forts along its line of communications. The second dry season would provide an opportunity for bringing up reinforcements, mainly white troops, who could be recruited from deserters sentenced to transportation and from civil prisoners; meanwhile, the force at Segu would be busy building boats for use as transports on the Niger. In the third dry season a small detachment would be sent down the river to Timbuktu to provoke an incident, whereupon the whole force would advance, capture the town, drive 'the cruel, bigotted and treacherous Moors into the desert and seize their trade'. The memorandum of this modern conquistador must surely be one of the most extraordinary documents in the archives of the British Colonial Office.[14]

Stevenson's plan was, for practical and for moral reasons, not acceptable to the Government. Accordingly, Sullivan sat down to work out a modified scheme, which would also make it possible for use to be made of the services of Park and of Beaver. Under this new plan Park was to lead an advance party of three hundred men up the Gambia, capturing the French post of Albreda on the way; he was to win over the Kings of Wuli and Bondou with presents and obtain permission to establish forts in their territories, explaining to these rulers that the war with France made it necessary to seize the French posts on the Senegal and the Faleme. (Was Sullivan, one wonders, not aware that these posts had been abandoned ruins for over half a century?) At this point Park was to detach a naval officer to trace the upper reaches of the Gambia by canoe and afterwards to explore either the upper Faleme or the road southwards to Labé in Futa Jallon.

Stevenson, in Sullivan's plan, was to lead the main force which was to follow up Park's advance and seize the post at Fort St Joseph. He was then to confer with Park as to the best means of conveying the portable gun-boat that he would have brought with him to the Niger. Once Park had embarked on the Niger he was 'to assume the character of an envoy from the British Government to the Kings of Segu, Tombuctoo and Housa'. In his actions he was to take care 'not to excite alarm but to conciliate the natives and the chiefs of the principal towns by paying for everything they may furnish', 'endeavouring everywhere to give the most favourable impression of the British character and power'. His object should be to obtain permission to establish factories at Segu, Timbuktu and other important towns. Meanwhile Stevenson was to establish forts in Bambuk and maintain the lines of communication to the Niger, 'keeping in his mind that a free and secure intercourse of trade with the interior is the great object to be attained'.

At the same time two other expeditions were to be undertaken. By the first a detachment of soldiers was to be sent to Sierra Leone to enable the Governor to establish communications with the towns of Labé and Timbo in Futa Jallon. The members of this mission were to take ploughs with them and teach the natives how to use them. The second was devised for Beaver's benefit. He was to take command of a small naval force to survey the coast and to re-establish a settlement at Bulama, buying for that purpose a hundred slaves who would be promised their freedom after seven years' work.[15]

By the spring of 1804 all the preparations for this ambitious enterprise were complete; but at the last moment, when some of the soldiers had already embarked, the expedition was countermanded on account of the fall of Addington's Government. In May Pitt again became Prime Minister and appointed Lord Camden to the Colonial Office. Some time must pass before the new Minister could review the plan approved by his predecessor. Park, waiting impatiently in London, was informed by the Colonial Office that there was no possibility of the expedition sailing before September. He was advised to spend the intervening time in acquiring some knowledge of Arabic. He returned to Scotland, taking with him as his teacher a Moor from Mogador, Sidi Ombach Boubi, who had recently come to London as interpreter to an ambassador from Egypt. Sidi Ombach, a rigorously devout Muslim, 'created no small sensation in the neighbourhood of Peebles and Selkirk'. 'Many stories,' one of Park's biographers discovered thirty years later, 'are still told of his peculiar habits and superstitious observances.' So a Moor came to excite as much curiosity among the natives of Scotland as a Scotsman had once excited among the Moors of the Western Sudan.[16]

On September 28 Camden wrote to Banks to say that an expedition on the scale originally planned was 'impracticable *now*'; but that he considered 'much might be gained by an expedition on a confined scale undertaken by a man of sense and experience'. For this purpose he had written to Park, asking him to come to London. As for the instructions, the revised enterprise bore 'so much the description of a Journey of Enquiry without any military attendance upon it', that he felt it would be better if Banks himself drew them up. Camden did not explain why the larger expedition had been abandoned; but, noting that he stressed the word *now*, one may guess that shortage either of money or of men provided the reason for the decision. Naturally one speculates on what would have happened had Sullivan's plan been put into action. The experience of the large British expedition to the Niger, maintained at great expense from 1815 to 1821, suggests an answer: the hostility of native rulers effectively blocked the paths to the interior.[17]

Park was with his family when he received Camden's summons; unable to face the poignancy of another farewell, he left on the pretext that he was making a short journey to Edinburgh. From there he wrote his parting letter. In London he presented Lord Camden with a long memoir giving details of the plan he proposed to follow. Two objects, he proposed to keep constantly in view: 'the extension of British Commerce and the enlargement of our Geographical Knowledge'. He would also 'turn his attention to the general fertility of the country, whether any part of it might be useful to Britain for colonization and whether any objects of Natural History, with which the natives are at present unacquainted, might be useful to Britain as a commercial nation'.

329

He would need a force of thirty European soldiers, six European carpenters and up to twenty Africans. Starting from the Gambia, he would strike across to the Niger by the shortest route, which passed through Fuladu. At Segu he would build two boats and sail down the river to its end. If the Niger terminated in a great lake at Wangara, as Rennell suggested, Park reckoned that he would be faced with two alternatives, either to strike northwards across the Sahara or southwards—this seemed the easier way—to the Bight of Benin. But he was inclined to think that Rennell was wrong. He had recently been in touch with a certain George Maxwell, a former African trader, who had spent many years on the Congo and had once worked out a plan for exploring that river, only the first hundred miles of whose course were known. Maxwell believed that the Congo and the Niger were one and the same river. Boiled down to its essentials, his theory was based on two obvious facts: the Niger was a great river with a beginning and no end, the Congo a river equally great with an end and no beginning. Park came to accept Maxwell's theory completely. There could be no doubt that if he proved it to be right he would have established a fact of incalculable importance. 'The expedition,' he concluded, 'though attended with extreme danger, promises to be productive of the utmost advantage to Great Britain. Considered in a commercial point of view, it is second only to the discovery of the Cape of Good Hope, and in a geographical point of view is certainly the greatest discovery that remains to be made in the world.'[18]

Shortly afterwards Park went down to Brighton to talk to Rennell. The veteran geographer refused to accept his arguments about the Congo and did his utmost to dissuade him from embarking on so exceptionally dangerous an enterprise. Sir Joseph Banks thought differently. 'I am aware,' he wrote in a lengthy comment on Park's Memoir, 'that Mr Park's expedition is one of the most hazardous a man can undertake but I cannot agree with those who think it is too hazardous to be attempted; it is by similar hazards of human life alone that we can hope to penetrate the obscurity of the internal face of Africa; we are wholly ignorant of the country between the Niger and the Congo and can explore it only by incurring the most frightful hazards.'[19]

In the last months of 1804 Park busied himself with the final preparations for the expedition. He secured the appointment of his young brother-in-law, Alexander Anderson, as second-in-command

17. Explorers: J. L. Burckhardt in Eastern Dress
From J. L. Burckhardt's *Travels in Nubia*, London, 1819

18. Incidents of exploration: 'Mr. Bruce enraptured at the Fountain
of the Principal Source of the Nile'
From Bruce's *Travels*, Halifax, 1846

19. Incidents of exploration: 'I saw with infinite pleasure the great object of my mission'—Mungo Park's first view of the Niger. From a late nineteenth-century edition of Park's *Travels*

20. Incidents of exploration: the death of Mungo Park

and arranged for another friend from Selkirk, George Scott, to be attached to the party as a draughtsman. The carpenters were recruited in England, but the soldiers were to be taken from the garrison at Goree. In order to make quite secure his position as leader of this military force he obtained from the Government a temporary commission as captain, with a lieutenancy for his brother-in-law. It was agreed that he should be allowed to spend up to £5,000 on the cost of the expedition. His own private interests he preserved by securing from the Government the promise of a large gratuity on his safe return or a pension to his family in the event of his death.

There were other important pieces of business to see to: the requistioning of stores and the arrangements for a ship to take the party to Goree. All these negotiations took time—and already the essential months of the dry season were slipping away. So serious was the delay that on December 18 Camden and Banks held a meeting to decide whether or not the expedition should be called off. They estimated that it would take Park four months from the time of leaving England to reach the Niger and another two months to prepare his ship; if he left at the beginning of January he should be ready to sail down the river at the beginning of July, before the rains, so they reckoned, had reached their height. But there were further difficulties over the stores and last-minute delays in obtaining permission to sail. It was not until January 31 that Park and his party sailed out of Portsmouth harbour aboard the troopship *Crescent*.[20]

PARK'S SECOND EXPEDITION

The first port of call was Santiago in the Cape Verde Islands, where forty-four donkeys and their fodder were purchased for the expedition. On March 28 the *Crescent* reached Goree. Major Lloyd, the garrison commander, suggested to Park that the best way of obtaining volunteers was to offer double pay on the journey and a discharge on their return; when a notice to this effect was posted almost the entire garrison volunteered to join the expedition. Park selected thirty-five soldiers and one of the officers, Lieutenant Martyn. He also took with him two sailors, who had offered to assist 'in rigging and navigating our *Nigritian man of war*'. It was, however, a faintly ominous sign that not one of the Africans in Goree could be induced to accompany the expedition. Among the English soldiers, delighted at the chance of escaping the tedium of garrison duty, there seems to

have been no premonition of the dangers that lay ahead; when the
the time of departure arrived 'they jumped into the boats in the
highest spirits and bade adieu to Goree with repeated huzzas'. The
soldiers on the West African stations were generally reputed to be
among the dregs of the British Army. This was not Park's opinion
of them: 'They are the most *dashing* men I ever saw,' he said in one
of his letters home at this time, 'and if they preserve their health,

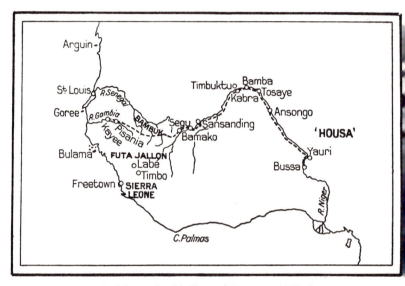

9. Mungo Park's Second Journey, 1805–6

we may keep ourselves perfectly secure from any hostile attempt on
the part of the natives.'[1]

Here indeed was the justification for his decision, so severely
criticized in view of what happened later, to take a fair-sized force
of Europeans with him. Such a force, Park argued, while not so large
as seriously to alarm the states through which he passed, would yet
be strong enough to deter any possible assailants. 'I have little
doubt,' he continued in the same letter, 'but that I shall be able, with
presents and fair words, to pass through the country to the Niger;
and if once we are fairly afloat, *the day is won.*' He had, however,
made two serious miscalculations: the first, that his men would be
able to do all the heavy work of handling the pack-animals themselves, for though he had secured the services of an excellent Man-

dingo guide named Isaaco and a few African servants, he was not able to recruit any regular drivers; the second, that his men would show the same exceptional resilience in meeting the hazards and discomforts of African travel that he had already proved himself to possess. But there was another even more serious mistake: he was setting out at the very worst time of year, when the dry season was coming to an end. Why on earth did he—who of all people knew the great practical difficulties that travelling during the rains involved— decide against remaining on the Gambia till the rains were over? There were certain rational arguments he could put forward: since he had told the Government he would set out without delay, a change of plans would hardly be welcome in Whitehall; it would be difficult to keep the soldiers, now that he had secured their services, usefully employed; but more potent than either of these reasons to a man utterly consumed by the purpose of his journey must have been the obsessive impatience to get started after years of aggravating delay.

The expedition left Goree on April 6 and sailed up the Gambia River to Kayee. From Kayee on April 27 they set out on the overland journey to the Niger. The first day's travelling revealed all too clearly the practical difficulties of managing a caravan of donkeys heavily laden with all the impedimenta of the expedition: tents, tools for boat-building, sacks of trade-goods—beads for the most part, elaborate presents for the more important rulers, fire-arms and a supply of food for the men and fodder for the animals. Some of the donkeys sat down and refused to budge, others kicked and bucked to free themselves of their loads, while some of the soldiers, exhausted by their exertions in the fierce midday sun, stole away from the line of march to rest, so that the caravan was broken up into several straggling groups. After the second day, which brought them to Pisania, for Park a place of many memories, it was decided to call a halt to buy more donkeys and to reorganize the loads. This work took longer than Park had expected, for not until six days had passed —and this was at a time when every day counted—were they able to set out again.

In the next three weeks they covered a distance of two hundred miles and were now, so Park reckoned, half-way to the Niger, and likely to reach the river within a month. Finding an opportunity to send letters back to the Gambia, he wrote a reassuring note to his wife. 'We all of us keep our health and are on the most friendly

333

terms with the natives. I have seen many of my old acquaintances and am everywhere well received. . . . We carry our own victuals with us, and live very well, in fact we have only had a pleasant journey, and yet this is what we thought would be the worst part of it.' In fact, the journey had not been as Park would have his wife believe. Two soldiers had gone down with dysentery, and one had died after an epileptic fit; at one town Isaaco, the guide, had been kidnapped and released only after a show of force; three days earlier the expedition's camp had been attacked by a swarm of bees and seven of the pack animals had been lost, either stung to death or disappeared completely into the bush. And yet, Park might think, if nothing worse than incidents such as these occurred all would be well; did he realize the falseness of his optimism in saying the worst part of the journey was already over? Ahead, as he well knew, lay the rocky and desolate country of Fuladu; and though no rain had yet fallen, one night the sky to the south-east had been lurid with the flashes of distant lightning—clear sign of the rains' approach.

Sure enough, a week later the first storm broke over them. Drenched to the skin, some of the soldiers began to sicken. Yet now it was impossible to call a halt, for they had reached a country veined with many streams flowing northwards to the Senegal—it seemed better to push on as fast as possible before the streams turned into torrents and their valleys into morasses. The next evening another storm struck them, before they had put up the tents. Within a few minutes the camping-ground was flooded three inches deep. A few hours later yet another storm burst over them. That night, so Park wrote in his diary, proved to be *the beginning of sorrow*. 'The rain had not commenced three minutes before many of the soldiers were affected with vomiting; others fell asleep and seemed as if half intoxicated.' 'I had proudly flattered myself that we should reach the Niger with a very moderate loss . . . but now the rain had set in, and I trembled to think we were only half-way through our journey.'

To avoid the uninhabited Jallonka wilderness, Park decided to make a detour to the north. The new route presented few advantages: there were still rivers to cross and the country was roughly littered with many rocky hills, their shapes—ruined castles, spires, pyramids —beguiling to the eye, their slopes wearing beyond words to travel over with a caravan of feverish men and overladen donkeys, for many of the soldiers were now too ill to walk and had to be mounted on the baggage animals, leaving to their already sickening comrades a double task. And this was not all: there were still the local inhabitants to be considered. In some villages they were well enough received; in others the natives, seeing the plight of the caravan, pilfered what they could. So it was necessary to keep a constant guard—and not only against men: the country was invested with dangerous animals—Park mentions lions and wolves (these latter must have been hyenas or wild dogs). Amid all these perils death started to work on their ranks: on June 17 two dying men had to be left behind; a few days later a soldier was drowned crossing a river; in the next week four sick men, tired of being driven on, left the caravan and were not seen again. On July 4 Isaaco was caught by a crocodile while swimming across a river; he succeeded in freeing himself by thrusting his fingers in the beast's eyes, but his leg was badly mauled. Fortunately, for his experience of the road was quite indispensable, he made a rapid recovery.

Through the whole of July the expedition struggled on. By the end of the month the death-roll had risen to twenty; the baggage animals with which they had started the journey had all either been lost or stolen, to be replaced by others locally purchased or hired; and some of the equipment had disappeared. Every night Park, though weak and giddy from fever, noted down the main incidents of the days' journey in his diary. Here is a typical passage:

July 19*th.*—Having purchased an ass in lieu of the one stolen, we left Nummaboo, which is a walled village, and proceeded onwards. Had two tornadoes; the last, about eleven o'clock, wetted us much, and made the road slippery. Two asses unable to go on. Put their loads on the horses and left them. Mr. Scott's horse unable to walk: left it to our guide. At noon came to the ruins of a town. Found two more of the asses unable to carry their loads. Hired people to carry the loads, and a a boy to drive the asses. Past the ruins of another town at half-past twelve, where I found two of the sick who had laid themselves down under a tree and refused to rise (they were afterwards stripped by the Negroes, and came naked to our tents next morning). Shortly after this, came to an ass lying on the road unable to proceed with its load. Put part of the load on my horse, which was already heavily loaded. Took a knapsack on my back. The soldier carried the remainder and drove the ass before him. We arrived on the banks of the Ba Woolima at half-past one o'clock ... [here it was necessary to build a primitive bridge, which took the better part of a day]. ... Our people being all so sickly, I hired the Negroes to carry over all the baggage, and swim over the asses. Our baggage was laid on the rocks on the East side of the river, but such was our weakly state that we were unable to carry it up the bank. Francis

Beadle, one of the soldiers, was evidently dying of the fever, and having in vain attempted, with the assistance of one of his messmates, to carry him over, I was forced to leave him on the West bank, thinking it very probable that he would die in the course of the night.

Reading these austere, laconic phrases, one has to make an effort to body them out with one's own imagination. However critical one may be of his judgement in setting out when he did, it is impossible to withhold admiration for the incredible, never-flagging energy, the quite indomitable spirit shown by Park in the direst of circumstances.

At last, on August 19, the party crossed the final ridge and saw below them the Niger 'rolling its immense stream along the plain'. 'The sight of the river promised,' so Park thought, 'at least an alleviation on our toils. But when I reflected that three-fourths of the soldiers had died on their march, and that in addition to our weakly state we had no carpenters to build the boats the prospect appeared somewhat gloomy. It however afforded me peculiar pleasure, when I reflected, that in conducting a party of *Europeans*, with immense baggage, through an extent of more than five hundred miles, I had always been able to preserve the most friendly terms with the natives.' 'In fact,' he went on, with a wilfully self-deluding optimism, 'this journey plainly demonstrates 1st that with common prudence any quantity of merchandize may be transported from the Gambia to the Niger without danger of being robbed by the natives, 2dly that if this journey be performed in the dry season, one may calculate on losing not more than three or at the most four men out of fifty.'

Now, however, as they struggled into Bamako on the Niger, their numbers were down to ten; George Scott was among those who had been left behind, and Alexander Anderson was so ill that he had to be carried in a litter. At Bamako they hired canoes and moved down the river to Marraboo, from where Issaco was sent forward to Segu with some of the presents for Mansong, still king—so Park must have been relieved to learn—of Bambara. Nearly a fortnight passed at Marraboo; during this time Park was ill with dysentery, the first occasion on which he mentions himself as suffering from this complaint; he achieved a violent cure through strong doses of calomel, which affected his mouth so badly that for six days he could neither speak or sleep. Meanwhile alarming rumours reached Marraboo to the effect that Mansong had killed Isaaco with his own hands and said he would do the same to all the white men who came

336

to Bambara. These were dispelled only by the arrival of one of Mansong's courtiers with six canoes for Park and his party.*

Paddling down the river, they stopped at a place somewhat short of Segu, where Isaaco later joined them. He reported that Mansong had said he would allow them to pass but that he seemed strangely afraid of the white man; Isaaco had noted that whenever he mentioned Park and his party the king 'immediately began to make squares and triangles in the sand before him with his finger.' The next day Mansong's chief minister, Modibinne, and four other high officials came to interview Park and to hear from his own mouth what had brought him to Bambara. In answer Park made a fluent and diplomatically phrased reply. He began by referring to Mansong's generous conduct to him on his first journey, conduct which had made his name much respected in the land of the white people. Now the King of the white people had sent him again to Bambara; if he could be sure of a good reception—he paused for their assurances—he would tell them the object of his journey. 'You all know,' Park went on, 'that the white people are a trading people; and that all objects of value, which the Moors and the people of Jinnie [Jenne] bring to Segu, are made by us. If you speak of a *good gun*, who made it? *the white people*. If you speak of a good pistol or sword, or piece of scarlet or baft, or beads or gunpowder, who made them? *the white people*. We sell them to the Moors; the Moors bring them to Timbuctoo, where they sell them at a *higher rate*. The people of Timbuctoo sell them to the people of Jinnie at a still higher price; and the people of Jinnie sell them to you. Now, the King of the white people wishes to find out a way by which we may bring our own merchandise to you, and sell everything at a much cheaper rate than you have them now. For this purpose, if Mansong will permit me to pass, I propose sailing down the Joliba to the place where it mixes with the salt water; and if I find no rocks or danger in the way, the white men's small vessels will come up and trade at Segu, if Mansong wishes it.'

* Before he left England Park had received a curious piece of information which threw some light on Mansong's attitude towards him at the time of his first visit to Segu. At the General Meeting of the African Association for 1804 a letter was read from a Mr Cahill, a merchant at Rabat in Morocco. Cahill said that he had met a Moor who had known Park at Sansanding. This man told Cahill that the King of Bambara had suspected Park either of being a spy sent by some Christian power to take a plan of the country with a view to conquering it or of being a magician, who by his charms might cause his death and be the ruin of his people.[2]

'Your journey is a good one,' Modibinne said simply in answer to this eloquent exposition, 'and may God prosper you in it; Mansong will protect you.' Then Park brought out all the presents intended for Mansong, including those entrusted to Isaaco, which the king had said he would prefer to receive more directly from the white man. They included a handsome silver-plated tureen, a pair of double-barrelled guns and also of pistols, both silver-mounted, a sabre in a scabbard of morocco leather and the inevitable bales of cloth—these were for the king. Suitable presents on a more modest scale were also made to the king's eldest son and to Modibinne and his companions. Both the quantity and the quality of the gifts made a deep impression. Modibinne then returned to Segu. Two days later he was back with Mansong's answer—a promise of protection in all his dominions and of conveyance to whichever town they might choose as a base for building their boat. In return for the presents, Mansong promised to send Park a good canoe, but he said nothing of wishing to interview the white man; so, as on his first journey, Park and his party passed Segu by and went on to Sansanding.

They reached Sansanding on September 27 and waited three weeks without a sign of the canoe appearing. In the meantime Park decided to sell off his surplus goods in order to accumulate a good supply of cowries. He opened shop in great style: 'such was my run of business that I was sometimes forced to employ *three tellers at once* to count my cash'. This unexpected competition was deeply resented by the regular traders of Sansanding; they offered Mansong a large sum in merchandise if he would seize the white men's baggage and either kill them or send them out of the country. At last the canoe that Mansong had promised arrived, brought by Modibinne. It proved to be half-rotten. Park demanded another and was sent one in no better state. However, by taking the sound parts of the two canoes and joining them together, he succeeded after eighteen days' hard labour with only one of the soldiers helping him, in changing the Bambara canoe into *His Majesty's Schooner Joliba*, a flat-bottomed boat, forty feet long and six feet wide.

While this work was in progress Dr Anderson, who had been sick for the last four months, died. 'No event which took place during the journey,' Park wrote in his journal, 'ever threw the smallest gloom over my mind till I laid Mr. Anderson in the grave. I then felt myself as if left a second time, lonely and friendless, amidst the wilds of Africa.' Since leaving Bamako, five of the soldiers had died

either of dysentery or of malaria. Martyn, the officer, was still alive
and so were three of the soldiers, but most of them were sick men.
Isaaco was about to leave them, so for guide and interpreter Park
engaged a certain Amadi Fatouma, a man with excellent qualifications, for he had visited all the countries as far as Bornu in the east
and Cape Coast in the south; he promised to take the party as far as
Kashna, after which, so he told Park, the river turned to the south.
To help paddle the boat Park procured three slaves.

On November 18 a message arrived from Mansong advising Park
to leave as quickly as possible, before the Moors who lived to the
east and whose compatriots in Bambara had been constantly hostile
to the white man, were warned of his coming. Park promptly set
about his final preparation. He rigged up an awning of bullock hides
as a protection against arrows in the event of any attack, bought a
large supply of provisions so that it would not be necessary to make
frequent halts to buy food, put the finishing touches to his journal
and wrote letters to his family, to Banks and to Camden. These,
with his journal, he entrusted to Isaaco to carry back to the coast.
To Camden he described the state of the expedition: 'I am afraid
that your Lordship,' he continued, 'will be apt to consider matters
as in a very hopeless state, but I assure you I am far from desponding.
. . . Though all the Europeans who are with me should die, and
though I were myself half dead, I would still persevere; and if I could
not succeed in the object of my mission, I would at least die on the
Niger.' The letter to his wife he left to the last; in it he did his best to
reassure her. 'The rains are completely over, and the healthy season
has commenced, so that there is no danger of sickness, and I still
have a sufficient force to protect me from any insult in sailing down
the river, to the sea. . . . I do not intend to stop nor land any where,
till we reach the coast, which I suppose will be some time in the end
of January. . . . I think it not unlikely but I shall be in England before
you receive this.' The letter was dated November 19. 'We shall sail,'
Park told his wife, 'the moment I have finished this letter.'

Martyn, too, took the opportunity of sending by Isaaco a letter
addressed to a friend named Megan. He struck with his first words a
different and, one may feel, a more realistic, if less presentable, note.

Thunder, Death and Lightning—the Devil to pay: lost by disease Mr.
Scott, two sailors, four carpenters and thirty-one members of the Royal
African Corps which reduces our numbers to seven out of which Doctor
Anderson and two of the soldiers are quite useless, the former from one

disease or other has been for four months disabled: we every day suppose he'll kick it . . . Capt. Park has made every enquiry concerning the River Niger and from what he can learn there remains no doubt but it is the Congo . . . Excellent living since we came here (August 22nd) the Beef and Mutton as good as was ever eat. Whitbreads Beer is nothing to what we get here.

This was written on November 1; a few days later he added a postscript.

Dr. Anderson and Wills dead since writing the within—my head is a little sore this morning—was up late last night drinking Ale in company with a Moor who has been at Gibraltar and speaks English—got a little tipsy—finished the scene by giving the Moor a damned good thrashing.[3]

THE DEATH OF MUNGO PARK

Isaaco reached the coast many months later. After nearly a year rumours of the expedition's progress down the Niger began to reach the coast. In September 1806 J. G. Jackson wrote to Banks that he had learnt from a correspondent in Mogador that Park had reached Timbuktu in March. This information was given in a letter sent across the desert by a Moorish trader living in Kabra, the port of Timbuktu. 'You will be much surprised to know from me,' this man had written, 'that a few days since a boat came to this place having Christians on board . . . they did not appear to be hostile but on the contrary they seemed peaceably inclined and inoffensive.' It was thought that the Christians wanted to trade, but no one had any communication with them and they returned to Jenne. Quite a different story was reported some months later by Court, an English merchant in Mogador, who had met a Moor recently returned from the Sudan. The Moor told him that the boat had been attacked by Tuareg at Timbuktu, as it had refused to stop and pay the customary tribute. Some time afterwards rumours were picked up from African traders on the Gambia that the expedition had met a disastrous end. Meanwhile it was long past the date which Park had given for his estimated arrival at the mouth of the Niger and not a line had been received from the explorer.[1]

The only way to clear up the mystery of the expedition's fate was to send an agent into the interior. As early as July 1806 Lloyd, the commander at Goree, had been officially instructed to send 'an intelligent negro' to pick up information about Park. No doubt

Lloyd found it impossible to find a suitable man; at any rate nothing seems to have been done for about three years. In 1809 the British at last succeeded in capturing the French colony on the Senegal. Shortly afterwards Maxwell, the Governor of Senegal, came across Isaaco, Park's valued guide; Isaaco agreed to go into the interior to gather news about Park. In October 1810 Isaaco reached Sansanding, where by a stroke of extraordinary chance he ran into Amadi Fatouma, Park's guide on his passage down the Niger. 'They are all dead; they are lost forever,' Amadi burst out, when he saw Isaaco. The story he had to tell is one of the great dramas of African exploration.[2]

The voyage of H.M.S. *Joliba* down the Niger had been far from peaceful. At five different places along the great bend of the river the boat had been attacked by hostile canoes, but the crew—Park, Martyn, three other Europeans, three slaves and Amadi—were so well armed, each man having fifteen muskets ready for action beside him, that every attack was beaten off. Martyn seems to have taken frantic delight in the work of killing. On one occasion, after a great number of their assailants had been mown down, Amadi, as he told Isaaco, took hold of Martyn's hand saying, 'Martyn, let us cease firing, for we have killed too many already'; on which 'Martyn wanted to kill me, had not Mr. Park interfered.'*

* Twenty years later Major Laing, on his way to Timbuktu, met a Tuareg who had been wounded by Park. 'How imprudent, how unthinking! I may even say how selfish it was in Park,' Laing wrote to a friend in England, 'to attempt to make discoveries in this country at the expense of the blood of the inhabitants, and to the exclusion of all after communication: How unjustifiable was such conduct.'

Fifty years later Heinrich Barth travelled through the country of the Niger bend and picked up many stories about Park's passage, one of them at least from an eye-witness, 'an old man with a very lively remembrance of Park' who gave 'an accurate description of his tall commanding figure and his large boat'. The fullest account was provided by Awab, a Tuareg chief of Timbuktu. Awab said that Park had first been attacked by the Tuareg below Kabra, the port for Timbuktu, where he had lost some time in trying to open communications with the people. The news of his arrival was passed on to another tribe of Tuareg, who attacked him with canoes at Bamba and again at Tosaye, where the river was only one hundred yards across. At Ansongo the boat stuck fast and the Tuaregs made yet another attack causing 'an immense deal of trouble and killing two of his Christian companions'.

Barth reckoned that it had been Park's policy 'to fire at anyone who approached him in a threatening manner'. It is obviously quite impossible

These affrays were not the only incidents on the journey. Twice they had to pass large armies camped on the banks of the river, one composed of Fulani, the other of Tuareg; on neither occasion were they molested. Twice they ran into herds of hippopotami and narrowly escaped being upset by the great beasts. The large store of provisions that they had taken with them made it unnecessary to make frequent stops; when a need for fresh food arose, Amadi was the only member of the party to go ashore.

Eventually—Amadi was not precise about the length of time taken on the journey—they came to Hausa country and reached the small state of Yauri on the left bank of the river. Amadi was not prepared to go any farther, so Park sent him ashore with presents for the chief of the village where he had landed and for the king of the country—Birnin Yauri, the capital, lying some distance from the river. The morning after Park had departed Amadi found himself under arrest; the King of Yauri considered that the white men had departed without giving him sufficient presents and held Amadi responsible for making a fool of him in this way.

> 'The next morning early [so Amadi's account continued] the King sent an army to a village called Boussa near the river side. There is before this village a rock across the whole breadth of the river. One part of the rock is very high; there is a large opening in that rock in the form of a door, which is the only passage for the water to pass through; the tide-current is here very strong. This army went and took possession of the top of this opening. Mr. Park came there after the army had posted itself; he nevertheless attempted to pass. The people began to attack him, throwing lances, pikes, arrows and stones. Mr. Park defended himself for a long time; two of his slaves at the stern of the canoe were killed; they threw everything they had in the canoe into the river, and kept firing; but being overpowered by numbers and fatigue, and unable to keep up the canoe against the current, and no probability of escaping Mr. Park took hold of one of the white men and jumped into the water; Martyn did the same, and they were drowned in the stream in attempting to escape.

There was one survivor, one of the slaves who remained in the canoe and called on the people to stop throwing their weapons; later this man found his way to Yauri and told Amadi his story.

to decide whether Park would have been able to sail down the Niger unscathed if he had behaved differently. But there can be little doubt that he was strongly influenced by his experiences among the Moors on his first journey and that the worst fate he could conceive for himself would be to fall once again into the hands of those merciless fanatics.[3]

Isacco returned to the coast in September 1811. His narrative was given as a postscript to Park's *Journal*, which was published by the African Institution in the beginning of 1815. To some people in England the circumstantial evidence surrounding Park's death seemed convincing enough; but many refused to believe that a man who had so successfully surmounted so many and great dangers could possibly be dead. The most popular theory was that he was being held captive by some African ruler; it was given new life by every rumour of a white man in the interior.* No one believed more ardently that Park was still alive than his wife and children. Mrs Park lived until 1840, yet never abandoned the hope that her husband might one day be found. His eldest son, Mungo, joined the Indian Army and died ten days after landing at Bombay. Thomas, the second son, brooded on the idea of going to Africa to look for his father. He joined the Navy, and in 1827 obtained three years' leave of absence to search for his father in the heart of Africa. He worked his way to Accra, where he made a point of avoiding the company of Europeans, settled in the African town and 'allied himself' to an African woman with a view to learning the language. After three months on the coast he set out for the interior, where he was struck down by a fatal attack of fever.[4]

A year earlier—though Thomas Park could not have known this at the time—the scene of his father's death had been visited by two British explorers, Hugh Clapperton and Richard Lander. Four years later Lander, accompanied by his brother John, came to Bussa again and made a special journey to Yauri to look for papers belonging to Park that the king was said to hold in his possession. Clapperton and Lander arrived in Bussa exactly twenty years after Park's death. The information that they received in answer to prolonged inquiries substantially confirmed Amadi's story, except in one particular:

* Rumours about Park were picked up as far away as Ethiopia. In 1812 Coffin and Pearce, two Englishmen living in Ethiopia, were told by a Muslim merchant that he had seen a strange white man in a large town in the interior of Africa, not far from Timbuktu. The white man looked about fifty years old and had a light-red beard; he lived in a common hut by himself, but took his food with the principal people; he said he was learning the language and had come from the west and was going east. He particularly asked the merchant if he could speak English. It was generally assumed that this could only be Park—in fact, it may well have been some Levantine trader. Coffin and Pearce would have gone in search of the stranger if the Ras, their master, had allowed them.[5]

Park's death had been caused not by the King of Yauri but by the people of Bussa. Of the various accounts that were received, the most convincing was given by a man in Nupe, who claimed to have been an eye-witness. He told Clapperton that Park's boat had come down the river just at the start of the Fulani *Jihad*—that religious crusade which developed into a war of conquest and established those light-skinned people as rulers of most of the central Sudan. When the King of Bussa learnt of the approach of the strange vessel with white men in it he assumed that they must be the advance guard of the Fulani Army coming to attack Bussa, summoned together his warriors and attacked the boat as it went past.*

Park's last journal was never recovered. Clapperton was told that the King of Yauri had given a book, which might have been the Journal, to an Arab merchant some ten years earlier; the Arab had been murdered by the Fulani and the book had disappeared. Lander, on his second visit, was more successful in recovering relics. In Yauri he obtained a double-barrelled sporting-gun that had formed part of Park's presents to the king. In Bussa he was given a magnificent robe made of rich crimson damask and covered with heavy gold embroidery which Park was said to have worn; he also saw an old nautical almanac which a man had picked out of the Niger after the wreck of Park's boat. The gun and the robe Lander, to his deep regret, had to surrender during the course of his adventurous journey down the Niger; the almanac was purchased in 1857 by another English traveller, Lieutenant John Glover. It now reposes in the museum of the Royal Geographical Society in London, the sole surviving relic of Park's second expedition.†[6]

Park's second expedition set the seal on his fame; the interweaving of heroism, of tragedy and of mystery could not fail to stir deeply

* This account disposes of the least credible part of Amadi's evidence. Bussa lies about forty miles distance from Yauri, Park and his party had at least a day and a half's start, so it would have been quite impossible for an army from Yauri, even if transported part of the way in canoes, to have taken up a position on the rocks at Bussa in time to intercept Park. It is possible that Amadi sought deliberately to put the blame for Park's death on the King of Yauri in revenge for the ill-treatment he had suffered at the king's hands. Another feasible explanation is that the King of Yauri sent canoes after Park, possibly even to warn him of the existence of rapids at Bussa, and that Amadi thought these canoes had caused his death.

† At least in England. In Nigeria the staff of office of the Emirs of Yauri is made from a silver-mounted walking-stick that belonged to Park and was recovered from the river.[7]

the imagination of Europe. Moreover, Park's own character compelled attention. 'He blended', wrote one of the earliest of his biographers, 'the virtues of a hero of romance—ardour of enterprise, generosity and contempt for danger—with the more sober, but still more valuable qualities of sagacity, calmness and good sense.' 'Perhaps no man of equally humble pretensions ever excited so general an interest among his countrymen or more powerfully moved their sympathy.' This was to forget Captain Cook; but if Park's practical achievements were infinitely less than those of the great Circumnavigator (or indeed of other African explorers), in the volume of his public fame he undoubtedly proved himself Cook's peer, joining him to become one of 'the heroes of British history.'[8]

In Africa Park's fame ran a different course. The story of that fantastic ship and its tall young commander spread through the length of the western and central Sudan. In 1823 a British officer, Major Denham, was at Kuka, the capital of Bornu. There he met a young Fulani who had come from Jenne. Often, at his father's house, the lad told Denham, he had heard people talking for a whole day at a time about the Christians who had come down the river from Segu in their large boat with guns fixed to its sides, many years ago before he himself had been born. Thirty years later, another explorer, Heinrich Barth, picked up many stories about Mungo Park as he travelled along the bend of the Niger, stories which 'proved what an immense excitement the mysterious appearance of this European traveller, in his solitary boat, had caused among all the surrounding tribes.'[9]

A few years ago an English traveller, Mr Richard Owen, set out to trace the route that Park had followed in the course of his expeditions, a journey that still requires ample qualities of fortitude and of endurance to complete. He 'found that to many West Africans Park has become a legendary and timeless character, an heroic figure, who once upon a time, had passed this way'. So, at the last, Africa and Europe join in honouring one, who, in his passionate and courageous quest for knowledge, is certainly worthy of so remarkable a fame.[10]

V

BRITAIN AND THE WEST COAST

THE DRAMA OF PARK'S second expedition and the mystery of his fate—as baffling to contemporaries as the disappearance of Colonel Fawcett to a later age—was for many Englishmen the only event connected with West Africa of which they were aware. Yet historically, except in so far as that inspiring, tragic, inconclusive narrative provoked to further endeavour, Park's second expedition was not of great importance. Much more significant for the future development of Britain's relationship with West Africa were certain lines of activity that took place between 1795 and 1815 of which most Englishmen must have been little aware: the consolidation of the colony of Sierra Leone, the beginnings of missionary enterprise, the first encounter between the European forts on the Gold Coast and the armed power of Ashanti, and the practical consequences of the abolition of the slave trade.

On the morrow of the French attack on Freetown in 1794 it would have needed some optimism to assert that the colony would not only survive but also grow stronger. Yet by 1810 it was clear that this had happened. In the intervening years Sierra Leone had moved from one crisis to another: in 1796 serious discontent among a group of the black settlers from Nova Scotia, intent on breaking away from the Company's rule, and inspired by the successful revolts in the West Indies; in 1800 an armed uprising, defeated by the providential arrival of a British ship; in 1801 a formidable invasion by the Temne, which, though defeated, served to discourage the settlers from making farms for themselves. By this time it was clear that, measured in terms of commercial profit, the colony had been a failure: expenditure was rising and the Company's capital diminishing. In 1800 the British Government had provided a subsidy of

346

£4,000; this sum was increased in subsequent years, until it became clear that the colony could survive only if it was brought entirely under the control of the Government. The Directors of the Company were the first to advocate this change, which was given Parliamentary sanction in 1807. On New Year's Day 1808 Sierra Leone came formally under the Crown; the date is one to be remembered as marking the establishment of the first Crown Colony—if the fiasco of Senegambia be excluded—in tropical Africa. The colony possessed one feature peculiarly auspicious for the future: men of colour were allowed in Sierra Leone a considerable measure of political freedom, in striking contrast to their position in other European colonies.

At the end of the eighteenth century the Catholic Church, even if its ardour seemed less intense, could look back on a long and noble history of missionary enterprise in many parts of Africa; but before the 1790s only a handful of Protestant missionaries had visited West Africa.* That decade, however, was distinguished by the founding of the several Protestant missionary bodies, the Baptist Missionary Society in 1792, the London Missionary Society, with offshoots in Glasgow and Edinburgh, in 1795, the Anglican Church Missionary Society in 1799, and in 1804 the interdenominational British and Foreign Bible Society. These were products of the same spirit that had inspired the Methodist movement, the Evangelical revival and the Abolitionist crusade.

Sierra Leone provided an obvious field for missionary endeavour, since Zachary Macaulay, Governor from 1793 to 1799, was himself an ardent Evangelical. Indeed, it was on Macaulay's suggestion that the first mission was launched. The remarkable account that Watt had given on the state of civilization in Futa Jallon led Macaulay to believe that a mission could be established in that country. He made arrangements for a party of Methodist lay preachers to be sent out. It was a disillusioning experience: few missionaries could have been

* The Moravian Brethren had sent missions to South Africa and to West Africa in 1737 and to Ethiopia in 1758. Between 1768 and 1770 nine European missionaries were sent by the Moravians to the Gold Coast; all of them died within a few months and the mission was abandoned. In 1751 Thomas Thompson, a missionary in the service of the Society for the Propagation of the Gospel, arrived on the Gold Coast. He returned to England in 1756, bringing with him three African boys. One of the boys, Philip Quaque, took Anglican orders and returned to the Gold Coast in 1766 as 'Missionary, Schoolmaster and Catechist'. He died in 1816.[1]

less suitable than these evangelizing British working-men and their wives. No sooner had they set foot at Freetown than one of the men went up to a quiet and dignified Muslim trader, and told him, brandishing his fist to emphasize his words, that Muhammad was a false prophet. As for the wives, 'to their astonishment,' Macaulay ironically recorded, 'Freetown resembled neither London nor Portsmouth; they could find no pastry cooks' shops, nor any ginger bread to buy for their children . . . if this was Africa, they would go no further!' They were soon on their way home.[2]

A year or two later the newly founded Missionary Societies of London, Edinburgh and Glasgow sent out six missionaries. Within twelve months three had died of disease, one had been murdered and two were invalided home. In 1804 the Church Missionary Society entered the field with two German missionaries. Thenceforward the current of Christian enterprise was never again interrupted. Formidable difficulties, as these early experiences had so clearly shown, remained to be overcome. Against the lethal climate there could be no sure protection, even though the experience of many traders had shown that it was not impossible to spend years on the Coast and return to tell the tale. Nevertheless, deliberately to face such a risk—and for no profit to oneself—required rare qualities of dedication. Evangelizing fervour in itself was not enough; to achieve his ends, a missionary needed to be both intelligent and practical, able to master an unwritten language, organize a school, build a house or run a farm. In such a demanding occupation naturally there would be many failures; it was the glory of the missionary movement, as it developed throughout Africa, that it did produce many noble and a few saintly men and women.[3]

At the beginning of the nineteenth century there were about twenty-five European forts strung along the Gold Coast, eleven Dutch, five Danish, the remainder British. The British forts were administered not by the Crown but by the Company of Merchants, which was assisted by a Government subsidy. The international anarchy in Europe might have provided an excuse, as earlier wars had done, for another round of petty skirmishing on the coast. Instead a tacit neutrality was preserved. European companies could not afford the expense or the risk of fighting one another when their own positions were so weak. 'It is necessary to keep black men of power in our pay that we may live in peace with the natives, who would otherwise molest us, knowing that we have not sufficient power to protect ourselves.' So wrote an official of the English company in 1774; the same policy held good forty years later. Indeed, by that time the position of the Europeans seemed even weaker than it had before, for they had recently been brought face to face with the most formidable power the Gold Coast had yet known, the kingdom of Ashanti.[4]

A century and a half earlier the Ashanti nation did not exist. It had its origin in a cluster of small states, little larger, indeed, than village communities, which had formed an alliance to defend themselves against their more powerful neighbours. These states were moulded into one nation by the statesmanlike ability and psychological genius—or, as the legends have it, the magical powers—of a priest, Anokye, and by the military prowess of the ruler, Osei Tutu. This movement took place towards the end of the seventeenth century. The Ashanti nation continued to expand after the death of its founders, but its centre of power was still far from the coast.* Between Ashanti and the sea lay the states of Akim and Assim and the federation of the Fante: these were the middlemen, who controlled for their own profit the trade that was so important to the Ashanti, for it supplied them, in exchange for slaves, with the firearms they needed for their constant campaigns. In such a situation conflict was inevitable. In 1765 the Ashanti defeated Akim and clashed with the Fante. In 1805 a major war broke out between the Fante and the Ashanti; the Fante were defeated and both a British and a Dutch fort taken by the victorious army. In 1811 and again in 1814 an Ashanti army ravaged the coast. At this point it might have been possible to drive all the Europeans into the sea. But to the Ashanti such a step would have presented no advantages, for it would have led to the destruction of a trade that provided them with essential commodities. As for the British, they found themselves drawn, in the course of their chequered relationship with the Ashanti, ever more deeply into the interior of the Gold Coast, to country where, at this time, no European had ever been known to set foot.[6]

While this new situation was emerging on the Gold Coast, the

* No European is known to have visited Ashanti before 1817, but from an early date European traders on the coast were aware of the importance of the new state. Thus in 1708 the Royal African Company's Chief Agent at Cape Coast Castle described the King of Ashanti as 'a great Governing Man in these parts' and stressed the value of sending him lavish presents to obtain his friendship.[5]

British Government had taken a decision whose ultimate consequences no one could have foreseen, for they were to involve Englishmen in direct action in many different parts of Africa and to provide one of the main justifications for the assumption of imperial responsibilities. In 1807 the Parliament at Westminster gave assent to a Bill which prescribed that 'all manner of dealing and trading' in slaves in Africa was to be 'utterly abolished, prohibited and declared to be unlawful'.

Seven years earlier the Abolitionist Movement had been at its lowest point. Clarkson, his health broken by his exertions, had retired from the struggle, the Abolitionist Committee had ceased to meet, Wilberforce alone, almost without allies, continued to raise the subject before an uninterested House. The enthusiasm generated for the crusade in the early nineties had been deflated by the war; patriotic Abolitionists accepted the argument that the reform be postponed until the war was over, while their opponents gleefully profited from the fact that some of the leading Abolitionists had expressed—like fellow-travellers in the Cold War—dangerously Jacobinical views.

By 1804 the climate of opinion showed remarkable signs of change. The West Indians were no longer united in opposing abolition. In the course of the war the more fertile islands belonging to the French and the Dutch had fallen into British hands. If they were developed by the import of fresh slaves it would be at the expense of the older British settlements, which could not face such competition. A section of the British planters began to see that the cessation of the slave trade might be to their own advantage. This was a crucial change. In the past supporters of the trade could always fall back on not unconvincing economic arguments; now these were undermined. Pitt, however, for the first time refused to support the motion for Abolition; utterly absorbed in the conduct of the war, working himself indeed to death in his lonely office, he could not accept the burden of renewed controversy. He died in January 1806. A new Government was formed with Fox as its most powerful member. Thus success was assured, for to Fox and to many of his supporters Abolition was a cause no less important than the struggle against Napoleon. When on February 23, 1807, the Bill received its second reading in the House of Commons, the majority in its favour, 283 to 16, was overwhelming.

The Abolitionists had won their battle. At the same time the

Directors of the Sierra Leone Company had handed over their responsibilities to the Government, but those who had been involved in the struggle for African rights knew how much there still remained for them to do. Different circumstances required a different organization. Accordingly, only three weeks after the royal assent had been given to the Abolition Bill the formation of a new body, the African Institution, was announced. Macaulay was the first Secretary, Henry Thornton the first Treasurer, other members of the Clapham Sect were, as one would expect, prominently represented; but the President and Patron of the Institution was a Royal prince, the Duke of Gloucester, and the Governing Council included the Archbishop of Canterbury and many members of the Cabinet. It was a remarkable indication of the way in which the Movement had gained the support of many of the most influential members of the Establishment. Equally remarkable was the opinion expressed at the inaugural meeting of the Institution: 'deeply impressed with a sense of the enormous wrongs which the natives of Africa have suffered in their intercourse with Europe; and from a desire to repair those wrongs, as well as from a general feeling of benevolence, [the meeting] is anxious to adopt such measures as are best calculated to promote their civilization and happiness'. Rarely can the guilt-complex of any nation have received so emphatic an expression.[7]

To encourage legitimate trade by collecting and diffusing information about the natural products and agricultural possibilities of the continent, 'to promote the instructions of Africans in letters and in useful knowledge', to stimulate the study of African languages, to proceed with the exploration of the interior 'not merely to gratify curiosity but to open sources for future intercourse': such were the purposes the founders of the Institution had in mind. With subscriptions bringing in nearly £3,000 in the first year—a much greater sum than the African Association was ever able to collect—tasks such as these would have been well within the Institution's powers. The Abolition of the slave trade had served, it was believed, to remove the barrier which has so long obstructed the natural course of 'social improvement' in Africa. Alas, the time had not yet come when the English supporters of African development could devote all their activities to positive ends. The slave trade was not yet dead. While it still flourished, the members of the African Institution were bound to spend by far the greater part of their resources on the struggle with the old evil.

The slave trade was not dead; it had not even been struck into decline; the years of its greatest activity lay indeed not in the past but in the future. When in 1810 British Commissioners visited the coast, they found evidence of an 'extent of evil compared with which the former supply of our West Indian settlements sinks into a trickle'. This was a virtuous exaggeration, but it emphasized the point the Commissioners were concerned to make—that since Abolition, conditions on the coast had got worse, not better. Statistics graphically illustrate this fact: in the eighteenth century, when the trade was at its height, the annual export of slaves was reckoned to be about 80,000, in 1815 the figure was put at 106,600, twenty years later it had risen to 135,000. That the slave trade should continue to flourish was hardly surprising; too many people were making money out of it. On the African side there were the powerful slave-merchants of the coastal states and their contacts in the interior; their lives revolved round the trade, which was sanctified by the practice of centuries. 'We tink trade no stop,' the King of Bonny, the richest of the Niger Delta states said to Captain Crow, an English slave trader, in 1807, 'for all we Ju-Ju-men tell we so, for dem say you country no can niber pass God A'mighty.' Across the Atlantic many of the West Indian markets might be closed, but Portuguese Brazil, the Spanish colonies of Central and South America, and the Southern States of North America were capable of absorbing an infinite number of cargoes of slave labour.[8]

Already by 1815 the broad outline of the strategy of the fight against the foreign slave trade was beginning to emerge. There was to be direct action by the British Navy. In 1808 two warships had been despatched to the West Coast to intercept slaving vessels; in 1810 the squadron was doubled in size, yet was still little more than a token force. Moreover, the British had no legal right to arrest vessels flying a neutral flag. It was therefore necessary to put pressure on other powers to outlaw the trade. The United States had abolished the trade in the same month as Britain; but the American Government was not able to enforce the new law. Meanwhile in France, Spain and Portugal the trade was still legal. In 1815 the powers assembled at the Congress of Vienna expressed their 'sincere desire of concurring in the most prompt and effectual execution of this measure [the Abolition of the Slave Trade] by all the means at their disposal'. It was to take years of hard and tedious diplomatic negotiation before all the powers of Europe could be persuaded to act in accordance with this declaration. The day on which the last slave-ship sailed from the West Coast still lay half a century ahead.[9]

'White man now come among us with new face, talk palaver we do not understand, they bring new fashion, great guns and soldiers in our country.' So a group of Chiefs, watching the growth of the colony of Sierra Leone, was recorded as saying in the first years of the century; they were more prescient than anyone at the time could possibly have realized. For to many British politicians and civil servants the problems of West Africa seemed in the next fifty years a distraction, an irritation, a liability which they would have been happy to shake off. Politicians and civil servants are never free agents. The pressure of the Humanitarians, so powerfully exerted, so skilfully deployed, involved the British Government ever more deeply in African affairs. In the moral ideas of a Wilberforce one may trace as surely, if more obliquely, as in the grandiose schemes of a Bonaparte, the roots of a new imperialism.[10]

THE AGE OF THE AFRICAN
ASSOCIATION—II 1802-15

I

THE AFRICAN ASSOCIATION 1802-15

THE YEARS BETWEEN 1798 and 1802, with the publication first of Park's, then of Hornemann's explorations, represent the apogee of the African Association. Never again was the Association able to claim such undisputed success; not for much longer could it monopolize the field, for Park's second expedition, despite its dismal ending, created a precedent for Government sponsorship of African exploration. But in the year 1802, with the glow of achievement quite undimmed, the Association seemed well set to procure even greater discoveries. Yet there were signs of weakness which were not apparent ten years earlier. Membership was falling: in 1799 Banks reported that of 143 members who had joined the Association in the last ten years, only 57 could be regarded as 'efficient'; of the remainder, 23 were dead, 42 withdrawn and 21 'doubtful'. Park and Hornemann gave the Association a boost; in the four years 1799–1802 35 new members joined. But in the next period of four years there were only 9 new members, and for the period 1807–10 an even more discouraging figure, 4. 'We have lost many subscribers,' Banks told Matra in 1800, 'on account of the vast increase in personal taxes on the rich.' Yet this was perhaps only part of the reason for the decline. Some of those who withdrew may well have reflected, even if unfairly, on the large element of failure—Ledyard dead, Lucas never leaving the coast, Houghton and Hornemann lost in the wilds—in the Association's schemes.[1]

There were changes too among those who formed the active core of the Association. Banks certainly was still there; his interest as keen as ever—but Africa was only one among the many affairs that claimed his attention and his time. Shortly after Beaufoy's death, when he had accepted the post of acting secretary, Banks had written to Park: 'I have so many things to do that in truth I should not have done it now, if it had not been that I had much expectation from you and was unwilling that your affairs should be conducted by anyone else.' Two years later he was appointed a Privy Councillor and given a seat on the Board of Trade, where he was involved in long and complicated discussions on plans for a reform of the coinage. He had been directly involved in the schemes for the establishment of the colony in New South Wales; now more continuously than any other public man of his time, he was caught up in the growing pains of the colony. Indeed, as his correspondence shows, he found himself having to give much more of his attention to Australia than he allowed to Africa. The Royal Society, with the multitude of contacts that it brought him in the world of science, took up as much of his time as ever. On his Lincolnshire estate at Reresby, where he regularly spent a few months each year, he maintained his reputation as an active and progressive landowner. And constantly he found himself, as the Chairman of many committees, called on to undertake new duties in the public cause. But the most grievous of his burdens was ill-health. He had suffered from gout for some years; but after 1804—he told the Association that year that 'from the infirm state of health he wished to resign the treasurership'—he was completely crippled. 'He lost the use of his lower limbs so completely as to oblige him to be carried or wheeled by his servants in a chair'; yet this infirmity, a close friend of his wrote afterwards, 'never disturbed his uniform cheerfulness.'[2]

Bryan Edwards, Beaufoy's successor, died in 1800. His place was filled by a friend of his, Sir William Young, a man with a scholarly and wide-ranging mind, who possessed, like Edwards, West Indian connections. In 1807 Young was appointed Governor of Tobago. The Rev. Dr Anthony Hamilton, the vicar of St Martin-in-the-Fields, who had taken over the Treasurership from Banks, reluctantly agreed to combine the two offices by acting as Secretary, until in 1811 ill-health and old age forced him to resign. His place as Secretary was taken by his more famous son, William, one of the rising stars of the Foreign Office. William Hamilton had spent ten years in the Near East, and had recently published an important work on Egypt. In 1809, at the age of thirty-two, he became Under-Secretary of State for Foreign Affairs. He remained as Secretary of the Association until 1822, when he went to Naples as Ambassador. The post of

Treasurer in these years was held first by Sir Thomas Metcalfe, then by the Earl of Hardwicke.[3]

Of the founder members of the Association, four—Beaufoy, Conway, Fordyce and Stuart—were dead by 1802; the Earl of Galloway had withdrawn, and Sinclair and Ferguson were regarded in 1799 as being among the 'doubtful'. The Saturday's Club had changed. For two years after 1794 there were no meetings, but in March 1796 a special meeting was held to revive it. New rules were drawn up: it was agreed that only those already members of the African Association could be considered for election, while the membership should be set at fifteen. Three years later there was a change in name; as 'the African Club', the society remained in existence at least until 1815, though only holding its dinners twice a year. The Committee had changed as much as the Club. In 1809, when its membership was increased to eight (Wilberforce being among the new members), there was only one other committee-man who could join with Banks in looking back on twenty years of service, Lord Rawdon, now Earl of Moira.[4]

In 1813 Moira was appointed Governor-General of Bengal. Shortly before he left England a special meeting was held in Banks's house for the purpose of introducing changes into the Constitution of the African Association. The Association had never felt the need of a titular head; but now it was resolved to request the Earl of Moira, 'whose attention to the business of the Annual meetings greatly facilitated the best interests of the Society', to accept the office of President, with the right to nominate a Vice-President during his absence from the country. At the same time 'the Noble President' was requested 'to establish in India an African Association', with a 'civil servant of rank and consequence' as its secretary.[5]

It seems unlikely that an Indian African Association was ever established. But it was not unreasonable to attempt to draw on the information that India, through its trading connections with the Red Sea and the East Coast, might provide on Africa. Indeed, in the same year, 1811, the East India Company sent one of its cruisers from Bombay on an exploratory mission along the East Coast from Cape Guardafui to Zanzibar. Captain Smee, the officer commanding, was instructed to obtain general information on that almost unknown coast, to examine with special attention any navigable stream—a report obtained in Muscat suggested that one of East African rivers might rise from the same source as the Nile—and to inquire after

Hornemann and Park, who might possibly have succeeded in crossing the continent. Intercourse between the British in India and East Africa developed very slowly. But when at last in the 1850s the interior of East Africa came to be explored, the leading part was taken by two British Army officers with Indian experience, Richard Burton and John Hanning Speke.[6]

II

THE APPROACH FROM THE SOUTH

HENRY NICHOLLS

BY 1800 THE ASSOCIATION HAD tried three routes into the interior
—from Cairo, from Tripoli and from the Gambia. In that year Banks
began to think about a fourth possibility, the route northward from
the Gold Coast; but, with Hornemann still in the field, the Association could not afford to send out another explorer. Three years later
Banks told Blumenbach, who had written to say that he had been
approached by three young men anxious to succeed Hornemann,
'I am at present inclined to an attempt from Calabar or some other
point on the coast of Guinea to visit *Gana* near the Lake Wangara,
which was, when the Portuguese made their discovery, the capital to
which the Gold and Ivory Coasts etc. were subject.' In 1804, when
Banks was able to report that the Association's finances were 'in
a flourishing state', the decision was taken to launch a mission along
this untried route. On June 4 the Committee instructed their Secretary
to gather information about Old Calabar and to examine the
qualifications of two new applicants, Mr Nicholls and Mr Fitzgerald.
Fitzgerald was interested only in South Africa, so Nicholls, of whose
previous career nothing has been recorded, was chosen. He was
'required to bestow serious consideration on the dangers and
difficulties of the enterprise', advised to study the travels of Park and
other writers with care, and allowed a salary of half a guinea a day
to start from June 9 and to be increased to a guinea from the day
he left for Africa.[1]

For advice on the West Coast, Sir William Young, the Association's
Secretary, turned to Archibald Dalzel. He could have found few
men better informed on African affairs, for Dalzel had spent thirty

years on the Coast and had been Governor of the English factories at both Whydah and Cape Coast. Dalzel talked first about Dahomey, the country he knew best. 'The Dahomans,' he told Young, were 'really a polished and hospitable people,' but it would be 'next to impracticable' to get beyond the capital, Abomey, 'not so much from any bad temper or indisposition of the inland people the Eyoes [the Yoruba of Oyo], but from the extreme jealousy of the Daho-mans and their government lest any intelligence be carried to the Eyoes, who are a most extended and powerful nation and who yearly come for tribute to the Dahomans and which their king readily pays in purchase of peace and quiet.' Bonny or Old Calabar seemed a much better starting-point; from either of them a traveller would be able to by-pass Dahomey and make a shorter cut to the Niger, while passing through countries and tribes still completely unknown. On Calabar, Dalzel added, it should be possible to obtain first-hand information before leaving England, for a number of the Calabaris came to Liverpool to learn English.[2]

On Dalzel's advice, Nicholls travelled up to Liverpool to talk to the traders who knew the Bight of Benin. Those he met advised him that Old Calabar was to be preferred to Bonny, as its people were 'more intelligent and civilized', many of them indeed being able to write 'tolerable English'. Unfortunately, there were no Calabar people in Liverpool at that time, but Nicholls's informants told him that even if there had been, he would not have learnt much from them, for most of them lived near the trading centre and knew nothing of the country 'even at a few leagues from the Coast'. They themselves, however, had heard of a place known as Newtown lying sixty miles up the Calabar river. Here three important native traders in gold dust, ivory and slaves had their residence, men of great influence, whose names were known over a wide area; from them the African traders of Calabar obtained their slaves. All the information that Nicholls had acquired in Liverpool seemed to indicate that Old Calabar was 'the place above all others best suited for inquiry in directions of the greatest interest, Northward by the Eyoe country to the river Niger . . . and Eastward to Darkulla and districts south of Darfur'; in the course of his journey Nicholls, so Young informed the next General Meeting, would 'have to pass over unexplored country probably covered with intermediate nations of the *vera Nigritia*, the Negro aborigines of Africa'. One thing, however, struck the Committee as surprising—why had none of the Liverpool traders ever made any

attempt to procure reliable information about the interior? 'It hath
been remarked, on a minute and careful inquiry,' Young told the
Committee, 'that all Europeans (and without one known exception),
who have hitherto visited or even for a length of time resided on
these coasts of Africa, have narrowed their views to trade and wholly
suppressed curiosity as of possible bad effect in raising jealousies
and suspicion to prejudice of their commercial concerns.'[3]

News that a ship was about to leave for Calabar caused Nicholls
to hasten his departure. Quickly he gathered the necessary equipment,
the trade-goods and the presents for the chiefs, at a cost of £450.
On November 1, 1804, he sailed from Liverpool.[4]

The Cross river, after the Niger the largest stream that flows into
the Gulf of Guinea, has a wide estuary 'well furnished', so Barbot
described it at the end of the seventeenth century, 'with villages and
hamlets all about'. A hundred years later eight or nine such settlements with a total population of about six thousand, lying on the
left bank of the estuary about fifty miles from the sea, formed the
trading community of Old Calabar. They had been founded during
the course of the seventeenth century by a branch of the Ibibio
people, who had come to be called *Efik*, a nickname derived from a
word meaning *to oppress*, because they prevented other tribes from
establishing direct trade relations with the Europeans. The Efiks
throve on this monopoly to become one of the most prosperous
communities on the West Coast. By the end of the eighteenth century
they were exporting barwood and ivory together with about two
thousand slaves a year—though the oppressive duties they insisted
on charging were losing them some trade to Bonny. Significantly
for the future, they were beginning to develop a trade in palm-oil.
Europeans were welcome in Calabar, so long as they kept their
distance: they were not allowed to establish factories on the shore,
and their ships often had to spend eight months or more in the river
before they had completed their cargo. 'The air in this river is very
malignant and occasions great mortality amoung our sailors that
make any long stay.' Did Nicholls flinch for a moment when he
read this remark of Barbot's? He might well have done so, for the
Committee had instructed him to spend up to a year in Calabar,
gathering information and making preparations for his journey.[5]

Nicholls landed at Duke Town, one of the settlements of Calabar,
on January 14, 1805. He hastened to present the letter of introduction
he had been given by a Liverpool merchant to one of the leading

traders of Duke Town, Egbo Young Eyambo, an elderly corpulent man with a pleasant face. Nicholls's first interview seemed singularly unpropitious. 'Why have you come here?' Egbo Young asked him. 'Do you come to build a fort as your people have done on the Gold Coast? Or perhaps you have come from Mr Wilberforce?' 'For neither of these purposes,' Nicholls replied. 'I have been sent by some great men in my country to try and find out dye-woods and another thing, to increase trade and do good for all Calabar.' Egbo Young was not satisfied; eyeing Nicholls 'with some little ferocity', he said, 'If you come from Mr Wilberforce, we will kill you.'

The next day, however, after he had absorbed the letter Nicholls had given him from the Liverpool trader, he was perfectly polite. Nicholls decided to be absolutely candid about his mission, saying that he had come 'to look at his country and to describe the beasts, birds, fishes and plants, and to write a large book about it.' Egbo Young was delighted with this explanation, shook Nicholls warmly by the hand and promised him every assistance, even to the point of forwarding him 'as far towards the interior as his people dare go without endangering their own safety'. He then began to talk about Captain Cook, part of whose *Voyages* he possessed, and said once again how happy he would feel in assisting Nicholls. The other great men of Calabar were no less co-operative, the two greatest traders, Ego Honesty and Duke Ephraim, being especially friendly. Both men impressed Nicholls deeply in character and appearance. Ephraim, reckoned to be 'by far the greatest trader', was a 'very elegant formed young man' with 'a very expressive countenance', while Honesty, reputed 'a very great warrior', had 'an extreme good-natured negro countenance' and a 'very commanding deportment'. During the next few weeks Nicholls met many other important men —Antera Duke, King Aqua, Jemmy Henshaw, Momo Dick, Otto Ephraim—and found that they all behaved 'as politely as English gentlemen'. He also cultivated the company of 'the middling traders', men whose work took them farthest up-country and who were therefore the most valuable sources of information. With them, as he reported, 'I am obliged to be very profuse with my rum.'

Meanwhile he was busy making notes on all that he saw around him: the narrow paths of Creek town 'lined with ripe pineapples, which send forth a most delicious odour'; the fetiches that adorned Ego Honesty's house—birds' skins, egg shells and human skulls; a manatee 'a most uncommon misshapen animal', something like a seal; 'the pretty jumble of furniture' that filled the double-storied house Duke Ephraim had set at his disposal, ranging from 'two large pierglasses, elegantly gilt and ornamented' to 'two handsome escritoire desks and two musical clocks'; the masked figure of the secret society known as Egbo, that enforced the law at Calabar, 'who runs about the town everyday', flogging those who had failed to pay their dues.

These details formed part of the account he gave of Calabar in a letter to the Association dated February 18. 'My health is very good,' he wrote in his last sentence, 'and I am in good spirits, no obstacle appearing to prevent me from eventually accomplishing my mission.' Two months later he was dead, 'a victim to the disease incidental to all European travellers on the coast'. Not one of his papers was recovered, for an English sea-captain with whom he was intimate at Calabar, and who might have preserved his possessions, died in Calabar shortly afterwards.[6]

Nicholls seems to have been an able man. If he had lived, what success would he have achieved? One can hardly believe that on the route that had been chosen for him he would have found it possible to penetrate deep into the interior, for after passing through the forest belt he would have entered the territory of the war-like Tiv, a people who showed themselves later in the century notoriously ill-disposed to European travellers. Indeed, there seems to be no record of any European going from Calabar to the Benue until all that country had been brought under British administration at the beginning of the twentieth century. For early nineteenth-century explorers Calabar was, like Darfur and Morocco, a cul-de-sac.

III

THE EASTERN SUDAN

J. L. BURCKHARDT

NICHOLLS'S DEATH WAS REPORTED to the General Meeting of
1807. At the same time the Treasurer was able to announce a balance
of £1,605—ample funds with which to support another traveller. It
was decided to investigate an application that had been received from
a certain Mr Eschauzier, an army officer in Sicily. But though both
his qualifications and his testimonials seemed excellent, he was under
the disadvantage of being unable to come to England to explain his
plans in person. In the spring of 1808 the Committee were glad,
therefore, to receive and on inquiry to accept the offer of service
made to them by a young Swiss gentleman, Johann Ludwig Burckhardt.[1]

Burckhardt was twenty-three years old. He came from one of the
wealthiest and most distinguished families in Basle, a family that had
been cruelly disturbed by the Revolution, for in 1797 his father had
been tried on a trumpery charge put up by the local Jacobins and
forced to leave the country. Young Burckhardt had completed his
education at the Universities of Leipzig and Göttingen. In 1805 a
relation, serving as a Quartermaster with the English forces, offered
to take him to London and set him on a profitable career. Burckhardt
leapt at this opportunity. He arrived in England in the summer of
1806. 'When one has once felt what freedom is,' he wrote to his
parents, 'then one realises that in our age this is the only country in
which one can breathe freely.' This devotion to England, so quickly
conceived, never left him—but it had to withstand some hard knocks.
He had arrived full of hope, aiming high and assiduously cultivating
his contacts with the Establishment in the expectation of being

366

offered a post in the Foreign Service. Not unnaturally, as an unknown young man, he met with a cool reception. But in 1807, through a Swiss lady who was acting as a governess to the family, he secured an introduction to Lord Bathurst, who recommended him to Canning, the new Foreign Secretary. Canning could do nothing for him; so Burckhardt turned to the possibility of employment in Russia, only to meet with another disappointment. Hitherto he had been supported by remittances from his family; but for a time these were held up, and in the autumn of 1807 he found himself with no prospect of a job, reduced to a state of real poverty. Yet the time—as he told his parents in one of his intimate and affectionate letters—was not without its lessons. It taught him the virtue of austerity and it made him turn for consolation to his Bible, one saying of Christ's striking him with particular relevance: *fast and pray*.[2]

Poor though he was, he still frequented the houses of the great, and among them Sir Joseph Banks's. He had brought with him on his arrival in England a letter of introduction to Banks from Professor Blumenbach, and had been regularly invited to the Sunday Assemblies in Soho Square. But it is clear from his letters that it was not until the hopes of regular employment faded that he turned to the idea of African exploration. It must almost certainly have been Banks who sowed the seed in his mind, though he counted among his friends at this time W. G. Browne, who could talk about African exploration with greater authority than anyone else in England. In February 1808 Burckhardt told his parents that he was thinking of accepting an engagement with the African Association. A month later he made the Committee a definite offer and found himself accepted.[3]

He had thought the matter out with remarkable penetration. His plan was to follow Hornemann's example, acquire so fluent a knowledge of Arabic that he could pass himself off as a Muslim trader and join one of the Saharan caravans in North Africa. Certainly there were dangers—but they were less, he reckoned, than a soldier would be called upon to face. He was confident that he was strong enough to resist the effects of the climate; as for the other difficulties, arising from the men he might encounter on his way, on a closer analysis and as his knowledge of Arabic increased, these tended to disappear. 'The dangers that await me,' he wrote to his parents explaining his decision, 'are not so innumerable as the name Africa may perhaps already seem to you to imply. With countries which are only half known, which have for centuries been almost completely unknown, simply because no one has felt the urge or dared to make the attempt to penetrate them, with countries such as these it could not possibly have happened otherwise; they have been and still are the subject of many stories.' How refreshing it is at any time to hear such sensible talk about Africa! 'The legends about wild cannibal tribes,' he went on, 'are absolute lies; unfortunately it is just rumours of this sort, listened to from childhood on, that have rooted themselves so deeply in our imagination.' Of his own motives he was equally sure. 'I want to be of some use in this world,' he wrote in the same letter, 'and I believe that when I come to leave it, this together with a certain virtue that repentance brings will be the only things I can take with me to the other side.' Personal fame had no attraction for him. 'I have not taken on this task, God knows, in order to be gaped at and pointed at on my return, but because in an age like this, when whole nations—my own among them—have given themselves up to a wretched, selfish, sensual absorption in the affairs of the moment, reeling round in circles of utterly unprincipled corruption, I can take heart in treading the same path as those who still think about and believe in the future, and because a proven strength and achievement in an individual is something that gives honour to his country and makes it the more esteemed by those who come after.'[4]

In the spring of 1808 Burckhardt, with the Committee's approval, went up to Cambridge and threw himself into preparations for his journey. There he laid the foundations of his knowledge of Arabic (he had the advantage of being by inclination something of a linguist, and already knew five European languages); there he toughened himself by taking long walks—he took the opportunity of a heatwave to make a thirteen-hour tramp across the unshaded Cambridgeshire fields—and by keeping to an austere diet; there he attended lectures on 'chemistry, astronomy, mineralogy, medicine and surgery'; there he began to let his beard grow and to practise the wearing of Oriental dress.[5]

By the end of January 1809 he was ready to leave. The members of the Committee, to whose friendliness and help he paid glowing tributes in his letters home, allowed him to draft his own instructions. It was agreed that he should go first to Syria, where there should be no danger of meeting any North African traders; there in the space of two years he should be able to acquire a sufficiently detailed knowledge of Arabic and of the manners of the people to be able to pass himself off as a Muslim. From Syria he should go to Cairo and join one of the caravans to Murzuk, where he would have to decide on the best route to the Sudan. In the Sudan itself no specific task was assigned to him: 'try your luck,' it was suggested, 'in pressing forwards, or to the Right or to the Left', letting 'neither rashness nor timid cautions influence your conduct'. For salary he was to receive, apart from £120 for his equipment and his passage, 10s. 6d. a day until he arrived in Cairo and £1 1s. a day thereafter for a period no exceeding six years, together with £150 to be made available for buying camels and trade-goods for his desert crossing. With these terms Burckhardt was completely satisfied; indeed, he reckoned that with the savings he would make, and with the money he would receive from a publisher on his return, he should be able to accumulate close on £2,000.[6]

Burckhardt left England on March 2 in a ship in the Malta convoy. He decided to pass himself off as an Indian Muslim with the name of Sheikh Ibrahim, bearing despatches from the East India Company to Barker, the British Consul and the Company's Agent at Aleppo. This disguise would secure him a measure of diplomatic immunity and at the same time serve to excuse his present 'irregularity of speech and manners'. He spent two months in Malta, living in the house of the harbour-master 'out of the way of intruders', for there were many Moorish merchants in Malta whom it was imperative to avoid—and, equally embarrassing, a Swiss regiment stationed on the island, several of whose officers were known to him personally.

Leaving Malta in a Greek ship at the beginning of June, Burckhardt found to his alarm and astonishment that among the few other passengers was a rich Tripoli merchant. His Arabic was still 'hardly intelligible', but this deficiency he covered by saying that he had lived in England from an early age and was now on his way home. When asked for a specimen of Hindustani, he replied in 'the worst dialect of Swiss German, which in its gutteral sounds may fairly rival the harshest utterance of Arabic'. Every evening the passengers met on deck to enjoy the cool breeze and to smoke their pipes. When called on for a story, Burckhardt obliged the company with 'the wonders of the furthest east'—the court of the great Mogul, suttee, the Great Wall of China, while the Tripoli merchant 'regaled us with the wonders of the Soudan, of one nation of speaking sheep, of another of necromancers, who lately defeated a whole army which the King of Bornou sent against them, etc. etc.' Soon Burckhardt and the Moor were on the most intimate terms, the rich man inviting Burckhardt to share his meals, while Burckhardt made himself useful in various ways.

After landing near Antioch, where the Aga and most of the townspeople suspected him of being a Frank, Burckhardt travelled with a caravan to Aleppo. In Barker, the British Consul, he found an obliging host and a real friend. It was no longer practicable to maintain his Indian disguise, so Burckhardt let himself be known as a travelling English merchant, while retaining his Muslim name and eastern dress; 'as it frequently happens that people coming to the Levant change their name,' he explained to the Association, 'nobody wonders at my being called with an oriental name'. Passing as an Englishman, he could enjoy complete security and at the same time continue his study of Arabic without arousing suspicion.[7]

Burckhardt spent two and a half years in Syria. It was, as his letters to his parents show, a happy time for him. In Aleppo he threw himself into his Arabic studies, started his collection of manuscripts and, as an exercise, prepared a translation of *Robinson Crusoe*. He also undertook three daring expeditions, first a fortnight in the tents of a Turcoman tribe, then a long tour through Palmyra, Damascus and Baalbek, finally a journey to the banks of the Euphrates, in the course of which he was set upon by robbers and stripped to the skin. Inclination induced him, necessity forced him to travel lightly. 'I put up every time in the dirtiest caravanserai,' he told his parents, 'take my cloak for a blanket, the earth for a mattress, eat with camel drivers, groom my own horse—but see and hear many things those who travel in comfort will never know.' 'Travelling alone in the desert has its own great charm, even though one is surrounded by people one cannot trust, deprived of the least comfort and plagued by the heat and by vermin,' so he wrote in another letter, launching into a lyrical description of the pleasures of that life: dawn in a desert camp, the halt in the heat of midday (he used the pretext of covering himself with his cloak at this time to to make notes of all that he had seen), the evening meal, the hospitable tents, the coffee passing round, stories and the singing of girls and overhead, as he wandered out of the camp, the magnificent canopy of the stars.[8]

In June 1812 he left Syria for Egypt, avoiding the beaten track through Jerusalem and Gaza and taking a route that lay through the almost unknown districts east of the Dead Sea. In this way, not without some danger from the Bedouin tribes, he came to visit the fabulous ruins of Petra, which no European had seen in modern times. To the Association he sent regular reports on all these expeditions, explaining that they were made 'as a general would take possession of any strong post on his way, even without any express commands to that purpose'.[9]

On his arrival in Cairo he found that there was in the city a caravan from the central Saharan oasis of Tuat. He decided not to join it, as he was not sufficiently well informed on African ways. 'I am extremely averse,' he told Banks at this time, 'to any hasty steps; they are the ruin of the traveller's health as well as of his plans.' Instead he acquired a small house in Cairo and set about preparing for a journey southwards to Dongola. Time had become a secondary consideration; his overall plan was to visit as many countries in the Sudan as possible. He started on this new expedition early in 1813, only to find that the Mamluk Beys, whom Muhammad Ali had driven out of the country, were troubling the borders of Upper Egypt, making it impossible for him to travel on alone. So he retired to Esne in Upper Egypt to wait until the caravan for Sennar should set out. He stayed in that dull little town almost a year, for the caravan was delayed, first by reports of robbers on the road, then of a famine in Sennar. 'I am almost dying of boredom,' he told his parents in the only letter he had a chance to send back. All the time he had to take care not to arouse suspicion; 'not wishing to be much known,' he wrote later, 'I kept as little company as possible, dressed myself in the poorest dress of an inhabitant of Egypt and spent as little money as I possibly could.' He had brought a servant with him from Cairo; but, deeming it safer to travel unaccompanied, he sent this man back. All he possessed when he joined the caravan was an ass, a store of provisions, the minimum of equipment and a very small sum of money. Yet he had already made up his mind to go from Sennar across to Massawa on the Red Sea and over to Mecca, returning to Cairo by way of the Hejaz; 'my journey through Arabia,' he told the Association, 'may probably qualify me better than anything else to future perilous travels in the Mohammedan world, nor will it, I hope, be devoid of some advantages to science.'[10]

The caravan route to Sennar cut across the great bend of the Nile by passing through the Nubian desert, where James Bruce had nearly met with disaster forty years earlier. For Burckhardt the ardours of the journey were much increased by his solitary and unprotected state. The Egyptian slave-merchants in the caravan accepted his story that he was a Turk from Syria searching for a relative, to to whom he had entrusted all his property, and who had disappeared on a trading mission to Sennar, but they suspected that he might be trying to encroach, as other Turks had done, on their trading-preserve and were determined to make his life unpleasant by treating him 'with neglect and even with contempt'. So he had to endure their taunts and their curses, to be always the last to fill his water bags at the wells, to submit to being driven out of the shade into the burning sun at the midday halts and always to wear himself out with the chores that others could entrust to their servants. And yet afterwards he could write of this experience: 'I was never in better health and spirits than during this journey, although its fatigues were certainly very great and much beyond my expectation.'[11]

On March 23, 1814, three weeks after they had set out, the caravan reached the district of Berber on the Nile, the northernmost province of Sennar, bound to the capital by the almost negligible ties of an occasional tribute. The people were Arabs of the Mirafab tribe, sedentary cultivators for the most part; Burckhardt formed the lowest opinion of them—'cheating, thieving, and the blackest in-gratitude are found in almost every man's character . . . infamous as the eastern races are in general, I have never met with so bad a people, excepting perhaps those of Suakin'. He refused the invitations to join them in their drinking bouts, parties where every man carried a sword and was quick to draw it. Instead he made himself as incon-spicuous as possible, living in the same house as the Egyptian traders and bearing as best he could their 'dirty villainous tricks', noting down surreptitiously all the while everything he could learn about the country.[12]

After a fortnight in Berber the caravan moved on to Shendi, after Sennar itself and Cobbe in Darfur the largest town in the eastern Sudan and, like Berber, virtually independent of Sennar. 'Commerce is the very life of society in these countries,' so Burckhardt wrote; nowhere could he be more conscious of this truth than in Shendi, for the town served as the cross-roads of all the trade-routes of the eastern Sudan. Here in the dusty, crowded market were rich Arab merchants from Suakin with cambric from Madras and coarse muslin from Bengal, with spices—cloves and ginger—and with sandal-wood to exchange for gold brought down from Ethiopia, for slaves and for the spirited Dongola horses. Irregularly, four or five times a year, caravans came from Kordofan and Darfur, bringing slaves from the Negro countries to the south and gum arabic and ostrich feathers, waterskins of ox-hide or of sheep-skin, and well-wrought wooden dishes. From Sennar caravans arrived more frequently, six hundred camels being needed for those that brought the corn without which

10. J. L. Burckhardt's Travels in Nubia, 1813–15

Shendi would have starved, others coming with cotton goods and leather work of excellent quality made in Sennar itself, with ivory and honey and rhinoceros horn and inevitably with slaves from Ethiopia—Galla women were in great demand in the seraglios of the Mamluks—and from the countries to the south. The Egyptian traders carried with them the produce of Europe and the Levant: *Sembil*, a species of Valerian, grown in North Italy and much esteemed both

373

as perfume and as medicine, soap from Palestine, hardware from Germany, a coarse blue cambric made in Egypt, cheap wooden beads of Egyptian manufacture and fine glass ones from Venice. All this and much more Burckhardt noted down, under the same perilous conditions as before, in a survey that runs to nearly fifty pages, a masterpiece of meticulous observation, to be equalled, among the writings of nineteenth-century explorers, only by Barth's great chapter on the trade and industry of Kano in the 1850s.[13]

Two reflections of relevance to Europe and the future struck Burckhardt while he was in Shendi. He noted that fire-arms were seldom seen, the traders fearing to import them lest they be seized by Bedouin chiefs on the road. 'With prudence and perseverance,' he thought, 'a very small body of European soldiers might make their way across these countries without opposition . . . single individuals attempting to make discoveries in the interior of this continent, through districts unfrequented by northern traders, will, I fear, always fall victims to their zeal and honourable ambitions; and if the sources of the Bahr el Abyadh [White Nile] are ever to be discovered, it must be by an armed force.' So half-prophetically he looked forward to the Egyptian armies led by English officers, by men such as Samuel Baker, pushing southwards to the great lakes, or even indeed to Stanley, leading his armed askaris through the forests of the Congo.[14]

His other reflection bore on the slave trade. Even if all the outlets on the coast were blocked, the trade would, he was convinced, continue in the interior. Only when 'Negroes shall become possessed of the means of repelling the attacks and resisting the oppression of their Mussulman neighbours', would slaving cease. This great work must, he argued, 'be effected by the Negroes themselves', though 'European governments may contribute to it by commerce and by the introduction among the Negroes of arts and industry, which must ultimately lead them to a superiority over the Mussulmans in war'. 'Europe,' he went on, 'will have done but little for the Blacks if the abolition of the Atlantic slave trade, which is trifling when compared with the slavery of the interior, is not followed up by some wise and grand plan, tending to the civilisation of the continent. None presents a fairer prospect than the education of the sons of Africa in their own country, and by their own countrymen, previously educated by Europeans.' But he was obliged to conclude these wise and prescient remarks with a gloomy, realistic warning;

'faint hopes, however, can be entertained that the attention of European governments will be turned towards the remote and despised Negroes, while selfishness and a mistaken policy have prevented them from attending to the instruction of their own poor'. So with half a century between them, Burckhardt stretches out a hand to Livingstone, to Kirk, to all those good and great men who fought for the redemption of Africa and whose achievements are the crowning glory, even as they are the only moral justification, of the age of Imperialism.[15]

From Shendi Burckhardt decided to strike across to the Red Sea. It would not have been difficult, he thought, to have reached Sennar and passed on to Gondar and Massawa; but this was a route Bruce had already mapped out. The path he proposed to follow to Suakin would break new ground for a European traveller and 'being full of difficulty and danger could only be undertaken by a traveller, who had already served a hard apprenticeship'. Though a little less arduous than the crossing of the Nubian desert, wells being more frequent, the Suakin road was more dangerous, lying as it did through the territory of Beja tribes, the Bisharein and the Hadendowa, noted for their inhospitality.[16]

In the caravan which Burckhardt joined was a party of pilgrims from Darfur and Bornu, the chief of whom might have stepped straight out of the pages of the *Canterbury Tales*. Haji Ali came from Bornu, 'had travelled as a slave trader in many parts of Turkey', lived for some years in Damascus and was now established in Kordofan, whence he made frequent journeys to Jedda. Being almost constantly occupied—even on the march—in reading the Koran, he had acquired a reputation of great sanctity; in fact, he was 'a complete bon vivant, whose sole object was sensual enjoyment', sought with his favourite concubine, who accompanied him on all his travels, and from the choicest delicacies that Shendi could provide, the sugar and the dates with which he had filled his sacks. Yet, as Burckhardt learnt later, he did not scruple, when short of cash, to sell as a slave a girl cousin from Bornu, whom he had met and married in Mecca. With Haji Ali and the other *Tekruri*, as the pilgrims from the Sudan were known, Burckhardt became familiar, if not intimate. He acquired from them a mass of detailed information on the caravan routes between Bornu and Sennar and was able to write an account of the pilgrim traffic in the eastern Sudan that has never been surpassed.[17]

The journey from Shendi to Suakin was accomplished without serious incident. But at Suakin Burckhardt found himself threatened with arrest on the charge of being a Mamluk spy. He had carried with him, without once showing it, a letter from Muhammad Ali, the Pasha of Egypt.* This he now reluctantly produced. At the sight of it the Aga cringed before him, provided him with food and secured him a free passage to Jidda. Arrived in Arabia, Burckhardt found it would arouse suspicion for him to travel in the humble garb he had worn in the Sudan; he therefore changed into 'the dress of a reduced Egyptian gentleman'. He hoped to visit the Yemen before making the pilgrimage; this plan had to be renounced, when he learnt that the Wahhabis, against whom Muhammad Ali was campaigning in person, controlled the roads to the south. The cost of living was so much higher in Arabia than in the Sudan that Burckhardt was compelled to apply to the Pasha for funds to maintain himself.[18]

Muhammad Ali had seen Burckhardt in Cairo and taunted him with his 'travelling madness'. He knew that 'Sheikh Ibrahim' was a European, thought that he was English and suspected him of being a spy, but he had not molested him, because he was afraid, Burckhardt thought, of the possible English reaction. But did the Pasha believe that 'Sheikh Ibrahim' was really a Muslim? Later, back in Egypt, Muhammad Ali told the British Consul that he knew perfectly well that 'Sheikh Ibrahim' was an imposter, but in the Hedjaz, after he had sent the Kadi of Mecca to question him, the Pasha seemed to believe 'Sheikh Ibrahim's' profession of faith. And what of that illustrious dignitary, the Kadi of Mecca, with whom Burckhardt said the evening prayer, taking 'great care to chaunt as long a chapter of the Koran' as he could remember? As the Kadi had come from Constantinople and was generally suspected of having been sent by the Sultan to report on the Pasha, Burckhardt surmised that he had accepted him as a Muslim, only in order to be able to charge the Pasha on his return with the unpardonable crime of allowing an infidel into the holy places. Thus through his own boldness and through this fortunate balance of power, Burckhardt was able to make the pilgrimage. As a result, he sent back to the African Association the most accurate and complete account that had ever

* Muhammad Ali, a Turk from Albania, ousted the Mamluks from power and was recognized as Pasha of Egypt in 1807. He was nominally subject to the Sultan of Turkey.

been received in Europe of the holy places of Islam. But he paid a heavy price for this achievement. Arabia was less healthy than the Sudan, the water being particularly bad; as a result, Burckhardt found himself prostrate in Medina with an attack of dysentery that lasted three months and nearly killed him. He had planned to follow the pilgrim road up through Arabia; now in his reduced state he had to content himself with the easier route by way of Jedda and the Red Sea, then overland from Cosseir to Cairo.[19]

He was back in Cairo in the summer of 1815 after an absence of two and a half years. Three months later, after a stay in Alexandria with his friend, the British Consul, Colonel Missett, he felt his health quite recovered. He could now hold himself in readiness for the last and greatest stage of his mission, the journey to the interior of Western Africa, confident that he was indeed better qualified than any of his predecessors. It was necessary to await the arrival of a pilgrim caravan from the Fezzan or the Maghrib. The time of waiting was most profitably spent: he wrote up the journals of his travels in Nubia and Arabia, added to his remarkable collection of Arabic manuscripts, interested himself in Egyptian antiquities and helped to secure for the British Museum that magnificent piece known as the Young Memnon, while an outbreak of plague in Cairo in the summer of 1817 gave him an excuse to leave the city and explore the Sinai Peninsula.[20]

In Cairo he lived comfortably but quietly. 'Experience has taught me,' he told his mother, 'that the smaller the circle of one's acquaintances, the deeper one's enjoyment of life.' 'I have reason to believe,' he had written half ironically of himself during his travels in Nubia, 'that I acquired the character of a hardy, active man, very selfish, stingy and attentive to his own interests.' This was certainly not the face that he presented to his European friends. It was, above all, the charm of his conversation that they noted—'the only conversable friend I had in Cairo,' Henry Salt, Missett's successor as Consul and himself a traveller of repute, said of him. 'I never talked with him without learning something,' wrote Turner, a young Foreign Office man. 'To an intimate acquaintance with the Arabic language,' Richardson, an English doctor who met him in 1817 wrote afterwards, 'he added a profound knowledge of the human heart and possessed such an affable manner of conversing with the world as gained him many friends.' To the pleasure of his conversation he added practical acts of kindness. Belzoni, a remarkable Italian, whom he had engaged to search for Egyptian antiquities, was greatly indebted to him and spoke of him afterwards with 'the deepest gratitude', while Turner remembered the pains he had taken in correcting a journal he had shown him. There can be no doubt that Burckhardt was a really good, kind and considerate man; yet his powers of sympathy were limited. 'I regret,' he had written during his Nubian travels, 'that I am compelled to represent all the nations in Africa, which I have yet seen, in so bad a light . . . they are all tainted more or less deeply with ill faith, avarice, drunkenness and debauchery.' This bitter judgement was the price he had to pay for the manner in which he travelled, the reaction to those jeers and insults he had steeled himself to endure in silence; and yet one may feel, for Burckhardt was good and great enough to be judged by the highest standards, that so categorical a statement reveals a flaw, a narrowness of heart, an inability to achieve that selfless understanding of other men's motives that is the foundation of wisdom, an understanding that Mungo Park, who had suffered even more than Burckhardt and was by nature a much less humble man, had shown himself to possess.[21]

In the autumn of 1817 a pilgrim caravan from the Fezzan at last arrived in Cairo; it was due to return from Mecca at the end of the year. This was the opportunity for which Burckhardt had been waiting; the accounts of his earlier journeys were now complete, he could be ready to leave at a moment's notice. Though eight years of travelling had left their mark on him—'my sallow emaciated face and my thick beard,' he had written in 1815, 'belong rather to a man of forty than to one of thirty-one'—his health since his recovery from his serious illness in Arabia had been reasonably good. Quite suddenly, at the beginning of October, he was struck down by a recurrence of dysentery. Within a fortnight he was a dying man. Among those who were with him in his last days was Henry Salt. 'I saw him,' Salt wrote afterwards, 'but a few hours before his death; and though he felt all the bitterness of the disappointment, he bore it with the noblest courage.' With a clear mind he made his will, making bequests to his servants and leaving all his Arabic manuscripts to Cambridge University, whose librarian, Dr Clarke, had become his friend nine years earlier. 'Say to my mother,' his voice was strained now with deep emotion, 'that my last thoughts have been with her. . . . The Turks will keep my body, I know it, perhaps you had better let them.' These words were his last; that night he died. His body was laid to rest with Muslim rites and in a Muslim grave.[22]

IV

GERMAN TRAVELLERS IN NORTH AFRICA

U. J. SEETZEN

IN THE YEARS WHEN Burckhardt was living in Syria, training himself to become an explorer, two Germans, Ulrich Jasper Seetzen and Heinrich Röntgen, had set themselves to reach the interior of Africa. They followed different paths, each acting entirely on his own initiative.

Seetzen, the son an innkeeper, was born in 1767. As a student at Göttingen, where he came under Blumenbach's influence, he responded eagerly to the intellectual stimulus of the new ideas of the age, not in politics but in science. Though trained as a doctor, his real interests centred on natural history and on technology, allied with a passion for travelling. These tastes he was able to gratify by setting himself up as a timber merchant. He read with eager, critical attention the latest works on African travel, and in 1799 worked out the project for a journey more ambitious than any hitherto undertaken by a European traveller: he would make his way through Turkey and Arabia to Malindi on the East Coast of Africa, whence he would cross the continent from east to west.[1]

By 1802 his preparations were complete. He started with nothing to support him but his own limited financial resources and a commission from the Duke of Gotha to collect material for his Oriental museum. Reaching Syria, he stayed in Aleppo for two years, to acquire a knowledge of Arabic and to make a collection of Oriental manuscripts and geological and botanical specimens for his princely patron. He was soon desperately short of money; but his success as a collector made him famous. The Czar of Russia sent him a thousand roubles, and the Duke of Gotha and other members of the ruling

379

houses of Germany contributed to his support. This enabled him to proceed with his plan. From Syria he travelled through Palestine to Egypt. He was accepted as a Muslim, though his practice of taking astronomical observations led many to regard him as a sorcerer. In Egypt Seetzen spent another two years, continuing to purchase manuscripts and obtaining from African travellers valuable accounts of the central Sudan.[2]

In 1809 Seetzen left Egypt to perform the pilgrimage. His sojourn in Arabia presented a new object for his attention, the little-known kingdom of Yemen, last visited by Niebuhr forty years before. In September 1811 he set out from Mocha on the Red Sea coast, travelling in state with a caravan of seventeen camels. Two days later he was found dead in mysterious circumstances. The matter was never fully cleared up, but it was generally believed that he had been poisoned on the orders of the Imam of San'a. He died then without embarking on the most ambitious stage of his great plan;* but his zeal as a collector produced results of lasting benefit to scholars, and his remarkable achievements as a traveller secured him an honoured place among European Orientalists.

HEINRICH RÖNTGEN

Heinrich Röntgen, born in 1787, was twenty years younger than Seetzen. He came of an adventurous and enterprising stock. His grandfather, as a young man, had been disappointed in his ambition to become a missionary in Nubia, and became the founder of a prosperous furniture factory which he passed on to his son, Heinrich's father. For young Röntgen, however, a career in industry had no attraction. While still a schoolboy, Africa had absorbed his thoughts. In 1807 he came as a student to Göttingen with the deliberate intention of preparing himself for a journey into the unknown interior. Naturally he took the first opportunity to introduce himself to Blumenbach.[1]

Blumenbach was greatly impressed by his intellectual and physical powers. 'I very soon found,' he wrote afterwards, 'that this worthy young man possessed a heaven-sent call to such an undertaking.' Few prospective explorers have possessed, indeed, so passionate a

* 'If he decides to go to Malindi,' Reichard, a German geographer, wrote of Seetzen, 'he will have to go through the Jaggas [Chaggas?] and will be eaten up by them. . . . Why will no one go through Benin—a country whose people have a very good reputation.'[3]

sense of destiny: 'Providence,' Röntgen unashamedly confessed, 'has marked me out for the discovery of Africa.' He planned to reach Ethiopia and strike westwards. At Göttingen he followed an elaborate course of training, which included the study of Arabic, a diet of raw meat and long tramps with a heavy load on his back.[2]

In 1809 he came to London. He hoped to attach himself to Henry Salt's mission to Ethiopia* or to obtain the support of the African Association. But Salt had already left, and the Association, having recently engaged Burckhardt, could not afford the expense of another traveller. Yet support of some kind was essential, for Röntgen had no resources of his own. By a stroke of good fortune, which he thoroughly deserved, he was given the opportunity of commending himself to influential members of London society. A young diplomat, Benjamin Bathurst—a distant relative of Lord Bathurst, the Cabinet Minister and future Colonial Secretary—had mysteriously disappeared while returning with despatches from Berlin. When his wife bravely decided to go to war-torn Germany to look for him, Röntgen chivalrously offered to act as her escort. Their search was without success. Bathurst's fate remained a mystery, though it was widely believed that he had been murdered by French soldiers.[3]

In the autumn of 1809 Röntgen returned with Mrs Bathurst to England and resumed his stringent course of training. His behaviour soon earned him some notoriety. 'A German Gentleman,' wrote an anonymous writer in the *Quarterly Review*, 'is now in England preparing to trace the steps of Mungo Park: for this purpose he has undergone the operation of circumcision . . . and, for some time past, accustomed himself to the spare and acrid diet of spiders, ants and grasshoppers! By way of seasoning himself to the burning sands of Africa, he sleeps, at nights, under a hedge in England in the month of December.' The same writer—who was, in fact, John Barrow, himself a traveller of distinction in South Africa and in China—later admitted that Röntgen showed himself 'indefatigable in the search for knowledge', 'utterly regardless of danger' and 'fired with a sense of glory'. Armoured by such intense conviction and encouraged by friends in high places, Röntgen set about canvassing subscriptions to finance his African journey. He was able to raise £350, of which £50 came from one of his own relations, amounts up to £10 from a large number of businessmen and smaller amounts from other well-wishers, including William Wilberforce.[4]

* For Salt's mission to Ethiopia in 1809, see p. 386.

By this time Röntgen had given up the idea of starting from Ethiopia and turned his attention to Morocco. It seems probable that he was led to change his plans after reading Jackson's recently published account of the country, with its detailed information on the caravan route to Timbuktu. The African Association had no part in his affairs, but, regarding it 'as a kind of headquarters for all African expeditions', Röntgen gave Sir Joseph Banks detailed information on the programme he had worked out. He would go to Mogador and spend a year there to master colloquial Arabic, sticking to European dress until experience had enabled him 'to support the usurped Character of a Mahommedan'. As soon as he had sufficient knowledge, he would go to Gibraltar, 'cast off my skin', let his beard grow, adopt Moorish dress and smuggle himself into Morocco. He would then join a caravan going to Timbuktu. From Timbuktu he would follow the Niger wherever it might lead. Should any accident befall him, he told Banks, he had instructed his friends to give the residue of his funds to the Association.[5]

In March 1811 Röntgen was in Mogador, where he found accommodation with a hospitable English merchant. 'At last I am in Africa,' he wrote to an English friend shortly after his arrival, 'and my whole frame trembles when I say "I am in Africa".' He was at once entranced and disconcerted by the life he saw around him. 'Most of the people look like a living Bible—their whole speech is poesy—but alas they have adopted many ways not mentioned in the Bible . . . I am convinced that their first article of religion is: whosoever pesters a Christian, will find a seat in heaven.' With quite extraordinary energy Röntgen applied himself to his task: 'I get up at four and never go to bed before eleven—every hour is spent either learning Arabic or making observations about the Muslim world, which I record in exact detail in my journal.'[6]

Röntgen had been only a few weeks at Mogador when a chance encounter led him to change his plans. There came as a gardener to the house where he was staying, a curious individual, a renegade, who claimed to have been born in Yorkshire of German parents. His story, if it can believed, was extraordinary. Eighteen years ago, when he was twenty, he had been caught on Malta by an English press-gang and forced to serve on an English ship. After a violent quarrel with an officer he had escaped the ship at Tetuan and become a Muslim. Since that time he had travelled far and wide, performed the pilgrimage, kept a coffee-house in Arabia and acted as gardener to a Pasha in Constantinople. To Röntgen it seemed proof of the workings of Destiny that he should have met with a compatriot so ideally suited to help him in his great enterprise. 'My genius,' he wrote to his brother, 'led him here.'

Röntgen himself had recently returned from Marrakesh, where he had seen a caravan preparing to leave for Timbuktu. He was so impressed with his rapid progress in Arabic that he decided to join such a caravan without delay. His new friend eagerly fell in with his plans; 'he jumped with joy at the opportunity of seeing the wonderful south of Africa'. When some of his friends at Mogador warned him to be on his guard against El Haji, the renegade, Röntgen rejected their advice.

To get from Mogador, where he lived as an English gentleman, to the starting-point for the desert caravans, where he would have to assume the character of a Muslim, presented serious practical difficulties, for it was essential to avoid rousing the suspicion of the Moroccan authorities. To cover his movements, Röntgen let it be known that he was planning to go to Gibraltar. Meanwhile he prepared Moorish dress, sewing the robes himself at night, with El Haji's assistance. In mid-July a party of English residents went on a trip out of Mogador. Röntgen joined them, but, when they were some distance from the town, suddenly announced that he was setting out on a longer journey. One of the Englishmen rode on with him until they came to a river, where El Haji appeared with two mules, the baggage and astronomical instruments. Before the Englishman left, Röntgen gave him a long letter for his brother; the date was July 21, the place 'my Rubicon'.[7]

Two or three months later a rumour reached Mogador that a Moor had been seen in Marrakesh attempting to sell a pocket watch which had evidently belonged to a European. The Moor was traced and the watch identified as one belonging to Röntgen. The Moor said he had found it on the corpse of a traveller lying in an advanced state of decay underneath a tree. It was generally believed in Mogador that El Haji had murdered Röntgen on the first night of their journey. Röntgen was known to have been carrying seven hundred dollars, so robbery would supply the motive. El Haji was never caught. He was said to have been seen again in another part of the country, but to have deliberately avoided intercourse.[8]

This, however, was not quite the end of the matter. In February 1814 Banks had a visit from William A'Court, a diplomat who had recently returned from an embassy to Morocco. He told Banks a curious story he had heard from the Vice-Consul at Tangier. The Vice-Consul said he had seen letters from Röntgen written in the spring of 1813 from Tafilalet, on the southern side of the Atlas. These stated that the supposed murder had been a strategem to fool those who had discovered his identity. The ruse had succeeded perfectly. He and his suspected 'murderer' were living in Tafilalet, where they had made contact with a couple of German renegades. No one suspected them of being Franks, and they were on the point of setting out for Timbuktu. 'After Timbuktu, whither?' Röntgen had written to his brother in his letter of July 1811. 'My heart is drawn ever further south towards Mosambique or the Cape.' Röntgen, according to the report the Vice-Consul had received, was 'in high spirits and firmly convinced that he is the instrument designed by Providence to disclose to the public the mysteries of the Soudan'. Was this new report true? Certainly the evidence relating to his murder had been circumstantial in the extreme; it would not after all, have been impossible to have planted his watch on the body of an unknown traveller. Whatever happened, nothing more was ever heard of him. Africa like an implacable goddess—so it must have struck the imagination of the romantic—had destroyed the latest of her devotees, rashly attempting to despoil her of her mysteries.*[9]

For Blumenbach Röntgen's end, following as it did the still un-explained disappearance of Hornemann, was a most grievous blow. He refused to send any more of his students to London. Not until after his death in 1840 did other German travellers achieve fame in the field of African exploration. Meanwhile the interest of German scholars in African geography was maintained.

* Another European with an ambition to reach Timbuktu came to Morocco about this time. He was a young Spaniard, Antonio Piloti, who had taken refuge in the country during the Peninsular Wars. He took to Moorish dress and was able to join the Emperor's guard. Thus established, he secretly offered his services as an explorer to the French Consul. His offer was turned down, but Delaporte, the French Vice-Consul, agreed to help him and made arrangements for him to obtain instructions from France. His behaviour aroused the suspicion of some of the Moors and Jews around the palace. He was denounced to the Emperor on a trumped-up charge and immediately beheaded. Not until 1830 did a brief account of his career appear in England.[10]

In 1803 C. G. Reichard, an academic geographer, put forward a remarkable theory. After examining all the accounts of the West Coast of Africa, he suggested that the country between the Rio de Rey and the Rio Formoso had the appearance of a great delta, similar in character to that of the Nile or the Ganges. This led him

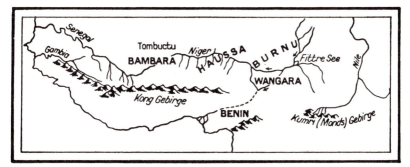

11. The Rivers of West Africa: according to Reichard, 1803

to conclude that the Niger on reaching Wangara ended not in a lake, as Rennell so fervently believed, but instead made a great bend to the south-west and pursued its course to the north-eastern extremity of the Gulf of Guinea. Reichard's views were first referred to by an English writer in 1815, in the Appendix to Park's *Journal*. They received very little attention at that time.[11]

V

ETHIOPIA

LORD VALENTIA AND HENRY SALT

IN DECEMBER 1808, WHILE THE members of the Committee of
the African Association were busying themselves with Burckhardt's
impending departure, they were approached with a suggestion
directing their attention to a part of Africa with which they had not
yet been concerned. The suggestion came from a young Mr Salt,
recently returned from a visit to Ethiopia and on the point of proceeding again to that country on an official mission. Salt told the
Committee that he had left in Ethiopia a servant, Nathaniel Pearce,
who had entered the service of the powerful Ras of Tigre. This man
might usefully be employed in making discoveries, possibly by
joining one of the caravans that came to 'the great mart' of Berbera
and 'returned to very distant inland countries'. At the same time
Salt himself was 'desirous to procure every information in his power
for the use of the Association'. The Committee were impressed by
Salt's manner and assurance. They agreed to place the considerable
sum of £500 at his disposal, and laid down the objects to which he
should give special attention—'the situation of the Chain of Mountains which is said to be not very distant from the country of Darfur,
where the parting of the waters that run some to the West, others to
the East, takes places', the source of the White Nile, the course of
the Niger and that 'vast lake' into which it was supposed to flow,
together with any information about the Somali and their trade and
about the Galla, 'represented as an active, intelligent and warlike
people'.[1]

Who was this Mr Salt? How had he come to make a name for
himself as an African traveller? Henry Salt was born in 1780, the

386

son of a 'highly respectable medical practitioner in the city of Lichfield'. Ambitious to become a portrait painter, he had attended the art schools of the capital. In appearance, tall, thin, gangling— these details came from his intimate friend and later biographer, J. J. Halls—in manner cheerful and lively, fond of the girls, fond of the pleasures of the table, he seemed the conventional art-student, even though as an artist he possessed only mediocre ability. Indeed,

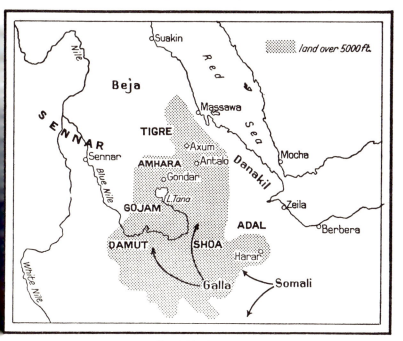

12. Ethiopia

in art there was little future for him, so it was a piece of extraordinary good fortune when he made the acquaintance, then won the friend-ship of an Irish peer, ten years his senior, George Annersley, Lord Valentia, to whom his uncle had once acted as tutor. Valentia, though reputed an eccentric (one of his foibles was to dress himself up as a Cherokee Indian), was in most ways the very opposite of Henry Salt, serious, self-important, extravagant and, since his wife had run away with a Guards officer, probably an unhappy man. Yet strangely the friendship that developed between these two was to be a shaping force in both their lives.[2]

In 1802 Valentia decided to make a Grand Tour of the East—Salt was bold enough to ask His Lordship to take him along as secretary and draughtsman. Valentia was surprised at this request, but yielded when Salt began to talk about 'the melancholy state of his prospects'. So they set out, rounded the Cape and arrived in India in splendid style, to be received by the Governor-General, that proud, lonely, disdainful man, Lord Wellesley, 'with great attention and civility'.[3]

After a year in India, after Calcutta and Benares and Colombo, Valentia's thoughts strayed to the Red Sea; why, he began asking, had not the western coast ever been properly charted or the commercial possibilities of Ethiopia explored? Wellesley was interested. 'At last I proposed to His Excellency that he should order one of the Bombay cruisers to be prepared to a voyage to the Red Sea; and I offered my gratuitous services to endeavour to remove our disgraceful ignorance.' His Excellency approved, but the expedition miscarried, when Captain Keyes of the *Antelope*, which had been put at His Lordship's disposal, refused to follow the dangerous Eritrean coast beyond Massawa. Six months later, with a new ship and a new commander, Valentia returned to the attack, but was unable, in the face of unfavourable winds, to sail beyond Suakin. In the meantime, letters had been exchanged with the ruler of Tigre (the Ethiopian province that overlooks the Eritrean coast), Ras Welde Selassie, the most powerful war-lord in the country, for the Imperial line at Gondar had reached the nadir of its fortunes. Gondar, however, through Bruce's great volumes (the latest work on Ethiopia, though they described the state of affairs thirty years past), still retained its lure, the feebleness of its shadowy Emperors not being realized. Valentia therefore decided to despatch a mission led by his secretary to the Ras and to the Emperor, whoever he might be.[4]

Why did not Valentia go to Tigre himself? 'His Lordship,' Salt said later, 'had too great a stake in life and was of too much importance to have his life risqued.' Salt himself must have been delighted to have command of the little expedition, which included three other Englishmen: Captain Rudland, an adventurous Indian army officer, a certain Mr Carter and Nathaniel Pearce. Pearce, a sailor on the *Antelope*, had deserted at Mocha, turned Muslim, found himself worse off than before and flung himself on Valentia's mercy. He was a natural rebel; the 'scandalous' story of his life would, so with obvious relish he once confessed to Salt, 'shame the devil!' Though not without some education, he had run away to sea at an early age, been captured by the French, escaped, joined up with a band of Breton rebels, narrowly escaped a revolutionary firing squad and, still little more than a boy, got safely back to England; taken to the sea again, been to India, the East Indies, China, made unsuccessful attempts at desertion in every country he had been in, been shipwrecked off South Africa, joined the *Antelope* under a Portuguese name and now, with apostasy added to desertion, acquired so black a name that it was impossible for him to return to England. He was still only in his mid-twenties, a tough, bold, hot-headed adventurer.[5]

Salt and his party left Massawa in July 1805. Four months later they were back. War-ridden Gondar they could not reach, but at Antalo they had spent many weeks in the company of the powerful old Ras. Welde Selassie had been perplexed by the arrival of this curious expedition, and many of his great men were glad to work on his suspicions; but he came at last to accept the sincerity of Salt's professions. 'An intercourse with the English, who are uncontrolled masters of the sea,' Salt pointed out, 'would enable the Ras to supply himself at once with whatever commodities he might want, and of a quality far superior to any that had hitherto found their way into his country.' ('There is a proconsular air about the sentence,' so Archbishop Mathew has relived the scene with that precise, dramatic and beautifully evocative imagination of his, 'and it has that happy ring of pride on pride which was long found useful in British dealings with despotic eastern rulers and their viceroys. In the draughty halls of Antalo there must have been a noble sound in the high claim to be "uncontrolled masters of the sea."')[6]

So Salt, Rudland and Pearce found themselves accepted as honoured guests: sitting by the Ras's side as he reviewed his troops, the cavalry galloping past in wild salute, their chiefs in splendid cloaks of embroidered damask flinging down with proud, defiant speech before ·their leader the hideous trophies that showed the manhood of the enemies they had slain; the evenings in high society, enjoying the company of 'ladies of rank'—'we had an opportunity of remarking in what a free and unreserved style the Abyssinians pass their time in private parties'; the constant games of chess in the palace at Antalo, the large coarse ivory chessmen, the cheers and eager advice flung in by the bystanders, the old Ras always winning. And away from the capital there was Axum, with its mysterious ancient obelisks and its cathedral, the holiest place in Ethiopia, that struck Salt as looking like nothing so much as 'the Gothic seats of noblemen in England': the strange ritual of the priests, the chanting and the 'jangling keys' and 'the violent gestures and grimaces'. So they rode among the hills of Tigre, 'in the quiet light and freshness of this lovely country', finding as other European travellers have done, echoes of home, here a plain densely cultivated that reminded Salt of the vale of Evesham, there 'woody hills and towering rocks, very similar in general character to some of the finer valleys in Derbyshire', while Rudland paused to go out after wild fowl with his gun, and Salt botanized or sketched the landscape. How sharp the contrast between these fresh highlands and the dusty bush of the Sudan, the stony desert of the Red Sea coast. How strange this whole world is, the ancient Christian ritual beside the barbaric rites, the peasant austerity set against the magnificent monuments of the past, different utterly from anything else in Africa. And always one is conscious of the shadow which Salt himself intensely felt of his great predecessor. He had been treading in Bruce's footsteps on the way up from Massawa. In Tigre he met many elderly men who remembered 'Yagoube' clearly. Alas, much that they had to say threw 'great doubt' on the veracity of certain parts of the earlier traveller's story.[7]

When the time came to leave, Pearce asked to be left behind. This was acceptable to all parties. The Ras said that after accompanying him on an expedition planned against Gondar he would be permitted to visit any part of the kingdom he chose. To this Pearce made reply that 'being an Englishman, he never knew what fear was; with which the Ras was much gratified; and answered that though very old, his own feelings were the same'. Pearce remained in Ethiopia thirteen years.[8]

'The direct communication between Abyssinia and other Christian nations,' Valentia announced on his return to England, 'may be considered as again opened, by the visit of Mr Salt to Tigre, after having been closed since the year 1558 when Soolimaun Basha conquered Massowah and deprived the Abyssinians of all access to the Red Sea.' But who in an England engaged in the sternest war of the country's history, against the most powerful conqueror Europe had ever known, could worry themselves about this remote and backward land? Undeterred and armoured with an aristocratic conceit, Valentia decided—one can put it best in the harsh jargon of the present age—to make himself a one-man pressure group. He talked about 'the extensive market' Ethiopia afforded 'to every kind of European manufacture'. He tried to stir the Directors of the East India Company into action. The Directors were shrewd businessmen, whose company had maintained a footing in the Red Sea for many years; they dismissed his plans as 'chimerical'. So Valentia brought his ideas before the general public. A merchant named Jacob was attracted and decided to send out a ship, on which His Lordship's own servant, Coffin, was to act as supercargo.[9]

Fortified by this success, Valentia now approached Canning, who had recently become Foreign Secretary. He dwelt especially on the political advantages of contact with Ethiopia to counterbalance French intrigue among the Wahhabis of Arabia. He suggested that an island on the Eritrean coast, to which he had given his own name, would make an excellent trading depot and allow Massawa to be by-passed. (It was true that Valentia Island belonged to the Nayib of Massawa; but if he refused to sell, then 'the hostilities he exercised against my boats'—there had been a tiff on Valentia's last visit—'would be a sufficient justification of any steps that might be taken to oblige him to comply'. How quickly Valentia had slipped into the wiles of imperialism!) Finally, he referred to the friendly letters that Salt had brought back with him, together with presents of 'fine Habesh cloth'. 'I took the liberty of suggesting that as His Majesty had been pleased to accept the presents of the Emperor'—they were in fact from the Ras, but that did not sound so imposing—'it was but decorous that some notice should be taken of them, when an English vessel was going direct to his ports.' Canning was unable to withstand this tiresome, rather crazy man; he accepted the idea of a mission and directed Valentia to choose the presents. Valentia decided on 'two pieces of curricle artillery' and other 'specimens of our finest manufacture', which would 'certainly impress the present monarch with a favourable idea of the power and riches of his new ally': the cost was £1,906. Nor did he forget his young friend. 'I pointed out Mr Salt as by far the most eligible person'; 'he was accordingly appointed'.[10]

This new appointment was extremely gratifying to Henry Salt. His intimate friends had noticed that though 'still frolicsome and eccentric', he had during his travels not only matured remarkably in manner, casting off 'the boyishness of his earlier days', but also developed an obvious and intense ambition. 'It will be hard on me,' he confessed to Halls, 'if I don't get a respectable niche in the temple of Fame before I'm finished'; 'he neglected nothing which seemed likely to ensure his final triumph'—an ambiguous comment, though Halls was too staunch a friend to imply the pejorative. How lucky he had been to have become Valentia's friend, Valentia with his grand, quasi-imperial dreams.[11]

Salt left England in January 1809. Nine months later, after a stay at Cape Town and an interesting month in Mozambique, he arrived in the Red Sea. Making Mocha, where the East India Company maintained a factory, his base, he sent messengers to the Ras and to Pearce to announce his arrival, and turned his mind to follow up the promise he had made to the African Association to secure information from the great market at Berbera. In Mocha he made the acquaintance of an elderly Arab, 'one of the best informed and most liberal minded Mahommedans I have ever been acquainted with', who turned out to be the commercial agent of the Sultan of Harar, in whose territory Berbera lay. Salt was assured that it would be quite possible to travel from Zeila on the coast to Harar and on through Galla country to Gondar. Indeed, he told the Association later that he had received very flattering letters from the Sultan of Harar inviting him to visit the country. This he himself was unable to do; but there was on Jacob's ship, the *Miriam*, a young man named Stuart, who was glad to take his place. Stuart sailed across the Red Sea to Zeila, only to receive a letter from the Sultan of Harar forbidding him to enter the country, as his chief men would not 'consent to the admission of a stranger'. However, he was able to accumulate a mass of valuable information, which was passed on to the African Association, though never published.[12]

Salt landed at Massawa in February 1810. Pearce had come down to meet him. Salt found him as tough and active as ever, completely fluent in the language of Tigre, and with 'a perfect insight into the manners and feelings of the Abyssinians'. Pearce had many new adventures to relate. He had lost favour with the Ras and been forced to lead a wandering life that had brought him to the heart of the Amhara country. On his return he had found the Ras assailed by many enemies, joined him, fought by his side, won general admiration for his reckless bravery and been restored again to high estate. He brought with him a hundred followers and sixty bearers belonging to the Ras, 'wild desperate young men', who provided for Salt a suitably imposing escort as they climbed the steep paths on to the high, cool plateau.[13]

Welde Selassie gave Salt the most cordial of welcomes, but refused for good reasons to allow the mission to proceed to Gondar. It was therefore to the Ras and not to the Emperor that Salt handed over the presents. These included, besides the artillery, a stained-glass window, a painting of the Virgin and a marble table. The ecclesiastical pieces gave the Ras particular pleasure. Salt helped him to arrange them in his favourite church, while Pearce played away on a hand-organ 'considerably out of tune' that had been sent up as a present by Rudland, now in charge of the East India Company's factory at Mocha. Delightful scene—how Valentia would have enjoyed it, how pleased he must have been when Salt told him that the Ras had given orders that 'a prayer should be offered up weekly for the health of His Majesty, the King of Great Britain' and that 'the effect produced by the presents on the minds of all classes became very apparent': 'the purity of our religion ceased to be questioned' and 'our motives for visiting the country were no longer doubted'.[14]

Salt spent three months in Tigre and would indeed have stayed longer, had the *Miriam* not been waiting for him at Massawa, each day adding to the owner's expense. By Welde Selassie he was treated with even greater attention than on his first visit. During one of their daily conversations the Ras told him candidly that many of the chief men, and especially the priests of Axum, had tried to turn him against the English, alleging that their purpose was to kill him and seize the country; 'I was not fool enough to regard these extravagances'. But the Ras had a practical reason for welcoming the English as friends. 'With the guns your king has sent me,' he told Salt, 'I will before long establish the Emperor in his right at Gondar and settle the religion of the country.' 'We all say this is right and the other is right in religious matters,' he went on, 'but I believe that we shall only wander about in the dark until we receive a lesson from you.' Here indeed in this modest avowal was a call to touch the hearts of Protestant churchmen in their growing consciousness of the needs of Africa as a field for missionary endeavour.[15]

In his instructions Salt had been directed 'to ascertain the present state of Abyssinian trade'. He did not explore this subject in the methodical and exhaustive manner that Burckhardt would have done, but he grasped the main points. Slaves, ivory and gold, the last being surrounded by much secrecy, were still—as they had been in the days of the Pharaohs—the only significant exports of the country. There was really nothing here to attract an English trader. The Ras realized this. At his last interview with Salt he 'professed his most anxious wish to encourage by every means in his power an intercourse with Great Britain', but at the same time he expressed 'with great sincerity his fears that the country which he commanded might not be able to supply any quantity of valuable commodities sufficient to compensate our merchants for engaging in so precarious a trade; more especially as the Abyssinians were not much acquainted with commercial transactions and the unsettled state of the provinces prevented the usual circulation of gold and other articles which are brought from the interior'. They talked all through the night on that last meeting; when at last it was time to go, 'the old man attended us to the door of his hall, where he stood watching us, with tears running down his face, until we were fairly out of sight.'[16]

On his return to England, Salt suggested to the Government that a point on the Eritrean coast be taken under the protection of the British flag. 'The advantages of this intercourse to the Abyssinians themselves would prove incalculably beneficial; it would open to them the means of improvement . . . introducing at the same time such an amelioration into their condition, as might lead perhaps ultimately to a diffusion of civilization, if not of Christianity, over a considerable portion of Africa.' The British Government could not afford to become dispensers of a questionable charity, especially when the cost of intercourse appeared to be so high, for the bill for Salt's mission reached the disagreeably large figure of £2,837 19s. 6d. No attempt was made, therefore, to follow up the mission.[17]

But if as a political venture it had achieved nothing, for Salt himself it was a great personal success. The African Association elected him an honorary member. He was given the entrée to London Society, being noticed even by the Prince Regent and invited to His Royal Highness's 'splendid entertainments'. The account of his mission, when at last an illness provided him with the leisure to write it, brought him over £1,000. Finally, when in 1815 the post of Consul-General in Egypt fell vacant, Salt was offered it at a salary of £1,700 a year.

After the gaiety of London and the adventures of Ethiopia the post at Alexandria, with all the chores of consular routine that it involved, proved a little dispiriting. Salt found distraction by throwing himself into the search for Egyptian antiquities. Indeed, through Hamilton's influence at the Foreign Office, he was officially encouraged to do so. He was urged on, too, by Sir Joseph Banks, who had helped him to obtain his present post and was one of the trustees of the British Museum.

Salt maintained his interest in Ethiopia and sent Pearce a regular present of £60 every year. In 1816 the old Ras, Welde Selassie, died. The country was immediately plunged into civil war, which brought Pearce and Coffin yet more desperate adventures. Two years later Pearce decided to leave the country. On his arrival in Egypt he was received by Salt with great affection and appointed major-domo at the Consulate. During this time he wrote an account of his extraordinary life in Ethiopia. It was impossible for him to return to England as he was still legally a deserter. Salt set to work to clear his name, Banks and Valentia appealed to the Admiralty, and Pearce was pardoned. But he never saw England again. A few days before he was due to sail for home he developed a serious fever, 'greatly aggravated by the mistaken and somewhat intemperate use of brandy' and died.[18]

Pearce's death was the first of many misfortunes that now came to cast a shadow over Salt's life. He suffered severely from an undiagnosed disease of the liver. His wife, an Italian girl, married in 1819 at the age of sixteen, died in child-birth five years later, leaving an only surviving daughter who was taken to live with grandparents in Italy. Shortly afterwards Salt lost his friend and colleague, Lee, the consul at Alexandria. Yet, though a sick man, suspecting that he had not long to live, and, since Lee's death, heavily overworked, Salt kept his courage up and his mind active in an admirable manner: poetized, painted, prepared a great work on Ethiopia, Egypt and Arabia (it was intended to establish his fame, but the manuscript was, by another cruel stroke of fate, completely lost), and proved himself to passing visitors the kindest and most entertaining of hosts, the habitual languor of his manner vanishing as he talked.

In 1827 Coffin arrived in Egypt, charged with a mission to England by the most powerful of the Rases to succeed Welde Selassie. Salt was now a mortally sick man. Coffin's arrival was the last happiness he knew. 'Where is Coffin?' he cried in his last illness. 'I like to see his honest English face beside me.' On October 29, 1827, in his forty-eighth year, Henry Salt died. His funeral service was read by a missionary, the Rev. Christian Keugler, who came from Basle on his way to Ethiopia. Keugler's mission had been organized, largely through Valentia's prompting, by the Anglican Church Missionary Society.[19]

In 1829 Keugler and two companions entered Ethiopia. The next year Keugler died, but the mission continued. Among those who served in Ethiopia was a German, J. F. Krapf, who visited parts of the country that had not been seen by any European since the days of the Portuguese. When in 1842 the Protestants were banned from Ethiopia Krapf transferred his activities to Mombasa on the East Coast. From there he and his colleague Rebmann made a number of journeys into the unknown interior and became the first Europeans to see the great snow mountains on the Equator, and to pick up reports of a great lake many hundred miles from the coast. These reports aroused such interest in London that the Royal Geographical Society, the successor to the African Association, organized an expedition to investigate them. The expedition was undertaken by two Indian Army officers, Richard Burton and John Hanning Speke. The great age of East African exploration had begun.

So the strands of scholarship and commercial interest and missionary zeal were interwoven, the links, the life-work of individual men, forged. By these ties Africa and Europe were to be drawn ever closer together. Yet how strange appear the workings of Providence, when one reflects that the friendship of a young English art student and an eccentric Irish peer served, in a by no means negligible way, to shape the course of history.

VI

1815

HISTORY'S TEXTURE IS SEAMLESS. Event breaks upon event ceaselessly as the waves of the sea. But the historian in his fallibility must impose artificial limits, beginnings, ends, breathing spaces. For the present study the year 1815 marks the most convenient point at which to pause. The date has the advantage of being one of the best known in European history but it is also of significance for Africa. With the conclusion of the Napoleonic War, Europeans, who for twenty years had expended a vast amount of energy in slaughtering one another on the battlefields of their own continent, could devote more money, thought and enterprise to other parts of the world. Within a year one can notice in Africa the consequences of this change. In North Africa a British and Dutch fleet bombarded Algiers to force that state to abandon its piratical practices. Egypt, under Muhammad Ali, its most efficient ruler for centuries, was beginning to appear as a country which wealthy tourists could visit without excessive discomfort. On the West Coast—and in the chancelleries of Europe—the British struggle against the foreign slave trade was being more energetically conducted. Finally, the British Government had decided to finance two expensive expeditions to solve the mystery of the Niger, one organized by the Colonial Office to proceed overland from Senegambia, the other, under the Admiralty's control, to push up the Congo.

So much for the future. As for the immediate past, looking back on the events of twenty-five years, an observer in 1815 might well reflect how little in the African scene had changed. Sierra Leone represented the only new foothold acquired by Europeans anywhere on the continent: it was a novel form of colony, a philanthropic experiment, innocent of any aggressive intent. As for the geography of

397

the interior, Europe was now a little better informed, but seldom had knowledge been gained at so cruel a price. Ledyard dead, Houghton dead, Park dead, Hornemann dead, Röntgen dead, Seetzen dead, Badia and Burckhardt shortly to die, all in the course of their exertions. Well might it appear to contemporaries suicidal to probe the mysteries of the 'dark continent'. And how much there was still unknown—one can have a convincing illustration of Europe's ignorance in one astounding fact. In the first decade of the nineteenth century, in the very years which have been considered here in such detail, the countries of the central Sudan were convulsed by the greatest revolution in their history, the Fulani *jihad*. Yet not one ripple of this great movement appears to have reached the Europeans on the coast; not one mention may be traced in the newspapers of Europe.

But if, in practical terms, comparatively little seemed to have happened, already, as this study has attempted to show, the seeds of change had been sown. The narrowly materialistic attitude towards Africa exhibited over the past three centuries by the supporters and beneficiaries of the slave trade had been challenged. A new, juster and more humane movement of opinion had made its power felt and indicated the possibility of a different approach to people less 'civilized' or—to avoid the moral innuendo of that epithet—technically less highly developed. The untapped wealth of Africa—its natural resources and its potential markets—was coming more insistently to attract the attention of men of affairs in the most powerful states of Western Europe. International interest involved the likelihood of international rivalry. Already there had been incidents to suggest that European powers might want to seize hold of parts of the continent, not because they were ambitious to impose their ideas on Africans, but because they felt they could not afford to allow the material advantages of a developing trade to fall into potentially hostile hands. Finally, there had come to be evolved through the energy and enthusiasm of a very few men, pre-eminent among them Sir Joseph Banks, a new form of organization for supporting geographical research, while the hard-won experience of a handful of brave young men had illuminated at once the practical difficulties and the evident possibilities of penetrating into parts of the interior of Africa where in the whole course of history no European was ever known to have set foot. A new movement in human affairs had been born. From now on, with every year that passed, Africa and Europe were to be drawn closer, and ever closer, together.

SOURCES AND REFERENCES

SOURCES

WORKS RELATING TO AFRICA PUBLISHED UP TO 1815

THIS IS NOT A COMPLETE bibliography but a list of all the more important works on Northern and Western Africa that were available for English readers up to the year 1815. It has been arranged chronologically in order to illustrate more clearly the growing interest in Africa. Works by foreign authors are given under the date of their first English translation. Some important works published in French or in German were never translated; they have been given under the date of their original edition. In the case of translated works the original title has not been given unless it differs substantially from the English version. In order to give some indication of the extent to which works on Africa were available throughout Europe, some information has been given about foreign translations. This information has been derived from the following sources:

1. British Museum Catalogue.
2. Cox, Edward G. *A Reference Guide to the Literature of Travel.* Vol. I. *The Old World.* University of Washington, Seattle, 1948.

Some of the works listed here are now extremely rare; all of them tend to fetch prices which put them out of the reach of all but the most opulent of private collectors or the most richly endowed institutions. This is frustrating for the ordinary reader, who cannot have access to a really good library. Readers of the eighteenth century were equally conscious of this frustration; hence the popularity of *Collections of Travels.* The two best contemporary *Collections* were those published by Astley in 1745 and by Pinkerton in 1808–14. A new institutional library trying to build up an *Africana* section with limited funds would probably be better advised to try to obtain one or other of these two works rather than to spend its money on the individual works published in the seventeenth and eighteenth centuries. For the general reader who wishes only to taste the works of the period the following historial anthologies may be recommended: Hodgkin, 1960 (Nigeria), Howard and Plumb, 1955 (West African Explorers), Perham and Simmons, 1945 (African Explorers), Wolfson, 1958 (Ghana).

Abbreviations

D	Dutch	L	Latin
Da	Danish	O	Original edition
E	English	P	Portuguese
F	French	S	Swedish
G	German	T	Translation
I	Italian		

All works published in London, unless otherwise stated.

5th century B.C.   Herodotus. *History.*
E.T. 1584. B.R. *The Famous Hystory of Herodotus.* New Edition, introduced by L. Whibley, 1924.
1709. Littlebury, I. *The History of Herodotus.*

1st century A.D.   Pliny. *Natural History.*
E.T. 1601. Holland, Philip. *The Historie of the World.*
1947–56. Rackham, H. Loeb Edition.

1st century A.D.   Strabo. *Geography.*
E.T. 1848. F.T. 1805. G.T. 1775.

2nd century A.D.   Ptolemy. *Geography.*
E.T. 1932. Stevenson, E. L. New York.

3rd century A.D.   Solinus. *Collectanea Rerum Memorabilium.*
E.T. 1587. Golding, A. *The excellent and pleasant work, of Iulius Solinus Polyhistor.*

12th century A.D.   al-Idrisi. *Geography.*
L.T. 1619. *Geographia Nubiensis.* Paris.
E.T. 1738. Moore, F. Passages relating to interior of Africa only, as appendix to *Travels.*
L.T. 1796. With commentary by J. M. Hartmann, Göttingen.
F.T. 1840. Jaubert, P. A. Paris.

15th century A.D.   Cadamosto. *Voyages*
I.O. 1507. In the Collection, *Paesi novamente retrovati,* Vicenza.
1550. In Ramusio's *Collection,* Venice.
E.T. 1745. Extracts in Astley's *Collection.*
1789. Richardson's *Collection.* Complete translation.
1937. Crone, G. R. Hakluyt Society.

1550–59   Ramusio, G. B. *Navigationi e viaggi.* Venice. 3 vols.

1552–1613   De Barros, João. *Asia.* Lisbon. New edition, Lisbon 1778.
I.T. 1554. In Ramusio's *Collection,* first part only.
No complete translation has ever been made into another European language.
E.T. 1745. Astley's *Collection.* Brief extracts only.
1937. Crone, G. R. Passages relating to West Africa.

1573–99   Marmol Caravajal, Luys del. *Descripcion General de Affrica.* Vol. I e II, Granada, Vol. III, Malaga.
F.T. 1667. 3 vols.

E.T. 1705. Extracts in Harris.

1589   Hakluyt, Richard. *The Principall Navigations, Voiages and Discoveries . . . of the English Nation.* 2nd ed., greatly expanded, 3 vols. 1598–1600. Reprinted, 12 vols. Glasgow, 1903–5. *Everyman's Library,* 9 vols. *World's Classics,* extracts, 1 vol.

1597   Lopez, Duarte. *A Report of the Kingdome of Congo.* I.O. 1591. Rome.
See also Hutchinson, 1881.

1598   Iohn Huighen van Linschoten. *Discours of Voyages unto ye East and West Indies.* D.O. 1596. New edition, Hakluyt Society, 1885.

1600   Leo Africanus. *A Geographical Historie of Africa.* Translated by J. Pory. New edition, edited by R. Brown. Hakluyt Society, 3 vols. 1896.
I.O. 1550. In Ramusio's *Collection.* Venice.
L.T. 1556. Antwerp.
F.T. 1556. Lyon.
1956. Edited by A. Épaulard, H. Lhote, R. Mauny and T. Monod. Paris.

1623   Jobson, Richard. *The Golden Trade or a Discovery of the River Gamba and the Golden Trade of the Aethiopians.* Reprinted, Teignmouth, 1904.

1625   Purchas, Samuel. *Hakluytus Posthumus or Purchas His Pilgrimes.* 4 vols. Reprinted, 20 vols. Glasgow, 1905–7.
Purchas included the following works relating to Africa; references are to the volumes of the 1905–7 edition.

      I.   Phoenician Voyages.
   II–IV.   Voyages to East Indies.
   V–VI.   Leo Africanus. (See Leo Africanus 1600)
     VI.   'Collection of things most remarkable, in the Historie of Barbarie, written by Ro. C.' Other accounts of North Africa. 'A description . . . of the golden Kingdome of Guinea. Translated out of Dutch'. 'The strange adventures of Andrew Battell sent by the Portugals prisoner to Angola' (See Ravenstein 1901)
'A report of the Kingdome of Congo'. (See Lopez 1597)
  VI–VII.   The Voyage of Sir Francis Alvarez . . . unto the Court of Prete Janni'. (See Beckingham and Huntingford 1961)
    VII.   'A Rutter of Don John of Castro, of the Voyage made from India to Zoez'. 'A briefe Relation of the Embassage, which the

Patriarch Don John Bermudez brought from the Emperor of Ethiopia'. (See Whiteway 1902)

IX. 'Collections out of the Voyage and Historie of Friar Joano dos Sanctos his Aethiopia Orientalis'. (See Axelson 1954)
'Larger observations of Master Richard Jobson, touching the River Gambra'. (See Jobson 1623)

1643 Jannequin, Claude. *Voyage de Lybie*. Paris.
E.T. 1745. In Astley's *Collection*.

1670 Ogilby, John. *Africa, being an Accurate Description*.

1670 Villault, Sieur de Bellefond. *A Relation of the Coasts of Africk Called Guinee*.
F.O. 1669.

1678 Vansleb, J. M. *The Present State of Egypt*.
F.O. 1677. G.T. 1792.

1682 Ludolphus, Job. *A New History of Ethiopia*. 2nd ed. 1684.
L.O. 1681, Frankfurt. F.T. 1684.

1684 Dapper, O. *Description de l'Afrique*. Amsterdam.
D.O. 1668. G.T. 1670.

1695 Manuel de Faria y Sousa. *The Portugues Asia*. Translated by J. Stevens.
P.O. 1666, 1674–5.

1696 Le Maire, J. *A Voyage to . . . Senegal and Gamby*. F.O. 1695.

1704 Churchill, A. and J. *A Collection of Voyages and Travels*. 4 vols.
Reprinted with 2 additional vols. 1732; new edition with 2 more vols., making 8 in all, edited by Thomas Osborne, 1745, 1752.

1704 Pitts, Joseph. *A True and Faithfull Account of the Religion and Manners of the Mahometans*. New eds., 1717, 1731, 1738.

1705 Bosman, William. *A New and Accurate Description of the Coast of Guinea*. 2nd ed., 1721.
D.O. 1704. F.T. 1705.

1705 Harris, John. *A Complete Collection of Voyages and Travels*, 2 vols. Revised and enlarged, 2 vols. 1744–48.

1709 Poncet, C. J. *A Voyage to Aethiopia*.
Reprinted, Hakluyt Society, edited by W. Foster, 1949.
F.O. 1700.

1710 Tellez, Balthazar. *The Travels of the Jesuits in Ethiopia*.
P.O. 1645. I.T. 1660. F.T. 1674, 1696. D.T. 1707.

1710 Krump, Theodor. *Hoher and Fruchtbarer Palm-Baum des Heiligen Evangelij*. Augsburg.

E.T. see Crawford, 1951.

1713   Ockley, S. (ed.). *An Account of South West Barbary . . . written by a person who has been a slave there.* F.T. 1726.

1725   Windus, John. *A Journey to Mesquinez.*

1727   Hamilton, Alexander. *A New Account of the East Indies.* 2 vols. Edinburgh. New ed., 1744.

1728   Labat, J. B. *Nouvelle Relation de l'Afrique Occidentale* 5 vols. Paris. E.T. Extensive extracts in Astley, 1745.

1730   Labat, J. B. *Voyage du Chevalier des Marchais en Guinée, Isles Voisines et à Cayenne.* E.T. Extensive extracts in Astley, 1745.

1732   Barbot, John. *A Description of the Coasts of North and South Guinea.* In Churchill's Collection, Vol. V.

1732   Phillips, Thomas. *A Journal of a Voyage made . . . along the Coast of Guiney to Whidaw.* In Churchill's Collection, Vol. VI.

1734   Bluet, Thomas. *Some Memoirs of the Life of Job, Son of Solomon, the High Priest of Boonda in Africa.*

1734   Snelgrave, William. *A new Account of some Parts of Guinea and the Slave Trade.* 2nd ed., 1754.

1735   Atkins, John. *A Voyage to Guinea, Brasil and the West Indies.* 2nd ed., 1737.

1735   Maillet, Benoit de. *Description de l'Égypte.*

1735   Lobo, Jeronymo. *A Voyage to Abyssinia.* Translated by Samuel Johnson. F.O. 1728. The work was translated by Le Grand from a Portuguese manuscript that has since disappeared; Le Grand added considerable additional material.

1738   Moore, Francis. *Travels into the Inland Parts of Africa. . . . to which is added Capt. Stibbs' Voyage up the Gambia in the Year 1723 to make Discoveries.* Moore also included an account of an expedition up the Gambia in 1660 and newly translated extracts from al-Idrisi and Leo Africanus.

1738   Shaw, Thomas. *Travels and Observations Relating to the Several Parts of Barbary and the Levant.* Oxford. 2nd ed., 1747: 3rd ed., 1808. F.T. 1743. G.T. 1765. D.T. 1773.

1739   Salmon, Thomas. *Modern History or the Present State of the Nations.*

1743–5   Pococke, Richard. *Description of the East.* 2nd ed., 1771. G.T. 1754. F.T. 1772. D.T. 1776.

1744   Smith, William. *A New Voyage to Guinea.* 2nd ed., 1745.

1745   'A British Merchant'. *The African Trade.* [Postlethwayt, Malachy.]

1743–7   Astley, Thomas. *A New General Collection of Voyages and Travels*. 4 vols.
F.T. 1746–68. Prévost, Abbé. *Histoire Générale des Voyages*. 18 vols. Paris.
G.T. 1747–74. Schwabe, J. J. *Allgemeine Historie der Reisen*. 14 vols. Leipzig.
Astley's Collection was intended to cover the whole world; Vols. II and III relate to Africa, but the rest of the collection was not completed. Prévost and Schwabe translated Astley's work and went on to complete the collection from other sources.

1747   Bowen, Emmanuel. *A Complete System of Geography ... of the Known World*. 2 vols.

1750   [Langier de Tassy.] *A History of the Piratical States of Barbary*.
F.O. 1725.

1757   Norden, F. L. *Travels in Egypt and Nubia*. New eds., 1780, 1792.
F.O. 1750–5, Copenhagen. G.T. 1779.

1758   Postlethwayt, Malachy. *The Importance of the African Expedition*.

1759   Adanson, Michael. *A Voyage to Senegal*.
F.O. 1757. *Histoire naturelle du Sénégal*.

1759   D'Anville, J. B. 'Dissertation sur les sources du Nil' and 'Mémoire concernant les rivières de l'interieur de l'Afrique'.
Mémoires de Littérature de l'Académie Royale des Inscriptions et Belles Lettres. Vol. XXVI. Paris

1760–1   Newbery, John. *The World Displayed*. New eds., 1767, 1774–8, 1790.

1766   Fenning, D. *A New System of Geography*. 3rd ed., 1771.

1767   Knox, John. *A New Collection of Voyages*. 7 vols.

1768   Lind, James. *An Essay on Diseases. Incidental to Europeans in Hot Climates*. 2nd ed., 1771; 6th ed., 1808.

1769   Römer, L. F. *Nachrichten von der Küste Guinea*. Copenhagen and Leipzig.
Da.O. 1769.

1778   Salmon, Thomas. *New Universal Geographical Grammar*. Edinburgh. 2nd ed., 1782.

1779   Middleton, C. T. *A New and Complete System of Geography*. 2 vols.

1781   Host, George. *Nachrichten von Marokos und Fes*.
Da.O. 1779.

1782   Sancho, Ignatius. *The Letters of the Late Ignatius Sancho, an African*. 2nd ed., 1783; 5th ed., 1803.

1785   Sparrman, André. *A Voyage to the Cape of Good Hope*. 2nd ed., 1786.

S.O. 1783. F.T. 1786, 1787.

1786   Smeathman, Henry. *Plan for a Settlement to be made near Sierra Leone.*

1787   Bankes, Thomas. *A New, Royal, Authentic and Complete System of Universal Geography.*

1787   Cugoano, Ottobah. *Thoughts and Sentiments on the Evil and Wicked Traffic of the Slavery and Commerce of the Human Species.*

1787   Savary, C. F. *Letters on Egypt.* 2 vols. 2nd ed., 1787; 3rd ed., 1799.

F.O. 1785–7.

1787   Volney, C. F. de. *Travels through Syria and Egypt.*

F.O. 1787.

1788   Benezet, A. *Some Historical Account of Guinea.*

1788   Chenier, L. de. *The Present State of the Empire of Morocco.* 2 vols.

F.O. 1787. *Recherches Historiques sur les Maures.*

1788   Falconbridge, Alexander. *Account of the Slave Trade on the Coast of Africa.*

1788   Isert, P. E. *Reise nach Guinea.* Copenhagen: New ed. Berlin and Leipzig, 1790.

F.T. 1793.

1788   Matthews, John. *A Voyage to the River Sierra Leone.* 2nd ed., 1791.

1788   Newton, John. *Thoughts upon the African Slave Trade.* Reprinted 1962: edited by B. Martin and M. Spurrell.

1788   Volney, C. F. de. *Considerations on the War with the Turks.*

F.O. 1788.

1789   Brisson, P. R. de. *An Account of the Shipwreck and Captivity of Mr de Brisson, with a Description of the Deserts of Africa from Senegal to Morocco.*

F.O. 1789, Geneva. G.T. 1799.

1789   Equiano, Olaudah. *The Interesting Narrative of the Life of Olaudah Equiano or Gustavus Vassa, the African* 3rd ed., 1790; 6th ed., 1793; 8th ed., 1794; other eds., 1809, 1814.

1789   Paterson, William. *A Narrative of Four Journeys in the Country of the Hottentots and Caffraria.* 2nd ed., 1790.

F.T. 1790.

1789   Richardson, W. *A General Collection of Voyages and Discoveries made by the Portuguese and Spaniards during the Fifteenth and Sixteenth Centuries.*

1789   Wadström, C. B. *Observations on the Slave Trade.*

1790   *Proceedings of the Association for Promoting the Discovery of the Interior Parts of Africa*

G.T. 1790.

Further reports were issued by the African Association in 1792, 1793 and 1797.

1790   Bruce, James. *Travels to Discover the Sources of the Nile.* 5 vols. Edinburgh and London. 2nd ed., corrected and enlarged by A. Murray, 8 vols. Edinburgh, 1805. Abridged edition by C. F. Beckingham. Edinburgh, 1964.
G.T. 1790–1. F.T. 1790–2.

1790   Le Vaillant, F. *Travels in the Interior Parts of Africa by Way of the Cape of Good Hope.* New ed. Perth, 1791; London, 1796.
F.O. 1790. G.T. 1790, 1792.

1791   Lemprière, William. *A Tour from Gibraltar . . . to Morocco.* 2nd ed., 1793; 3rd ed., 1800; new ed., 1813.
G.T. 1792, 1798.

1791   Poiret, J. L. M. *Travels through Barbary.*
F.O. 1789. G.T. 1789.

1791   Sierra Leone Company. *Substance of the Report of the Court of Directors.* Further reports were published in 1794, 1796, 1796, 1801, 1804, 1808.

1792   Niebuhr, Carsten. *Travels through Arabia and Other Countries of the East.*
G.O. 1772, Copenhagen. F.T. 1776.

1792   Saugnier and Brisson. *Voyages to the Coast of Africa.*
Saugnier—F.O. 1791. Brisson—F.O. 1789.

1793   Dalzel, Archibald. *The History of Dahomey.*

1794   Falconbridge, Mrs A. M. *Narrative of Two Voyages to the River Sierra Leone.* 2nd ed., 1802.

1794   Lalande, J. *Mémoire sur l'Interieur de l'Afrique.* Paris.

1794–5   Wadström, C. B. *Essay on Colonization. . . . Particularly Applied to the Western Coast of Africa.* 2 vols.

1795   Thunberg, C. P. *Travels in Europe, Africa and Asia.* 2nd ed., 1795.
S.O. 1788. F.T. 1794. G.T. 1792.

1798   *Proceedings of the Association for Promoting the Discovery of the Interior Parts of Africa. Containing an Abstract of Mr. Park's Account. . . . Abridged by Bryan Edwards. Also, Geographical Illustrations of Mr. Park's Journey and of North Africa at large by Mr. Rennell.*

1799   Browne, W. G. *Travels in Africa, Egypt and Syria.* 2nd ed., 1806.
D.T. 1800. F.T. 1800. G.T. 1801.

1799   Bruns, P. J. *Neue systematische Erdbeschvreibung von Afrika.* 6 vols. Nuremburg.

1799   Leyden, John. *A Historical and Philosophical Sketch of the Discoveries and Settlements of Europeans in*

Northern and Western Africa at the Close of the Eighteenth Century. Edinburgh.

G.T. 1802.

1799   Park, Mungo. *Travels in the Interior Districts of Africa.* 2nd and 3rd eds., 1799. Often reprinted, latest edition in Everyman's Library.

F.T. 1800. G.T. 1800.

1799   Sonnini de Manoncour, C. N. S. *Travels in Upper and Lower Egypt.* New eds., 1800, 1807.

F.O. 1799. G.T. 1800, 1802.

1800   Wharton, Richard. *Observations on the Authenticity of Bruce's Travels.* Newcastle.

1800–3   Institut d'Égypte. *Memoires sur l'Egypte.* 4 vols. Paris.

1801, 1804   Barrow, John. *An Account of Travels into the Interior of Southern Africa.* 2nd ed., 1806.

1801   Damberger, C. F. *Travels through the Interior of Africa from the Cape of Good Hope to Morocco.*

G.O. 1800.

1802   Denon, Vivant. *Travels in Upper and Lower Egypt.* Another ed., 1803.

F.O. 1802.

1802   Golbéry, S. M. X. de. *Travels in Africa.* Another ed., 1803.

F.O. 1802 *Fragments d'un Voyage en Afrique.*

G.T. 1803.

1802   Hornemann, Frederick. *The Journal of Frederick Hornemann's Travels from Cairo to Mourzouk.*

F.T. 1802. G.T. 1802. Hornemann's Journal was written in German, so the German edition contains the original text, together with other translated material. New edition, Bovill 1964.

1802   Labarthe, P. *Voyage au Sénégal.* Paris.

G.T. 1802.

1802   *African Researches or the Proceedings of the Association for Promoting the Discovery of the Interior Parts of Africa.* Vol. II.

Issued for members of the Association and containing 'Transactions and Correspondence, 1799–1801' and Hornemann's Journal, with other material by Sir Wm. Young, Major Rennell and William Marsden.

Further reports were issued by the African Association in 1805, 1807, 1808, 1810.

1803   Labarthe, P. *Voyage à la Côte de Guinée.* Paris.

G.T. 1804.

1803   Winterbottom, Thomas. *An Account of the Native Africans in the Neighbourhood of Sierra Leone.* 2 vols.

1805   Beaver, Capt. Philip. *African Memoranda; Relative to an Attempt to Establish a British Settlement on the Island of Bulama.*

1806   Durand, J. B. L. *A Voyage to Senegal.*
F.O. 1802. G.T. 1804.

1807   Corry, J. *Observations upon the Windward Coast of Africa.*

1807–24   African Institution. *Annual Reports.*

1808   Clarkson, Thomas. *History of the Rise, Progress and Accomplishment of the Abolition of the African Slave Trade by the British Public.* 2nd ed., 1839.

1808   Hamilton, William. *Remarks on several Parts of Turkey. Part I: Aegyptica.*

1808   Murray, Alexander. *Account of the Life and Writings of James Bruce.* Edinburgh.

1808–14   Pinkerton, John. *A General Collection of the Best and Most Interesting Voyages and Travels in all Parts of the World.* 17 vols.
Africa is covered in Vols. 15 and 16.

1809–28   *Description de l'Égypte.* 9 Vols. of text and 10 of plates Paris.
2nd ed., 24 vols., 1821–27.

1809   Jackson, James Grey. *An Account of the Empire of Morocco.* Enlarged eds., 1811, 1814.

1809   Valentia, George Viscount. *Voyages and Travels to India, Ceylon, the Red Sea, Abyssinia and Egypt.* Two editions, one quarto with Salt's illustrations, the other octavo, without illustrations, both 3 vols., an additional volume being made up of engravings by Henry Salt. 2nd ed., 1811.
F.T. 1813. G.T. 1811.

1810   *Proceedings of the Association for Promoting the Discovery of the Interior Parts of Africa.* 2 vols. Reprint of proceedings 1788–1809.

1812   Meredith, Henry. *Account of the Gold Coast of Africa.*
F.T. 1824.

1814   Salt, Henry. *A Voyage to Abyssinia.*
F.T. 1816.

1815   Park, Mungo. *Journal of a Mission to the Interior of Africa . . . to Which is Prefixed an Account of the Life of Mr. Park.*
F.T. 1820.
In later editions the Journal was published in the same volume as the *Travels* of 1799.

    The following works, though published after 1815, were all written before that date:

1816   Ali Bey. *Travels in Morocco, Tripoli, Cyprus, Egypt, Arabia, Syria and Turkey.*
F.O. 1816.

1817   (Tully.) *Letters written during a ten year Residence at the Court of Tripoli . . . in the Possession of the Family of the late Richard Tully*. 3rd ed., 1819. New ed. with introduction by S. Dearden. 1957.

1819   Burckhardt, J. L. *Travels in Nubia*. 2nd ed., 1822.

1820   Jackson, James Grey. *An Account of Timbuctoo and Housa . . . by El Hage Abd Salam Shabeeny . . . to which is added Letters Descriptive of Travels through West and South Barbary and across to the Mountains of Atlas.*

1822   Burckhardt, J. L. *Travels in Syria and the Holy Land.*

1829   Burckhardt, J. L. *Travels in Arabia*. 2 vols.
           F.T. 1835.

1830   Burckhardt, J. L. *Notes on the Bedouins and Wahhabys.*

1830   Burckhardt, J. L. *Arabic Proverbs.*

Maps

Between 1600 and 1800 nearly a hundred different maps of Africa were printed: a full list is given in Tooley, 1952. Many of these maps have been reproduced in Yusuf Kamal, *Monumenta Cartographica Africae at Aegypti*. Cairo. Vol. V. 1951.

OTHER WORKS

This is not a complete list of all works consulted but only of those mentioned in the references.

For further information four detailed bibliographies are available.

THE CAMBRIDGE HISTORY OF THE BRITISH EMPIRE
Vol. I. *The Old Empire to 1783*. Cambridge, 1929. Bibliography, pp. 824–88.
Vol. II. *The Growth of the New Empire 1783–1870*. Cambridge, 1940. Bibliography, pp. 885–1004.

INTERNATIONAL AFRICAN INSTITUTE
African Bibliography Series: West Africa. Compiled by Ruth Jones. 1958.

PARGELLIS, S., and MEDLEY, D. J.
Bibliography of British History: 1714–1783. Oxford, 1951.

AHMED, J. H. *The Intellectual Origins of Egyptian Nationalism*. 1960.

ANDERSON, M. S. 'Great Britain and the Barbary States in the Eighteenth Century'. *Bulletin of the Institute of Historical Research*. Vol. XXIX. 1956.

ANIS, M. 'British Travellers' Impressions of Egypt in the Eighteenth Century'. *Bulletin of the Faculty of Arts*, Cairo University. Vol. XIII. 1951.

ANON. *Sir Joseph Banks and the Royal Society*. 1844.

ARBERRY, A. J. *British Orientalists*. 1943.

ARISTOTLE. *Meteorologica*. (Loeb ed.)

AXELSON, E. *South African Explorers*. 1954.

AXELSON, E. *South-East Africa, 1488–1530*. 1940.

BARBOUR, K. M. *The Republic of the Sudan*. 1961.

BARTH, H. *Travels and Discoveries in North & Central Africa*. 5 vols. 1857–58.

BARROW, J. *Sketches of the Royal Society Club*. 1849.

BEAGLEHOLE, J. C. (ed.). *The Journal of Captain James Cook*. Vol. I. 1768–71. Cambridge. 1955.

BEAGLEHOLE, J. C. (ed.). *The Endeavour Journal of Joseph Banks 1768–1771*. 2 vols. Sydney. 1962.

BEAZLEY, C. R. *The Dawn of Modern Geography*. 3 vols. 1897.

BECKINGHAM, C. F., and HUNTINGFORD, G. W. B. *Some Records of Ethiopia, 1593–1646: Being Extracts from the History of High Ethiopia . . . by M de Almeida*. Hakluyt Society. 1954.

BECKINGHAM, C. F., and HUNTINGFORD, G. W. B. *The Prester John of the Indies . . . written by Father Fransisco Alvarez*. Hakluyt Society. 2 vols. Cambridge. 1961.

[BELOE, W.] *The Sexagenarian or the Recollection of a Literary Life*. 2 vols. 1817.

BELZONI, G. *Narrative of the Operations and Discoveries . . . in Egypt and Nubia*. 1820.

BENNETT, N. R. 'Christian and Negro Slavery in eighteenth century North Africa'. *Journal of African History*, Vol. I. 1960.

BERNARD, A. *Afrique Septentrionale et Occidentale*. Vol. XI in *Géographie Universelle*. Paris. Part I, 1937; Part II, 1939.

BERTHELOT, A. *L'Afrique Saharienne et Soudanaise—ce qu'en ont connu les Anciens*. Paris. 1927.

BLAKE, J. W. *Europeans in West Africa, 1460–1560*. Hakluyt Society. 2 vols. 1942.

BLAKE, J. W. *European Beginnings in West Africa, 1454–1587*. 1937.

BLUMENBACH, J. F. *Anthropological Treatises, with a Memoir by K. F. H. Marx*. 1865.

BRADBURY, R. E. *The Benin Kingdom and the Edo Speaking People of South Western Nigeria*. International African Institute. 1957.

BOAHEN, A. A. *The British Penetration of the Sahara and Western Sudan*. Ph.D. Thesis, London University. Unpublished. 1959.

BOAHEN, A. A. 'The African Association, 1788–1805'. *Transactions of the Historical Society of Ghana*, Vol. 5. Legon. 1961.

BOAHEN, A. A. *Britain, the Sahara and the Western Sudan, 1788–1861*. Oxford. 1964.

BOTSFORD, J. B. *English Society in the Eighteenth Century as Influenced from Overseas*. New York. 1924.

BOVILL, E. W. *The Golden Trade of the Moors*. 1958.

BOVILL, E. W. *Missions to the Niger—I. The Journal of F. Hornemann and the Letters of A. G. Laing*. Hakluyt Society. Cambridge. 1964.

BOWDICH, T. E. *Mission from Cape Coast Castle to Ashantee*. 1819.

SOURCES AND REFERENCES

BOWDICH, T. E. *An Account of the Discoveries of the Portuguese in the Interior of Angola and Mozambique*. 1824.

BOXER, C. R. *Four Centuries of Portuguese Expansion*. Johannesburg. 1961.

BRIGGS, L. Cabot. *Tribes of the Sahara*. 1959.

BROOKS, E. ST. J. *Sir Hans Sloane*. 1954.

BROUGHAM, LORD. *Lives of Men of Science who Flourished in the Time of George III*. 1845.

BUCHANAN, K. M., and PUGH, J. C. *Land and People in Nigeria*. 1958.

BUNBURY, E. H. *History of Ancient Geography*. 2 vols. 1879.

BURCKHARDT-SARASIN, C., and SCHWABE-BURCKHARDT, H. *Scheik Ibrahim-Johann Ludwig Burckhardt. Briefe an Eltern und Geschwister*. Basle. 1956.

BURTON, R. F. *The Lands of Cazembe*. 1873.

BYNG, J. *The Torrington Diaries*. Edited by C. B. Andrews. 3 vols. 1934–36.

CAILLIÉ, R. *Travels through Central Africa to Timbuctoo*. 2 vols. 1830.

CAMERON, H. C. *Sir Joseph Banks*. 1952.

CAPOT REY, R. *Le Sahara Français*. Paris. 1953.

CARRÉ, J. M. *Voyageurs et Ecrivains Français en Egypt*. Vol. I. 1517–1840. Cairo. 1932.

CASTRIES H. DE, *Les Sources Inédites de l'Histoire du Maroc. Ser. I—Dynastie Saadienne. Archives et Bibliotheques d'Angleterre*. 3 vols. Vol. I. Paris. 1918.

CHARLES-ROUX, F. *Bonaparte: Governor of Egypt*. Translated by E. W. Dickes. 1937.

CHESTERFIELD, LORD. *Letters to His Son*. Edited by C. Strachey. 2 vols. 1901.

CHURCH, R. J. HARRISON. *West Africa*. 1957.

CLAPPERTON, H. *Journal of a Second Expedition into the Interior of Africa*. 1829.

CLARIDGE, W. W. *History of the Gold Coast and Ashanti*. 2 vols. 1915.

COLERIDGE, S. T. *Collected Letters*. Edited by E. L. Griggs, Vols. III and IV. Oxford. 1959.

COLLINS, A. S. *Authorship in the Days of Johnson*. 1927.

COUPLAND, R. *The British Anti-Slavery Movement*. 1933.

COUPLAND, R. *East Africa and its Invaders*. Oxford. 1938.

COUPLAND, R. *Wilberforce*. 1923.

CRAWFORD, O. G. S. *Ethiopian Itineraries, c. 1400–1524*. Hakluyt Society. Cambridge. 1958.

CRAWFORD, O. G. S. *The Fung Kingdom of Sennar*. Gloucester. 1951.

CRONE, G. R. *The Voyages of Cadamosto*. Hakluyt Society. 1937.

CULTRU, P. *Histoire du Sénégal de XVe Siècle à 1870*. Paris. 1910.

CUNNISON, I. 'Kazembe and the Portuguese, 1798–1832' in *Journal of African History*. Vol. II. 1961.

CURTIN, P. D. *The Image of Africa*. University of Wisconscin. 1964.

D'ARBLAY, MADAME (Fanny Burney). *Memoirs of Dr Burney*. 3 vols. 1832.

DAVIDSON, B. *Black Mother*. 1961.

DAVIDSON, B. *Old Africa Re-discovered*. 1959.

DAVIES, K. G. *The Royal African Company*. 1957.

DEARDEN, S. (ed.). *Tully's Ten Years Residence at the Court of Tripoli*. 1957.

DE LA RONCIÈRE, C. *La Découverte de l'Afrique au Moyen Age. Mémoires de la Société Royale de Géographie d'Egypte*. 3 vols. Cairo, 1924–27.

DE LA RONCIÈRE, C. 'Une Histoire du Bornou au XVIIe Siècle par un Chirugien Français captif a Tripoli.' *Revue de L'Histoire des Colonies Françaises*. Vol. VII. Paris. 1919.

DELAFOSSE, M. *Haut-Sénégal-Niger*. 3 vols. Paris. 1912.

DELCOURT, A. *La France et les Etablissements Français au Sénégal, 1713–1763*. Paris. 1952.

DENHAM, D., CLAPPERTON, H., and OUDNEY, W. *Narrative of Travels and Discoveries in Northern and Central Africa*. 3rd ed., 1828.

DIKE, K. O. *Trade and Politics in the Niger Delta, 1830–1885*. Oxford. 1956.

DONNAN, E. *Documents Illustrative of the History of the Slave Trade to America. Vol. I, 1441–1700. Vol. II, Eighteenth Century*. Washington, D.C. 1931.

DUFFY, J. *Portuguese Africa*. 1959.

DUPUIS, J. *Journal of a Residence in Ashanti*. 1824.

DUTOT, S. *De l'Expatriation*. Paris. 1840.

DYKES, E. A. *The Negro in English Romantic Thought*. Washington, D.C. 1942.

FAGE, J. D. *An Atlas of African History*. 1958.

FAGE, J. D. *An Introduction to the History of West Africa*. Cambridge. 1955.

FAGE. J. D. *Ghana. A Historial Introduction*. University of Wisconsin. 1959.

FAIRCHILD, H. N. *The Noble Savage*. New York. 1928.

FERGUSON, J. (ed.). *Letters of George Dempster to Sir Adam Ferguson*. 1934.

FISHER, G. *Barbary Legend*. Oxford. 1957.

FITZGERALD, W. *Africa*. 9th ed., 1961.

FORDE, D. (ed.). *Efik Traders of Old Calabar*. 1956.

FOSTER, W. *The Red Sea and Adjacent Countries*. Hakluyt Society. 1949.

FURBER, H. *Henry Dundas*. 1931.

FYFE, C. H. *A History of Sierra Leone*. 1962.

GIBBON, E. *Miscellaneous Works*. 5 vols. 1814.

GIBBON, L. G. *Niger: The Life of Mungo Park*. Edinburgh. 1934.

GRAY, J. M. *A History of the Gambia*. 1940.

GRAY, R. 'The Archives of Propaganda Fide as a Source for the History of West Africa'. *Third Conference of African History and Archaeology*. London. 1961.

GREENBERG, J. H. *Studies in African Linguistic Classification*. New Haven. 1955.

GROVES, C. P. *The Planting of Christianity in Africa*. Vol. I. 1948.

GWYNN, S. *Mungo Park and the Quest of the Niger*. 1934.

H.B. *The Life of Mungo Park*. Edinburgh. 1835.

HAGBERG, K. *Carl Linnaeus*. Translated by A. Blair. 1952.

HAIR, P. E. H. 'Beaver on Bulama'. *Boletin Cultural da Guiné Portuguesa*. Bissao. Vol. XV. 1960.

HALLETT, R. (ed.). *The Records of the African Association, 1788–1831*. 1964.

HALLS, J. J. (ed.). *The Life and Adventures of Nathaniel Pearce*. 2 vols. 1831.

HALLS, J. J. *The Life and Correspondence of Henry Salt*. 2 vols. 1834.

HARLOW, V. T. *The Founding of the Second British Empire*. 1952.

HASTINGS, A. C. G. *The Voyage of the Dayspring*. 1927.

HEAWOOD, E. *A History of Geographical Discovery in the Seventeenth and Eighteenth Century*. 1912.

HERSKOVITS, M. J. *Dahomey*. 2 vols. New York. 1938.

HODGKIN, T. *Nigerian Perspectives*. 1960.

HOLT, P. M. *A Modern History of the Sudan*. 1961.

HOOKER, J. D. *Journal of the Rt. Hon. Sir Joseph Banks during Capt. Cook's First Voyage, 1768–1771*. 1896.

HOTBLACK, K. *Chatham's Colonial Policy*. 1917.

HOWARD, C., and PLUMB, J. H. *West African Explorers*. 1951.

HOWARD, J. E. *Letters and Documents of Napoleon*. Vol. I. 1961.

HUNT, L. *Autobiography*. 3 vols. 1850.

HUTCHINSON, M. (ed.). *A Report of the Kingdom of Congo . . . from the Writings of Duarte Lopez*. 1881.

ILCHESTER, EARL OF (ed.). *The Journal of Elizabeth, Lady Holland*. 2 vols. 1908.

JACKSON, B. D. *Linnaeus*. 1923.

JOHNSON, G. W. *A History of English Gardening*. 1829.

JOHNSON, H. H. *Liberia*. 2 vols. 1906.

JONES, A. C. M., and MONROE, H. *A History of Abyssinia*. Oxford. 1935.

JONQUIERE, C. DE LA. *L'Expedition d'Egypte*. 5 vols. Paris. 1899–1907.

JULIEN, C. A. *Histoire de L'Afrique du Nord*. 2nd ed. Paris. 1952.

KIMBLE, G. H. T. (ed.). *Esmeraldu de Situ Orbis by Duarte Pachecho Pereira*. Hakluyt Society. 1937.

KLINGBERG, F. J. *The Anti-Slavery Movement in England*. New Haven. 1926.

KNUTSFORD, LADY. *The Life and Letters of Zachary Macaulay*. 1900.

KRUSE, DR F. *Ulrich Jasper Seetzens Reisen*. 3 vols. Berlin. 1854–55.

LANDER, R. *Records of Captain Clapperton's Last Expedition in Africa*. 2 vols. 1830.

LANDER, R. and J. *Journal of an Expedition to Explore the Course and Termination of the Niger*. 3 vols. 1832.

LEVI-PROVENÇAL, E. *Histoire de l'Espagne Musulmane*. 3 vols. Leyden. 1950–3.

LEYDEN, J. *Poems and Ballads, with a Memoir by Walter Scott*. Kelso. 1858.

LHOTE, H. *Les Touaregs du Hoggar*. 2nd ed. Paris. 1955.

LINDROTH, S. 'Adam Afzelius' in *Sierra Leone Studies*. June 1955. Freetown.

LITTLE, T. *Egypt*. 1958.

LLOYD, C. *The Navy and the Slave Trade*. 1949.

LOCKHART, J. G. *Memoirs of the Life of Walter Scott*. 1836–38.

LOKKE, C. L. *France and the Colonial Question. A Study of Contemporary French Opinion, 1763–1801*. New York. 1932.

LOUDON, J. C. *Encycloapeadia of Gardening*. 1835.

LYNAM, E. (ed.). *Richard Hakluyt and his Successors*. Hakluyt Society. 1946.

LYON, G. F. *A Narrative of Travels in Northern Africa*. 1821.

MACKENZIE-GRIEVE, A. *The Great Accomplishment*. 1953.

MACPHERSON, D. *Annals of Commerce*. 4 vols. 1805.

MARKHAM, C. R. *Major James Rennell and the Rise of Modern English Geography*. 1895.

413

SOURCES AND REFERENCES

MARKHAM, C. R. (ed.). *Book of the Knowledge of all the Kingdoms . . . written by a Spanish Franciscan in the XIVth Century.* Hakluyt Society. 1912.

MARTIN, B., and SPURRELL, M. *The Journal of a Slave Trader (John Newton) 1750–1754.* 1962.

MARTIN, E. C. *The British West African Settlements, 1750–1821.* 1927.

MAS LATRIE, M. L. DE. *Les Relations des Chrétiens avec les Arabes de l'Afrique Septentrionale au Moyen Age.* Paris. 1866.

MASSON, P. *Histoire des Établissement et du Commerce Française dans l'Afrique, Barbaresque, 1560–1793.* Paris. 1903.

MATHEW, D. *Ethiopia.* 1947.

MAUGHAM, R. *The Slaves of Timbuktu.* 1961.

MAUNY, R. *Tableau Géographique de l'Ouest Africain du Moyen Age.* Dakar. 1961.

MOOREHEAD, A. *The Blue Nile.* 1962.

MURDOCK, G. P. *Africa. Its People and their Culture History.* New York. 1959.

MURRAY, H. *Historical Account of Travels and Discoveries in Africa.* 2 vols. 1818.

MALTE-BRUN, C. *Précis de la Geographie Universelle.* 5 vols. Paris. 1810–7.

OLIVER, R., and FAGE, J. D. *A Short History of Africa.* 1962.

OWEN, R. *Saga of the Niger.* 1961.

PAHDE, A. *Der Erste Deutsche Afrikaforscher.* Hamburg. 1895.

PERHAM, M., and SIMMONS, J. *African Discovery.* 1945.

PINDAR, PETER. *Peter's Prophecy.* 1788.

PINKERTON, J. *Literary Correspondence.* 2 vols. 1830.

PLAYFAIR, R. L. *Travels in the Footsteps of Bruce in Algiers and Tunis.* 1877.

PLISCHKE, H. *Johann Frederick Blumenbachs Einfluss auf die Entdeckungsreisenden seiner Zeit. Abhandlungen der Gesellschaft der Wissenschafen zu Göttingen, Philologisch-Historische Klasse.* Dritte Folge, No. 20. Göttingen. 1937.

PLUMB, J. H. *England in the Eighteenth Century.* 1950.

PORTER, R. K. *Travels in Georgia.* 2 vols. 1822.

POSTLETHWAYT, M. *Britain's Commercial Interest.* 1757. 2nd ed., 1759.

POSTLETHWAYT, M. *The Universal Dictionary of Trade and Commerce.* 4th ed., 1774.

PRIESTLEY, M., and WILKS, I. 'The Ashanti Kings in the eighteenth century'. *Journal of African History.* Vol I. 1960.

PRIESTLEY, M. 'The Ashanti question and the British: eighteenth-century origins'. *Journal of African History.* Vol. II. 1961.

PROTHERO, R. E. (ed.). *Private Letters of Edward Gibbon.* 2 vols. 1896–97.

RAVENSTEIN, E. G. (ed.). *The Strange Adventures of Andrew Battell in Angola.* Hakluyt Society. 1901.

RICHARDSON, R. *Travels along the Mediterranean.* 2 vols. 1822.

ROBERTSON, C. G. *Chatham and the British Empire.* 1946.

ROBINSON, R., GALLACHER, J., and DENNY, A. *Africa and the Victorians.* 1961.

ROSE, J. H. *The Life of Napoleon I.* 2 vols. 1910.

ROUSSIER, P. 'Les derniers Projets et le dernier Voyage de Dominigo Badia'. *Revue Africaine.* Vol. LXXI. Algiers. 1930.

RUTHERFORD, H. *Sir Joseph Banks and the Exploration of Africa.* Unpublished Thesis. California. 1949.

RYDER, A. F. C. 'The Portuguese in West Africa'. *Third Conference of African History and Archaeology.* London. 1961.

SAINTOYANT, J. *La Colonisation Française sous l'Ancien Regime.* 2 vols. Paris. 1929.

SAINTOYANT, J. *La Colonisation Française pendant la Revolution, 1789–1799.* 2 vols. Paris. 1930.

SAINTOYANT, J. *La Colonisation Française pendant la Période Napoléonienne, 1799–1815.* Paris. 1931.

SCHEFER, C. *Instructions Générales données de 1763 à 1870 aux Gouverneurs et Ordinnateurs des Établissements Français en Afrique Occidentale.* 2 vols. Paris. 1921.

SCHULTESS, E. *Africa.* 1961.

SINCLAIR, J. *Memoirs of the Life and Works of Sir John Sinclair.* 2 vols. 1837.

SMEE, T. 'Observations during a voyage of research on the East Coast of Africa'. *Transactions of the Bombay Geographical Society.* Vol. VI. 1844.

SMYTH, W. H. *The Life and Works of Captain Philip Beaver.* 1829.

SOUTHERN, LADY. *The Gambia.* 1952.

SPARKS, J. *Memoirs of the Life and Travels of John Ledyard.* 1828.

STONE, T. G. 'Journey of Cornelius Hodges in Senegambia, 1689–90'. *English Historial Review.* Vol. XXXIX. 1924.

SYKES, N. *Church and State in England in the Eighteenth Century.* 1934.

TAUXIER, L. *Histoire des Bambaras.* Paris. 1942.

TERRASSE, H. *Histoire du Maroc.* 2 vols. Casablanca. 1949. Abridged edition. Casablanca. 1952.

THEAL, G. M. *Records of South Eastern Africa.* 9. vols. Cape Town. 1898–1903.

THOMSON, J. *Mungo Park and the Niger.* 1890.

THOMSON, T. *History of the Royal Society.* 1812.

TOOLEY, R. V. *Maps and Mapmakers.* 2nd ed. 1952.

TRIMINGHAM, J. S. *Islam in West Africa.* 1959.

TUCKER, A. N., and BRYANT, M. A. *The Non-Bantu Languages of North-Eastern Africa.* 1956.

TURBERVILLE, A. S. (ed.). *Johnson's England.* 2 vols. Oxford. 1933.

TURNER, W. *Journal of a Tour in the Levant.* 3 vols. 1820.

ULLENDORF, E. *The Ethiopians.* 1960.

URVOY, Y. *Histoire de l'Empire du Bornou.* Paris. 1949.

URVOY, Y. *Histoire des Populations du Soudan Central.* Paris. 1936.

VOLLKOMMEN, M. *Die Quellen Bourguignon d'Anvilles für seine kritische Karte von Afrika.* Münchener Geographische Studien. Munich. 1904.

WADDINGTON, G., and HANBURY, B. *Journal of a Visit to some Parts of Ethiopia.* 1822.

WALPOLE, R. *Travels in various Countries of the East.* 1820.

WARD, W. E. F. *A History of Ghana.* 2nd ed. 1958.

WATSON, S. *The Reign of George III.* 1960.

415

WESTERMANN, D., and BRYANT, M. A. *Languages of East Africa.* 1952.

WHITEWAY, R. S. *The Portuguese Expedition to Abyssinia, 1541–5 . . . as narrated by Castanhoso.* Hakluyt Society. 1902.

WILLIAMS, E. *Capitalism and Slavery.* Chapel Hill, North Carolina. 1944.

WILLIAMSON, J. A. *Cook and the Opening of the Pacific.* 1946.

WOLF, A. *A History of Science, Technology and Philosophy in the Eighteenth Century.* 2nd ed. 1952.

WOLFSON, F. *Pageant of Ghana.* 1958.

WOOD, A. C. *A History of the Levant Company.* 1932.

REFERENCE WORKS

Biographie Universelle. Paris.

Complete Baronetage. Exeter.

Complete Peerage.

Dictionary of National Biography.

Encyclopaedia Britannica. 2nd ed. 1778. 11th ed. 1911.

Encyclopaedia of Islam. Leyden.

PERIODICALS

Allgemeine Geographische Ephemeriden. Weimar. 1798–.

Annual Register. 1758–.

Edinburgh Review. 1802–.

Gentleman's Magazine. 1731–.

Monatliche Correspondenz zur Beforderung der Erd-und Himmels-Kunde. Gotha. 1802–.

Quarterly Review. 1809–.

MANUSCRIPTS

Guides to manuscript material

    Cambridge History of the British Empire. Vol. II. Bibliography.

    Dawson, W. R. (ed.). Bibliography. *The Banks Letters, a Calendar of the Manusacript Correspondence of Sir Joseph Banks, preserved in the British Museum, the British Museum (Natural History) and other Collections in Great Britain.* 1958.

BRITISH MUSEUM

Sir Joseph Banks: Letters	Add MSS. 33977–80; 8096
Mungo Park: Letters	Add MSS. 37232

BRITISH MUSEUM (Natural History)

Sir Joseph Banks: Letters	Dawson Turner Copies

PUBLIC RECORD OFFICE

Foreign Office Records:

Abyssinia	F.O.1
Morocco	F.O.52
Tripoli	F.O.76
Tunis	F.O.77

Colonial Office Records:

African Exploration	C.O.2
West African Settlements	C.O.267

ROYAL BOTANICAL GARDENS, KEW
  Sir Joseph Banks: Letters   B.C. 1 and 2
ROYAL GEOGRAPHICAL SOCIETY
  African Association   Minute Books for the:
         Committee, 1788–1809
         General Meetings, 1789–1831
         Saturday's Club, 1788–1815
         Photostat Copies: originals in
         Cambridge University Library
  Sir Joseph Banks: Letters and Papers   The Sutro Papers: papers and
         letters relating to Africa and
         the African Association 1788–
         1820
         Photostat copies: originals in
         Sutro Library, University of
         California, San Fransisco

REFERENCES

Abbreviations

A.A.   African Association.
A.A. Ctee.   African Association Committee—Minute Book.
A.A.G.M.   African Association General Meeting—Minute Book.
A.A.S.C.   African Association Saturday's Club—Minute Book.
B.C.   The Banks Collection of Letters in Royal Botanical Gardens
         Library, Kew.
B.L.   *The Banks Letters.* Calendar edited by W. R. Dawson.
B.M.   British Museum.
B.U.   *Biographie Universelle.*
D.N.B.   *Dictionary of National Biography.*
D.T.C.   Dawson Turner Copies of Banks's letters in British Museum
         (Natural History).
E.I.   *Encyclopaedia of Islam.*
P.A.A.   *Proceedings of the African Association.* 1810.
R.A.A.   *Records of the African Association.* Edited by R. Hallett.
         1964.
S.P.   The Sutro Papers of Sir Joseph Banks.

THE AFRICAN SETTING

I. BACKGROUND

1. *The Land*

For evocative descriptions of African landscapes the eighteenth- and nineteenth-century travellers are unsurpassed. For comprehensive geographies there are a number of excellent modern works: Fitzgerald 1961 on Africa; Bernard 1937 on North Africa; Capot Rey 1953 on the Sahara; Harrison Church 1957 on West Africa; Buchanan and Pugh 1958 on Nigeria and Barbour 1961 on the Sudan. The work of modern photographers should not be ignored: Schultess's pictures (1961) of Africa are outstanding.

1. Fitzgerald 1961, 373.
2. Lind 1771 (2nd ed.), 47–9; *D.N.B.*: Lind. For other interesting comments on the climate of West Africa: Jobson 1623 (1904 ed.), 161–2; Bosman 1705, Letter VIII.
3. Curtin 1964, 71–3.

2. *The People*

Murdock 1959 provides the most recent and the most comprehensive survey. The geographers, mentioned above, have useful chapters on the people of their respective areas; to them should be added Briggs 1959, on the tribes of the Sahara. The bibliographies produced by the International African Institute are the best guide to the literature about individual peoples. On languages the handbooks prepared by the Institute are the best introductions; they contain beautifully clear maps. On language classification, Greenberg 1955 is widely accepted. On Islam in West Africa, Trimingham 1959.

II. THE STATES OF NORTHERN AND WESTERN AFRICA IN THE EIGHTEENTH CENTURY

Oliver and Fage 1962 provide the best introduction to African History; Bovill 1958 and Davidson 1959 and 1961 are also to be recommended for the general reader. There are two good introductions to regional history: Julien 1952 on North Africa and Fage 1955 on West Africa. On individual African countries there are now a number of excellent histories: Terrasse 1949 on Morocco (abridged ed., 1952); Holt 1961 on the Sudan; Jones and Monroe 1935 and Ullendorf 1960 on Ethiopia; Urvoy 1949 on Bornu and 1936 on the Central Sudan; Ward 1958 and Fage 1959 on Ghana; Fyfe 1962 on Sierra Leone; Hodgkin 1960 on Nigeria, and Gray 1940 on the Gambia. The *Encyclopaedia of Islam* contains many useful articles on the Muslim states and cities of Africa. Fage's *Atlas of African History* is an indispensable work.

1. The word 'anarchy' as applied to Morocco is a Europocentric expression; for a brief, profound and sympathetic sketch of Berber institutions, Terrasse 1952, 25–36.
2. Fisher 1957 provides a salutary corrective to conventional European ideas about Barbary pirates.
3. For a fuller discussion of Wangara, Bovill 1958, 191–202.

III. AFRICAN IDEAS ABOUT EUROPE

1. de Tassy 1750, 83.
2. Tully 1819, II 355.
3. Niebuhr 1792, II 240–1.

4. Ludolphus 1684, 356–8.
5. Cadamosto 1789, 56–7.
6. Newton 1788 (1962 ed.), 107; Park 1799, ch. xxiv; Smith 1745, 266.
7. Bowdich 1819, 261–2.
8. Hakluyt 1904, VII 91.
9. Job's story is given in Bluet 1734; his return to the Gambia, Moore 1738, 202.
10. Dupuis 1824, 100; Park 1799, ch. xxi.
11. Equiano 1793, 4.
12. Browne 1806, 224.
13. Tully 1819, II 51–4.
14. al-Idrisi's account of England is given in his Seventh Climate, ch. ii.

EUROPE'S KNOWLEDGE OF AFRICA IN THE EIGHTEENTH CENTURY

I. POPULAR CONCEPTIONS

Curtin 1964, 27–57, provides an excellent study, more detailed than that attempted here, of 'the Africans' "Place in Nature".'

1. Chesterfield 1901, I 116; *D.N.B.:* Stanhope.
2. Salmon 1782, 634.
3. Bankes 1787, Preface.
4. Crone and Skelton in Lynam 1946, 66.
5. For a survey of 'English Collections of Voyages and Travels 1625–1846', Crone and Skelton in Lynam 1946.
6. Dapper 1686, Preface; *D.N.B.:* Ogilby.
7. Bowen 1747, I viii, ix.
8. Middleton 1779, I 241; Salmon 1739, vi; *D.N.B.:* Salmon.
9. Bowen 1747, II 377.

II. SAHARA AND SUDAN

1. *Classical Writers*
Bunbury's *History of Ancient Geography*, though first published in 1879, is still the best general introduction. Classical knowledge of the Sahara and the Sudan has been studied in great detail by Berthelot.

1. Herodotus, II 32; 1584 trans., 154–6 (this translation only covers the first two books).
2. Lhote 1955, 68–72.
3. Herodotus, IV 183; 1709 trans., I 436.
4. On the Roman penetration of the Sahara: Bovill 1958, 31–49.
5. Pliny, *Natural History*, V 5; Lhote, 113–15.
6. Ptolemy (1932 trans.), I 8; Lhote, 115–17; Bovill 1958, 40.
7. Pliny, V 10 (Loeb ed.): V 8–9 (1601 trans.).
8. Lhote 1955, 117–21.
9. Murray 1818, I 29.
10. Pliny, V 8 (1601 trans.).
11. Pliny, VIII 25 (1601); VIII 29–30 (Loeb). In the description of the

mantichora there is an obscurity in the text which makes it uncertain whether Pliny meant that the creature was to be found in India or Africa.

12. Pliny, II 68. Cf. Aristotle, *Meteorologica*, II 5; Strabo, *Geography*, II 2.

13. Solinus, ch. 4 (1583 trans.); Beazley 1897, 243–72. A copy of de Mornas's map exists in the King George V Memorial Museum, Dar-es-Salaam; there is no copy to be found in the British Museum or in the Royal Geographical Society, London.

2. *Arab Geographers*

Bovill, 55–65, provides a useful brief introduction to the Arab geographers; further information on individual geographers may be found in *E.I.* Hodgkin 1960 gives extracts from Arab geographers relating to the area now lying within the borders of Northern Nigeria. A complete translation of al-Idrisi's work is to be found in a French edition, 1840. Pory's translation of Leo Africanus was reprinted by the Hakluyt Society in 1896, ably edited by R. Brown. This edition has now been out-dated by a new French edition, edited by Épaulard, with notes by Monod, Lhote and Mauny; this is based on the French translation of 1556, a more accurate version than Pory's.

1. Gibbon 1814, V 192–3: 'An Inquiry into the supposed Circumnavigation of Africa by the Ancients'.

2. The quotations from al-Idrisi are all from Moore's translation, 1738.

3. On Leo's life: Épaulard 1956, I vi–ix.

4. Leo, Book I: Brown 1895, I 151–5, 187.

5. Leo, Book I: Brown, I 128; Maugham 1961, 120–1.

6. Leo, Book VII: Brown, III 824–6; Bovill, 89; Épaulard, II 467 n.

7. Leo, Book I: Brown, III 822–34.

8. Leo, Book I: Brown, I 187–8.

9. Leo, Book I: Brown, III 1096.

10. Leo, Book VII: Brown, III 819.

III. GUINEA

1. *The Portuguese*

Blake's two works form the standard introduction to the Portuguese in West Africa; Boxer's *Four Centuries of Portuguese Expansion* is a concise and lucid survey.

1. *Esmeraldo de Situ Orbis* was written c. 1510 but not published in Portugal until 1895, English trans., Hakluyt Society, 1937.

2. The translations are all taken from the earliest complete English translation contained in *A General Collection of Voyages and Discoveries made by the Portuguese and Spaniards*, 1789; a modern translation by G. R. Crone was published by the Hakluyt Society in 1937. Richardson 1789, 62, 64, 70.

3. Richardson 1789, 57–8.

4. Herodotus, IV 196: 1709 trans., I 442; Crone 1937, xvi, 23.

5. A complete translation of de Barros's *da Asia* into another language

has still to be made. Fortunately the passages relating to West Africa have been translated by Crone and are contained in his edition of Cadamosto.

6. de Barros, I ii 3–4; Crone 1937, 124–7.
7. Bradbury 1957, 20.
8. de Barros, I ii 6–8; Crone, 128–41.
9. de Barros, I ii 12; Crone, 142–5.
10. de Barros, I ii 12; Crone, 146–7.
11. Villault 1670, 88–9.
12. Murray 1818, I 59; Ryder 1961; Axelson 1940, Appendix V contains much interesting information about the Portuguese archives.

2. *The English, the French and the Dutch*

The second and third volumes of Astley's *Collection* (1745) contain abridgements of most of the works mentioned in this chapter. Shorter extracts are given in Wolfson 1958 and Hodgkin 1960.

1. Hakluyt 1903, XI 23, VI 148–9.
2. Bosman 1705, Preface; Barbot 1732, 13.
3. Labat (1660–1738) had been a missionary in the West Indies and had written a famous account of those islands. For his career, *B.U.:* Labat.
4. Le Maire 1696, 47; Barbot 1732, 82, 138, 235, 359; Adanson 1759, 40.
5. Barbot 1732, 34, 359; Bosman 1704, 117; Smith 1745, 195.
6. Moore 1738, 120; Phillips 1732, 219; Smith 1745, 248, 244.
7. Barbot 1732, 110; Dalzel 1793, xix.
8. Dalzel 1793, 166, 218.
9. Herskovits 1938, II 55; Davidson 1961, 214.
10. Barbot 1732, 187.
11. Barbot 1732, 463 map.
12. Barbot 1732, 362, 375–6.
13. Snelgrave 1734, 55–9.
14. Snelgrave 1734, 79–80; Smith 1745, 135–7; Labat 1730, II 273–82.
15. Dapper 1686, 245; Barbot 1732, 168.
16. Barbot 1732, 229.
17. Dapper 1686, 246, 253; for comments on Dapper's reports of the tribes of the Liberian hinterland, Johnson 1906, I 86–90.
18. Ward 1958, 76.

IV. AVENUES INTO THE INTERIOR

1. *The English on the Gambia*

Gray's *History of the Gambia* is an exhaustive work, making use of a mass of material contained in English archives. Lady Southern's book, whose historical chapters are little more than an abridgement of Gray, is better suited for the general reader.

1. Southern 1952, 31; Gray 1940, ch. i; Golbéry 1803, II 110.
2. On the tribes there is a mass of material in Astley 1745, II 254–303; Gray 1940, 325–8.
3. Hakluyt 1903, VII, 90–9.
4. Hakluyt 1903, VII 88–9, 99–102.

5. The account which Jobson wrote of his experiences, *The Golden Trade*, published in 1623, is an exceedingly rare book; the British Museum does not possess a copy. A facsimile edition was published in 1904. Lengthy extracts are given in Howard and Plumb. Additional material on Jobson has been discovered by Gray 1940, 26–35.

6. Gray 1940, 26–8; Purchas 1905, I 75.

7. Gray 1940, 72–4; Vermuyden's account is given in Moore 1738, Appendix III.

8. On 'Tarra' see the articles in *E.I.*: Atar and Moors.

9. Hodges's account has been reprinted by Stone 1924; see also Gray 1940, 96 n., 184; Labat 1728, IV 277–9, V 7–11.

10. The Committee's recommendations are reprinted in Donnan 1931, II 250–6.

11. Stibbs's account is given in Moore 1738.

12. Curtin 1964, 89–94.

2. The French on the Senegal

Labat 1728 is the most important contemporary work; extracts are translated in Astley 1745. Labat has been criticized by Cultru 1910. Golbéry 1803 is the best description of Senegal in the second half of the eighteenth century. Cultru 1910 and Delcourt 1952 have examined the archive material.

1. Golbéry 1803, I 125, 127.

2. Hakluyt 1903, VII 91.

3. Le Maire 1696, 58–9; Cultru 1910, 117.

4. Astley 1745, II 66–74; Labat 1728, III 333–73.

5. Astley 1745, II 145–6; Labat 1728, IV 110–12.

6. Astley 1745, II 147; Labat 1728, IV 22–7.

7. Astley 1745, II 148–58; Labat 1728, IV 32–58.

8. Delcourt 1952, 169–74.

9. Cultru 1910, 208–12; Golbéry 1803, I 276–362.

V. WESTERN AFRICA

1. *Cartographical Impressions: 1500–1750*

There is no single work on the history of African cartography. Of the many good general works on cartography, Tooley 1952 is particularly useful, as it contains a list of all the maps on Africa known to have been published between 1500 and 1750. Yusuf Kamal's *Monumenta Cartographica Africae* is a truly princely work; it contains reproductions of most, though not all, of the early maps of Africa.

1. On the work of Delisle and d'Anville, Vollkommen 1904.

2. *B.U.*: d'Anville.

3. D'Anville's two articles on African geography, 'Dissertation sur les sources du Nil' and 'Mémoire concernant les rivières de l'intérieur de l'Afrique', were both published in *Mémoires de Littérature de l'Académie Royale des Inscriptions et Belles Lettres*, 1759, XXVI.

SOURCES AND REFERENCES

VI. EXPLORERS WITHOUT RENOWN. EUROPEANS IN THE SAHARA
AND THE SUDAN: THIRTEENTH–EIGHTEENTH CENTURIES

De la Roncière's work, *La Découverte de l'Afrique au Moyen Age*, was published in Cairo in three volumes (1924–27) as part of the *Mémoires de la Société Royale de Géographie d'Égypte*.

1. Bovill 1958, 111; de la Roncière 1924, I 108–12. The reference to the journey of an unknown European occurs in a work written by Ramon Lull, the great Spanish missionary, 1283.

2. Bovill 1958, 113–14; de la Roncière 1924, I 102–9, 114–15.

3. The documents relating to Anselm d'Ysalguier are printed in de la Roncière 1927, III 1–5; for criticism of the story, Mauny 1961, 463.

4. Malfante's letter is given in the original Latin in de la Roncière 1924, I 143–60; Crone 1937, 85–90, gives an English translation.

5. De la Roncière 1924, I 161–3.

6. Imbert's account is given in de la Roncière 1924, I 164–8.

7. De la Roncière 1919, 73–88.

8. Masson 1903 quotes reports from the following consuls: Lemaire 1686, 177; Delalande 1698, 178; De Lancey 1766, 604–5; D'André 1770, 606–11. A report from an English consul, Fraser 1767, is given in Macpherson 1805, IV 468.

9. The account of this expedition was found in a manuscript in the Convent of the Propaganda Fide in Tripoli; it was brought to the notice of John Barrow probably by Captain W. H. Smyth and published as a footnote to a review of various books about Africa in the *Quarterly Review* January 1818, XVIII 375. I am indebted to Mr D. B. Ellison of the Northern Nigerian Administrative Service for first bringing this account to my attention, and to Dr Richard Gray of the School of Oriental and African Studies, University of London, for information derived from the Vatican archives about the report secured by the Catholics in Cairo.

VII. OTHER PARTS OF AFRICA

1. *Barbary*

Julien 1952 contains a useful guide to European writers on the Barbary states during the seventeenth and eighteenth centuries.

1. Chenier 1788, Preface; de Tassy 1750, iii, 246, 261–2; Poiret 1791, 329; Ockley 1713, 36, 110.

2. Postlethwayt 1774, 'Barbary'; Bovill 1958, 182.

3. Shaw 1808 (3rd ed.), I 462; Host 1781, 160; Bennett 1960, 60. Anderson 1956 describes British relations with the Barbary states during the eighteenth century.

4. Marmol Caravajal, a Spaniard who spent several years as a prisoner in North Africa, published a *Description of Africa* in 1573; this work supplemented Leo's account.

5. De Tassy 1750, 264.

2. *Egypt*

Carré 1932 provides an excellent account of French travellers in Egypt. For English travellers there is only the brief article by Anis 1951. Biographies of all the French travellers mentioned are given in *B.U.*, of all the English travellers in *D.N.B.*

1. Wood 1932, 166; Carré 1932, I 82.
2. Carré 1932, I 39–75.
3. Wood 1932, 165–74.
4. Carré 1932, I 80–103; Volney 1787, II 497.
5. Carré 1932, I 107–15.

3. *Nubia, Sennar and the Nile*

1. Leo, Book VII. Poncet's account has been reprinted by the Hakluyt Society: Foster 1949.
2. Crawford 1951, 196–288.
3. Ptolemy, IV 8; Bunbury 1879, II 347–8, 612–18; d'Anville 1759, 'Dissertation sur les sources du Nil'.

4. *Ethiopia*

Accounts of European relations with Ethiopia are given by Jones and Monroe 1935, Mathew 1947 and Ullendorf 1960.

1. Some fifteenth-century accounts of Ethiopia by European travellers have been translated by Crawford 1958.
2. Alvarez's account of the 1520 mission has been edited by Beckingham and Huntingford 1961.
3. The account of da Gama's expedition has been edited by Whiteway 1902. Ethiopian chronicle quoted by Whiteway 1902, xxxvii.
4. Foster 1949, 124–5.
5. Ullendorf 1960, 9; *B.U.*: Ludolf.

5. *The Congo, Angola and Mozambique*

Duffy 1959 is the best introduction in English to the Portuguese colonies south of the equator. Davidson 1959 and 1961 contain useful chapters.

1. Duffy 1959, 5.
2. Duffy 1959, 10–13; Lopez, edited by Hutchinson 1881, 73; Davidson 1961, 138–9.
3. Duffy 1959, 22.
4. Astley 1745, III 265; Duffy 1959, 48–73; 96; Bowdich 1824, 7.
5. Axelson 1954, 14; al-Idrisi, Climate I, Section 8.
6. Axelson 1954, x; Axelson 1940, ch. xv; Duffy 1959, 107.
7. Duffy 1959, 36–8.
8. Duffy 1959, 41–8, 82–5, 109–12.
9. Duffy 1959, 188–9; Hutchinson 1881, Lopez's map.
10. Burton 1873, 29.
11. Duffy 1959, 190–2; Burton 1873 contains Lacerda's and Baptista's journals; Cunnison 1961.
12. Hutchinson 1881, xxi.
13. Ravenstein's edition of Battell's *Adventures* (1901) contains an excellent history of the Portuguese in Angola.
14. Axelson 1954 contains extracts from dos Santos; Lancaster's narrative, Hakluyt 1904, VI; Coupland 1938; Theal's nine volumes, 1898–

1903, contain translations of the principal Portuguese works on S.E. Africa.

6. *South Africa*
1. Axelson 1954, xiii–xiv.
2. Astley 1745, III 322; *B.U.*: Thunberg, Sparrman and Le Vaillant; *D.N.B.*: Paterson.

7. *Asia and the Americas*
Heawood 1912 provides a comprehensive account of the development of geographical knowledge in the seventeenth and eighteenth centuries. The contemporary *Systems of Geography* reveal the extent of Europe's knowledge of particular areas.

VIII. THE CAUSES OF IGNORANCE
1. Rennell in P.A.A. I 211–12; Church 1957, 151. Howard and Plumb 1951, Introduction, and Davies 1957, 4–6, provide a more realistic assessment of the reasons for Europe's ignorance.
2. Postlethwayt 1774, 'Africa'.
3. De Barros, *da Asia*, I 3 xii, translated by Boxer 1961, 26–7.
4. Hunt 1850, II 285.
5. C.O. 267/6. Board of Trade to Pitt, November 23, 1758.
6. *Encyclopaedia Britannica* 1778, 'Africa'.
7. On missionary enterprise in the eighteenth century, Groves 1948; on the Capuchins in West Africa, Gray 1961.
8. Lobo, translated by Johnson, 1735, chapter 2.

THE BONDS OF INTERCOURSE
I. FUNDAMENTALS
2. *The African Trade*
1. Macpherson 1805, IV 153.
2. Postlethwayt 1745, 4–6; Anon, *A Treatise upon the Trade of Great Britain to Africa*, 1772, quoted by Martin 1927, 1.
3. Williams, 1944, 52, 63; Donnan 1931, II 630.
4. *Journal of a Slave Dealer: A View of some Remarkable Axcedents in the Life of Nics. Owen on the Coast of Africa and America from the year 1746 to the year 1757*, edited by E. C. Martin, 1930, 97–8, quoted by Williams 1944, 36.
5. Postlethwayt 1758, 59, 85, 96; Postlethwayt 1745, 35; Postlethwayt 1759, II 218.
6. *D.N.B.*: Postlethwayt; S.P. 749. Commander James Lucas Yeo to J. W. Croker, May 12, 1817.

3. *War and Politics*
1. Defoe, quoted in Plumb 1950, 21; Robertson 1945, 24.
2. Postlethwayt 1759, II 202; Postlethwayt 1758, 3; Hotblack 1917, 32.

3. C.O. 267/12. The memorial of Thos. Cumming, 26.1.1758; Hotblack 1917, 27–43.

4. For the history of Senegambia, Martin 1927, 57–103; Gray 1940, 234–75; for an eye-witness account of the fall of Fort St Louis: C.O. 276/18. J. C. Schotte to Lord Germaine, 29.3.1779.

5. C.O. 267/12. Worge to Pitt, 14.1.1760, 14.7.1760. Worge to Egremont, 16.2.1762; C.O. 267/13. O'Hara to Conway, 28.5.1760.

6. Macpherson 1805, III 375.

7. On the peace negotiations in 1783, Harlow 1952, 102–3.

II. THE CURIOSITY OF THE AGE

1. *The Cosmopolitan Spirit*

1. Trevelyan in Turberville 1933, I 3; Wolf 1952, 27.

2. More information on the works mentioned here only by their titles is given by Dykes 1942, a study of the Negro in English literature.

3. Hodgkin 1960 reprints Equiano's account of Ibo village life.

4. *D.N.B.*: Sancho; Sancho 1782, I xiii.

5. Hodgkin 1960, 157–9; Sancho 1782, I 70, II 4.

6. Sancho 1782, I xvi.

7. No detailed study of English Orientalists has yet been made; Arberry 1943 provides a brief sketch; all the scholars mentioned here are given in *D.N.B.*

2. *The Produce of the Tropics: Interests Practical, Aesthetic and Scientific*

1. Botsford 1924, 49–78.

2. Loudon 1835, 351–2; Johnson 1829, 152.

3. On Linnaeus, Jackson 1923 and Hagberg 1952; the articles on 'Linnaeus', 'Botany' and 'Zoology' in *Encyclopaedia Britannica*, 11th edition, clarify Linnaeus's achievement and influence.

4. Hagberg 1952, 105.

5. Johnson 1829, 147–52.

6. *D.N.B.*: Solander.

3. *The Circulation of Ideas*

1. Collins 1927, 232.

2. *Encyclopaedia Britannica*, 11th edition, article on 'Encyclopaedias'; Johnson, *The Idler*, No. 7, quoted by Collins 1927, 248.

3. Thomson 1812, 1, 351–2, 552.

4. Thomson 1812, 5.

5. Birrell quoted by Brooks 1954, 181; *D.N.B.*: Ashmole.

6. On Sloane, Brooks 1954.

III. THE INFLUENCE OF GREAT MEN

1. *James Cook*

1. Bruce 1805, I 20; Beaglehole 1955, xxi.

2. On Dampier and his successors, Williamson's chapter on 'Exploration and Discovery' in Turberville 1933.

3. Cameron 1953, 319. Banks to Count Lauragais, 6.12.1771.

4. P.A.A. I 3, (R.A.A. 42).

5. Golbéry 1803, I 3–4.

2. *James Bruce*

Bruce's *Travels* in the complete editions of 1790 and 1805 has the disadvantage for the modern reader of being the bulkiest of all the great works of African exploration. A number of abridged editions were published in the first half of the nineteenth century; a new abridgment edited by C. F. Beckingham appeared in 1964. Moorehead 1962, 18–43, provides a vivid sketch of Bruce, but it is surprising that one of the greatest of African explorers should never have been made the subject of a full-length modern biography.

1. Bruce 1805, I 2.

2. Murray 1808, 13–16.

3. *D.N.B.*: Wood.

4. Murray 1808, 28–9.

5. *D.N.B.*: Murray; Mathew 1947, 150–2.

6. Murray 1808, 31.

7. D'Arblay 1832, I 300, 309; Murray 1808, 80–3, 129–34.

8. Playfair 1877, 287–8.

9. Murray 1808, 59.

10. Bruce 1805, V 269, I 70.

11. Murray 1808, 114–15.

12. Murray 1808, 118; Prothero 1896, II 226. Sheffield to Gibbon, 21.9.1790; *D.N.B.*: Bruce (the article was written by Richard Garnett).

13. For Bruce's interest in the African Association, B.L. 179 and Murray 1808, 284–5.

3. *Joseph Banks*

In his lifetime Banks published little—and nothing relating to Africa. This is not surprising when the extent of his correspondence is considered. W. R. Dawson, the leading authority of Banks's letters, reckons that his total correspondence may have amounted to 100,000 documents and letters—an average of fifty letters a week during the course of his working life. Banks kept his correspondence meticulously filed; so it might have come down to posterity but for a disastrous sale in London in 1886. Today Banks's letters are to be found in the libraries scattered throughout three continents. Dawson has traced 7,000 letters in the United Kingdom and given summaries of them in his *Calendar*, a great work to which scholars in many fields will be indebted for generations to come, and which has proved indispensable for the present study. The largest collections of Banks's letters in England are held by the British Museum, the British Museum (Natural History), the Royal Society and the Royal Botanical Gardens at Kew. To these must now be added photostat copies of Banks's letters and papers relating to Africa, presented to the Royal Geographical Society by the Sutro Library, California, which holds the originals. The Sutro papers were made the subject of an unpublished thesis, *Sir Joseph*

Banks and the Exploration of Africa, by Homer Rutherford, a copy of which is held by the British Museum (Natural History). At a time when the Sutro Papers were not available in England, Dr Rutherford's thesis opened my eyes to the pre-eminent role played by Banks in supporting African exploration. At the same time Dr A. A. Boahen drew my attention to Banks's early contacts with Africa (Boahen 1959, 1961). The existing information on Banks's contacts with Africa is now published in R.A.A. (Hallett 1964).

1. Beaglehole 1955, cxxxvi.
2. Cameron 1952, 297.
3. Beaglehole 1955, cxii.
4. Beaglehole 1955, cxxxvi.
5. The translation of Cuvier's speech to the French Academy of Science in 1821 is taken from an anonymous work, *Sir Joseph Banks and the Royal Society*, 1844, 67–8.
6. Cameron 1952, 29; Hooker 1896, 185. The complete text of Banks's journal on his expedition with Cook has recently been edited by Beaglehole 1962.
7. *Middlesex Journal*, 31.8.1771, quoted by Beaglehole 1955, 655; Linnaeus to Ellis, quoted by Cameron 1952, 44.
8. Beaglehole 1955, cxiii.
9. 'Peter Pindar', *Peter's Prophecy*, 1788, 22; Cameron, 248.
10. Pindar 1788, 22; Cameron 1952, 248.
11. *Travels in England, Scotland and the Hebrides*, 1799, I 46, quoted by Cameron 1952, 170–1.
12. Cameron 1952, 252–3.
13. On Masson, *D.N.B.*, B.L. 590–1, (R.A.A. 271); on Brass, B.L. 151, 202, (R.A.A. 273).
14. B.C. 1/131. De Ponthieu to Banks, 29.5.1783 (B.L. 680, R.A.A. 273).
15. B.M. Add. MSS 8096/331–2. Isert to Banks, 13.1.1785 (R.A.A. 273–4); Bruce, B.L. 179, (R.A.A. 271–3); B.M. Add. MSS 33978/97. Thompson to Banks, 23.1.1787 (R.A.A. 274); Matra, B.L. 592–9.
16. On Matra, Beaglehole 1955, cclvi–viii; Matra's official correspondence is in F.O. 52/7—13.

IV. THE ANTI-SLAVERY MOVEMENT

1. On the cult of the Noble Savage, Fairchild 1928; *D.N.B.*: Day; Fairchild, 145–8; Day, *The Dying Negro*, 1775, 7.
2. Clarkson 1808, I 469–70.
3. Coupland 1923, 143; Walpole quoted by Klingberg 1926, 91 n.

V. THE INTEREST OF EUROPE

2. *Paul Isert*

1. *B.U.*: Isert; Isert 1788; Isert to Banks, 13.1.1785.
2. Wadström 1794, II 176, 316; Claridge 1915, I 223.
3. Tully 1819, I 215, 218.

3. *C. B. Wadström*

1. *B.U.*: Wadström; on the Swedenborgian interest in Africa, Lindroth 1955.
2. Wadström 1794, II 179–87.
3. Memoir of Wadström by Helen Maria Williams, *Annual Register*, 1799, 322.
4. Wadström 1794, I 23–4.
5. Williams's Memoir.

4. *J. F. Blumenbach*

An English translation of Blumenbach's principal works, together with Marx's Memoir, was published by the Anthropological Society of London in 1865.

1. Marx in Blumenbach 1865, 6–7.
2. Blumenbach 1865, 21.
3. Blumenbach 1865, 98, 302.
4. Coleridge 1959, III 79; Blumenbach 1865, 312.

THE AGE OF THE AFRICAN ASSOCIATION: I
1788–1802

I. THE FIRST YEARS: 1788–90

The reports of the African Association were published at irregular intervals between 1790 and 1810. A complete edition of all the reports was published in 1810; it is referred to here as P.A.A. Additional information on the Association is provided by the Association's Minute Books (originals in the University Library, Cambridge, photostat copies in the Royal Geographical Society), and by the correspondence and papers of Sir Joseph Banks. All available material of any importance relating to the Association has been printed in *The Records of the African Association, 1788–1831*, edited by Hallett 1964, referred to here as R.A.A. For another account of the African Association, Boahen 1964, 1–28.

1. *The Founding of the African Association*

1. Biographies of the founder members of the Association are given in *D.N.B.*, *Complete Peerage* and *Complete Baronetage*; R.A.A. 12–15, 42–7.
2. Rawdon is described as a 'conceited, solemn coxcomb' in the Journal of Elizabeth Holland: Ilchester 1908, I 165.
3. On Ferguson, Ferguson 1934, xxi–xxiii.
4. For a sympathetic study of Watson, Sykes 1934, 332–78.
5. Sinclair 1837, I 76–8, 202–8.
6. Boahen 1961 draws attention to the scientific interests of the members of the Saturday's Club; the details are taken from the biographies in *D.N.B.*
7. P.A.A. I 9–11; R.A.A. 46–7.
8. P.A.A. I 3–8; R.A.A. 45. The British Museum possesses a copy of the *Plan* of the Association printed as a special four-page brochure.

9. P.A.A. I 441; R.A.A. 14 n.
10. On the Dilettanti Society, Cust 1898.

2. *The First Explorers: John Ledyard in Cairo*
Material quoted here is given more fully in R.A.A. 48–62.
1. P.A.A. I 3–8.
2. *D.N.B.*: Lucas; P.A.A. I 19–20; A.A. Ctee, 13.6.1788, 17.6.1788;
S.P. 97. Note in Beaufoy's hand about Lucas, n.d.
3. B.M. Add. MSS. 33978/228. Matra to Banks, 13.2.1789.
4. P.A.A. I 43–4.
5. Sparks 1828; *D.N.B.*: Ledyard.
6. Sparks, 301, 396; P.A.A. I 18.
7. A.A. Ctee, 26.6.1788.
8. P.A.A. I 21; S.P. 4. Ledyard's expenses; S.P. 70. Lucas's expenses;
A.A. Ctee, 26.6.1788; S.P. 6–7. Extracts by Banks of letters from Ledyard,
Alexandria, 9.8.1788, and from Baldwin, n.d.
9. P.A.A. I 23–41; Sparks, 424.

3. *The First Explorers: Simon Lucas in Tripoli*
Material quoted here is given more fully in R.A.A. 63–9.
1. Tully 1819, I 1–4.
2. On the history of Tripoli, *E.I.*: Tripoli; Dearden 1957, Introduction.
3. F.O. 76/4. Lucas to Nepean, 12.11.1788; P.A.A. I 48.
4. Tully, I 111, II 1–6; P.A.A. I 50–65; F.O. 76/4. Lucas to Nepean,
8.12.1788.
5. F.O. 76/4. Lucas to Nepean, 8.12.1788; P.A.A. I 58–9.
6. P.A.A. I 78–80.
7. P.A.A. I 74–6.
8. P.A.A. I 112, 125, 128, 174, 175.
9. Details of Lucas's later career are in F.O. 76/5; D.T.C. IX 293.
Hornemann to Banks, 3.10.1799.

4. *Widening Contacts: Ben Ali and Swediaur; Consular Reports*
Material quoted here is given more fully in R.A.A. 70–84.
1. P.A.A. I 82; A.A. Ctee, 12.6.1789; D.T.C. VI 184. Beaufoy to Banks,
23.7.1789; S.P. 81. Thomson to Rawdon, 10.6.1789.
2. *B.U.*: Swediaur; B.L. 738. Letters from Swediaur to Banks,
1782–85; D.T.C. VI 190. Beaufoy to Banks, 23.7.1789; A.A. Ctee, 6.8.1789,
2.4.1790; S.P. 41. Swediaur's terms; S.P. 83. Precis by Banks of letter
from Dodsworth about Ben Ali's disappearance, 6.8.1789; S.P. 43. Note
about Swediaur's illness. Swediaur's name is sometimes spelt as Schwe-
diaur.
3. F.O. 52/7. Sydney to Barbary Consuls, 6.10.1788; F.O. 52/8. Matra
to Sydney, 28.3.1789 (S.P. 39. Banks's copy of Matra's letter).
4. F.O. 77/3. Traill to Sydney, 1.2.1789 (S.P. 51. Banks's copy of Traill's
letter).
5. A.A. Ctee, p. 30, separate entry, not part of minutes of a meeting.

SOURCES AND REFERENCES

5. The African Association: Organization, Finance and Membership

1. On the finances of the Association, R.A.A. 34–6, 264–70. The Sutro Papers contain a mass of material on the finances of the Association up to 1795, including a 'General Statement of the Receipts and Expenditure from 1789 to 1795', S.P. 364.

2. A.A.S.C., 21.6.1788, 25.4.1789; S.P. 55. List of members attending General Meeting, 30.5.1789.

3. Details of attendances are given in the Committee's Minute Book; S.P. 11, 22, 81. Letters from Rawdon; S.P. 431. Edwards to Ivatts, 25.8.1797.

4. The organization and membership of the Association is described and analysed in more detail in R.A.A. 15–25; for a full list of members with brief biographies, R.A.A. 264–70.

5. Watson 1960, 337–8.

6. *Gentleman's Magazine*, 1790, LX ii 633–6; P.A.A. I 199–205.

7. *D.N.B.*: Rennell; Markham 1895

II. THE APPROACH FROM THE WEST: 1790–99

1. Shabeni's Story: Timbuktu and Housa

Material quoted here is given more fully in R.A.A. 103–19.

1. Shabeni's account is referred to briefly in the Association's report for 1792, P.A.A. I 239; the full account was published by Jackson 1820; Sinclair 1837, I 204.

2. D.T.C. VIII 48. Matra to Banks, 5.8.1793; D.T.C. X 263. Matra to Banks, 18.10.1793.

3. Matra to Banks, 5.8.1793, 17.10.1793; P.A.A. I 258–9.

4. P.A.A. I 258.

2. Daniel Houghton

Material quoted here is given more fully in R.A.A. 120–40.

1. A.A. Ctee, 5.7.1790.

2. *D.N.B.*: Houghton; S.P. 187. Houghton's 'Memorial to the King's Most Excellent Majesty', applying for a pension, and giving details of his career; C.O. 267/18. References to Houghton's service at Goree; C.O. 267/20. Houghton to Townsend, 24.2.1783; S.P. 13. Musgrave to Banks, 18.7.1789.

3. A.A. Ctee, 18.12.1790.

4. S.P. 422. Dufaud to Banks, 9.6.1796; S.P. 186. Mrs Houghton to A.A., 26.5.1792; A.A. Ctee, 18.12.1790, Beaufoy's instructions to Houghton.

5. P.A.A. I 241–54.

6. P.A.A. I 318–22.

7. P.A.A. I 524.

8. P.A.A. I 300–2.

9. P.A.A. I 263–84.

10. S.P. 279–93. Letters and papers about Mrs Houghton; A.A.G.M., 31.5.1794, 13.6.1795, 27.5.1797.

3. The Consul in Senegambia

Material quoted here is given more fully in R.A.A. 141–57.

1. P.A.A. I 302–4; A.A.G.M. 26.5.1792.

2. S.P. 231. Beaufoy to Banks, n.d.; A.A.S.C., 25.5.1793, Brodie's election to A.A.; C.O. 267/10. Banks to Dundas, 24.12.1795, mentioning Brodie; on Brodie's relationship with Dundas, Furber 1931.

3. A.A.G.M., 26.5.1793; C.O. 267/10. Beaufoy's 'Remarks on the expediency of appointing a consul to Senegambia', 26.6.1793; copies of all the available correspondence relating to the Consul in Senegambia were written in A.A. Ctee, 6.3.1796.

4. S.P. 225. Beaufoy to Banks, 27.6.1793; A.A. Ctee, 6.3.1796, Willis's plan.

5. P.A.A. I 304.

6. S.P. 11. List of volunteers; for Dickson's contacts with Banks, B.L. 265.

7. *Transactions of the Linnean Society*, 1797, III 33, Park's paper; Park 1799, chapter 1; A.A. Ctee, 23.7.1794; P.A.A. I 304–5.

8. Thomson 1890, 175, 43–4, 165; Park 1815, iv, lxxxviii.

9. S.P. 314. Beaufoy to Banks, 17.10.1794: C.O. 267/10. Willis to Huskisson, 18.4.1795.

10. A.A. Ctee, 6.3.1796, 24.3.1796, 22.4.1796. The minutes contain the correspondence relating to the winding up of the scheme for a Consul in Senegambia.

4. Mungo Park

An authoritative biography of Mungo Park has not yet been written; none of the existing biographies make use of all the available material. The first memoir of the explorer was written by J. Wishaw and printed as the introduction to the Journal of Park's second expedition (Park 1815). Both Wishaw and the anonymous H.B., Park's second biographer (1835), drew on information from Park's friends and relations. Thomson's biography (1890) has the advantage of being written by one who was himself an explorer; it contains some new material. Gwynn 1934 is a sound straightforward account. Gibbon 1934 is a romantic impression, of interest because the author was able to read some letters of Park in private hands, even though he was allowed neither to quote the letters nor even to mention the owner's name.

The few documents belonging to the African Association and relating to Park's first mission are given in R.A.A. 157–71.

1. From this point the narrative follows the course of Park's *Travels*. As there are so many editions of this book and as quotations should prove easy to locate, detailed references have not been given.

2. Tauxier 1942 provides the most detailed history of the Bambara Kingdoms.

5. Park's Achievement

1. D.T.C. XI 88. Park to Banks, 26.9.1798; D.T.C. XI 81. Banks to Moss, Under-Secretary of State, 21.9.1798; D.T.C. XI 77. Dickson to

Banks, 20.9.1798; B.L. 647. Other letters between Banks and Park; D.T.C. XI 84. Edwards to Banks, 24.9.1798; D.T.C. XI 181. Edwards to Banks, 30.1.1799.

2. S.P. 478. Nicol to Banks, 7.5.1799; S.P. 463. Park's account with African Association.

3. Ilchester 1908, I 172; Gibbon 1934, 254, quoting the description of Park having the 'dignity of his Niger kings' but infuriatingly failing to give the source; Park 1815, iv, lxxxviii.

4. A.A.G.M., 25.5.1799; the version in P.A.A. II 1–6 is somewhat abridged.

III. THE APPROACH FROM THE NORTH: 1797–1802

1. *Frederick Hornemann*

A new edition of Hornemann's *Journal* of his journey from Cairo to the Fezzan, first published in 1802, has been prepared for the Hakluyt Society by E. W. Bovill. Much of the material quoted here is given more fully in R.A.A. 171–91. Additional information on Hornemann is to be found in Pahde 1895, Plischke 1937 and Bovill 1964, 3–38.

1. D.T.C. X i 50. Blumenbach to Banks, 4.5.1796; D.T.C. X i 91. Hornemann to Banks, 7.12.1796.

2. A.A.Ctee, 3.6.1796.

3. A.A.Ctee, 20.3.1797.

4. Cameron 1952, 212–13; S.P. 497–503. Banks's correspondence with Charretié.

5. Plischke 1937, 87. Hornemann to Heeren, 26.6.1797; D.T.C. X i 163. Hornemann to Banks, 12.7.1797.

6. B.L. 427. Hornemann to Edwards, 21.9.1797 and 18.10.1797; P.A.A. II 7. Hornemann to Edwards, 31.8.1798.

7. S.P. 431. Hornemann to Banks, 18.10.1797.

8. P.A.A. II 7. Hornemann to Edwards, 31.8.1798; Bonaparte on the Bedouin, quoted by Charles-Roux 1937, 100.

9. Hornemann 1802, 21; D.T.C. XI 64. Hornemann to Edwards, 2.9.1798.

10. Charles-Roux 1937, 241–2.

11. The account of Hornemann's experiences between Cairo and Murzuk are taken from his *Journal* (1802). The *Journal* was first printed in P.A.A. II.

12. Hornemann wrote an account of the Fezzan and 'A Memorandum containing various information respecting the Interior of Africa', both of which were printed with his journal. On the Fezzan, P.A.A. II 132–51; on the Tebu, 187–91; on the Tuareg, 192–5; on Bornu, 189–200; on Hausa, 196–8; on the Niger, 201–3.

13. Plischke 1937, 88. Hornemann to his mother, 19.10.1799; D.T.C. XI 265. Hornemann to Banks, 19.8.1799.

14. D.T.C. XI 324. Hornemann to Banks, 29.11.1799.

15. B.L. 429. Hornemann to Banks, 6.4.1800; Plischke 1937, 90. Hornemann to his mother, 6.4.1800.

16. P.A.A. II 320, 363, 421.

17. Lyon 1821, 132–3.

18. Denham and Clapperton 1828, II 296.

2. *J. G. Jackson and others in Morocco*

1. On Morocco in the eighteenth century, Julien 1952, 242–6; on Mogador, Terrasse 1949, 298–9.

2. Jackson, 1820, 67.

3. C.O. 267–10. Jackson's Memorandum, 12.12.1795; S.P. 435–40. Banks's correspondence with Jackson; R.A.A. 277–8.

4. D.T.C. X i 173. Jackson to Willis,–.9.1797; D.T.C. XI 173. Matra to Banks, 24.1.1799.

5. S.P. 450. Matra to Banks, 4.8.1798; D.T.C. XI 68, Matra to Banks, 7.9.1798.

6. D.T.C. XI 300. Matra to Banks, 5.11.1799.

7. D.T.C. XII 28. Banks to Matra, 4.2.1800; B.M. Add. MSS. 33980/231. Matra to Banks, 4.4.1800; B.M. Add. MSS. 33980/256. Matra to Banks, 1.12.1800; R.A.A. 279.

8. S.P. 624. Jackson to Banks, 29.6.1804; S.P. 626. Banks to Hawkesbury, 29.6.1804; D.T.C. XVI 320. Jackson to Banks, 21.9.1806.

9. The prospectus is given with other interesting material in Jackson 1820, 247–58.

IV. THE ENTERPRISE OF OTHERS

1. *The Sierra Leone Company*

Fyfe 1962 is the authoritative history of the colony.

1. *D.N.B.*: Hanway.

2. Smeathman 1786, 9.

3. Martin 1927, 108; Sierra Leone Company 1791, 54; the list of shareholders is given in Wadström 1794, II 341.

4. *D.N.B.*: Falconbridge; for a sketch of Mrs Falconbridge, Mackenzie-Grieve 1953.

5. The only published account of Watt and Winterbottom's journey is in the Sierra Leone Company's Report for 1794, 134–43. A manuscript copy of Watt's Journal is in the Library of Rhodes House, Oxford.

6. D.T.C. IX 91. Gray to Banks, –.7.1794; R.A.A. 275–7.

7. On Banks's association with Afzelius, B.L. 6–8, R.A.A. 275; D.T.C. IX 193. Banks to Gray, 16.2.1795.

8. Lindroth 1955; Fyfe 1962, 42–3.

2. *The Bulama Association*

Beaver published his journal and other documents in 1805. Beaver's biography was written by Smyth in 1829. Wadström 1794 provides some additional material including a list of subscribers. See also Hair 1960.

1. Beaver 1805, xii–xiv.

2. Beaver, i.

3. Beaver, 48.
4. Beaver, 495.

3. *W. G. Browne in Darfur*

Browne's Travels were published in 1799, with a slightly revised second edition in 1806. *D.N.B.* lists the sources for his biography.

1. B.L. 176. Browne to Boylston, 30.1.1792, passed on to Banks.

2. For Browne's letters from Egypt to Pinkerton, a literary man and the author of a great variety of works, including some on geography, Pinkerton 1830, I.

3. Burckhardt 1819, 349.

4. For a critical review of Browne, Wharton 1800.

5. This important chapter was extended and revised in the edition of 1806; Browne 1806, 531–2.

6. Browne 1806, 528.

7. D.T.C. XII 258–66. Browne to Banks, 22.9.1801; on Banks's association with Browne, R.A.A. 278.

8. On Browne's character, Beloe 1817, II 59–60, and Walpole 1820, 162–84; on his death, Porter 1822, I 268–73, and Walpole 1820, 181.

9. Walpole 1820, 184.

V. THE AFRICAN ASSOCIATION'S ACHIEVEMENT

Some of the material quoted here is given more fully in R.A.A. 246–56.
1. P.A.A. II 305.
2. P.A.A. II 306–8.
3. Park 1799, chapter 8.
4. P.A.A. II 268–82; S.P. 441–2. Jackson to Willis, 10.8.1800.
5. P.A.A. I 537, 533, 421–5; Jackson 1820, 40.

6. Rennell's maps were published with the African Association's *Proceedings* in 1790, 1798 and 1802.

7. Scott's *Memoir*, first published in the *Edinburgh Annual Register* 1811, reprinted in Leyden 1859.

8. Leyden 1859, 14–15 (Scott's *Memoir*).

9. Leyden 1859, 33–4 (Scott's *Memoir*); *D.N.B.*: Leyden.
10. P.A.A. II 3–7; Cultru 1910, 295–6.
11. P.A.A. II 327.
12. P.A.A. II 328.
13. *Edinburgh Review*, 1802, I 137.
14. *Annual Register*, 1800, 222.

THE ROOTS OF IMPERIALISM

II. FRANCE AND AFRICA

Saintoyant's three volumes provide a useful introduction to French colonialism in every part of the world up to 1815.

SOURCES AND REFERENCES

1. *Senegal*
   1. Cultru 1910, 217–45; Rubault's journey is described in Dufand 1802, 270–346.
   2. Saugnier 1792.
   3. Blanchot's instructions are given in full in Schefer 1921, I 181–92.
   4. Cultru 1910, 277–91.
   5. On the development of French colonial ideas, Lokke 1932.
   6. Talleyrand's paper is given in Dutot 1840, 324–38.
   7. Lokke 1932, 179–82.

2. *Egypt*
   Charles-Roux's *Bonaparte: Governor of Egypt* is a most stimulating work for any student of colonialism; it contains a useful bibliography on the Egyptian expedition.
   1. For French interest in Egypt before 1789, Lokke 1932, 90–101.
   2. Volney's pamphlet, *Considerations on the War with the Turks*, appeared in an English translation in 1788; for the passages relating to Egypt, 74–83.
   3. Lokke 1932, 186; Rose 1910, I 175.
   4. Talleyrand's Memorandum is printed in de la Jonquière 1899, I 15 and summarized in Charles-Roux 1937, 1–3; the ideas behind the Expedition are eloquently expounded by Fourier in his Preface to the *Description de l'Égypte*: Planches d'Antiquité, I xxxv.
   5. The hyperbole was made by H. A. L. Fisher; for a shrewd comment, Howard 1961, I xix.
   6. Little 1958, 53–4; Howard 1961, I 246. 'Proclamation to the People of Egypt', 2.7.1798.
   7. Charles-Roux 1937, 29, 353.
   8. Charles-Roux 1937, 58, 174.
   9. Charles-Roux 1937, 4–14.
   10. Charles-Roux 1937, 142–51.
   11. P.A.A. II 10. Hornemann to Edwards, 31.8.1798; on al-Attar, Ahmad 1960, 5–6.
   12. Saintoyant 1931, 149.

III. SPAIN AND MOROCCO

The Adventures of Ali Bey
   Ali Bey's *Travels* 1816 contain no hint as to the real purpose of his mission, which was not revealed until Roussier 1930 discovered in the French archives his memoir, 'Colonisation de l'Afrique' and published it *verbatim*. Roussier also traced from official French documents the history of Ali Bey's last expedition.
   1. General ideas on Spanish colonization in North Africa in Badia's memoir, Roussier 1930, 92–3.
   2. The description of Ali Bey's physical appearance was given to Burckhardt in Aleppo in 1810 by two Persian dervishes, Burckhardt 1819, xxxiii; F.O. 52/12. Matra's despatch, 6.6.1804, describing local reactions to Ali Bey.

436

3. F.O. 52/12. Matra's despatch, 6.6.1804; F.O. 52/13. Matra's despatch, 29.1.1805.

4. On Badia's early career, *B.U.*: Badia.

5. Roussier 1930, 94–6.

6. For a report on Badia in England, *Allgemeine Geographische Ephemeriden*, 1803, XI 100.

7. D.T.C. XIII 239. Banks to a Consul in North Africa, 29.8.1802; F.O. 52/12. Matra's despatch, 6.6.1804; B.L. 598–9. Matra's correspondence with Banks.

8. Roussier 1930, 100.

9. F.O. 52/12. Matra's despatch, 6.6.1804.

10. Badia's account in his Memoir of his adventures in Morocco, Roussier 1930, 100–11.

11. F.O. 52/12. Matra's despatch, 6.6.1804.

12. F.O. 52/13. Matra's despatch, 29.1.1805.

13. Burckhardt 1819, xxxiii.

14. Roussier 1930, 67–8, 110–12.

15. Roussier 1930, 69–79.

IV. BRITAIN AND THE NIGER

Some of the material quoted here is given more fully in R.A.A. 211–17.

1. D.T.C. XI 233. Banks to Hawkesbury, 8.6.1799 (also in C.O. 2/1).

2. C.O. 267/18, material on Goree, 1800–6.

3. Park 1815, xxxii. Park to Banks, 31.7.1800.

4. Thomson 1890, 179. Park to his wife, 12.3.1801.

5. D.T.C. XII 265. Park to Banks, 13.10.1801.

6. Golbéry 1803, I 56.

7. C.O. 2/1. Banks to Sullivan, 1.8.1802.

8. C.O. 2/1. Beaver to Sullivan, 14.8.1802.

9. C.O. 2/1. Macaulay to Sullivan, 4.9.1802. Rennell to Sullivan, 17.10.1802.

10. C.O. 2/1. Sullivan's memorandum, n.d.

11. D.T.C. XIV 161. Banks to Park, 10.10.1803; D.T.C. XIV 162. Park to Banks, 20.10.1803; D.T.C. XIV 163. Banks to Park, 26.10.1803.

12. Park 1815, xxxiv; Lockhardt, *Life of Scott*, chapter 13.

13. Gray 1940, 287, states that Stevenson was commandant at Goree; this is a mistake, as the commandant at Goree was Lt.-Col. Fraser, C.O. 267/18.

14. C.O. 2/1. Stevenson to Sullivan, 10.3.1804; C.O. 2/1 contains other letters from Stevenson, the earliest dated 13.1.1804.

15. C.O. 2/1. Sullivan's memorandum, n.d.

16. H.B. 1835, 174–5; Park 1815, xxxvii.

17. B.M. Add. MSS. 37232/54. Camden to Banks, 28.9.1804.

18. Park 1815, xxxix–xlvii; B.M. Add. MSS. 37232/56. Maxwell to Park, 12.10.1804.

19. D.T.C. XIV 242. Banks's comment on Park's memoir.

20. D.T.C. XV 24. Banks's notes on his conference with Camden, 18.12.1804.

2. *Park's Second Expedition*

1. The details of Park's journey are taken from his Journal (Park 1815). Some of the later editions of Park's *Travels* contain a version of the Journal that has been substantially abridged. Papers relating to Park's stay at Santiago and Goree are contained in C.O. 2/2.

2. P.A.A. II 322–5.

3. B.M. Add. MSS. 37232/63. Martyn to Megan, 1.11.1805.

3. *The Death of Mungo Park*

1. D.T.C. XVI 320. Jackson to Banks, 21.9.1806; B.M. Add. MSS. 37232/69. Court to Banks, 2.12.1806.

2. C.O. 267/18. Windham to Lloyd, 12.7.1806; Park 1815, 173–219, Isaaco's narrative.

3. Laing's letter is quoted in Barth 1858, V 202 n.; Barth's references to Park, Barth 1858, IV 453, 505, V 162, 180, 201–2, 245.

4. Thomson 1890, 243–245.

5. This story was passed on to the African Institution by the Rev. Robert Chetfield, a Cambridgeshire clergyman, who had received the news from his brother in Bombay: S.P. 712. Chetfield's letter, 21.5.1813.

6. Clapperton 1829, 104, 123, 132, 134–5; Lander 1830, I 144–9; Lander 1832, II 6–8, 12–13, 132, 140 (Bussa), 35–38 (Yauri); Hastings 1927, 190.

7. Owen 1961, 165.

8. H.B. 1835, 286–7.

9. Denham 1828, II 384–6; Barth 1858, IV 505.

10. Owen 1961, 92.

V. BRITAIN AND THE WEST COAST

Two chapters in the *Cambridge History of the British Empire*, Vol. II— 'British Enterprise in Tropical Africa' by A. P. Newton, and 'The Abolition of the Slave Trade' by R. Coupland—provide an introduction to the development of British interests in West Africa.

1. For early Protestant missionaries in West Africa, Groves 1948, 172–7 and Ward 1958, 200–3.

2. Knutsford 1900, 122.

3. For a review of missionary activity in West Africa up to 1815, Groves 1948, 197–218.

4. Ward 1958, 146.

5. Priestley 1961, 47.

6. On the rise of Ashanti, Ward 1958, 116–26, 137–61; Priestley and Wilks 1960, Priestley 1961.

7. African Institution, *Report*, 1807, 65–9.

8. *Report of the Commissioners sent to investigate some of the Settlements and Forts on the Coast of Africa, Parliamentary Papers*, 1816, VII ii, 122; for statistics on the slave trade, Lloyd 1949, 5, 61, 255; *Memoirs of the late Captain Crow*, 1830, 137, quoted by Lloyd 1949, 3.

9. Coupland 1933, 155.

10. Corry 1807, 127, quoted by Dike 1956, 15; on British attitudes to West Africa, 1815–80, Robinson, Gallacher and Denny 1961, 27–33.

THE AGE OF THE AFRICAN ASSOCIATION: II
1802-15

I. THE AFRICAN ASSOCIATION: 1802-15

Some of the material quoted here is given more fully in R.A.A. 258–63.
1. S.P. 453–5. List of members, 25.5.1799; details of new members from A.A.S.C.; D.T.C. XI 28. Banks to Matra, 4.2.1800.
2. S.P. 389. Banks to Park, n.d. (1795?); Barrow 1849, 41.
3. *D.N.B.*: Young, Hamilton.
4. S.P. 400. Revival of Saturday's Club, minutes of meeting, 19.3.1796.
5. S.P. 706. Meeting of the African Association, –.2.1813.
6. Smee 1844.

II. THE APPROACH FROM THE SOUTH. HENRY NICHOLLS

The material quoted here is given more fully in R.A.A. 191–210.
1. S.P. 622. Banks's notes for A.A.G.M., 31.5.1800; A.A.G.M., 29.5.1803. Banks to Blumenbach, n.d.; A.A.G.M., 28.5.1804; A.A. Ctee., 4.6.1804, 9.6.1804.
2. A.A. Ctee, 2.8.1804.
3. A.A. Ctee. Information brought by Nicholls from Liverpool, pp. 207–11.
4. A.A. Ctee. Nicholls's expenses, p. 227.
5. Barbot 1732, 382–4; Forde 1956.
6. P.A.A. II 384–414. Nicholls's letter from Calabar, 15.2.1805.

III. THE EASTERN SUDAN. J. L. BURCKHARDT

Burckhardt's letters to the African Association were published in the introduction to his *Travels in Nubia*, 1819. His letters to his family in Switzerland have been edited and published by his descendants, C. Burckhardt-Sarasin and H. Schwabe-Burckhardt in 1956 (they are referred to below as *Briefe*). Burckhardt's accounts of his travels were published from his journals after his death: Nubia 1819, Syria 1822, Arabia 1829.

Some of the material relating to the African Association is given more fully in R.A.A. 218–24.
1. A.A.G.M., 30.5.1807, 22.6.1807; A.A. Ctee., 21.3.1808.
2. Burckhardt 1819, iii–iv; *Briefe*, 64–95.
3. A.A. Ctee., 21.3.1808.
4. *Briefe*, 94–112, especially letters of 1.5.1808, 15.8.1808.
5. Burckhardt 1819, v; *Briefe*, 109–12.
6. A.A. Ctee., 20.1.1809; *Briefe*, 112–14.
7. Burckhardt 1819, vi–xxv; *Briefe*, 115–19.
8. Burckhardt 1819, xxv–xliii; *Briefe*, 119–39; Burckhardt 1822.
9. Burckhardt 1819, xlii, xliv–xlvii.
10. Burckhardt 1819, xlvii–lvii, 164–8; *Briefe*, 145–8.

11. Burckhardt 1819, 169–209.
12. Burckhardt 1819, 210–57.
13. Burckhardt 1819, 277–323.
14. Burckhardt 1819, 288.
15. Burckhardt 1819, 344–5.
16. Burckhardt 1819, 359.
17. Burckhardt 1819, 364–6, 406–15.
18. Burckhardt 1819, 453; Burckhardt 1829, I 5, 7.
19. Burckhardt 1829, I 134–6, 150–2, II 140–4.
20. Burckhardt 1819, lix–lxxxvi; *Briefe*, 148–87.
21. Burckhardt 1819, 366, 443; Halls 1834, II 20; Richardson 1822, I 161–2; Turner 1820, II 357–8; Belzoni 1820, 6.
22. *Briefe*, 20; Burckhardt 1819, lxxxvi–lxxxiv.

IV. GERMAN TRAVELLERS IN NORTH AFRICA

1. U. J. Seetzen
1. On Seetzen's career, Kruse 1854; the plan for his journey is printed in *Monatliche Correspondenz*, 1802, VI.
2. *Monatliche Correspondenz*, 1809, XIX (Darfur), 1810, XXI ('Mobba' —i.e. Wadai and countries to the West).
3. *Monatliche Correspondenz*, 1811, XXIV 183, quoted by Plischke 1937, 47.

2. Heinrich Röntgen
1. For the fullest account of Röntgen's career, Plischke 1937, 42–7.
2. Blumenbach in *Monatliche Correspondenz*, 1811, XXIV 467, quoted by Plischke 1937, 43.
3. Plischke 1937, 44; *D.N.B.*: Benjamin Bathurst.
4. *Quarterly Review*, February 1810, III 201, April 1817, XXXIV 321–3; Plischke 1937, 44; S.P. 677. König to Banks, n.d. giving details of Röntgen's supporters.
5. Plischke 1937, 44; S.P. 678. Röntgen to Banks, 20.11.1810; for Banks's association with Röntgen, R.A.A. 281–3.
6. Plischke 1937, 95–8. Röntgen to an English lady, 2.4.1811.
7. Plischke 1937, 99–102. Röntgen to his brother, 21.7.1811, describing his stay in Mogador; *Quarterly Review*, April 1817, XXXIV 321–3, accounts obtained from English merchants.
8. Plischke 1937, 45.
9. S.P. 714. Banks's notes on A'Court's statement, 14.2.1814.
10. Caillié 1830, II 361–2.
11. Reichard's theory was first advanced in an article in the *Monatliche Correspondenz*, May 1802, V 402–15, expanded in an article in the *Allgemeine Geographische Ephemeriden*, August 1803, XII 157–67 summarized by Malte Brun 1813, IV 653, and first presented to English readers in Park 1815, cxxi.

V. ETHIOPIA. LORD VALENTIA AND HENRY SALT

Salt's account of his first mission to Ethiopia is given in Valentia 1809, of his second mission in Salt 1814. His biographer, Halls 1834, supplies further details. F.O. 1/1 contains official correspondence on the second mission. For Salt's connection with the African Association, R.A.A. 224–230.

1. A.A. Ctee., 26.12.1808.

2. Halls 1834, I 1, 15, 45–7, 60–2; Mathew 1947, 109.

3. Halls 1834, I 63; Mathew 1947, 114–16.

4. Valentia 1809, II 1–5.

5. Farington's *Diary*, IV 38, quoted by Mathew 1947, 121; on Pearce's early life, Halls 1831, I 1–35.

6. Valentia 1809, III 39; Mathew 1947, 126.

7. Salt's experiences in Ethiopia, Valentia 1809, II 441, III 258; his comments of Bruce, Valentia 1809, III 209–11; Mathew 1947, 121–8.

8. Valentia 1809, III 145.

9. Valentia 1809, III 261, 275–6.

10. Valentia 1809, III 276–78; F.O. 1/1. Valentia's 'Observations on the Trade of the Red Sea', 13.9.1808.

11. Halls 1834, I 135–7.

12. Salt 1814, 131–3, 498; A.A.G.M., 25.5.1811.

13. Pearce's account of his adventures is given in Halls 1831, I.

14. Salt 1814, 266–7.

15. Salt 1814, 363.

16. Salt 1814, 383–4, 425–6.

17. Salt 1814, 497–8; details of the mission's expenses, F.O. 1/1.

18. Halls 1831, I 53.

19. There is much information on Salt's life in Egypt in Halls 1834, II.

INDEX

Abbreviations: A.A. – African Association; E – English; F – French; G – German; P – Portuguese.

Figures in italics after the names of certain peoples, places or states refer to the number of the map or maps on which they are shown.

Abd-ar-Rahman, Sultan of Darfur, 279–80
Abd-ar-Rahman, Haji, Foreign Minister of Tripoli, 200
Abdsulem, Mulay, of Morocco, 315, 318
Abolitionists, 138, 182, 187, 270, 350
Abomey, 362
Accra, *2*, 12, 185, 343
A'Court, W., E diplomat, 383
Adal, *12*, 112
Adamawa, 7, 47
Adanson, M., F traveller in Senegal, 68, 172, 404
Addington, H., member of A.A., 214
Admiralty, British, 158
Adrar, 21
Afonso, Mani-Congo, 115
African, Africans: *and Europe:* acquiring European dress, language, etc., 30, 116, 365; Europeans 'a small tribe with red skins', 33; geographical ideas about, 33; visiting Europe, 31, 34, 147, 362
    attitudes to Europeans: demanding presents, 90, 222, 232–3; suspicious and hostile, 83, 89, 128, 221, 235, 239, 279, 337; welcoming and friendly, 81, 88, 115, 223, 233, 241, 272, 338
    impressions of white men: bringing 'new fashion', 353; cannibals, 241; causing unhappiness, 31; 'formidable but ignorant heathens', 30; legends about, 31; magical beings, 30; magicians, 337; monsters, 99; strange, 232
    qualities ascribed to by Europeans: barbarous and cruel, 69, 71–2; brutal, compared to beasts, 37, 42, 58; careless and stupid, 37, 57–8, 69, 70; civil and good-natured, 57, 69, 70, 81, 88, 272; crafty, fraudulent, 70, 74, 378; gay and happy, 60, 71, 233; indolent, 70; not different from Europeans in 'characteristic feelings', 233; not disagreeable, 70; not to be despised on account of colour, 70; poor, 60; sensual, gluttonous, 70, 378 *see also* Muslims, attitude to Christians; slave trade, African reactions to abolition of
African Association (Association for Promoting the Discovery of the Interior Parts of Africa); achievement of, 285, 289, 290, 293; and Bonaparte, 262; clerk: *see* Ivatts; committee, 196, 359, 368; explorers: *see* Burckhardt, Hornemann, Houghton, Ledyard, Lucas, Nicholls, Park, Salt; finances, 202, 211, 361, 366; foundation of, xiv, 196; and India, 359; informants: *see* Ben Ali, Dalzel, Dodsworth, Magra, Matra, Traill, Shabeni; membership, 212–4, 357; president, 359, *see also* Rawdon; prospective explorers, 220, 227, *see also* Crammond, Eschauzier, Fitzgerald, Jackson, Swediaur, Walwyn, Weales; records of, 429; reports, 215, 243, 262, 357, 405–8; rules of, 196; secretary, 196, 212, 243, 358, *see also* Banks, Beaufoy, Edwards, Hamilton A., Hamilton W., Young; and Sierra Leone Company, 273; and Spain, 292; treasurer, 196, 212, 259, *see also* Banks, Hardwicke, Metcalfe
African Institution, 351, 408
Afzelius, A., Swedish naturalist, 274
Aga Muhammad, Egyptian Mamluk, 203
Agades, *1*, *3*, *7*, 22, 54, 103
Agadir, *8*, 97, 100, 265
Agisymba, 47, 92
Ahmad al-Mansur, Sultan of Morocco, 101

Air, 4, 21, 210–11
Akan, 10
Akim, 349
Alaska, 123
Albreda, 2, 142, 299, 327
Alcazar, battle of, 101
Aleppo, 164, 369–70, 379
Alexandria, 1, 108, 112, 253, 278, 394
Algeria, 4
Algiers, 1, 17, 28, 101, 105–7, 160, 162, 166, 397
Ali, Fulani host to Hornemann, 262
Ali, Browne's agent in Darfur, 278
Ali, Haji, of Bornu, 375
Ali, King of Ludamar, 235–6
Ali Bey, see Badia, Domingo
Ali Karamanli, Pasha of Tripoli, 206
Alkalawa, 218
Allen, A. R., 262
Allgemeine Geographische Ephemeriden, 291
Almoravids, xiv
Alvarez, F., P traveller in Ethiopia, 114, 401, 410
Amadi Fatouma, Park's guide, 339–42
Amazon, river, 124
America, exploration of, 123–4, 130–1
Amhara, Amharic, 1, 12, 10, 12, 24, 114
Amir Sultan, King of Legibbilli, 143
Ammonium, see Siwa
al-Andalus, xiii
Anderson, Ailie, see Park, Mrs
Anderson, Alexander, Park's brother-in-law, 330, 336, 338–9
Anderson, Dr, Park's father-in-law, 228–9, 246
André, d', F consul in Tripoli, 102
Angola, 116–17, 125, 130, 132
Annual Register, 153, 289, 293
Anokye, priest of Ashanti, 349
Anson, G., E admiral and circum-navigator, 42, 130
Ansongo, 9, 341
Antalo, 12, 389
Antera Duke, Calabar trader, 364
Antioch, 370
Anti-Slavery Movement, 177–83; see also Abolitionists
Appolinaire, F agent in Bambuk, 88
Aquapim, 186
Arab, Arabic: geographers, xvi, 51–9; language, 12–13, 148–9, 247, 251, 267, 311, 368, 382; people, 10, 12; see also Bedouin
Arabia, 371, 376–7, 379
architecture, 14, 16
Ardra, 75
Arguin, 2, 63, 79, 86, 142
Aristotle, 50

Arma, 25; see also Moroccans in Timbuktu
Arrhenius, Swedish traveller in West Africa, 187
Ashanti, 1, 63, 79, 86, 142
Ashmole, E., E collector, 154–5
Asia, exploration of, 122, 130–1
Asiatic Society of Bengal, 149
Askia Muhammad, Songhai Emperor, 54, 56
Assim, 349
Astley, T., E publisher, 40, 62, 120–2, 399, 404
Aswan, 10, 278
Asyut (var. Assiut), 6, 22
Atar (var. Tarra), 83
Atkins, J., E ship's surgeon and writer, 68, 403
Atlas, 4, 17, 49
al-Attar, Hasan ibn Muhammad, Egyptian scholar, 308–9
Augila, 1, 258
Australia (*Terra Australis*), 130, 132, 157
Axum, 12, 389, 393
Aylesbury, Countess of, member of A.A., 213
al-Azhar, 308–9

Badagry, xvi
Badia, Domingo, *alias* Ali Bey, Spanish traveller in Morocco, 310–19, 398, 408, 436
Baguirmi (var. Bagherme, Gaoga), 1, 7, 24, 58
Bahr-al-Ghazal, 7, 281
Baker, S., E explorer, 374
Bakkannee (? Bokani), 262
al-Bakri, Arab geographer, 51–2
Balbus, Cornelius, Roman general, 47
Baldwin, G., E consul in Egypt, 202, 253
Bamako, 5, 9, 240, 336
Bamba, 9, 341
Bambara: people, 1, 10, 11; kingdom, 4, 5, 7, 11, 25, 90, 242, 246; see also Kaarta, Segu; trade of, 88, 210; reports on, 96, 288; Park in, 233–9, 246, 336–9
Bambuk: 2, 9; equated with Wangara, 23, 59; French in, 88–91, 96; gold of, 129, 230; Hodges in, 83, 130; Houghton in, 222–3; proposal for English consul in, 225–7, 325
Bankes, T., E geographer, 42, 405
Banks, Sir Joseph: career and character, 167–76, 350; importance of, 138, 398; and Africa, 173–6, 185, 198; and African Association, 193–8, 212, 220, 229, 243, 357; and Australia,

INDEX

85, 173, 358; and Badia, 313; and Blumenbach, 250–1, 361; and Browne, 277, 282–3; and Bruce, 166, 175; and Burckhardt, 367, 371; and Colonial Office, 324; and Cook, 158, 169–71, 174; and Dilettanti Society, 198; and France, 252; and George III, 170, 174; and Hornemann, 250–3, 261–2; and Houghton, 220; and imperialism, 244, 321–2; and Isert, 175, 185; and Jackson, 265–7, 340; and Ledyard, 200–1; and Linnaeus, 170; and Matra, 175, 200, 265–6, 313; and Park, 227–8, 242–5, 322–3, 326, 329–31, 339, 358; and Röntgen, 382–3; and Royal Society, 171–2, 213, 358; and Salt, 394; and Sierra Leone Company, 273–4; and Solander, 152, 169; and Swediaur, 209, correspondence of, 427–8

Banu Hilal, 21
Banu Sulaim, 21
Baptist missionaries, 347
Baptista, Angolan *pombeiro*, 120
Baqqara, 10, 24
Barbary, 37, 104–7; *see also* Algiers, Morocco, Tripoli, Tunis
Barbauld, Capt., E army officer, 229
Barbot, James, F trader in West Africa, 121
Barbot, John or Jean, F trader in West Africa, 67–8, 70, 74–5, 128, 363, 403
Barclays, members of A.A., 214
Bardeoa, 54
Barker, E consul in Syria, 369–70
Barnes, E governor of Senegambia, 145
Barracunda Falls, 2, 78, 81–3, 221
Barreto, F., P general, 118
Barros, J. de, P historian, 62–5, 96, 128, 400
Barrow, J., E traveller, 382
Barth, H., G explorer, 188, 341, 345, 374
Batavia, 9, 169
Bathurst, Earl, Colonial Secretary, 367, 382
Bathurst, B., E diplomat, 381
Battell, A., E traveller in Angola, 120, 401, 414
Beaglehole, J. C., quoted, 156, 167, 169, 171
Beaufoy, H., secretary of A.A.: and Ben Ali, 209; and Browne, 277; and consul in Senegambia, 225–6, 229; and foundation of A.A., 194–8, 214; and Houghton, 221, 223; and Ledyard, 200–1; and Lucas, 200; and Shabeni, 217, 268; death of, 242–3; quoted, 159, 216
Beaufoy, M., member of A.A., 214

Beaver, P., E naval officer, 274–6, 324, 327–8, 407
Bedouin Arabs, 20–1, 106, 254, 256
Bedwell, W., E orientalist, 148
Beechey, F. W., E naval officer, 159
Behring, Capt., Russian explorer, 123
Beja, *1*, 10, 20, 375
Bellefond, Villault de, F traveller in West Africa, 65, 67, 402
Belzoni, G. B., Italian archaeologist in Egypt, 377
Bemoy, Wolof ruler, 63
Ben Ali, Moroccan trader, 209–12, 219
Bencoolen, 9, 149, 225
Bengal, 9, 149
Benguela, 119
Benin: Kingdom and city, *1*, 26, 70, 74–5; E in, 66–7; on European maps, 93; human sacrifice in, 72; missionaries in, 131; P in, 62, 65; Reichard and, 380
Ben Nasser, Moroccan chief, 266
Benown, *5*, 235–6
Benue, river, *1*, 6–7, 260, 365
Berber people, 10, 12
Berber, Nubia, *10*, 372
Berbera, *12*, 386, 392
Bermudez, J., P traveller in Ethiopia, 113, 401–2
Berthollet, C. L., F scientist, 254, 306
Bilad-al-Djarid (Biledulgerid), 37
Bilad-as-Sudan; see Sudan
Bilma, 22
Birmingham, 140, 178–9
Birrell, A., quoted, 154
Bisharein, *10*, 375
Bissagos, 276, 301
Blaeu, Dutch cartographer, *3*, 92
Blanchot, F governor of Senegal, 300
Blake, William, 146
Blemmyes, 49
Blumenbach, J. F., G ethnologist: importance of, 188, 190; interest in Africa, 189–90, 291, 384; and African Association, 250, 291; and Banks, 250–1, 361; and Burckhardt, 367; and Hornemann, 250–1; and Röntgen, 380; and Seetzen, 379; and von Zachs, 291
Boahen, A. A., xx, 428
Bonaparte, Napoleon: and Badia, 318; expedition to Egypt, 110, 254, 302–6; and Hornemann, 254, 262; and imperialism, 352; and Senegal, 300, 324
Bondou, *5*, 26, 32, 222, 232, 242, 327
Bonny, *1*, 26, 126, 362
Bordeaux, 184
Borgu (*var.* Bourgou, Burgu), 25, 95, 211

445

Bornu (*var.* Borno, Bornou, Burnu, Dar Bornou): empire of, *1*, *3*, *4*, *6*, *7*, *11*, xiv, 22–4, 200, 216; Christian slaves in, 101–2; Hornemann in, 260–2; Leo Africanus in, 57–8; Lucas on, 205–8; pilgrims from, 375
Bornu, prince of, 34
Bosman, W., Dutch trader on Gold Coast, 41, 67, 132, 402
Boswell, James, 157
Botany Bay, 85
botany, study of, 151–2, 168, 172
Bovill, E. W., quoted, 97–8
Bowdich, T. E., E consul in Ashanti, 126
Bowen, E., E geographer, 41–2, 404
Brakna Moors, 86
Brandenbergers, 188
Brass, 26
Brass, W., E gardener, 175, 198
Brevedent, de, Jesuit missionary, 110
Bristol, 140
Bristol, Earl of, member of A.A., 213
British Museum, 155, 394
Brodie, A., E politician, 225
Broughton, W. R., E naval officer and explorer, 158
Browne, W. G., E explorer in Darfur, 33, 132, 256, 276–86, 367, 406
Bruce, James, traveller in Ethiopia: career and character, 159–67; European contacts, 184, 190; influence of, 138; literary sense, 248; quoted, 156; self-financed, 132, 198, 276; Banks and, 175; Browne and, 277, 279, 281; Burckhardt and, 371, 375; Salt and, 388–90; *Travels*, 406, 427
Brue, A., F governor of Senegal, 41, 68, 87–91, 144, 199
Bruns, P. J., G scholar, 291, 406
Bubaker, 236
Bucknor Sano, Gambian trader, 80
Buffon, F naturalist, 189
Bulama: island, *9*, 274–6, 328; Association, 187, 215, 275–6, 301, 324–5, 434
Burckhardt, J. L., G explorer in service of A.A., 166, 188, 247, 279, 318, 366–78, 381, 393, 398, 409, 439
Burke, Edmund, 153, 182
Burney, Fanny, quoted, 162
Burton, R. F., E explorer, 248, 360, 396
Bute, Earl of, member of A.A., 152, 213
Bussa (*var.* Bousa), *4*, *9*, 95, 342–3
Byng, J., Viscount Torrington, quoted, 162

Ca' da Mosto, A. de (Cadmosto), 29, 41, 60–2, 400

Cahill, E merchant in Morocco, 336
Caiado, A., P trader in Mozambique, 118
Caillié, R., F explorer, 132, 247, 273
Cairo: European traders in, 109–10; explorers in – Browne, 278, 281, 283; Bruce, 164–5; Burckhardt, 369, 371; Hornemann, 251–6; Ledyard, 201–3; Seetzen, 377–8; French occupation of, 304–8; reported river connection with Timbuktu, 286; trade of, 112
Calabar, *1*, xvi, 26, 30, 361–5
Call, Sir J., member of A.A., 214
Cambridge, University of, 148, 214, 368, 378
Camden, Earl, Colonial Secretary, 328, 331
Cameron, H. C., quoted, 173
Cameroons, 5, 6, 8
Canada, 124
Canning, G., Foreign Secretary, 367, 391
Canorfa, 102
Cão, Diego, P explorer, 115
Cape of Good Hope, 117, 119, 121–2, 198, 384
Cape Verde, 86, 187
Capuchins, 117, 121, 131
Carr, E. H., quoted, xxi
Carré, J. M., quoted, 107
Carron iron-works, 160
Carter, Salt's companion in Ethiopia, 388
Carthaginians, 44, 161, 218
cartography, European, 92–5, 97; *see also* D'Anville, Ptolemy, Rennell, Reichard
Carysfoot, Earl of, member of A.A., 194–6
Castell, E., E orientalist, 149
Catholic missionaries, 131, 147; *see also* missionaries
Cayor, 60
Cazembe, 120
Ceuta, *8*, 100, 312
Chad, lake (*var.* Zad), *1*, 7, 260
Chamba, 24
Chambers, E., E encyclopaedist, 153
Chambonneau, F trader on Senegal, 87
Chandos, Duke of, 84
Charretié, J., F diplomat, 252
Chenier, L. de, F consul in Morocco, 106, 405
Chesterfield, Earl of, quoted, 37
Chichoa, 118
China, 122–3, 132
Choiseul, Duc de, 302
Cholmondeley, Earl of, member of A.A., 213

Christians: in North Africa, 97, 102; *see also* missionaries, slaves
Christian VI of Denmark, 108
Christiansborg, *2*, 185
Church Missionary Society, 347–8, 395
Church, R. J. Harrison, quoted, 125
Churchill, A and J., E collectors of travels, 40, 402
Clapham Sect, 351
Clapperton, H., explorer, xv, xvi, xxi, 126, 128, 159, 263, 347
Clarke, Dr, E librarian, 378
Clarkson, J., E governor of Sierra Leone, 271
Clarkson, T., E abolitionist, 180–2, 271, 350, 408
climate, 7–9, 215
Cobbe (modern Kobbai), *6*, 279–80, 372
coffee, 150, 186
Coffin, W., Valentia's servant, 391, 395
Colaço, J., P agent in West Africa, 64
Colbert, 108
Coleridge, S. T., 146, 190
collections of travels, 39–40
Compagnon, F agent in Bambuk, 89, 129
Conakry, 8
Congo: kingdom, 31, 115–16, 120–1, 130, 132; river, 7, 115, 329, 397
convict settlement, 85
Conway, General, member of A.A., 193–7, 359
copper, 99, 121
Cornwallis, Lord, 219
Cosseir (modern Quseir), 377
Courland, Duke of, 82
Coutts, T., member of A.A., 214
Cowper, William, 140
Crammond, E traveller, 211
Crawford, O. G. S., 111
Crone, G. R., quoted, 39
Cross, river, 363
Crow, Capt., E trader in West Africa, 352
crusades, 28, 107
Cuanza, river, 117
Cugoano, O., Fante writer, 147, 405
Cumming, T., E merchant, 143
Curtin, P. D., quoted, 9–10
Cuvier, F scientist, quoted, 170
Cydamus; *see* Ghadames
Cyrenaica, *1*, 4, 20, 162
Cyrene, 45

Daer, Lord, member of A.A., 213
Dagomba, *1*, 25, 262
Dahomey, *1*, 6, 26, 68, 70–1, 131, 362
Dakar, 86
Dalrymple, E., E adventurer, 275–6

Dalzel, A., E trader in Dahomey, 72, 140, 361–2, 406
Daman Jumma, African trader, 234–7
Damascus, 318, 370
Damberger, C. F., G imposter, 291, 407
Dampier, W., E sailor, 156
Danakil, *1*, *12*, 24
D'Anville, J. B., F cartographer, *4*, 48, 94–5, 111, 123, 128, 404
Dapper, O., Dutch geographer, 41, 67, 402
Daradus, river, 95; *see also* Senegal
Darb-al-Arba'in, *6*, 22, 278
Darfur: kingdom, *1*, *6*, 5, 24; Browne in, 132, 277–81, 286–7; cul-de-sac for explorers, 280, 365; ideas about Europeans in, 33; Ledyard and, 203
Dar Kulla, *6*, 362
Dasibari, 46–7
Davidson, B., quoted, 72
Day, T., E writer, 178
Debo, lake, 6
Debundscha, 8
Defoe, Daniel, 142, 177–8
Dei, Benedetto, Florentine merchant, 100
Delaporte, F vice-consul in Morocco, 384
Delisle, F cartographer, 93
Demba, Park's servant, 231, 235–6
Denham, D., E explorer, xv, 248, 344
Denkera, 76
Denon, V., F artist in Egypt, 307, 407
Description de l'Égypte, 367–8, 408
Detroye, F army officer in Egypt, quoted, 255–6
D'Ghies, Muhammad, of Tripoli, 252–4, 266
Dias, B., P explorer, 117
Dickson, J., Park's brother-in-law, 227–8, 242–3
Dickson, W., E writer, 187
Dieppe, 86
Dilettanti, Society of, 154, 198
disease, 9, 127
Dodsworth, E trader, 209–11, 219
Dolomieu, F geologist in Egypt, 307
Dongola, *6*, *10*, 112, 371
Dramanet, 88
Drake, Sir Francis, 130
Dufaud, C., Houghton's companion, 220–1
Duke Ephraim, Calabar trader, 364
Duke Town, Calabar, 363
Dundas, H., Secretary of State, 225–6, 233
Dupuis, J., E consul in Ashanti, 33
Dutch: in West Africa, 26, 86; in South Africa, 102, 115, 121–2

East Africa, 117, 121, 359, 379, 396
East India Company, English, 109, 123, 359, 369, 391–2
Edinburgh Review, 292
Edwards, B., secretary of A.A., 212, 243–4, 358
Efik, 364
Eghalir, 211
Egbo, 364
Egbo Young Eyambo, Calabar trader, 364
Ego Honesty, 364
Egypt: people, 10, 12; government of, 20; *see also* Mamluks; attitude to Europeans in, 28, 107, 202; European travellers in, 108–10; explorers in, *see* Cairo: explorers in; French expedition to, 302–9; Salt as consul in, 394
Encyclopaedia Britannica, 153; quoted, 129
English: in East Africa, 121; in Egypt, 108–9, 304; on the Gambia, 78–85; in Morocco, 105–6; in Senegambia, 143–5; in South Africa, 119; in West Africa, 26, 128, 346–53
Equiano, O., Ibo writer, 33, 147–8, 405
Eschauzier, E army officer, 366
Esne, *10*, 371
Etearchus, King of Ammon, 45
Ethiopia: land, *12*, 5, 37; kingdom, 24, 132; Europeans in, 29, 111–14, 125, 130, 343; Browne and, 277–8; Bruce in, 164–5; Röntgen and, 381–2; Salt in, 386–90
eunuchs, 210–11
European Magazine, quoted, 288
Evangelicals, 179
Ewe, 10
exploration: as Europocentric expression, xvii; significance of, xvii; motives behind, xviii, 129–31; organization of, 131, 398

Falconbridge, A., E surgeon in Sierra Leone, 271
Falconbridge, Mrs, 271, 406
Faleme, river, *5*, 7, 87, 89, 221, 299, 328
Fante, *1*, 26, 349
Farim, Bambuk chief, 89
Faria y Sousa, M. de, P historian, 121, 402
Fatetenda, Wuli, 226
Fatima, wife of Ali of Ludamar, 245
Fatteconda, Bondou, 232
Felup, 69, 78
Ferbanna, Bambuk, 223
Ferguson, A., member of A.A., 194–5, 359
Ferlo, 297

Fernandez, A., P explorer in Mozambique, 118, 129
Fez, *1*, *8*, 315
Fezzan: kingdom tributary to Tripoli, 20; trade routes of, *1*, 22, 102, 216; country of Garamantes, 46; Burckhardt and, 377–8; Catholic missionaries in, 103; de Haslien and, 186; Hornemann in, 251, 253–4, 258–62, 288; Leo Africans and, 54; Lucas and, 200, 205–8
firearms, 216, 226, 272, 374, 393
Fitzgerald, E traveller, 361
Flaccus, Septimius, Roman general, 47
Flinders, M., E naval officer and explorer, 159
Fordyce, Sir W., member of A.A., 194–6, 209, 359
forest, West African, 5, 126
Fort St Joseph, *2*, 88–9, 223, 300, 328
Fort St Pierre, 89
Fox, C. J., 182, 350
Franklin, Sir J., E naval officer and explorer, 159
Fransiscans, 97, 110
Freetown, *9*, xvi, 271–2, 346–8
French: and Algiers, 105; attack on Freetown, 271; and Badia, 319; and Egypt, 108–9, 254–5, 302–8; and Senegal, 86–91, 129–30, 142, 299–300, 323, 328; and slave trade, 352; and Tripoli, 352
Frendenburgh, G renegade, 253, 256–7, 260
Fuladu, 330, 334
Fulani (*var.* Foulahs, Fulbe etc.): people, *7*, 10, 11, 13, 32, 78, 342; kingdoms of, 25, 64, 272–3, *see also* Futa Jallon, Futa Toro; *jihad*, 344, 398
Fullarton, Col., member of A.A., 213
Fung, 10, 13, 24
Fur, 10
furniture manufacture, 150
furs, 130, 200
Futa, 64
Futa Jallon, 6, 25, 272–3, 288, 328, 346
Futa Toro, 25, 300

al-Gabarti, Egyptian scholar, 308
Gabba (? Kabba), 211
Gabi, *see* Kebbi
Galam (*var.* Kajaaga), *5*, 86–90, 144, 242–3, 299
Galla, *1*, *12*, 10, 24, 132, 164, 166, 386
Galloway, Earl of, member of A.A., 194–7, 359
Gama, C da, P commander in Ethiopia, 113
Gama, Vasco da, 117

Gambia, river: course, *1*, *2*, *4*, 6, 7, 78; A.A. and, 209, 216, 226; equated with Niger, *3*, 59; English on, 68, 78–85, 96, 129; Houghton and, 219–20; Park and, *5*, *9*, 230–1, 241, 333; people of, 26, 78–9, 126; proposed convict settlement on, 85; proposed English agent on, 325, 327
Gao (*var.* Gago), 25, 57–8, 79, 98
Gaoga, *see* Baguirmi
Garamantes, *3*, 46–7
gardening, 150–1
Garnett, R., quoted, 167
Garrick, David, 147
Geesh, 6
Ge'ez, 114, 161
Genoese, 105, 259
Gentleman's Magazine, 153, 215
geography, popularity of, 39, 41
German: explorers, *see* Burckhardt, de Haslien, Hornemann, Krapf, Röntgen, Seetzen; interest in Africa, 290–1, *see also* Blumenbach, Reichard; renegades, 384, *see also* Frendenburgh, Haji
Ghadames, 22, 46, 54, 210–11
Ghana (*var.* Gana): empire of, xiv, 23, 52–3, 97; on European maps, *4*, *7*, 59, 287, 361; modern, 6
Ghat, *1*, 22, 211
Gibbon, Edward, 51, 166, 214
Gibraltar, *8*, 105, 128, 383
Gingiro, *4*, 95, 102
Giorback, 211
Gisborne, T., member of A.A., 214
Gloucester, Duke of, President of African Institution, 351
Glover, J., E naval officer, 344
Goatpans (Aegipans), 49
Gobir (*var.* Guber), *1*, *4*, 25, 58, 95, 211, 218
Godoy, Spanish minister, 213
Goes, de, Jesuit traveller, 123
Gojam, *12*, 24
Golbery, S, X. M. de, F traveller in Senegambia, 78, 85, 159, 323–4, 407
gold: *European expeditions to obtain:* English, 81–2, 85, 216, 226, 245, 265, 321, 327; French, 89–90; Portuguese, 76, 117–18; Swedish, 187
  trade in: Bambuk, 83, 89–90, 129; Bornu, 57; Carthaginians and, 61; Ethiopia, 372, 393; Gambia, 81–2, 85; Gold Coast, 76, 128, 130; Mali, 61, 98; Monomotapa, 117–18, 121, 129; Timbuktu, 56, 217; West Africa, 23, 61, 99, 210, 265, 362

Gold Coast: Brass on, 175; European forts on, 26, 7, 966, 348; gold in, 23, 76, 128, 130; Isert on, 175, 185; relations of Africans with Europeans on, 30, 69, 128, 133, 349; Park and, 239
Gondar, *1*, *12*, 24, 111, 164–6, 374, 388–90, 393
Gonja, *1*, 262
Goree, *2*, 86, 142–3, 145, 226, 299, 300, 322, 331–3, 340
Gotha, Duke of, 379
Göttingen, University of, 189–90, 250–1, 366, 379–80
Grafton, Duke of, member of A.A., 213
Grain Coast (*var.* Pepper Coast), *2*, 26
Gran, Ahmad ibn Ibrahim, Somali leader, 112–13
Granada, 100
Gray, J., E official of Sierra Leone Company, 273
Greaves, J., E orientalist, 108
Greeks in Africa, 44, 259
Guinea, 37
Gum Coast, 144–5
gum senegal, 86, 130, 150
Hadendowa, *10*, 375
Haji, El, G renegade, 382–4
Hakluyt, R., E collector of travels, 39, 66, 79, 121, 401
Halifax, Lord, Secretary of State, 161–2
Halls, J. J., E biographer, 387, 391
Hamilton, A., E trader in Indian Ocean, 121, 403
Hamilton, Rev. A., secretary of A.A., 358
Hamilton, W., secretary of A.A., 358, 394, 408
Hanway, J., E philanthropist, 269
Harar, *1*, *12*, 24, 112, 393
Hardwicke, Earl of, treasurer of A.A., 359
Harris, J., E collector of travels, 40, 153, 402
Harwood, Professor, member of A.A., 214
Haslien, Baron de, G traveller, 186
Hasselquist, Swedish botanist, 152
Hastings, Marquess of; *see* Rawdon
Hausa: kingdoms, *1*, xiv, 25, 58, 96, 208, 263, 321; *see also* 'Housa'; language, 12–13, 58; people, *1*, xiv, 10, 25, 259
Hawkesbury, Lord, later Earl of Liverpool, Secretary of State, 267
Hawkins, W., E merchant and sailor, 66
Heeren, A. H. L., G historian, 251

Henry the Navigator, 65, 131
Herodotus, Greek historian, xvi, 44–6, 61, 215, 258, 285, 400
Heyne, C. G., G scholar, 251
hides, 82
hippopotamus, 49
history, African: myths about, xiii; study of, xv, 418; *see also* Ludolphus
Hobart, Lord, Colonial Secretary, 326–7
Hodges, C., E trader, 82, 127, 130
Hoggar (*var.* Ahaggar), 4, 21–2
Hombori, 5
Hornemann, F., G explorer in service of A.A., 166, 188, 208, 247, 250–63, 265–6, 285–6, 357, 361, 367, 384, 398, 407
Hosein of Darfur, 280
Host, G., Danish consul in Morocco, 106, 404
Houghton, D., Irish explorer in service of A.A., 219–24, 227, 231, 233–4, 357, 398
Houghton, Mrs, 220, 223
'Housa' (*var.* Houssa, Haussa), 7, 9, 218–9, 227, 231, 238; *see also* Hausa
human sacrifice, 72
Hunt, Leigh, quoted, 128
Hunter, J., member of A.A., 214
Huntingdon, Earl of, member of A.A., 213
Husainid Deys of Tunis, 20

Ibadan, xiii, 8
Ibibio, 10, 363
Ibn Battuta, Arab traveller, 51
Ibn Khaldun, Arab historian, 51
Ibo, *1*, xiv, 10, 26, 74
Ibrahim, Sheikh, *see* Burckhardt, J. L.
Idah, 26
al-Idrisi, Arab geographer, 23, 34, 51–3, 94–5, 117, 199, 287, 400
Ifat, 112
Igala, *1*, 26
Igbirra, 25
Imbert, P., F slave, 101
Imhammed, Shereef from the Fezzan, 206–9
imperialism, European, xvii, 245, 297–8, 303, 322, 375, 398
Institut National, 252, 301, 306, 313
Institut d'Égypte, 307
Islam, expansion of, xiii, 13, 88, 283; *see also* Muslim
Isaaco, Park's guide, 333–43
Isert, P., G traveller in West Africa, 175, 185–6, 191, 405
Issabo, 75

Italians: merchants in North Africa, 97, 111, 205, *see also* Florentines, Genoese, Venetians; cartographers, 98
Ivatts, T., clerk to A.A., 211
ivory, 82, 122, 210, 362–3, 393
Ivory Coast, *1*, 6, 26
Iyasu I of Ethiopia, 24

Jaboe, 75
Jackson, J. G., E merchant in Morocco, 265–8, 340, 382, 408
Jacob, W., E merchant, 391
James I of England, 80
James II of England (Duke of York), 82
James Island, *2*, 82, 143, 325
Jannequin, C., F traveller in Senegal, 67, 402
Jarra, *5*, 234, 236
Jefferson, Thomas, 201–3
Jekyll, J., E biographer, 147
Jemmy Henshaw, Calabar trader, 364
Jenne, 13, 25, 57, 340
Jesuits, 29, 113–14, 123, 131
Jews in North Africa, 98, 102, 205
Jidda, *1*, *10*, 164, 376
Joag, 232
Joao II of Portugal, 62–5, 112, 115, 131
Job ben Solomon, prince of Bondou, 32, 403
Jobson, R., E trader on Gambia, 41, 67, 129, 131, 401
Johnson, Park's servant, 231, 237–9
Johnson, Samuel, 40, 144, 146, 153
Joliba, *see* Niger
Jos, 5
José, Angolan *pombeiro*, 120
Jones, Sir W., E orientalist, 149, 290
Juba, Berber king, 47
Judar, Moroccan general, 101
Jukun, 25
Jumbo, 233
Jupiter, Ammon, temple of, 256, 277, 285

Kaarta (*var.* Karta), *1*, *5*, *7*, 25, 233–8 246
Kabra, *9*, 340–1
Kajaaga, *see* Galam
Kakundy, 272
Kamalia, *5*, 240–1
Kamchatka, 123
Kanem, xiv, 23, 52
Kano (*var.* Cano), *1*, *3*, *7*, *8*, 11, 25, 57–9
Kanuri, 10, 12, 13
Karamanlis of Tripoli, 20, 205
Karfa Taura, Gambian trader, 240–1, 247

Kasson, *5*, 26, 232–3
Katsina (*var.* Cassena, Kashna): kingdom of, *1*, *3*, *4*, *7*, 25; Catholic missionaries in, 103, 129; Hornemann in, 251, 261–2; Leo Africanus in, 57–8; learned men of, 13; Park and, 339; Rennell and, 288; trade of, 22, 211
Kawar, *1*, 22
Kayee, *9*, 332
Kaynura, 89
Kayor, 26
Kebbi (*var.* Gabi), 25, 95, 260
Kekia, 95
Keugler, C., G missionary, 395
Kew, Royal Botanical Gardens, 152
Keyes, Capt., E naval officer, 388
Kiewiet, C. A. de, quoted, xxi
Kilwa, 117
Kimbundu, 117
King Aqua, Calabar trader, 364
Kingsley, Mary, E traveller in West Africa, 248
Kirk, Sir John, E consul in Zanzibar, 375
Komadugu Yobe, river, 7, 45
Kong, Mountains of, *7*, 288
Koniakori, *5*, 233
Kormachi, 95
Krapf, J., G missionary and explorer, 396
Kufra, 22, 164
Kuku, 52–3, *see also* Gao
Kumbi Saleh, 52, 59

Labat, J. B., F writer, 68, 84, 87, 403
Labé, *9*, 273, 328
Labillardière, F explorer, 252
Lacerda, F. J. de, P explorer, 119–20
Lafayette, 201
Lagos, 26
Laidley, Dr, E trader on Gambia, 221–3, 227, 231, 234, 242
Laing, A. G., E explorer, 211, 340
Lalande, J. J., F scientist, 252, 406
Lamlem, river, *4*, 95; country, *7*; *see also* Lemlem
Lander, J., E explorer, xv, 248
Lander, R., E explorer, xv, xvi, 128, 343
Langley, E trader on Gambia, 81
Ledyard, J., American explorer in service of A.A., 200–3, 215, 277, 357, 398
Lee, E vice-consul in Egypt, 395
Legrand, F writer, 110, 403
Leibnitz, 109
Le Maire, Sieur, F traveller in West Africa, 67, 69, 87, 402

Le Mesurier, P., member of A.A., 214, 275
Lemlem, 53
Lemprière, W., E traveller in Morocco, 106, 406
Leo X, Pope, 54
Leo Africanus, Moorish traveller: on Barbary, 106; career and writing, 53–9, 96, 208, 259; cartographers and, 92, 94, 199, 211; editions of, 41, 51, 401; on Nubia, 110; on Wangara, 23
Lettsom, Dr, member of A.A., 214
leucricota, 49
Levi-Provencal, E., xiv
Leyden, J., Scottish orientalist, 289–90
Liberia, 6, 77
Libya, 3, 4, 44, 46
Lind, J., E medical writer, 9, 171, 404
Linnaeus, C., Swedish botanist, 151–2
Linschoten, J. H. van, Dutch traveller, 121, 401
Lister, E slave-owner, 179
Littleton, E trader on Gambia, 221
Liverpool, Earl of, 321
Liverpool, traders of, 31, 139–4, 362–3
Livingstone, David, 120, 375
Llandaff, Bishop of, Richard Watson, member of A.A., 194–6, 212
Lloyd, Major, E commandant at Goree, 331, 340–1
Lobi, 23, 61
Lobo, J., Jesuit missionary in Ethiopia, 114, 132, 403
Locke, John, 177
London, 140, 153, 275, 366
London Missionary Society, 347–8
Logone, river, *1*, 7, 260
Lopez, D., P trader in Congo, 120, 401
Lorenzo the Magnificent, 100
Lotus plant, 285
Loughborough, Lord, member of A.A., 213
Louis XIV of France, 106
Luanda, 116
Lucas, 'Abyssinian', 64
Lucas, S., E consul in Tripoli and explorer in service of A.A., 199–200, 202, 204–9, 215, 217, 219, 251, 259, 261, 277, 288, 357
Ludamar (Oulad Mbareck), *5*, 233–5, 246
Ludolf (Ludolphus), J., G scholar on Ethiopia, 114, 402
Lugard, Lord, 305
Lyon, G. F., E explorer, 159

Macaulay, Z., E governor of Sierra Leone, 271, 324–5, 351
Macdonagh, E consul in Tripoli, 262

Macks, Quarter-Master, 266
Madoc, L., E merchant in Morocco, 79
Magallon, F consul in Egypt, 302
Magra, P., E consul in Tunis, 176, 225
mahogany, 150
Maillet, B. de, F consul in Egypt, 108, 403
Majorcan cartographers, 92, 98
Malade, Bambara trader, 90
Malfante, A., Genoese merchant, 98–100
Mali (*var.* Melli), *3, 7*, xiv, 23, 56–7, 61, 63–4, 75–6, 92, 98
Malindi, 118, 379
Malta, Maltese, 205, 303, 369, 382
Mamluks: in Egypt, 20, 203, 303–6, 371, 376; in Fezzan, 258–9
Mamprussi, 25
Manchester, 140, 143, 275
Mandara, *1*, 24
Mandi Mansa, ruler of Mali, 63
Mandinga, *3*, 76
Mandingo, *1*, 10–11, 13, 26, 30, 33, 75, 78, 83, 88, 248
Mansa Musa, emperor of Mali, 56
Mansong, King of Segu, 238, 246, 336–8
mantichora, 49
Manuel I of Portugal, 116
Marees, P. de, Dutch trader in West Africa, 67, 401
Maria, Carlo, Italian missionary, 103
Marrakesh, *8*, 12, 97, 100, 315, 317, 383
Marsden, W., E orientalist and member of A.A., 149, 214
Martin, J., member of A.A., 214
Martyn, Lt., E army officer, 331, 339–42
Massawa, *1, 10, 12*, 20, 164, 167, 371, 375, 388–92
Masson, F., E botanist, 175, 198
Masudi (*var.* Meshudi), Arab geographer, 59
Maternus, Julius, Roman general, 47
Mathews, D., quoted, 162, 389
Matra, J. M., E consul in Morocco, 175–6, 200, 210, 265–6, 311–16
Mauritania, 83
Maxwell, G., E trader on Congo, 330
Mecca, *1, 10*, 123, 199, 201, 318–19, 330, 371, 376
Medina, Arabia, *10*, 377
Medina, Wuli, *5*, 221–2
Mediterranean, 3–4, 97
Meknes (*var.* Mequinez), *8*, 313, 315
Melek Musa, Darfur official, 280
Melilla, *8*, 312–14
Mende, *1*, 10
Mesurata, 207
Metcalfe, Sir T., treasurer of A.A., 359

Methodist missionaries, 347
Mexico, 124
Michael, Ras of Tigre, 164–5
Middleton, C. T., E geographer, 42
Middleton, Sir C., later Lord Barham, member of A.A., 214
Miller, E geographer, 42
Mirafab, 372
missionaries, Christian: as explorers, 130–1; in Congo, 115–16; on Gold Coast, 347; in Katsina, 102–3; in Mozambique, 118; in Nubia, 110; *see also* Capuchins, Catholics, Fransiscans, Jesuits, Methodists, Protestants, etc.
Missett, Col., E consul in Egypt, 371
Mobidinne, Bambara official, 337–8
Mocha, *12*, 380, 388, 393
Mogador, *8*, xvi, 264–5, 315, 340, 382–3
Mogadishu, 117
Moira, Earl of, member of A.A., 214; *see also* Rawdon, Lord
Mombasa, 117, 121, 396
Momo Dick, Calabar trader, 364
Monge, G., F scientist, 254, 306
Monomotapa, 118, 121, 129
Montagu, Duke of, 32, 147
Montaigne, 178
Montesquieu, 177
Montlinot, F colonialist, 301
Moon, Mountains of (Montagnes de la Lune, Kumri (Monds) Gebirge), *4, 6, 7, 11*, 111
Moore, F., E trader on Gambia, 41, 51, 70, 85, 199, 403
Moors, *1*, 10, 12, 13, 21, 69, 143, 234–9, 247–8, 339
Moravian Brethren, 247
Mornas, de, F cartographer, 50
Moroccans: in Senegal and Mauritania, 83, 89; in Timbuktu, 23, 25, 79, 90, 101, *see also* Arma
Morocco: land, *1, 8*, 4; kingdom, 16–17; Europeans and, 28, 79, 104–6, 125, 130, 365; Badia in, 310–17; Houghton in, 219; Jackson in, 264–8; Matra in, 176; Röntgen in, 382–4
mosquito, 10, 127
Mossi (*var.* people of Moses), 10, 13, 25, 63–4, 96, 130
Muhammad Ali, Pasha of Egypt, 107, 308, 371, 376, 397
Muhammad, Sidi, Sultan of Morocco, 17, 264
mulattos, Portuguese, 65, 80, 117
Murray, Alexander, Scottish scholar, 162–3, 406, 408
Murray, Hugh, quoted, 48
Murzuk, *1*, 22, 251, 258–61, 369, 378

Muscat, 359
Musgrave, Sir W., member of A.A.,
220
Muslim: *attitude to Christians:* in Darfur, 279; in Egypt, 29, 107, 202, 254;
in North Africa, 28, 105; other, 32,
283; *see also* African: attitudes to
Europeans
disguise adopted by explorers:
Burckhardt, 367, 369–72, 376,
378; Hornemann, 253–4, 256–7,
263; proposed by Jackson, 265;
Röntgen, 383; Seetzen, 380
Mweru, lake, 120

Nachtigal, G., G explorer, 188
Namaquas, 122
Nantes, 184
Nasamonians, 45
Navy, British, 352
Neave, Sir R., member of A.A., 214
Nelson, Admiral Lord, 303–4
Nerico, river, 78
Nero, Roman Emperor, 111
Nettico, river, 83
New South Wales, 322–3
Newton, J., E abolitionist, 30, 181, 405
Newtown, Cross river, 362
Ngola, 117
Niebuhr, C., Danish traveller, 28–9,
380, 406
Nicholls, H., E explorer in service of
A.A., 361–5
Nicol, G., E publisher, 244
Niger, river (*var.* Joliba, Nile of the
Negroes):
actual course, 1, 6–7
exploration of: African Associa-
tion and, 219, 226, 245–6, 321,
362; British Government and,
325, 327, 397; Hornemann and,
260, 286; Houghton and, 224;
Jackson and, 286; Park and,
5, 9, 231, 238–9, 285, 330, 332–
44; Portuguese and, 65; Romans and, 46–7; Röntgen and,
382; Salt and, 386
theories about: ending in lake, 7,
287, 330; ending in Bight of
Benin, 11, 287, 385; flowing
eastwards to Egypt, 45, 47–8,
99, 286; flowing westwards to
Atlantic, 3, 52, 58–9, 85, 87,
94, 202, 208; joined to Congo,
330, 348; D'Anville, 4, 95;
Herodotus, 45; al-Idrisi, 52;
Maxwell, 330; Pliny, 47–8;
Reichard, 11, 385; Rennell, 7,
287, 330
Nigeria, xiii, xiv, 3, 11

Nigritia, 37, 43, 362
Nile, river (Blue Nile, White Nile or
Bahr-al-Abiad);
course: 1, 10, 7
exploration of: Browne and, 277,
281; Bruce and, 165; Burckhardt and, 374; inquiries about
in East Africa, 359; Paez and,
111; Roman centurions and,
111; Salt and, 386
theories about source of: Browne,
6, 285; Bruce, 165; D'Anville,
4, 111; Herodotus, 45; al-
Idrisi, 52; Pliny, 47–8; *see also*
Niger; flowing eastwards to
Egypt
noble savage, 138, 177
Norden, F., Danish naval officer and
traveller in Egypt, 108, 404
Nordenskiold, A., Swedish mineralo-
gist in Sierra Leone, 274
North, F., member of A.A., 213
North African or Sudan Company, 267
Northumberland, Duke of, member of
A.A., 175, 213
North-West Passage, 132
Nuba, 10
Nubia, 1, xvi, 10, 20, 102, 108, 110,
112, 377, 380
Nunez, Rio, 272
Nupe (*var.* Nyffe), 1, 7, 25, 260
Nyika, 127

Ockley, S., E orientalist, 148–9, 403
Oedoba, 75
Ogané, 62
Ogilby, J., E geographer, 41, 402
O'Hara, E governor of Senegambia,
144–5
Omani Arabs, 119
Ombach Boubi, Sidi, Park's tutor in
Arabic, 329
Ophir, 81, 117
Oran, 100
Orange, river, 122, 199
oriental studies, 148–9
Osei Tutu, King of Ashanti, 349
ostrich feathers, 210
Otto Ephraim, Calabar trader, 364
Oudney, W., E explorer, xv
Owen, N., E slave-dealer, 140–1
Owen, R., quoted, 345
Owen, W. F., E naval officer and ex-
plorer, 159
Oyo, 1, 26, 72, 75, 96
Ozoro Esther of Ethiopia, 165

Pacific Ocean, 156–8
Paez, Jesuit traveller in Ethiopia, 111,
165

Paine, Tom, 177
Paley, Dr, 177
palm-oil, 363
Paradis, Venture de, F orientalist, 307
Paris, 165, 184
Park, Mrs, 246, 323, 343
Park, Mungo: biographies of, 432;
    first expedition, 227–49, 285, 288;
    second expedition, 130, 322–3, 326–
    57; and Badia, 313; mentioned, 120,
    128, 361, 378, 381, 398; quoted, 30,
    33; *Travels*, 247–9, 407, 408
Park, Mungo, junior, 343
Park, Thomas, 343
Parry, W., E naval officer and ex-
    plorer, 159
Paterson, W., E traveller in South
    Africa, 122, 198, 405
Pearce, N., E sailor and adventurer in
    Ethiopia, 343, 386–90, 395, 412
pegasi, 49
Pepper Coast, 69; *see also* Grain Coast
Periera, Pachecho, P navigator, 60,
    420
Persia, 123
Petra, 371
Phillips, T., E ship's captain in West
    Africa, 68, 70, 403
pilgrims: Christian, 108; Muslim, 374
Piloti, A., Spanish traveller in Morocco,
    384
Pindar, Peter, E satirist, quoted, 171–2
piracy, 17, 97, 101, 105–7
Pisa, 100
Pisania, 5, 221, 231, 333
Pitt, William, Earl of Chathim, 128,
    142–3
Pitt, William, the Younger, 181–2, 214,
    226, 328, 380
Pitt, W. M., member of A.A., 214
Playfair, R. L., E consul in Algiers, 163
Pliny, xvi, 46–50
Pococke, R., E traveller in Egypt, 108,
    403
Poiret, Abbé, F botanist in North
    Africa, 40, 62, 406
Polo, Marco, 122
pombeiros, 120, 132
Poncet, C. J., F traveller in Ethiopia,
    110, 113, 402
Ponthieu, de, E merchant in Antigua,
    175, 198
Pope, Alexander, 177
Porsinari, 100
Portuguese: archives, 66; in Congo and
    Angola, 115–17; in East Africa, 117–
    21; in Ethiopia, 112–13, 396; in
    North Africa, 26, 28, 100–1; and
    slave trade, 352; and West Africa,
    26, 31, 60–66, 76, 79, 80, 127

Pory, J., E translator, 51, 401
Postlethwayt, M., E economist, 139,
    141, 403, 404, 414
Prester, John, 62, 111–12, 115, 119,
    130–1
Prévost, Abbé, F collector of travels,
    40, 62, 404
Priestley, J., E scientist, 171
Prince of Wales, later Prince Regent
    and George IV, 194, 394
Propaganda Fide, 102
Protestant missionaries, 131, 138, 347,
    393; *see also* Baptists, Church
    Missionary Society, London Mis-
    sionary Society, Methodists, Society
    for Propagation of the Gospel
Ptolemy, Claudius, Greek geographer,
    xvi, 46–50, 95, 111, 400
Pulteney, W., member of A.A., 194–6
Purchas, S., E collector of travels, 40,
    81, 108, 114, 120, 401–2
Pythagoras, Greek scientist, 56

Quakers, 179, 214
Quaque, P., African Christian on Gold
    Coast, 347

Rabelo, Rodrigo, P agent in West
    Africa, 63
rainfall, 7–8
Rainolds, R., E trader in West Africa,
    79, 86
Raleigh, Walter, 124
Ramusio, G. B., Italian collector of
    travels, 39, 62, 92, 114, 400
Rawdon, Lord, later Earl of Moira and
    Marquess of Hastings, member of
    A.A., 193–5, 212–3, 359
Rebmann, G missionary and explorer
    in East Africa, 396
Red Sea, 109, 112, 123, 278, 374, 388–
    92
Reichard, C. G., G geographer, *11*,
    380, 385
Reinel, Pero, P agent in West Africa,
    64
renegades, 101, 106, 384; *see also*
    Frendenburgh
Rennell, J., E geographer: career, 215;
    geographical essays, 215, 243, 285;
    maps, 7, 288; and Niger, 287, 385;
    and Browne, 282; and Bruce, 166;
    and Park's second expedition, 324–5,
    330
rice, 150
Richardson, R., E traveller in Egypt,
    377
Rio de Morte, 9
Rio Grande, *7*, 59, 324–5

rivers of West Africa, 6–7, 125–6; *see also* Benue, Gambia, Niger, Senegal, Volta
Robespierre, 201
Rohlfs, G., G explorer, 164, 188
Romans in Africa, 44, 46–7
Rombulo, P., Italian traveller in Ethiopia, 112
Rome, 165, 184
Roncière, C. de la, 96
Röntgen, H., G explorer, 166, 267, 379–82, 398
Royal African Company; *see* trading companies
Royal Society, 154–5, 171
Rousseau, J. J., 177
Rubault, F agent on Senegal, 299
Rudland, Capt., E traveller in Ethiopia, 388–9, 393
Rupert, Prince, 81–2
Russians in Siberia, 123, 158
Ryder, A. F. C., quoted, 66
Rzevuski, Count, Polish traveller in Syria, 319

Sahara (*var.* Zaara): geography of, *1*, 4–5; people of, 21, *see also* Moors, Tebu, Tuareg; European ideas about, 38, 125; Herodotus on, 45; Hornemann in, 258–62; Leo Africanus on, 54–5; medieval European travellers in, 97–100; Portuguese in, 64; Ptolemy on, 48; Romans in, 46; Saugnier in, 299
sahel, 5
as-Saheli, Andalusian architect, 56
St Albans Club, 195
St Albans Tavern, 193–6
St Domingo, 183
St Louis, *2*, *9*, 86, 88, 143–5, 299–300
Salawi, Moroccan vizier, 315, 317
Sale, G., E orientalist, 148
Salesia, Severino di, Italian missionary in North Africa, 103
Salmon, T., E geographer, 39, 42, 403, 404
salt, 22, 61, 99
Salt, H., E traveller in Ethiopia and consul in Egypt, 377–8, 381, 386–96, 408
Sancho, I., African writer, 147–8, 404
Sandys, G., E traveller in Egypt, 108
Sansanding, *5*, *9*, 338
Sansom, P., E merchant and member of A.A., 209
Santiago, Cape Verde Islands, 331
Santos, J. dos, P missionary in East Africa, 121, 402
São Salvador, 116
São Tomé, 116
Sarakole, 26, 87–8

Saturday's Club, 193, 195, 212, 358
Satyrs, 49
Saugnier, F traveller, 299–300, 406
Savary, C. F., F traveller in Egypt, 109–10, 302, 405
Scott, G., Park's companion, 331, 336, 339
Scott, Walter, 289–90, 326
Sebastian, King of Portugal, 79, 118
Seetzen, U. J., G traveller, 379–80, 398
Sefuwa, ruling dynasty of Bornu, 23
Segu (*var.* Sego), *1*, *5*, *7*, *9*, 25, 288, 327–30, 337
Sena, 118
Senegal, river: course, *1*, 6–7, 85; English on, 144–5, 321–2, 328, 341; French on, *2*, 31, 85–91, 96, 129, 299; regarded as part of westward-flowing Niger, *3*, 59, 87, 94; D'Anville on, *4*, 95; Golbéry on, 85; Labat on, 68; Wadström on, 187
Senegambia, E colony of, 143–4, 347, 397
senna, 210
Sennar, *1*, *6*, *10*, *12*, 24, 110, 165–6, 201, 280, 371–3
Shabeni, Moroccan merchant, 217, 287, 409
Shakespeare, William, 146
Shari, river, *1*, 7, 260
Sharp, G., E abolitionist, 179–81, 270
Shaw, T., E traveller in North Africa, 106, 150, 161, 403
Sheffield, Lord, member of A.A., 166
shilluk, 24
Shuwa Arabs, 10, 13
Siberia, 122–3, 132, 158, 201
Sierra Leone: geography of, *1*, 6; peoples of, 26, 77; English colony of, 183, 269–74, 346–7, 397; exploration from, 271–3, 328; French and, 143, 271, 301
Sierra Leone Company, 183, 187, 270–5, 325, 346–7, 351, 406
Sijilmassa, 97
Silla, *5*, 239
silver, 118
Silviera, G. da, P missionary in Mozambique, 118
Simbing, 223, 234
Sinai, 108, 377
Sinclair, Sir J., member of A.A., 193–6, 217, 358
Siwa, *1*, 44–5, 256, 277–8
skelton, R. A., quoted, 39
slaves: *African*: in England, 179; in Egypt, 203, 278; Park and, 241–2 *European*: in Algiers, 106; in Bornu, 101; in Morocco, 104; in Timbuktu, 101

trade in: Atlantic, 23, 26, 30, 130, 139, 179, 352; Calabar, 363; Congo, 116; Eastern Sudan, 203, 278, 372–3; Ethiopia, 393; French and, 300; Gambia, 221, 241

abolition of trade in: abolitionist movement in England, 179–83, 350–3; African reactions to, 72, 352–3, 364; Burckhardt and, 374; Park and, 249; Sierra Leone Company and, 272

Sliman, Mulay, Emperor of Morocco, 264, 314

Sloane, Sir H., E collector, 32, 155

Smeathman, H., E naturalist, 269, 405

Smee, Capt. T., E naval officer in East Africa, 359, 415

Smith, Adam, 177

Smith, W., member of A.A., 214

Smith, William, E surveyor in West Africa, 68–9, 75, 403

Smyth, W. H., E naval officer, 159

Snelgrave, W., E ship's captain in West Africa, 68, 75, 128, 403

Société de L'Afrique interieure et des Découvertes, La, 292

Society for Propagation of the Gospel, 347

Sofala, 117–18, 121

Solander, D. C., Swedish botanist, 152, 158

Solinus, Latin geographer, 50, 400

Somali, *1, 12,* 10, 12, 24, 386

Songhai, *1,* xiv, 10, 13, 23, 25, 101

Sonnini de Manoncour, C. N. S., F traveller in Egypt, 110, 407

South Africa, 115, 121–2, 130, 132

Spain, 292, 310–17, 352

Spaniards, 26, 28, 79, 100, 124, *see also* Badia, Piloti

Sparrman, Swedish naturalist in South and West Africa, 122, 152, 187, 198

Speke, J. H., E explorer in East Africa, 360, 396

spices, 112, 130

Stael, van der, Dutch governor in South Africa, 121–2

Stanley, H. M., explorer, 126, 374

Stevenson, Col., E army officer, 327–8

Stibbs, B., E explorer on Gambia, 84

Strabo, Greek geographer, 50, 400

Strapfoots, 49

Strong, J., African slave, 179

Stuart, A., member of A.A., 194–5, 212, 359

Stuart, Salt's companion, 392

Suakin, *1, 10, 12,* 20, 372, 376, 388

Sudan (*Bilad-as-Sudan*): definition of, 5; landscape, 5; climate, 8; Arab geographers and, 52, 54–5; *for* Central Sudan *see* Bornu, Hausa; *for* Eastern Sudan *see* Baguirmi, Darfur, Sennar, Wadai; *for* Western Sudan *see* Bambara, Mali, Songhai, Timbuktu

Suez, 109

sugar, 130, 139, 150

Sullivan, J., E official in Colonial Office, 324–5, 327

Susu, *1,* 10, 77, 274

Swahili, traders, 118

Swedenborg, E., doctrines of, 174, 186–7

Swediaur, F. X., Swedish doctor, 209–10, 212

Swein, 278–9

Swift, Dean, 93

Syria, 318–19, 368–70, 380

Systems of Geography, 41, 153

Tacitus, Roman historian, 178

Tafilelt (*var.* Tafilalet), *8,* 384

Tahiti, 170

Talleyrand, F statesman, 301–3

Tambacunda, 299

Tamerlane, 112

Tanezrouft, 7

Tangier, *8,* 175, 210, 264, 310, 314

Taodeni, *1,* 22

Tassy, Langier de, F writer on North Africa, 106–7, 404

tea, 150

Tebu, *1,* 11, 12, 21, 54, 259, 267

technicians, Europeans: in Congo, 116; in North Africa, 105–6

Tecla Haimanot, Emperor of Ethiopia, 165

Teghaza, 22, 61

Tekrur, 52–3, 64

tekruri, 374

Tellez, B., P writer on Ethiopia, 114, 402

Temalo, 64

Temissa, 258

Temne, 346

Tenda, 80

Tennyson, A., quoted, 129

Terga, 54, *see also* Tuareg

Terrasse, H., quoted, 264

Tete, 118, 120

Tetuan, 382

Thompson, E trader on Gambia, 80

Thompson, Capt., E naval officer, 270

Thomson, Dr, 209

Thornton, H., E abolitionist, 351

Thunberg, C. P., Swedish traveller in South Africa, 122, 152, 406

Tibesti, *1*, 4, 21, 22, 208, 259
Tibet, 122–3
Tigre, *12*, 24, 390, 393
timber, 129, 150
Timbo, 9, 272, 328
Timbuktu (*var.* Tombotu, Tombuctoo, Tombut, Tombutu):
  early European contacts with: cartographers and, *3*, *4*, 93, 98; Dei in, 100; French attempts to reach, 90, 95; Imbert and, 101; Jobson and, 80; Leo Africanus on, 55–6; Portuguese and, 64; renegades in, 101; reports on, 90, 99; *see also* Moroccans in Timbuktu
  explorers and: African Association and, 7, 209, 216, 219, 227; British Government and, 321, 327–8; Caillié and, 132; Gray and, 273; Hornemann and, 261; Houghton and, 221–4; Jackson and, 264–8, 286; Park and, *9*, 231, 238–9, 340–2; Röntgen, 383–4; Saugnier and, 299
  trade of: with Galam, 88; with Fezzan, 102; with North Africa, 22, 61, 76, 79
Tiv, 365
Tiemcen, 99
Togoland, 6
Tom, King, Chief in Sierra Leone, 271
tomato, 150
Tombaconda, 80
Torrid Zone, 50, 128, 208
Tosaye, *9*, 341
trade, traders: *area and routes:* Calabar, 363; Central Sudan, 211; Congo, 116; Darfur, 278, 280; East Africa, 117–18; Eastern Sudan, 372–4; Egypt, 108, 203; Ethiopia, 393–4; Gambia, 79–85, 223; 'Housa', 218; Morocco, 105, 264; Sahara, *1*, 22, 54, 61, 79, 99, 210, 265, 267; Senegal, 86–91, 299; South Africa, 122; Tripoli, 102; West Coast, 30, 76, 139; Western Sudan, 57, 61, 210
  African: Angolan, 120; Calabar, 364; Egyptian, 203, 278–80; 373; Gambian, 80–1, 221, 231, 239–40; Mandingo, 75, 83, 88; Moors, 239; Muslims in East Africa, 117; North Africans in Sudan, 57; Swahili, 118
  European: Dutch, 67; English, 66, 67, 79–85, 105, 139–42, 144–5; French, 67, 86–91, 299; Italians, 97–100, 108; Jews, 98; Portuguese, 65, 79, 80; in West Africa, 30, 76

goods: see firearms, gum, gold, ivory, salt, slaves
other references: African Association's interest in, 209, 216–17, 225–6, 227, 244–5, 321; British Government and, 393; Cadamosto on, 60; and exploration, 129–30; and imperialism, 297, 301, 321; Jackson on, 265, 267; legitimate, 270, 351; silent, 61
Tradescant, J., Dutch collector, 155
trading companies: Company of Merchants, 143, 145, 348; English on Gambia, 80–1; French on Senegal, 86–7; Royal African Company, 84
Traill, R., E consul in Tunis, 210
Trarza Moors, 86
trek-boers, 132
Trevelyan, G. M., quoted, 146
tribe, definition of, 10–11
Tripoli: government of, 20, 204–6; attitude to Europeans in, 28; Europeans in, 95, 97, 101–3; Bruce in, 163; de Haslien in, 186; Hornemann in, 252–3, 260, 263; Lucas in, 200, 206–9, 260–1
Tripolitania, 4
tropical crops, 150
Tuareg, *1*, *12*, 21, 25, 46, 54, 98–9, 340–2
Tuat, *1*, 22, 54, 99, 371
Tuckey, J. K., E naval officer and explorer, 159
Tully, R., E consul in Tripoli, 206, 208
Tully's sister-in-law, E writer on Tripoli, 28, 204–6, 408–9
Tunis, J, 20, 22, 28, 98, 100, 105, 160, 162, 210
Tunisia, 4, 10
Turks: in Egypt, 109, 304; in North Africa, 17, 20, 101, 205; Browne and, 284
Turner, W., E traveller in Egypt, 377–8

Ullendorf, E., quoted, 114
United States of America, 352

Valentia, Lord, George Annersley, E traveller in Red Sea, 387–93, 395, 408
Valentia Island, 391
Vancouver, G., E naval officer and explorer, 158
Vansleb, J. M., G traveller in Egypt, 108, 402
Venice, Venitians, 97, 105, 112, 374
Venus, transit of, 154, 157, 164
Vermuyden, Col., E explorer on Gambia, 82
Vincent, St, de Paul, 106

Violaine, F agent in Bambuk, 90
Volney, C. F. de, F traveller in Egypt, 109–10, 302, 405
Volta, river, *1*, 7, 23

Wadai (*var.* Dar Bergoo), *1*, *6*, 10, 22, 24, 203, 280
Wadan, 64
Wadström, C. B., Swedish traveller and abolitionist, 185–8, 274, 301, 406
Wahhabis, 318, 391
Walpole, Horace, 171, 182, 193
Walwyn, E traveller, 211
Wangara (*var* Guangara), *3*, *4*, *7*, *11*, 23, 52, 59, 287, 330, 361, 385
Warri, 26, 126
Watson, Richard; see Llandaff, Bishop of
Watt, E official in Sierra Leone, 271–3, 347
Waugh, E traveller in Morocco, 266
wax, 221
Weales, Surgeon, E traveller in Morocco, 266–7
Weddell, J., E navigator and explorer, 159
Wedgwood, J., member of A.A., 214
Welde Selassie, Ras of Tigre, 388–90, 392–5
Wellesley, Lord, Governor-General of India, 388
Wesley, John, 180
West Indies, 139–40, 151, 178–9, 185, 301, 327, 350
Wheeler, C., E trader in West Africa, 70

'White Man's Grave', 26, 68, 143
Wilberforce, W., E abolitionist, 181, 194, 214, 350, 353, 363, 380
Wilkins, C., E orientalist, 149
Wilkinson, J., member of A.A., 214
Williams, E., quoted, 139
Willis, J., E consul in Senegambia, 225–30, 265
Winterbottom, E official in Sierra Leone, 272–3
Wolof, *1*, 10, 13, 26, 60, 69, 78–9
Wood, R., E traveller, 161–2
Worge, E governor of St. Louis, 144
Wuli (*var.* Woolli), 26, 221, 226, 231, 327

yale, 49
Yatenga, 25
Yauri (*var.* Yaorri, Yaouri), *4*, *9*, 25, 95, 211, 342
Yemen, 29, 380
Yoruba, xiii, 10, 26, 75, 361
Young, Sir W., secretary of A.A., 292, 313, 358, 361
Ysalguier, A. d', medieval F traveller, 98–9

Zaara, see Sahara
Zachs, von, G scholar and editor, 290
Zambezi, river, 118–20
Zamfara, *1*, 23, 25, 57–9, 208
Zanzibar, 121, 359
Zaria (*var.* Zeg-zeg), *1*, xiv, 25, 58
Zoffany, W., E artist, 171
Zuila, 258

DATE DUE